Black Stats Matter

Black Stats Matter

*Integrating Negro League Numbers
into Major League Records*

PHILIP LEE

Foreword by Larry Lester

McFarland & Company, Inc., Publishers
Jefferson, North Carolina

Frontispiece: *Crossed Bats* by David Hagen
(courtesy David Hagen, hagenillustration@gmail.com, IG @hagenillustration

LIBRARY OF CONGRESS CATALOGUING-IN-PUBLICATION DATA

Names: Lee, Philip, 1968– author. | Lester, Larry, writer of foreword.
Title: Black stats matter : integrating Negro League numbers into Major League records / Philip Lee ; foreword by Larry Lester.
Description: Jefferson, North Carolina : McFarland & Company, Inc., Publishers, 2023 | Includes bibliographical references and index.
Identifiers: LCCN 2023013562 | ISBN 9781476688343 (paperback : acid free paper) ∞
ISBN 9781476647012 (ebook)
Subjects: LCSH: Negro leagues—History. | African American baseball players—Statistics. | Baseball players—United States—Statistics. | Baseball—Records—United States. | Major League Baseball (Organization)—History. | Discrimination in sports—United States. | BISAC: SPORTS & RECREATION / Baseball / Statistics | SOCIAL SCIENCE / Ethnic Studies / American / African American & Black Studies
Classification: LCC GV875.N35 L44 2023 | DDC 796.357/640973—dc23/eng/20230419
LC record available at https://lccn.loc.gov/2023013562

BRITISH LIBRARY CATALOGUING DATA ARE AVAILABLE

ISBN (print) 978-1-4766-8834-3
ISBN (ebook) 978-1-4766-4701-2

© 2024 Philip Lee. All rights reserved

No part of this book may be reproduced or transmitted in any form or by any means, electronic or mechanical, including photocopying or recording, or by any information storage and retrieval system, without permission in writing from the publisher.

Front cover image: Josh Gibson (Baseball Hall of Fame, Cooperstown, NY)

Printed in the United States of America

*McFarland & Company, Inc., Publishers
Box 611, Jefferson, North Carolina 28640
www.mcfarlandpub.com*

To LARRY DOBY,
for the brilliance of his play in two different worlds,
from which flowed the idea for this book—
and for his personal kindness to me on April 19, 1997;

to WOODROW T. "WOODY" PETERSEN,
my Grandfather,
the best pitcher who ever threw me a knuckleball;

and to GILLIAN,
for everything else that matters:

to you, I dedicate this book.

A Note on Abbreviations

This book uses a number of words and phrases repeatedly, and it would be disastrous for the reading flow to spell them out in full each time they're used. The abbreviations you'll see most often are:

- **AL** American League—the junior Major League, founded 1901
- **AP** Associated Press
- **ASG** Major League All-Star Game
- **GG** Gold Glove award, given annually to the top NL and AL fielder at each position
- **GM** General Manager
- **HoF** Baseball Hall of Fame
- **MLB** Major League Baseball
- **MVP** Most Valuable Player award
- **NEA** Newspaper Enterprise Association
- **NgL** Negro Leagues, founded 1920
- **NL** National League—the original or senior Major League, founded 1876
- **OPS** On-Base Plus Slugging—a useful shorthand tool for evaluating a player's offense
- **RoY** Rookie of the Year award
- **SABR** Society for American Baseball Research
- **TSN** *The Sporting News*
- **UP/UPI** United Press International
- **WAR** Wins Above Replacement—today's most common metric for weighing a player's total value

Further abbreviations are introduced as required.

For innings pitched, ".1" means ⅓ of an inning, and ".2" means ⅔ of an inning. For example, in 1929 Satchel Paige pitched 185.2 innings, or 185⅔ innings.

Contents

A Note on Abbreviations	vi
Foreword by Larry Lester	1
Introduction: Statistical Justice	3

Part I. Arguments

1. "Disgraceful Baseball"	11
2. What Constitutes a Major League?	31
3. The Dam Trickles Open	39
4. Statistical Variance Across Leagues and Eras	54
5. Mr. James's 23 Tests	65
6. Arguments Against Statistical Integration	86
7. Re-Writing the Record Books	96
8. Josh Gibson vs. Ruthsrecord	103
9. Monte Irvin: Half in One World, Half in Another	106
10. Willard Brown: The Chance That Wasn't a Chance	109
11. Roy Campanella: The Fallacy of Equivalency	113
12. Luke Easter: The Toughest Case to Prove	125
13. Larry Doby: Five-Tool Superstar	141
14. The Greatest	147
15. My Inner Circle: The Top 73 Players in American Baseball History	157
16. Two Down, One to Go	164
17. Wrapup: What's Fair Is Fair	167
A Personal Postscript	168

Part II. Reference

18. Negro Leaguers in the Hall of Fame	173
19. Negro Leagues All-Time Teams	175
20. The Negro Leagues All-Star Register	177

21. A Proposed Major Leagues Organizational Chart	269
22. A Proposed Negro Leagues Team Roster	273
23. Negro League and Early MLB Team Failures	285
24. Negro Leaguers Who Played in the Majors	298
25. Short Notes on Diverse Subjects	305
26. A Long Note: Major League Baseball vs. the Truth	315
Acknowledgments	327
An Open Letter to Atlanta's Ownership and Management	329
Chapter Notes	331
Bibliography	345
Index	359

Foreword

by Larry Lester[*]

In the words of opera soprano singer Leontyne Price, "Accomplishments have no color"—and like Price, this narrative by Philip Lee hits all the high notes. Originally from Minnesota but now a citizen of Great Britain, Lee holds three University diplomas with top honors and has won several essay contests. With a conversational rather than an academic tone, Lee advances his propositions of why Black Stats Matter.

This is not a sci-fi movie about cloning White stars into Black stars, or about a parallel universe. Lee brilliantly credentials the Black inhabitants of the baseball planet. As a mega fan of big-game Bill James's sabermetric work, Lee takes us on an unprecedented connect-the-dots journey.

Let's note that the Major Negro Leagues employed the same rules as the Major White Leagues. Both ordered their gloves, caps and uniforms from Rawlings, Spalding or Wilson and their bats from the Louisville Slugger factory. What's more, their teams played on the same diamonds in Comiskey Park, Forbes Field, Griffith Stadium, the Polo Grounds and Yankee Stadium, among other parks. They shared fundamentally the same script, in other words—there was just a different cast of characters, some of whom were a shade darker than the hide of a dirty baseball.

The "What Constitutes a Major League?" chapter in particular is an eye opener, as Lee reveals how historians accommodate several oddities and snafus in early baseball—fielders with mirrors, hidden baseballs in the outfield grass, walks counted as hits, non-regulation bats and gloves—that, were they part of Black baseball, might be cited as evidence of less-than-major-league quality. (He argues that the Union Association and the American Association are more accurately described in just that way.) It is here that Lee offers the most compelling analysis of the statistical anomalies of the white leagues before the turn of the century.

The selected what-if profiles of Monte Irvin, Willard "Home Run" Brown, Roy Campanella, Larry Doby and Luke Easter provide more unanswered truths as to what might have been if racial barriers never existed. The compiled testimonials about the greatness of Luke Easter's batting prowess are alone worth the price of the book.

Perhaps Lee's most controversial essay is about Roy Campanella, in which he

---

[*]*Author, historian, and chairman of SABR's Negro Leagues Research Committee. www.LarryLester42.com*

challenges the legitimacy of Major League Equivalencies (MLEs) that value Black players at four-fifths of major league white players. A must-read.

The greatest-of-all-time chapter is more an interesting conversation than a statistical challenge for the reader. Somehow, Lee dodges Hammerin' Hank Aaron in this pool of excellence; however, a personal favorite, Wilber "Bullet Joe" Rogan, does appear in his "inner circle" of relatively underrated players.

Hopefully, Lee's premise will allow some doubters to embrace the facts and stats of the Black leagues. Talent cannot be measured by the amount of melanin in a person's skin, or the lack thereof, and Lee asks that we look not at these players' Black bodies but at their bodies of work. He provides lots of statistical models, tables and analyses for validation of the Negro Leagues' business model. Don't laugh—do the math!

Sports fans' thinking will evolve now that Negro League players have been officially recognized as major league talents, and *Black Stats Matter* will be part of the conversation and debates. Batter up!

Introduction
Statistical Justice

Let me tell you a story about the world as it is, and as I'd like it to be.

My formative years were spent in an American town whose population happened to be almost exclusively white. My otherwise conservative, backwards-looking high school was fortunate in its librarian, who ensured that his shelves were stocked with books banned routinely in other American schools. These shelves I browsed every day, often in preference to my schoolwork.

Many of these oft-banned books were written by Black Americans. The writers of the Harlem Renaissance came to obsess me; I drank in Ralph Ellison, Jean Toomer and Langston Hughes—and then I found Richard Wright, whose *Native Son* was the first book ever to hypnotize me, to transport me to another time and place as only a great book can. Later I discovered *The Ethics of Living Jim Crow* and realized the social import of Wright's work; but at the time, for me, it was just good writing.

Of Mice and Men was the wrong vessel to introduce my young mind to Steinbeck's brilliance. Once I got my hands on Ellison's *Invisible Man*, I couldn't understand why they'd taught us that Steinbeck junk (*ah, the ignorance of youth*) in preference to this visionary, hallucinatory masterpiece. It had nothing to do with Black or white; to me, *Man* was better-written than *Men*.

Looking back, I realize I'd been taught nothing—literally nothing—by or about Black writers by my WASP-centric teachers. Perhaps I'd been seeking to fill a gap in my education I didn't consciously perceive.

Besides reading, my other youthful passion was baseball. As with many fans, a major part of my love of the game was the wonder I felt for its one and a half centuries of history and continuity. Baseball talk on TV was all about modern players, so to educate myself about the game's past, I'd journey to my local library and pore through the pages of Macmillan's *Baseball Encyclopedia*. Over time, Babe Ruth and Ty Cobb became every bit as alive to me as Rickey Henderson and Cal Ripken.

I shared my enthusiasm for the achievements and numbers of these legends with my baseball-loving Grandfather, who'd seen them all in the flesh. I knew he'd been a semi-pro pitcher, a damn good one too, but imagine my awe when I learned (not from him—he was too modest to tell the tale) that he'd struck out Ted Williams in a World War II inter-service game. Ted freaking Williams!

In my reading I'd occasionally stumble across a player named Josh Gibson, but the *Encyclopedia* had no statistics for him—which, in baseball terms, was akin to saying he'd never existed. Satchel Paige I knew as a verbal wit—I loved "Don't look back, something might be gaining on you," and "Keep the juices flowing by jangling gently as you move," which appealed to my sense of the absurd the same way that Monty Python did—but when I looked him up in the trusty *Encyclopedia*, his Major League numbers didn't seem that impressive.

And then I discovered the Negro Leagues, and another hidden world was opened to my view. As with the writers of the Harlem Renaissance, the culture that surrounded me had taught me nothing about this vital facet of American history.

I took to wearing a Homestead Grays cap everywhere I went. And one day, as I was out for a stroll, a Black man told his friends, in a stage whisper I could easily hear: "Hey look, it's a white dude with a Grays cap."

My first instinct was to say, "What's wrong with a Grays cap? They were the most dominant team in baseball history, nine pennants in a row, and Josh Gibson and Buck Leonard were the Babe Ruth and Lou Gehrig of the Negro Leagues." (The numbers weren't available then to back up that last assertion, but Negro League veterans all said it, and I assumed it was true.)

But I hesitated: maybe it *was* weird, me being a white dude and all, to be sporting a Grays cap. Maybe it was culturally appropriative.

And then I thought: No, because I've seen plenty of Black dudes wearing Yankees caps, and in their glory days the Yanks were whiter than snow.

In the world as I'd like it to be, Ellison and Steinbeck are both taught in American high schools, Grays caps and Yankees caps are worn by Black dudes and white dudes alike, and when talk turns to baseball, Gibson springs to mind as readily as Ruth.

My goal in writing this book is to make the greats of the Negro Leagues come to life for a new generation of fans, not through their biographies—others have done this better than I could—but through their numbers, just as Ruth and Williams came to life for me as a boy. I want to see these diamond greats remembered with the same sense of awe as the greats of the Majors, celebrated in the same breath, woven co-equally into the warp and weft of our society.

* * *

More than in any other sport, numbers are the language of baseball. The mathematical analysis of baseball, dubbed "sabermetrics" by Bill James, dominates media and public discussion of the game. Who deserves the MVP Award? Who belongs in the All-Star Game? Are the right players in the Hall of Fame? These debates always center around numbers.

Black stars who played before 1947 have until now been excluded entirely from these discussions—and that's not right. As John Thorn and Pete Palmer observe, "Baseball may be loved without statistics, but it cannot be understood without them. Statistics are what make baseball a sport rather than a spectacle; what make its past worthy of our interest as well as its present."[1]

William Brashler notes that "even in a sport like baseball, where statistics are kept and memorized with stupefying fastidiousness, records of the Negro leagues were haphazardly assembled if at all…. So-called official eyes were never trained on the Negro Leagues, a blindness which did not say that the game or its stars didn't exist, just that they didn't count for very much."²

In declaring on December 16, 2020, that the Negro Leagues would at long last be recognized as major leagues, organized baseball took an enormous step towards acknowledging that the Negro Leagues and its stars *do* count. But this step hasn't been met with universal approval or agreement.

The opinion generally expressed in baseball circles for many years has been that while the top Negro Leaguers could have starred in any league, most NgL players were not quite the equivalent of their Major League counterparts; that the Negro Leagues were closer in quality to, say, triple-A or Japanese baseball than to the Majors. A representative example of this opinion was offered in 2017 by former Hall of Fame researcher Eric Enders: "The Negro Leagues are variously described as anywhere between Nippon Pro Baseball and AA quality. That would put them in the range of 0.75–0.90 [75 percent to 90 percent of the quality] of MLB. I suspect the truth is they come in at both ends of this spectrum at different times in history." This belief continues to cast its pall over perceptions of the Negro Leagues.³

Some commentators posit that to merge incomplete NgL records with (supposedly) complete MLB records is an insult to Black players excluded from the Majors. "Baseball should have taken the honest road," argues ESPN's Howard Bryant, "which would be to carry its stain [of segregation] and leave the tattered, piecemeal records of the various Negro Leagues as a historical reminder of its own destructiveness." Unfortunately, this argument can also be read to infer that inequality then necessitates inequality now. "Josh Gibson should not be acknowledged as a major league batting champ," writes Bryant, "because Josh Gibson never played in the major leagues. His statistics were never considered on par with the big leagues because Major League Baseball did not respect the institution of the Negro Leagues."⁴

Others cite the inferiority of NgL record-keeping as justification for opposing statistical combination. Cory Franklin writes, "Negro League players could never have been major leaguers, not because of talent but because the very racism that kept them outside the major leagues means their statistics cannot be retrofitted…. Player records were an afterthought and poorly maintained. It has taken baseball archivists years to recreate these statistics, which are admittedly incomplete and often inaccurate. They can't be simply grafted on to MLB records, no more than we could listen to the sound of cornetists Chet Baker (white) and King Oliver (Black) playing together."⁵

Still others bemoan the discarding of unrecorded games and unofficial barnstorming contests from Negro Leaguers' résumés. "If we simply say that Josh Gibson and the Yankees' Tony Lazzeri each hit 18 homers in 1933," writes Owen Poindexter, "we erase both whatever Gibson homers were not recorded and the institutionalized segregation that kept the two from playing on the same fields against the same players. Meanwhile, it's easier to trust Lazzeri's total…. Deeming certain incomplete numbers 'official' puts a stamp of certainty on these stats that can't possibly exist, and it risks *diminishing* mythic heroes like Gibson in the process."⁶

The core argument of this book is that **Negro League statistics from 1920 to 1948 are 100 percent equivalent to Major League statistics from 1876 to today.**

It's my purpose to convince you, the reader, through a combination of contemporary evidence, sequential reasoning, and a sense of what's right and just, that the players and numbers of the Negro Leagues should be regarded as Major in precisely the same way that we regard the players and numbers of the National and American Leagues.

* * *

In their 1981 book ranking the 100 greatest ballplayers of all time, Lawrence Ritter and Donald Honig lamented their inability to include Negro League players: "There is no doubt that a book purporting to represent the greatest ballplayers of all time should include them…. In their cases we are unable to document what we know to be true."[7]

John Thorn and Pete Palmer expressed similar regrets in 1984 when ranking the 200 greatest players: "Alas, their feats were recorded in fragmentary fashion."[8]

"When you discuss Negro Leaguers," wrote Rob Neyer in 2000, "it's not easy to distinguish the great from the merely good. There simply isn't much statistical evidence regarding Negro League players. The teams didn't play nearly as many official league games as the white major leaguers did, and some of the stats are missing even from the games that did count."[9]

"The fascination of player rankings," observed Bill James in 2001, "is that, if you work meticulously through the arguments, you can achieve the illusion of great accuracy. If we were to try to mix Ray Dandridge, Oliver Marcell, and Newt Joseph in with Clete Boyer, Ron Santo, and George Brett we would not only be unable to sustain the illusion of great accuracy, we would destroy it such as it exists now."[10]

These words were valid when written, because the numbers weren't available; they lay hidden in box scores buried in the archives of newspapers that had long since gone out of print. But today this obstacle no longer exists. Thanks to the efforts of the tireless researchers at *seamheads.com*, we have objective, verified numbers for the whole of the period 1920–1948—numbers that can be used as a basis for comparison and analysis.

Negro League players can no longer be called, in the parlance of Mr. Ellison, invisible men. When John Holway began his groundbreaking research in 1970, the Hall of Fame library held "one thin manila folder marked 'Negro,'" as Holway remembered. "In America's national baseball library, half the history of baseball was missing!" But today there are hundreds of books on the Negro Leagues and on individual players. Thirty-three Negro League players, executives and pioneers, plus 10 men who played in both the Negro Leagues and the Majors, are enshrined in the Baseball Hall of Fame.[11]

Yet the invisibility of their achievements is still cemented in custom and practice. As Eric Garcia McKinley observes, "The history of baseball statistics is enmeshed in the history of race in baseball…. [*The Official Encyclopedia of Baseball*] covered the Negro Leagues in the section 'Outside Professional Baseball.' They fit the Negro leagues in between sandlot play and softball…. Later editions relegated discussion of Negro Leagues to a 'Features' section. Doing so cast them as novelties—located side-by-side with essays on spitball pitchers and players who wore glasses."[12]

To frame the issue in harsh and deliberately jarring terms, Major League stats have been at the front of the bus, and Negro League stats have been at the back.

The painstaking compilation of Major League statistics by hand, as practiced by a handful of pioneering sabermetricians in the 1970s, revolutionized the record-keeping of the game, and in time revolutionized the game itself. The work done by Seamheads.com and now embraced by Baseball Reference.com, the premier provider of baseball's historical numbers, has the potential to initiate a second revolution: a revolution of statistical justice, wherein the great Black players of bygone years stand shoulder to shoulder with their white peers, and each new generation of fans marvels at the exploits of Gibson, just as they do at the exploits of Ruth.

* * *

To date, Negro Leagues commentary and analysis has been based mostly on numbers and stories conveyed by word of mouth. Rob Neyer sums up the problem: "You'll often hear that so-and-so hit 73 home runs in a single season, but those big numbers always include games against all competition: semi-pro teams, amateur teams, whatever."[13]

Negro League teams played far more exhibition games than official league contests. Josh Gibson's Hall of Fame plaque credits him with "almost 800 home runs." Hilton Smith's plaque claims that he's "credited with 20 or more wins in each of 12 seasons with the Kansas City Monarchs" and cites "a near-perfect 25–1 mark in 1941." Such numbers are anecdotal; they have little or no hard statistical evidence behind them. Proper evaluation of Negro Leaguers can't be based on figures like these.

We shouldn't blame the plaque makers; they did the best they could with the information they had, which wasn't much. But today we live in an age awash in information. In this book (with rare exceptions that are scrupulously noted), only inter-league statistics from 1920 to 1948, researched and verified by Seamheads, are used for comparison and analysis.

A further critique from Mr. Neyer: "If you must resort to hundreds of hours of socio-economic and demographic research to justify a player's Hall of Fame qualifications, something's wrong." I agree 100 percent. A major purpose of this book is to move discussion of the Negro Leagues from an anecdotal to an analytical level, from stories to stats.[14]

I'll use a variety of methods to *prove* that Negro Leaguers were professionals in every sense of the word—that they were in fact more professional, and by far, than entire leagues whose numbers are enshrined in the Major League canon. I'll cite plenty of reasons in support of, and plenty of evidence for, the assertion that the Negro Leagues were Major League Baseball's peer in every respect.

We'll examine the origins of what I call statistical segregation, a purposefully provocative descriptor of a shameful practice. We'll see how it came to pass that three generations of ballplayers were excluded from Major League playing fields—and from Major League record books. We'll see how the post–1947 dismantling of the color line was willfully delayed, and tell the stories of players whose historical image has been suppressed by segregation's messy aftermath. Heroes will be praised, villains shamed.

"Baseball people generally are allergic to new ideas," wrote Branch Rickey; "we are slow to change." True combination of Major and Negro League statistics will have many ramifications for the way we look at the history of the game. Changes will be made to the record books—changes that will likely encounter resistance from traditionalists. Well, Jackie Robinson encountered resistance from traditionalists too.[15]

* * *

Before we plunge headlong into the specifics of *why* Major League and Negro League statistics should be fully integrated, it might be instructive to review *how* they became unstuck in the first place: how the Major Leagues became the Caucasian Leagues, and how Black players were forced to play in a separate (though ultimately equal) league of their own.

We'll begin the journey where baseball segregation began: with the sordid maneuverings of a talented, famous, and morally corrupt nineteenth-century superstar by the name of Anson.

Part I

ARGUMENTS

1

"Disgraceful Baseball"

Adrian "Cap" Anson's Hall of Fame plaque describes him as the "greatest hitter and greatest National League player-manager of [the] 19th century." He won four batting titles, was the first player to reach 3,000 hits, and at the time of his retirement was the all-time leader in games, at-bats, runs scored, hits, and doubles. Even today, over a century after his retirement, he ranks fourth in runs batted in. He helped introduce numerous innovations to the game, including, on May 20, 1880, the first-ever use of a pitching rotation. No player prior to Ruth was as universally revered, and no player before Ruth was more instrumental in securing baseball's place as America's national pastime.

That's the good bit. Depending on which historian you believe, Anson was also the principal architect of segregation in baseball. Or not.

Pioneering Negro Leagues historian Robert Peterson, for instance, wrote that "Anson's animus towards Negroes was strong and obvious. But that he had the power and popularity to force Negroes out of baseball almost singlehandedly ... is to credit him with more influence than he had, or for that matter, than he needed. For it seems clear that a majority of professional baseball players ... opposed integration in the game."[1]

In the years since Anson did (or didn't) lead the charge in forcing Black players from the field, a debate has raged among historians regarding his degree of culpability for this tremendous moral crime. One means of examining the question is to chronologize the key events of the times through the lens of contemporary evidence, with particular focus on a man whose path intertwined regularly with Anson's, much to his sorrow: Moses "Fleetwood" Walker.

Prelude to Jim Crow Baseball

Even before the 1871 formation of the National Association (precursor to the National League), a de facto ban on Black players was observed throughout baseball's higher levels. In December 1867 the Philadelphia Pythians, one of the early all–Black baseball clubs, sent their vice-president Raymond Burr (no relation) to apply for membership at the annual general meeting of the National Association of Base Ball Players (NABBP). Burr was allowed neither to argue his case nor to file a formal membership application.

Through nuanced verbiage, the official report of the meeting denied even the presence of a Black team representative: "It is not presumed by your committee that any club *who have applied* are composed of persons of color, or any portion of them; and the recommendations of your Committee in this report are based upon this view, and they unanimously report against the admission of any club which may be composed of one or more colored persons." (Emphasis mine.)[2]

In defense of the NABBP's logic in turning away the Pythians (alone among 266 applicant clubs), the *DeWitt Base Ball Guide for 1868* claimed that "if colored clubs were admitted there would be in all probability, some division of feeling, whereas, by excluding them no injury could result to anybody." In the language of the *Guide*, "colored" people were not "anybody."[3]

As Supreme Court Chief Justice Robert Taney had written nine years earlier in his astonishing *Dred Scott* decision, Black Americans were "regarded as beings of an inferior order, and altogether unfit to associate with the white race either in social or polit-

Adrian "Cap" Anson, the famed 19th-century player-manager who was also, unfortunately, a man of influence within the game (Jefferson R. Burdick Collection, Metropolitan Museum of Art).

ical relations, and so far inferior that they had no rights which the white man was bound to respect.... No one of that race had ever migrated to the United States voluntarily [*sic*]; all of them had been brought here as articles of merchandise [*sic*].... It is obvious that they were not even in the minds of the framers of the Constitution when they were conferring special rights and privileges upon the citizens.... It is impossible to believe that these rights and privileges were intended to be extended to them.... [The 'African race'] is not, by the institutions and laws of the State, numbered among its people."[4]

Such thinking permeated white American society in this era. The fledgling game of "base ball" was no exception.

In the spring of 1878, a 20-year-old Black position player and pitcher named John "Bud" Fowler began a 22-year odyssey through organized (i.e., white) baseball. The focus of this narrative is the triumph of Jim Crow in the Major Leagues, so while Fowler's life is worthy of a book in and of itself, I won't recount his story in detail here, though he does reappear in the narrative. For our purposes it's sufficient to note that Fowler, and not Jackie Robinson, made the first-ever appearance by a Black man in organized baseball.

1. "Disgraceful Baseball"

The peripatetic Bud Fowler, who as the earliest known Black professional traveled throughout the country in pursuit of a career, moving from team to team whenever his race wore out his welcome (National Baseball Hall of Fame and Museum, Cooperstown, N.Y.).

The only Black player known to have appeared in a Major League game prior to 1884 did so through subterfuge. A Brown University student named William Edward White, once a slave but now passing in society as a white man, appeared for the National League's Providence Grays on June 21, 1879, as a substitute for the injured Joe Start. He hit a single in four at-bats, stole two bases and scored a run, and vanished back into the mists of obscurity.

In August 1881, Moses "Fleetwood" Walker, a law student who caught for Oberlin College's baseball squad, played several games with the Cleveland Whites, a semi-professional team fielded by the White Sewing Machine Company. When the team arrived in Louisville, Kentucky, in the early morning hours of August 21 prior to a game against the Eclipse baseball squad, the Saint Cloud Hotel turned Walker away; before the game itself, "players of the Eclipse Club objected to Walker playing on account of his color."[5]

As this is the first recorded instance of racial prejudice preventing a player from taking the field in organized baseball, it's worth recounting in detail. Per the August 22 *Louisville Commercial*:

> Louisville is the first city whose base ball club has refused to allow [Walker] to play. He is well educated and probably more intelligent than sixteen out of the eighteen players. His parents are highly respectable and wealthy citizens of Cleveland.... When the [Whites] club arrived they were informed that he could not play in the games here. Yesterday West, the

William Edward White, the first Black man to play Major League baseball (courtesy *Brown Daily Herald*).

first baseman, began at catcher, but one inning was sufficient to demonstrate that he could not catch.... The crowd raised a yell for "Walker," and, after much persuasion, he came out.... A member of the Eclipse players [second baseman Fred Pfeffer] left the grounds and refused to play if the "objectionable Negro" was allowed to stay. After much talk it was agreed that he should not play, and he started for his coat and collar, of which he had divested himself upon entering the field. He had about reached them when Charles Fuller rushed up and endeavored to eject him summarily from the park.

Presumably, Mr. Fuller tried to eject Fleet from the park by physical force. The crowd seems to have been generally on Walker's side—but in this era, in this city, he could not have defended himself from Fuller without risk of being lynched. Fortunately,

> Some gentlemen standing near interfered and prevented this, so [Walker] took a seat among the crowd, and watched the game throughout.

The August 22 account of events in the white-owned *Courier-Journal* gives insight into the *lack* of bias faced by Walker, on the field, from the fans, and from the local press:

Moses "Fleetwood" Walker was Major League Baseball's second Black player, though he may be as well remembered for the events that ended his short-lived big league career and established the color line in baseball.

Walker ... has earned the reputation of being the best amateur catcher in the Union [League]. He has played against the League clubs, and in many cases with other white clubs, without protest.... As he passed before the grand stand, he was greeted with cheers, and from the crowd rose cries of "Walker, Walker!".... When it was seen that he was not to play, the crowd cheered heartily and very properly hissed the Eclipse club.... If Walker had caught, it is probable the Eclipse would have been defeated.... The Clevelands acted foolishly in playing. They should have declined to play unless Walker was admitted and entered suit for gate money and damages. They could have made their point because it was understood that Walker was catcher, and no rules provide for the rejection of players on account of "race, color, or previous condition of servitude" [the language of the 15th Amendment, ratified 11 years earlier]. The crowd was anxious to see Walker play, and *there was no social question concerned*. [Emphasis mine.]

That's an important event, an event we can't overlook when discussing the road to baseball segregation—but it's equally important to note that there's no record of any on-field racist acts against Walker during the next two years.

Like the Black pioneers of the 1940s and '50s who followed in his footsteps,

Walker did face discrimination at his team's hotels—but the Oberlin law student didn't take it lying down. "In certain cities the ball club visited, Fleet Walker was refused admission to hotels with the ball team, because of his color and he entered suit against several hotels for the discrimination because of his race and color."[6]

In the spring of 1882 Walker transferred from Oberlin to the University of Michigan, becoming the first Black athlete to play for any Michigan team. Like Jackie Robinson, who on July 6, 1944, accepted a court martial (which he won) by refusing to move to the back of a military bus, Walker was destined to become an integration pioneer on multiple fronts. His burgeoning baseball skills were about to carry him into professional baseball—and into contact, and conflict, with Cap Anson.

The Events of 1883–84

In mid–1883 Walker abandoned his academic career and signed as a catcher with the Northwestern League's Toledo Blue Stockings, becoming the first acknowledged Black player in high-level organized baseball. Before he could make his on-field debut, the League's executive committee met on March 14. "A motion was made by a representative from Peoria that no colored player be allowed in the league," reported the March 15 *Toledo Daily Blade*. "It is well known," continued the *Blade*, "that the catcher of the Toledo club is a colored man. Besides being a good player he is intelligent and has many friends. The motion which would have expelled him was fought bitterly and finally laid on the table [i.e., defeated]."

(References to Walker's keen intellect recur constantly in press articles of the time. This mirrors the impression Jackie Robinson made on sportswriters of his own day; for example, Stanley Woodward's *New York Herald Tribune* column for May 9, 1947, noted that Jackie's "intelligence and degree of education are far beyond that of the average ball player." Perhaps superior intelligence was a prerequisite for the men who dared to defy the color line.)

Walker's presence in the International League was regarded by the sporting press as a novelty, his skin color as a sort of disability he'd successfully overcome. "Columbus has a deaf-mute [pitcher Ed Dundon] and Cleveland a one-armed pitcher [Hugh Daly]," noted the July 22 *Sporting Life*; "Toledo a colored catcher [Walker] and Providence a deaf center fielder [the hard-of-hearing Paul Hines, who used an ear trumpet]; and yet these men can earn about $2,000 per annum apiece."

On August 10, prior to a Toledo exhibition game against the Chicago White Stockings, Chicago player-manager Cap Anson declared that his team would refuse to take the field if Walker was in the lineup. Toledo manager Charlie Morton stood his ground, retorting that he was starting Walker (who, nursing a sore hand, had been scheduled to take the day off) in right field, and warning Anson that Chicago would forfeit its share of the gate receipts if his team declined to take the field.

According to the August 11 *Daily Blade*, this is when Anson said: "We'll play this here game, but won't play never no more with the n----- in."

(There are certain words in the historical record which I must report for the sake of accuracy, but I decline to spell them out in their entirety. Doing so profits no one. I'm not judging anyone else's choice; that's just me.)

Walker started the game but, as the November 25, 1888, *Brooklyn Daily Eagle* observed, "was not in condition to play" and "retired in the first inning." The *Eagle* noted that "Anson ... is very particular about playing against respectable players who happen to be colored, [but does] not hesitate to play against the dirtiest white ball player and rough in the fraternity."

John R. Husman cites this incident as the beginning of "an open, blatant, and successful effort to bar Black players from Organized Baseball." It's perhaps more accurate to say that this was the first blow in a sustained effort by Anson, and by others who later flocked to his banner, to maintain the racist status quo.[7]

As with the incident of August 1881, the local white-owned press *defended* Walker, contrasting him sardonically with the skills, behavior, and intelligence of Anson and his crew:

> [Fleet Walker] is a gentleman and a scholar, in the literal sense.... It was not stated that Walker, being a "n-----," might contaminate the select organization of visitors, but that was the only inference to be drawn from the announcement. The New Yorks, Metropolitans, Columbus and St. Louis clubs, organizations outside of the [Northwestern] League, had played with Walker against them and had experienced no unpleasant results save as his excellent play had militated against them, but the Chicago club was of more delicate fiber, more susceptible to deleterious influences and hence could not play ... [Walker] is the superior intellectually of any man in the Chicago club. He differs from the "kicking" players in that he is a gentleman on or off the ball field.... As a ball player he is the equal of any of the visitors here yesterday. He has won the respect of all with whom he has been brought in contact.... As to the Chicago club, it is a fact not to be disputed that it contains a greater proportion of the "bum" element than any ball club in America.[8]

Walker was clearly headed for the Majors; the February 25, 1883, *Trenton Evening News* told its readers that "he has grit unsurpassed, stands up to the hottest pitching without trouble and cannot be excelled at throwing rapidly to the bases.... [He] excited wonder wherever he played." For the 1884 season he signed with the American Association's Toledo Blue Stockings, where he was joined later for four games by his brother Weldy, who had played with Fleet at Oberlin College. The year 1884 was the only one prior to 1947 in which persons who self-identified as Black played in the Major Leagues.

In March 1884, Anson's Chicago squad formally threatened to cancel their July 25 exhibition game against Toledo if Walker took the field, and insisted on a written promise that he would not do so from Charlie Morton. Chicago's Treasurer-Secretary John Brown (oh! the irony in that name!) sent a demand letter to Morton: "The players do most decisively object.... I have no desire to replay the occurrence of last season, and must have your assurance to that effort [*sic*]."[9]

Just before the game, White Stockings president and part-owner Albert Spalding wrote directly to Anson, pleading with him not to follow through on the threat to boycott; but the issue had already been rendered moot on July 12 when Fleet was benched with a fractured collarbone.

Howard W. Rosenberg, who first discovered Brown's letter, speculates that

Spalding's personal note might show that Anson was the only prominent Chicago player to stand against Walker. There's another possibility too: that Spalding recognized Anson as the ringleader, and thought that if he could bring Anson around, other objectors would fall in line. Either way, as in August 1883, all evidence points to Anson as the instigator.[10]

In Walker's Major League debut on May 1 and again on May 3—both games played, unhappily, in Louisville—

> the spectators hissed him and otherwise insulted him because he was colored…. Walker, as has been said before, is one of the most reliable men in the club, but his poor playing in a City where the color line is drawn so closely as it is in Louisville, is not to be wondered at, and should not be counted against him. Many a good player, under less aggravating circumstances than this, has become "rattled" and unable to play. It is not creditable to the Louisville management that it should permit such outrageous performances on its grounds.[11]

Like his better-known brother, Weldy Walker was both a collegian and a Major Leaguer, having played in the American Association in 1884.

Walker soldiered on in the face of increasing hostility from opponents and Southern fans—and from at least one of his teammates. He was hit by a team-high six pitches in just 42 games; his regular battery-mate Tony Mullane refused to talk to him or take signals from him, and constantly threw unannounced pitches to cross him up. "I had it in for him," Mullane told the January 11, 1919, *New York Age*. "He was the best catcher I ever worked with, but I disliked a Negro and whenever I had to pitch to him I used to pitch anything I wanted without looking at his signals…. That season he caught me and caught anything I pitched without knowing what was coming." (This from a person who the April 9, 1884, *Sporting Life* described as "a man of the most sordid nature.") Not surprisingly, Walker led all American Association catchers with 72 passed balls, most of them on pitches thrown by Mullane.

Despite this treatment, Walker played such brilliant overall defense that the same issue of the *New York Age* observed, "Toledo once had a colored man who was declared by many to be the greatest catcher of the time and greater even than his contemporary, [Hall of Famer and consensus greatest 19th century catcher William] 'Buck' Ewing."

On September 5, four supposed residents of Richmond, Virginia—signing names that never appeared on any Richmond census—wrote Morton this letter:

> DEAR SIR: We the undersigned, do hereby warn you not to put up *Walker*, the negro catcher, the evenings that you play in Richmond, as we could mention the names of 75 determined men who have sworn to mob Walker if he comes on the ground in a suit. We hope you will listen to our words of warning, so there will be no trouble; but if you do not, there certainly will be. We only write this to prevent much blood shed, as you alone can prevent.[12]

Toledo released Walker on September 22, ending his Major League career, though he continued to play in the high minors. From the perspective of playing winning baseball, Walker's release made no sense at all: the September 25 *Fort Wayne* (IN) *Daily News* opined that "to his fine work last year much of the success of the Toledo club was due none will deny." Fleet hit .263 for Toledo, the second-highest average on the team; the team's other catchers, James "Deacon" McGuire and John "Tug" Arundel, hit .185 and .085.

Walker's final appearance for Toledo on September 4 was the last by a Black player in the Majors for more than half a century.

The Events of 1886

Despite Walker's release by Toledo, the door to the Majors was not yet barred to talented Black players. On June 29, 1886, the *Trenton Daily True American* reported that "Messrs. [Charlie] Mason and [Bill] Sharsig, of the Athletic, (Phila.) were here yesterday endeavoring to engage [Cuban Giants catcher Arthur] Thomas, but he declined." (Don't be deceived by the "Cuban" prefix added to many Black team names; "Cuban" was a kind of code, a shorthand way of telling fans that a team played professional-quality Black baseball.) Thomas opted instead to jump the following year to the Baltimore Lord Baltimores of the short-lived League of Colored Base Ball Players, one of several pre–1920 attempts by Black entrepreneurs to organize viable professional leagues.

The September 8 *Sporting Life* reported that "New York has been seriously considering the engagement of [George] Stovey, Jersey City's fine colored pitcher. The question is would the [National] League permit his appearance in League championship games?"

Stovey never made it to the Majors. The key question for the purposes of this chronology is, why not? In his pioneering 1907 *History of Colored Base Ball*, Hall of Famer Sol White recounts a story which, if true, is one of the most damning indictments of Cap Anson's legacy:

> Were it not for this same man Anson, there would have been a colored player in the National League in 1887. John M[ontgomery] Ward, [outfielder and team captain] of the New York [Giants] club, was anxious to secure Geo. Stovey and arrangements were about completed for his transfer from the Newark club, when a brawl was heard from Chicago to New York. The same Anson ... made strenuous and fruitful opposition to any proposition looking to an admittance of a colored man into the National League.[13]

White's account is one of two contemporary references to the incident known today. The other is an interview with Jersey City manager Pat Powers in the February 13, 1892, *Cleveland Gazette*. Powers recounted the surrounding events in exact and convincing detail:

> During the season of 1886 ... Mike Tiernan's arm gave out, and I didn't have any one to put in the box. The next day we were to play Newark, and the championship depended on the game.... By luck I happened to think of a colored pitcher named Stovey in Trenton, a fellow with very light skin, who was playing on the Trenton team. It was my game to get him to Jersey City in time for the game. I ... went down to Stovey's house, roused him up, and got his consent to sign with Jersey City. Meanwhile some Trenton people got onto the scheme and notified the police to prevent Stovey from leaving town. I became desperate. I worked a member of "Trenton's finest" all right, and finally hired a carriage, and, amid a shower of missiles, drove Stovey to a station below, where we boarded a train for Jersey City....
>
> When I marched my men on the field the public was surprised, and Tom Day, Tom Burns, [Tommy] Tucker, [Bill] Greenwood, and [John] "Phenomenal" Smith, of the Newark team, gave me the laugh.... Stovey was put in to pitch for the home team, and dropped the Newarks out in one, two, three order. The game ended with the score 1 to 0 in Jersey City's favor, and Stovey owned the town.
>
> The same season [1886] the New York [Giants] had a fighting chance to win from Chicago, and Walter Appleton, of the New York club, was very much in favor of having Stovey sent to Chicago to pitch the last four decisive games. In fact, a deal was fixed between Appleton, the Jersey club, and Stovey to this end. Stovey had his grip packed and awaited the word, but he was not called owing to the fact that Anson had refused to play in a game with colored Catcher Walker at Toledo, and the same result was feared in Stovey's case.

It's possible, as some have argued, that Sol White's accounting of these events was wrong, and that Anson wasn't directly involved in hampering Stovey's career. But selective questioning of White's accuracy on this lone issue would seem to derive from preconceived bias; as Jerry Malloy observes, "White's text ... has withstood the scrutiny of subsequent historical research. Contemporary coverage, especially in the Black press, pretty much confirms White's version of most events and testifies to his credibility and reliability as a historian."[14]

In Walker's May 17, 1924, obituary in the *Cleveland Gazette*, Cleveland Blues treasurer George W. Howe relates that he "would [have sent] to Toledo [probably in 1884] for Fleet to catch for the local team, which sorely needed a good backstop at the time, but for objections raised by Anson of the Chicago club." Here is an instance, documented by first-person testimony, in which Anson did make "strenuous and fruitful opposition to any proposition looking to an admittance of a colored man." It would in fact have been out of character for Anson *not* to have intervened to prevent Stovey from joining the Giants.

Anson's personal intervention against Stovey seems to have been accepted as fact among white sportswriters decades before Sol White's version of events gained popular currency. (Only five original copies of *History of Colored Base Ball* are known to exist today, and the book wasn't reprinted until 1995.) In the November 1, 1945, *Sporting News*, Fred J. Bendel reported that "John Montgomery Ward, famous lawyer and shortstop, then head of the New York Giants, tried to buy Stovey. But Anson spotted the deal and blocked it." In the February 20, 1971, *Sporting News*, Bob Fowler wrote that "Anson screamed and stomped until Toledo got rid of Walker. When the New York Giants tried to purchase Stovey's contract, he fell into a swoon. Shamelessly, baseball placated him."

Even if Anson didn't intervene personally, Powers's account confirms an unpleasant truth which Anson's defenders tend to downplay or even deny: that his public stance against Walker in 1883 and 1884 was sufficient, in and of itself, to deter Major League owners from signing Black ballplayers.

When Stovey instead joined Walker on the Newark Little Giants roster in November, the March 21, 1887, *Baltimore Sun* predicted, "Geo. W. Stovey, pitcher of this year's Newarks, is a colored man. There is a prospect that the Newarks and Jersey City clubs may get into a fight over him." This sad prediction was more prescient than its author could have dreamed.

The Decisive Events of 1887–88

Black participation in high-level nineteenth-century baseball reached its apex in 1887. George Stovey, Bud Fowler, and four other Black players joined Walker on International League rosters. Every National League team played at least one exhibition game against IL teams with one or more Black players on their rosters.

On April 7, the New York Giants and Newark Little Giants met at the Polo Grounds in an exhibition contest, with Walker and Stovey both appearing for Newark. The April 8 *Newark Daily Journal* reported that Giants manager Jim Mutrie "made an offer to buy the 'Spanish Battery' [i.e., Stovey and Walker], but [Newark] Manager [Charley] Hackett informed him they were not on sale" (indelicate phrasing to say the least). Here is evidence that Walker was playing at Major League levels three years after his release by Toledo—and that despite a growing wellspring of prejudice, the door to the Majors was potentially open to Black players as late as April 1887.[15]

Violence now reared its ugly head on the ballfield. Baseball tactics were still in flux in these formative years. Anson's teammate Michael "King" Kelly is credited with many innovations, both on and off the field: he was the first player to be routinely sought for his autograph, the first to publish an autobiography, and the first to achieve fame outside baseball, pursuing a vaudeville career during the off-season. But "Kelly's greatest invention," wrote future Hall of Famer Johnny Evers in the May 4, 1910, *Pittsburgh Press*, "was the famous 'Chicago slide,' now used by every good base runner. This slide, it is conceded by the veterans of Anson's famous White Stocking infield, was the invention of Kelly, although every man on the team used it with great success until it became the trademark of the White Stockings." His hook slide into second base was so iconic that in 1889, "Slide, Kelly, Slide" became the first recording to be recognized as a #1 hit song; a movie of the same title was released in 1927.

While there's no evidence that Kelly shared Anson's overt racism, his signature move did have sinister roots. In the March 23, 1889, *Sporting News* an un-named player described the violence that Black players endured in IL play, including the vicious precursor to Kelly's slide:

> While I myself am prejudiced against playing in a team with a colored player, still I could not help pitying some of the poor Black fellows that played in the International League. [Bud] Fowler used to play second base with the lower part of his legs incased [sic] in wooden guards. He knew that about every player that came down to second base on a steal had it in for him,

and would, if possible, throw the spikes into him. He was a good player, but left the base every time there was a close play in order to get away from the spikes.

I have seen him muff plays intentionally, so that he would not have to try to touch runners, fearing that they might injure him. [Frank] Grant [who also wore wooden shin guards] was the same way. Why, the runners chased him off second base. They went down so often trying to break his legs or injure him, that he gave up his infield position the latter part of [1887] and played right field....

About half the pitchers try their best to hit these colored players when at the bat.... One of the International League pitchers last season pitched for Grant's head all the time. He never put a ball over the plate, but sent them straight and true, right at Grant.

Infielder Ned Williamson confirmed the origins of the Chicago slide in an October 24, 1891, *Sporting Life* interview:

> No, ball players do not burn with a desire to have colored men on their team. It is, in fact, the deep seated objection that most of them have for an Afro-American professional player that gave rise to the "feet first" slide.... The haughty Caucasians of the [IL] were willing to permit d-----s to carry water to them or guard the bat bag, but it made them sore to have the name of one in the batting list. They made a cabal against [Frank Grant] and incidentally introduced a new feature into the game. The players of opposing teams made it their special business in life to "spike" this brunette Buffalo. They would tarry at second when they might easily have made third, just to toy with the sensitive shins of this second baseman. The poor man played in two games out of five perhaps; the rest of the time he was on crutches. To give the frequent spiking of the d---- an appearance of accident the "feet-first" slide was practiced. The negro got wooden armor for his legs.... [White players] filed their spikes and the first man at second generally split the wooden half cylinders. The colored man seldom lasted beyond the fifth inning, as the base-runners became more expert. The practice survived long after the second baseman made his last trip to hospital. And that's how Kelly learned to slide.

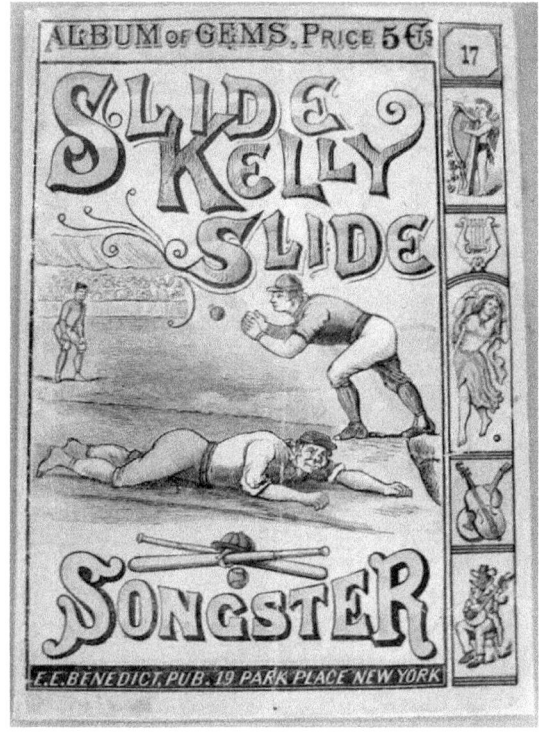

Sheet music for "Slide, Kelly, Slide," which celebrates the feet-first slide popularized by Mike "King" Kelly. According to Kelly's teammate Ned Williamson, the slide originated in the International League as a means of injuring Black second baseman Frank Grant (courtesy Oak Knoll Books).

Violence against Black players took many forms. The April 11, 1891, *Sporting Life* reported that in an un-dated 1887 game, "when [Ed] Crane [of the Toronto Canucks] went down to steal second Grant got squarely in front of him. Crane was going like the wind. He ducked his head after measuring the distance and caught Grant squarely in the pit of the stomach with his shoulder. [Grant] went up in the air and

A movie poster for *Slide, Kelly, Slide* (MGM, 1927) includes Hall of Famer Harry Carey.

when he came down he looked as if he had been in a threshing machine. They took him home on a stretcher, and he didn't recover for three weeks. 'The crowd came near to mobbing us,' said [Toronto manager Charley] Cush[man], 'but there were no more d-----s in the League after that.'" (Cushman's name will recur in unflattering contexts as we proceed.)

White players also openly sabotaged their Black teammates. On May 26, under the headline "DISGRACEFUL BASEBALL," the *Toronto World* remarked that three of Robert Higgins's teammates seemed to deliberately muff plays in his May 25 pitching debut, leading to a crushing 28–8 defeat: "The infield of the [Syracuse] Stars … are from the Southern League, and dislike to play with colored folks. For no other reasons than these can the wretched work of [Charles "Lefty"] Marr, [Henry "Red"] Bittman and [Ollie] Beard be accounted for in yesterday's game. They seemed to want the Torontos to knock Higgins out of the box, and time and again they fielded so badly that the home team were enabled to secure many hits after the side should have been retired. In several instances these players carried out their plans in a most glaring manner…. The unsuccessful efforts of [Higgins] to throw out [Mike Slattery] at second were most amusing. No less than ten times did Higgins make the effort … but Bittman and Beard were not disposed to assist Higgins to any great extent."

The next day, ignoring (or excusing) the white players' undermining of their teammate, the *World* ran a more pointed headline: "The Colored Ball Players Distasteful." The accompanying editorial twisted the knife: "A number of colored players are now in the International League, and to put it mildly their presence is distasteful to the other players.... The chief reason for [John] McGlone's refusal to sign with Buffalo this season is that he objected to playing with Grant." McGlone was a career .195 hitter, Grant a future Hall of Famer—but it was Grant who the *World* considered "distasteful."

On June 1, *Sporting Life* asked its readers: "How far will this mania for engaging colored players go? At the present rate of progress the International League might ere many moons change its name to 'Colored League.'" With schizophrenic racist logic, the same issue breathlessly reported Binghamton's signing of "Another Colored Phenomenon," William Renfro, who "come[s] splendidly recommended and may prove a valuable acquisition." On June 2, Renfro lost his pitching debut 7–6, an 11-inning complete game in which he allowed zero earned runs; every run against him resulted from errors committed by his teammates. The June 2 *Binghamton Daily Leader* noted that "the 'Bings' did not support Renfroe [*sic*] yesterday, and many think that the shabby work was intentional."

On June 5, Doug Crothers and Hank Simon refused to sit for a Syracuse team portrait with Bob Higgins. In reporting on the event, the June 11 *Sporting News* opined that "a new trouble has just arisen in the affairs of certain of the baseball associations. It seems to have done more damage to the International Association than to any other we know of. We refer to the importation of colored players into the ranks of that body." On June 9 Renfro managed to eke out a 12–8 win against the all-Black Cuban Giants, despite his Binghamton teammates allowing all but one of the Giants' eight runs to score on errors.

In contrast to their general condemnation of Black players in high-level baseball, the white press stood solidly behind Walker, whose intelligence and charisma seem to have overawed many a sportswriter. In replying to an anonymous *Hamilton* (Ontario) *Spectator* writer who referred to Walker as "the c--- catcher," the June 18 *Sporting News* editorialized that "the man who wrote it is without doubt Walker's inferior in education, refinement and manliness."

On June 27, William Dilworth and Milt "Buck" West asked Binghamton management for their release, saying they didn't want to play with Renfro and Fowler. After that day's game, West convinced eight other players to sign a petition stating their refusal to play "if the colored players, who have been the cause of all our trouble, are not released at once."[16]

Fowler asked for his own release on June 30, doubtless under tremendous pressure; both he and Renfro were let go on July 7. Binghamton's top brass may not have wanted Fowler around, but they had sufficient respect for his abilities to make him agree not to sign with any other IL club as a condition of his release. The *Binghamton Daily Leader*, which had reacted to Renfro's June 9 victory over the Cuban Giants by suggesting "watermelons on the home plate" for "the simmerian [*sic*] visitors," celebrated the pair's departure with its July 13 headline: "Gone c---s—Fowler and Renfroe [*sic*]."[17]

On the morning of July 14, International League owners met secretly at Genesee House in Buffalo, and by a 6-to-4 vote agreed to ban new contracts with Black players. Owners fielding exclusively white teams voted in favor, while those with at least one Black player voted against. The Binghamton team, which had released Fowler and Renfro seven days earlier, cast the decisive vote in favor of segregation.

The July 15 *Newark Daily Journal* reported: "The question of colored players was freely discussed. Several representatives declared that many of the best players in the league are anxious to leave on account of the colored element, and the board finally directed Secretary [C.D.] White to approve of no more contracts with colored men."

The *Daily Journal* recognized the historic importance of this meeting in its headline "The Color Line Drawn in Base Ball"—but in reality the line had been in place since at least December 1867, and now, in the face of its stiffest-ever challenge, owners sought to reaffirm the segregationist status quo.

Later that same day, Anson's explicit objections forced Walker and Stovey to sit out Newark's game against Chicago. Anson had sent a telegram to Newark manager Charlie Hackett, stating that Chicago wouldn't play if Stovey and Walker took the field.

"Stovey was to have pitched for Newark, but he complained of sickness," claimed the July 15 *Newark Evening News*, "and so [Mickey] Hughes was substituted." On July 17 the *Newark Sunday Call* exploded this sham alibi: "Stovey was expected to pitch in the Chicago game. It was announced on the ground[s] that he was sulking, but it has since been given out that Anson objected to a colored man playing. If this be true, and the crowd had known it, Mr. Anson would have received hisses instead of the applause that was given him when he first stepped to the bat." The July 19 *Toronto World* confirmed Anson's instigation of the events of the day: "Hackett intended putting Stovey in the box against the Chicagos, but Anson objected to him playing on account of his color."

July 14, 1887, then, is the day that Jim Crow was firmly and irrevocably entrenched in organized baseball—and as with the 1883 and 1884 incidents that started the ball rolling downhill, Cap Anson was the prime instigator of the key on-field event of the day. His refusal to allow his team to play if Black opponents took the field transformed the owners' de jure ban on future contracts into a de facto ban on Black players already under contract.

The night before a scheduled September 12 exhibition game between the St. Louis Browns and the Cuban Giants, eight St. Louis players delivered a petition to owner Chris Von der Ahe declaring that they did "not agree to play against negroes tomorrow. We will cheerfully play against white people at any time, and think, by refusing to play, we are doing what is right." One of the signatories, center fielder Curt Welsh, had played with the Walker brothers in Toledo three years earlier without objection—but now, in 1887, open displays of racist hostility had become normalized. Von der Ahe cancelled the game; segregation won the day.[18]

George Stovey quit the IL for the lower-level New England League after 1887, despite setting a league record that stands to this day with 34 wins. Stovey's rationale for departure is not recorded, but it's safe to assume his exit wasn't voluntary.[19]

On May 23, 1888, came an incident that revealed the degree of pressure and fear now felt by Black ballplayers when they entered an International League ballpark. No single reporter seems to have captured all the events of the day, and newspaper accounts contradict each other on numerous small details—for instance, it's unclear whether the incident happened in the third or fourth inning—so any reconstruction is necessarily somewhat speculative. I'm happy to be contradicted by any scholar with superior documentation, but for this book I've done my best, using the words of dueling reporters' accounts:

> [Joe] Battin, the Syracuse third baseman, called upon Umpire [Billy] Hoover to remove a number of boys and men who had got over the east fence adjoining the grand stand.... Battin had heard one of the crowd call out, "Look at that negro," referring to Walker, who was sitting on the visiting players' bench [judging by Battin's actions, I'm guessing the word used was harsher than "Negro"] ... Battin insisted on having the field cleared, and Hoover called upon Manager [Charley] Cushman to do it.... Cushman ordered them out, and with them catcher Walker, who was on the Stars' bench without uniform.... [Walker] did not relish the treatment, and after getting off the field got into a wordy war with the Toronto manager, which was subsequently renewed with others after Cushman had returned to the bench. The controversy between Walker and the crowd waxed hotter, and at one time it looked as if he was in danger of being assaulted.... Just outside the ball field he flourished a loaded six-chambered revolver and talked of putting a hole in some one in the crowd. He was promptly arrested.[20]

A portrait of Fleet Walker that ran in the *Waterbury* (CT) *Evening Democrat*, March 15, 1888.

Clearly, Walker, who brought a gun into this and doubtless other ballparks, now feared for his life—and judging by the actions of the fans, his fear was justified. "If the hoodlums in the Toronto audience had one-third the gentlemanly qualities that Walker possesses," insisted the May 30 *Sporting Life*, "there would never be a disturbance at ball games."

By now only three Black players were left standing in the IL—and that was too many for some. Shortly after his confrontation with Walker, the June 11 *Toronto Daily Mail* reported that Charley Cushman "is said to be engineering a scheme to have colored players ousted from the International Association. Cushman's scheme will hardly go," opined the *Mail*; "there are only three colored men in the association—Grant, of Buffalo, and Higgins and Walker, of Syracuse—and they behave themselves very nicely."

In the end, it was not Cushman but Cap Anson who delivered what was perhaps the finishing blow to the integration of high-level organized baseball when, on September 27, his vocal objections once again forced Walker to sit out against Chicago.

Anson's intolerance was by now so universally known within the sports fraternity that no national white newspaper bothered to report the incident. We know of it today thanks to reporting by local and Black-owned newspapers. "Big Anson at once refused to play the game with Walker behind the bat on account of the Star catcher's color," wrote the September 28 *Syracuse Evening Herald*; the Black-owned *Cleveland Gazette* for October 20 commented that "the big bully Anson … clings to his barbarous notions, and refused to play against a nine which has a colored member." One wonders how many similar incidents were lost to history because the white press neglected to record them.[21]

Weary of the unrelenting pressure, Robert Higgins quit the IL at the end of 1888. Frank Grant, who had hit a team-leading .346 for Buffalo, was released under threat of a team strike. Fleet Walker, uniquely supported by the white sporting press, survived the exodus and carried on for a final year; but with skills visibly eroding, he was released by Syracuse on August 23, 1889, ending the seven-year integration of high-level organized baseball.

More than 70 Black players appeared in otherwise all-white leagues in the 19th century, and Bud Fowler, a truly great ballplayer, continued to appear on mixed-race rosters with lower-level clubs as late as 1899; but the next appearance by a Black player in the high minor leagues was Jackie Robinson's Montreal Royals debut on March 17, 1946.

How the Evidence Stacks Up— and at Whom It Unerringly Points

It can't be claimed, as does Kevin B. Blackistone, that Cap Anson "erected the color barrier in baseball," or that he was "the acknowledged leader of the segregation forces already at work in the game." A de facto color line was in place long before 1883. A strong current of opinion formed against Black players' participation in the mid–1880s; this current was fed by Anson, but also by other players, owners, fans, and a national sporting press that turned against them with vehemence. There's a documented instance, predating Anson's initial outburst by two years, in which Fleet Walker was forced to withdraw from a semi-professional game due to the color of his skin. Numerous racist acts that didn't involve Anson were aimed at Walker and other Black players.[22]

But it's equally wrong to downplay Anson's role. The historical record leaves no doubt that Anson was the prime mover of the 1883 and 1884 incidents that gave momentum to the Jim Crow movement within baseball, the 1887 incident that formalized the ban against Black players, and the 1888 incident that helped drive the final nail into the coffin. Prior to Anson's actions there was no mass agitation against Black players, and—much more importantly—no recognized and respected advocate against them. Once he'd made his stance clear, violence against Black players escalated to near-lethal levels.

Anson's first public demonstration against Walker took place in October 1883. Bear in mind that the March 1883 motion to bar Blacks from the Northwestern

League was *defeated*, and that Walker was reported by the contemporary press to have "many friends" within the League fraternity.

Anson, the biggest star of his day, was unique in his willingness to act repeatedly on sentiments that others undoubtedly shared. He instigated multiple public incidents against Walker and George Stovey, intervened personally to prevent Walker's return to the Majors with the Cleveland Blues, and probably intervened to prevent Stovey from advancing to the Majors.

Baseball wasn't the only pro sport to impose color lines. From 1915 to 1937 no Black man was allowed to fight for the heavyweight boxing title; from 1934 to 1946 no Black man was allowed so much as a tryout for the National Football League. But baseball led the pack by decades. As the April 11, 1891, *Sporting Life* remarked, "Probably in no other business in America is the color line so finely drawn as in base ball. An African [sic] who attempts to put on a uniform and go in among a lot of white players is taking his life in his hands."

Fleet Walker was not only a fine ballplayer, but a brilliant and enormously complex man. Deprived of his principal source of income on the baseball diamond, he re-made himself as a successful businessman, writer, and inventor. His improvements to early motion picture cameras earned him three mechanical patents; a fourth patent was granted for his proposed improvements to US Army artillery shells.

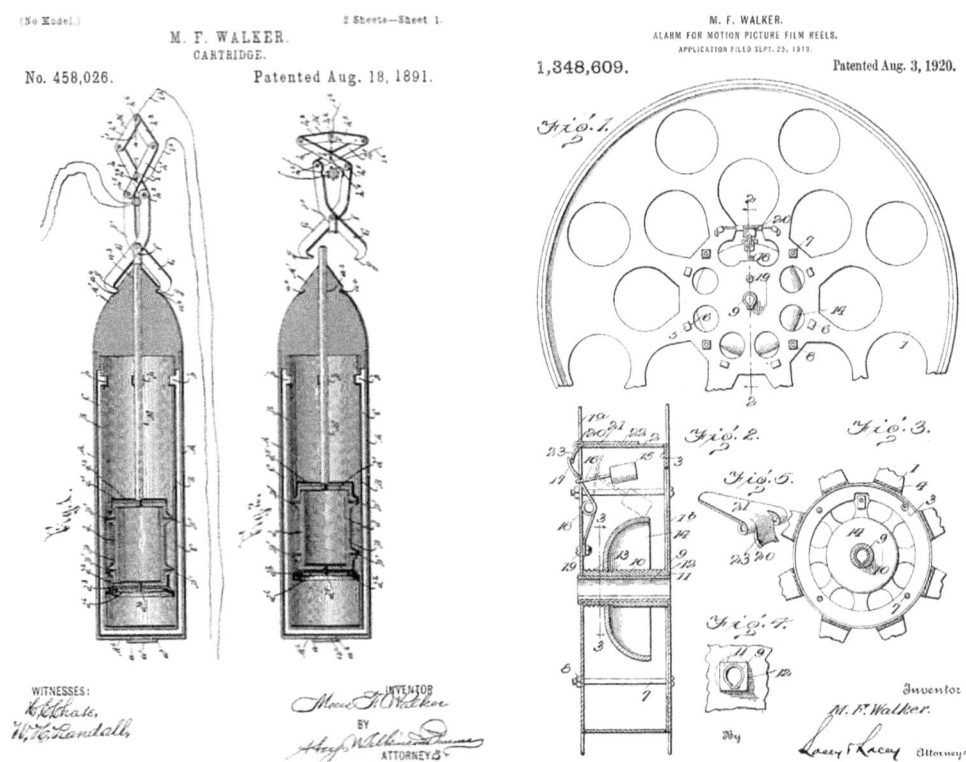

Left: An artillery shell patent granted to M.F. Walker, August 18, 1891. *Right:* One of the three motion picture camera patents granted to M.F. Walker, August 3, 1920 (both photographs United States Patent and Trademark Office).

Walker also founded and edited a short-lived newspaper devoted to Black issues, wrote a book on Black nationalism that presaged Marcus Garvey's public pronouncements by more than a decade—and served a year in prison for mail fraud. He was so well-spoken, and so well-liked and respected by people of all races, that in 1891, after killing a white man in a street brawl, he claimed self-defense and charmed his all-white jury into an outright acquittal. In 1891!

Anson, meanwhile, won election to the post of Chicago city clerk in April 1905 on the strength of his fame as a player—and, explicitly, his fame as a proud racist. Under the headline "Capt. Anson Campaigns as Foe to Race Suicide," the March 18 *Chicago Tribune* remarked that "Anson is not following the lead of the head of his ticket [Edward Dunne, subsequently elected Mayor of Chicago] and confining his speeches to municipal ownership and the street car question. The captain does not pretend to be especially well versed on these topics, and so is leaving them alone. He is devoting his oratory to the question of race suicide." The Captain's ignorance extended beyond his racial bigotry; the April 6 *Boston Globe* prophesied that "with Adrian C. Anson as city clerk of Chicago, the score will be well kept"—but his tenure, tarnished by multiple scandals, was a disaster.[23]

After the election, the Chicago wire services reported that "[Anson's] popularity personally was beyond doubt a potent help to the Democrats, who seemed to hugely appreciate his campaign statistics designed to prove that the Democracy, at least in Chicago, are the original and only genuine opponents of race suicide." Anson was far from unique among white politicians of his era in campaigning on the theme of race suicide; President Theodore Roosevelt, among others, publicly embraced the theory—but here was the Captain again, on the wrong side of history.[24]

Anson found multiple outlets to spew his race hate. His 1906 autobiography *A Ball Player's Career* makes no mention of Fleet Walker or the other Black players whose careers he helped to destroy; but Anson does relate the story of Clarence Duval.

The White Stockings' mascot Clarence Duval, whom Anson paraded about as a clown (courtesy Mastro Auctions).

Duval was what we might call today a

little person, a talented and charismatic man. Nineteenth-century American society offered few places for someone like Duval, even without his physical disadvantage; his natural refuge was entertainment; and so, he accepted a position as Cap Anson's clown.

Verona Jarbeau, the actress for whom mascot Clarence Duval "deserted" Cap Anson. Photograph by Benjamin J. Falk (Jerome Lawrence and Robert E. Lee Theatre Research Institute, Ohio State University).

> Clarence was a little d---- that I had met some time before while in Philadelphia … a little c--- whose skill in handling the baton would have put to the blush many a bandmaster of national reputation. I had togged him out in a suit of navy blue with brass buttons, at my own expense, and had engaged him as a mascot. He was an ungrateful little rascal, however, and deserted me for Mlle. Jarbeau, the actress….
>
> When I got back to the car I found the little "c---" there, and ordered him out, but the boys interceded for him…. The little c--- did not prove to be much of a mascot for Chicago that afternoon…. The contract that he was made to sign … carried such horrible penalties with it in case of desertion that it was enough to scare the little d---- almost to death…. Outside of his dancing and his power of mimicry he was, however, a "no account n-----," and more than once did I wish that he had been left behind.[25]

The idea that an ignorant bigot like Anson could lead the charge in forcing a polymath like Walker out of his chosen profession would be laughable if it hadn't actually happened. Sol White painted the man and his role quite accurately: "His repugnant feeling, shown at every opportunity, toward colored ball players, was a source of comment throughout every league in the country, and his opposition, with his great popularity and power in base ball circles, hastened the exclusion of the Black man from the white leagues."[26]

In deference to his wishes, Jackie Robinson's original Hall of Fame plaque spoke only of the brilliance of his playing career, but in 2008 the plaque was amended to add his role in shattering the color barrier that Anson fought so hard to enforce. Kevin Blackistone argues that Anson's plaque should be amended too. That's an important and necessary step in my view, an acknowledgment that's long overdue.

But were it within my power, I would go a step further.

Anson did more damage to baseball than anyone has ever done to any American sport. His venom helped deny generations of Black ballplayers their rightful places in the Major Leagues. He did more damage to baseball than the Black Sox cheaters, more than Pete Rose's gambling, more than the steroid abusers.

Perhaps Anson's place as the principal architect of baseball's greatest shame would have been taken by someone else. Perhaps. But Anson actually did it. I for one cannot forgive him for this, and if it were possible, in this age of Colin Kaepernick and George Floyd, of Charlottesville and "good people on both sides," he's the one man I would kick clean out of the Hall of Fame, gaudy statistics be damned.

2

What Constitutes a Major League?

It's commonly argued that the Negro Leagues were closer in quality to triple-A minor league baseball than to the Major Leagues. In response to that argument, let's examine the early Major Leagues—the structure Mr. Anson was so anxious to keep "pure"—with a critical eye.

In early MLB, batting and pitching statistics were compiled under laughable rules:

- From 1876 through 1886, batters could instruct the pitcher to throw a "high ball" or a "low ball." (Seriously.)
- From 1876 through 1883, pitchers weren't allowed to throw overhand.
- From 1887 through 1892, hitters could use bats with a flat side, like a cricket bat. (Imagine Babe Ruth with a flat-sided bat …)
- From 1876 through 1882, fielders could retire a batter by catching a foul ball after it bounced.
- From 1876 through 1880, rather than calling a strike on a good pitch that a batter let go past without swinging, umpires could give the batter a "warning."
- From 1876 through 1888, between five and nine balls were required for a batter to draw a walk; the number went down or up almost every year.
- In 1876, walks were counted as outs; in 1887 they were counted as hits.
- Throughout the 1870s and early 1880s, most fielders made plays with their bare hands.
- From 1876 through 1881, many games were umpired by local men hired by the home team on the day of the game.

The records of this era are often farcical. In 1876 a ball landing anywhere in fair territory was counted as a ball in play, even if it then bounced foul. Ross Barnes hit .429 that year by instructing the pitcher to throw "low balls" and then bouncing the ball from fair to foul territory. When the rule was changed in 1877, his average plummeted 157 points to .272. Despite building the whole of his success on a cheap tactic that was promptly outlawed, Barnes is credited today as the 1876 National League batting champion.

The 1887 batting championship was also awarded in dubious circumstances. For that one year only, walks were counted as hits—and by this strange rule, Cap Anson won the batting title at .421. In 1968, 81 years after the event, the Special

Baseball Records Committee changed the rule retroactively, dropping Anson's average to .347 and stripping him of the title.

In contrast to Major League Baseball's primitive, inconsistent mess, the Negro Leagues used recognizably modern rules from their first game to their last—but NgL numbers were excluded from MLB record books.

The way the early game was played on the field was equally primitive. Fielding mistakes were not just common, but expected[1]:

- On May 21, 1878, Ed Nolan of the Indianapolis Blues threw a two-hitter against the Milwaukee Grays, but barely eked out the win, 6–5, thanks to 11 Indianapolis errors and passed balls.
- In the 1885 World Series, the St. Louis Browns and Chicago White Stockings collected 102 errors in seven games, scoring 17 earned runs against 55 unearned. (St. Louis forfeited Game 2 when the team left the field to protest an umpire's ruling—and then, when they won Game 7 to create a 3–3–1 tie between the teams, they claimed they'd actually won the championship because their Game 2 forfeit somehow didn't count.)
- On June 21, 1890, the Chicago Pirates' Charles "Silver" King pitched a no-hitter against the Brooklyn Ward's Wonders—which he lost, 1–0, on eight errors by his teammates.
- On May 11, 1892, Baltimore defeated St. Louis 5–3; the May 21 *New York Clipper* remarked that "a curious feature was the fact that all of the runs scored were earned."
- On October 8, 1900, the Chicago Cubs and Cincinnati Reds combined for 25 errors in a single game.

Numerous hazards prevailed in early MLB play, from cheating opponents to self-sabotaging teammates, from over-zealous fans to unusual objects on the field:

- On June 17, 1885, John "Phenomenal" Smith's teammates, taking offense at his brash personality, deliberately wrecked his Brooklyn Grays pitching debut. Shortstop George "Germany" Smith committed seven errors in the 18–5 loss; catcher Jackie Hayes added two more errors, plus five passed balls.
- On April 29, 1887, the right fielders of the New York Giants and Philadelphia Quakers fielded their positions on an

A balls and strikes counter. In the early Major Leagues, the only constant was change (courtesy Legendary Auctions).

outdoor stage built for the play *Nero*, wearing rubber-soled shoes in case rain made the stage slippery.
- On August 12, 1887, the Philadelphia Quakers' Gus Weyhing hit what should have been a triple against Cleveland. Right fielder Bob Hogan cleverly kicked the ball into the on-field set of the play *The Fall of Babylon*, and Weyhing's triple was transformed into a ground-rule double.
- Local rules allowed fielders in some parks to go into the crowd to retrieve a batted ball. On July 20, 1894, the Pittsburgh Pirates' Elmer Smith punched several fans while trying to retrieve a ball that would win the game for the Cincinnati Reds—but was ultimately prevented from reaching the ball by a Reds fan wielding a pistol.
- Throughout the 1890s, the Baltimore Orioles employed every dirty trick in the book. They dazzled opposing fielders with mirrors. They hid spare baseballs in the outfield grass (kept long for this purpose) to throw back to the infield on close plays. They pushed, tripped, spiked, and physically held onto opposition baserunners.
- On the Fourth of July, 1900, the Philadelphia Phillies more or less deliberately threw both games of a doubleheader against the Chicago Cubs when thousands of gun-toting Cubs fans invaded Wrigley Field, loosing off volleys of live ammunition to intimidate the visitors. (It worked like a charm.)

If an over-capacity crowd showed up for an early MLB game, teams seated the overflow in the outfield—with game-altering consequences:

- On September 29, 1885, the Chicago Cubs hit five triples against the New York Giants by lofting balls into temporary seats in left and right field.
- On May 30, 1895, a huge crowd at the already diminutive Baker Bowl shrank the outfield so severely that Cincinnati right fielder Charles "Dusty" Miller was able to throw out four runners at *first base*. Sixteen doubles were hit in the game, almost all lost in the overflow crowd.
- On June 9, 1901, Cincinnati's tiny League Park was overrun by 17,000 fans. The Reds and New York Giants played a 25–13 game featuring 31 hits, including 13 doubles, mostly ground-rule. Nineteen runs were scored in one 2½-inning stretch.
- An on-field crowd probably decided the 1907 AL pennant race. On September 30, in the 14th inning of a 9–9 tie that was supposed to be the first game of a doubleheader, the Philadelphia Athletics' Harry Davis hit one into the overflow crowd in left center. Davis's hit would ordinarily have been a ground-rule double, but a policeman in the overflow impeded the Detroit Tigers' Sam Crawford as he went for the ball (accidentally or purposefully, no one knew) and the umpire called interference, placing Davis on first instead of second. Danny Murphy then hit a long single that would have driven in Davis as the winning run, had he been on second. Instead, the game was called on account of darkness as a 17-inning tie, and the second game was never played. The Tigers went on to win the AL pennant over the Athletics by a 1½-game margin.

At times, the appellation "Major League" was little more than a joke:

- On July 14, 1888, the Brooklyn Bridegrooms forfeited to the Kansas City Cowboys in the ninth inning of a 5–4 game, after a Brooklyn player overheard Cowboys manager Sam Barkley *order* substitute umpire Jim Donahue to call a Brooklyn runner out.
- On June 29, 1889, Cap Anson was allowed to swing with "a large sized fence rail," reaching base on an error by Abram "Hardy" Richardson.[2]
- On October 22, 1889, in Game 3 of the World Series, the Brooklyn Bridegrooms were up 8–7 through 8½ innings. In the bottom of the ninth the New York Giants loaded the bases with one out—whereupon umpire John Gaffney called the game on account of darkness and declared Brooklyn the winner.
- On August 22, 1894, the Chicago Colts' Bill Lange went to the plate against the New York Giants with a five-foot, ten-inch long theater-prop "bat," and reached base on Jack Doyle's error at first.
- And of course there's the 1919 World Series, deliberately thrown by the Chicago "Black Sox," the numbers of which were compiled under totally fraudulent conditions, but which are nonetheless included in official Series records.

Early home runs are a catalog of primitivism unto themselves:

- On May 21, 1880, Lipman "Lip" Pike was credited with a home run when the ball landed in the Niagara River. Right fielder Lon Knight couldn't retrieve it in time to throw Pike out—even though Knight used a rowboat.
- On July 4, 1884, Tom O'Brien was credited with a home run when the ball buried itself in an on-field heap of dirt.
- On August 22, 1886, Willie "Chicken" Wolf was credited with a home run when a dog attacked Abner Powell as he tried to retrieve the ball.
- On June 1, 1891, Cap Anson was credited with a home run when outfielder Ed Delahanty became physically stuck in the doorway of a storage shed.
- On June 24, 1892, Tom Brown was credited with a home run when Cap Anson was chased away from the ball by a horse. (Perhaps the steed, seeing Anson, thought it was chasing another horse's ass…)
- On September 10, 1892, Jimmy McAleer was credited with a home run when Hugh Duffy couldn't dislodge the ball from a tomato can. (There's some dispute among baseball historians about whether this incident actually occurred. I believe it did—garbage dumps often formed the perimeter of early outfields—and September 10, 1892, is the date I believe it happened.)
- On May 10, 1897, Jack Doyle was credited with a home run when the ball bounced up the rungs of a ladder leaning against the outfield wall.
- On October 6, 1906, George Stone was credited with a home run when Ty Cobb and Matty McIntyre let the ball roll past them, because they didn't like pitcher Ed Siever and wanted him to lose the game.

- On June 27, 1911, John "Stuffy" McInnis was credited with a home run when he suddenly stepped into the box and swung at Ed Karger's warm-up pitch.

Every one of these home runs is in the Major League record books.

Search as you might, you'll find no tales of Negro Leaguers fielding on theater stages, or fending off attacks from dogs and horses. Which data set is more deserving of inclusion?

Early MLB umpires, when they weren't making absurd calls like these, were being physically assaulted. SABR's Larry R. Gerlach tells us that "umpires were routinely spiked, kicked, sworn at and spit upon by players, while fans ('kranks' as they were then called) hurled curses, bottles and all manner of organic and inorganic debris at the arbiters. Mobbings and physical assaults by players and patrons alike became commonplace; police escorts were familiar and welcome sights to the men in blue." At least one umpire, Andy Gifford, carried a knife while he called games.[3]

And then there are the amateurs. From at least May 17, 1877, when a man named John Brockway walked out of the stands in Cincinnati to umpire a game when the official umpire left early, and continuing through at least 1905, amateurs were seen on MLB playing fields, sometimes being invited onto the field directly from the stands. A few of the more egregious examples:

- On July 12, 1890, a local Brooklyn boy named "Lewis"—that's all we know, just "Lewis," no first name recorded—was allowed to pitch for the Brooklyn Ward's Wonders. In three innings he surrendered 13 hits, seven walks and a wild pitch for a total of 20 earned runs. "Lewis" "retired" with an ERA of 60.00.
- On September 17, 1890, the Philadelphia Athletics disbanded, selling or releasing all of their professional players. A squad comprised of 22 amateurs finished the season as the Athletics, compiling a record of 0 wins and 22 losses. All of these men are listed on Baseball Reference with question marks by their names; five are known by their (questionable) last names only. "Sterling" allowed 12 runs on 16 hits and four walks in his sole five-inning outing; "Al Sauter" hit .098 in 52 plate appearances.
- On October 18, 1912, when the Detroit Tigers went on strike to protest Ty Cobb's suspension for attacking a fan, nine local amateurs and two coaches played a full game as the Tigers, losing to the Athletics by a score of 24 to 2.

Every one of these men is listed at Baseball Reference as a Major League player.

Ty Cobb's career began in 1905, when amateurs were still taking the field. Cobb is credited without qualm or asterisk as the all-time MLB leader in batting average. How confident are we that his .366 average was compiled under professional conditions?

Early Major League baseball, which was counted in the official record, was *vastly* less professional than Negro Leagues baseball, which wasn't counted in the official record.

* * *

It's not just early NL and AL play that clearly falls below Negro League standards. Let's take a look at the four leagues other than the AL and NL that historians and statisticians acknowledge as early Major Leagues.

First there's the American Association (AA), which competed from 1882 to 1891 and, prior to the American League's incorporation in 1901, represented the National League's principal competition for the status of top (white) North American league.

Not a single AA regular has been elected to the Hall of Fame. The first seven World Series were held between NL and AA teams, with the AA winning one, losing four and drawing two: not a promising mark of quality. These World Series are today labelled exhibitions, their statistics excluded from official Series records—an odd disavowal of a so-called Major League. In 1891, the final year of the league's existence, the NL champion Boston Beaneaters flat-out refused to play the AA champion Boston Reds, forcing the cancellation of that year's Series.

The dubious numbers compiled by AA players are found today in Major League record books.

Next we have the Union Association, which played only the 1884 season. Founded by millionaire Henry Lucas, who signed all the best available players for his own team, the league was a lopsided, uncompetitive mess from the start. Lucas's team, the St. Louis Maroons, won 94 games and lost 19 for an .832 winning percentage. (To put this into perspective, the best-ever record by a NL or AL team was posted by the 1906 Chicago Cubs, who went 116–36 for a .763 winning percentage.)

Four of the UA's eight teams folded before the season was through; another team changed cities in the middle of the year. Representatives of just two teams showed up for a meeting to plan the 1885 season, whereupon the whole freak show collapsed.

The Negro Leagues sent Hank Aaron, Ernie Banks, Willard Brown, Roy Campanella, Larry Doby, Monte Irvin, Willie Mays, Minnie Miñoso, Satchel Paige and Jackie Robinson to the Majors—to name *just the Hall of Famers*—despite the glacial pace of integration (discussed in the next chapter), which left dozens of quality NgL players to wither on the vine. Former Negro Leaguers earned seven Rookie of the Year Awards, 135 All-Star Game selections and 12 MVPs. Mays and Aaron are legitimate candidates as the greatest ever to don a Major League uniform.

From its 272 players, the UA produced a grand total of 14 men who managed to play regularly in other Major Leagues, including one (marginal) Hall of Famer, Tommy McCarthy, who hit .182, .185 and .186 in successive NL follow-up seasons.[4]

Jack Glasscock split his 1884 season between the UA, where he hit .419, and the NL, where he hit .249. His instant plunge from stardom to mediocrity is a solid indicator of the inferior competition Glasscock faced in the UA—but his numbers from both leagues are credited equally towards his Major League totals.

Alone among UA teams, the Maroons (they of the .832 winning percentage) survived the collapse of the league to join the NL, playing two seasons in St. Louis, then three more as the Indianapolis Hoosiers, before finally folding. In their five years in the NL, this most professional of all UA teams posted a record of 225 wins, 400 losses, for a scintillating .360 winning percentage.

In every conceivable respect, the Negro Leagues were a model of professionalism

Federal League players demonstrate the "professional" quality of their "Major League" ballfield (courtesy Froelich Collection, Missouri Historical Society).

in comparison with the UA—but UA numbers were counted as Major League stats, and NgL numbers were not.

Next up was the Players' League, which played only the 1890 season before collapsing. The PL was the brainchild of John Montgomery Ward, who sought to create an alternative to the contractual stranglehold that Major League owners imposed on their players.

Unlike the AA or UA, the PL was packed with legitimate stars, including 15 future Hall of Famers: Jake Beckley, Dan Brouthers, Charlie Comiskey, Roger Connor, Ed Delahanty, Hugh Duffy, William "Buck" Ewing, James "Pud" Galvin, Ned Hanlon, Tim Keefe, Michael "King" Kelly, Connie Mack, "Orator" Jim O'Rourke, Charles "Old Hoss" Radbourn and John Montgomery Ward. Players felt free to abandon their existing NL contracts and jump to the PL—exactly the situation that later plagued the NgL. Certainly the PL had the top-tier talent to be described as a major league, but it lacked the decisive element of long-term economic stability—again like its NgL counterparts. And again, PL numbers were recorded as official Major League stats.

Finally we have the Federal League. Unlike the UA or the PL, the FL had a bit of staying power, three seasons' worth from 1913 to 1915, the latter two being counted by the encyclopedias as Major League seasons. Once again, lack of economic stability exacted its toll. FL owners sued Major League Baseball to break its monopoly status, but had the misfortune to have their suit assigned to Judge Kenesaw "Mountain"

Landis, who twice helped preserve MLB's status as America's national pastime: first by delaying the FL's antitrust suit in his courtroom while the League died a financial death, and later, in his capacity as Commissioner of Baseball, by banning the Black Sox for life, thereby restoring public confidence in the integrity of the game. (As we shall see, Landis also significantly delayed the integration of baseball—but hey, once crisis at a time.)

The online National Pastime Museum reports that the top ten stars of the FL lost 88 percent of their WAR value in their first two years after moving to the Majors—and no less than 99.6 percent of their value if we exclude a single player, Benny Kauff. That doesn't sound like a Major League to me. Nonetheless, FL records for 1914 and 1915 are in the Major League record books.[5]

Every organizational evil ascribed to the Negro Leagues—league instability, uneven scheduling, teams disbanding in mid-season, contract jumping, failure to meet payrolls, etc., etc.—is equally well ascribed to the early Majors. To be fair, the PL was stocked with legitimate stars, but the NgL featured more Major League–caliber players than the AA, the UA, and the FL combined, and more Hall of Famers than all four leagues put together.

Taking into account, then, the ludicrous rules under which early MLB numbers were compiled, the distinctly unprofessional quality of early MLB play, and the marginal character of multiple whites-only leagues classed as Major, the quality-of-play argument against counting the Negro Leagues as Major Leagues is … what, exactly?

3

The Dam Trickles Open

There's a false impression, conveyed unintentionally by the media and by capsule histories that mention key events in passing or omit them altogether, that Jackie Robinson's 1947 Major League debut ended baseball segregation. Nothing could be further from the truth.

It's important to realize that dozens, possibly hundreds, of Major League–caliber players never got a shot at the Majors—or even the minors—thanks to the snail's pace of post–Jackie Robinson integration, which made *Brown v. Board of Education*'s "all deliberate speed" seem like the final lap at Le Mans.

From 1920 to 1944 baseball's affairs were overseen by Kenesaw Landis, a crusty traditionalist with no interest in disturbing the segregated status quo. Landis delayed the integration of baseball through a combination of deliberate inertia and occasional overt acts.

Many historians debate whether Landis was actively racist, or dispute the degree of his racism. David Kaiser decries the idea of Landis, "a man of great integrity," being "a key foe of integrating organized baseball" as a "myth," asserting that "the owners, not Landis, had effectively banned Black Americans from organized baseball, and it was up to them to do something about it." Landis biographer and former SABR president David Pietrusza writes that "the image of Kenesaw Landis as … an unyielding racist who prevented the game's integration" is "a convenient image" that "oversimplifies the issue." (To be fair, Pietrusza also notes that the tendency of some historians to paint Landis as the sole villain "exculpates the rest of baseball for its actions, inactions, and attitudes.")[1]

Norman L. Macht goes so far as to assert that "there is no documentation of anything racist Landis ever did or said in or out of baseball." But that's not true. There's broad agreement among baseball historians that sometime around October 1923, Landis took action to ban complete Major League teams from barnstorming against Black teams or wearing their MLB uniforms while they played—because, as all accounts agree, *the Black squads were humiliating the white teams*.[2]

(The date of Landis's action is variously cited; I believe October 1923 corresponds most logically with surrounding events. In that month, Black teams went 8–3–1 against white opposition, a fact Landis couldn't abide. Today, the fact that Negro Leaguers weren't playing against "real" white baseball teams is cited as a reason why Black vs. white statistics can't be trusted as measures of competitiveness. Racism then begets racism now.)

When white All-Star squads were hammered by Black competition, Landis was equally willing to intervene. After the NgL champion Kansas City Monarchs took three straight from the Dizzy Dean All-Stars in May and June 1942 while out-scoring them 25 to 5, Landis arbitrarily cancelled a fourth game scheduled for the Fourth of July, on the purported grounds that the games were out-drawing MLB contests.

(Landis was not the first MLB authority figure to issue a race-related ban. In 1909 the Detroit Tigers, winners of three consecutive AL pennants, lost eight of 12 games to mixed-race Cuban teams; in 1910 the World Series-champion Philadelphia Athletics lost six of 10 to the Cuban Giants. The Giants began billing themselves as "champions of the world"—which, by rights, they were.³

On January 7, 1911, the National Commission [forerunner to the Commissioner's office] comprising Cincinnati Reds general manager August "Garry" Herrmann, AL president Byron "Ban" Johnson—an appropriate moniker, that—and NL president Tom Lynch—another unsettling soubriquet—enacted rule 691: "Hereafter it will not be permissible for the major league club winning the world's championship series to participate in any exhibition games[,] the victorious club being required to disband immediately after the series has been completed."⁴

In 1913 Johnson spelled out the explicitly racist nature of the new rule, while also implying that the pennant-winning MLB teams which had been thrashed in Cuba were really just pickup squads: "We want no makeshift club calling themselves the Athletics to go to Cuba to be beaten by colored teams."⁵)

Those who credit Landis with being pro-integration are mistaking words for deeds. Certainly he made the right noises with his mouth.

Kenesaw Landis, perhaps contemplating the idea of Black players in the Majors (courtesy MEARS Online Auctions).

In the October 1, 1938, *Chicago Defender*, Brooklyn manager Burleigh Grimes, who'd just guided his team into a 69-80 toilet, told Al Monroe, "I would rather lose the pennant than to have Negro players on my ball club." Grimes was fired at the end of the season, and in the August 5, 1939, *Pittsburgh Courier*, Brooklyn Dodgers shortstop and rookie skipper Leo Durocher took an astonishingly progressive tack with Black reporter Lester Rodney:

> I've seen plenty of colored boys who could make the grade in the Majors. Hell—I've seen a million! I've played against some colored boys out on the coast who could play in any big league that ever existed. About two years ago I played against Josh Gibson in Cincinnati and found out that everything they say about him is true, and then some.... There are plenty of colored players around the country who should be in the big leagues

right now. However, that decision is not up to the managers. Personally, I have a liberal attitude toward the Negro ball player.... I certainly would use a Negro ball player if the bosses said it was all right.[6]

The bosses, of course, never did say it was all right; and so, on May 23, 1942, Rodney printed a scathing open letter in the *Daily Worker*, laying the onus for continuing segregation at the feet of Kenesaw Landis:

> The first casualty lists have been published. Negro soldiers and sailors are among those beloved heroes of the American people who have already died for the preservation of this country and everything this country stands for—yes, including the great game of baseball. So this letter isn't going to mince words....
>
> You, the self-proclaimed "Czar" of baseball, are the man responsible for keeping Jim Crow in our national pastime. You are the one who by your silence is maintaining a relic of the slave market long repudiated in other American sports. You are the one who is refusing to say the word which would do more to justify baseball's existence in this year of war than any other single thing. You are the one who is blocking the step which would put baseball in line with the rest of the country, with the United States Government itself....
>
> [Black sailor and Navy Cross winner] Dorie Miller, who manned a machine gun at Pearl Harbor when he might have stayed below deck, has been honored by a grateful people. The President of our country has called for an end to discrimination in all jobs.... You haven't a leg to stand on. Everybody knows there are many Negro players capable of starring in the big leagues....
>
> Bill McKechnie, manager of the Cincinnati Reds, set the tone for all the managers when he said, "I could name at least 20 Negro players who belong in the big leagues and I'd love to have some of them on the Reds if given permission." If given YOUR permission, Judge Landis....
>
> The American people are waiting for you. You're holding up the works. And the first casualty lists have been published.

Stung badly by this frontal assault, and by an alleged statement from Durocher that a "grapevine understanding or subterranean rule" was barring Blacks from the Major Leagues, Landis fired back to reporter Joe Cummiskey on July 17, 1942, by telephone: "There is no rule—formal, informal or otherwise—that says a ball player must be white. There is nothing to prevent one player or the full limit of 25 players being colored on any baseball team.... I insist there's no law now or ever against it." The next day he told the International News Service that "Negroes have not been barred from baseball by the commissioner and never have been during the 21 years I have served as commissioner," and in a press conference at Wrigley Field declaimed that "there is no rule, formal or informal, or any understanding—unwritten, subterranean or sub-anything—against the hiring of Negro players by the teams of Organized Ball."[7]

The press and the public—excepting perhaps the Black community, who had been listening to empty promises from white authority figures since 1865 and can be excused a certain cynicism—took Landis at his word. His comments produced headlines like the July 18 *Daily Worker*'s "Landis's OK on Negro Stars is a Great Democratic Victory for All America" and the July 25 *Pittsburgh Courier*'s "Commissioner Landis' Emancipation Proclamation—'Negro Players Are Welcome.'"

Modern biographers also tend to interpret Landis's statements as a concession in the direction of integration. For example, Larry Moffi, who agrees that "[Landis] did his part to keep [baseball] free of African Americans," cites the Judge's public declarations as evidence that "four years before Rickey signed Robinson to a Montreal Royals contract, Landis did open the door to integration just a crack."[8]

But having mollified his critics with a spate of speechifying, Landis *did* nothing.

Well, okay, he convened a meeting—one and a half years later!—on December 3, 1943, ostensibly to hear the opinions of prominent Black leaders on the continuing segregation of baseball. John H. Sengstacke, in particular, spoke with uncommon eloquence against the status quo.

- *Paul Robeson, stage and screen performer and civil rights activist:*

    I have played with Southern boys in football. At first they wouldn't play, but at the end of the game every man shook my hand. When I went out to play pro in Akron, years later, the first fellows that greeted me were fellows from the South.... There is no question about the quality of the ball players; there are plenty of them around.

- *John Sengstacke, president of the Negro Newspaper Publishers Association and publisher of the* Chicago Defender*:*

    Organized baseball's unwritten, but effective, practice of exclusion against some players because of their color helps to spread the [Nazi] "master race" theory among Americans on a mass basis.... The forces of hate, at home and abroad, are hard at work. But we do not believe they will ever succeed in selling racism to Americans who have purchased democracy and their right to be free men through blood, sweat and tears.... No organization, truly representative of the American philosophy of fair play, can justify any bars, either psychological or real, which are predicated on color, race, creed or national origin.[9]

- *Ira Lewis, publisher of the* Pittsburgh Courier*, the weekly newspaper of record for Black America*:

    Your Honorable Commissioner has stated that there is no written law barring Negro players from participation in organized baseball. We thank Judge Landis for this statement.... But we believe, however, that there is a gentleman's agreement that no Negro players be hired. I ask you, gentlemen, in the name of the America we all love, in the name of the democracy that we associate with the word "America," that you undo this wrong; that you do away with this mean precedent, this gentlemen's understanding and agreement, and let our national pastime be a game for all the boys of America.

Following these impassioned pleas, Howard Murphy, secretary of the Negro Newspaper Publishers Association, proposed a series of concrete steps that MLB could take immediately, foremost among which was "that a joint statement be issued by this body declaring that Negroes are eligible for trials and permanent places on your respective teams." Landis did no such thing.

The lack of interest in what the speakers were saying was palpable. Questions were called for, but none were asked—though Landis did interrupt Ira Lewis's statement to insist yet again that "there is no haymow rule or subterranean rule or understanding" preventing MLB teams from hiring Black players.

After the speakers left the room, the meeting carried on for another 64 pages of transcript with nary a syllable uttered on the subject of integration. Landis was about to close proceedings when Branch Rickey (bless his little cotton socks) pressed the issue—and forced Landis to reveal his true motives:

> **MR. RICKEY:** Mr. Commissioner, are we to understand that the report from this meeting, in response to the delegation that came in here today, is to be simply that the matter was not considered?
> **COMM. LANDIS:** No, no. The announcement will have to be that it was considered—and *my recollection now is that it was considered, and you gentlemen all remember that it was considered; you each participated in the consideration of it*—and that no action was taken on it….
> **MR. RICKEY:** Is it in order for a club to say that this is a matter requiring not only our League consideration, but joint consideration, and that the club itself is not able to give any further statement than it has now given?….
> **COMM. LANDIS:** I don't think anybody ought to say that. We can't say that…. If any of you gentlemen want to hire a Negro player, you are as much as liberty to do that as you are to sign up any other player, be he in human form. *That is our whole theory, and we must keep away from the other idea.* [Emphasis mine.]¹⁰

Messrs. Robeson, Sengstacke, Lewis and Murphy might as well have been talking to a brick wall. Landis never had the slightest intention of acting on what he heard in that room. The meeting was a farce, a put-on, a contrivance for show rather than substance.

The public, sadly, took Landis's "theory" as a sign that the times were changing. The Commissioner's Office was bombarded by telegrams supporting the abolition of the color line—and demonstrating how effective Landis's sham meeting had been in hoodwinking American public opinion:

> **AMERICAN YOUTH FOR DEMOCRACY:** WE CONSIDER YOUR DECISION TO DISCUSS DISCRIMINATION IN BASEBALL HIGHLY COMMENDABLE
> **COLLEGE STATION POST OFFICE EMPLOYEES:** COMMEND YOU ON YOUR PATRIOTIC ACTION IN OPENING FLOOR TO DISCUSSION OF NEGROES IN BASEBALL
> **HOTEL AND CLUB UNION:** YOUR ACTION PLACING MATTER OF NEGRO BALL PLAYERS ON AGENDA IS MOST COMMENDABLE
> **INTERNATIONAL WORKERS ORDER:** ENDORSE YOUR STEPS TAKEN TO PERMIT DISCUSSION ON SIGNING NEGRO PLAYERS FOR MAJORS
> **UNITED OFFICE AND PROFESSIONAL WORKERS OF AMERICA:** WE HAIL YOUR STAND IN PUTTING ON AGENDA FOR BOTH LEAGUES THE CASE OF NEGRO PLAYERS…. WE SUPPORT YOUR PATRIOTIC AND DEMOCRATIC BELIEFS THAT THEY BE GIVEN EQUAL OPPORTUNITY REGARDLESS OF RACE COLOR OR CREED¹¹

It's questionable, to put it mildly, whether Landis held any such beliefs. At any rate, as before, he *did* nothing.

During World War II Major League teams were so desperate for live (white) bodies to put on the field that in 1945 the St. Louis Browns played Pete Gray, a thirty-year-old man missing his right arm, who hit .218 and slugged .261 in 77 games.

This isn't to knock Pete Gray, who served as an inspiration to a generation of wounded veterans returning from World War II. But to play him while talents like Josh Gibson watched from the outside was a slap in the face to every American. "How do you think I felt," exclaimed Chet Brewer, "when I saw a one-armed outfielder?"¹²

Kenesaw Landis was as two-faced as they come. Only his death made change possible. A handful of whites—like Branch Rickey, Clyde Sukeforth, Stan Musial,

Pee Wee Reese, Vern Stephens and Steve Gromek—emerge from this divisive era as heroes. Landis does not.

* * *

Landis was far from alone in rejecting integration. The opinion expressed openly and explicitly by white team owners, general managers, and sports reporters was not just that Black players were unwanted, but specifically that they were inferior to white players. Further, they insisted that this opinion was shared by Black America.

The typical response of executives and team owners to the idea of an MLB color line was outright denial. "I do not recall one instance," insisted NL president John Heydler in 1933, "where baseball has allowed either race, creed or color to enter into the question of the selection of its players." When sports reporters questioned the absence of Black players on MLB ballfields, owners insisted this was a temporary state of affairs; in 1938, Senators owner Clark Griffith told Sam Lacy: "There are few big league magnates who are not aware of the fact that the time is not far off when colored players will take their places beside those of the other races in the major leagues." Sounds great, doesn't it?—but Griffith didn't integrate the Senators until September 1954, more than eight years after Jackie opened the door.[13]

On July 16, 1942, Leo Durocher continued to express sentiments ahead of his time when he told reporter Tom Meany, "I have no prejudices against any ball player on account of race or religion. After all, we're all Americans. As long as I am manager I'll play the best 25 players I can get." But Durocher went on to contradict his positive 1939 assessment by disparaging the professional quality of the contemporary NgL: "Personally, I have seen only one colored player in recent years of major-league caliber. He's a shortstop named [Silvio] Garcia, whom I played against in Cuba. I played against Satchel Paige and other fine Negro stars years ago, but I think those men are too old to play in the major leagues now."[14]

Leo the Lip can be forgiven for thinking Paige was past it; he thought Satch was merely human, and bound by the biological limits imposed by Father Time on every other pitcher who ever lived. But Josh Gibson was active in the NgL at the time ... and Buck Leonard, and Monte Irvin, and Roy Campanella ... none, apparently, of "major-league caliber" in Leo's judgment.

Durocher and Landis's open remarks on Black players stirred up considerable controversy, to which others in organized baseball responded with vehemence. In the July 18 *New York Herald Tribune*, Pittsburgh Pirates president William Benswanger flatly denied the existence of an MLB color line: "There is not and never has been, to my knowledge, anything to ban Negroes from baseball. I know nothing of any agreement in the major leagues to ban Negroes." "Our scouts have never recommended a Negro player," asserted Chicago Cubs GM James Gallagher in the same issue, adding helpfully: "Personally, I think everybody in this country should be doing something of more value to the nation as a whole than stirring up racial hatred."

Dodgers president Leland "Larry" MacPhail chipped in—camouflaging his opinions as the purported views of NgL team owners—in the July 28 *Newark*

Star-Ledger: "The way they look [at] it is that there aren't too many players of major league caliber in the Negro National and American Leagues, so, if they should lose their best players to the majors, their own clubs would be hurt at the gate."

In the same day's *Newark Evening News* MacPhail made it clear that these were in fact his personal views, though he insisted he was merely heeding the Black consensus: "There is no real demand for Negro baseball players.... How many of the best players in the Negro circuit do you suppose would make the National or American Leagues? Very few.... I have talked with some of the leading Negroes. Ask them what they think of breaking down the custom.... If we were to raid [NgL] clubs it would mean many tryouts for boys who would not make the big-league grade in our circuit."[15]

Having embarrassed himself in the eyes of history, MacPhail proceeded to undercut the lies of the Commissioner and his fellow team owners: "Judge Landis was not speaking for baseball when he said there is no barrier; there *has* been an unwritten law tantamount to an agreement between major league clubs on the subject of avoiding the racial issue." (Emphasis mine.)

There it was, at long last, in the open for all to see. By the admission of one of their own number, MLB owners did have a "subterranean rule" barring Black players from the Majors.

But no remediative action was taken, by President Roosevelt, the Congress, or anyone else. The United States was too busy fighting for liberty overseas to concern itself with civil rights at home.

J.G. Taylor Spink, publisher of *The Sporting News*, took it upon himself to speak for Black America, editorializing on August 6, 1942, that "there are agitators, ever ready to seize an issue that will redound to their profit or self aggrandizement, who have sought to force Negro players on the big leagues.... There are some colored people who take a different view, and they are entitled to their opinions, but they are not looking at the question from the broader point of view, or for the ultimate good of either race or the individuals in it. They ought to concede their own people are now protected and that nothing is served by allowing agitators to make an issue of a question on which both sides would prefer to be left alone."

In the March 29, 1945, *Sporting News*, Larry MacPhail claimed that "I have been saying for 15 years that there should be no discrimination in any American sport"; but later that year he showed his true colors in a document submitted to New York City Mayor Fiorello LaGuardia's Committee on Unity: "There are few, if any, negro players who could qualify for play in the major leagues at this time. A major league player must have ... the technique, the coordination, the competitive aptitude and the discipline usually acquired only after years of training in the smaller [i.e., minor] leagues." Of course, such training was unavailable: "I do not believe anything can be accomplished by signing negro players for small minor league clubs. To give tryouts to players whom you do not intend to employ," MacPhail insisted, oblivious to the irony, "is sheer hypocrisy." He then extended a hopelessly conditional olive branch: "If and when the negro leagues approve, *and other difficulties can be overcome*, I personally favor the adoption of some plan under which a limited number of negro players ... might advance to the majors or big minors." (Emphasis mine.) For "if and when ... other difficulties can be overcome," read: Hurry up and wait.[16]

The catch-22 identified by MacPhail was summed up by Cleveland part-owner Alva Bradley's pretzel logic in an October 24, 1945, AP interview: "Colored players have never been discriminated against in the major leagues. They have simply never been able to get into the minor leagues to get the proper training for major league competition."

Branch Rickey, of all people, denied the existence of MLB-ready Black players *after* he'd signed Jackie Robinson. The October 25, 1945, *Boston Globe* revealed Rickey's view that Jackie "should be able to play for Brooklyn after the proper schooling. He isn't ready now and I don't think there is a Negro player anywhere who is ready. If I thought he was ready I would have signed him to a Dodger contract." Rickey went further in the November 11 *Sporting News*: "[Jackie] is not now major league stuff and there is not a single Negro player in this country who could qualify for the National or American leagues…. There isn't a single Negro player of major league class."

On November 1, 1945, in an unsigned editorial probably penned by J.G. Taylor Spink, *The Sporting News* asserted that "there is not a single Negro player with major league possibilities…[Jackie] Robinson, at 26, is reported to possess baseball abilities which, were he white, would make him eligible for a trial with, let us say, the Brooklyn Dodgers' Class B farm at Newport News, if he were six years younger…. The waters of competition in the International League will flow far over his head."[17]

With Jackie performing brilliantly in the Majors, Rickey continued to express doubts about Black professionalism, stating in the July 16, 1947, *Sporting News* that "I don't believe too many [Black players] will make good, not enough for distribution around the National and American leagues." Bill Veeck concurred in the July 30 *Sporting News*: "With [Larry] Doby, Jackie Robinson, Willard Brown and Henry Thompson already under big league contracts, the cream of the colored crop has been taken…. For the present, there is no possibility that Negro players will be arriving in wholesale numbers in the majors."

This opinion, which ran contrary to the facts on the ground, seems to have affected Rickey's professional judgment. In 1946 Brooklyn assigned pitcher Don Newcombe to a minor-league slot. Newk, who'd posted a 2.60 ERA for the Newark Eagles in 1945, dominated Class B competition with a 14–4, 2.41 campaign, but Rickey left him in the lower minors for 1947, where he dominated again (19–6, 2.91). For 1948 he was belatedly promoted—not to the Majors but to triple–A, where he went 17–6, placed fourth with a 3.14 ERA, and pitched a no-hitter and one-hitter in back-to-back games. Still Rickey cast public doubt on his ability to pitch in the Majors. "He's a major league pitcher right now as far as ability goes," opined the Mahatma to Sam Lacy in the April 20, 1949, *Sporting News*, "but there is something else…. Don hasn't matured in keeping with his physical development. I have a personal interest in all my boys and I would hate to see him come up too soon." When Newk was finally promoted to the Majors in 1949, he went 17–8, 3.17, led the NL in strikeouts per 9 innings, tied for the league lead with 5 shutouts, finished 8th in MVP voting and walked away with the Rookie of the Year award. It's hard to avoid the suspicion that Rickey's doubts about Newcombe's "maturity"—an aspersion all-too-commonly cast on Black athletes—cost Newk a solid chunk of his Major League career.

Some in baseball who ought to have known better continued to doubt the existence of MLB-quality Black talent for years afterwards. In May 1949, Hall of Famer Connie Mack told *Ebony* magazine that "I have been advised that there are not many Negro boys playing baseball." Hall of Famer Bob Feller—whose Cleveland teammates Larry Doby and Satchel Paige had been instrumental in winning the 1948 pennant—opined in the same issue that "there will be no avalanche of Negroes into the major leagues mainly because there are few Negro ball players today who can make the grade."

Durocher, Veeck, and Rickey, at the least, were intelligent, progressive men. So from what well of inner blindness could such opinions have sprung?

There can be only one answer. Racist tropes, overt or covert, admitted or denied, were woven so thoroughly into the fabric of American society that they caused otherwise admirable people to deny the evidence of their own eyes.

* * *

On August 27, 1946, a secret report on the post–World War II problems facing baseball was issued to MLB team owners by six men: Yankees president and general manager Larry MacPhail, NL president Ford Frick, AL president William Harridge, Cardinals majority owner and president Sam Breadon, Cubs owner and president Phil Wrigley, and Red Sox owner and president Tom Yawkey. The MacPhail Report outlines, among other goals, "methods to protect baseball from charges that it is fostering unfair discrimination against the Negro by reason of his race and color."

The Report, which its authors never dreamed would be exposed to public scrutiny, is an exemplar of Jim Crow logic in full flower. It first denies that racism exists in organized baseball, then dredges up an array of lame excuses for preserving the status quo, reaffirms the supposed inferiority of Black ballplayers, and dips its toes into the murky waters of "separate but equal" and "there goes the neighborhood":

> Certain groups in this country … are conducting pressure campaigns in an attempt to force major league clubs to sign Negro players…. These people who charge that baseball is flying a Jim Crow flag at its masthead—or that racial discrimination is the basic reason for failure of the major leagues to give employment to Negroes—are simply talking through their individual or collective hats…. Professional baseball, both Negro and white, has grown and prospered over a period of many years on the basis of separate leagues…. If Negroes participate in major league games[,] the preponderance of Negro attendance in parks such as Yankee Stadium, the Polo Grounds, and Comiskey Park could conceivably threaten the value of the major league franchises owned by these clubs…. Comparatively few good young Negro players are being developed. This is the reason that there are not more players who meet major league standards in the big Negro leagues…. The Negroes who own and operate [NgL] clubs do not want to part with their outstanding players—no one accuses them of racial discrimination…. The Negro Leagues rent their parks in many cities from clubs in organized baseball[, and] club owners in the major leagues are reluctant to give up revenues amounting to hundreds of thousands of dollars every year…. This is not racial discrimination.[18]

MLB owners approved the Report by a vote of 15 to 1, with Branch Rickey (of course) casting the lone dissenting vote.

I'll have much more to say on this damning document later in the book. For now it's sufficient to note that with the threat of integration looming on the horizon, MLB owners were willing to go beyond their long-standing "subterranean rule" and codify segregation as official (though secret) Major League policy.

* * *

Belief in the inferior quality of Negro Leagues players persists to this day. Probably the most pervasive opinion I encountered in my research was that the average NgL player was closer to minor league than Major League quality.

There's some heavy-duty racism at the foundation of this assumption—unconscious in virtually every case, expressed by intelligent people of good will, but racist nonetheless. It's a depressingly common view.

Let's go with the argument for the moment to see if it bears up under scrutiny.

The first Black player admitted to the Majors in the 20th century was Jackie Robinson, a Rookie of the Year, batting titlist, stolen base champion, MVP, and inner-circle Hall of Famer.

The second was Larry Doby, a home run and RBI champion and Hall of Famer.

The fourth was Willard Brown, an inner-circle Hall of Famer.

The sixth was Roy Campanella, an RBI champion, three-time MVP, inner-circle Hall of Famer, and reasonable candidate as the greatest catcher in MLB history.

The seventh was Satchel Paige, an inner-circle Hall of Famer and reasonable choice as the greatest pitcher of all time.

The eighth was Minnie Minoso, a stolen base champion and Hall of Famer.

The ninth was Don Newcombe, a Rookie of the Year, wins and WHIP champion, Cy Young Award winner and MVP.

The tenth was Monte Irvin, an RBI champion, .394 postseason hitter and Hall of Famer.

The twelfth was Sam Jethroe, a Rookie of the Year and stolen base champion.

The seventeenth was Willie Mays, a Rookie of the Year, batting titlist, home run and stolen base champion, two-time MVP, inner-circle Hall of Famer, and consensus pick as the greatest Major League player of all time.

That's four Rookies of the Year, one Cy Young Award, seven MVP Awards and eight Hall of Famers among the first 20 Black Major Leaguers of the 20th century—plus the consensus greatest player ever—plus the possible greatest catcher—plus the possible greatest pitcher.

There's no intake of players at any point in MLB history, not a single draft, not a single expansion, that approaches this level of accomplishment, despite often drawing from larger pools of potential talent.

This tally doesn't include other high-quality MLB players among the first twenty, like Luke Easter (the 11th) or Sam "Toothpick" Jones (the 20th).

Nor does it include immortals like Hank Aaron and Ernie Banks, nor future MVPs like Elston Howard and Maury Wills, who climbed to the Majors from later iterations of the Negro Leagues.

Nor does it include men like defensive master Ray Dandridge, who won minor league Rookie of the Year and MVP honors in 1949 and 1950, or shortstop Artie Wilson, a two-time NgL batting champion who racked up five 200-hit seasons in the minors—players who would have been given proper Major League trials by any reasonable system of promotion. (According to Jonathan Fraser Light, Wilson, who collected 264 hits in the 1950 PCL, may have been sent down by the New York Giants in 1951 after a mere 19-game trial to make room for Willie Mays, in observance of an unwritten rule that no MLB team could have more than two Black players on its roster.)[19]

The players who did manage to get in could *play*. The NL Rookie of the Year Award was swept by ex–Negro Leaguers for five years running, 1949 through 1953:

- 1949: Don Newcombe
- 1950: Sam "The Jet" Jethroe
- 1951: Willie Mays
- 1952: Joe Black
- 1953: James "Junior" Gilliam

Besides these five, Jackie Robinson won the first-ever Rookie of the Year award in 1947, given to the top rookie in all of MLB, and Minnie Miñoso won the AP's AL Rookie of the Year award in 1951.

None of these men were truly rookies, of course; all were veterans of professional baseball, which explains the immediacy and magnitude of their MLB impact.

Let's further test the proposition that the NgL lacked professional-quality players by building a scratch team from just the first 20 Negro Leaguers to make the Majors. That's a ridiculously small pool from which to draw, but we'll give it a try:

- C: Roy Campanella (RBI title, 8× All-Star, 3× MVP)
- 1B: Luke Easter (missed 1952 AL home run title by 1)
- 2B: Jackie Robinson (RoY, batting title, 2× stolen base titles, 6× All-Star, MVP)
- SS: Artie Wilson (2× NgL batting titles, 4× NgL All-Star)
- 3B: Minnie Miñoso (3× triples titles, 3× stolen base titles, 7× All-Star, 3× Gold Glove)
- LF: Monte Irvin (RBI title, All-Star)
- CF: Willie Mays (RoY, batting title, 3× triples titles, 4× home run titles, 4× stolen base titles, 20× All-Star, 12× Gold Glove, 2× MVP)
- RF: Larry Doby (2× home run titles, RBI title, 7× All-Star)
- PH: Willard Brown (4× NgL batting titles, 5× NgL home run titles)[20]
- PR: Sam Jethroe (RoY, 2× stolen base titles)
- UT: Bob Boyd (4× .300 hitter)
- UT: Harry Simpson (2× triples titles, All-Star)
- #1 starter: Don Newcombe (RoY, wins title, strikeout title, 3× BB/9 titles, 2× WHIP titles, 4× All-Star, Cy Young, MVP)
- #2 starter: Sam Jones (wins title, ERA title, 3× strikeout titles, 2× H/9 titles, 4× K/9 titles, 2× All-Star)
- RP: Satchel Paige (more games, wins, and strikeouts than any pitcher in history)

… Think that team might win a pennant or two?

In fact, when you think it through, you might conclude that this team, which we'll call the Pioneers, would consistently defeat the 1927 New York Yankees, a team boasting six Hall of Famers that's generally considered the greatest baseball squad ever assembled. Willie Mays is a fine counterbalance to Babe Ruth, and while Lou Gehrig shines above any other individual player, the Pioneers come out ahead with ease on a position-by-position matchup:

- C, Roy Campanella vs. Pat Collins: An inner-circle Hall of Famer vs. a journeyman receiver. Advantage Pioneers in a blowout.
- 1B, Luke Easter vs. Lou Gehrig: Easter's severely underrated historically, but the Iron Horse is the greatest first baseman of all time. Advantage Yankees in a blowout.
- 2B, Jackie Robinson vs. Tony Lazzeri: Lazzeri's good, even very good, but Jackie's a top-four all-time second baseman. Big advantage to the Pioneers.
- SS, Artie Wilson vs. Mark Koenig: A Negro Leagues All-Star and two-time batting champion vs. a journeyman shortstop. The Pioneers in a blowout.
- 3B, Minnie Miñoso vs. Joe Dugan: Dugan is solid but unspectacular, Miñoso's a stolen base champion and superior defender who won multiple Gold Gloves as an outfielder. Another big advantage to the Pioneers.
- LF, Monte Irvin vs. Bob Meusel: We'll call this one a draw, though in my view Irvin was much the greater athlete and all-around player. Meusel did have a fine '27 season, and I want to try to limit the influence of my freely admitted personal bias on the result.
- CF, Willie Mays vs. Earle Combs: Combs is one of the most overrated players of all time, a relatively low–OBP contact hitter and lousy base stealer with a dreadful throwing arm, whereas Mays ... well, as Jim Murray wrote: "The first thing to establish about Willie Mays is that there really is one." The Pioneers in a blowout.[21]
- RF, Larry Doby vs. Babe Ruth : I'm the biggest Larry Doby fan walking this Earth, but it's the Bambino and the Yankees in a blowout.
- #1 starter, Don Newcombe vs. Waite Hoyt: These guys were about equal at their peak, but Hoyt has the considerably greater career. Hoyt was 6–4, 1.83 in World Series play, Newk was 0–4, 8.59. Big advantage to the Yankees.
- #2 starter, Sam Jones vs. Herb Pennock: Like Hoyt, Pennock leads by an enormous margin on longevity—but unlike Newk, Jones holds a clear edge on peak value with an ERA title and four consecutive SO/9 crowns. Pennock was another World Series monster for the Yanks, 5–0, 1.95 in World Series play, while Jones never got a shot at the postseason.... I think we've got to call this one for the Yankees.
- RP, Satchel Paige vs. Wilcy Moore: Wilcy had his one and only great year in 1927, but career-wise it's a walk-away blowout for Satch. In my view, having Satch on the roster has to be counted as an advantage to the Pioneers.
- PH / PR / UT: The '27 Yankees had a relatively weak bench; the Pioneers' bench, drawn from a tiny player pool, is sparse but *loaded*. Advantage Pioneers.

That's seven advantages to the Pioneers, four to the Yankees, and one draw. Breaking it down further:

Team power: Surprisingly, despite the presence of the greatest one-two punch in MLB history, the advantage probably goes to the Pioneers. Mays has Ruth's power, and while Gehrig is the only other serious bopper for the Yankees, the Pioneers can draw on Campy, Doby, Easter and Irvin, notable power hitters all.

Team speed: The Pioneers in a blowout. Mays, Miñoso and Robinson, plus Jethroe off the bench, are all winners of multiple stolen base crowns.

Team defense: The Pioneers in a blowout. Easter is weak at first base, but Campanella is probably the greatest defensive catcher of all time, Mays might be the greatest defensive center fielder, Jackie's a truly great glove man at literally any position he's placed, and Doby, Miñoso and Wilson are all above-average defenders. Ruth was a decent right fielder at this time, but really, the Yankees have nothing comparable to bring to the field.

Even if you disagree with the conclusion that the Pioneers would consistently defeat the 1927 Yankees, it has to be obvious they'd give the Yanks a helluva scrap.

So much for the argument that "there isn't a single Negro player of major league class."

Now consider: The Pioneers are drawn from the first 20 Negro Leaguers admitted to the Majors—*the only Negro Leaguers to be given Major League trials in the first half-decade of integration*, 1947 to 1951. That's an average of just four players a year.

Further, *six years in*—through the end of the 1952 season—*only six of 16 Major League teams had given a Black player a trial*. Not until 1959, 12 years after Jackie's debut, had every MLB team given at least one Black player a chance.

And so, the question becomes: If a team of such superlative quality can be drawn from just the first 20 Negro Leaguers to reach the Big Show—a process that took half a decade, and admitted the tiniest fraction of available Black talent—what about the players who never made it?

The stagnant pace of integration left behind *dozens* of Negro League All-Stars.

The slim margin of economic stability the NgL had managed to achieve by 1947 vanished almost overnight. Players, owners, umpires, coaches—anyone and everyone who earned their living via the NgL—were ruined utterly. With just one exception (the New York Cubans, whose owner, Hall of Famer Alex Pompez, secured their informal admittance to the New York Giants' farm system), NgL teams weren't offered entry into the MLB major- or minor-league structure. Top players were snatched up by MLB teams with minimal compensation to NgL owners, and sometimes with no compensation at all.

Branch Rickey, an admirable figure in so many ways, was a real hard-nose when it came to raiding NgL teams without compensating their owners. On October 25, 1945, Clark Griffith criticized Rickey to an AP reporter for signing Jackie without compensating the Kansas City Monarchs: "While it is true that we have no agreement with Negro leagues—National or American—we still can't act like outlaws in taking their stars. We have no right to destroy them…. If Brooklyn wants to buy Robinson from Kansas City that is all right, but contracts of Negro teams should be respected by organized baseball." Rickey responded heatedly to the AP the same day: "Negro baseball is in the zone of a racket. Clark Griffith notwithstanding, *I have not signed a player from what I regard as an organized league.*" (Emphasis mine.)[22]

As NgL pitcher Dave Barnhill remembered, "The fans followed that one man [Jackie Robinson] instead of following the rest of the teams, so the league folded.... Just pulled the league down completely. The fans stopped going to the ball games.... We had to give it up." "The livelihoods, the careers, the families of 400 Negro ballplayers are in jeopardy," Newark Eagles co-owner Effa Manley said bitterly in 1948, "because four players were successful in getting into the major leagues."[23]

Hundreds of players never got the chance to prove their worth in the Majors. An entire generation of Black ballplayers was wiped from baseball's collective consciousness.

A handful of Negro Leaguers were accorded shots at the Majors, a few more were given roster spots in the minors—but the minor leagues were thoroughly segregated too. As late as 1961, 16 years after Jackie's Montreal debut, the Class AA Southern Association still refused to admit Black players. Minor league star Nate Peeples had appeared in two Southern Association games in 1954, but the Atlanta Crackers released him under pressure from other League teams. Channeling the ghost of Kenesaw Landis, Crackers officials issued a statement insisting that "the door was still open for Negroes in the league." The SA—a befitting acronym—collapsed financially after the 1961 season as a direct consequence of their Jim Crow stance, which kept Black patrons away from their ballparks. In effect, they inflicted a Montgomery bus boycott on themselves.[24]

In a very real way, NgL players of the 1940s had it far worse than Negro Leaguers of the '20s or '30s. For the vast majority of NgL players of the '40s, integration was a disaster. It wiped out their leagues, and with their leagues went their means of putting bread on their families' tables.

How many potential All-Stars, how many Gold Glove winners and Hall of Famers and World Series heroes, were lost to history this way?

We can never know.

* * *

The charming opinions expressed in the MacPhail Report are no mere relic of the past. Let's let the almost exclusively white Major League elite tell the story:

Minnesota Twins owner Calvin Griffith, 1978—"Any Blacks around? I'll tell you why we came to Minnesota. It was when I found out you only had 15,000 Blacks here.... We came here because you've got good, hardworking white people here."[25]

Los Angeles Dodgers GM Al Campanis, 1987—"I truly believe that [Blacks] may not have some of the necessities to be, let's say, a field manager, or perhaps a general manager.... I don't say all of them, but they certainly are short."[26]

Cincinnati Reds owner Marge Schott, 1992—"I once had a n----- work for me.... I would never hire another n-----. I'd rather have a trained monkey working for me than a n-----."[27]

3. The Dam Trickles Open

Think things are okay today? Jackie Robinson broke the Major League color barrier in 1947. Nineteen years later, on April 11, 1966, Emmett Ashford became the first Black MLB umpire; and on February 25, 2020, Kerwin Danley became MLB's first Black umpire crew chief—54 years after Ashford called his first MLB game, and 73 years after Jackie's ascent.

Major League Baseball has a long way to go. A key component of its long-overdue reckoning is statistical integration.

4

Statistical Variance Across Leagues and Eras

MLB players from different eras are compared routinely through their numbers, despite the fact that the game has changed repeatedly and profoundly. The MLB single-season record for batting average, .440 by Hugh Duffy, is a useful signpost for this discussion.

From 1876 to 1880 the distance from the front of the pitcher's box (there was as yet no mound) to the plate was 45 feet; from 1881 through 1892 it was 50.

Prior to the 1893 season the distance from the mound to the plate was increased to today's standard of 60 feet 6 inches, and for the next five seasons batters feasted as never before. In 1894 Hugh Duffy set the record for single-season batting average at .440, a mark that's stood for 129 years. The National League batted a collective .309; George "Tuck" Turner hit .418, Sam Thompson .415, Ed Delahanty .405, Billy Hamilton .403.

Post–World War II players who have chased a .400 average—Rod Carew with .388 in 1977, George Brett with .390 in 1980, Tony Gwynn with .394 in 1994—have never approached within 45 points of Duffy's mark.

Do higher single-season averages make Duffy, Turner, Thompson, Delahanty and Hamilton *greater* hitters than Carew, Brett and Gwynn? Of course not. It's commonly accepted that today's batters play in conditions that don't permit them to compile such high averages.

Does the fact that Duffy & Co. played in conditions far more favorable to hitting for average make them *lesser* hitters? Again, the argument is self-evident nonsense. They did the best they could within the constraints of their time, just like Carew, Brett and Gwynn.

Now fast-forward to 1968. The pitchers had taken charge, and Carl Yastrzemski topped the American League with a minuscule .301 average. The league as a whole batted .230; only one other AL batter, Danny Cater, reached .290. Yaz's league-leading mark was eight points below the *league-average* hitter of 1894.

Were Duffy & Co. greater hitters in 1894 than Yaz in 1968? Not at all; in fact, it's self-evident that hitting .400 in the 1894 National League was a lesser achievement than hitting .300 in the 1968 American League.

Does Yaz's batting title somehow count for less than Duffy's? Duffy's 1894 is the highest-ever mark by a league leader, Yaz's 1968 the lowest; both topped their respective leagues, and that's how the record books read.

4. Statistical Variance Across Leagues and Eras

Browse any website or open any encyclopedia devoted to Major League stats and you'll find Brett, Carew, Duffy, Gwynn and Yaz, all listed together. The fairness of the arrangement is never questioned.

Some folks, including baseball professionals, can't accept the logic that old-time numbers aren't better just because they're bigger. Joe Morgan dismissed the idea that he was a greater second baseman than Rogers Hornsby because Morgan hit .271 and Hornsby hit .358. Broadcaster Joe Miller told Morgan, a devout student of baseball history, that Bill James had rated him above Hornsby, and Morgan replied: "Well, how could that be? He hit .400 and 42 home runs, and I'm hitting .325 and 27 homers." Well, Joe, you *were* a greater player than Mr. Hornsby, far greater, for lots of reasons; you were deceived by the unequal eras in which you played.[1]

No professional sport reflects on its past with awe like baseball does. Modern fans speak in wonder of Ty Cobb's .366 lifetime batting average, a record that's stood for over a century—not because modern hitters aren't as skillful as the hitters of Cobb's day, but because the conditions of the game have changed.

The consensus top all-around player in the game today is Mike Trout. The Millville Meteor hit .291 in his 2019 MVP campaign. Was Trout, as a hitter, 149 points worse than Hugh Duffy in 1894?

It's not just batting average that varies wildly with context and era. As Houston third baseman Alex Bregman said that same year:

> If I wanted to hit .300, I'd hit .300. It's an OPS game, though. It's about driving the baseball and getting on base, walks and extra-base hits.... Batting average is an old stat that doesn't matter. It's OPS, runs created, WAR. Look at Mike Trout's numbers. There are guys that hit .340. Mike Trout is hitting, what, .300 on the dot? I'd rather have Mike Trout's numbers with all the walks and the damage than the guy who hits .340.[2]

One reason many consider Babe Ruth the greatest ever is his career OPS mark of 1.164, much the highest that any batter has compiled. Even a steroid-fueled Barry Bonds couldn't reach the Babe's heights in this respect. Ruth piled up a lot of that mark in the 1920s, a decade more favorable to Ruth's style of play than any other. Is that fair to Hank Aaron, Mickey Mantle and Willie Mays, who played through the pitcher-dominated 1960s? We never ask the question.

The National League leader in slugging for 1919, Hi Myers, slugged .436; three years later, Rogers Hornsby slugged .722. Was the National League of 1919 less of a professional league because its slugging leader finished 286 points lower than the 1922 leader—or had conditions fundamentally changed?

The same illusions apply to pitching. In 1880 Tim Keefe led the NL with an 0.86 ERA; in 1950 Early Wynn led the AL with 3.20. In 1884 Charles "Old Hoss" Radbourn led the NL with 60 wins; in 2006 six pitchers tied for the NL lead with 16. In 1888 three AL pitchers tied for the AL lead with one (retroactively awarded) save apiece; in 2008 Francisco Rodriguez led the AL with 62.

Fielding, too, is subject to illusions of context. In 1884 Walter Hackett led UA second basemen with an .855 fielding percentage; in 2002 Mike Bordick led the AL with .998. In 1930 Chuck Klein led NL right fielders with 41 assists; in 1948 Taft "Taffy" Wright led the AL with 8.

The high-offense Major League totals of the 1890s, 1920s-30s and 1990s are accepted as part of the statistical base, as are the low-offense totals of the 1900s and 1960s. Major League batters once played in the hitters' paradise that was the Baker Bowl, and play today in atmospherically buoyed Coors Field; their numbers are included in the Major League canon without caveat.

The game is in a constant state of flux. As it changes, the statistical performances required to lead a league change too. But it's all Major League baseball.

* * *

A .400 batting average is a special mark, achieved by only a handful of Major Leaguers. Even Ruth never reached that particular height.

Here are the Major League players who hit .400+ in a single season:

1876: Ross Barnes, .429
1884: Fred Dunlap, .412
1887: James "Tip" O'Neill, .435; Pete Browning, .402
1894: Hugh Duffy, .440; George "Tuck" Turner, .418; Sam Thompson, .415; Ed Delahanty, .404; "Sliding" Billy Hamilton, .403
1895: Jesse Burkett, .405; Ed Delahanty, .404
1896: Jesse Burkett, .410; Hughie Jennings, .401
1897: "Wee" Willie Keeler, .424
1899: Ed Delahanty, .410
1901: Nap Lajoie, .426
1911: Ty Cobb, .420; "Shoeless" Joe Jackson, .408
1912: Ty Cobb, .409
1920: George Sisler, .407
1922: George Sisler, .420; Rogers Hornsby, .401; Ty Cobb, .401
1923: Harry Heilmann, .403
1924: Rogers Hornsby, .424
1925: Rogers Hornsby, .403
1930: Bill Terry, .401
1941: Ted Williams, .406

That's 28 MLB seasons in 66 years—unless we include the statistics of the National Association (NA), 1871–75, which SABR and Retrosheet regard as a major league, in which case there are 35 seasons in 71 years:

1871: Levi Myerle, .492; Cal McVey, .431; Ross Barnes, .401
1872: Ross Barnes, .430; Davy Force, .418; Cap Anson, .415
1873: Ross Barnes, .431

The top NgL single-season batting average is .463 by Juan "Tetelo" Vargas in 1943. This beats Hugh Duffy's official Major League record of .440 in 1984, but falls short of Levi Myerle's .492 in the 1871 National Association. Vargas had 136 plate appearances, Myerle 132. Retrosheet and SABR regard Myerle as a Major Leaguer.

I don't know that I agree—but I do know it's ridiculous to count NA marks and not count NgL marks.

Early MLB provides many examples of skillful batters posting big numbers within short seasons—exactly as in NgL play; yet even within a 154-game framework, MLB batters compiled 13 .400 seasons.

Now for the Negro Leaguers who hit .400+ in a single season[3]:

1920: Cristóbal Torriente, .411
1921: Oscar Charleston, .422; Charlie Blackwell, .402
1923: Oscar "Heavy" Johnson, .406
1924: Wilber "Bullet Joe" Rogan, .411; Oscar Charleston, .405
1925: Oscar Charleston, .427; Edgar Wesley, .404; John Beckwith, .404
1926: George "Mule" Suttles, .425
1927: Charles "Chino" Smith, .457; Roy Parnell, .422; Ernest "Jud" Wilson, .422
1929: Chino Smith, .451; Herbert "Rap" Dixon, .415; Jud Wilson, .404
1930: Jud Wilson, .433; Chino Smith, .417; James "Biz" Mackey, .414; Willie Wells, .411; Mule Suttles, .409
1931: Jud Wilson, .415
1934: Knowlington "Buddy" Burbage, .438; Ray Dandridge, .432; Bert Johnson, .417
1937: Josh Gibson, .417
1938: Walter "Buck" Leonard, .415; Harry Williams, .409
1939: Bill Hoskins, .403; Josh Gibson, .402
1940: James "Cool" Papa Bell, .437
1943: Josh Gibson, .466; Tetelo Vargas, .463
1944: Artie Wilson, .421
1948: Artie Wilson, .437; Willard Brown, .400

That's 36 .400 seasons in 29 years, a considerably greater relative frequency than was achieved in the Majors. The top number of MLB .400 seasons in an equivalent period was 18 in 28 years, 1884 to 1912.

It's axiomatic in the study of statistics that greater deviation from league norms—for instance, a greater number of players posting averages far above the league—tends to indicate a lesser quality of play. For seasons of the same length, that's unquestionably true. But Negro League seasons were much shorter than Major League seasons, with many fewer at-bats—and smaller sample sizes also produce greater deviations from league norms.

Consider:

- Two Major Leaguers (Burkett and Sisler) and two Negro Leaguers (Mackey and Wilson) hit .400 twice.
- Three Major Leaguers (Delahanty, Cobb and Hornsby) and three Negro Leaguers (Charleston, Smith and Gibson) hit .400 three times.
- One Major Leaguer (Barnes) and one Negro Leaguer (Wilson) hit .400 four times.
- In MLB's top single season (1894) and in the NgL's top single season (1930), five players batted .400.

- In MLB's top four-year period (1894–97) and in the NgL's top four-year period (1927–30), each produced ten .400 seasons.

Uniformity of peak performance indicates that while optimum conditions prevailed in the NgL for a longer period than in MLB, early MLB and the NgL featured similar .400-friendly conditions.

* * *

Now let's look at power. A single-season MLB slugging percentage of .700 can be termed historic; it's been achieved just 36 times:

1871: Levi Myerle, .700
1920: Babe Ruth, .847
1921: Babe Ruth, .846
1922: Rogers Hornsby, .722
1923: Babe Ruth, .764
1924: Babe Ruth, .739
1925: Rogers Hornsby, .756
1926: Babe Ruth, .737
1927: Babe Ruth, .772; Lou Gehrig, .765
1928: Babe Ruth, .709
1930: Babe Ruth, .732; Lewis "Hack" Wilson, .723; Lou Gehrig, .721; Al Simmons, .708
1931: Babe Ruth, .700
1932: Jimmie Foxx, .749
1933: Jimmie Foxx, .703
1934: Lou Gehrig, .706
1938: Jimmie Foxx, .704
1941: Ted Williams, .731
1948: Stan Musial, .702
1956: Mickey Mantle, .705
1957: Ted Williams, .735
1994: Jeff Bagwell, .750; Frank Thomas, .729; Albert Belle, .714
1996: Mark McGwire, .731
1997: Larry Walker, .720
1998: Mark McGwire, .753
1999: Larry Walker, .710
2001: Barry Bonds, .863; Sammy Sosa, .737
2002: Barry Bonds, .799
2003: Barry Bonds, .749
2004: Barry Bonds, .812

The names on this list are the ones you'd expect, with the exception of Levi Myerle, who posted the only .700 season of the dead-ball era. As with his .492 average, this achievement is attributable to small sample size.

Ruth's dominance from 1920 to 1931 is astonishing, nine .700+ seasons in 12 years. That's a strong point in favor of the proposition that he, and not Ted Williams, is the greatest MLB hitter of all time. Surely Ruth and Gehrig in 1927 are the most fearsome one-two punch in MLB history.

Note the performance spike in 1994, the only season since 1930 in which more than two players achieved a .700 slugging mark. Here's evidence that sample size impacts peak performance: a players' strike shortened the 1994 schedule, which reduced players' at-bats, which in turn boosted peak performances. The nearest MLB run at a .400 season since Ted Williams, Tony Gwynn's .394, also occurred in 1994.

We can raise the MLB total from 36 to 41 seasons by adding part-season performances. Ordinarily, if a hitter is slugging .700 he's going to be allowed to play more than part-time, but MLB history features a smattering of brilliant but injury- or war-shortened seasons. With a minimum of 100 plate appearances—a number in line with full-time play in many NgL seasons—we can add five more entries to the MLB list:

1953: Ted Williams, .901 slugging in 110 PA
1955: Ted Williams, .703 slugging in 416 PA
1993: Mark McGwire, .726 slugging in 107 PA
2000: Mark McGwire, .746 slugging in 321 PA
2005: Mike Jacobs, .710 slugging in 112 PA

The surprising name here is Mike Jacobs. It's not an aberration—the guy could mash; he hit 32 homers in 2008, but couldn't hold down a long-term job in the Majors.

Now for the Negro Leagues:

1921: Oscar Charleston, .736
1922: Heavy Johnson, .715
1923: George Scales, .738; Heavy Johnson, .722; "Candy" Jim Taylor, .712; Norman "Turkey" Stearnes, .710
1924: Oscar Charleston, .780
1925: Oscar Charleston, .776; John Beckwith, .738; Edgar Wesley, .715
1926: Mule Suttles, .877; Martin Dihigo, .737; Turkey Stearnes, .716
1928: Rap Dixon, .701
1929: Chino Smith, .870; Rap Dixon, .722
1930: Mule Suttles, .817; Chino Smith, .726
1931: John Beckwith, .714; Jud Wilson, .707
1932: Josh Gibson, .711
1934: Josh Gibson, .783
1937: Josh Gibson, .974; Buck Leonard, .729; "Wild" Bill Wright, .728
1938: Josh Gibson, .733; Buck Leonard, .727
1939: Josh Gibson, .824; Buck Leonard, .780
1941: Josh Gibson, .754
1943: Josh Gibson, .867

That's 31 .700 seasons for the NgL to 36 (or 41) for the Majors. Clearly, Gibson and Leonard deserved their contemporary billing as the Black Ruth and Gehrig.

Three factors in NgL slugging data are at variance with MLB stat lines. First, while there are a smaller number of .700+ seasons in NgL play, they occur, as did .400 averages, with greater relative frequency, 31 in 29 years vs. 21 in the top 29-year MLB stretch. Second, there are nine NgL seasons in which more than one player posts .700+ slugging, vs. four such seasons in MLB. Third, the top four NgL seasons—Gibson's .974 in 1937, Suttles's .884 in 1926, Smith's .870 in 1929, and Gibson's .867 in 1943—all eclipse the top three MLB seasons: Bonds' .863 in 2001, Ruth's .847 in 1920 and Ruth's .846 in 1921.

All of these factors are attributable to small sample size. Suttles had 116 PAs in 1926 and Gibson 183 in 1937, vs. Bonds' 664 in 2001. Gibson did accumulate 302 plate appearances in 1943, when he surpassed Bonds' single-season slugging record by four points, but that's still less than half of Bonds' PAs. (Use of inferior balata-cored baseballs during World War II had a negative effect on MLB and NgL batting numbers, making Gibson's 1943 batting prowess all the more remarkable.)

The same holds true for on-base percentage and OPS. The highest NgL single-season OBP is Gibson's .560, again in 1943, which falls short of Barry Bonds' .609 in 2004 and .582 in 2002, but beats Ted Williams's best, .553 in 1941. The two highest NgL OPS figures are both by Gibson (surprise!), 1.474 in 1937 and 1.427 in 1943; both top the four best MLB marks, by Bonds (1.422 in 2004), Bonds (1.381 in 2002), Ruth (1.379 in 1920), and Bonds (1.379 in 2001).

Small sample sizes can produce astonishing results. Any semi-serious baseball fan knows that Ted Williams was MLB's last .400 hitter. The fact that stands out for me, though, is that he actually hit .400 three times—his famous .406 in 1941, and also .400 in 1952 and .407 in '53, in fragmentary stints just before and after he left for the Korean War. Had the Splinter been able to sustain his 1953 performance over a full season, he would have broken the MLB record for single-season slugging, ranked second all-time in OPS, and tied Barry Bonds for the highest OPS+. Most players, deprived of nearly two years' experience and then thrust into the lineup without benefit of spring training, would have struggled. Williams feasted—and showed us what a great hitter can do within the bounds of a small sample. (In the examples that follow, numbers printed in **bold** indicate stats that would break an all-time MLB single-season record when extrapolated to 162 games.)

Ted Williams, 1953

G	PA	AB	R	H	2B	3B	HR	RBI	BB	SO	BA	OBP	SLG	OPS	OPS+
37	110	91	17	37	6	0	13	34	19	10	.407	.509	.901	1.410	268
Per 162	482	398	74	162	26	0	57	149	83	44	.407	.509	**.901**	1.410	**268**

Here's another great hitter mashing a small sample:

Josh Gibson, 1937

G	PA	AB	R	H	2B	3B	HR	RBI	BB	SO	BA	OBP	SLG	OPS	OPS+
39	183	156	60	65	13	7	20	73	25	–	.417	.500	.974	1.474	278
Per 162	760	648	**249**	**270**	54	29	**83**	**303**	104	–	.417	.500	**.974**	**1.474**	**278**

Given the sample sizes of Negro League seasons, it's surprising that NgL players didn't smash every calculated MLB single-season record. The truth of this becomes evident when we compare NgL performances with another set of small sample sizes: great *months* posted by Major League batters. Here's a by no means exhaustive sample of great months by MLB hitters compiled just in the years since Jackie broke the color barrier—performances that stand shoulder to shoulder with the finest Negro League seasons:

Ted Williams, July 1957

G	BA	SLG	OPS
28	.440	.893	1.472
Per 162	**.440**	**.893**	**1.472**

Norm Cash, June 1961

G	HR	SLG
30	14	.901
Per 162	76	**.901**

Reggie Jackson, June 1969

G	HR	RBI
26	14	37
Per 162	**87**	**231**

4. Statistical Variance Across Leagues and Eras

Rod Carew, June 1977			
G	H	3B	BA
28	54	8	.486
Per 162	312	46	.486

George Brett, July 1980				
G	H	2B	RBI	BA
21	42	12	25	.494
Per 162	324	93	193	.494

Tony Gwynn, June 1987		
G	H	BA
25	44	.473
Per 162	285	.473

Frank Thomas, May 1994				
G	R	BA	SLG	OPS
25	39	.452	.988	1.581
Per 162	253	.452	.988	1.581

Jeff Bagwell, July 1994		
G	HR	RBI
24	11	29
Per 162	74	196

Juan Gonzales, July 1996			
G	HR	RBI	SLG
27	15	38	.917
Per 162	90	228	.917

Ken Griffey, Jr., July 1996		
G	HR	RBI
18	11	30
Per 162	99	270

Larry Walker, April 1997							
G	R	H	HR	RBI	BA	SLG	OPS
23	29	41	11	29	.456	.911	1.449
Per 162	204	289	77	204	.456	.911	1.449

Mark McGwire, May 1998			
G	HR	RBI	SLG
26	16	32	.907
Per 162	100	199	.907

Sammy Sosa, June 1998		
G	HR	RBI
27	20	40
Per 162	120	240

Albert Belle, July 1998			
G	HR	RBI	SLG
26	16	32	.941
Per 162	100	199	.941

Todd Helton, May 2000						
G	R	H	HR	BA	SLG	OPS
23	32	42	11	.512	1.000	1.588
Per 162	225	296	77	.512	1.000	1.588

Barry Bonds, April 2004					
G	BB	BA	OBP	SLG	OPS
23	39	.472	.696	1.132	1.828
Per 162	275	.472	.696	1.132	1.828

Ichiro Suzuki, August 2004		
G	H	BA
28	56	.463
Per 162	324	.463

Albert Pujols, April 2006				
G	HR	RBI	SO	BA
25	14	32	.914	1.423
Per 162	91	207	.914	1.423

David Ortiz, July 2006		
G	HR	RBI
26	14	35
Per 162	87	218

Ryan Howard, August 2006		
G	HR	RBI
29	14	41
Per 162	78	229

Alex Rodriguez, April 2007		
G	HR	RBI
23	14	34
Per 162	99	239

Bryce Harper, May 2015		
G	HR	SLG
26	13	.884
Per 162	81	.884

Ryan Zimmerman, April 2017			
G	HR	RBI	SLG
24	11	29	.886
Per 162	74	196	.886

Giancarlo Stanton, August 2017				Aaron Judge, September 2017				J.D. Martinez, September 2017			
G	HR	RBI	SLG	G	HR	RBI	SLG	G	HR	RBI	SLG
29	18	37	.899	27	15	32	.889	24	16	36	.970
Per 162	101	207	.899	Per 162	90	192	.889	Per 162	108	243	.970

Some of these month-long "seasons" put Gibson's 1937 in the shade. There's not a player in this group who wouldn't have smashed at least two all-time MLB records if they'd sustained this level of production for an entire season—and these months correspond with the length of most full Negro League seasons. Each of these performances was compiled against the highest possible level of professional pitching and fielding; no one questions the legitimacy of the numbers. (Except, perhaps, in the case of steroid-fueled performances—but that's a different topic.)

Mine is not the only study that shows results like these. ESPN's Bradford Doolittle compiled a list of 25 MLB hitters who've batted .400+ over a half-season (82 games) since 1945, with George Brett hitting .476 over 82 team games in 1980.[4]

Viewed in the context of small sample size, the sometimes stratospheric single-season calculated stats put up by Negro Leaguers become more comprehensible—and again we find that NgL offensive data falls within historical norms of MLB play.

* * *

NgL performances tend to line up neatly with stat lines from earlier or later eras of MLB—but sometimes the parallel with contemporary MLB is quite exact.

In the six-year span 1920 to 1925, which saw both the advent of the Negro Leagues and the beginning of the MLB live-ball era, the top hitter in the Negro Leagues was Oscar Charleston. In that same span of years the top AL hitter was Babe Ruth, the top NL hitter Rogers Hornsby. Charleston's record is beautifully in scale with Major League accomplishments over the same period. *(See the following table.)*

- Over a concurrent six-year span, Charleston hit .400 three times, as did Hornsby.
- Hornsby batted .397 overall, Charleston .389, Ruth .360.
- Ruth posted an OBP of .497, Hornsby .467, Charleston .465.
- Ruth's slugging was .747, Hornsby's .666, Charleston's .665.
- Ruth's OPS was 1.245, Hornsby's 1.133, Charleston's 1.130.
- Ruth's OPS+ was 217, Charleston's 206, Hornsby's 200.

Overall, we have to rate Ruth the #1 batsman in professional baseball, and also the #1 player, over this six-year span—no surprises there. (Just for laughs, he also posted a 3–0 win-loss record as a starting pitcher in this same frame.) But Charleston and Hornsby produced startlingly similar offensive results. The only real difference is that Hornsby's performance was accepted into the Major League record books and Charleston's wasn't.

4. Statistical Variance Across Leagues and Eras

Oscar Charleston, 1920–25

Yr	G	AB	R	H	2B	3B	HR	RBI	SB	CS	BB	SO	BA	OBP	SLG	OPS	OPS+	HBP
1920	92	346	80	122	20	11	5	59	20	–	37	–	.353	.418	.517	.936	176	2
1921	77	284	104	123	17	12	15	91	32	–	41	–	.433	.512	.736	1.248	250	5
1922	101	401	105	150	25	18	19	102	21	–	41	–	.374	.433	.668	1.102	193	1
1923	84	308	68	112	25	6	11	94	25	–	48	–	.364	.453	.591	1.043	168	2
1924	54	205	63	83	22	5	15	63	20	–	28	–	.405	.476	.780	1.257	254	–
1925	71	255	97	109	23	3	20	97	17	–	51	–	.427	.523	.776	1.299	228	–
	479	1,799	517	699	132	55	85	506	135		246		.389	.465	.665	1.130	206	10

Rogers Hornsby, 1920–25

Yr	G	AB	R	H	2B	3B	HR	RBI	SB	CS	BB	SO	BA	OBP	SLG	OPS	OPS+	HBP
1920	149	589	96	218	44	20	9	94	12	15	60	50	.370	.431	.559	.990	185	3
1921	154	592	131	235	44	18	21	126	13	13	60	48	.397	.458	.639	1.097	191	7
1922	154	623	141	250	46	14	42	152	17	12	65	50	.401	.459	.722	1.181	207	1
1923	107	424	89	163	32	10	17	83	3	7	55	29	.384	.459	.627	1.086	187	3
1924	143	536	121	227	43	14	25	94	5	12	89	32	.424	.507	.696	1.203	222	2
1925	138	504	133	203	41	10	39	143	5	3	83	39	.403	.489	.756	1.245	210	2
	845	3,268	711	1,296	250	86	153	692	55	62	412	248	.397	.467	.666	1.133	200	18

Babe Ruth, 1920–25

Yr	G	AB	R	H	2B	3B	HR	RBI	SB	CS	BB	SO	BA	OBP	SLG	OPS	OPS+	HBP
1920	142	458	158	172	36	9	54	135	14	14	150	80	.376	.532	.847	1.379	255	3
1921	152	540	177	204	44	16	59	168	17	13	145	81	.378	.512	.846	1.359	238	4
1922	110	406	94	128	24	8	35	96	2	5	84	80	.315	.434	.672	1.106	182	1
1923	152	522	151	205	45	13	41	130	17	21	170	93	.393	.545	.764	1.309	239	4
1924	153	529	143	200	39	7	46	124	9	13	142	81	.378	.513	.739	1.252	220	4
1925	98	359	61	104	12	2	25	67	2	4	59	68	.290	.393	.543	.936	137	2
	807	2,814	784	1,013	200	55	260	720	61	70	750	483	.360	.497	.747	1.245	217	18

Given his superior baserunning, fielding, postseason play and clubhouse presence, it's clear that Charleston, and not Hornsby, was the Number Two man to Ruth for the period 1920–25.

Shouldn't the record books, the All-Decade teams, and—especially—the consciousness of the average fan, all reflect this fact?

5

Mr. James's 23 Tests

In describing (and dismissing) the Union Association's recognition as a Major League, Bill James's *New Historical Baseball Abstract* offers eight *structural* tests by which the professional quality of a league can be measured:

1. Stability.
2. Competitiveness.
3. Quality players.
4. Size of cities.
5. Ballparks.
6. Attendance.
7. Major league media coverage.
8. A structure to attract talent.

Later in the *Abstract* James lists 14 primarily *statistical* tests, 12 of which are relevant to the present discussion (two of the statistical tests—condition of the field, and average attendance and seating capacity of the game location—are repetitive of numbers 5 and 6 and are therefore omitted here):

9. Hitting by pitchers.
10. The average distance of the players, in age, from 27.
11. The percentage of players who are less than six feet tall or more than 6'3".
12. Fielding percentage and passed balls.
13. Double plays.
14. Usage of pitchers at other positions.
15. The percentage of fielding plays made by pitchers.
16. The percentage of games that are blowouts.
17. The use of players in specialized roles.
18. The average distance of teams from .500.
19. The percentage of games that go nine innings.
20. The standard deviation of offensive effectiveness.
21. The standard of record-keeping.
22. The percentage of managers who have 20 years or more experience in the game.

A final test is mentioned elsewhere in the *Abstract*:

23. The common success of teenagers, and in particular teenaged pitchers.

That's 23 tests of professional quality in total. Let's begin by examining the NgL in the light of James's structural tests[1]:

1. STABILITY.

There are three issues here: league stability, team stability, and contract stability.

The National League was formed from the remnants of a previous league that some consider professional, the National Association, whose teams never did settle on a common schedule, or even a fixed number of games to be played by each team:

National Association Games Played			
Year	Most GP	Least GP	Difference
1871	33	19	174%
1872	54	9	600%
1873	59	6	983%
1874	70	47	149%
1875	79	13	608%

To anyone versed in Negro League team records, NA variations in games played will look familiar. The 1920 Negro National League was a new organization with the same start-up troubles of the 1871 National Association, along with systemic racism.

The National League never fully lost league stability from the day of its founding in 1876, though it had to fight off challenges from five competitor leagues over the next 40 years. The rival American League, which at first raided the NL for players, was simply absorbed into the existing MLB structure, where it thrives to this day; four other all-white major leagues collapsed completely. MLB faced down the last of its serious competitors, the Federal League, in 1915 after a two-year challenge.

Andrew "Rube" Foster founded the original Negro National League (NNL) in 1920. The Eastern Colored League (ECL), created to complement the NNL and establish a two-league structure like the NL and AL, endured six years from 1923 to 1928 before folding. The ECL's successor, the American Negro League (ANL), lasted a single year, folding after the 1929 season. World events then intervened: the Great Depression led directly to the 1931 collapse of the original NNL. The Negro Southern League (NSL) and East-West League (EWL) were formed from the rubble, but after a single year the EWL folded completely and the NSL returned to minor league status.

Illustrative of NgL teams' struggle for survival in this era, the Homestead Grays, most famous and iconic of all Black teams, were forced to declare five different NgL affiliations in as many years, as leagues coalesced and collapsed around them:

1929: American Negro League (ANL)
1930: Eastern Independent Clubs (EAS)
1931: Independent (IND)
1932: East-West League (EWL)
1933: Negro National League II (NN2)

The NgL achieved league stability 14 years after its founding, despite the intervention of the Depression and the refusal of most American banks to extend loans to Black Americans. The formation of the NN2 in 1933 and the Negro American League (NAL) in 1937 created the stable two-league structure NgL owners and teams had been striving for since 1923. The NgL faced down its only serious rival, the Mexican League (MEX), in 1941 after a two-year challenge.

(Mexico had attractions for NgL stars beyond the enormous salaries offered by MEX owners. As Willie Wells told Wendell Smith in the May 6, 1944, *Pittsburgh Courier*: "I've found freedom and democracy here, something I never found in the United States. I was branded a Negro in the States and had to act accordingly. Everything I did, including playing ball, was regulated by my color. They wouldn't even give me a chance in the big leagues because I was a Negro, yet they accepted every other nationality under the sun. Well, here in Mexico I am a man. I can go as far in baseball as I am capable of going."

Canada appealed to Black players for the same basic reasons, though there was no organized professional structure to aspire to as there was in Mexico. "They loved it," remembers Jay-Dell Mah, a batboy for semi-pro teams in Saskatchewan. "They felt it was a breath of fresh air because they didn't have to sneak into the back door through the kitchen to get something to eat at a restaurant."[2])

In its various incarnations, the NgL lasted more than twice as long as the American Association, the Union Association, the Players' League and the Federal League *combined*. It was by far the most robust and durable challenge to MLB supremacy in North America. Perhaps the two-league NN2-NAL structure would ultimately have enjoyed multi-decade stability and success akin to the two-league NL-AL structure, but the breaking of the color barrier led to the NgL's almost immediate collapse as a viable financial proposition.

Monte Irvin put it best: "The raw talent of the players was generally major-league caliber, but in other ways, the leagues were not at that level. The owners had a loosely formed league and they stayed together, but they were not very well organized."[3]

Next is *team* stability. Of 59 Negro League franchises affiliated with one or more leagues in the NgL's 29-year existence, 25 teams lasted four or more consecutive years; 29 teams (49 percent) folded after a single year or less of play.

Similarly, of 81 franchises affiliated with one or more leagues in the first 30 years of NA and MLB play, 1871–1900, no less than 73 teams (90 percent) folded, 39 of them after a year or less. The eight teams that survived are with us today.[4]

In sum, the NgL was a less stable league structure than the NL-AL combine, but more stable than any other challenger to MLB supremacy. By contrast, *team* instability plagued both MLB and the NgL for three decades—the difference being that MLB alone had the opportunity to outgrow its early struggles.

Lastly there's *contract* stability. It's true that Negro Leaguers, including the great players, had a tendency to flit from team to team, and neither NgL players nor owners considered themselves particularly bound by contracts. But these same conditions prevailed in early MLB. All five of the National League's competitors—the AA, the UA, the PL, the AL and the FL—freely raided the NL for talent; the players themselves often broke their contracts and jumped leagues for a fatter paycheck.

And so, while the stability argument favors MLB, it does so by no decisive margin, as early MLB had teething troubles of its own.

2. COMPETITIVENESS.

Within a year of the founding of its second league, the NgL established a Colored World Series. The four Series that followed, 1924–27, featured three different winners. This successful inter-league championship series ended with the collapse of the ECL.

In 1942, six years after the founding of the NAL, a new Negro World Series was established; this time five different winners emerged from seven Series, 1942–48. The end of this second run of Series marks the end of the NgL's generally acknowledged status as a Major League.

In MLB, the American Association staged seven World Series with the NL, 1884–90, but these contests are not regarded as true World Series today, nor are their records included in the post-season statistical base. These Series were not very competitive, with NL teams winning four, losing one and drawing two.

From 1903 onwards the NL and the AL have held the World Series contests we know today, which at times have been far from competitive. From 1936 to 1964 the Yankees participated in more than three-quarters of all World Series, 22 of 29, winning 16, or 55 percent of all Series held in that 29-year stretch.

I see no reason to declare the NgL any less competitive than MLB.

3. QUALITY PLAYERS.

The presence of 43 Hall of Famers in the NgL, and the sheer impact of the handful of NgL players who made it to the Majors, decides this question strongly in favor of NgL professionalism.

4. SIZE OF CITIES.

The Negro Leagues played in far more cities, and far more *big* cities, than MLB in the same era.

From 1903 to 1952, MLB teams were concentrated in just seven northeastern states: Chicago (Illinois), Boston (Massachusetts), Detroit (Michigan), St. Louis (Missouri), Brooklyn and New York City (New York), Cincinnati and Cleveland (Ohio), Philadelphia and Pittsburgh (Pennsylvania), plus Washington, D.C. The team located farthest south didn't make it past the Mason-Dixon Line.

The NgL had top-level teams in all of these cities except Boston—plus teams in Birmingham (Alabama), Jacksonville (Florida), Atlanta (Georgia), Indianapolis (Indiana), Kansas City (Missouri), Louisville (Kentucky), Atlantic City and Newark (New Jersey), Columbus, Dayton, and Toledo (Ohio), Harrisburg (Pennsylvania), Memphis and Nashville (Tennessee), Houston (Texas), and Milwaukee (Wisconsin).

The NgL has the superior claim—and by far—as the great *national* pastime.

5. BALLPARKS.

The NgL had one world-class, purpose-built stadium dedicated specifically to Negro Leagues play. Greenlee Field, which hosted the Pittsburgh Crawfords from 1932 through 1938, is commonly recognized as the finest independent ballpark of its era anywhere in the United States.

Unlike Gus Greenlee, most NgL owners didn't have personal funds sufficient to finance the construction of world-class stadiums; nor did they have access to capital held by white-owned banks, which was readily available to MLB owners. And so, almost every NgL team used Major League stadiums, every chance they got. "Before some of us got the opportunity to play in Major League baseball," remembered Larry Doby, "we had played in stadiums like Yankee Stadium, and the Polo Grounds, and

Ebbets Field, and Comiskey Park, and Griffith Stadium." When NgL owners couldn't get MLB stadiums, they'd try to rent high minor-league parks. MLB owners gladly pocketed the rental income, even as they cynically denied these same players the chance to wear their uniforms.[5]

For a rundown of the quality of other NgL parks, I turned to Seamheads co-founder and Negro Leagues ballpark expert **Kevin Johnson**, who offers this original essay:

> In the 1920s, Negro League teams mostly played in wooden ballparks they either built or rented, but they were close to MLB quality:
>
> 1. Chicago's Schorling Park had been a major league facility for the White Sox. The White Sox upgraded to Comiskey, but Schorling/South Side was still a fine facility, at least in the 1920s.
> 2. Kansas City's Muehlebach Field was brand new, and was used by the A's and Royals decades later.
> 3. St. Louis's Stars Park and Detroit's Mack Park were small fields but could hold up to 10,000 fans, and were not much smaller in size than Philadelphia's Baker Bowl, home of the Phillies from 1895 to 1938.
> 4. Both Birmingham's Rickwood Field and Memphis's Lewis Park/Martin Park in Memphis had Major League dimensions.
> 5. Hilldale Park in Darby, Pennsylvania, had MLB dimensions and held large crowds.
> 6. Washington Park in Indianapolis was a Major League park also, having been used by the Federal League's Brooklyn Tip-Tops.
> 7. Baltimore's Maryland Park and Atlantic City's Bacharach Park were run down from a facility perspective, but the fields themselves were of at least high minor league dimensions.
> 8. Catholic Protectory Oval (CPO) in the Bronx and whatever park the Cleveland franchise was playing in during a particular season were the only truly non-major league parks.
>
> In the 1930s, parks like Greenlee and Michigan's Hamtramck Stadium were built, and other teams transitioned to more renting of MLB parks. CPO was no longer used, and Cleveland teams started playing in League Park. Franchises that couldn't rent a high minor league or MLB park, like the St. Louis Stars, typically didn't survive.
>
> In the 1940s, Negro League teams were consistently playing in MLB parks or modern high minor league parks. But in 1948, the last year of the NgL's Major League status, teams could no longer afford renting MLB stadiums, and started barnstorming or otherwise struggling to find parks to play in.
>
> So from a batting/pitching balance perspective the fields were generally *not* substandard. However, even when playing in MLB parks, Negro League teams had to play without the fields being cut or manicured as they were for MLB games, so fielding in the Negro Leagues was impacted by the ballparks vs. MLB fielding quality.
>
> —*Kevin Johnson*

While official NgL fields may not have been universally up to MLB standards of the *same* era, they were vastly superior to many early MLB parks, which weren't far removed from farm fields. As official MLB historian John Thorn observes, "The

Top: Exposition Park, Pittsburgh, 1910s (courtesy Pittsburgh City Photographer Collection, University of Pittsburgh). *Above:* PNC Park, Pittsburgh, 2010s (Pixabay).

playing fields themselves were often an adventure; outfielders, some playing without walls behind them, had to contend with slopes, trees, swamps, lakes and dangerous debris left over from the garbage dumps some ballparks were built upon." At Bennett Park, where the Detroit Tigers played their home games from 1901 through 1911, cobblestones stuck up through the playing field, injuring players and causing balls that struck them to carom in bizarre directions.[6]

There's no disadvantage for the NgL to be found here.

6. ATTENDANCE.

Negro League events often out-drew analogous MLB events—this despite Blacks comprising slightly less than 10 percent of the total US population in the period 1920–48. The NgL East-West Game out-drew the MLB All-Star Game by 11,485 in 1942, 19,785 in 1943, 16,658 in 1944.

NgL attendance success helped fuel Kenesaw Landis's antagonism towards the Black leagues—and was a major motivator for MLB owners contemplating integration. "Branch Rickey was a top businessman," remembered Buck O'Neil. "He had seen us play before 50,000 in Comiskey Park, you understand? We had played in Yankee Stadium with 40,000 people. So he knew—here's a new source of revenue."[7]

Larry Doby agreed: "We would play in Yankee Stadium ... and you'd have like 40[,000], 45,000 people. That's why sometimes I think, and I think a lot of people think the same way, that [Chicago Cubs president Phil] Wrigley saw more than just players. And that's business, you know. You get 40,000 Afro-Americans in the stadium, even if it's only a dollar a head, that's $40,000."[8]

7. MAJOR LEAGUE MEDIA COVERAGE.

MLB enjoyed vastly more mainstream (i.e., white) press coverage than the NgL—but as this was 100 percent attributable to racist mass-media indifference, it's hard to construe this as a point against NgL professionalism.

8. A STRUCTURE TO ATTRACT TALENT.

NgL teams had an elemental advantage over their MLB counterparts in finding new players: they travelled non-stop, playing against local talent across the eastern United States and seeing the best un-signed Black players in action. NgL teams also benefited from what Satchel Paige called the "Bama grapevine," a tremendous word-of-mouth network that brought talented players to the attention of NgL owners.[9]

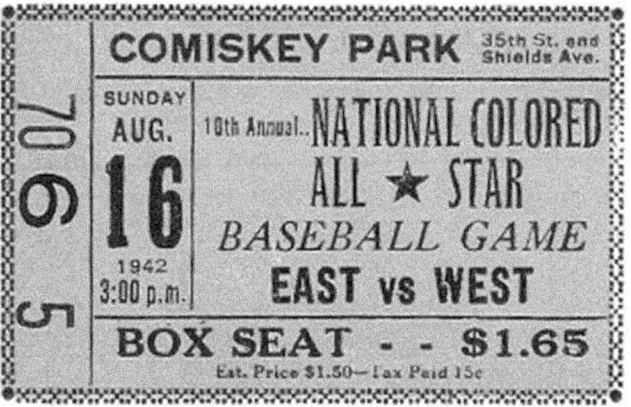

A ticket for the 1942 East-West Game, played in MLB's Comiskey Park.

This compares favorably with the first 40 years

of MLB practice. As Mr. James tells us: "The networking system by which the Negro Leagues identified and developed talent was certainly far more sophisticated than nineteenth century baseball.... It is absolutely amazing how many minor league organizations in that era (1900–1920) didn't know a baseball player from an opera singer." In August 1905, Detroit Tigers manager Bill Armour left his team in mid-season to personally scout the East Coast for players to replace the coterie of drunken sots that infested his roster.[10]

So, in respect of James's eight structural tests, there's a minor advantage for MLB in league stability; otherwise, the NgL's looking pretty good.

Next, addressing James's statistical tests:

9. Hitting by Pitchers.

If what James means is the raw hitting ability of certain pitchers, then certainly "Bullet Joe" Rogan and "Cyclone" Joe Williams could rake with the best of them. If what he means instead is the ability of pitchers to change positions and fashion themselves into great position players, Martin Dihigo and James "Cool Papa" Bell made successful transitions.

But couldn't Babe Ruth hit a little too? How about George Sisler, or "Smoky" Joe Wood? Wes Ferrell was often used as a pinch hitter. John Montgomery Ward compiled 2000 hits *and* 100 wins. Plenty of MLB pitchers converted successfully to full-time position players: Stan Musial, Rube Bressler, Francis "Lefty" O'Doul. And this isn't solely a phenomenon of the past: just look at Shohei Ohtani.

But I think what Mr. James means is how pitchers hit as a group. I can't run my usual comparisons between the NgL and early MLB, as MLB records for batting by position exist only from 1918 forwards. Still, we'll do our best:

MLB hitting by pitchers				NgL hitting by pitchers		
1920–29	1930–39	1940–49		1920–29	1930–39	1940–48
.203	.192	.173	BA	.219	.213	.205
.243	.232	.214	OBP	.269	.257	.251
.258	.241	.213	SLG	.292	.277	.262
.501	.473	.427	OPS	.560	.533	.513

In both leagues we see a steady decline in hitting by pitchers in every calculated category. NgL stats for 1940–48 run very close to MLB stats for 1920–29.

However, if we change the parameters of the comparison to hitting by pitchers vs. the league average, the results change sharply:

MLB pitchers' hitting relative to league average				NgL pitchers' hitting relative to league average		
1920–29	1930–39	1940–48		1920–29	1930–39	1940–48
–.082	–.087	–.087	BA	–.057	–.062	–.065
–.104	–.111	–.116	OBP	–.070	–.081	–.085
–.138	–.158	–.153	SLG	–.092	–.108	–.106
–.242	–.269	–.269	OPS	–.162	–.189	–.191

There's a significant gap in favor of MLB in this data.

Based on other early MLB data I analyzed for this section, I strongly suspect that nineteenth-century MLB pitchers' hitting stats deviated from league norms much more narrowly than NgL stats, both by raw numbers and relative to league averages—but I can't prove it; the data points don't exist for early MLB play.

Small roster sizes meant that NgL pitchers often had to play other positions. This may have prompted NgL owners and managers to favor pitchers who could hit well—but again, I can't prove it.

Therefore, frustratingly, I must interpret this data as a *disadvantage* for NgL professionalism.

10. THE AVERAGE DISTANCE OF THE PLAYERS, IN AGE, FROM 27.

To examine this and the following question, I compared NgL and MLB players for 1920, the founding year of the Negro Leagues.

For NgL players there's a typical data gap; nonetheless, thanks to the remarkable reconstructions performed by Seamheads, we know the ages of 236 of 289 players (82%) and the height of 175 (61%). For MLB, Baseball Reference has the ages of all 494 players and the height of 492.

The average age of an NgL player for 1920 is exactly 27.0, vs. 26.7 for MLB. If we pro-rate ages by the number of plate appearances per player, the average age for the NgL is 27.5; the average for the MLB, 26.7.

I'm calling this one a dead-even draw between the NgL and MLB, and therefore a point in the NgL's favor.

11. THE PERCENTAGE OF PLAYERS WHO ARE LESS THAN SIX FEET TALL OR MORE THAN 6'3".

MLB enjoys a distinct advantage here. In 1920, 35.2 percent of MLB players fall between 6'0" and 6'3", vs. 23.4 percent of NgL players, a 50 percent gap.

Strangely, if we prorate the results by number of plate appearances, the percentage drops sharply for both leagues, but still favors MLB 23.8 percent to 15.0 percent, a 59 percent gap.

With other tests, I've searched for comparisons between the NgL and earlier eras of MLB—but that can't apply here, because the human population itself becomes taller with each passing generation, which biases comparison of heights between eras.

It's possible that Black poverty relative to whites caused nutrition standards for NgL players to be lower than for MLB players—but a lot of white boys from poor farming and immigrant families played in MLB in the 1920s, so this cause-and-effect scenario can be nothing but speculation.

In 11 tests, this is the first definite, irrefutable disadvantage we've seen for the NgL.

12. FIELDING PERCENTAGE AND PASSED BALLS.[11]

Passed ball data isn't available for NgL play—but fielding percentage is:

MLB fielding percentage by decade

NA	1876–80	1880–89	1890–99	1900–09	1910–19	1920–29	1930–39	1940–49
.837	.884	.905	.931	.953	.961	.968	.971	.973

NgL fielding percentage by decade

1920–29	1930–39	1940–48	Overall
.951	.956	.955	.953

NgL fielding percentages compare nicely with MLB fielding percentages for the period 1900–09.

By this measure, MLB was more professional than the NgL for the period 1910–1948—but the NgL was more professional in its first three decades, or 1920–1948, than MLB was for the period 1876–1899.

13. DOUBLE PLAYS.

The NgL consistently maintained a much higher rate of double plays per nine innings than *any* era of MLB:

MLB double plays per 9 innings

NA	1876–80	1880–89	1890–99	1900–09	1910–19	1920–29	1930–39
.058	.064	.073	.086	.070	.080	.104	.108

1940–49	1950–59	1960–69	1970–79	1980–89	1990–99	2000–09	2010–19
.110	.116	.102	.106	.104	.104	.106	.098

NgL double plays per 9 innings

1920–29	1930–39	1940–48	Overall
.196	.161	.190	.183

This measure is skewed, though, by varying offensive levels in different eras, which affect the number of baserunners per nine innings. Double plays per baserunner are a more context-neutral measure—but the result of the comparison remains the same: MLB has never caught up with the NgL's ability to turn two:

MLB double plays per baserunner

NA	1876–80	1880–89	1890–99	1900–09	1910–19	1920–29	1930–39
.044	.055	.057	.060	.056	.062	.073	.076

1940–49	1950–59	1960–69	1970–79	1980–89	1990–99	2000–09	2010–19
.081	.088	.084	.083	.082	.079	.080	.080

NgL double plays per baserunner

1920–29	1930–39	1940–48	Overall
.148	.143	.135	.155

The NgL passes this test with flying colors.

14. USAGE OF PITCHERS AT OTHER POSITIONS.

See number 17 below.

15. THE PERCENTAGE OF FIELDING PLAYS MADE BY PITCHERS.

High putout totals by pitchers are tied closely to the conditions of dead-ball era baseball, in which batted balls had a strong tendency to stay on the ground. It's no coincidence that MLB fielding plays by pitchers exceeded 6 percent every year from 1895 through 1929, the first year that home runs outnumbered triples—but in all the years since 1929, triples outnumbered homers only once (1931), and fielding plays by pitchers topped 6 percent only once (1933).

Although its ranks included first-class sluggers, the NgL never fully embraced the live-ball era. Homers outnumbered triples in only six of 29 seasons: 1925–26, 1929, 1935–36 and 1939. Correspondingly, NgL fielding plays by pitchers dipped under 7 percent only five times through 1939: 1925, 1929–30 and 1935–36, aligning with four of the six seasons in which homers outnumbered triples.

NgL fielding data for 1925 is very limited, confined to independent play only—but within that limited data set, fielding plays by pitchers accounted for 6.35 percent of total fielding chances. For the 1940s we have only three seasons' worth of NgL fielding data; all three seasons place under 7 percent.

MLB percentage of fielding plays by pitchers

NA	1876–80	1880–89	1890–99	1900–09	1910–19	1920–29	1930–39	1940–49
5.74%	5.88%	5.83%	6.37%	7.54%	7.28%	6.47%	5.76%	5.67%

NgL percentage of fielding plays by pitchers

1920–29	1930–39	1940–48	Overall
7.96%	7.05%	6.62%	7.46%

The percentage of fielding plays by 1920s NgL pitchers was higher than in any MLB decade, a potential point against NgL professionalism for that period. However, NgL play for the decade 1930–39 corresponds roughly with the MLB decade 1910–19, while NgL data for the subsequent decade 1940–48 corresponds roughly with MLB data for the subsequent decade 1920–29. We see a steady improvement over time in both NgL and MLB data.

Both NgL double play percentages (a professional positive) and fielding plays by pitchers (a professional negative) run higher than MLB totals through the 1940s. This probably correlates to the fact that NgL on-base and slugging rates were higher than MLB dead-ball rates, but lower than live-ball rates:

MLB vs. NgL on-base, slugging, and OPS rates by era

	MLB Dead-Ball	NgL	MLB Live-Ball*
OBP	.317	.338	.340
Slg	.342	.380	.388
OPS	.658	.717	.728

*1920–48 only.

NgL play was essentially a hybrid of pre–1920 MLB, with a full arsenal of small-ball tactics on display (but with more baserunners per inning), and post–1920 MLB, with home runs supercharging the offense (but with less extra-base power).

This is the #1 reason why NgL play doesn't compare readily with any one specific MLB era: the NgL played its own unique brand of the game. I wish I'd been there to see it; their combination of basepath daring and long-ball slugging sounds pretty damn entertaining.

I believe that when all elements of the argument are considered, the NgL passes this test.

16. THE PERCENTAGE OF GAMES THAT ARE BLOWOUTS.

There are two methods of looking at this question. The first is to pick an arbitrary number of runs by which a team can win a game and call any win by that margin or greater a blowout. I've chosen eight runs; here are the results:

*MLB wins by 8+ runs as a percentage of games played
(insufficient data exists for NA play)*

1876–80	1880–89	1890–99	1900–09	1910–19	1920–29	1930–39	1940–49
20.3%	16.1%	16.6%	8.3%	6.1%	9.3%	10.4%	8.3%

NgL wins by 8+ runs as a percentage of games played

1920–29	1930–39	1940–48	Overall
11.3%	12.4%	13.0%	12.1%

NgL numbers fall between the highs of nineteenth-century MLB and the lows of twentieth-century MLB, clearly at a professional level.

Another method is to define a blowout as any win by more than twice the league average of runs scored per game, which allows the definition to rise and fall with league offensive levels. If teams in a given league regularly score five runs a game, it's probably going to take a 10-run win to awe the fans, whereas if teams struggle to put three runs on the board, a six-run win is mighty impressive.

*MLB wins by 2× the league average of runs
per game as a percentage of games played
(insufficient data exists for NA play)*

1876–80	1880–89	1890–99	1900–09	1910–19	1920–29	1930–39	1940–49
6.8%	5.7%	3.5%	7.0%	4.9%	4.1%	4.8%	4.8%

*NgL wins by 2x the league average of runs
per game as a percentage of games played*

1920–29	1930–39	1940–48	Overall
4.0%	4.4%	5.7%	4.6%

By either method, NgL data corresponds beautifully with MLB data.

17. THE USE OF PLAYERS IN SPECIALIZED ROLES.

NgL rosters were much smaller than MLB rosters, 14–16 players vs. 24–25, a matter of basic economics. Being able to handle more than one position was a necessity for most NgL players. It follows that NgL players were *required* to be more versatile athletes than MLB players.

Consider the first wave of NgL stars to cross over to the Majors. Jackie Robinson won the 1940 NCAA long jump championship, and is to this day the only four-letter athlete in UCLA history; Larry Doby was a four-sport, 11-letter monster in high school, and in January 1948 became the first Black man to play top-level professional basketball; Monte Irvin, too, was a four-sport, 16-letter high school phenom. All three arrived in the first wave of Negro Leaguers to play in the Majors.

Apart from boxing, baseball was the one pro sport in which great Black athletes knew they could earn a living prior to 1947. I doubt very much whether the heavy concentration of superior multi-sport athletes in the 1940s NgL was accidental—and I'd be willing to bet that a similar concentration existed in earlier iterations of the NgL and other Black leagues.

Overall, I think the athletic and multi-positional ability of so many NgL players has to be interpreted as an *advantage* over their MLB counterparts.

18. THE AVERAGE DISTANCE OF TEAMS FROM .500.

As both the NgL and nineteenth-century MLB suffered tremendous team and league instability, we'd expect to see NgL teams sitting about the same distance from .500 as early MLB teams—and that's what we find. All three NgL decades fall in the MLB range for 1876–89; the NgL distance for 1930–39 is exactly the same as the MLB distance for 1880–89.

NA and MLB average team distance from .500

NA	1876–80	1880–89	1890–99	1900–09	1910–19	1920–29	1930–39	1940–49
35.5%	27.9%	21.6%	19.1%	18.1%	15.7%	16.0%	10.6%	14.0%

NgL average team distance from .500

1920–29	1930–39	1940–48	Overall
24.4%	21.6%	22.4%	23.4%

In none of its three decades does the NgL come within 10 points of the distance from .500 compiled by NA teams.

Another test passed by the NgL.

19. THE PERCENTAGE OF GAMES THAT GO NINE INNINGS.

This question is unfortunately unanswerable at present. As Negro Leagues data is systematized by Seamheads researchers, it might be addressable in future.

20. THE STANDARD DEVIATION OF OFFENSIVE EFFECTIVENESS.

This was the hardest of Mr. James's tests for me to answer. I asked the man himself what, exactly, he meant by "the standard deviation of offensive effectiveness." His reply: "I don't have a standing opinion on it. It's just something that I would decide how to measure if I was in the practice of measuring it."[12]

And so, the ball being in my court, I devised a method; it may not be how Mr. James would tackle the problem, but I've done my best. For each decade of MLB and NgL play I chose to examine the weighted standard deviation of batters' OPS, this being the core statistic that correlates best with actual runs scored.[13]

A large percentage of players whose OPS runs well above league averages is a strong indicator of a lower-level league, because low levels of competition allow true professionals to stand out from the pack.

Here's a simplified rule of thumb by which to judge whether a StDev indicates a true outlier from normal performance:

- A standard deviation (StDev) of 0 is league average.
- A StDev of 1 is a minor outlier.
- A StDev of 2 is a major outlier.
- A StDev of 3 or more is a freak aberration.

The distorting effect lesser leagues can have on a player's numbers is illustrated by Hall of Famer Nap Lajoie, who played 21 seasons from 1896 to 1916. In 1901 Lajoie joined the Philadelphia Athletics of the nascent American League, which had played the previous season as a minor league. For that one year, Lajoie was one of the greatest hitters who ever lived; his king-sized performance is a core reason why many historians discount the professional quality of the 1901 American League.

Single-season bests posted by Nap Lajoie, 1901 vs. other years in Lajoie's career

	Career high	Career 2nd place	Difference
Runs scored	145 (1901)	113 (1898)	32 runs
Home runs	14 (1901)	9 (1897)	56%
BA	.426 (1901)	.383 (1910)	43 points
OBP	.463 (1901)	.444 (1910)	19 points
Slg	.643 (1901)	,569 (1897)	74 points
OPS	1.106 (1901)	.984 (1902)	122 points

Lajoie's 1901 can be compared to an average Nap Lajoie season from the other 20 years of his career with the aid of StDevs:

StDev of Nap Lajoie's 1901 vs. career averages

	1901 season	Average season, 1896–00 + 1902–16	StDev
BA	.426	.333	2.3
OBP	.463	.375	2.0
Slg	.643	.456	2.2
OPS	1.106	.831	2.4

StDevs confirm that Lajoie's 1901 is a major outlier as compared to the rest of his career. This is directly attributable to the lesser quality of the competition he faced in the just-turned-Major American League.

Not all outlier seasons result from inferior competition; sometimes a player is simply locked in for a season; but if we see large numbers of Lajoie-type outliers occurring consistently in a league, that's a solid indicator that the league is populated by a sprinkling of professionals surrounded by lesser-caliber athletes.

Here's a table of the frequency of high StDevs in OPS among MLB batters who qualify for hitting titles:

5. Mr. James's 23 Tests

NA and MLB OPS StDevs by decade,
1871–1949 (qualifying batters only)

Decade:	NA	1876–79	1880–89	1890–99	1900–09	1910–19
Qualifying batters:	256	205	941	808	849	895
StDevs of 2+:	11	5	38	18	29	37
StDevs from 1 to 2:	30	30	105	100	92	90
Total StDevs of 1+:	16.0%	17.1%	15.2%	14.6%	14.3%	14.2%

Decade:	1920–29	1930–39	1940–49
Qualifying batters:	864	866	820
StDevs of 2+:	33	31	27
StDevs from 1 to 2:	73	83	79
Total StDevs of 1+:	12.3%	13.2%	12.9%

StDevs of 1+ account for a surprisingly low 16 percent of qualifying batters in the NA, 17 percent in the 1870s, 15 percent in the 1880s, 14 percent for 1890–1919, and 12–13 percent for 1920–49. Based on my other studies of early MLB data, this declining pattern over time is what I expected to see.

But when I extended the study to include the 1950s, the pattern changed sharply:

MLB OPS StDevs by decade, 1876–1959
(qualifying batters only)

Decade:	1876–79	1880–89	1890–99	1900–09	1910–19
Qualifying batters:	205	941	808	849	895
StDevs of 2+:	5	38	18	29	37
StDevs from 1 to 2:	30	105	100	92	90
Total StDevs of 1+:	17.1%	15.2%	14.6%	14.3%	14.2%

Decade:	1920–29	1930–39	1940–49	1950–59
Qualifying batters:	864	866	820	788
StDevs of 2+:	33	31	27	29
StDevs from 1 to 2:	73	83	79	95
Total StDevs of 1+:	12.3%	13.2%	12.9%	15.7%

StDevs leap upwards in the 1950s—and one part of the reason is that ex–Negro Leaguers compiled large numbers of standout high-offense seasons, which pushed the overall MLB StDev higher than in any decade since the 1880s.

Ex-NgL players accounted for 26 percent of all 1950s qualifying seasons with StDevs of 1+:

1950: Roy Campanella, Larry Doby, Jackie Robinson (3 of 16)
1951: Roy Campanella, Larry Doby, Monte Irvin, Minnie Miñoso, Jackie Robinson (5 of 10)
1952: Larry Doby, Jackie Robinson (2 of 13)
1953: Roy Campanella, Monte Irvin, Jackie Robinson (3 of 15)
1954: Willie Mays, Minnie Miñoso (2 of 11)
1955: Hank Aaron, Ernie Banks, Roy Campanella, Willie Mays (4 of 12)

1956: Hank Aaron, Willie Mays, Minnie Miñoso (3 of 15)
1957: Hank Aaron, Ernie Banks, Willie Mays (3 of 10)
1958: Hank Aaron, Ernie Banks, Willie Mays (3 of 11)
1959: Hank Aaron, Ernie Banks, Willie Mays (3 of 8)

(Frank Robinson also compiled a high-StDev OPS in 1959, but Frank never played in the NgL.)

By the end of 1951, only 20 ex–Negro Leaguers had played even a single game in the Majors—yet ex–NgL players comprised half of all 1951 batters with standout StDevs.

League splits reinforce the notion that ex–NgL players were responsible for rising MLB StDevs. The NL integrated much more quickly and completely than the AL; ex–Negro Leaguers received 49,400 plate appearances in 1950s NL play vs. 26,934 in the AL, a difference of 83 percent. We'd therefore expect to see a higher StDev in the NL than in the AL—and sure enough:

1950s OPS StDevs (qualifying batters only)

	1950–59 NL	1950–59 AL
Qualifying batters:	414	374
StDevs of 2+:	17	12
StDevs from 1 to 2:	55	40
Total StDevs of 1+:	**17.4%**	**13.9%**

From the 1950s through the 1970s, MLB StDevs rose to 1880s levels, and then, from the 1980s through the 2010s, fell again to 1890–1919 levels.

MLB OPS StDevs by decade, 1950–2019 (qualifying batters only)

Decade:	1950–59	1960–69	1970–79	1980–89	1990–99
Qualifying batters:	788	983	1264	1411	1422
StDevs of 2+:	29	30	34	28	46
StDevs from 1 to 2:	95	122	169	175	166
Total StDevs of 1+:	**15.7%**	**15.5%**	**16.1%**	**14.4%**	**14.9%**

Decade:	2000–09	2010–19
Qualifying batters:	1577	1435
StDevs of 2+:	49	53
StDevs from 1 to 2:	178	159
Total StDevs of 1+:	**14.4%**	**14.8%**

I'm not going to attempt to analyze why this happened, as innumerable variable factors creep into the equation: the increasing dominance of Black superstars, sure, but also multiple league expansions (three in the 1960s alone), the designated hitter rule, the steadily increasing use of relievers, strike-shortened seasons, video replay, performance-enhancing drugs, weight and nutrition training, keyhole and

Lasik surgery, PITCHf/x and FIELDf/x, etc. Any supposition on my part is no better than guesswork.

Now let's look at figures for the NgL:

NgL OPS StDevs by decade, 1920–48 (qualifying batters only)

Decade:	1920–29	1930–39	1940–48
Qualifying batters:	1142	697	731
StDevs of 2+:	41	25	27
StDevs from 1 to 2:	123	66	76
Total StDevs of 1+:	14.4%	13.1%	14.1%

These numbers fit nicely into the MLB continuum from 1890 to 1919, and again from 1980 to 2019.

Unlike the other studies contained between these covers, I'm not wholly confident in this one; I *think* the study shows NgL play meeting MLB standards, but am prepared to be proven wrong by those better versed in weighted standard deviation than I.

In the absence of superior evidence, my answer to question 20 is a qualified Yes for NgL professionalism.

21. THE STANDARD OF RECORD-KEEPING.

This is the NgL's Achilles' heel. If NgL teams had been able to afford in-house statisticians—or if the white press had taken the slightest interest in NgL play—the good folks at Seamheads wouldn't have to put forth such Herculean exertions to reassemble their records. But that's impossible to construe as a mark against the professionalism of NgL *players*.

22. THE PERCENTAGE OF MANAGERS WHO HAVE 20 YEARS OR MORE EXPERIENCE IN THE GAME.

For this comparison I examined league numbers from the first year of each decade through the 1940s. In compiling these numbers I assumed that by 20 years of experience, James means professional experience. (Obviously I relaxed my standards for the first decade of organized baseball.)

MLB managers with 20+ years' experience in professional baseball

1876	1880	1890	1900	1910	1920	1930	1940
13%	10%	8%	20%	71%	69%	81%	83%

NgL managers with 20+ years' experience in professional baseball

1920	1930	1940*
20%	47%	33%

*1940 data is based on 20 of 25 NgL teams only, as 5 MEX teams were managed by men for whom we have virtually no biographical information of any kind.

As with the percentage of games which are blowouts, NgL numbers fall neatly between the lows of nineteenth-century MLB and the highs of twentieth-century MLB.

23. THE COMMON SUCCESS OF TEENAGERS, AND IN PARTICULAR TEENAGED PITCHERS.

James isn't commenting on the *presence* of teenagers in pro baseball. Teenagers have always been a feature of MLB. In 115 consecutive seasons from 1871 to 1985, at least one teenager took the field as a pro every year. The youngest was Joe Nuxhall, who made his debut aged 15 years, 10 months and 11 days in 1944. As recently as 1955–56, at least two 16-year-olds, Alex George and Jim Derrington, pitched in Major League games.

Rather, what James sees as evidence of an increase in the quality of play over time—a thesis with which I agree—is the decreasing *success* of teenagers. He cites the following figures:

1880–1889: 8 teenaged 20-game winners
1890–1899: 2 teenaged 20-game winners
The entire 20th century: 1 teenaged 20-game winner[14]

In studying this issue, I couldn't use winning 20 games as a measure of success, as NgL pitchers won 20+ games a total of six times in the league's entire history: Jim Jeffries (21) in the 1922 NNL; James "Nip" Winters (20) in the 1924 ECL; Willie Foster (21) in the 1927 NNL; Stuart "Slim" Jones (20) in the 1934 NN2; and Willie Jefferson (22) and Andy Cooper (21) in the 1940 MEX. (This book considers the MEX a Negro League for the 1940 and 1941 seasons only; my reasoning is explained in "A Proposed Major Leagues Organizational Chart.")

So instead I examined the biographical details of every NgL pitcher who threw 20+ innings in a single season. We lack birthdates for a significant minority of NgL players, but among the majority for whom we do possess biographical data, here are the 39 instances in which a teenaged pitcher pitched 20+ innings in any Negro League season from 1920 to 1948:

Teenage pitchers who threw 20+ innings in any NgL season

(an asterisk next to the pitcher's name indicates
that this pitcher also competed in MLB)

Year	Pitcher	Age	IP	ERA
1920	Bill Holland	19	25.1	5.33
1921	*(none)*			
1922	Joe Strong	19	66.2	5.27
1923	Martin Dihigo	18	33.1	4.05
	Willie Foster	19	70.0	1.74
	Edward "Eli" Juran	19	45.2	4.93
1924	Roosevelt Davis	19	121.2	4.29
	Martin Dihigo	19	49.0	2.39
1925	Chet Brewer	18	32.1	7.52
	William "Steel Arm" Tyler	19	171.2	4.14
1926	Chet Brewer	19	121.1	2.37
1927	*(none)*			

Year	Pitcher	Age	IP	ERA
1928	Richard Cannon	18	55.2	7.92
	Herb Thomas	18	37.0	5.84
1929	Thomas Albright	19	48.1	6.52
	Herb Thomas	19	43.2	8.04
	Richard Cannon	19	34.1	4.19
1930	(none)			
1931	Tom Parker	19	35.0	11.31
1932	Roy Welmaker	18	20.0	5.85
	Slim Jones	19	25.0	3.96
1933	(none)			
1934	Leon Day	18	103.2	4.34
1935	Leon Day	19	76.1	3.30
	Johnny Taylor	19	74.1	2.78
	Willie Burns	19	62.0	7.84
1936	Willie Burns	19	62.0	7.84
1937	(none)			
1938	(none)			
1939	Willie Hutchinson	18	25.0	3.60
1940	Willie Hutchinson	19	33.0	2.73
	Bill Barnes	19	20.2	10.89
1941	Wilmer Fields	18	24.1	4.81
	Connie Johnson*	18	22.0	2.45
	Fred Hobgood	19	62.0	5.08
1942	Connie Johnson*	19	30.1	2.97
1943	Tite Figueroa	19	60.1	3.43
	Larry Kimbrough	19	27.0	7.33
1944	Don Newcombe*	18	42.1	3.83
1945	Don Newcombe*	19	67.0	2.42
	Archie Hinton	19	36.0	6.25
	Amos Watson	19	25.1	5.68
1946	Vibert Clarke*	18	22.1	6.45
1947	Vibert Clarke*	19	36.0	2.75
1948	Clyde Golden	19	55.0	4.58

If we roughly define "poor" as an ERA above 4.50, "average to good" as an ERA between 3.00 and 4.50, and "very good" as an ERA under 3.00, we find:

19 poor seasons

11 average to good seasons

9 very good seasons

These nine very good seasons were split among eight pitchers. Let's take a closer look at these teenage phenoms:

- **Willie Foster**, a Hall of Famer who compiled an NgL career record of 126–60 with a 2.57 ERA;
- **Martin Dihigo**, a Hall of Famer who could do it all, a 46–35 pitcher and 143 OPS+ hitter;

- **Chet Brewer**, a solid, rotation-anchor type pitcher with a 24-year career, 70–60 with a 3.23 ERA (Brewer bombed at age 18, but came back strongly at age 19);
- **Connie Johnson**, who later went 40–39, 3.44 in the Majors; and
- **Don Newcombe**, who later earned NL Rookie of the Year, Cy Young and MVP honors.

That's five men who belonged in the Big Show, teenager or no.

The three remaining "very good" seasons were posted by Johnny Taylor, who was solid in his nine-year NgL career (34–30, 4.23); Vibert "Webbo" Clarke, most of whose Negro League experience falls after 1948 and who pitched briefly in the Majors; and Willie Hutchinson, the only true outlier in the group, a sort of spot starter for seven so-so years.

That really is a talented group; it shouldn't be surprising that they made their way to the Show at a tender age. Most teams in history would take them gladly as the core of their pitching staff. This isn't a group of teenagers stumbling randomly into the NgL; this is young talent scouted, evaluated as worthy, and promoted by NgL managers and owners—just like the hundreds of teenagers who played in the Majors.

Also, it can't be said that this group exceeds the performances of top MLB teenagers: not nineteenth-century seasons like John Montgomery Ward's 1879 (47–19, 2.15) or Nat Hudson's 1888 (25–10, 2.54), nor early twentieth-century seasons like Jake Weimer's 1903 (20–8, 2.30) or "Smoky" Joe Wood's 1909 (11–7, 2.18) or Raymond "Rube" Bressler's 1914 (10–4, 1.77), nor post–World War II seasons like Wally Bunker's 1964 (19–5, 2.69) or Gary Nolan's 1967 (14–8, 2.58) or Dwight Gooden's 1984 (17–9, 2.60), all achieved at age 19.

Here's a complete list of the teenaged pitchers who led any NgL league in any statistical category:

- In 1923, age 19, Hall of Famer Willie Foster led NgL Independent teams with a .750 win-loss percentage, a 1.74 ERA, 46 strikeouts, a 0.887 WHIP, 6.2 hits per 9, 6.7 strikeouts per 9, and a 3.83 strikeout-to-walk ratio. Foster is an all-time immortal who went on to claim four more ERA crowns and compile a 12–7, 2.54 postseason record, so it shouldn't be too surprising that his NgL impact was immediate and tremendous.
- In 1935, age 18, Hall of Famer Leon Day led the NN2 with 62 strikeouts and 5.4 strikeouts per 9.
- In 1942, age 19, future Major Leaguer Connie Johnson led the NAL with 7.0 strikeouts per 9.

…And that's it.

Well, how about the Majors?

- In 1874, age 18, Tommy Bond led the NA with 0.1 walks per 9 and a 5.25 strikeout-to-walk ratio.
- In 1878, age 18, John Montgomery Ward led the NL with a 1.51 ERA. The next year, age 19, he led the NL with 47 wins, a .712 win-loss percentage, 239 strikeouts, and a 6.64 strikeout-to-walk ratio.

- In 1890, age 19, Amos Rusie led the NL with 341 strikeouts, 7.2 hits per 9, 5.6 strikeouts per 9, and 3 home runs allowed in 548.2 innings.
- In 1938, age 19, Bob Feller led the AL with 240 strikeouts, 7.3 hits per 9, and 7.8 strikeouts per 9. He also broke the MLB single-game strikeout record, punching out 18 Detroit Tigers (including two fans of 58 home run-hitter Hank Greenberg) on October 3.
- In 1964, age 19, Wally Bunker led the AL with a .792 win-loss percentage.
- In 1967, age 19, Gary Nolan led the NL with 8.2 strikeouts per 9.
- In 1984, age 19, Dwight Gooden led the NL with 276 strikeouts, a 1.073 WHIP, a 1.69 FIP, 6.6 hits per 9, 0.3 home runs per 9, and 11.4 strikeouts per 9—a performance every bit as dominant as Willie Foster's 1923.

By the lights of this final test, the Negro Leagues were at least the equal of, and possibly superior to, the Majors.

* * *

Of Mr. James's 23 tests, one can't be applied to NgL play because of a lack of data. Of the remaining 22 the NgL passes 16, with a 17th receiving a qualified Yes—and of the five No's, four come with caveats:

- League stability—which is all about access to capital, a commodity in short supply for Black entrepreneurs of the era;
- Hitting by pitchers—which, based on the other tests presented above, I'm reasonably certain would redound to the NgL's advantage if pre–1918 MLB data were available;
- Record keeping and press coverage—neither of which, in this case, have anything to do with quality of play; and
- Player height. I'll leave you to draw your own conclusions on that one.

And again we must ask: What's the case *against* the Negro Leagues being regarded as Major Leagues? Where are the compelling arguments *against* statistical integration?

6

Arguments Against Statistical Integration

Let's look at a sampling of the arguments that skeptics might cite in opposing statistical integration. (I'm not just setting up straw men to knock them down; each of these arguments is one I've read or heard more than once in discussions of the Negro Leagues.)

1. Tradition. Things should stay as they've always been.
2. Negative assumptions about the professionalism of the NgL as a league structure.
3. The presence of All-Stars and Hall of Famers in the NgL doesn't necessarily prove that other NgL players were MLB quality.
4. NgL hitting and pitching stars didn't have to face Major League opposition.
5. The numbers in the NgL database are unreliable compared to MLB numbers.
6. NgL statistics are too incomplete to draw meaningful conclusions.
7. NgL statistics often don't resemble MLB stats from the same year or era.
8. Thanks to their short seasons, NgL players could put up huge numbers on the basis of a great but short run, or a lucky streak.
9. Combination of NgL and MLB statistics will distort the all-time leaderboards beyond recognition.

Addressing these points in turn:

1. TRADITION. THINGS SHOULD STAY AS THEY'VE ALWAYS BEEN.

Lots of undesirable things are traditional. The segregation of baseball was traditional. I think, in this instance, that tradition can safely be dispensed with.

2. NEGATIVE ASSUMPTIONS ABOUT THE PROFESSIONALISM OF THE NGL AS A LEAGUE STRUCTURE.

Histories of Negro Leagues play can be a distressing read. Low salaries, small rosters, all-night drives between games, sleeping on buses or in fleabag lodgings, shortages of bats and other basic equipment, salaries that were pennies on the Major League dollar, un-met payrolls, contract-jumping, league collapse, on and on: these conditions don't sound professional.

The 1976 film *The Bingo Long Traveling All-Stars & Motor Kings*, which likely constitutes many fans' sole visual impression of the NgL, did the image of the Black leagues no favors. Roster-jumping in the NgL was attributable to the never-ending quest for enough money to survive—but in *Bingo Long* the title character, a Satchel Paige–type showman, invites his All-Star buddies to jump ship on their current teams, to which all agree without once asking about money. (As Sol White advised in 1907, "The colored ball player should always look before he leaps.")[1]

Later, Bingo tries to sell his teammates on a contractual agreement by displaying ignorance that would never have emerged from the mouth of the savvy Satchel (who was, at various points in his career, the best-paid baseball player in America, Black or white): "The man is guaranteeing us two hundred dollars. You slice that eleven ways, that comes out to about … uh … uh … uh … a lot of money!"[2]

Elsewhere the film seems to imply that shucking and jiving somehow made white communities' racism go away, or at least muted it sufficiently to make it tolerable. Perhaps it sometimes did—but this first-hand account by Buck O'Neil describes a commonplace aspect of NgL barnstorming overlooked (for the sake of comedy, I'm sure) by *Bingo Long*:

> It was terrible, really, in some spots. We got in the ballpark once in Macon, Georgia, and I got the stuff off the bus and went into the dugout and here's the Wizard of the Ku Klux Klan. They're going to march on that field. So you know, when the Ku Klux Klan was marching that means all Black people, you closed your windows, you brought the shades down and all. So he says "You boys aren't going to play here tonight. We're going to march here tonight." I say "Yes sir." So we get back on the bus and go on.[3]

Even if professionalism is conceded, the conditions under which Negro Leaguers plied their craft seem analogous to minor league baseball—which leads, inevitably, to a subconscious denigration of the quality of Negro Leagues play.

Such conditions were imposed by the straitened economic circumstances of the NgL, not by any dearth of professionalism. It's somewhat miraculous that with no access to the resources of the Majors other than the use of MLB ballparks (for which they had to pay in cash), the Negro Leagues managed to survive, in one form or another, for three decades.

The economic collapse of the organized NgL league structure in 1931 didn't transform its stars into minor league-caliber players; rather, it deprived them (temporarily) of the chance to display their talents in an organized league, as systemic racism barred them from the only North American league with real economic stability. Also, it can't be stressed enough that this same instability prevailed in the early Major Leagues.

I suspect there's another factor at work here too. When we see team names like the Indianapolis Clowns and watch the antics of the Bingo Long All-Stars, our brains rebel; we conjure up images of other "clowns," like the Harlem Globetrotters.

What people tend to forget about the Globetrotters is that they can *play*. It's true that the Trotters mostly stage comedic exhibitions, but throughout their long history they've also played against—and consistently crushed—US collegiate champion and All-Star teams, European national and All-Star teams, and national Olympic squads. They began in 1927 as a serious barnstorming team, compiling a 101–16 inaugural record; in 1948 they defeated the Minneapolis Lakers, reigning champions of the NBL (precursor to the NBA), shocking the basketball world. In 1950, four former Trotters—Earl Lloyd, Nat "Sweetwater" Clifton, Chuck Cooper, and Hank DeZonie—broke the NBA color barrier. (They weren't the first Black men to play pro basketball, though; as we'll see later, that honor belongs to Larry Doby, who, like Fleet Walker and Jackie Robinson, was an integration pioneer on multiple fronts.) Wilt "The Stilt" Chamberlain played two years with the Trotters, 1958–59, before going on to shatter every NBA scoring record.

From 1971 to 1995 the Trotters won 8,829 consecutive games against all comers. It took a 15-for-16 shooting performance from retired NBA Hall of Famer Kareem Abdul-Jabbar to lead his All-Star squad to a victory over the Trotters by a single point—whereupon the Trotters reeled off another 1,270 straight wins. In 2003 they whipped the defending national collegiate champion Syracuse Orange, leading the NCAA to ban such contests to prevent further humiliation. (Sound familiar?)

Whatever might be said about their clowning, the Trotters can *play*. And so could the Indianapolis Clowns.

(Mind, MLB has had clownish team names of its own: the Toledo Maumees, the Worcester Ruby Legs, the Boston Buffeds, the Pittsburgh Stogies, the Houston Colt .45s—I wonder how that one would go over today?—and my personal favorite, the Cleveland Infants.)

3. THE PRESENCE OF ALL-STARS AND HALL OF FAMERS IN THE NgL DOESN'T NECESSARILY PROVE THAT OTHER NgL PLAYERS WERE MLB QUALITY.

In other words, Stan Musial played for the Rochester Red Wings, but that doesn't make the Red Wings a Major League–quality team.

This is a false analogy. When Musial played well for Rochester he was quickly promoted to the Majors, whereas the Negro Leagues were the highest possible destination for Black players from the time of their formation to the advent of Jackie Robinson. For Oscar Charleston and Pop Lloyd there was no higher league to which to aspire; they had already reached the top, where they were surrounded by the cream of Black baseball in America.

As Joe Posnanski puts it, "If you ever find yourself wondering about the quality of the players in the Negro Leagues, think about this: If Aaron, [Billy] Williams and [Willie] McCovey had been born 20 years earlier, all three of them would have spent their primes in the Negro Leagues, and their stories would be told as legend."[4]

Monte Irvin agreed: "Oscar Charleston was the Willie Mays of his day. Nobody ever played center field better than Willie Mays. Suppose they had never given Willie a chance, and we said that, would anybody believe there was a kid in Alabama who was that good? Or there was a Black guy in Atlanta [Mr. Aaron] who might break Babe Ruth's home run record? No."[5]

Here's another way to examine the question of whether NgL players were generally of MLB quality: From 1920 to 1948, how did NgL and other all–Black teams perform against white competition?

The answer, no matter which source you consult, is: Very well indeed.

SABR's Ted Knorr has tackled the proposition that Negro Leaguers played Major League–quality baseball. One of his arguments centers on the win-loss

6. Arguments Against Statistical Integration

records of NgL and other all–Black teams against all-white baseball squads. To Knorr's figures I've added an earlier version of John Holway's research.

Historian	Games	W	L	WPct
John Holway *(version quoted by Knorr)*	156	89	67	.571
"Bench 5" *(a poster at Baseball Fever)*	242	132	110	.545
Scott Simkus	243	128	115	.527
John Holway *(earlier version)*	436	268	168	.615
Ken Burns	518	309	209	.597
William McNeil	880	614	266	.698

Originally compiled by Ted Knorr, as quoted in Petersen (ed.),
The Negro Leagues Were Major Leagues

Clearly these records were compiled from widely divergent source materials— but they all show Black teams out-performing white teams.

Now, thanks to the unparalleled data source provided by Seamheads, we can use verified box scores from 1920 to 1948 to compile a record with historical rigor.

All-white team	Year(s)	Vs. all–Black teams:					
		W	L	T	WPct	RS	RA
St. Louis Cardinals	1920	2	2	0	.500	18	12
New York Giants		0	1	0	.000	1	4
Stengel All Stars		5	1	0	.833	19	15
Joe Judge's All Stars		2	2	0	.500	11	12
St. Louis Cardinals	1921	4	1	0	.800	38	22
Philadelphia Athletics		3	2	0	.600	32	34
Detroit Tigers	1922	1	2	0	.333	21	19
O'Neill's All Stars		2	0	0	1.000	14	9
American Stars		0	1	0	.000	0	4
Philadelphia Athletics	1923	1	2	0	.333	16	15
St. Louis Browns		1	2	0	.333	23	22
Detroit Tigers		1	1	1	.500	12	9
Major League All Stars		0	3	0	.000	4	9
Tierney's All Stars		0	1	0	.000	5	7
Philadelphia Athletics	1924	1	1	0	.500	11	10
American League All Stars	1926	2	7	0	.222	25	34
American League All Stars	1927	4	2	0	.667	28	21
American League All Stars	1928	4	4	0	.500	44	49
American League All Stars	1929	2	5	0	.286	30	46
American League All Stars	1930	1	3	0	.250	26	22
Max Carey's All Stars	1931	0	3	0	.000	12	32
Major League All Stars II	1932	2	5	0	.286	41	50
Hornsby's Major League Stars	1936	1	4	0	.200	13	22
Major League All Stars III	1937	3	1	0	.750	17	21
Dressen's All Stars	1945	4	0	0	1.000	17	5
Bob Feller's Major League All Stars	1946	9	4	0	.692	68	49
Overall record		**55**	**60**	**1**	**.478**	**547**	**555**

By the lights of the most reliable data set ever compiled, from 1920 to 1948 Black teams won 60 and lost 55 against white teams, posting a .522 winning percentage and out-scoring the white squads 555 to 547.

Excluding the many white All-Star teams that competed against Black teams, complete MLB squads did out-score all–Black teams 172–147, but posted an exactly equal record against them: 14 wins, 14 losses and 1 draw.

For NgL players to be considered Major League quality, they don't have to be better than MLB players, or even exactly equal; rather, they have to show that they were solidly and consistently competitive against MLB-quality opposition. Even in the least generous interpretation possible, the records prove exactly that.

(In a verifiable Black-vs.-white semi-pro contest held on June 21, 1925, the all–Black Wichita Monrovians defeated the obviously all-white Wichita Klan No. 6, 10–8. No kidding. According to the June 21 *Wichita Beacon*, "strangle holds, razors, horsewhips, and other violent implements of argument will be barred.... The umpires have been instructed to rule any player out of the game who tries to bat with a cross.")

4. NgL HITTING AND PITCHING STARS DIDN'T HAVE TO FACE MAJOR LEAGUE OPPOSITION.

The opposite is also true: MLB hitting and pitching stars didn't have to face Negro Leagues opposition. Would Babe Ruth have slugged .847 in 1920 if his opposition had included Cyclone Williams? As Satchel Paige observed, "I could have knocked a few points off of those big, fat lifetime averages." It's hypocritical to accept Ruth's marks, yet simultaneously reject Josh Gibson's because he never faced Lefty Grove.[6]

5. THE NUMBERS IN THE NgL DATABASE ARE UNRELIABLE COMPARED TO MLB NUMBERS.

This assertion, which I've heard and seen expressed countless times by well-meaning fans, is based on a false premise. Major League records themselves are hardly definitive.

Did Tim Keefe win 341 games as the Elias Bureau says, 342 as Baseball Reference claims, or 346 as his Hall of Fame plaque has it? Did Babe Ruth drive in 145 runs in 1926, or 146, or 149, or 150, or 151, or 155? Did Cap Anson collect 3,012 career hits, or 3,081, or 3,418, or 3,435, or 3,479? Each of these figures is cited as accurate by one authority or another.

In 2005 MLB spokesperson Rich Levin acknowledged that "there's no official record book. I can't give you a good reason as to why. We've discussed it at times, but it hasn't progressed past that."[7]

Ty Cobb, holder of a number of important career records, is a perfect illustration of the dilemma this creates for the baseball historian. Did he bat .366, as *Total Baseball* purports, or do we accept .367, as given by the Macmillan *Encyclopedia*? Did he score 2,245 runs or 2,246? Did he have 4,189 hits in 11,440 at-bats, or 4,191 in 11,434?

When Cobb sat out the final two games of the 1910 season to preserve his fourth consecutive batting title, St. Louis Browns manager Jack "Peach Pie" O'Connor, who hated the very ground Cobb walked on, instructed third baseman John "Red" Corriden to move back to the outfield grass each time Napoleon "Nap" Lajoie came to bat in the Browns' season-finale doubleheader against the Cleveland Naps. (At this time the Naps were named after their biggest star…. My, but I enjoy the nicknames of this era.) Lajoie, who trailed Cobb by a handful of points in the batting race, proceeded to slap seven easy bunt singles down the third base line.

Convinced they'd cheated Cobb out of the title, the Browns sent Nap a congratulatory telegram. But the official league statisticians screwed up: they counted a Cobb 2-for-3 box score twice, and awarded him the batting title anyway.

And then in 1978 Pete Palmer discovered the mistake, and Lajoie was retrospectively awarded the batting title—yet some sources still credit Cobb as the 1910 batting champion. Baseball Reference splits the difference and credits both with the 1910 title, despite listing Lajoie with an average one point higher.

So did Cobb win 12 batting titles, as the Hall of Fame asserts and as he went to his grave believing? Or did he win 11, as the Elias Bureau has it? Or is it 10, as cited by various books and websites? Or perhaps 9, as MLB.com used to show? That's a pretty basic question, and there's no definitive answer.

The most important Major League records are not immune to revision. In the run-up to Barry Bonds' record-breaking 2002 season, the addition of two walks to Ted Williams's 1941 tally altered the all-time mark for single-season On-Base Percentage—obviously a highly important record—from .551 to .553.

As Rob Neyer notes, "Baseball statistics are approximations…. If the stats are wrong for players like Ruth and Williams, whose careers have been studied as much as anybody's, how many stats are wrong for everybody else? The answer, of course, is 'A lot of them.'"[8]

6. NgL statistical samples are too incomplete to draw meaningful conclusions.

This statement, true in the past, no longer obtains. Thanks to Seamheads researchers, more than enough verified numbers are now in place, for the whole of the NgL's 29-year existence as a professional league, to enable reasoned comparisons and judgments.

While NgL statistics are not as complete as MLB data for the same era, they approximate the completeness of early MLB data. From 1876 through 1883 we have no MLB numbers for stolen bases, caught stealing, intentional walks (batters or pitchers), hit by pitch (batters or pitchers), grounded into double plays, sacrifice hits, or sacrifice flies—but the statistics that do exist are accepted as part of the canon.

The baseball community has a choice: it can lament the incomplete nature of the NgL data set, or proceed with analysis on the firmest possible footing. Interpretation of NgL data will no doubt present sabermetricians with a fresh set of challenges. The sabermetric community has never shied from challenges.

7. NgL statistics often don't resemble MLB stats from the same year or era.

… And why should they?

It's crucial to understand that Negro Leagues numbers for, say, the 1920 season may not be precisely equivalent to Major League statistics for the same year—but that they *are* equivalent to MLB norms *for other years and eras*. This is probably the most important point I'll make in this book.

In 1920, the National League had been around for 45 years, the American League for 20. By contrast, the Negro National League was a brand-new creation, more analogous in terms of structure, scheduling, ballfields, equipment, scouting, coaching, umpiring, and in every other respect to the infant NL of 1876—or even the infant National Association of 1871—than to the mature NL of 1920.

Jeremy Beer asserts that "Negro leagues teams, on the whole, were not as good as Major League teams," citing two reasons: relative lack of depth (explicable at least in part by smaller rosters), and the fact that "top-tier Negro leagues players saw their stat lines diminish when they went to the Majors." Mr. Beer is comparing NgL stats to MLB stats of the same era. NgL numbers of any era are more comparable to those of MLB players of the 1890s, the 1920s and the 1930s. Larry Doby's NgL-leading .743 slugging in 1947 is much higher than his AL-leading .541 in 1954—but that .743 would slot beautifully into MLB play from 1922 through 1934.[9]

Then there are the wild variations seen in NgL league-leading counting stats. Every Negro League regular, without exception, engaged in vast amounts of what Scott Simkus calls "outsider baseball": playing as many games as possible, as often as possible, against as many different opponents as possible, through all twelve months of the year. Money, not team loyalty, was the determinant factor. This invariable practice led to enormous disruptions in team scheduling.

Huge variations in games played per season in the Negro Leagues can be disorienting for the average fan, who's used to looking at orderly rows of 154- and 162-game seasons. Mule Suttles led the Negro National League with 130 RBI in 1926, and led again with 36 RBI in 1931: a 94-RBI swing.

That's not something fans are used to seeing—unless they're versed in early MLB history, in which case it's nothing they haven't seen before. Deacon White led the 1877 NL with 49 RBI, Sam Thompson led the 1887 NL with 166: a 117-RBI swing.

The NL and AL themselves aren't always directly comparable within the same year, or decade, or era. In the 1910s the AL won eight World Series, the NL won two; in 1919 Hi Myers led the NL with .436 slugging, Babe Ruth led the AL with .657—a ridiculous 221-point gap. Obviously the 1910s AL was superior in quality to the 1910s NL; but this disparity is never interpreted by historians or statisticians to mean that the NL merits its Major League status less than the AL, or the AL less than the NL.

Sabermetrics assumes that both leagues are professional-quality and compensates for these differences in its formulas. And so it must be with Negro Leagues data.

8. Thanks to their short seasons, NgL players could win hitting and pitching titles on the basis of a great but short run, or a lucky streak.

In this argument, small sample size is conflated with random success. There's a degree of overlap to be sure; it's true that a player might enjoy a sustained hot streak and win a one-off batting crown. That's a strong reason why I believe it's inadvisable to mix MLB and NgL *single-season* records.

But there's nothing random about, say, the career-long dominance of Josh Gibson. If short sample sizes were responsible for Gibson's success, we'd see a mixture of seasons with huge numbers and seasons with lesser numbers—but that's not the case. Gibson had a great year every year. The *lowest* OPS of his career was .917, one of three full seasons (of 16 total) in which his OPS dipped below 1.000. That's not random. His lowest single-season batting average was .311, his lowest slugging percentage .527—numbers that would represent career highs for the majority of players who ever donned a professional uniform.

In light of this machine-like consistency, should it really be surprising that Gibson secures multiple places among the all-time leaders?

9. Combination of NgL and MLB statistics will distort the all-time leaderboards beyond recognition.

For players who played in both the NgL and MLB, this isn't a major consideration. When a player's NgL and MLB statistics are combined, each NgL season, thanks to its smaller sample size, has much less impact on combined career totals than each MLB season.

Here's a hypothetical example: Player A compiles a .300 batting average on 150 hits in 500 NgL at-bats, then .250 on 1250 hits in 5000 MLB at-bats. The resulting combined average of .255 (1400 H / 5500 AB) is five points above Player A's Major League average, 45 points below his Negro League average. The total is adjusted upwards, but not distorted beyond recognition.

Players who played in the NgL only do make substantial changes to the career leaderboards, as we'll see presently; but the outcome is a blend of white and Black players in the top spots—presumably the same result that would've occurred anyway had Black players competed in MLB from the start.

* * *

Probably the most thoughtful, multi-layered argument against statistical integration I've heard was articulated by famed sportscaster Bob Costas:

> Very often, if you're in general sympathy or agreement with a cause, then you're supposed to just nod in assent with anything that's presented under the heading of that cause…. The Negro Leagues derive their meaning from the injustice that was imposed upon them, and from everyone involved triumphing over that injustice. We can't learn enough about the Negro Leagues. I think I've read every book and watched every documentary that's been made about it. It's a glorious story; it's an important part of big league history. But you can't automatically just blend those stats with big league stats. Which is not to say that the Negro Leagues weren't as good; in some cases they were better than their contemporaries among white Major Leaguers. But a generation or two down the road, if that's all you're looking at, you will have lost the meaning of the Negro Leagues. The truth is that at various times, there were three or four different Negro Leagues operating simultaneously. And even the researchers, who have done an exhaustive job, haven't been able to track down all the stats. They've got Josh Gibson with 113 home runs. By legend he had about 800. You know the old saying: When the facts and legend collide, print the legend. In this case the legend is almost certainly closer

> to the truth. Why should a few at-bats that a 17-year-old Willie Mays had in 1948 for the Birmingham Black Barons lower his lifetime batting average from .302 to .301?[10]

Meaning no disrespect to Mr. Costas, who's definitely on the side of the angels, let's unpack his argument point by point:

> The Negro Leagues derive their meaning from the injustice that was imposed upon them, and from everyone involved triumphing over that injustice.... A generation or two down the road, if [statistics are] all you're looking at, you will have lost the meaning of the Negro Leagues.

Why must the choice be mutually exclusive? Why can't we learn about Negro Leagues history *and* incorporate NgL accomplishments into the record books? In today's climate of ever-increasing scrutiny of past and present racial injustice, I don't think the fact of baseball segregation will somehow fall through the cracks.

> At various times there were three or four different Negro Leagues operating simultaneously.

It's true, for instance, that the NNL, the ECL, and a handful of independent Black teams operated at the same time. But by the same logic, the National and American Leagues count as separate leagues, and at various times the UA, the PL and the FL operated as third leagues within the MLB structure—yet we happily incorporate their numbers into the professional database. There's no reason why the leagues comprising the NgL should be treated any differently.

> Even the researchers who have done an exhaustive job haven't been able to track down all the stats.

We've discussed this point, haven't we? First, the fact that the white sporting press didn't report NgL numbers is no reason to perpetuate the injustice fostered by their negligence; second, Major League stats themselves can hardly be described as definitive.

> They've got Josh Gibson with 113 home runs. By legend he had about 800. You know the old saying: When the facts and legend collide, print the legend. In this case the legend is almost certainly closer to the truth.

I'm not sure where Mr. Costas got the figure of 113 homers for Josh; Baseball Reference has 165 and I've got 234, but that's a side issue. The "old saying" comes from John Ford's 1962 film *The Man Who Shot Liberty Valance*: "This is the West, sir. When the legend becomes fact, print the legend." Well, this isn't the West anymore. We have hard numbers now. True statistical integration acknowledges Gibson as capturing several important Major League records, and I can't see how that could be interpreted as somehow diminishing Josh's standing among the greats of the game.[11]

> Why should a few at-bats that a 17-year-old Willie Mays had in 1948 for the Birmingham Black Barons lower his lifetime batting average from .302 to .301?

Because, sir, this system treats pre–1948 Black and white players equally for the first time ever. This is no insult to Mr. Mays—it is in fact the opposite: an acknowledgment that the game he and his contemporaries were forced to play by MLB racism was professional baseball. Somehow I can't see the Say Hey Kid objecting to this; I can't say with any certainty how he'll feel, but I'm guessing he'll approve. (Please do feel free to drop me a line, Mr. Mays, and let me know what you think.)

Some players' calculated stats decrease as a result of combination, though there are no enormous swings. Roy Campanella loses a bit of his historic slugging edge on other MLB catchers—and that's fair, because his place in history should be based on his experience in *all* professional leagues.

The introduction of NgL players does roil the MLB calculated career leaderboards. The very history of the game, as embodied in its numbers, is altered radically. Players who toiled in segregated obscurity, with names unknown to the average fan, leap to prominence decades after their careers came to an end.

I call that Justice.

7

Re-Writing the Record Books

True and total integration of MLB and NgL career statistics has profound consequences for the all-time leaderboards. Let's start with a big one:

The leader in career batting average isn't Ty Cobb, but Josh Gibson at .369.

This change will likely be opposed by purists who cherish Cobb's sacrosanct .366 average as the all-time high—even though it used to be .367, before the underlying data set was corrected by diligent research.

For the purists, it gets worse:

The career leader in slugging average isn't Babe Ruth at .690, but Gibson at .706.

Gibson was essentially Ruth and Cobb rolled into one, a devastating hitter for average and power (.337 isolated power, second all-time to Ruth's .348). His plate selectivity was also elite (.452 OBP, good for fifth all-time), though not quite the equal of Ruth's (.473, second all-time).

Any doubts as to whether Gibson was the greatest right-handed hitter in baseball history, and by far, is lain to rest by these figures. Thoughts that Mike Piazza, the greatest batsman among MLB catchers, was anywhere near Gibson's level as a hitter can also be discounted.

* * *

Combination of *single-season* NgL and MLB records is discouraged by two factors inherent in the nature of NgL play. The first of these factors is schedule length.

The concept of standard deviation (StDev) is quite straightforward. If a batter hits .300 with a StDev of .030, this means that the hitter's true ability tends to lie within a range of .030 below (.270) to .030 above (.330) the mark he actually posted. Where he ends up within that .270–.330 range is largely a matter of luck. If the batter's StDev decreases to .020, then his range of his true ability tends to narrow to a range of .280 (.020 below) to .320 (.020 above).

The more plate appearances a batter has, the lower the standard deviation.

It's like the probability inherent in flipping a coin. If I flip a coin once and it comes up heads, it's not correct to say there's a 100 percent chance it will come up heads on the next flip, because the sample size is too small. If I flip the coin ten times and it comes up heads six times, it's still not correct to assess the odds at 60 percent, because the sample size, while larger, is still pitifully tiny. (The StDev in those ten flips is .155, meaning that the true odds tend to lie somewhere between 44.5 percent and 75.5 percent—and we know that's correct, because the true odds are 50 percent, which falls within the predicted range.)

To get an accurate idea of the odds of the coin coming up heads on a given flip, we'd need to flip the coin thousands of times, until the StDev of the event approaches zero. (Because chance is involved, the StDev never truly reaches zero.)

Batting is much the same. Luck dictates that a hitter with true .300 ability, playing in a season of just 100 at-bats, might hit as low as .235 or as high as .365 with a StDev of .065. Increase the at-bats to 600 and the range narrows to .281–.319 with a StDev of .019. Longer schedules decrease standard deviation—and, by so doing, decrease the impact of luck.

NgL teams and leagues never achieved sufficient economic success to match the longer schedules of their MLB counterparts of the same era—and they faced other obstacles to scheduling stability too. Because money was a serious and constant problem for every NgL owner and team, teams sometimes couldn't pay their players' salaries on time; players sometimes jumped teams when they got a better offer elsewhere; teams sometimes cancelled officially scheduled games in favor of better-paying exhibition matches.

Josh Gibson, one of the greatest *Major League* hitters of all time (courtesy Josh Gibson Foundation, www.joshgibson.org).

As a consequence, NgL scheduling varied wildly; teams suddenly appeared, then folded just as suddenly; entire leagues crashed in and out of existence (just as in early MLB; not until 1884 did NL and AA teams play as many as 100 games in a season, and the AA folded completely in 1891). NgL hitting and pitching titles are therefore more likely to be influenced by luck than MLB titles won in many more plate appearances or innings.

The second factor that discourages combination of single-season records is the unique nature of NgL play relative to other professional leagues.

In 1886, American Association pitcher Matt Kilroy struck out 516 batters in 583 innings. His dominance was so extreme that for the 1887 season, MLB changed its rules to require four strikes instead of three to notch a strikeout.

By modern standards, 583 innings pitched is as absurd as "four strikes and you're out." The record books reflect this, and instead credit Nolan Ryan's 1973 mark of 383 Ks in 326 innings (marks that still appear extreme to the modern eye) as the all-time record. We've selected Ryan's mark over Kilroy's because Ryan and Kilroy were playing in different eras, under different conditions. I suspect the "all-time record" will eventually be lowered again, as the game moves towards rigid pitch counts for starters and ever-increasing reliance on relievers.

The last 600-inning season came in 1892, the last 400-inning season in 1908, as the ultra-dominant role of the starting pitcher was steadily scaled back. The top 273 single-season totals for innings pitched were all achieved prior to the dawn of the live-ball era. Pitchers can't throw like that anymore because the constant home-run threat forces them to pitch at the top of their game all the time, to every batter in the lineup; they can't cut back on their velocity for an inning or two, as they could before Ruth showed the world how to consistently launch long flies into the bleachers.

Pre-1920 and post–1920 MLB were different forms of the game. The NgL, too, was practicing its own unique brand of the game. And it's all Major League baseball.

* * *

Combining NgL and MLB *counting* stats doesn't make much of a dent in established MLB history.

The NgL's top home run hitter, Josh Gibson, tallied 234 homers in official league play—a mind-boggling total for just 3751 plate appearances, but good for a 280th-place tie on the MLB leaderboards. No one else is over 200 homers; the second-place man, Turkey Stearnes, ties for 388th with 189 bombs. In all likelihood, is that going to bother anyone? Will we hear a chorus of complaints that the inclusion of Gibson and Stearnes' NgL numbers has corrupted the home run leaderboards?

Other counting leaderboards fare the same. Willie Mays picks up nine runs scored (increasing his career total from 2062 to 2071) and eight RBI (from 1903 to 1911), but stays in seventh and twelfth place, respectively, on the all-time lists. Again, is this likely to offend anyone?

Actually, I concede that some purists *will* be offended by any change to the all-time leaderboards—in which case, I refer them to the numerous changes made to cherished MLB records by researchers digging through old-time box scores. The diligence of modern research makes changes like these inevitable, and I say that the benefits of this improved knowledge should be extended to NgL players, just as to their MLB counterparts.

* * *

Calculated stats are an altogether different animal from counting stats. Calculated batting leaderboards change radically through career combination.

High standard deviations discourage combination of NgL and MLB single-season records, but StDevs are no obstacle to combination of calculated career statistics. In a sample comprised of thousands of at-bats, StDevs shrink to much less significant proportions.

Here's a chart expressing the standard deviation of a .300 batting average in various numbers of at-bats:

StDevs of a .300 batting average with increasing numbers of at-bats

At-bats	Hits	Average	STDEV
50	15	.300	.065
100	30	.300	.046
150	45	.300	.037
200	60	.300	.032
250	75	.300	.029
300	90	.300	.026
350	105	.300	.024
400	120	.300	.023
450	135	.300	.022
500	150	.300	.020
550	165	.300	.020

At-bats	Hits	Average	STDEV
600	180	.300	.019
1,000	300	.300	.014
2,000	600	.300	.010
3,000	900	.300	.008
4,000	1200	.300	.007
5,000	1500	.300	.006
6,000	1800	.300	.006
7,000	2100	.300	.005
8,000	2400	.300	.005
9,000	2700	.300	.005
10,000	3000	.300	.005

When I assert that Josh Gibson's .369 career batting average tops Ty Cobb's .366, a look at StDevs reveals that their ability as contact hitters was more or less equal. (Overall, Gibson was much the superior hitter; Cobb had excellent power for the dead-ball era, leading in slugging eight times, but Gibson marshalled genuine Ruthian power and near–Ruthian plate discipline.) Gibson's .369 was achieved in 3099 at-bats, Cobb's .366 in 11440. Gibson's StDev is .009, Cobb's is .005, indicating that Gibson's range of true ability was probably in the .360–.378 range and Cobb's was probably .363–.373. The figures overlap; Gibson's range was potentially higher or lower than Cobb's actual performance, Cobb's potentially higher or lower than Gibson's. Which man won through to become the all-time batting leader was largely a matter of chance—but it's Gibson who wound up with the edge.

In the April 7, 1939, *Washington Post*, Walter Johnson told Shirley Povich that "there is a catcher that any big league club would like to buy for $200,000. I've heard of him before. His name is Gibson. They call him 'Hoot' Gibson, and he can do everything. He hits that ball a mile. And he catches so easy he might just as well be in a rocking chair. Throws like a rifle. Bill Dickey isn't as good a catcher. Too bad that Gibson is a colored fellow."

Carl Hubbell concurred: "I've seen a lot of colored boys who could make it up here in the big leagues. First of all, I'd name this big guy Josh Gibson, the catcher. He's one of the greatest backstops in the history of baseball, I think. Boy—how he can throw! There seems to be nothing to it when he throws. He just whips the ball down to second base like it had a string on it. He's great, I'm telling you. Any team in the big leagues could use him right now."[1]

If Josh Gibson wasn't a *professional* baseball player, who was?

There's no sound reason why Gibson's career marks shouldn't stand alongside those of Cobb, Ruth, and Bonds.

And if Gibson, why not others?

* * *

When Negro League and Major League calculated career records are combined into a seamless whole, players unknown to today's average fan spring to prominence—and rightly so.

As a standard for inclusion on the batting charts below, I've diverged from Baseball Reference, which uses standard MLB minimums, and set a minimum of 2000 plate appearances for NgL players, vs. 3000 for MLB hitters. 1,964 MLB batters racked up 3000+ PAs against just 29 NgL batters—an unacceptably small number for 29 years of Major League–level play. Even when we expand the NgL pool by including hitters with 2000+ PAs, just 85 hitters qualify. I considered moving the marker down to 1500 PAs (124 qualifiers), but that threshold produces leaderboard entries for NgL batters who appear nowhere in the top 20 in any counting category, a result that strikes me as unsound in the context of such a limited data set.

For NgL pitchers I used a threshold of 700 innings pitched (64 qualifiers), vs. the MLB threshold of 1000 innings pitched; at the 1000-inning level only 34 NgL pitchers qualify, vs. 1,246 MLB pitchers.

I've set thresholds dictated by the soundest logic I could muster. Professional statisticians may or may not agree with my choices. But I will make this point:

Holding NgL players to MLB standards for plate appearances and innings pitched, when segregation and *segregation only* prevented almost all of them from reaching these standards, is as ridiculous as Bowie Kuhn's attempt to segregate Negro League Hall of Fame inductees because they didn't play 10 seasons in MLB. "We can't make them real members," lamented Kuhn, "because they don't qualify under the rules."[2]

Any system that excludes a player like Josh Gibson because he doesn't "qualify under the rules" is self-evidently absurd. As Jackie Robinson said of Kuhn's proposal: "Rules have been changed before. You can change rules like you change laws. If the law's unjust…."[3]

Combined career leaders through the end of the 2020 season

	Batting Average	
1	**Josh Gibson**	**.3692**
2	Ty Cobb	.3662
3	Rogers Hornsby	.3585
4	**Jud Wilson**	**.3576**
5	**Oscar Charleston**	**.3571**
6	Shoeless Joe Jackson	.3558
7	**Dobie Moore**	**.3496**
8	**John Beckwith**	**.3495**
9	Lefty O'Doul	.3493
10	**Turkey Stearnes**	**.3466**
11	Ed Delahanty	.3458
12	**Wild Bill Wright**	**.3454**
13	**Buck Leonard**	**.3450**
14	Tris Speaker	.3447
15t	Billy Hamilton	.3444

	On-Base Percentage	
1	Ted Williams	.4817
2	Babe Ruth	.4739
3	John McGraw	.4657
4	Billy Hamilton	.4552
5	**Josh Gibson**	**.4519**
6	**Buck Leonard**	**.4478**
7	Lou Gehrig	.4474
8	Oscar Charleston	.4398
9	**Jud Wilson**	**.4363**
10	Bill Joyce	.4349
11	Rogers Hornsby	.4337
12	Ty Cobb	.4328
13	Jimmie Foxx	.4283
14	Tris Speaker	.4279
15	Eddie Collins	.4244

7. Re-Writing the Record Books

Batting Average		
15t	Ted Williams	.3444
17	Dan Brouthers	.3424
18	Babe Ruth	.3421
19	Dave Orr	.3420
20	Harry Heilmann	.3416

On-Base Percentage		
16	Ferris Fain	.4241
17	Dan Brouthers	.4234
18	Max Bishop	.4230
19	Shoeless Joe Jackson	.4227
20	**George Scales**	**.4224**

Slugging Percentage		
1	**Josh Gibson**	**.7064**
2	Babe Ruth	.6897
3	Ted Williams	.6338
4	Lou Gehrig	.6324
5	**Turkey Stearnes**	**.6143**
6	**Mule Suttles**	**.6107**
7	Jimmie Foxx	.6093
8	Barry Bonds	.6069
9	Hank Greenberg	.6050
10	**Oscar Charleston**	**.5999**
11	**John Beckwith**	**.5950**
12	Mark McGwire	.5882
13	**Buck Leonard**	**.5873**
14	Manny Ramirez	.5854
15	Mike Trout	.5821
16	Joe DiMaggio	.5788
17	Rogers Hornsby	.5765
18	Larry Walker	.5652
19	Albert Belle	.5638
20	Johnny Mize	.5620

On-Base Plus Slugging		
1	Babe Ruth	1.1636
2	**Josh Gibson**	**1.1593**
3	Ted Williams	1.1155
4	Lou Gehrig	1.0798
5	**Oscar Charleston**	**1.0427**
6	Barry Bonds	1.0512
7	Jimmie Foxx	1.0376
8	**Buck Leonard**	**1.0351**
9	**Mule Suttles**	**1.0172**
10	Hank Greenberg	1.0169
11	Rogers Hornsby	1.0103
12	Mike Trout	.9996
13	**John Beckwith**	**.9982**
14	Manny Ramirez	.9960
15	Mark McGwire	.9823
16	Mickey Mantle	.9773
17	Joe DiMaggio	.9771
18	Stan Musial	.9757
19	Frank Thomas	.9740
20	**Jud Wilson**	**.9724**

Adjusted OPS+		
1	Babe Ruth	206
2	**Josh Gibson**	**205**
3	Ted Williams	191
4	Barry Bonds	182
5	**Oscar Charleston**	**179**
6	**Buck Leonard**	**179**
7t	Rogers Hornsby	175
7t	Mike Trout	175
9	**Turkey Stearnes**	**174**
10	Mickey Mantle	172
11	Dan Brouthers	171
12	Shoeless Joe Jackson	170
13	Ty Cobb	168
14	**Mule Suttles**	**167**

Adjusted ERA+		
1	Mariano Rivera	205
2	**Satchel Paige**	**191**
3	**Dave Brown**	**169**
4	**Bullet Joe Rogan**	**160**
5	**Ray Brown**	**159**
6	**Cyclone Williams**	**161**
7	Clayton Kershaw	158
8	**Hilton Smith**	**157**
9	Pedro Martinez	154
10t	Jacob deGrom	150
10t	Jim Devlin	150
12	Lefty Grove	148
13t	Walter Johnson	147
13t	Hoyt Wilhelm	147

Adjusted OPS+		
15	**Cristóbal Torrente**	**166**
16t	Pete Browning	163
16t	Jimmie Foxx	163
16t	Mark McGwire	163
16t	Dave Orr	162
20t	Hank Greenberg	159
20t	Stan Musial	159

Adjusted ERA+		
13t	Dan Quisenberry	146
16	**Willie Foster**	**143**
17t	Roger Clemens	143
17t	Ed Walsh	146
17t	Smoky Joe Wood	146
20	Addie Joss	143

Negro Leaguers make from four to eight appearances on each of these combined top-20 charts. The greatness of players like John Beckwith and Jud Wilson is set forth with crystal clarity, enshrined in numbers that stand with the greatest MLB players of any era. Which is the point of the exercise.

The dominance of the top NgL starters is revelatory: six Negro Leaguers among the top eight OPS+ slots, with Satchel Paige trailing only the amazing Mariano Rivera for the best mark in baseball history. Even if we arbitrarily knock, say, 10 percent off these numbers for some unknown bias that causes top NgL starters to rate well in OPS+, Satch has no peer among starting pitchers.

Josh Gibson's name appears repeatedly at or near the top of every offensive chart. Truly, Gibson is Ruth's NgL analogue (or is it the other way around?), and clearly the greatest player in Negro Leagues history.

Other NgL appearances on Top 20 leaderboards include:

- *Isolated power:* Josh Gibson 2nd (.3371), Mule Suttles 11th (.2732), Turkey Stearnes 16th (.2677)
- *Secondary average*: Josh Gibson 5th (.5019), Oscar Charleston 18th (.4409)
- *At-bats per home run:* Josh Gibson 4th (13.41)
- *WHIP:* Satchel Paige 6th (1.0346)
- *Hits per 9 innings:* Dave Brown 14th (7.1719)

8

Josh Gibson vs. Ruthsrecord

In his original *Historical Abstract*, Bill James refers to "Ruthsrecord," the absurd agglomeration of all-time bests posted by Babe Ruth as he re-wrote not just baseball's record books, but the very nature of the game.[1]

The eponym "Ruthian" has come to describe not only the power behind an especially long home run or the numbers posted by a great slugger, but the accomplishments of any master of sport. The Babe had a best-selling candy bar named after him, though the Curtiss Candy Company, in a clever royalties dodge, claimed the Baby Ruth was named after President Cleveland's daughter. (Curtiss's ruse was undermined by their erection of an illuminated Baby Ruth sign near the landing spot of Ruth's "called shot" home run in the 1932 World Series.) His mystique was so complete that on at least one occasion during World War II—and I promise this will be the only use of the word in this book—when American soldiers taunted their Japanese foes with shouts of "Fuck the Emperor!," the Japanese shouted back, "Fuck Babe Ruth!" Not George Washington or FDR, not Humphrey Bogart or Clark Gable, not even Uncle Sam; no, it was the Babe who Japanese fighting men selected as the symbol of everything beloved by America and Americans.[2]

Ruth's mythic status has an impact on the core argument of this book. If we integrate Negro League career statistics fully into the Major League canon, and in so doing acknowledge that Josh Gibson out-slugged Ruth .706 to .690, aren't we re-writing a cherished page in our history? Aren't we robbing Ruth of his hallowed place in our society?

But wait! Just because Gibson *out-slugged* Ruth doesn't necessarily make him a greater *slugger* than Ruth. There are many measures of power-hitting prowess on which the two can be compared:

Most runs scored titles: Ruth, 8 to 5
Most home run titles: Gibson, 13 to 12
Fewest at-bats per home run: Ruth, 11.8 to 13.5
Most RBI titles: Gibson, 9 to 5
Most bases on balls titles: Ruth, 11 to 2
Most total bases titles: Gibson, 8 to 6
Highest batting average: Gibson, .369 to .342
Most batting titles: Gibson, 3 to 1
Highest OBP: Ruth, .474 to .451
Most OBP titles: Ruth, 10 to 6

Gibson and Ruth—will they finally be recognized as slugging peers by Major League Baseball?

Highest slugging average: Gibson, .706 to .690
Most slugging titles: Ruth, 13 to 9
Highest isolated power: Ruth, .348 to .337
Highest OPS: Ruth, 1.164 to 1.157
Most OPS titles: Ruth, 13 to 8
Highest OPS+: Ruth, 206 to 205
Most OPS+ titles: Ruth, 12 to 8

Ruth and Gibson were the most feared sluggers of all time in their respective leagues; each set every league slugging record; each consistently launched the longest home runs of his time; each hit for a high average; each was adept at drawing walks. But on the weight of the evidence, Ruth shows up as a slightly greater slugger than Gibson—and overall, a slightly greater hitter too, a fact underscored by Ruth's razor-thin edge in OPS+, 206 to 205.

The magic of Gibson comes from the fact that he put up Ruthian numbers from the catcher's slot—and that he was right-handed. No catcher comes close to Gibson in any of these measures, and only Jimmie Foxx and Hank Greenberg, plus perhaps a young Frank Thomas and Albert Pujols, approach (but cannot match) Gibson's prowess among right-handed batters.

Yet again we see that nothing in top Negro Leagues performances is significantly out of scale with long-established Major League records. We're not re-writing our history; rather, we're acknowledging a facet of that history which to this day is suppressed by racist tropes that survived the triumph of Jackie Robinson, the Dream of Martin Luther King and the advent of the modern statistical revolution. We're filling in the blank spaces in a portrait that till now has been only partially painted.

Perhaps, if our society hadn't been fundamentally diseased, Gibson's legend

Babe Ruth, posing happily with a group of his fellow human beings in 1925.

would shine as brightly as Ruth's. We'll never know. But it's not too late to honor the man's accomplishments properly, to set them side by side with Ruth's for the wonderment of a new generation of fans.

"He would have been fine with it," said Ruth's daughter Julia when Hank Aaron captured her Dad's all-time home run record. "Daddy used to always say, 'Records are made to be broken.'" In 2014 Julia also revealed that Ruth was refused a managerial position in the Majors because MLB owners were convinced he'd stock his team with Black players. "Daddy would have had Blacks on his team, definitely," said Julia. "I remember his talking about Satchel Paige. Daddy thought Satchel Paige was great."[3]

I think it's safe to assume that among those who might support the idea of recognizing Josh Gibson as baseball's all-time leader in slugging, the Bambino himself would be at the head of the line.

9

Monte Irvin

Half in One World, Half in Another

"Regarded as one of Negro Leagues' best hitters."
—Monte Irvin's Hall of Fame plaque

"I'm not going to try to rate Monte Irvin, since his career is half or two-thirds in one world, half or one-third in another."
—Bill James[1]

In this and the following chapters I examine the careers of men who serve as examples of the damage done by segregation to the historical reputation of Black superstars. This comparatively brief profile of Monte Irvin is intended to illustrate one of the most egregious injustices caused by statistical segregation: both a player's Negro Leagues numbers *and* his wartime service were made to disappear.

The disconnect between the Hall of Fame's thumbnail evaluation of Monte Irvin on the one hand and James's inability to rate his career with precision on the other is emblematic of the fate of players whose careers were split by the color line.

Now, James *said* he wasn't going to rate Irvin, and didn't give him a specific numbered ranking among the 100 greatest left fielders—he numbered him "XX" instead—but he did stick his Irvin comment between the 18th and 19th slots on his list of left fielders, implying at least an approximate placement on James's part. So, with the aid of combined career statistics, let's find out if Irvin is worthy of a top-20 all-time ranking.

* * *

Monte Irvin's Major League career was solid but not historically great. He posted All Star–caliber offensive seasons in 1950–51 and 1953, with a good but injury-riddled stint in 1952. His RBI title and third-place finish in 1951 MVP voting, plus a .394 average in two World Series, are really all he's got to sell in terms of Hall of Fame credentials. His 125 OPS+ is decent but not spectacular, below the level of most HoF left fielders. The average fan, seeing Irvin's name on the Hall of Fame roster and then consulting his record in *Total Baseball*, might be excused for wondering what all the fuss was about.

The most important fact to be gleaned from perusal of his MLB stat line is that his first full season came when Irvin was 31 years old, past the prime of most professional athletes.

Irvin had a greater impact in the Negro Leagues than he did in MLB, as one would expect because he was a younger man, posting All-Star–caliber offensive seasons in 1940–41 and again in 1946-47-48. He hit for almost precisely the same average in NgL postseason play (.395) as he did in MLB postseason play (.394).

Irvin's 1943-44-45 seasons, ages 24 through 26, were lost almost entirely to military service; he played just eight games during the war. As with Ted Williams, Irvin posted high-quality years both before and after his war service, and we can safely assume that these missing years would have been All Star–caliber offensive seasons.

Fifty-four Negro League players served in the US armed forces in World War II; others served their nation in vital wartime industries. Because the color line was broken three years after the war ended, most of these players suffered a double injustice at the hands of baseball's record-keepers: not only did their NgL play go uncounted, but their war service vanished as well.

To judge by his page in *Total Baseball*, Monte Irvin's great NgL seasons and three years of military service might never have happened.

Though Irvin himself held no hopes for reaching the Majors as a young man—"you could not even think of making it," Irvin told Lew Freedman in 2006; "the doors were closed"—Newark Eagles owner Effa Manley asserted that "Monte was the choice of all Negro National and American League club owners to serve as the No. 1 player to join a white Major League team." As it turned out, it was July 1949 before Monte got his chance, his best years long behind him.[2]

"I got home on September 1, 1945," remembered Irvin. "In October I started playing right field for the Newark Eagles. I had been a .400 hitter before the war. I became a .300 hitter after the war…. The war had changed me mentally and physically…. I was never the same guy that I was when I went in. I had lost my timing, and I was three years older…. Sometimes I think, 'Nobody saw me when I could really play.' I guess it's human nature to think that way. You know, I've tried not to think about it. But sometimes you can't help it."[3]

Combining Irvin's NgL and MLB records raises his OPS+ from 125 to 135, a jump that takes him, in historical terms, from marginal to well-deserved Hall of Famer. Here are MLB-only Irvin and combined-stats Irvin in comparison with other Hall of Fame left fielders:

HoF Left Fielder	OPS+	HoF Left Fielder	OPS+
Ted Williams	190	Fred Clarke	133
Stan Musial	159	Charles "Chick" Hafey	133
Ed Delahanty	152	Carl Yastrzemski	130
Ralph Kiner	149	Zack Wheat	129
Willie Stargell	147	Leon "Goose" Goslin	128
Jesse Burkett	140	Jim Rice	128
Monte Irvin (NgL+MLB)	**135**	Rickey Henderson	127
Joe Medwick	134	**Monte Irvin (MLB only)**	**125**
Joe Kelley	134	Tin Raines	123
"Orator" Jim O'Rourke	134	Henry "Heinie" Manush	121
Al Simmons	133	Lou Brock	109
Billy Williams	133		

This exercise lifts Irvin much closer to where we'd expect to see him based on his historical reputation. He doesn't crack the pantheon of Inner Circle greats, but he's right up there. Where he should be.

Is it so improbable that the greats of the Negro Leagues deserve to be ranked with the greats of the white Major Leagues? Is it so unlikely that Monte Irvin was a greater hitter, in the context of his own place and time, than Joe Kelley or Fred Clarke or Chick Hafey?

"Why did they think we could not play?" asked Irvin as an older man. "That's always been my question when I think back to the Negro Leagues. The ball was the same size. The bats weighed the same. The fields were no smaller. Why did they think we could not play?"[4] That's Irvin's question, and it's unanswerable. My question is this: The ball was the same size. The bats weighed the same. The fields were no smaller. Why, then, do some continue to argue that the majority of Irvin's professional career should count less, or differently, than his time in the Majors?

10

Willard Brown

The Chance That Wasn't a Chance

Consult *Total Baseball* under the letter B and you'll find that Willard Brown's professional career consisted of a .179 average in 21 games, with three doubles and a single home run.

Check his combined stat line in this book and you'll see a .349 professional hitter, winner of four batting titles and five slugging crowns. You'll also see nine years at the end of his record filled with minor and foreign league stats. Those rows should be crowded with Major League hitting heroics. As much as anyone who ever played the game, Willard Brown was shafted by the glacial pace of Major League integration.

He was hurt by other factors too: the unwillingness of managers and owners to give great Black players a proper shot at a Major League roster, their eagerness to send those players down at the slightest sign of struggle, and—especially—Major League Baseball's indifference to racist behavior by fans, players, coaches, managers, and owners alike.

Brown was one of the highest-impact hitters ever to play the game. His dominance with the Kansas City Monarchs from 1937 to 1948 is reminiscent of abbreviated-career monsters like Hank Greenberg and Johnny Mize: seven titles in hits, six in doubles, six in triples, five in home runs, eight in RBI. Towards the end of this paralyzing run of offensive potency he was given his "chance" by the St. Louis Browns. Twenty-one games, one game-winning home run and one smashed bat later, he was gone for good.

Brown joined the St. Louis Browns on July 19, 1947, two days after Hank Thompson integrated the team; both arrived without prior notice from general manager Bill DeWitt. Manager Herold "Muddy" Ruel immediately complained to DeWitt that he didn't want them on the team. "The gloom that pervaded the dressing room and bench of the Browns," commented Dent McSkimming in the July 21 *St. Louis Post-Dispatch*, "was thick enough to make one gasp for air.... It was very apparent the majority of players were determined they would just go through the motions.... The two Negro boys were there, in uniform, but few teammates spoke to them and they had to pair off together to get their own pre-game warmup."[1]

Throughout their tenure with the Browns, almost all of their white teammates gave Brown and Thompson the silent treatment. With the sole exception of All-Star shortstop Vern Stephens, no white player would train with them. "No one on the club would have anything to do with us," Thompson told the April 18, 1950, *Washington Afro-American*. "They wouldn't speak to us, and they wouldn't even warm up with us. If Brown wasn't around and I asked another player to warm up with me he'd just shake his head." In one game Brown split his cleats making an outfield play, and asked if anyone would loan him a pair—but no one would, so Brown played the final inning wearing a single shoe.[2]

In the Negro Leagues, Brown had used a heavy 40-ounce bat to rack up his enormous numbers. "I could've brought my bat with me [to the Browns]," he remembered in 1985, "but the Monarchs said, 'You don't need no bat. They furnish you bats in the major leagues.'" The Browns provided bats all right, but not to Brown's specifications: they were "33 inches, pitchers' bats," and Brown was forced to hunt the clubhouse and dugout for old bats that suited his style and stance.[3]

On August 13, appearing as an eighth-inning pinch-hitter with St. Louis down a single run, Brown walked to the plate with a bat with a broken knob, abandoned by outfielder Jeff Heath. "I could use that bat because it was 36 inches and kind of heavy," recalled Brown, who had taped the remnants of the knob back on—but the plate umpire wouldn't allow him to proceed until he removed the tape.[4]

And so, Brown went to the plate with his remnant of a second-hand broken bat, and smacked a go-ahead inside-the-park two-run homer off Hal Newhouser—the first home run by a Black player in AL history.

Willard Brown, who was nicknamed "Home Run" by, of all people, Josh Gibson (courtesy Ray Doswell and the Negro Leagues Baseball Museum).

But upon Brown's return to the dugout, Jeff Heath grabbed the remains of his former bat. "Heath was going to see I wasn't going to use it no more.... He took the bat and hit it on the dugout. Tore it all to pieces in splinters in the dugout.... You don't want it no more because you broke the knob off. And then I hit a home run, and you best break the bat. He did that."

The Browns did nothing about this. Muddy Ruel uttered not a word; no coach upbraided Heath for his publicly expressed wish to see his teammate fail; there was no recrimination, no benching, no telling-off at the post-game press conference; not so much an admonitory whisper in Jeff Heath's ear.

Maybe it's just me, but isn't it obvious that any *real* prospect, in whose success the Browns were properly invested, would have been provided with the type of bat he preferred as a matter of course? (Not to mention more than one pair of shoes.) The one and only time Brown got his hands on a heavy bat in the Majors, he hit an inside-the-park home run—whereupon the bat was taken away from him. Said Brown in classic understatement: "I wasn't used to that kind of baseball."[5]

St. Louis road secretary Charlie DeWitt later said that Heath was expressing superstition rather than racist intolerance when he broke the bat. "[Heath] would not have minded if Brown had got a single," claimed DeWitt, "but he had used up one of the bat's home runs." This is revisionist nonsense. The bat was *broken*; Heath had *thrown it away*. Unlike Brown, Heath had a ready supply of heavy bats supplied by the club; he didn't have to make use of a cast-off bat with a broken knob. A promising rookie had hit a home run with it, and by splintering that bat, Heath spoke for the team in wishing him ill.[6]

Through this incident, and others which doubtless eluded history's scribes, Brown saw exactly what level of investment the St. Louis Browns were willing to put into his chances at success. It was like being locked in a classroom with a bullying peer while a cohort of teachers and students looked on with tacit approval, if not outright applause. Willard Brown was twenty times the player Jeff Heath was, but Heath had Right—er, White—on his side.

Brown never collected another hit in the Majors. A handful of extraordinary men, like Jackie Robinson and Roy Campanella, could take the absurd pressure, the racist bombardment falling on their unprotected shoulders in this watershed year of 1947, and thrive—and some men, like Larry Doby and Willard Brown, could not, at least at first. That didn't make them lesser ballplayers, and it certainly didn't make them lesser men. What it made them was human.

As Frank Robinson remembered: "This is why some Blacks made it and some didn't, other than talent. If you could not overcome, you were going to fail." Doby and Brown initially buckled under the pressure, as you and I likely would have under the same horrific circumstances. Doby got another shot the following year, and Brown did not.[7]

Compare Brown's "chance" with, say, the chance given another power-hitting prospect, Mike Schmidt, who in his first two years in the Majors was allowed to appear in 145 games, in which he hit .197 with .367 slugging. Schmidt had posted one promising season in Triple-A ball; the Phillies knew he had power and an excellent glove, so they let him flounder and flail until he found his Hall of Fame groove. Willard Brown had a long, proven track record of dominant power hitting in a professional setting, but was allotted 21 games in which to demonstrate his worth.

Hank Thompson, who hit .333 over his final nine games, was released by St. Louis on August 23, the same day as Brown. When he asked why, Browns GM Bill DeWitt looked him in the eye and said, "There are some things I can't discuss with you, Hank." As Thompson later observed, "We both knew what those things were." The Browns would not employ another Black player until Satchel Paige joined the team four years later.[8]

We can't know with certainty what heights Willard Brown might have reached in the Majors given a proper chance—but he left us some powerful clues:

- In the 1947–48 PRWL he ran away with the Triple Crown with a 27/86/.432 slash line, also leading in runs scored and slugging and setting the single-season record for home runs.
- In the 1948 NAL he put up an MVP-type performance, hitting .404 and leading the league in hits, doubles, homers, RBI, total bases, slugging percentage, OPS and OPS+.
- In the 1948–49 PRWL he hit .323 and led the league with 18 homers.
- In the 1949 NAL (a year generally considered to be beyond the scope of NgL professional play), he led the league in total bases, RBI, batting average and slugging percentage, presumably also leading in OPS+.[9]
- In the 1949–50 PRWL he won his second Triple Crown with a 16/97/.354 slash line, also leading in slugging and setting the single-season record for RBI.

That's three titles in batting and four in home runs, four slugging championships, two Triple Crowns, and at least three probable MVPs in the four years following his demotion.

The call to the Majors never came.

In 1950, now age 35, Brown began an eight-year journey through the minor and Mexican leagues, hitting .352 with the Border League's Ottawa Nationals. Many of these numbers are lost to history, but those that survive make it clear that the man could still rake: as the Texas League's first everyday Black player he slashed 23/108/.310 in 1953, 35/120/.314 in 1954 and, at age 40, 19/104/.301 in 1955.

Brown's "chance" had come and gone years before. Unlike Luke Easter, who nearly won the AL home run crown in just 127 games in 1952 (but was nonetheless demoted twice after sluggish starts), Brown was never given the opportunity to establish a Major League track record. His prospects of promotion at this late hour were vanishingly small.

The question is, should he have been in the minors in the first place? The answer is clearly No. The factors that leveraged him so quickly out of Major League Baseball—an abbreviated trial, a hair-trigger demotion and, especially, a display of unbridled and unpunished racial animosity by a teammate—had nothing to do with his ability.

So why, then, was Brown's career batting average—any hitter's most easily identifiable measuring stick and most basic claim on the awareness of the average fan—recorded as .179? Was this fair? Was it just?

Willard Brown hit .349 in professional play, not .179. History deserves the whole of his story, not a tiny, discouraging fragment viewed through a haze of racist tropes which have stained our society from that day to this.

11

Roy Campanella

The Fallacy of Equivalency

The Hall of Merit (HoM), probably the top Internet site for high-level discussions of baseball history, held a vote in 2008 to determine the greatest players of all time at each position. At catcher, Josh Gibson won in a blowout; no surprise, as the HoM electorate is uncommonly well-educated on Negro Leagues history. But the electorate also ranked Roy Campanella 10th among catchers, well outside what might be described as the Inner Circle of the Hall of Merit—and by extension, the Inner Circle of the Hall of Fame. At least one HoM voter left him off the ballot entirely.

Now, this is a group vastly more knowledgeable on baseball history than the average fan; several posters are published authors in the field, and two, Kevin Johnson and Gary Ashwill, are respectively the co-founder of Seamheads and its chief Negro Leagues researcher. So if their opinion (which I believe has since changed) was that Campanella was a mid-tier Hall-of-Famer at best, surely the average fan's opinion is no higher. Today's sports media tends to lionize Johnny Bench and Yogi Berra as the definition of a great catcher.

I see Campanella as an Inner Circle catcher, in the same elite class as Berra and Bench. I believe the disconnect between the popular assessment and mine stems from a variety of factors, including an underestimation of the dominance of Campanella's defense at all levels of play, an underestimation of his games-played totals and quality of play in Negro League baseball, and—in the case of the Hall of Merit—a severe underestimation of Campanella's NgL power hitting as expressed by Major League Equivalencies (MLEs).

Hall of Merit posters Eric Chalek and Chris Cobb are acknowledged experts at calculating MLEs, used by baseball analysts to predict future MLB performance and to prevent lower-level performances from overshadowing Major League numbers from the same era. MLEs work very well for conversion of minor-league and Japanese-league stats to Major League-equivalent numbers.

But use of MLEs to posit how NgL players "would have" performed in the Majors, while well-intentioned, is the wrong thing to do, for a variety of reasons, and Roy Campanella is a case study in why.

There's no single conversion formula that could ever gain universal acceptance among fans, scholars, and historians. At the Hall of Merit, different systems are used to evaluate the same set of NgL players, and though each system uses the same base of hard, objective data, each calculation produces different results.

Chalek and Cobb revise and perfect their formulas relentlessly; but no matter how skilled the analyst, no matter how subtle the equation, *there's no equivalency formula that rises above the accuracy of an educated guess.* In an age where hard numbers are readily available, there's no more need for guessing.

The Inner-Circle Case for Roy Campanella

Part 1: Power

Campanella's MLB power hitting was historic. He established Major League career records for slugging percentage (.500) and isolated power (.224) by a catcher; in the 65 years since his retirement, only Mike Piazza has surpassed either mark. Campy still holds three of the top 12 single-season slugging marks by a catcher. He set the single-season record for catcher's home runs with 40 in 1953 (a record that stood for 43 years) and set the career record for catchers with 17.38 at-bats per home run (again, a figure surpassed only by Piazza).

Clearly, then, Campanella was an elite power-hitting catcher, one of the greatest ever—but his equivalencies painted the opposite picture. Compared with other Hall of Merit live-ball catchers, Campanella's career equivalencies, as a stand-alone player, ranked *dead last* in slugging, at .397 (Cobb) or .391 (Chalek).[1]

Individual seasons fared no better. In 1943 Campy finished second in the Mexican League in home runs (one behind the league leader) and fifth in doubles, with a batting average 18 points above league average—but his equivalent slugging was translated to .376 (Chalek) or .375 (Cobb). In 1944 he slugged .582 in NgL play, just six points behind Josh Gibson's .588—but Campy was credited with equivalent slugging of .411 (Chalek) or .419 (Cobb) against Gibson's .556 (Chaleeko and Cobb).

Combining his equivalencies with his actual MLB totals dragged Campanella's all-time rank in slugging among catchers from third down to 12th (Cobb) or 15th (Chalek). There can't be any serious doubt that these rock-bottom equivalencies contributed to his low ranking by Hall of Merit voters.

Player	AB	TB	Slg
Josh Gibson (actual NgL performance)	3134	2214	.706
Josh Gibson (Cobb MLE)	6627	3941	.595
Mike Piazza	6911	3768	.545
Roy Campanella (actual MLB performance)	**4205**	**2101**	**.500**
Roy Campanella (combined MLB + NgL performance)	**4944**	**2460**	**.498**
Charles "Gabby" Hartnett	6432	3144	.489
Roy Campanella (actual NgL performance)	**739**	**359**	**.486**
Bill Dickey	6300	3062	.486
Lawrence "Yogi" Berra	7555	3643	.482
Mickey Cochrane	5169	2470	.478
James "Biz" Mackey (actual NgL performance)	3668	1747	.476
Johnny Bench	7658	3644	.476

Player	AB	TB	Slg
Ivan Rodriguez	9592	4451	.464
Carlton Fisk	8756	3999	.457
William "Buck" Ewing	5365	2444	.456
Quincy Trouppe (actual NgL performance)	1174	534	.455
Roy Campanella (actual MLB + Cobb MLE)	**7777**	**3518**	**.452**
Joe Torre	7874	3560	.452
Cal McVey	2513	1123	.447
Roy Campanella (actual MLB + Chalek MLE)	**8303**	**3702**	**.446**
Gary Carter	7971	3497	.439
Ted Simmons	8680	3793	.437
Bill Freehan	6073	2502	.412
Roy Campanella (Cobb MLE)	**3572**	**1417**	**.397**
James "Deacon" White (retired 1890)	6624	2605	.393
Biz Mackey (Cobb MLE)	8275	3249	.393
Roy Campanella (Chalek MLE)	**4098**	**1601**	**.391**
Charlie Bennett (retired 1893)	3821	1480	.387
Roger Bresnahan (retired 1915)	4491	1690	.377
Biz Mackey (Chalek MLE)	7036	2515	.357
Quincy Trouppe (Chalek MLE)	7195	2568	.357

In terms of actual performance, Campanella out-slugged both Berra and Bench in both Negro League and Major League play—but according to his equivalencies, Campy's combined career ranked above three dead-ball catchers, plus two other Negro League catchers also subjected to equivalencies, and below every other catcher on the list.

Note also that Campanella's actual Negro League slugging was lower that his Major League slugging—in the same ballpark, but lower. (Sorry; I have an affection for tattered, tawdry puns.) Rather than inflating his totals to some absurd height, statistical integration lowers Campy's combined slugging average.

The problem with application of equivalencies to NgL play is generalized. Biz Mackey was knocked down from .476 actual slugging to .357, Quincy Trouppe from .456 to .357; the two were listed dead last, behind even the MLB dead-ball catchers. Mackey's actual slugging is a shade higher than Johnny Bench's, .4763 to .4758, but equivalency pegged him at .357, 119 points lower.

Josh Gibson lost 111 points of slugging by equivalent analysis. Everyone who saw Gibson play—everyone!—compared him favorably with monsters like Ruth, Gehrig, and Foxx; but according to his equivalencies he was 14 points below Foxx, 37 points below Gehrig, and no less than 95 points below the Babe: still fearsome, obviously, but not quite in their class. Foxx, not Gibson, comes out as the top right-handed slugger of all time. This conclusion flies in the face of contemporary evidence.

Considering the problem from another angle, from 1949 to 1956, *all* of Campanella's actual MLB isolated power figures were higher than *any* equivalent figure. Only in his final season did he post an ISO lower than his highest projected equivalency.

Year	League	ISO
1953	Actual Major League performance	.299
1950	Actual Major League performance	.270
1951	Actual Major League performance	.265
1955	Actual Major League performance	.265
1949	Actual Major League performance	.211
1954	Actual Major League performance	.194
1952	Actual Major League performance	.184
1956	Actual Major League performance	.175
1941	*Projected MLE (Negro National League)*	*.167*
1940	*Projected MLE (Negro National League)*	*.146*
1957	Actual Major League performance	.145
1943	*Projected MLE (Mexican League)*	*.124*
1944	*Projected MLE (Negro National League)*	*.122*
1945	*Projected MLE (Negro National League)*	*.177*
1939	*Projected MLE (Negro National League)*	*.110*
1942	*Projected MLE (Negro National League)*	*.104*

Equivalencies implied that Campy hit at dead-ball power levels in the Negro Leagues, then suddenly transformed into a record-breaking slugger in the Majors. The proposition is absurd.

Worse, combining equivalencies with MLB numbers dragged down Campy's combined totals much further than they should have—because equivalencies not only downgrade Negro League performance, they also add thousands of "equivalent" at-bats at a level vastly below actual, proven MLB performance.

In the years since they posted these numbers, Chalek and Cobb have revised and improved their methods and results. But frankly (and meaning no disrespect to the important work done by these analysts in advancing public recognition of Negro Leagues superstars), any equivalency is an estimate, pure and simple—an estimate that may or may not be accepted by other analysts, who may have figured equivalencies of their own. This promotes instability in the data set and renders sustained analysis impossible.

We don't seek equivalencies for early Major League numbers; we accept them as they are within the context of their time and place. Frederick "Cy" Williams hit 5 homers in 1917, 41 homers in 1923—not because he'd suddenly blossomed into a fearsome power hitter, but because the live-ball era dawned in the middle of his career. His figures for 1917 and 1923 are both included in Williams's accepted career batting line. We don't adjust Cy's 1917 numbers upwards to account for the dead-ball era, or seek a dead-ball equivalency for 1923; rather, we look at the whole of the record, with an understanding that the time and place within which Williams performed had changed. And so it is, or should be, with the statistics of the Negro Leagues.

More on this later; first, you need to know more about this prodigy of nature named Campanella. Using the Hall of Merit's own words and arguments, let's examine further components of Campy's claim to a place in the Inner Circle.

Part 2: Defense and Durability

In the Hall of Merit thread on Yogi Berra, Eric Chalek presents his "reductive view of catcher defense in today's game," with which I agree 100 percent:

—A lot of catcher assists (non-stolen base ones that is) are discretionary, throwing guys out on bunts or on dinkers. The catcher waves off the pitcher and takes the throw.
—Catcher putouts have very little meaning. Mostly they are strikeouts or high popups around the plate.
—Plate blocking is important, but it comes up about once a month.
—The variation of pitcher-handling and game-calling a game has been pretty thoroughly debunked by Keith Woolner (and probably others too), and catcher ERA is a poor measure of working with pitchers.
—Wild pitches and passed balls are much rarer today than ever and are extremely dependent on the repertoire of the pitching staff.
There are two things that today's catcher must be good at: gunning down runners and catching a lot of innings despite getting dinged up a bit…. The real difference in catchers is in their arms and their footwork.[2]

Taking Chalek's criteria for catcher excellence point by point, let's start with "gunning down runners." Campanella holds the career record for caught-stealing percentage at 57.4 percent. He wiped out more than half of all baserunners attempting to steal against him in eight of his ten MLB seasons, a fact perfectly well known while he was active; this suppressed the number of attempted steals and hit-and-runs opposing managers were willing to try against him—and this deterrent effect, in and of itself, had game-altering defensive value. Campy's caught-stealing rate was 18 percent above league average, best of all time; he faced 34 percent fewer base-stealing attempts than league average, also the best mark ever. (In case you're curious, Ivan Rodriguez is second in both categories at 17 percent and 32 percent respectively.)

An arm of such strength and accuracy confers other defensive advantages too, such as an increased risk of pickoffs and the smaller leads risked by baserunners, which suppresses opponents' stealing and scoring opportunities. Phil Rizzuto, wiped out twice by Campy in Game 4 of the 1949 World Series, remarked: "I was never picked off third base in my career, and Campanella made it look easy."[3]

Chalek's second criterion concerns durability, and here again Campanella stands virtually without peer. He and Yogi Berra set parallel MLB records by catching 100+ games in nine consecutive seasons. Campy caught 76.3 percent of his team's total games, a mark which easily broke Mickey Cochrane's record of 72.9 percent and ranks third today. He also displayed tremendous durability on a game-to-game basis: he ranks #1 among Hall of Merit live-ball catchers with 8.56 innings caught per appearance, #2 in completing 90.6 percent of his games caught.

Campanella is therefore a superb exemplar—one of the best all-time—of "catching a lot of innings despite getting dinged up a bit."

Chalek's third criterion is footwork. It's striking how consistently Campy's contemporaries mention not only his arm, but also his gracefulness and economy of motion, his dexterity and nimbleness afoot. The June 6, 1953, edition of *Life* described him as "quick despite his casual air"; the August 8, 1955, *Time* as a player who "never makes an unnecessary move"; the February 10, 1958, *Time* as "an athlete of grace." "More than one observer," wrote Tom Meany in his 1950 book *The Artful Dodgers*, "has likened [his] quickness to that of a cat. He can pounce on bunts placed far out in front of the plate and he gets his throws away with no lost motion."[4]

Mickey Cochrane praised Campy's "remarkable agility, his powerful throwing arm, and the disdainful confidence with which he pegged to any base at any time, never fearful of throwing the ball away.... There's no doubt in my mind he's the best in [the National] League." Bill Dickey told Sam Lacy in the April 22, 1950, *Washington Afro-American* that "he's easily one of the smoothest receivers of his generation, has an excellent arm.... It makes me feel pretty good to have him say he learned something from me."[5]

Campanella therefore ranks at or near the top in all three of Chalek's criteria for modern catcher defense—and there's plenty of favorable evidence beyond these criteria.

Range factor (calculated by dividing putouts plus assists by defensive games played) contains too many illusions to paint an accurate season-by-season picture of catcher defense: strikeouts are credited as catcher putouts; assist totals increase as catchers on bad teams face more stolen-base attempts; the size of home-park foul territory influences a catcher's opportunities to record outs via popups. However, range factor does have an aspect I've not seen mentioned in discussions of catcher defense: consistent predictive career value.

In the Hall of Merit thread on election results for the all-time greatest catchers, poster Ron Wargo (a.k.a. "ronw") divided Major League catchers into three groups by the quality of their defense, as perceived by Win Shares and fielding runs above average (FRAA1)[6]:

Excellent: Johnny Bench, Charlie Bennett, Yogi Berra, Gary Carter, Bill Dickey, Buck Ewing, Gabby Hartnett.
Great: Roy Campanella, Mickey Cochrane, Carlton Fisk, Bill Freehan, Deacon White. (Wargo added the caveat that Campanella and Cochrane have excellent rates, but poor FRAA1 ratings due to perceived short career length. I'll expand on Campy's true career length in the next section.)
Poor: Roger Bresnahan, Cal McVey, Ted Simmons, Joe Torre.

Adding Hall of Merit electees Ivan Rodriguez to the Excellent group and Mike Piazza to the Poor group for completeness, the following trend is observable in single-season range factor leaderboards:

- All eight catchers in the Excellent group, and all five catchers in the Great group, led their leagues in range factor at least once, and
- None of the five catchers in the Poor group ever led their leagues in range factor.

Sustained dominance in range factor has consistent predictive value. Every live-ball catcher who led his league in range factor four or more times was a superior defender: Campanella, Cochrane, Dickey, Johnny Edwards, Jerry Grote, Bill Killefer, Yadier Molina, and John Roseboro.

In sum, in the live-ball era there's a reliable predictive correlation between high single-season range factors and excellent catcher defense. Not all great defensive catchers have consistently high range factors, but live-ball catchers with consistently high range factors are always rated as great defensive catchers.

Like his caught-stealing rate, Campanella's dominance of range factor is historically unparalleled. His 5.98 career range factor is 1.32 points better than league average, the widest margin in history. He led the NL in range factor per game eight consecutive years (1948–55) and nine times overall (add 1957), and in range factor per nine innings seven consecutive years (1948–54) and eight times overall (add 1957). All of these figures stand today as Major League records.

In each of Campanella's MLB seasons, Brooklyn pitchers led the NL in strikeouts, a strong bias in his favor. However, Brooklyn's run of consecutive league-leading strikeout totals began the same year Campy took over catching duties, and some measure of credit should be accorded to his pitch-calling and -framing. (This is especially true in the case of Campanella, who had a sterling reputation as a handler of pitchers; as Carl Erskine remarked, "If you shook off Campy, you had to explain it to Walter Alston.")[7]

Other catchers have had similar strikeout-heavy pitching-staff advantages at various points in MLB history, but none, in 147 years of play, has matched Campanella's dominance in range factor behind the plate.

Consistent with excellent range, Campanella had a reputation for very soft hands. He "allows very few passed balls," said *Life* in 1953; "a high pitch does not even make Campy rise out of [his] crouch." This contemporary impression is borne out by the numbers. Among Hall of Merit catchers Campanella ranks fourth in passed ball prevention with just .0473 per game and .0498 per nine innings, and fifth in wild pitch prevention with .1851 per game and .1946 per nine innings. He is one of four Hall of Merit live-ball catchers never to lead his league in passed balls; in fact, he never finished higher than third in MLB passed balls or wild pitches in any season, despite routinely leading his league—often by multi-hundred inning margins—in innings caught.

At least one form of extended analysis shows Campy as the #1 all-time defensive catcher. Bill James's Defensive Winning Percentage takes many variable factors into account, including, for catchers, team strikeouts and walks, catcher assists, runners thrown out, errors, passed balls, and stolen bases allowed. James writes: "We have Campanella rated, as a defensive player, at 55–6, a winning percentage of .896. I believe that's the fourth- or fifth-highest percentage I've ever seen [at any position].... The mean Winning Percentage for [the 109 catchers who have caught 1,000+ games since 1900] is .681, with a Standard Deviation of .070. There are two catchers in history who are 2 standard deviations above the norm...: Roy Campanella and Yadier Molina."[8]

There is therefore a multi-faceted, evidence-based argument that Roy Campanella was the greatest defensive catcher in baseball history.

Still, for the sake of this analysis, let's err on the side of conservatism and place him somewhere in the top five. I can't see how any lower ranking is possible.

So: historic slugging, historic durability, historic defense—but wait ... there's more.

Part 3: Contemporary Reputation and the Great Intangible—Segregation

Campanella was a star literally everywhere he played (or should I say, everywhere he was *allowed* to play) for a span of sixteen years:

- 1941: NN2 All-Star
- 1942: NN2 All-Star *(yes, 1942—see below)*
- 1943: MEX All-Star
- 1944: NN2 All-Star
- 1945: NN2 All-Star
- 1946: NENL MVP
- 1947: IL MVP
- 1948: *(season split between AAA and MLB)*
- 1949: NL All-Star
- 1950: NL All-Star
- 1951: NL All-Star and MVP
- 1952: NL All-Star
- 1953: NL All-Star and MVP
- 1954: NL All-Star
- 1955: NL All-Star and MVP
- 1956: NL All-Star

That's 13 All-Star selections and five MVPs in a 16-year span. Every audience that saw him play thought he was one of the very best around, for a very long time.

A large proportion of this reputation hinged on the contemporary view of his defense. In 1947 Campanella's highest placement on any IL offensive leaderboard was 14th place in RBI. 14th place, behind two of his own teammates, is hardly an argument-starter for MVP. It was Campy's defense, not his hitting, that stood him above the rest of the league in the eyes of the voters. Buffalo Bisons manager Paul Richards, himself a former top-notch MLB defensive catcher, told the June 12 *Pittsburgh Courier* that Campy was "the best catcher in the business—Major or Minor Leagues.... If [Rickey] doesn't bring that guy up, he might as well go out of the Emancipation business."

Campanella's MLB impact was immediate and sensational. Ty Cobb opined that "Roy Campanella will be remembered longer than any other catcher in baseball history.... When they look for players to put in the Hall of Fame, they'll have to start with Roy Campanella." ("I appreciated that," Campy said, "coming from such a man.") Tris Speaker agreed: "Of all the men playing baseball today, the one they will talk about the most twenty or thirty years from now will be Campanella."[9]

Some Hall of Merit posters have questioned whether Campy deserved various of his three NL MVPs. When debating their season-by-season merit, posters should recognize that voters of the time were weighing not only a catcher putting up .300/30/100 slash lines for pennant-winning teams, but also what many of them regarded as the finest defensive catching they'd ever seen.

The adversity underpinning Campanella's stardom in the minors and majors cannot be overstated. He produced at historic levels under pressure as intense as any athlete has ever faced.

In 1946 Campy integrated the New England League (and won the MVP); throughout 1947 he was the only Black player in the International League (and won the MVP); when finally promoted in 1948, he was the sixth Black player to appear in the Majors in the 20th century—whereupon, following Branch Rickey's pre-arranged plan, he was "demoted" to the American Association, specifically to integrate the final segregated Triple-A circuit.[10]

It's important to understand that racially motivated maneuvering cost Campanella playing time in both the NgL and MLB, and that this lost time unjustly hinders his legacy. It should also be understood that Campy was clearly ready not just to play in, but to star in, the Majors by 1941 at the latest.

Campanella was a prodigy of a type rarely seen in any era, playing with a semi-pro team of 14-to-20-year-olds at age 13 thanks to his precocious size and ability. He debuted with the independent Bacharach Giants in 1937 at age 15 and almost immediately jumped to the Negro National League's Washington (later Baltimore) Elite Giants, where, in an invaluable apprenticeship, he served as backup catcher to Hall of Famer Biz Mackey for two years. When Mackey jumped to the Newark Eagles halfway through the 1939 season, Campy took over as starting catcher at age 17; the Elites went 12–13 before Campy took over full-time catching duties but 13–8 after, earning a spot in the NN2 playoffs. In the ensuing Championship Series against the Homestead Grays, Campy hit .353 with a homer and six RBIs to help the Elites win their only NgL title.

Prior to the 1941 East-West Game, the NAL squad schemed to take advantage of the 19-year-old's supposed rawness by running wild on the basepaths. Campy gunned down lead runner Tommy Sampson on an attempted sacrifice bunt in the second, threw out Howard Cleveland trying to steal in the fifth, and threw out Jimmy Crutchfield trying to steal in the ninth. This defensive display, which earned him game MVP honors, captured the attention of interested parties outside NgL circles.

As a young man, Campy didn't believe he'd ever reach the Majors: "I had little faith that these bars would ever come down, at least in my lifetime. The color line in the Major Leagues did not take a man's talent into account. As far as I was concerned the big leagues were as far away as Siberia." But in July 1942 (not 1943 as is sometimes reported; the corrected timeline shows that Campanella was viewed as prospective MLB material by qualified observers at age 20), Nat Low, sports editor of the Communist, pro-integration *Daily Worker*, convinced Pirates owner William Benswanger to defy the color line and offer Campy, pitcher Dave Barnhill, and second baseman Sammy Hughes an August 4 tryout at Forbes Field.[11]

Campanella seemingly had good cause to trust Benswanger, who'd responded to a question from Lester Rodney in 1939 by writing, "If it came to an issue, I'd vote for Negro players. There's no reason why they should be denied the same chance that Negro fighters and musicians are given." As Rodney observed: "Coming from an owner, that was a breakthrough statement." When asked about the impending tryouts, Benswanger told a UP reporter: "We will give any man—white or colored—a chance, when asked. I have not changed from my original position that any player, regardless of race, will be considered for a position on the Pirates."[12]

Under pressure from others within baseball's power structure, all offers for tryouts were rescinded—but not before Campy, rightly expecting at minimum a spot on a minor league roster, had jumped ship on the Baltimore Elite Giants. He missed games and was suspended briefly for league-jumping upon his return to the Elites.

A few weeks later the NN2 suspended him again, this time for playing in an NAL charity game for the substantial fee of $200—$15 more than he later earned for each full month at Nashua—without permission. He was fined $250 and removed from his place, already awarded by the owners (the "fan vote" of the time being a sham) on the roster of the 1942 East-West All-Star game.

Infuriated and broke, Campanella jumped to the Mexican League's Monterey Industrials for the remainder of 1942 and all of 1943. The Elites had to waive the $250 fine, which Campy refused to pay, to regain his services for 1944—and it was worth it.

Rollo Wilson wrote in the October 7, 1944, *Philadelphia Tribune* that "this year I rate the young Philadelphia receiver over Gibson, because his game has advanced while Josh's has declined." In selecting his 1944 "All-American baseball team" for the December 16 *Pittsburgh Courier*, Grays owner Cumberland Posey also opted for Campy over his more famous rival: "We placed Campanella over Gibson…. Even with Gibson in perfect shape, it is a close race between him and Campanella."

Campy justified these high rankings by placing second in the 1944 NNL batting race at .388. (His equivalency, by the way, credits him with a .301 average, 87 points under his actual performance.) With his spectacular defense, Campanella would have been a strong choice, had the award existed, for NN2 MVP.

1945 was better still, as Campanella led the NN2 with 48 runs scored, 16 doubles, 43 RBI and 32 walks, and captured the batting championship at .385. He also won the NN2 OBP crown at .479, out-performing Jackie Robinson, who led the NAL at .449. Certainly Campy would have won the NN2 MVP for 1945.

When Bill James opined that Campy "wasn't as dominant a player in Black baseball as he was in the National League" and that "most of his time in the Negro Leagues was more analogous to a training period than to an indefinite extension of his Major League career," he was writing in an era when concrete numbers didn't exist—but today we can see that Campy was as dominant in the Negro Leagues as he was in the Majors.[13]

It's possible that Campanella, not Jackie Robinson, would have been Branch Rickey's choice to break the MLB color barrier if only he'd said "Yes" to Rickey. (Walter O'Malley confirmed, "It got down to two men, Jackie and Roy Campanella"; longtime Dodgers scout Clyde Sukeforth added, "We were all in on scouting Campanella, you couldn't go wrong there…. There was never any question about his ability.") Having been burned by Benswanger, Campy turned down a direct offer from Rickey because he was convinced Rickey wanted his services for the Brooklyn Brown Dodgers, a team in the short-lived, all–Black United States League co-created and co-financed by Rickey.[14]

Later in life Campanella said, "I felt bad. Not that Jackie had signed, it didn't matter to me who was number one. I felt bad that I had said no to Mr. Rickey"—but at the time, when told by Jackie that Rickey had signed him to play for Montreal, Campy exclaimed (as quoted by Dick Young): "Well, I'll be darned. What a dumb boy I am."[15]

(I'm willing to bet that the language used by Campy was a tad more, um, *mature* than Mr. Young dared to reproduce in 1952. This quote stands in stark contrast to another Campanella line: After Rex Barney blew a potential no-hitter by shaking off Campy's signals, Campy snarled at him, as quoted by Barney himself: "Don't you *ever* shake me off again. You *know* I'm smarter than you are. And I've always *been* smarter than you are. And I'll always *be* smarter than you are. Pitchers don't know a Goddamn thing. That's why they have catchers.")[16]

Campanella served his time in the minors not for seasoning, but specifically to integrate the leagues to which he was assigned. Emil "Buzzy" Bavasi, who in 1946 was business manager of the Nashua Dodgers, remembered that "he was the best player in the [New England] League. Nobody could touch him." Nashua's skipper Walter Alston confirmed that "Roy of course was better than a Class B player. But he knew why he was there. He was part of Rickey's plan to begin integrating baseball. He knew he was going to start something important." Campy's two minor league MVP years should be regarded as equivalent to All Star-caliber Major League seasons.[17]

Part of Campanella's 1948 season, too, was lost to Major League play through Rickey's color-line manipulations. The Dodgers brought Campy to spring training (Joe Posnanski describes him at this moment as "already, certainly, the best catcher in the world") and put him on the bench, then in the outfield, then at third base—anywhere but catcher. Rickey had forbidden Leo Durocher to play Campy at catcher for fear that the quality of his play would lead to fan demands that he play the full season with the Dodgers, thereby hindering Rickey's plan for Campy to integrate the American Association.[18]

Campanella's appearance in the Dodgers' opener on April 20 was the first by a Black catcher in MLB play since Fleet Walker's swan song on September 4, 1884; in his sole plate appearance that day, the Giants' Ken Trinkle welcomed him, Jackie Robinson–style, by drilling him in the ribs. After seeing play in just three of Brooklyn's first eight games, Campy was "sent down" to the all-white American Association. Sick of the machinations and badly wanting his long-deferred Major League roster spot, Campanella groused at the move—"I'm no crusader, I'm a ballplayer," he said—but he did as he was asked, and lit up the Triple-A circuit with .325-.432-.715 batting in 35 games.[19]

61 games in, with the Dodgers floundering at 27–34, Campy was "promoted," and proceeded to gun down 67 percent of opposing baserunners over the remainder of the year, including 12 in a row over his last 21 games. So immediate and visceral was his impact that he received MVP votes while playing in just 83 Major League games. As with 1946 and '47, 1948 should be regarded as equivalent to an All-Star-caliber Major League season.

While clearly necessary for the advancement of integration in baseball, Rickey's social engineering project likely cost Brooklyn a spot in the World Series. As with the 1939 Elite Giants, Campanella's second-half presence transformed Baltimore's fortunes. Following his promotion the Dodgers went 57–36: 50–23 in games he started at catcher, 7–13 in games he didn't. It seems probable that Campy's presence over the course of the full season would have brought home the pennant.

* * *

Roy Campanella was every inch as much a pioneer as Jackie Robinson, and should be acknowledged, remembered, and honored as such. He integrated the New England League, integrated the American Association, and served for a full year as the lone Black face of the International League. With Don Newcombe he formed the first all–Black battery in MLB history. In 1946, when Walter Aston was ejected from a Nashua game, Campy became the first Black man to manage white players at any level of organized baseball—and won the game for Nashua by selecting Newcombe as a surprise pinch hitter.

"Robinson proved he could play on the biggest stage," writes Bryan Soderholm-Difatte, "…but the success and progression of Campanella and Newcombe in the minor leagues was just as important in the long run—for the Dodgers, for baseball, even for America." As Martin Luther King told Newcombe: "You'll never know what you and Jackie and Roy did to make it possible to do my job."[20]

But let's be clear: Campanella doesn't require pioneer credit to be recognized as an inner-circle Hall of Famer (and Hall of Meriter). All he needs is proper credit for what he actually was from 1941 to 1948: the best catcher at any level of baseball.

So, if Campy's top five in defense, *and* top three in power, *and* set new standards for catcher durability, *and* had All-Star seasons across a span of sixteen years, *and* won five MVPs at the various levels of play he was allowed to access … well then, does he belong in 10th place, or 12th, in the all-time Hall of Merit catcher rankings?

I can see an argument for second place, behind only Gibson, but I personally see third as correct, behind Berra (my MLB pick: durability, underrated defense, superior plate selectivity, and clockwork year-to-year offensive consistency that neither Campy nor Bench could match—plus ten rings) but ahead of Bench (Campy had superior power and, at minimum, comparable defense).

Campy can't be the greatest catcher ever—nor can Berra or Bench—because they shared the planet with Josh Gibson. But Campy deserves recognition as one of the four best catchers who ever played the game. And I think, given his nature, that a place in the top four would be just fine with him.

Roy Campanella's career was brought to cruel and sudden end by a car crash on January 28, 1958. He spent the rest of his life in a wheelchair. But after a period of initial and wholly comprehensible bitterness, no one ever again heard him complain.

12

Luke Easter

The Toughest Case to Prove

Luscious "Luke" Easter belongs in the Hall of Fame. And yes, Luscious really is his first name.

As a young man Luke played for a truly great team that didn't document its batting statistics. Then World War II intervened; he was 31 years old before he appeared in a league that recorded even the most fragmentary numbers. At age 33 he finally made the Majors, but despite showing ample long-ball power he was demoted to the minors, where he continued to display obvious Major League–ready power for over a decade.

Luke's case for the Hall of Fame is exceptionally difficult to document. He has almost no statistics for many of what were likely his peak seasons, and his MLB career was cut artificially short.

In the absence of most of the evidence I'd cite ordinarily for a player of his caliber, the Hall of Fame case for Easter must be assembled from many pieces of fragmentary evidence—some complete, some incomplete; some concrete, some circumstantial. But consider what famed prosecutor Vincent Bugliosi wrote about circumstantial evidence:

> Circumstantial evidence is not like a chain. You could have a chain spanning the Atlantic Ocean, consisting of millions of links, and with one weak link that chain is broken.
> Circumstantial evidence, to the contrary, is like a rope. And each fact is a strand of that rope. And as we add strands we add strength to that rope. If one strand breaks, the rope is not broken.[1]

Put another way, a circumstantial case can stand on part of its evidence. It's possible to concur with points A, C and D while dismissing point B, and still agree with the ultimate conclusion.

Bearing this in mind, here follows my argument for Luke Easter to be inducted into the Baseball Hall of Fame.

Point 1: Luke Easter was playing professional-quality baseball by 1935, at age 19.

(Luke's career is almost always reported as beginning in 1937, but his name first appears in a Titanium Giants lineup in the May 10, 1935, St. Louis Argus.)

SABR's Justin Murphy writes that Easter "played outfield and first base and batted cleanup for the St. Louis Titanium Giants, [which] had become an elite club ... regularly winning 90 percent of their games." Very few statistics survive, but the May 31, 1935, *Argus* identifies Easter as one of four players in the Giants' "Murderers' Row," the June 12, 1936, *Argus* as "the home run king of the Giants"—suggesting strongly that he was an exceptional power hitter from the start.[2]

Besides Easter, the Giants' roster in those years featured former and future Negro Leaguers Jesse Askew, Herbert "Doc" Bracken, Earl "Lefty" Bumpus, "Little" Eli Chism, "Big" John Chism, Frank "Tenny" Edwards, Johnny Hundley, NAL All-Star Sam "The Jet" Jethroe, NAL All-Star John Lyles, St. Louis Amateur Baseball Hall of Famer Carl Whitney, and Ed "Pep" Young. Some of these men played for the Giants and Negro Leagues teams in the same years (not an unheard-of occurrence among cash-poor Black players)—and the Giants themselves played regularly against NgL teams; "in [1940] ... [Easter] saw action against every team in the Negro American League" (August 12, 1949, *St. Louis Star and Times*).[3]

As might be expected from the composition of their roster, the Giants overwhelmed most of the independent teams they played; in 1938 they racked up 102 runs on 113 hits over a 10-game stretch. But they defeated the professional teams they played with the same clockwork regularity, albeit by more moderate scores. In 1940 the Giants went 6–0 vs. Negro American League teams, including a 3–2 victory over the Kansas City Monarchs, who were 30–10–2 in NgL play en route to their second of four consecutive NAL championships.

One does not bat cleanup for a .900 team that routinely defeats professional competition if one cannot hit consistently and prodigiously. These hits included plenty of long balls; Joe Posnanski tells us that "he hit so many impossibly long home runs ... that teammates would sit on the bench and argue what was his longest."[4]

At 6'4" and 240 pounds, Luke Easter was an imposing figure in the batter's box. After returning from World War II, Easter caught the eye of Bill Veeck, and despite advanced age, he proved to be an extra-base machine at every stop (including the Majors) in professional baseball (courtesy Hake's Auctions).

Illustrating the lack of knowledge (which persists today) of Easter's pre–World War II career, Gordon Manning wrote in the August 5, 1950, edition of *Collier's* magazine that Easter's .363 PCL performance "wasn't a bad record for a fellow who never played much baseball before 1946." Topps's Luke Easter baseball card for 1954 made a more definite assertion: "Strange as it seems, Luke never played baseball before 1946!"

Here, then, is the answer to those who ask why Easter never appeared in organized ball until age 31: He did. And he was very, very good.

Point 2: Easter has documentable external markers as an All Star–caliber player as early as 1938 and as late as 1957, encompassing a 20-year span.

In 1938, 1939 and 1940, years for which we have almost no statistics, the *St. Louis Argus* selected Easter for its East-West All-Star Games. (He stroked a game-winning 2-RBI double in the 1939 contest.) Here is concrete, pre–World War II evidence of Easter being recognized as a top-echelon player.

Nine years later he was selected to the NgL East squad for both 1948 East-West Games. In 1948/49 he was named Puerto Rican Winter League MVP; in 1952 he was named the AP's American League Outstanding Player; in 1954/55 he was named Mexican Pacific Coast League MVP; in 1957 he was named International League All-Star and MVP.

That's a 20-year span during which Easter was cited at various points as being an All Star–caliber player. Only seven players in MLB history can match that, all elite superstars: Hank Aaron, Al Kaline, Willie Mays, Stan Musial, Pete Rose, Ted Williams, and Carl Yastrzemski.

Point 3: As Easter can be documented as a high-level player from 1935 to 1941, he's entitled to credit for his war service from 1942 to 1945.

Easter was drafted into the Army on June 22, 1942, but was honorably discharged on July 3, 1943, due to ongoing complications from a broken ankle and wrecked knee resulting from a car smash in the spring of 1941—the first of many times his knee would plague him. From 1943 through 1945 he performed war industry labor at a Portland shipyard and a Chicago chemical plant.

It appears that Easter played no baseball during the war years, almost certainly for lack of opportunity. This was, or should have been, his absolute prime: the years he missed were ages 27 through 30. As Bill James asks, "Who could miss four key years out of his youth, and still make the majors? A few guys did; a lot of people didn't." Luke Easter was one of the few.[5]

Point 4: Easter placed among league leaders in markers for power in every league for which statistics survive.

The following list of top-3 finishes should have many more entries—but for a number of the leagues in which Easter played, statistics are fragmentary or totally lost, making calculated comparisons impossible.

- 1946 Hawaiian Fall League:
    ◊ 1st in home runs
- 1947 Negro National League:
    ◊ 3rd in isolated power
- 1947/48 Venezuelan League:
    ◊ 1st in home runs
- 1948 Negro National League:
    ◊ 1st (tied) in home runs, 3rd in slugging percentage, 3rd in OPS, 2nd in OPS+, 2nd in isolated power, 2nd in extra bases on long hits, 2nd in home runs per game, 2nd in at-bats per home run
- 1948/49 Puerto Rican Winter League:
    ◊ 1st in batting average, 1st in slugging percentage, 1st in doubles, 1st in triples, 3rd in home runs, 1st *(estimated)* in isolated power
- 1949 Pacific Coast League *(insufficient at-bats to qualify for league titles)*:
    ◊ 1st in batting average, 1st in slugging percentage, 1st in OPS, 1st in isolated power, 2nd in secondary average, 1st in at-bats per home run, 1st in home runs per game
- 1951 American League:
    ◊ 3rd in at-bats per home run, 2nd in home runs per game
- 1952 American League:
    ◊ 2nd in home runs *(missing the AL lead by 1)*, 2nd in isolated power, 1st in at-bats per home run, 1st in home runs per game
- 1954 International League *(insufficient at-bats to qualify for league titles)*:
    ◊ 2nd in batting average, 1st in slugging percentage, 1st in OPS, 3rd in at-bats per home run, 1st in home runs per game
- 1954 Pacific Coast League *(insufficient at-bats to qualify for league titles)*:
    ◊ 2nd in isolated power, 2nd in at-bats per home run, 1st in home runs per game
- 1954/55 Mexican Pacific Coast League:
    ◊ 2nd in batting average, 1st in home runs
- 1955 American Association:
    ◊ 3rd in isolated power, 2nd in secondary average, 2nd in at-bats per home run
- 1955/56 Puerto Rican Winter League:
    ◊ 1st in home runs
- 1956 Internaional League:
    ◊ 1st in home runs, 1st in slugging percentage, 1st in total bases, 2nd in extra-base hits, 1st in extra bases on long hits, 1st in isolated power, 2nd in secondary average, 1st in at-bats per home run, 1st in home runs per game

- 1957 International League:
  - ◊ 1st in home runs, 1st in slugging percentage, 1st in OPS, 1st in total bases, 1st in extra-base hits, 1st in extra bases on long hits, 1st in isolated power, 1st in secondary average, 1st in at-bats per home run, 1st in home runs per game
- 1958 International League:
  - ◊ 2nd in home runs, 2nd in slugging percentage, 2nd in OPS, 2nd in total bases, 2nd in extra-base hits, 2nd in extra bases on long hits, 2nd in isolated power, 2nd in secondary average, 2nd in home runs per game, 2nd in at-bats per home run
- 1960 International League *(insufficient at-bats to qualify for league titles)*:
  - ◊ 3rd in slugging percentage, 1st in secondary average

This run of dominant power statistics begins *immediately* on Easter entering documentable play at age 31, and carries on through age 44—and that's a sure indicator that he hit for tremendous power in his twenties as well; because insofar as I can determine, there's no example (excepting the transition to the live-ball era and the 1990s steroid abusers) of a player showing substantially more power in his thirties and forties than he did in his twenties.

Point 5: The huge numbers of independent and exhibition home runs ascribed to Easter are not anecdotal; they were documented contemporaneously in the press.

Extensive independent play was part and parcel of the Negro Leagues experience. The following Gibsonesque numbers from independent games can be mostly or fully documented via contemporary press accounts:

- 1946: 62 home runs in independent games, plus 12 more in Hawaiian Fall League play[6]
- 1947: 43 home runs in ca. 100 independent games, plus 5 more in NN2 play[7]
- 1948: 58 home runs in independent games, plus 5 more in NN2 play[8]

Easter also hit for tremendous power in exhibition play:

- 1949: 4 home runs (and minimum .789 slugging) in 38 exhibition at-bats[9]
- 1953–54: 20 home runs in 33 exhibition games with Jackie Robinson's All-Stars[10]

Given his documented power levels in organized league play, these numbers should come as no surprise.

The July 24, 1946, *Cincinnati Enquirer* described Easter as "Negro baseball's leading home run hitter"; the September 24 *Honolulu Advertiser* as "the Negro 'Babe Ruth'"; the October 21 *Connellsville* (PA) *Daily Courier* as "home-run king of colored baseball." Josh Gibson, Willard Brown and Buck Leonard were all active in 1946—making these press assertions quite eye-opening.

Point 6: Comparisons with MLB Hall of Famers

I see Easter as comparable to Willie McCovey and Willie Stargell. All three men were tall, left-handed power hitters. Like Stargell, Luke was physically big (though overall, Easter was the biggest of the three—contemporary newspapers often described him as "the giant Negro"—and probably the strongest as well). Like McCovey, Easter had enormous shoulders; also like McCovey, Easter's size and lack of foot speed made him a minus defender.

Contemporary press accounts show that Easter had Stargell's tremendous bat speed. ("Bobby Doerr ... put a glove on one of Luke's larrups," wrote Gordon Manning in 1950; "the force of the blow spun Doerr around like a top.") All three hit screaming line drives for tremendous distances. All three were plagued by injuries that suppressed their plate appearances throughout their careers. All three faced fierce racism at the outset of their careers—though, as Easter's MLB career began closer in time to Jackie's debut, the racism he faced presented more of a systematic obstacle to his progression.[11]

Easter himself said in 1972 that "I definitely think I would have hit 714 easily.... I would have broken the record of 61 home runs in a season, too." As with McCovey, I think that's true, but only if either man had been consistently healthy. Given his history of constant injuries, I think Easter would more likely have compiled career totals in the McCovey range, 500 to 550 career home runs.[12]

Point 7: A primitive calculation of power production for a full MLB career

(I wrote the subjective estimate above before figuring the following ...)

This is much the least of the points I'll make, but as it seems that no one's tried it, I'll give it a go. Carefully worked estimates are impossible—there's far too much missing data—but here's a (very!) crude estimate based on Easter's proven Major League production.

From 1950–52, the only full seasons of MLB play for which we have data, Easter played 85.7 percent of his team's games and averaged a superb 93.6 percent of the home run production of the annual AL leaders on a per-game basis.

Given the following assumptions—

- Easter would have been injury-plagued throughout his career, averaging just 132 games (85.7 percent) per year, and would have missed all of 1941 and half of 1953 due to injury (as he actually did).

12. Luke Easter

- He would have debuted in 1937 at age 21 (this may be conservative, as he was considered a prodigy by all who saw him; Stargell debuted at 21, McCovey at 22).
- He would have played a total of 21 seasons (McCovey and Stargell played 22 and 21 in the Majors, 26 and 24 in organized ball), losing 1942–45 to war service.
- He would have retired in 1960 at age 44 (which is definitely conservative: he hit .302 that year with a .313 secondary average that would have led the IL with sufficient at-bats, and he slugged .512 in the 1961 IL, .514 in 1962).

—we can roughly project Easter's home runs using the following model:

- 20 percent below his 1950–52 average for 1937 and 10 percent below for 1938, when he was a young man learning the game.
- At his average for 1939–40.
- Inactive due to injury for 1941, and due to war service for 1942–45.
- 10 percent above for 1946 at age 30, a peak year for most athletes.
- 20 percent above for 1947–49, when he reached his first identifiable peak in power.
- His actual MLB totals for 1950–52, plus half credit for his 1952 minor league home runs (on the assumption that if he'd had a proven MLB track record and the Cleveland organization had believed in him, he wouldn't have been demoted for a slow start).
- At his average for 1953–54, with 1953 credited as half-time play only.
- 10 percent above for 1955, 20 percent above for 1956–57, and 10 percent above for 1958, when he reached his second identifiable peak in power.
- 20 percent below for 1959–60, his decline years, with 1960 credited as half-time play only.

This rough methodology produces a total of 614 home runs in 1981 games (McCovey and Stargell played 2,588 and 2,360).

If we add 1942–45 as years of full-time play (assuming 20 percent below his average for 1942, when he was coming back from a full year lost to injury; 10 percent below for 1943, when he was plagued by recurring problems from his 1941 injury; and 10 percent above for 1944–45 at ages 28 and 29, peak years for most athletes), Easter tallies 701 homers in 2,508 games.

I've done my best to be realistic with the methodology, but it's the crudest of estimates. I make no especial claims for accuracy—except to say that I believe the career total is high, but the seasonal totals are often low.

This time period encompasses some low-power environments (1944–45 with the balata ball, with league leaders popping just 22 and 24), but includes many more high-power environments, especially 1955–60, and some monster individual seasons (58 from Greenberg and 50 from Foxx in '38, 52 from Mantle in '56). In the midst of this home run plenty, with league leaders hitting 40+ eleven times, my estimate shows Easter topping 40 just four times. In reality, in the various leagues in which he played, Easter won seven home run titles, led eight times (that we can document—there were almost certainly more) in home runs per game, and came within a hair's breadth of wresting the 1952 AL title from Larry Doby despite time in the minors. I think it's common sense to assert that Easter would have challenged for multiple AL home run titles.

Using every fragment of information I could unearth on Easter's career, I've managed to document 655 home runs and 1886 RBI against all levels of competition. Now, consider that Josh Gibson's Hall of Fame plaque credits him with "almost 800 home runs in league and independent baseball," and that Easter hit cleanup for a top-shelf independent team for seven years prior to World War II…

It's not just possible, but likely, that Big Luke hit more homers against all competition than Gibson's "almost 800."

Point 8: The race barrier severely suppressed the length of Easter's MLB tenure.

Cleveland was slow in bringing Easter to the big show, and quick to send him down. As Gordon Graham wrote in the April 6, 1949, *Lafayette Journal and Courier*, "Three years of hitting over .350 and showering home runs over the land, wasn't enough to earn him a tumble…. Easter had to keep up his slugging in a winter league south of the border before Cleveland finally took hold."

The batting averages cited by Graham were correct—evidence that Easter's post–World War II exploits were known to at least some in contemporary baseball circles. One suspects, with good historical cause, that a white player with similar credentials would have had his red carpet to MLB rolled out long before.

When Easter was promoted to the Majors in 1949 he became the 11th Black player in twentieth-century MLB, the third for Bill Veeck's relatively enlightened Cleveland franchise after Larry Doby and Satchel Paige. When Paige was released at the end of the 1949 season, Easter and Doby were the only Black players left standing in the American League. Sam Jethroe, the 12th Negro Leaguer to make the Majors, was the only ex–NgL player signed to a Major League contract in all of 1950.

For many years after 1947, organized baseball was a hostile, lonely place for the pioneers who made the transition from the Negro Leagues. Following a 1949 game against Boston, an un-named Cleveland player remarked: "It's a good thing Luke can keep his temper. I don't know what I'd do if I had to take what he did." "You just carry half the world," Easter once said to Larry Doby; "I'll take care of the other half."[13]

Easter was demoted to the minors in 1954, where he overpowered pitchers for more than a decade—this despite hitting .303 in part-time play in 1953 and 31 homers the year before. His demotion was apparently motivated in part by racism; according to Larry Doby, Cleveland manager Al Lopez had discovered that Easter was dating a white woman, and Lopez didn't like it. (To be fair, Cleveland did win 111 games that year, and it's impossible to fault the World Series performance of Easter's replacement at first, Vic Wertz—but we have to wonder: Could Mr. Mays have roped in a Luke Easter blast the way he famously snared Mr. Wertz's drive in Game 1?)[14]

In 1957 Easter became the first Black player for the IL's Buffalo Bisons since Frank Grant in 1888, and in 1969 became the first Black coach in Cleveland history. It's incidental to the central point—but as A.S. "Doc" Young wrote: "History cannot ignore the fact that Big Luke was an important contributor to the cause of integration. His most important donation was proof that when an athlete hits home runs and plays a Titanic game, fans quickly lose sight of his color."[15]

("Big Luke" is the nickname by which Easter should be known to history. I read hundreds of contemporary press accounts while researching this chapter, and the majority used the sobriquet "Big Luke.")

BASEBALL   BASEBALL

LUKE EASTER'S ALL-STARS
vs.
Negro American League All-Stars
2:30 P.M. Saturday, October 21st
LA GRAVE FIELD
(Special Reserved Section for White Spectators)

An ad from the October 20, 1953, *Fort Worth Star-Telegram* promoting an exhibition game to be held the next day. Note the parenthetical comment at bottom; for once, Jim Crow's shoe was on the other foot.

Point 9: Despite Easter's willingness to play through injuries that would have finished most players, he was demoted twice to the Minors—and ultimately left there—though his play was clearly Major League–caliber.

It's well known that Easter was hobbled by injuries throughout his career; what's less well known is his willingness to play through extreme pain. Both his legs were wrapped fully to suppress swelling while he played. As we've seen, his 1941 ankle and knee injuries were so severe that they prompted the Army to grant him a medical discharge two years later. In the final exhibition game of 1949 he chipped his right knee in a basepath collision with Larry Doby. "[It hurts] all the time," Easter said in June; "even when I step on the brakes of my car; even when I go upstairs." He nonetheless soldiered on to play brilliantly in 80 PCL games—including playing through an early June hit-by-pitch when a fastball smashed directly into his injured knee—before finally relenting to surgery in July.[16]

Easter took up mountain climbing during the winter of 1949 to strengthen his knee, but successive spring trainings proved lethal to him. On April 9, 1950, he suffered a separated shoulder when he collided with centerfielder Bob Kennedy going after a fly ball. On March 6, 1951, he suffered a chip-fracture in his left elbow in a basepath collision with Bob Prentice; on April 28 he tore the cartilage in his left knee, and on November 26 had the cartilage surgically removed. In 1952 spring training he hurt his right knee yet again, and used a custom-made leather brace through at least April. Throughout his Major League tenure he had his left knee drained regularly; Easter called it "getting my oil changed."[17]

On April 18, 1953, Easter's foot was broken by a fastball from Lou Kretlow. Eyewitness Harry Grayson wrote that the bone "snapped like a twig broken from frost." Trainer Wally Bock remembered: "I went to check and saw his metatarsal bone was broken. He wanted to keep on playing. I can't recall a player with more courage." Knowing Cleveland was struggling without him, he defied doctors' orders and came back a week early.[18]

The Cleveland organization—and, from 1951 onwards, manager Al Lopez—never really believed in Easter. When they looked at him they saw not a promising power hitter but an old, injured man.

Despite posting an excellent 1950 rookie campaign (28/107/.280) and leading Cleveland in homers and RBI in 1951 (27/103/.270), Cleveland sent Easter down to the American Association in June 1952 for a prolonged slow start (.208, but with 11 homers in 63 games, tied for third in the AL)—something they likely wouldn't have done to a player with a "proven" track record. Clearly the fans had a different opinion of him than Cleveland management, as he received 300,000 All-Star votes prior to his demotion. He was called back up after shredding the AA with six homers and .340-.450-.720 hitting in 14 games and, despite the lost time, missed the AL home run crown by a single bomb, finishing with a 31/97/.263 slash line. I think it can be safely stated that his demotion cost him not just his third consecutive 100-RBI season, but the AL home run title too. He was named the AP's 1952 AL Outstanding Player and placed second in AP voting for AL Comeback Player of the Year. In 1953 he hit .303 in 68 games; the AP wrote that Cleveland "lost the pennant April 18. That's the date big Luke Easter broke his foot."[19]

Luke's inability to stay on a Major League roster in 1954 is attributable not to poor play, but to over-caution about Easter's age and health. After just six pinch-hitting appearances he was sent down for good—in spite of which, Cleveland players voted him a half-share of their World Series purse, showing, as with the fans in '52, an opinion of the big man that differed from that of the top brass.

No amount of league-dominant hitting would ever have been sufficient to bring him back up. For years to come, Easter's slugging drew huge crowds to minor league ballparks across North America. They'd never seen anything like him. From 1954 to 1956 he led three different leagues (the Mexican PCL, the PRWL and the IL) in home runs, and in 1957, age 41, led the IL in literally every power category it's possible to calculate.

"Babe, I'm not worried," Easter would say to his wife Virgil. "Somebody needs a good hitter." But he never got the call.[20]

Point 10: Easter does extremely well on the Keltner list.

In his 1994 book *The Politics of Glory*, Bill James proposed a list of 15 standards for Hall of Fame selection, known colloquially as the Keltner list. Baseball analysts often use the list as a shorthand method to evaluate a player's Hall of Fame credentials. Two of James's questions don't apply in Big Luke's case, but the other 13 do, so let's see how the big man fares.[21]

1. *Was he ever regarded as the best player in baseball? Did anybody, while he was active, ever suggest that he was the best player in baseball?*

Not the best *player*, no, though he did have multiple MVP-caliber seasons in various leagues. (The best *home run hitter*, yes, over many years and many leagues.)

2. *Was he the best player on his team?*

Yes. Easter was the best player on many of the minor- and foreign-league teams on which he played—and that's germane, because he shouldn't have been anywhere but the Majors in the first place. Luke was the biggest star and most popular player in IL history, and caused a turnstile-busting sensation in the PCL, the PRWL, the Venezuelan League, and the Mexican PCL.

3. *Was he the best player in baseball at his position? Was he the best player in the league at his position?*

Yes. Easter was selected as the top first baseman in Eastern Black independent ball by the *St. Louis Argus* for 1938-39-40. Given his Gibsonesque power numbers, he basically has to be considered the top independent first baseman for 1946-47-48. He's demonstrably the best first baseman in the Venezuelan League (1947/48), the PRWL (1948/49), the PCL (1949), the MPCL (1954/55), the AA (1955), and the IL (1956-57-58). He's also a reasonable candidate as the best AL first baseman for 1952, him or Ferris Fain.

4. *Did he have an impact on a number of pennant races?*

Only two. In 1948 his power hitting helped propel the Homestead Grays to the Negro World Series, and in 1957 his MVP performance led the Buffalo Bisons to the IL Championship.

Easter played in five rounds of playoffs in those two years, his teams winning four. He hit .467 with a triple and a grand slam in the 1948 NgL semi-finals and smacked three homers in the 1957 IL semis.

5. *Was he good enough that he could play regularly after passing his prime?*

Lord yes.

6. *Is he the very best baseball player in history who is not in the Hall of Fame?*

Excluding the steroid abusers, yes, I believe he is.

7. *Are most players who have comparable statistics in the Hall of Fame?*

Easter's case is unique; the question cannot apply.

8. *Do the player's numbers meet Hall of Fame standards?*

As above.

9. *Is there any evidence to suggest that the player was significantly better or worse than is suggested by his statistics?*

Yes, mountains of it; see the rest of this chapter.

10. *Is he the best player at his position who is eligible for the Hall of Fame?*

Yes, and by far in my view.

11. *How many MVP-type seasons did he have? Did he ever win an MVP award? If not, how many times was he close?*

Easter had eight MVP-caliber seasons that we know of, which is plenty. He won the 1948/49 PRWL MVP, the 1954/55 MPCL MVP, and the 1957 IL MVP. With 62 and 58 homers respectively, he was presumably the MVP of independent baseball for 1946 and 1948. He was also a strong MVP candidate in the 1947/48 Venezuelan League, hitting .341 with a league-leading 8 homers; in 1947 independent ball with 43 homers; and in the 1956 IL, hitting .306 with 105 walks and leading the league in home runs, RBI, total bases, slugging and OPS.

12. *How many All-Star-type seasons did he have? How many All-Star games did he play in? Did most of the players who played in this many All-Star games go into the Hall of Fame?*

Easter's only official All-Star selections came in 1938-39-40, 1948, and 1957, in three different leagues. That's a 20-year spread—and there are *no* eligible players who appeared in All-Star games as much as 20 years apart who are *not* in the Hall of Fame. I think we've got to give the man a Yes on this one.

13. *If this man were the best player on his team, would it be likely that the team could win the pennant?*

Certainly, considering that he'd probably lead the league in home runs.

14. *What impact did the player have on baseball history? Was he responsible for any rule changes? Did he introduce any new equipment? Did he change the game in any way?*

Easter was the 11th Black player in modern MLB, the Buffalo Bisons' first twentieth-century Black player, and Cleveland's first-ever Black coach; I think he deserves a measure of pioneer credit for this.

15. *Did the player uphold the standards of sportsmanship and character that the Hall of Fame, in its written guidelines, instructs us to consider?*

Absolutely, straight down the line. A contemporary remembers: "I'll never forget the kindness Luke Easter and Larry Doby showed me, after I had broken my elbow [in the 1950 All-Star Game] and nobody was sure I'd be able to play again…. The nurse told me there were two men downstairs who said they were ballplayers and would like to come to see me. Immediately, the door opened and it was Doby and Easter. Tears came into my eyes as I was so happy to see that they had taken the time to come to see Ted Williams."[22]

So, of the 13 Keltner criteria that apply to Easter's case, Big Luke comfortably meets 11. That sounds like a Hall of Famer to me.

Point 11: *A chorus of contemporary voices, including multiple Hall of Famers, cited Easter as one of the greatest power hitters of all time.*

Sure, it's anecdotal—but this is how we've built images of the great white players of the 1800s. Buck Ewing's reputation as possibly the greatest player of the 19th century rests not on his numbers, which are okay, but almost entirely on the awe in which he was held by his contemporaries. That's how we can enhance our image of Easter too. It's another strand in the rope. Besides, as Bill James observed in 1981: "Good sabermetrics respects the validity of all types of evidence, including that which is beyond the scope of statistical validation."[23]

♦ *Joe Astroth:* "The greatest home run hitter since Babe Ruth.... There is no one alive who can hit a ball for distance with Luke Easter."[24]

♦ *Del Baker:* "For sheer ability to knock a ball great distances, I've never seen anybody better than Easter. And I'm not excepting Babe Ruth."[25]

♦ *Dick Barrett:* "He put the fear of the Lord into us Seattle pitchers."[26]

♦ *Chet Brewer:* "He hit the ball on top of the lights. Three innings later a car went by and backfired, and the radio announcer said that was Luke Easter's home run coming down. He put the fear of God in those pitchers."[27]

♦ *Cucú Cabrera:* "[Josh] Gibson's homers went 500 feet, as did Easter's.... Every blast Easter connected ... was at least 20 feet above the fence."[28]

♦ *Jim Colzie:* "I got one low in Terre Haute one night, and the damn thing was still going up when it left the park at the 375 sign."[29]

♦ *Bob Feller:* "The two most powerful men I ever saw at the plate were Babe Ruth and Luke Easter."[30]

♦ *Wilmer "Red" Fields:* "Luke hit it into the [Polo Grounds] center-field stands, and that's 487 feet away. He hit it like a shot. And it went up in there. It didn't stop at the fence."[31]

♦ *Frank Finch (TSN):* "The other players, the sportswriters, goober salesmen and fans rivet their eyes on the batting cage to watch Luke powder the ball.... I've seen only three other batters paid that singular compliment—Ted Williams, Stan Musial and Ernie Lombardi."[32]

♦ *Harry Grayson (NEA Sports Editor) in 1952:* "Easter means as much to [Cleveland] as Joe DiMaggio did with the Yankees." *Grayson in 1953:* "Easter is to [Cleveland] what Willie Mays was to the Giants."[33]

- *Hank Greenberg:* "I knew Luke had it after watching him the first time he batted.... I thought the big guy was as great as anything I'd ever seen."[34]

- *Fred Haney:* "I wish they'd get him out of here before he kills every infielder in the Coast League."[35]

- *Ralph Houk*: "Easter's powerful swing resulted in hitting the ball as far as, or farther than, Mickey Mantle."[36]

- *Hal Lebovitz (Cleveland Plain Dealer)*: "With his power, no telling how many records he would have broken. He had more power than anyone I ever saw."[37]

- *Ed Lopat:* "Easter gives you the willies. When he walks up there with that bat you get the feeling you're pitching uphill."[38]

- *Bob Matthews*: "One day he might hit a ball so hard that it would knock down a light tower."[39]

- *James McGee (San Francisco News-Call Bulletin)*: "The greatest home run hitter in the history of baseball who will never make the record books. Maybe he might have been the greatest ever, record book or not."[40]

- *Buck O'Neil:* "How many home runs could Luke Easter have hit? Shoot. As many as he wanted."[41]

- *Joe Overfield (Buffalo Bisons historian)*: "The blow cleared the right-field light tower ... crossed Woodlawn Avenue, soared 30 feet over a two-story dwelling, struck the roof of a house on Emerson Place ... and finally came to rest in the street." (The house's owner told *Sports Illustrated* that "I thought for sure someone had dropped an atom bomb on the roof.")[42]

- *Jimmie Reese (San Diego coach)*: "Easter is the only player I ever saw who can hit a baseball as far as Babe Ruth."[43]

- *Dino Restelli:* "He hit a ball over the right field fence, and the street behind it, into a park.... The guy was phenomenal."[44]

- *Frank Robinson:* "He was awesome. I was a player from the sandlots myself. I was amazed by his strength and power."[45]

- *Jim Schlemmer (Ohio sportswriter)*: "Luke hit Sal Maglie's pitch over the right centerfield fence for an unmeasurable distance.... The ball left the park at the 373 foot sign but it was then higher than the scoreboard and appeared still to be climbing."[46]

- *Eladio Secades (Cuban sportswriter)*: "[The] most spectacular [hitter] we have seen since the days of Josh Gibson."[47]

- *Earl Sheeley:* "The greatest power hitter I've seen at first since Lou Gehrig."[48]

- *Rick Smith (San Diego sportswriter):* "Easter rattled outfield walls, dented passing autos and smashed windows in a distant freight shed."[49]

- *Wendell Smith:* "The successor to Josh Gibson, the greatest home run hitter in the history of Negro baseball."[50]

- *Bill Starr (owner of San Diego's triple-A club):* "The greatest hitter I've ever seen, and I don't exclude Ted Williams, another pretty good man at the plate who got his start in San Diego."[51]

- *Gayle Talbot (AP):* "Luke Easter … is hitting the ball up among the passing jets."[52]

- *Bob Thurman:* "He hit it halfway up the stands, about 500 feet. The thing about it—it was a line drive."[53]

- *Hollis Thurston (Cleveland scout):* "He swung on the first ball pitched to him and it travelled at least 450 feet. It was the longest drive I had ever seen at that park. Hank [Greenberg] looked at me and didn't say a thing. He grinned."[54]

- *Bill Veeck:* "[Luke] could hit the ball as hard and as far as Babe Ruth."[55]

- *Ted Williams:* "I thought so much of him as a person and a player…. He was a big, powerful guy and could hit the ball a mile."[56]

- *An anonymous Cleveland sports reporter:* "The only player I've ever seen in the big leagues who can make the pitcher duck on a home-run ball."[57]

- *Another Cleveland sports reporter:* "That ball could kill a man when it goes through the [pitcher's] box that way."[58]

- *The Associated Press:* "Able to hit a baseball as far—or farther—than anybody in the major leagues."[59]

- *The Harrisburg (PA) Telegraph*: "Has established a reputation for home-run hitting in the [Negro] American League comparable to joltin' Josh Gibson's in the National League."[60]

- *The Montgomery Advertiser:* "Unquestionably the best long ball hitter to come up to Negro big-time baseball since the advent of Catcher Josh Gibson."[61]

- *The Pittsburgh Courier:* "No fence appears to be too long for him to loop one over."[62]

- *The Sporting News:* "The greatest natural hitter the Coast League has seen since Ted Williams."[63]

- *United Press International:* "One of the greatest natural hitters ever to perform on the Western slope.…

Luke Easter, shown here in the late 1950s as a member of the Triple-A Buffalo Bisons, for whom he regularly demonstrated his prodigious power (courtesy of John Boutet).

This is the place where such great batsmen as Joe DiMaggio, Ted Williams, Paul Waner and many others got their start. But that's the kind of company Easter travels in."[64]

* * *

Luke Easter battled through systemic racism, war service, and excruciating injuries to win seven home run titles in the various leagues in which he played—six that we can account for; thousands of his at-bats are lost to history. He put up multiple All-Star and MVP-caliber seasons over a span of 20 years. A chorus of voices from the Major Leagues and the sporting press described him as one of the greatest power hitters ever.

Which brings me back to where I began:

Luscious "Luke" Easter belongs in the Hall of Fame. And yes, Luscious really is his first name.

13

Larry Doby

Five-Tool Superstar

No baseball book of mine would be complete without a profile of my all-time favorite player in any sport, Lawrence Eugene Doby.

The Negro Leagues produced two types of superstars in its 29 years of tenuous existence. Some, like Willie Mays and Roy Campanella, were young enough and gifted enough to follow Jackie's trail to the Majors; others, like Josh Gibson and Pop Lloyd, spent their careers in the relative obscurity of the NgL despite their obvious greatness. Neither group quite encompasses Larry Doby.

Press commentary on Doby's 1998 Hall of Fame election focused on his breaking the American League color barrier three months after Jackie made his NL debut. Little was written about his prowess as a player, and those articles that did mention his relatively short MLB career bore an almost apologetic tone. Doby's status as a pioneer, it was implied, alone propelled him through the doors of Cooperstown.

Doby rose to stardom in the NN2 and then rose again in the AL, becoming MLB's first great Black slugger. He didn't play long enough in either the Negro or Major Leagues to compile the career numbers we usually associate with greatness, but there can be no doubt that he was a great player. Doby was an offensive and defensive dynamo whose qualities and achievements were not fully appreciated in his own time; a man who today's sportswriters, armed with sabermetric thinking and analysis, would single out as the complete package.

* * *

Doby was the most famous high school athlete in New Jersey in the late 1930s and early 1940s, earning eleven letters in four different sports—baseball, basketball, football, and track and field—and playing baseball with the semi-pro Camden Giants. In 1942 he made his NgL debut as a second baseman with the Negro National League's Newark Eagles and batted .309, 58 points above league average. On June 12 he collected six hits in a single game.

He followed up this solid rookie campaign with a .301 average in 1943, 22 points above league; his slugging shot from .432 to .553 and his OPS from .796 to .973, both figures ranking third in the NN2. Already, at age 19, the game-breaking power that would characterize his career was coming to the fore.

After a single game Doby's 1944 season was interrupted by Uncle Sam, and he traded 1944 and 1945 for active duty in the US Navy. He starred for a segregated

Great Lakes Naval Training Station basketball team and hit .342 for an all–Black Great Lakes baseball team. This squad played twice against the famous (all-white) Great Lakes squad, the greatest military team ever. It's possible, then, that Doby played against my Grandfather, Woody Petersen, who signed with Cleveland in 1941, but chose the Navy after Pearl Harbor and pitched for Great Lakes during the war.[1]

In 1946 Doby reclaimed the Eagles' second base slot and hit .366, third in the NN2 and 100 points above league. He led the NN2 with 85 hits, 10 triples, 138 total bases and a 1.036 OPS, finished second to Josh Gibson with .595 slugging, and tied Gibson for the OPS+ title at 184. Displaying his versatility in both East-West Games, he stroked three hits, drew a walk, stole a base, scored twice, and drove in a run on a sacrifice fly. No official award was made, but by my evaluation, Doby would probably have beaten out Gibson as Negro National League MVP.

The Eagles captured the 1946 NN2 pennant, snapping a North American-best streak of nine consecutive pennants by Gibson's Homestead Grays. In the Negro World Series Newark defeated Satchel Paige's heavily favored Kansas City Monarchs in seven games, with Doby providing his share of the spark: he hit just .227 but led both teams with nine walks for a .452 OBP, scored seven runs and drove in five, stole three bases, and fielded the final two putouts of the decisive game.

Roy Campanella, scouting the Negro World Series for Branch Rickey, singled out Doby and Monte Irvin as players ready to make an immediate Major League impact. In the end Rickey set his sights on Jackie Robinson, a brilliant, unarguable choice; but subsequent events would prove Campanella a prophet.

Clyde Sukeforth also had an eye on Doby. "Oh, you had to like Doby," Sukeforth recalled; "he could run and he had real good power.... [*Pittsburgh Courier* sportswriter] Wendell Smith called me and said that Doby was going to be signed by someone else, but he'd prefer Brooklyn. So I spoke to Mister Rickey, but he said, 'By all means, let him go over to the other league. It will help the movement.'"[2]

Doby spent the 1947–48 offseason barnstorming with Jackie Robinson's All-Stars and playing winter ball with the Senadores (Senators) de San Juan of the Puerto Rican Winter League, hitting .349 and placing second in the PRWL with 12 homers. In the 1947 NN2 campaign he hit .354, 85 points above league, and tied for second with 8 homers. He left the NgL circuit early to make American League history, but his .743 slugging, 1.182 OPS and 220 OPS+ would all have topped the NN2 over the full season. On May 9 he blasted three homers in one game.

With Jackie Robinson performing spectacularly for the Montreal Royals and poised to break the MLB color barrier, Doby was an obvious candidate for the Majors. Jackie broke the NL color barrier on April 15; 11 weeks later, Cleveland owner Bill Veeck selected Doby to break the AL barrier. "I'm not going to sign a Negro player and send him to a farm club," Veeck had told the *Pittsburgh Courier*'s Bill Nunn in late 1946. "I'm going to get one I think can play with Cleveland. One afternoon when the team trots out on the field, a Negro player will be out there with it." This plan, while admirable from a moral perspective, deprived Doby of the adjustment period accorded to Robinson, who played a full year in the minors prior to his Brooklyn debut.[3]

As a fitting coda to his NgL stardom, Doby homered in his final Negro Leagues at bat on the Fourth of July 1947. Veeck announced his signing the next day, and he made his first appearance in a Cleveland uniform within 24 hours of his NgL finale.

Cast in the unfamiliar role of pinch-hitter, Doby struggled miserably through Cleveland's final games of 1947. Every aspect of his life was suddenly dominated by segregation. "Number one," Bill Veeck told him, "you're not gonna be able to stay with the team. Number two, you're not gonna be able to eat with the team. Number three, when you ride the bus, you're not gonna be able to get off the bus with the team." Opposing players tormented him non-stop. "I was on the bench," remembered the Philadelphia Phillies' Lou Brissie, "and heard some of my teammates shouting things at Larry, like, 'Porter, carry my bags,' or 'Shoe-shine boy, shine my shoes,' and well, the N-word, too. It was terrible." "I was called the N-word so much," remembered Doby, "that it got to the point that I didn't hear it."[4]

One incident haunted him for life. "I remember sliding into second base, and the fielder spitting tobacco juice in my face…. It really got to me. I never forgot it." Typical of the man, Doby refused, then or ever, to name the player who defiled him. However, in a 1987 interview he said in passing that the player was a shortstop; Jerry Izenberg later reported that the spitter was a "Philadelphia shortstop." Doby appeared against Philadelphia six times in 1947, strictly as a pinch hitter: July 11, 12, 22 and 23, August 26, and September 14. He reached base only in the July 11 game, on an error by the man who played short for Philadelphia in all six games. We can therefore pinpoint the date of the incident as July 11, 1947, and name Eddie Joost as the player who spat in Doby's face.[5]

For his second big-league game on July 6, player-manager Lou Boudreau assigned Doby to first base, but incumbent first baseman Eddie Robinson refused to lend him his glove. As with a 40-ounce bat and a second pair of cleats for Willard Brown, the club itself didn't bother to provide a first baseman's glove. Nor did they help him secure decent housing in a new and unfamiliar city; Doby told Ira Berkow that after a game, "you'd really like to be with your teammates, win or lose, and go over the game. But I'd go off to my hotel in the Black part of town, and they'd go off to their hotel."[6]

After the season, Doby found relief from the pressure by again touring the nation with Jackie Robinson's All-Stars. He also found time to play several games with the Paterson Crescents of the American Basketball League (ABL), the first-ever major pro basketball league. When he made his ABL debut on January 3, 1948, Doby integrated his second professional sports league in a span of six months.[7]

In the run-up to the 1948 MLB season, Doby benefited from the attentions of two Hall of Fame coaches. Tris Speaker tutored him on the finer points of the transition from second base to center field, while Hank Greenberg showed him the elements of a Major League power swing. Doby responded by hitting .301 with 14 homers as Cleveland challenged for the AL pennant. On May 8 came the first of his memorable long blasts, an estimated 450-foot rocket that cleared the right field wall at Griffith Stadium, eclipsing the distance of a legendary 1926 shot by Babe Ruth. "The ball soared over the centerfield fence," wrote John Hollis, "took two bounces, [and] came to rest in the high weeds that border the railroad tracks a good city block distant."[8]

In the final 20 games of the season Doby went on a .396 tear, 45 points higher than any other Cleveland player, as Cleveland tied the Red Sox for the AL flag. In a one-game playoff against Boston he stroked two doubles to help his team clinch its first pennant in 28 years, and then, in the World Series, as his teammates hit a collective .183, Doby starred as a one-man wrecking crew, leading Cleveland in hits, total bases, batting average, on-base percentage, slugging and OPS. His RBI single off Warren Spahn won Game 2, and his solo homer off Johnny Sain—the first by a Black player in MLB World Series play—sealed Boston's fate in Game 4.

World Series MVPs weren't awarded until 1955, but it's a safe bet that had it existed, Doby would have won it in 1948. He had now starred for two World Series winners in three years, at two different key defensive positions, in two different professional leagues. He and teammate Satchel Paige were the first Black Major Leaguers to win World Series rings.

A post–Game 4 photograph of winning pitcher Steve Gromek embracing Doby sparked comment and controversy throughout the land; it was the first image widely circulated in the United States showing Black and white sportsmen fraternizing as equals. "When Steve went back to his home in Michigan," Doby later recalled, "some of the people asked him, 'What are you doing, hugging *him*?'"[9]

"My dad got all kinds of resentment about that picture," remembered Gromek's son Greg. "Some of his friends really reacted negatively. They said things that were sort of shocking to him.... He even got death threats."[10]

It was taxing for certain; but Steve Gromek, who said in 1998 that "color was never an issue for me," lived long enough to be remembered more generously than the fools who called him names.[11]

Doby's World Series heroics were a foretaste; the best was yet to come. Al Lopez, manager of Cleveland's pennant-winning 1954 squad, once pointed at him and said, "There's the guy who makes the difference. Without him..."—whereupon Lopez pointed his thumb at the ground. Over the next eight seasons, 1949 through 1956, Doby wielded the complete, multi-faceted attack so highly prized in the modern game, hitting 20+ home runs each year, drawing 90+ walks six times and driving in 100+ runs five times. His offensive excellence over this span was comparable, perhaps, to Andrew McCutchen in his prime[12]:

- In 1950 Doby's .326 average, 25 homers and 98 walks generated AL bests with a .442 on-base percentage, .986 OPS, 156 OPS+ and 6.2 offensive WAR. *The Sporting News* selected Doby over Joe DiMaggio and Duke Snider as the top MLB center fielder for 1950.
- On August 2, 1950, he hit three home runs off Washington's Connie Marrero, becoming the only man with three-homer games in both Negro League and Major League play.
- In 1952 he led the AL with 32 home runs, 104 runs scored, .541 slugging, 163 OPS+, 6.5 offensive WAR and 7.1 total WAR, becoming the first-ever Black Major League home run champion. On June 4 he hit for the cycle.
- In 1954, powering a club that won 111 games, he topped the AL again with 32 home runs and added a league-leading 126 RBI, finishing second to Yogi Berra in the AL MVP race

- He was selected to each All-Star squad from 1949 to 1955, igniting a game-winning rally in the 1954 contest with an eighth-inning, pinch-hit homer off Gene Conley—the first home run by a Black player in MLB All-Star play.

Doby's ability to drive towering blasts out of any ballpark evoked respect and fear throughout the American League. Here's a representative sequence from 1949:

- On April 6, in exhibition play, he hit a home run 434-plus feet to center in Houston's Buffalo Stadium. Only Hack Wilson had previously touched the straightaway center field seats with a fair ball.
- On May 19 he crushed a home run 460 feet to center in Yankee Stadium. Those seats hadn't been reached since Lou Gehrig's titanic blast in the 1928 World Series.
- On May 25 he launched a ball 500-plus feet over Griffith Stadium's right-center field wall, out of the park and onto a distant rooftop. In the stadium's 51-year history as a Major League and Negro League ballpark, the other men to top the center field wall were Babe Ruth, Mickey Mantle, and Ted Williams.

Having played just one game as an outfielder in the Negro Leagues, Doby was at first a raw defender in the Majors, but quickly transformed himself into an exceptional defensive player who, as Arnold Hano wrote, "knows what a center fielder can do." In 1948, his first season as an outfielder, he led the AL with 14 errors, but two years later led AL center fielders with a .987 fielding percentage. In 1954 he tied the then–AL record with just two errors in 153 games, and from July 19, 1954, to August 12, 1955, accepted 421 chances without an error, setting a new AL outfield record with 164 consecutive errorless games.[13]

On July 31, 1954, at Cleveland Stadium, Doby made a wall-climbing, Spider-Man catch to rob the Senators' Tom Umphlett of a sure home run. Hall of Famer Jay "Dizzy" Dean, covering the game for radio, exclaimed in his uniquely Southern-fried manner: "That was the greatest catch I ever saw, as a player or as a broadcaster. It was the greatest catch I ever saw in my whole life. I saw Terry Moore and Lloyd Waner make some great ones, but they was routine compared to this one." Winning pitcher Art Houtteman agreed, telling Doby, "I wanted to thank you for that catch. As long as I live I'll never forget the greatness of that play."[14]

On May 14, 1956, two years before the AL mandated the use of batting helmets, Doby began wearing a Little League helmet at the plate. This innovation was born of necessity, and points to a bitter truth: Doby's status as a pioneer exacted a lasting toll. "To say I had it easy because of [Jackie Robinson] is silly. I came in 11 weeks after he did…. You didn't hear much about what I was going through, because the media didn't want to repeat the same story…. The crap I took was just as bad. Nobody said, 'We're gonna be nice to the second Black.'… The things I was called did hurt me. They hurt a lot. The things people did to me, spitting tobacco juice on me, sliding into me, throwing baseballs at my head…. I was raised to respect people. I found out that all people are not raised that way…. Jack and I went through a lot of the same things. I'd be lying if I said I didn't want people to remember that."[15]

Doby experienced a decline in home run power in 1957 and 1958, though his overall play was still sound, and decided to call it quits after a sub-par, injury-riddled 1959 season. He made a brief comeback attempt in 1962 with Japan's Chuinichi Dragons, but 10 home runs later he hung up his spikes for good. He then undertook a series of roles with major, minor, and foreign league teams beginning in 1969—minor league instructor, batting coach, first base coach, Venezuelan winter league manager—culminating in his appointment as manager of the Chicago White Sox on June 30, 1978, becoming MLB's second Black skipper after Frank Robinson.

Doby was a legitimate MLB Rookie of the Year candidate in 1948, and an MVP contender five times, in 1946, 1947, 1950, 1952 and 1954. I'll go so far as to say I think Doby *would* have won the 1946 NN2 MVP and 1948 World Series MVP had they been awarded, and *should* have won the 1952 AL MVP over Bobby Shantz. In 1950 Phil Rizzuto's dazzling double-play prowess and 200 hits for the pennant-winning Yankees was hard to beat, and Berra's win in 1954 is easy to explain: he and Roy Campanella were re-defining what great catchers could do. But in '52 Doby led the league in runs scored, home runs, slugging, OPS+ and WAR, drew 90 walks and, for the sabermetrically-minded among you, also led the AL in WPA, WPA/LI, RE24 and REW; in other words, he had the greatest game-winning impact per at-bat of any AL player. But these advanced metrics were unknown in 1952—and besides, Shantz won 24 games, and the writers loved their pitching wins. (Doby led the AL in those same four advanced metrics in 1950 too, but no one was going to take the MVP from the Scooter that year.)

Doby broke color barriers in pro baseball and pro basketball. He was the first Black Major Leaguer to hit 20 homers in a season, the first to hit 30, the first to win a home run title, the first to homer in a World Series, the first to homer in an All-Star Game. He set records on defense and awed crowds with tremendous shots to seldom-reached corners of storied ballparks. Lawrence Eugene Doby was a five-tool superstar.

* * *

I met Larry Doby in 1997, when the campaign to secure him Hall of Fame recognition was in full swing. Having read that he was speaking at a Negro Leagues conference in a neighboring state, I gladly made the drive to meet the man I regarded as the most underrated player of all time. After the conference a crowd formed around him, seeking his signature on programs and baseball cards; before I could reach him, his entourage signaled that it was time for him to go.

As he made his way toward the exit, I tapped him on the shoulder. Doby was an old man; his face showed marks of weariness from the events of the day; but when I asked him if he would sign my poster, he wrapped his arm around my shoulder and bestowed on me a bright and genuine smile. The smile of an elder spokesman for a bygone time, generously bestowed upon a representative of a younger generation that regarded him as a hero; the smile of a neglected giant who marched in the vanguard of a cause greater than one man's quest for the Hall of Fame, greater than the sport he played: greater even than the confines of the Nation he served so well.

14

The Greatest

With apologies to Muhammad Ali, there are seven realistic candidates for the title of The Greatest Player in Baseball History: **Barry Bonds**, **Oscar Charleston**, **Josh Gibson**, **Willie Mays**, **Babe Ruth**, **Honus Wagner**, and **Ted Williams**. You'll see the occasional nomination for someone else now and again—a Cobb here, a Mantle there—but these are the seven who are mentioned consistently in baseball literature as the best of all time.

The popular, man-in-the-street choice has long been the Babe, whereas at this moment in history, the sportswriting and analytical consensus has settled on Willie Mays. Both opinions can inform us; neither is necessarily definitive.

Let's rate these players by the traditional five tools—hitting for average, hitting for power, basepath speed, fielding, and throwing arm—and add a few more comparative categories: ability to get on base, longest sustained peak performance, longevity, durability, postseason performance, playing a key position, distance above peers at the same position, and intangible additions or subtractions to a player's game.

- *Hitting for average:*

All of these men are high-average hitters except for Mays, whose .301 lifetime average is hardly a blemish, but not quite on the same level as the others. Gibson, Charleston and Ruth are a cut above the rest, but as raw batting average is an overrated stat, it's not a major distinction.

- *Ability to get on base:*

Ted Williams wins this one comfortably, with Bonds, Charleston, Gibson and Ruth in the zone of dominance, but not at Williams's level. On-base percentage is not an especial strength of Mays or Wagner's game.

Irrespective of league or era, getting a man on base is the hardest thing for any offense to do, and Williams is the ultimate master of the art. This is Teddy Ballgame's #1 credential to be considered The Greatest.

- *Hitting for power:*

In terms of raw isolated power, Gibson and Ruth easily top this list. Wagner, rooted in the dead-ball era, was the only one of the seven who didn't have significant home run power; he had good power for his era though, leading the NL in slugging six times, though with a top figure of only *(only!)* .573.

It's important to note that Bonds' post–2000 power explosion coincides exactly with well-documented proofs of steroid abuse.[1]

Before we leave hitting behind, we should note that of the four top hitters in baseball history—Bonds, Gibson, Ruth and Williams—only Gibson is right-handed. There can be no doubt that Josh Gibson is the greatest right-handed hitter of all time.

- *Basepath speed*:

This is a tough one... The one player in this group who may have had game-breaking, Rickey Henderson–type speed, Oscar Charleston, has no caught-stealing data for his career, and is impossible to evaluate on a scalar basis with players who do. In almost all cases, raw steals totals aren't that valuable without accompanying figures for caught stealing; Charleston and Cool Papa Bell may be the prime exceptions to this rule.

Wagner is the leader by far in raw number of steals, and also won the most stolen base titles with five. However, caught-stealing data is missing for most of his career, and he played in an era when teams routinely risked steal attempts in less than break-even situations. For the two seasons for which we do have data, Honus was 33 for 59 (56 percent), well below the break-even point.

Ruth was vain about his speed, but was not a great base stealer, never swiping as many as 20 in a season and going 110-for-227 (48 percent) in seasons for which we have data. He famously made the final out of the 1926 World Series trying to steal second—in a one run game, with Bob Meusel (.315) at bat and Lou Gehrig (.313 with 83 extra-base hits and 105 walks) on deck. For all his awesomeness in other facets of the game, this is not a man who can be described as even a "good" baserunner. (He did however successfully steal home 10 times in his career. Only the Babe.)

Williams was an excellent baserunner as a young man, but not a gifted base stealer. Gibson racked up a few steals, actually quite a few for a catcher, but not an elite number—and as with Charleston, we lack caught-stealing data.

That leaves Mays and Bonds. Mays stole 338 bases at a 77 percent clip, Bonds stole 514 at a 78 percent clip—a clear advantage for Bonds. In the context of his own era, Mays was a higher-impact base stealer, winning four consecutive stolen base titles, 1956–59, though also leading in caught stealing twice; Bonds never led in either category. I see this one as a draw, and declare Mays and Bonds in a tie for best basepath speed, with a significant Probably to Charleston.

- *Longest sustained peak performance:*

Mays, with Charleston close but definitely behind. The Say Hey Kid led the NL in triples, batting, slugging and OPS in 1954, and led the NL in walks and OBP in 1971. That's an eighteen-year span bookended by seasons in which Mays led the NL in multiple offensive categories—and he led in plenty of categories in between.

- *Defense:*

Bonds, Charleston, Mays and Wagner are runaway winners here. Honus was either the best-ever defensive shortstop or second only to Ozzie Smith, which is no cause for shame; Bonds and Mays are considered to be among the all-time best left- and center fielders; Charleston is routinely described as Mays's equal, playing shallow like Tris Speaker and running down virtually everything hit over his head.

By the evidence, Gibson was a good solid catcher but not historic, though he was a slab of granite when it came to blocking the plate; Pittsburgh Crawfords manager Harold "Hooks" Tinker remembered, "He was built like sheet metal. If you ran into him it was like you ran into a wall." Ruth was a very good right fielder as a younger man, not so much as he gained weight. Williams was unreliable, not because he couldn't field—clearly he could—but because on occasion he didn't care, and it was hard to tell just when that might happen. Hitting was Teddy's thing, and he demonstrated this though his fielding.[2]

- *Throwing arm:*

We've got to give Charleston significant points here, as all authorities agree he could throw from deep center field with the best of them. Bonds led six times in assists from left field, and though Mays led only once from center, he was universally considered to have a superior arm.

Wagner had a decent arm, but made the majority of plays at second himself; Williams had a very good arm when he could be bothered to care, which isn't *quite* the same thing as having a very good arm, full stop; Gibson had a good solid throwing arm to go with his good solid defense; none approached the level of Barry, Oscar or Willie. The young Ruth could bring it from right field, but Bonds, Charleston and Mays are the clear winners here.

- *Longevity:*

Charleston wins this one in a blowout, tying Nolan Ryan and (ironically) Cap Anson with 27 pro seasons. (If we include years played in Japanese professional leagues, Ichiro Suzuki holds the all-time record with 28 seasons played—one of the many world records he enjoys.)

None of these men were wimps though; Gibson is low man with 17 seasons, damn solid for a catcher, and the other five all played between 18 and 22 pro seasons. Williams played 19, but lost three full seasons to World War II, plus chunks of two other years to Korea.

- *Durability:*

All of these men were quite durable season to season with the exception of Williams as an older man; none were iron men. The top men are Charleston with three games-played titles (albeit in relatively short NgL seasons) and Mays with five top-5 seasons in games played, but there's no decisive edge here.

- *Postseason performance:*

By far the easiest call in this exercise. Bonds stumbled badly in most of his postseason appearances, but did have one outstanding postseason in 2002. Williams, too, stumbled in his only appearance on the big stage, but he was nursing an elbow injury that left him unable even to swing a bat until the day before Game 1, so we can give him a pass. (Typical of Teddy, he declined to use the injury as an excuse for his poor performance.) Mays wasn't that great for the most part, but he did win a ring *and* make what's widely considered the greatest Series catch ever in '54, which also happened to save the game, so he gets a plus by his name. Gibson hit well below his regular-season power levels in NgL postseason play, but won rings in '43 and '44, hitting very well in '39 when the Grays lost and again in '44 when they won, so he gets a plus too. Honus was another OK postseason hitter, but played well in the one Series his team won in 1909: another plus. Charleston hit very well in his only playoff appearance in '35, which his team won: a plus for Oscar too.

Then there's the Babe, who's on another planet from the mortals above, winning seven rings. Not only was he brilliant as a hitter (.326-.470-.744, smashing three home runs in one Series game in 1926 *and* in 1928), he was also virtually untouchable as a pitcher (3–0 win-loss, 0.87 ERA, 0.935 WHIP, 29.2 consecutive scoreless innings).

Notwithstanding being thrown out to end the '26 Series, Ruth is not only the greatest postseason performer on this list, but the greatest of all time. It's a major cornerstone of his myth, and a huge factor in his case to be named The Greatest.

- *Playing an important defensive position:*

The players on this list who manned key defensive positions were, in order of defensive importance, Gibson at catcher, Wagner at shortstop, and Charleston and Mays in center field. Charleston, Mays and Wagner all get boosts by this method for playing brilliant defense at key positions.

- *Distance above peers at the same position:*

This is where Gibson and Wagner come into their own. Charleston and Mays can be compared directly with Cobb and Mantle, and some fans still question which of these men was the greater center fielder (I don't, but to each their own). Ted Williams, while possibly the finest hitter in baseball history, has to contend in left with not just Bonds but also Stan Musial, and Musial and Bonds were both better *all-around* players than Teddy. (I once told my Grandfather that Musial collected 1,815 hits at home and 1,815 on the road, and that he'd scored 1,949 runs and driven in 1,951. Grandpa pondered this for a moment, then said: "Now *that's* a ballplayer.")

In right field Ruth has to compete with Hank Aaron, who surpassed Ruth's career numbers in virtually every category, could also mash in the postseason, and was a superior baserunner and defender to boot. Ruth was also a great pitcher, which elevates him into another category entirely—but viewed strictly as a position player, Aaron holds his own.

Gibson towers over all other catchers, and Wagner towers above all other shortstops. There's never been a shortstop who could hit with Honus; Ozzie Smith is at or slightly above his level defensively, but not remotely equivalent as an offensive force. Gibson has only Piazza near him as a hitter, and not that near—and Gibson runs rings around Piazza on defense. There are better defenders than Gibson, but none come within a country mile of his hitting. Josh and Honus have no peers at their positions.

- *Intangible additions or subtractions to a player's game:*

Wagner lifted weights in the off-season; he may have been the only player of his era who did. This obviously contributed to the excellence of his play and, like fellow workout enthusiast Stan Musial, to his durability and longevity. Big points to Honus.

(Big points to Stan the Man too. Musial's Cardinals of the 1960s came closest in their time to forging a team with no racial animus, and the Man deserves his share of credit for that. Hank Aaron: "Musial was one of my favorite ballplayers, because he treated everybody the same—Black or white, superstar or scrub—and he genuinely loved the game." Willie Mays: "He was a true gentleman who understood the race thing and did all he could.... I never heard anybody say a bad word about him, ever.")[3]

Ruth's conditioning was famously awful; according to legend, he once ate 12 hot dogs and drank eight bottles of soda between doubleheader games and was promptly hospitalized. Even if the tale is apocryphal, the fact that his contemporaries believed it speaks volumes about the Babe. Not such big points to Ruth.

The Babe does, however, earn a massive bonus for his pitching. I'm not sure if modern fans always appreciate what a dominant pitcher he was. In 1916 he went 23–12, leading the AL with a 1.75 ERA and 9 shutouts. I realize this is the dead-ball era we're talking about, but he didn't allow a *single home run* in 323.2 innings. He followed this up in October with a 14-inning World Series complete game, allowing one miserly run (ironically, an inside-the-park solo home run) in a 2–1 victory. It's clear that Ruth could've been a dominant starter for years to come; if only he hadn't been so damn good at sailing long flies into the bleachers....

Gibson was respected and well-liked by his teammates. Charleston and Mays were known for the intensity and enthusiasm with which they played the game, Williams not so much unless the lumber was in his hands, though he became a much nicer man as the years went by. Williams *does* get big points from this author for unexpectedly calling for Negro Leagues representation in the Hall of Fame in his own Hall induction speech.

Wagner and Ruth, then, come out on top in the intangibles department, with Williams earning an honorable mention for his comments on the Negro Leagues, this being a book *on* the Negro Leagues.

Bonds, though, was clubhouse cancer. This may have been a consequence of compulsive steroid ingestion, which notoriously corrodes the temper—but that's a lifestyle choice.

In the August 27, 2001, issue of *Sports Illustrated*, Rick Reilly noted that in the Giants' locker room, Bonds had his own "p.r. man, masseur, flex guy, weight trainer, three lockers, a reclining massage chair and a big-screen television that only he can see." Reilly quotes Bonds's teammate Jeff Kent as saying, "On the field, we're fine. Off the field, I don't care about Barry and Barry doesn't care about me. Or anyone else." Bonds is an all-time great player, but I can't take him seriously when it comes to talk of being The Greatest.[4]

Conclusions

Summing up the advantages in each category:

- Hitting for average: Charleston, Gibson and Ruth, but the margin over the others is narrow.
- Ability to get on base: Williams, with Bonds, Charleston, Gibson and Ruth also showing well.

- Hitting for power: Gibson and Ruth—but all except Wagner measure extremely well, and even Honus does all right.
- Basepath speed: Bonds and Mays, plus probably Charleston.
- Longest sustained peak: Mays.
- Defense: Bonds, Charleston, Mays and Wagner.
- Throwing arm: Bonds, Charleston and Mays.
- Longevity: Charleston.
- Durability: Charleston and Mays, but there's no decisive edge.
- Postseason play: Ruth.
- Play at an important defensive position: Charleston, Mays and Wagner, and to a lesser extent Gibson.
- Distance above peers at the same position: Gibson and Wagner.
- Intangibles: Ruth for pitching, Wagner for conditioning; an honorable mention to Williams for his Hall acceptance speech; a big minus to Bonds for being carcinogenic.

I'm going with a three-way split decision:

- The greatest *baseball player* is Babe Ruth. With his pitching and postseason credentials included, it really can't be anyone but the Babe.
- The greatest *position player* is Josh Gibson. No peer at catcher, no one close—and unlike Honus, Gibson has elite plate discipline and light-tower power.
- The greatest *all-around player* is Willie Mays. At their peaks Charleston was Mays's equal in power, speed, defense and durability, and got on base more, but Willie has a longer run of peak/prime years, 18 (1954–71) to Oscar's 16 (1918–33)—and don't forget, Mays deserves peak credit for 1953 too, when he was serving his Nation, because he won the freaking MVP the next year. As George Martin said of Lennon and McCartney, "I couldn't put a cigarette paper between them"—but in the final analysis, I think it has to be Mays.[5]

* * *

"I didn't see the first two.
What makes you think I'm going to hit a third one?"
—John "Mule" Miles, who sat down after just two strikes thrown by
The Greatest Pitcher in Baseball History[6]

Originally I'd planned to work through a similar exercise to name The Greatest Pitcher—until I found that no matter whose names I put forward, no matter which tests I proposed, the same name kept recurring, at or tied for the top position in every category. There's no serious doubt in my mind that **Satchel Paige** is the greatest professional pitcher of all time.

First, let's establish that Satch's place as the greatest NgL pitcher is unchallengeable. He holds the lowest ERA in NgL history, the lowest WHIP, the highest rate of strikeouts per 9 innings, the best strikeout-to-walk ratio. The distance in strikeouts per 9 between Satch and the second-place hurler, Johnny Taylor, is more than five times greater than the distance between Taylor and the tenth-place pitcher, Willie Foster.

To deflate a popular canard, many writers point to the April 19, 1952, *Pittsburgh Courier* poll that named "Cyclone" Joe Williams, not Satch, as the best-ever NgL pitcher. Cyclone had died the previous year, and a Roberto Clemente–like outpouring of sentiment buoyed his posthumous reputation among the voters. I rate Cyclone as second only to Satch among NgL pitchers, but he was definitely second: Satch bests him by wide margins in win-loss percentage (.648 to .590), ERA (2.24 to 2.97), ERA+ (212 to 161), WHIP (0.997 to 1.144), hits per 9 (7.0 to 8.6), home runs per 9 (.2029 to .2499), strikeouts per 9 (8.3 to 6.1), and strikeout-to-walk ratio (4.15 to 3.52).

The evidence for Satch as the greatest professional pitcher irrespective of league is just as overwhelming. His combined professional ERA+ of 191 soars past the nearest MLB starter, Clayton Kershaw at 158; the ERA+ of the closest serious challengers as greatest pitcher ever, Lefty Grove and Walter Johnson, stand at 148 and 147. (Jacob deGrom is likely headed for Kershaw country too, but he'll still finish far short of Satch.) Satch's longevity exceeds Grove or Johnson or Warren Spahn; his pinpoint control equals Cy Young or Christy Mathewson or Greg Maddux; his fastball is easily a match for Sandy Koufax or Randy Johnson or Roger Clemens.

His fastball! Hitters spoke of the buzzing sound the ball made as it rocketed past them, strongly indicating a speed well in excess of 100 miles per hour. As a point of reference, Steve Dalkowski, frequently cited as the fastest pitcher of all time, threw the ball "so hard that it made a loud buzzing sound," according to his high school coach. Cal Ripken, Sr., wrote that "if you were to take the radar gun that's used today and put it on Steve, I think it would've shown him to be throwing the ball somewhere in the neighborhood of 115 miles an hour."[7]

Dizzy Dean, who barnstormed with Paige many times, wrote in his idiosyncratic fashion in 1938: "I know whose [sic] the best pitcher I ever saw and it's Satchel Page [sic].… My fastball looks like a change of pace alongside that little pistol bullet old Satchel shoots up to the plate.… Satchel Page with those long arms is my idea of the pitcher with the greatest stuff ever I see." Carl Hubbell affirmed that "Paige has the fastest ball I've ever seen"; Buck Leonard called him "the fastest pitcher I've ever seen, Black or white"; Ted "Double Duty" Radcliffe said that "catching Satchel is like trying to catch a freight train barreling at you with the brakes gone bad"; William "Judy" Johnson recalled, "It was like trying to hit a bullet.… He was head and shoulders above everyone else."[8]

Bob Feller stated flatly that "the prewar Paige was the best pitcher I ever saw"; Mickey Cochrane declared, "I guarantee he'd be a 30-game winner in the majors"; Bill Veeck called him "the best pitcher I've ever seen" and said that he had "the best fastball I've ever seen and the best control." Joe DiMaggio, who asserted multiple times that "Paige is the greatest pitcher I ever batted against," exclaimed: "His fast ball? Say, when he fires it the catcher gets nothing but ashes!… After I got a hit off Satchel I knew I was ready for the big leagues." (After the February 7, 1936, exhibition game in which Joltin' Joe got his hit, Yankees scout Ed Bessick telegraphed business manager Ed Barrow: "DIMAGGIO ALL WE HOPED HE'D BE. HIT SATCH ONE FOR FOUR." DiMaggio hit .332 with 29 homers for the Yankees that year.)[9]

From 1901 to 1933, the single-game strikeout record for MLB pitchers stood at 16. On April 29, 1929, Satch struck out 17 Cuban Stars; on May 5 he whiffed 18 Nashville Elite Giants in 14 innings; on July 14 he fanned 17 Detroit Stars.

When the annual Denver Post Tournament allowed Black players to participate for the first time in 1934, Satch struck out 44 batters in 28 innings; in 1935 he blew away a record 60 batters in 39 innings, yielding just 6 walks; in 1936, 20 years before batting helmets were made mandatory in the Majors, a Texas team donned helmets when it came their turn to face Satch—and who could blame them? Satch pitched for a different team in each of these three tournaments, and each time his team took home the title.

Satch retained his ability to blow the ball past hitters despite pitching absurd numbers of games and innings. On the Fourth of July 1934, in the first game of a doubleheader, Satch threw a 17-strikeout no-hitter against the Homestead Grays, then pitched an inning of middle relief in the second game, punching out his 18th batter of the day. In the 1942 Negro World Series Satch pitched in all four games (two as a starter, two in relief) as the Grays swept the Monarchs, going 2–0 plus a save with a 2.20 ERA and 0.857 WHIP and striking out 18 in 16.1 innings—one of the greatest postseason performances of all time.

Even as a senior citizen, Satch could bring it. Pitcher Bill Monbouquette, who was there for Satch's final MLB appearance at age 59 (in which he pitched three scoreless innings, allowed one hit and no walks, and—of course—struck out a batter) said, "They weren't using radar guns in those days, but I'd guess he was getting it up there about 86, 88 miles an hour."[10]

Unlike the ultra-fast but ultra-wild Dalkowski, Satch had impeccable control—maybe the best ever. As a barnstormer he would set up a wooden board behind home plate and drive nails into it, or pitch between the labels of two bats standing upright six inches apart on the plate, or line up soda bottles at the plate and knock them over one by one. In his 1948 tryout for Cleveland he threw 50 pitches, 46 of them for strikes. "He made his living by throwing the ball to a spot over the plate the size of a matchbook," said Cool Papa Bell—and that wasn't hyperbole: Clint Courtenay, who caught Satch in the Majors in 1952 and '53, remembered, "You hear about pinpoint control, but Paige is the only man I've ever seen who really has it. Once he threw me six strikes out of 10 pitches over a gum wrapper."[11]

Satch maintained his greatness against the highest levels of competition. In NgL All-Star Games he was 3–1 with an 0.86 ERA, zero home runs allowed, and 22 strikeouts in 21 innings; as an NgL star throwing against white Major Leaguers (Seamheads-verified games only), he was 3–2 with a 2.36 ERA, one home run allowed (0.2381 HR/9), and 55 strikeouts in 42 innings.

He performed just as brilliantly in unverified games against top opponents. Dizzy Dean won the 1934 National League MVP with a 30–7, 2.66 performance, followed by a 2–1, 1.73 World Series display—but on a post-season barnstorming tour Satch defeated him four games out of six. "In a dozen games against this Paige we never beat him," said Jimmy Wasdell. "He beat Paul and Dizzy Dean one night, 1–0, and we got only one hit off him. I was the only minor leaguer on our club."[12]

A major component of the man's genius, which I've not seen mentioned elsewhere, was his ability to prevent home runs. Satch allowed a combined NgL and MLB career total of 0.3198 homers per nine innings. While 276 pitchers rank ahead of him on the all-time tables, all but seven retired more than 20 years before Satch's final MLB season in 1953 (not including his 1965 swan song with Kansas City): Jack Quinn, Jake Miller, and Hall of Famers Urban "Red" Faber and Eppa Rixey, who retired in 1933; Hall of Famer Burleigh Grimes, who retired in 1934; Adolfo "Dolf" Luque, who retired in 1935; and Al Hollingsworth, the lone post–World War II name on the list, who retired in 1946. Most of Satch's home run-preventing value stems from his otherworldly 0.2029 NgL performance—but his MLB performance from age 42 on, 0.5483, is still far superior to that of any pitcher active today; the closest, the brilliant Clayton Kershaw, is a gaping .1499 behind.

His longevity ices the cake:

- In the 1927 NNL (age 21), Satch went 7–2 with a 2.39 ERA.
- In the 1934 NN2 (age 28), he went 13–3 with a 1.54 ERA.
- In the 1939 PRWL (age 33), he went 19–3 with a 1.93 ERA, setting records that stand today for wins and strikeouts.
- In the 1944 NAL (age 38), he went 6–3 with an 0.72 ERA.
- In the 1948 AL (age 42), he went 6–1 with a 2.48 ERA. As Cleveland beat Boston by a single game, it's safe to say that the oldest-ever MLB rookie propelled his team into the World Series.
- In the 1952 AL (age 46), as a spot starter he went 4–2, including a 12-inning 1–0 shutout; as the league's premier long reliever he led the AL with 8 wins, 35 games finished and 100 innings pitched, and with 10 saves missed the league lead by one. That's my pick as the greatest season by any player aged 43 or older in MLB history.
- In the 1956 IL (age 50), he went 11–4 with a 1.86 ERA.
- In the 1961 PCL (age 55), he pitched 25 innings with a 2.88 ERA.
- In the 1965 AL (age 59), he pitched three innings with a 0.00 ERA.

No one can match that five-decade run; no one comes close. There's no precedent for it, in the Majors or otherwise. J.G. Taylor Spink, never a proponent of Black players, opined in the July 14, 1948, *Sporting News* that "to bring in a pitching 'rookie' of Paige's age casts a reflection on the entire scheme of operation in the major leagues. To sign a hurler at Paige's age is to demean the standards of baseball in the big circuits." When the 42-year-old Paige demeaned the Chicago White Sox on August 13 and 20 with back-to-back shutouts, allowing eight hits and one walk in 18 innings, Spink's voice was curiously silent.

Satch pitched far more total games—pro, semi-pro, foreign league, exhibition, barnstorming—than any pitcher in history. "I'd have played every day of the year if I could," he said, and often he pitched more than once a day; his sometime roommate Larry Doby explained that "he owned an airplane.... He'd pitch three innings in Newark in the Negro Leagues and make himself a thousand dollars, like a one o'clock game; three o'clock game in Philadelphia, make another thousand dollars; a night game in Washington, make another thousand dollars." In 1935 his personal diary showed him pitching in 153 games; in 1953 his count was 169—57 in the Majors, 112 in independent ball before and after his MLB release. In 1947, reporter Burton Hawkins cited him as "pitching steadily since 1924, appearing in more than 100 games a year.... In 1940 he pitched in 134 games, within 20 of a complete schedule of a major league club." And the man pitched for 41 years.[13]

Satch himself estimated that he won 2,000 lifetime games. Excluding barnstorming contests and counting only the 714 games for which we have verifiable records, Satch compiled a 301–193 record (plus 47 saves) for a .684 win-loss percentage, superior to that posted by any MLB 300-game winner—this despite opposing teams routinely scheduling their top aces to pitch against him. (Some readers may consider this comparison unfair, as it includes games against all levels of opposition. I cite the figure only to illustrate Satch's dominance over all comers. Against strictly top-level competition—NgL and MLB—he compiled a 131–87 mark for a still-elite .601 win-loss percentage.) Given that barnstorming made up the vast majority of his un-recorded experience, and that, as all accounts agree, he generally overwhelmed his barnstorming opponents, his personal estimate of 2,000 wins is not only reasonable, it may be an understatement.

I looked at the evidence as objectively as I could, and couldn't see a decisive argument for any candidate over the Methuselah of baseball. Congratulations, Satch, and remember—go very light on vices such as carrying on in Heaven: the angelic ramble ain't restful.

* * *

These, then, are my picks as The Greatest. Perhaps you don't agree. You probably have your own choice, or choices.

And isn't that what baseball is all about?

15

My Inner Circle

*The Top 73 Players
in American Baseball History*

Here's my take on the very best players in American baseball history, an Inner Circle for the Hall of Fame if you will. (I say "American" in deference to Sadaharu Oh, Shigeo Nagashima, and the many great players who displayed their brilliance on the other side of the Pacific.) I'm a small–Hall kind of guy, and my selections are occasionally idiosyncratic. You're probably going to disagree with several of my picks and a whole big bunch of my omissions, and that's okay with me; it'll give readers of this book one more thing to talk about.

Michael Bates writes that "the list of baseball's best seems to have become calcified in the public consciousness, supported by stats, and is unbudgeable…. We have the answers, or at least a set that are generally agreed upon, so why bother asking the question when the only debate we get left with is about Josh Gibson, Satchel Paige, and where the rest of the Negro Leaguers would stack up. And even that question is largely unknowable."[1]

Obviously I don't agree with that last bit, but Mr. Bates makes an important point: most all-time teams to date have excluded or badly under-represented NgL players. That's one of the many reasons I wrote this book.

I've condensed the argument for each player to a single line. My primary consideration is career value, but spectacular multi-year peaks, contemporary opinion, and historical impact also get their due. At each position, the player I regard as the all-time best is marked with a bullet point; at Starting Pitcher I selected a lefty and a righty. Dishonorable Mentions are awarded for a) wagering on the outcome of games and b) being Adrian Anson.

I very much wanted to arrange this list so that the criminally under-sung Hammerin' Hank would place as the #1 right fielder—but if I shift the Babe to multi-position, where he kinda deserves to be on account of his pitching, he obscures the triumph of the astonishing **Bullet Rogan**, the greatest multi-position threat in baseball history. Rogan would hit cleanup while playing first, second, left, right, or center, unless he was whipping you as that day's starter, and probably he was managing his team at the same time. As a hitter he won a batting title; as a pitcher he led his league in wins twice, ERA twice, strikeouts per 9 three times; as a manager he guided his teams to three first-place finishes. Everyone knows the Babe and the Hammer, but comparatively few know the Bullet, so right field it is for George Herman. That's the trouble with Ruth: he tends to come out #1 no matter where you put him ... sorry Mr. Aaron, it wasn't for want of trying.

I encourage you to create your own Inner Circle—and hopefully there'll be more Negro Leaguers in it than there would have been before. If so, I've achieved at least part of my purpose.

Catcher

Johnny Bench: 389 homers, phenomenal defense, fabulous arm, a vital cog in the Big Red Machine
Yogi Berra: 14 pennants, 3 MVPs, solid defense, the most consistent of the great MLB catchers
Roy Campanella: power, world-class defense, three MVPs, multiple All-Star pick in the NgL and in MLB
Mickey Cochrane: .320 career average and .419 career OBP, excellent defense, one of history's best W/K ratios

The astonishing Wilber "Bullet Joe" Rogan (Library of Congress).

• **Josh Gibson**: caught like Freehan or Fisk and hit like Ruth, shares Buck Leonard's 9 straight pennants
Biz Mackey: .332 hitter, 3 titles in hits, he and Campanella were the defensive masters among NgL catchers
Mike Piazza: didn't have the D of the other top-flight catchers, but the best-hitting receiver not named Gibson
Honorable Mention: Gary Carter, Bill Dickey, Buck Ewing, Carlton Fisk, Bill Freehan, Gabby Hartnett, Joe Mauer, Ivan Rodriguez, Louis Santop

First Base

Jimmie Foxx: a hair below Gehrig as a hitter, but only a hair: less average (.325) but more power (534 taters)
• **Lou Gehrig**: a .340/.447/.632 hitter with tremendous power and plate discipline who played every game

Buck Leonard: a true Inner Circle giant, 1.033 OPS, 178 OPS+, an unmatched 9 consecutive pennants

Albert Pujols: NL Triple Crown winner for the 2000s, superb fielder, only his late decline keeps Gehrig at #1

Mule Suttles: .338 career hitter who launched 500-foot blasts, the East-West Game's greatest performer

Honorable Mention: Jeff Bagwell, Dan Brouthers, Miguel Cabrera, Luke Easter, Willie McCovey, Mark McGwire, Johnny Mize, Eddie Murray, George Sisler, Ben Taylor, Frank Thomas, Jim Thome—Dishonorable Mention: Cap "Race Suicide" Anson

Second Base

Eddie Collins: the Spahn of hitters: produced decades of interchangeable, high-performance .300 seasons

Rogers Hornsby: a poor fielder and colossal jerk, but from 1921 to 1925 he averaged .402 with long-ball power

• **Joe Morgan**: power, speed, W/K ratio, Gold Gloves, the Big Red Machine: a multidimensional game-winner

Jackie Robinson: .410 career OBP, devastating baserunner, brilliant defender—and an American hero to boot

Honorable Mention: Roberto Alomar, Craig Biggio, Rod Carew, Bingo DeMoss, Charlie Gehringer, Bobby Grich, Nap Lajoie, Bill Mazeroski, Ryne Sandberg, Lou Whitaker

Shortstop

John Henry Lloyd: 6 titles in batting, 5 in slugging, nicknamed "the Black Wagner"—and Honus was flattered

Cal Ripken, Jr.: the consecutive games, the shortstop home run record, 3,184 hits, a cannon arm

Alex Rodriguez: 3,115 hits, underrated defender—but how many of those 696 homers were propelled by 'roids?

Ozzie Smith: the greatest defender at the most crucial defensive position, brilliant W/K ratio, 580 steals

Arky Vaughan: his .385 in '35 was worthy of Honus—and he posted 11 other .300 seasons besides

• **Honus Wagner**: towers above all other shortstops, an unmatchable combination of defense and 3,415 hits

Willie Wells: defense near Ozzie and Honus's range, .333 career hitter, 5 titles in doubles, greatest-ever Cuba star

Honorable Mention: Luke Appling, Ernie Banks, Joe Cronin, George Davis, Derek Jeter, Grant Johnson, Barry Larkin, Alan Trammel

Third Base

Wade Boggs: a high-damage combination of huge hit and walk totals, excellent hot-corner defense

George Brett: 3,154 hits, 665 doubles, batting titles in 3 different decades, underrated glove man

Eddie Mathews: rivals Schmidt as the greatest power hitter at third, out-homered Aaron in Brewtown

• **Mike Schmidt**: holds every major power-hitting record—and many major defensive records—at 3B

Jud Wilson: not on the defensive level of the others here, but .358 hitting and 3 batting titles secures him a place

Honorable Mention: Home Run Baker, John Beckwith, Ken Boyer, Ray Dandridge, Darrell Evans, Stan Hack, Chipper Jones, Graig Nettles, Brooks Robinson, Ron Santo, Pie Traynor

Left Field

Barry Bonds: all-time records in HR and walks, excellent range and arm, #1 if he'd kept the needles out of his butt

Rickey Henderson: all-time leader in runs and steals, 4th in times on base, greatest leadoff man ever

• **Stan Musial**: .333 hitter, 3,630 hits, 725 doubles, solid defense and extreme, multi-decade durability

Ted Williams: .344 hitter, 521 homers, 6 batting titles, 2 Triple Crowns, his .482 career OBP is tops all-time

Honorable Mention: Jesse Burkett, Ed Delahanty, Goose Goslin, Minnie Miñoso, Tim Raines, Manny Ramirez, Willie Stargell, Carl Yastrzemski

Center Field

Cool Papa Bell: NgL career leader in runs, hits, and steals, 4 titles in walks: the NgL's Rickey Henderson

Willard Brown: .349 average, vicious line-drive hitter, 6 titles in doubles, 5 HR titles and 5 OPS+ championships

Oscar Charleston: spectacular defender, monster arm, ultra-durable, .357 hitter with game-breaking power

Ty Cobb: 12 (11?) batting titles, 8 slugging crowns, 892 steals: the man could do everything but smile

Joe DiMaggio: .325 hitter, all five tools, ultra-graceful center fielder, the Series was his bread and butter

• **Willie Mays**: 660 homers, 4 titles in steals, total domination on defense, greatest Series catch ever in '54

Mickey Mantle: .421 career OBP, 536 homers, above-average defense—plus 14 pennants

Tris Speaker: .345 hitter, 792 doubles, his CF glove was known as "the place where triples go to die"

Turkey Stearnes: .347 hitter, 2 batting crowns, 6 titles in triples, 6 in home runs, .417 postseason hitter

Honorable Mention: Richie Ashburn, Larry Doby, Ken Griffey, Jr., Sliding Billy Hamilton, Pete Hill, Monte Irvin, Spottswood Poles, Duke Snider, Cristóbal Torriente—and, already, Mike Trout

Right Field

Hank Aaron: all-time leader in HR and RBI, 3,771 hits, underrated top-notch defender, #1 at most positions

Mel Ott: .414 OBP, 6 titles in home runs, 6 in walks, homered more at home but average was higher on the road

Frank Robinson: 586 homers, '66 Triple Crown, a shorter career but 100 percent the offensive equal of Aaron and Mays

• **Babe Ruth**: out-homered every *team* in baseball in 1920, two 20-win seasons and an ERA title as a pitcher

Ichiro Suzuki: so many world records: 28 years, 3,604 games, 4,367 hits; the greatest defensive OF I ever saw

Honorable Mention: Roberto Clemente, Sam Crawford, Tony Gwynn, Reggie Jackson, Al Kaline, Paul Waner, Dave Winfield—Dishonorable Mention: at .356 with power, Joe Jackson would be a Shoe-in for this list if he hadn't sold his soul to the Devil

Designated Hitter

• **Edgar Martinez**: simply the best-hitting DH ever, .312 average with long-ball power and bucketfuls of walks

David Ortiz: the epitome of DH power, then tripled that power in the World Series, post–Marathon Boston hero

Multi-Position

Martin Dihigo: would sometimes play all 9 positions in NgL games, a .319 hitter and 46–38 pitcher

Hank Greenberg: MVPs at first and in left field, 4 HR titles, led AL by 51 RBI over #2 man Gehrig in '35

Paul Molitor: 3,319 hits, 605 doubles, 504 steals, played every position except pitcher and catcher

• **Bullet Rogan**: 122–53, 2.68 as a pitcher, .333/.407/.513 as a hitter, 284–166 as a manager: a baseball polymath

Robin Yount: 3,142 hits, high-percentage base stealer, an MVP at short followed by an MVP in center field

Honorable Mention: Sam Bankhead, Junior Gilliam, Harmon Killebrew, Gil

McDougald, Double Duty Radcliffe—Dishonorable Mention: Pete "I Have Never Bet on Baseball" Rose*

Starting Pitcher

Pete Alexander: 373 wins, 5 titles in ERA, 6 in wins, 7 in innings, 6 in strikeouts, 5 in WHIP

Roger Clemens: 354 wins and 7 ERA titles, but he wants us to believe his wife was injecting 'roids and he wasn't

Willie Foster: 126–60, 2.57 in NgL regular-season play, plus 12–7, 2.54 and 3 rings in the post-season

Bob Gibson: Mr. Clutch, lowest modern ERA in 1968, 7–2 and hit 2 homers in Series play, 2x Series MVP

• **Lefty Grove**: 9 ERA titles, 5 titles in win percentage, 300 wins + 108 in the high minors, most dominant MLB pitcher ever

Randy Johnson: 4 ERA and 9 strikeout titles, 10.6 Ks per 9 innings, his 2001 Series was among the best ever

Walter Johnson: 417 wins, 110 shutouts, 4 ERA titles in the dead-ball era and 1 more in the live-ball era

Clayton Kershaw: 158 ERA+, 5 ERA titles, 3 in wins, 3 in strikeouts, 4 in WHIP—and the man's not done yet

Sandy Koufax: 5 straight ERA titles, 2x Series MVP, the only man to rival Grove's dominance over a given span

Greg Maddux: 355 wins, masterful control and defense, rivals Spahn as the most consistent winner of all time

Pedro Martinez: 5 ERA titles, 6 WHIP crowns, his technical perfection was mesmerizing to watch

Christy Mathewson: 9 titles in K/W ratio, the only man to stand up against Hal Chase and the Black Sox

• **Satchel Paige**: 191 ERA+, 8 strikeout and 12 K/W titles, 41-year durability: the greatest pro pitcher ever

Tom Seaver: Maddux's principal rival as the greatest modern pitcher, won 311 games with some awful teams

Warren Spahn: 363 wins, 382 modern-era CG, an endless procession of high-performance 20-win seasons

Cyclone Williams: pinpoint control, 6 ERA titles, 5 WHIP titles and 7 K/W titles in pre–NgL and NgL play

Cy Young: mind-boggling durability, most games started, most innings pitched, brilliant control—and 511 wins

Honorable Mention: Dave Brown, Ray Brown, Steve Carlton, Bob Feller, Whitey Ford, Juan Marichal, Kid Nichols, Cannonball Redding, Max Scherzer

Relief Pitcher

Goose Gossage: 115 relief wins, an ERA at least one full run under league average in 11 different seasons

- **Mariano Rivera**: 559 saves, 1.000 WHIP, 0.70 October ERA, redefined the meaning of Excellence for relievers

    Hoyt Wilhelm: 147 ERA+, the greatest-ever long reliever and first man widely recognized as a relief ace

    Honorable Mention: Dennis Eckersley, Trevor Hoffman, Firpo Marberry, Dan Quisenberry, John Smoltz

16

Two Down, One to Go

Some baseball writers advocate dozens of Negro Leaguers for the Hall of Fame. My original manuscript for this book advocated a modest three (3) NgL players for the Hall—but events overtook my prose in December 2021 when, to my surprise and delight, the Veterans Committee elected two of my proposed enshrinees.

The first of my advocacies was for **Orestes "Minnie" Miñoso**. The man played baseball non-stop, summer and winter alike, for *32 years* from 1942 to 1973—not including MLB cameos in 1976, 1980, 1993 and 2003—amassing 4,126 games, 4,438 hits, 751 doubles, 193 triples, 389 home runs, 2,485 runs scored and 2,223 RBIs in a range of leagues spanning North and Central America. (He certainly amassed bigger numbers than this, but these are the totals I can verify.) Between the Negro, Major, and Mexican Leagues he racked up 16 All-Star selections.

Minnie hit .300+ twice in the NgL and eight times in the Majors, once in the white minors, nine times in Mexican leagues, and three times in Cuban pro ball. (These weren't empty .300 averages; he broke the White Sox career record for home runs in 1956 and didn't relinquish it until 1974.)

For those of you keeping track at home, that's 23 .300+ seasons in organized baseball. The official record-holder is Ty Cobb with 22.

Just to round things out, Minnie hit .308 in four NgL East-West Games, .300 in eight MLB All-Star Games, .333 in the 1947 Negro World Series, and .356 in two Caribbean World Series.

Like Craig Biggio, fellow excellent defender and master of small-ball tactics, Minnie found numerous ways to help his teams. He held the AL career record for hit by pitch for 27 years (1959–85) and still holds the MLB record with 10 titles in hit by pitch. Considering that he also won four Cuban League hit-by-pitch titles, it's safe to assume that his small-ball attack was effective in every league in which he played.

Here's a summary of MLB offensive and defensive titles won by Minnie, 1951–61:

- 1951: triples, steals, hit by pitch
- 1952: steals, hit by pitch
- 1953: steals, hit by pitch, LF games, LF double plays
- 1954: triples, total bases, hit by pitch, LF assists, LF double plays, LF range factor, LF Total Zone Rating
- 1955: stolen base percentage, LF games, LF putouts, LF assists, LF double plays
- 1956: triples, hit by pitch, LF games, LF putouts, LF assists
- 1957: doubles, hit by pitch, LF games (won LF Gold Glove)

- 1958: hit by pitch, LF games, LF assists
- 1959: hit by pitch, LF putouts, LF assists, LF Total Zone Rating (won LF Gold Glove)
- 1960: hits, hit by pitch, sacrifice flies, games played, LF games, LF putouts, LF assists, LF double plays (won LF Gold Glove)
- 1961: hit by pitch, sacrifice flies

The man could hurt you at the plate, on the basepaths, and in the field.

Minnie was elected to the Cuban Hall of Fame, the Mexican Hall of Fame, and the Caribbean Series Hall of Fame. Then pour some integration credit on top, as Minnie integrated the White Sox *and* was the first-ever Black Latin player in the Majors…

More so even than Larry Doby or Monte Irvin, Minnie Miñoso's historical image as a brilliant ballplayer was suppressed by the timing and glacial pace of integration. His call to the Hall was long overdue.

My second Hall advocacy was for **John "Buck" O'Neil**. The phrase "pioneer credit" was invented for men like him.

Buck played in the NgL and other Black leagues for 21 years (1933–55), earning two East-West Game selections and hitting a combined .369 in four NgL playoff

Buck O'Neil in 1997, speaking to an audience at St. Cloud State University about Jackie Robinson and Baseball's Great Experiment (courtesy St. Cloud State University Archives).

series. He compiled a first-place 53–27–1 record as manager of the 1948 Monarchs, plus a 273–186 record in post–1948 NgL play (1949–55). He scouted for the Chicago Cubs for 36 years (1953–88) and coached for 10 years for the Cubs (1962–65) and the Kansas City Royals (1989–94)—the first Black coach in MLB history.

That's 62 years of continuous engagement with professional baseball—and he was just getting started on his life's calling. More than any other person, Buck became the face of the Negro Leagues to multiple generations. He was instrumental in securing Hall of Fame recognition for dozens of NgL players.

Buck was devastated when the Negro Leagues Committee turned him down by a single vote; he believed that he had earned a place in the Hall of Fame. Now, 101 years on from the founding of the Negro Leagues, the Hall finally gave the man his due.

The final player for whom I intended to advocate, and the only one among the three who hasn't yet received baseball's highest accolade, is **Luscious "Luke" Easter**. Luke's case isn't as obvious as Mr. Miñoso's or as self-evidently just as Mr. O'Neil's, but I believe the standard of proof has been met.

I argued for Easter's candidacy at length in the body of the book, and won't repeat my long-form analysis here. But I'll say this: Weighing the evidence in sum, I rank Easter the same way I'd rank Willie McCovey and Willie Stargell. I consider this a conservative ranking. McCovey and Stargell are obvious, no-brainer Hall of Famers. And so I assert that despite having the toughest case to prove, Big Luke, too, deserves a plaque of his own.

In case the Hall is looking for some text for his plaque, here's my suggestion:

LUSCIOUS EASTER
"BIG LUKE"

INDEPENDENT TEAMS, 1935–41, 1946;
HOMESTEAD, N.N.2 1947–48; CLEVELAND, A.L. 1950–54;
MINOR LEAGUE, FOREIGN, AND WINTER TEAMS 1947–49, 1954–64

POSSIBLY THE GREATEST LONG-BALL HITTER EVER TO PLAY ORGANIZED BASEBALL, THIS GENTLE GIANT EMPLOYED TREMENDOUS BAT SPEED, PLATE DISCIPLINE, AND AN UNRIVALLED HOME-RUN STROKE TO TERRIFY PITCHERS ACROSS NORTH AMERICA. HIT 74 INDEPENDENT AND NEGRO LEAGUE HOME RUNS IN 1946, 48 IN 1947, 63 IN 1948. OVERCAME INJURIES AND PREMATURE DEMOTIONS TO AMASS 86 HOMERS AND 307 RBI IN JUST 3 FULL AL SEASONS, NEARLY CAPTURING 1952 HOME RUN CROWN DESPITE TIME IN MINORS. WON HOME RUN TITLES IN MULTIPLE MINOR AND FOREIGN LEAGUES: THE HFL (1946), VPBL (1948/49), MPCL (1954/55), PRWL (1955/56), AND IL (1956 AND 1957). SMASHED ATTENDANCE RECORDS IN PARKS THROUGHOUT NORTH AND CENTRAL AMERICA AND BECAME THE MOST POPULAR PLAYER IN BUFFALO BISONS HISTORY. HIT THE ONLY HOME RUN TO CLEAR THE CENTER-FIELD SCOREBOARD AT BUFFALO'S OFFERMAN STADIUM, JUNE 1957. NAMED INDEPENDENT ALL-STAR FOR 1938-1939-1940, PRWL MVP FOR 1948/49, AP OUTSTANDING AL PLAYER FOR 1952, MPCL MVP FOR 1954/55, IL MVP FOR 1957.

Two down, and one to go.

17

Wrapup
What's Fair Is Fair

I've presented the logical and statistical arguments for statistical integration first, as they're the more important, but there's another argument for integration: social justice.

Baseball has never come to terms with its past. Everything we love about the game—the history and continuity, the brotherhood of great players stretching back more than a century, the statistical record cherished by fans as in no other game—is sullied by the stain of segregation.

Statistical segregation prior to 2020 was as complete as physical segregation prior to 1947. Talented Black players plied their craft in the Negro Leagues only because systemic racism excluded them from the Majors. To deny their achievements is to deny their humanity.

It's time to affirm that Negro Leaguers were professionals in every possible sense of the word. It's time to embrace not only their achievements but their numbers too, and allow these diamond giants to stand shoulder to shoulder with their Major League peers.

We owe them no less.

A Personal Postscript

I've read about, and studied the statistics of, many hundreds of ballplayers since my youth, but Roy Campanella is the player I most regret not having seen in person. Such a big man, and yet so light on his feet! The stories about his fielding bring to my mind's eye an infinitely more athletic version of Oliver Hardy, who could dance a tarantella with Stan Laurel as though gravity did not obtain.

My Grandfather was also a powerful, strapping man, six foot five and 270 pounds. He was an independent-league star in the late 1930s and early '40s, striking out 14 batters per game and averaging .310 with the bat. He signed a pro contract with Cleveland, but after Pearl Harbor he walked into the Navy without a second thought, walking out 29 years later as director of Naval Recruiting for the midwestern United States.

In researching this book I stumbled across a possible Navy connection between Grandpa and Larry Doby. Grandpa was an honest and forthright man who couldn't see the logic in segregation or racial prejudice; in this respect he was decades ahead of most of his white contemporaries, and if anyone in the whole of the Navy would have welcomed Doby to Great Lakes, it would have been him.

My Grandfather (top left) with his 1938 Iowa barnstorming squad (author's collection, with thanks to Elsa Petersen and Rhoda Senkler).

I spent many a happy afternoon in the Wrigley and Comiskey bleachers with this genial colossus, who'd seen them all from Ruth to Trout. (The greatest player he ever saw: Willie Mays; the greatest pitcher: Bob Gibson.) The love of baseball that flowed from him found its way into my blood, and stays with me today.

Grandpa died in January 2016, and I never got to ask him about Roy Campanella. I wish I had. Rest in peace, Grandpa.

Part II

REFERENCE

18

Negro Leaguers in the Hall of Fame

This list explains itself. I will note, though, that there are some harsh positional imbalances among the Negro Leaguers in the Hall of Fame, more so than for their white counterparts; the list tells the story.

Players are listed at the position where they played the most professional games, with one exception: Ernie Banks played more games at first, but earned his MVPs at shortstop, and that's where I've put him.

(See chart on the following page.)

Negro Leaguers in the Hall of Fame

CENTER FIELD (8)
James "Cool Papa" Bell
Inducted 1974

Oscar Charleston
Inducted 1976

Willie Mays
Inducted 1979

Larry Doby
Inducted 1978

Norman "Turkey" Stearnes
Inducted 2000

Willard Brown
Inducted 2006

Pete Hill
Inducted 2006

Cristóbal Torriente
Inducted 2006

LEFT FIELD (2)
Monte Irvin
Inducted 1973

Minnie Miñoso
Inducted 2022

RIGHT FIELD (1)
Hank Aaron
Inducted 1982

SHORTSTOP (3)
Ernie Banks
Inducted 1977

John Henry "Pop" Lloyd
Inducted 1977

Willie Wells
Inducted 1997

SECOND BASE (2)
Jackie Robinson
Inducted 1962

Ulysses "Frank" Grant
Inducted 2006

THIRD BASE (3)
William "Judy" Johnson
Inducted 1975

Ray Dandridge
Inducted 1987

Jud Wilson
Inducted 2006

FIRST BASE (3)
Walter "Buck" Leonard
Inducted 1972

George "Mule" Suttles
Inducted 2006

Ben Taylor
Inducted 2006

LEFT-HANDED PITCHER (2)
Willie Foster
Inducted 1996

Andy Cooper
Inducted 2006

RIGHT-HANDED PITCHER (7)
Leroy "Satchel" Paige
Inducted 1971

Andrew "Rube" Foster
Inducted 1981

Leon Day
Inducted 1995

"Cyclone" Joe Williams
Inducted 1999

Hilton Smith
Inducted 2001

Ray Brown
Inducted 2006

José Méndez
Inducted 2006

MULTI-POSITION (2)
Martin Dihigo
Inducted 1977

"Bullet" Joe Rogan
Inducted 1998

CATCHER (4)
Roy Campanella
Inducted 1969

Josh Gibson
Inducted 1972

James "Biz" Mackey
Inducted 2006

Louis Santop
Inducted 2006

MANAGERS & PIONEERS (6)
Effa Manley
Inducted 2006

Alex Pompez
Inducted 2006

Comberland "Cum" Posey
Inducted 2006

Sol White
Inducted 2006

J.L. Wilkinson
Inducted 2006

John "Buck" O'Neil
Inducted 2022

19

Negro Leagues All-Time Teams

The following chart lists six all-time Negro Leagues teams, as selected by:

- Buck O'Neil (an undated, hand-written list held by the Hall of Fame);
- Cumberland Posey (two teams: the first selected in 1933, the second undated but apparently selected later);
- The *Pittsburgh Courier* (printed on April 9, 1952);
- The Negro Leagues Baseball Museum (selected 1993); and
- An "ultimate all-time Negro League all-star team," compiled in 2001 by a group of 57 Negro Leagues experts under the auspices of author William F. McNeil. McNeil was the first to compile the lists presented here, to which I've added Buck O'Neil's undated list.

The statistical record of every player who appears on these lists is found in the next section.

(See chart on the following page.)

Negro Leagues All-Time Teams

	Buck O'Neil (no date)	Cumberland Posey (earlier list, 1933)	Cumberland Posey (later list, no date)	Pittsburgh Courier (1952)	Negro Leagues Baseball Museum (1993)	Ultimate All-Time Team (2001)
C	Josh Gibson James Greene	Josh Gibson Biz Mackey	Josh Gibson Biz Mackey	Josh Gibson Biz Mackey	Josh Gibson Biz Mackey	Josh Gibson Biz Mackey
1B	Buck Leonard	Ben Taylor Buck Leonard	Buck Leonard	Buck Leonard Ben Taylor	Buck Leonard Mule Suttles	Buck Leonard Mule Suttles
2B	Newt Allen	Sammy Hughes	Martin Dihigo	Jackie Robinson Bingo DeMoss	Piper Davis Newt Allen	Sammy T. Hughes Newt Allen
SS	Willie Wells	John Henry Lloyd	John Henry Lloyd Willie Wells	John Henry Lloyd Willie Wells	Willie Wells Artie Wilson	Willie Wells John Henry Lloyd
3B	Ray Dandridge	Jud Wilson	Ray Dandridge	Oliver Marcelle Judy Johnson	Ray Dandridge Judy Johnson	Ray Dandridge Judy Johnson
LF	Cool Papa Bell	Cristóbal Torriente Oscar Charleston Pete Hill	Cristóbal Torriente Oscar Charleston Pete Hill	Monte Irvin Pete Hill	Cool Papa Bell Willard Brown Oscar Charleston Sam Jethroe Turkey Stearnes Martin Dihigo	Cool Papa Bell Oscar Charleston Turkey Stearnes Cristóbal Torriente Wild Bill Wright
CF	Oscar Charleston			Oscar Charleston Cool Papa Bell		
RF	Ted Strong			Cristóbal Torriente Chino Smith		
UT IF/OF		Dick Lundy Chester Brooks	Dick Lundy Chester Brooks	Martin Dihigo Sam Bankhead John Beckwith Newt Allen Clint Thomas		Martin Dihigo Sammy Bankhead
P	(No pitchers selected)	Cyclone Williams Cannonball Redding Eustaquio Pedroso Bullet Rogan Satchel Paige Dave Brown	Cyclone Williams Cannonball Redding Eustaquio Pedroso Bullet Rogan Satchel Paige Dave Brown	Cyclone Williams Satchel Paige Bullet Rogan John Donaldson Willie Foster Dave Brown Cannonball Redding	Satchel Paige Leon Day Hilton Smith Cyclone Williams Bullet Rogan Ray Brown	Satchel Paige Willie Foster Cyclone Williams Bullet Rogan Ray Brown Leon Day Hilton Smith

Originally compiled by William F. McNeil for his 2001 book Cool Papas and Double Duties: The All-Time Greats of the Negro Leagues.

20

The Negro Leagues All-Star Register*

Herein you'll find complete batting and pitching statistics for the greats of the Negro Leagues. Their numbers are presented in the basic style of Baseball Reference, with modifications (detailed below) to accommodate the nature of NgL statistics.

In the Seamheads system, everything is listed together: play vs. Negro League, Major League, minor league, winter league and foreign league competition, playoff numbers, All-Star numbers, the lot. Given their goal—to cover every aspect of play among players excluded from the Majors—that's a sound methodology.

In this book, though, only professional-level regular-season play is counted towards regular-season stats. No games are included from leagues that can't be classed as Major League quality; statistics for minor, semi-pro, winter, Central and South American, pre–1920 and post–1948 Black leagues, exhibition games, and barnstorming play are all excluded. Mexican League numbers are also excluded, with the important exception of 1940–41. (My argument for including these two years within the Major League canon is spelled out in the introductory text to "A Proposed Major League Organizational Chart.") As per Baseball Reference, playoff and All-Star numbers are presented in separate summaries.

Extra rows are added to the career summary for players who played in both the NgL and in MLB, to offer both separate tallies and a combined professional total for NgL and MLB stats. Further:

- I've omitted a number of standard statistical categories for both hitters and pitchers where data sets are almost non-existent for NgL play; there's no value in printing columns of blank space.
- For years in which a player played in leagues whose statistics can't be included in the professional record, the corresponding row reads, "Played in unrecorded [Black / independent / Mexican / Cuban / Japanese / etc.] league," as appropriate. (See Ray Dandridge's record for a representative example.) This doesn't necessarily mean there are no surviving statistics for these leagues, because sometimes there are; in such cases, the numbers can't be included within the database because they don't meet the standards of professional North American play.

---

*This section could not exist without core numbers from the Seamheads statistical base, reproduced by kind permission of Gary Ashwill.

- For years that a player was trapped in the minors by the treacle pace of integration, or by the fact that Black players were often not given a proper shot at the Majors, the corresponding row reads, "Played in minor leagues (Integration)."
- For each year a Black player was forced to play in a league whose stats can't be included in the professional database, and also for years given to military service, a (+1) is added to the right of Years Played. For example, Roy Campanella's record reads "18 Yrs (+3)" to reflect his year of military service and his two years trapped in the minors by the vagaries of the integration process.

I believe this last change to Baseball Reference's standard format is necessary to accurately describe the careers of players trapped in the limbo between the Negro Leagues and the Majors. Check out Artie Wilson's record to see why: there's a yawning chasm at the end of his career that would be filled with Major League hitting statistics if he'd stood on the right side of the color line. We're not crediting him with the numbers he compiled in the minors, because that would degrade the integrity of the database; rather, we're acknowledging in a symbolic way that even after we incorporate his NgL numbers in the official record, a substantial part of the man's career was lost to segregation.

I advocate that Baseball Reference adopt this change for all players who lost full seasons to military service. For example, Ted Williams's record should read, "19 Yrs (+3)," in recognition of his service to his Nation from 1943 to 1945.

Some players with combined Major League and Negro League records, like Monte Irvin, see their calculated career stats go up as a result of combination—and some, like Willie Mays, see their calculated stats go down. Mays gains a (+3) for his year of military service and two post–1948 years in the Negro Leagues, and adds a handful of runs and RBI for his 1948 NgL experience, but loses a point each from his career batting average, on-base percentage and slugging average, falling from .302-.387-.557 to .301-.386-.556. His numbers would rise rather than fall if we could include his .311 performance in the 1949 Negro Leagues and his .330 in 1950—but we can't, because the post–1948 NgL is generally conceded to have lost its status as a Major-quality league.

Martin Dihigo and Bullet Rogan, brilliant as both batsmen and pitchers, receive two entries apiece in the Register. Pitchers are pretty thin due to broad expert consensus on a handful of top names, so I added records for Rube Foster, who founded the NgL and was a damn good pitcher in his spare time, and Don Newcombe, who stands with Robinson, Doby and Campanella as a signal figure of the integration movement. Alone among the four, Newk didn't receive his own chapter, so I honor him this way instead.

For four players—Willard Brown, Luke Easter, Minnie Miñoso and Satchel Paige—I've compiled extended records that include every game I could locate for that player: not just NgL and MLB games, but also minor league, Mexican, Caribbean, Cuban, independent, exhibition, and any other games I could find. In Big Luke's case, my argument requires every scrap of supporting data I can provide; for Willard,

Minnie, and Satchel, an NgL- and MLB-only stat line paints a woefully incomplete picture of their amazing multi-decade careers. (That's generally true of all pre–1947 Black players, of course, but the dent in these four careers is especially egregious.) Consider Willard Brown: Besides being one of the greatest hitters in NgL history, Brown was *the* greatest hitter in Puerto Rican Winter League history. In my view, any proper accounting of his career has to include those numbers.

In two cases—Larry Doby in the 1947 NN2, and Luke Easter in the 1954 IL—I've awarded offensive titles although plate appearance totals are low. Both players left their respective leagues for reasons related to the race barrier: Doby because he was selected to integrate the AL, Easter because he was shuffled from the AL to the IL to the PCL after his premature, partly racism-driven demotion to the minors.

I've also added to Easter's batting record through what I call *inferred data recovery*. Common sense tells us that for batter records where runs scored and/or RBI data is missing for a given year, a minimum of one run and one RBI can be credited for each home run. This might seem an inconsequential addition—but when applied to an extended career record, encompassing every possible source of data, the results can be startling: Easter gains 185 runs scored and 239 RBI by this method.

Fifty-nine of the 63 players listed here appear on one or more of the NgL All-Time Teams listed in the previous section. The exceptions are Luke Easter, who can't be evaluated by ordinary methods; Rube Foster and Don Newcombe, added for reasons enumerated above; and Buck O'Neil. Buck was a very good player, but his fame rests on his unchallenged status as the ambassador and public face of the Negro Leagues for multiple generations. O'Neil, Alfred "Slick" Surratt and Larry Doby are the only Negro Leaguers I've been privileged to meet, and Buck was really nice to me, and it's my damn book.

Newton "Newt" Allen
Standard Batting

Year	Age	Tm	Lg	G	AB	R	H	2B	3B	HR	RBI	SB	BB	BA	OBP	SLG	OPS	OPS+	TB	HBP	Awards
1923	22	KCM	NNL	33	115	21	35	1	2	0	10	2	10	.304	.370	.348	.718	89	40	2	
1924	23	KCM	NNL	73	298	52	77	8	3	2	32	11	28	.258	.328	.326	.654	101	97	3	
1925	24	KCM	NNL	80	322	67	93	9	11	2	47	12	33	.289	.355	.404	.759	111	130		
1926	25	KCM	NNL	78	306	52	76	11	6	1	40	20	26	.248	.311	.333	.645	71	102	2	
1927	26	KCM	NNL	87	329	52	107	18	3	2	35	11	29	.325	.380	.416	.796	115	137	0	
1928	27	KCM	NNL	74	295	43	81	13	4	2	39	19	23	.275	.331	.366	.697	96	108	2	
1929	28	KCM	NNL	74	295	65	98	27	6	3	54	23	24	.332	.382	.495	.877	127	146	0	
1930	29	KCM	NNL	67	278	35	101	15	6	2	35	10	20	.363	.408	.482	.890	140	134	1	
1931	30	KCM	NNL+IND	45	173	40	54	6	6	2	32	4	21	.312	.390	.480	.870	132	83	1	
		TOTAL																			
		SLS	NNL	26	104	21	32	4	3	1	18	3	13	.308	.385	.433	.817	109	45	0	
		KCM	IND	19	69	19	22	7	3	1	14	1	8	.319	.397	.551	.948	167	38	1	
1932	31	TOTAL	EWL+IND	53	202	40	57	5	1	3	36	11	22	.282	.356	.361	.717	95	73	1	
		HG	EWL	37	140	25	35	4	1	0	25	4	16	.250	.327	.357	.684	87	50	0	
		KCM	IND	16	62	15	22	1	0	3	11	7	6	.355	.420	.371	.791	114	23	1	
1933	32	KCM	IND	6	21	4	5	1	0	0	2	3	0	.238	.333	.286	.619	88	6	0	
1934	33	KCM	IND	7	29	4	5	1	0	0	2	1	2	.172	.226	.207	.433	37	6	0	
1935	34	KCM	IND	11	43	5	12	3	1	0	5	2	1	.279	.326	.395	.721	97	17	0	
1936 *	35	KCM	IND	11	43	11	11	3	2	0	7	1	3	.256	.333	.419	.752	103	18	2	EWA
1937 *	36	KCM	NAL	54	205	36	64	6	4	2	40	11	19	.312	.382	.410	.791	125	84	4	EWA
		TOTAL	NAL	51	194	32	61	6	4	1	37	11	15	.314	.376	.402	.778	121	78	4	
		KCM	NAL	3	11	4	3	0	0	1	3	0	4	.273	.467	.545	1.012	198	6	0	
		CAG	NAL																		EWA
1938 *	37	KCM	NAL	35	132	25	36	7	0	1	20	4	13	.273	.338	.348	.686	91	46	0	
1939	38	KCM	NAL	47	167	19	37	5	0	0	19	1	11	.222	.270	.251	.521	53	42		
1940	39	KCM	NAL	22	76	11	20	2	0	0	8	1	5	.263	.309	.289	.598	88	22		
1941 *	40	KCM	NAL	32	122	22	34	3	1	0	11	3	12	.279	.343	.320	.663	109	39		EWA
1942	41	KCM	NAL	24	92	14	28	2	2	0	7	0	7	.304	.354	.326	.680	115	30		
1943 *	42	KCM	NAL	37	142	16	34	5	0	0	6	6	10	.239	.289	.275	.564	80	39	0	NSA
1944	43	KCM	NAL	26	89	10	21	3	0	0	9	1	5	.236	.277	.270	.546	75	24		
1947	46	CIC	NAL	13	35	3	11	0	1	0	5	0	1	.314	.333	.371	.705	133	13	0	
23 Yrs			NgL	989	3809	647	1097	159	57	22	501	151	330	.288	.348	.377	.725	103	1436	18	
162 Game Avg.			Pro	162	624	106	180	26	9	4	82	25	54	.288	.348	.377	.725	103	235	3	
22 Yrs		KCM	NNL+NAL+IND	910	3519	594	1016	151	52	17	450	144	296	.289	.347	.376	.723	103	1322	18	
1 Yr		HG	EWL	37	140	25	35	4	1	0	25	4	16	.250	.327	.357	.684	87	50	0	
1 Yr		SLS	NNL	26	104	21	32	4	3	1	18	3	13	.308	.385	.433	.817	109	45	0	
1 Yr		CIC	NAL	13	35	3	11	0	1	0	5	0	1	.314	.333	.371	.705	133	13	0	
1 Yr		CAG	NAL	3	11	4	3	0	0	1	3	0	4	.273	.467	.545	1.012	198	6	0	
9 Yrs			NNL	592	2342	408	700	106	44	15	310	111	206	.299	.358	.401	.759	107	939	10	
8 Yrs			NAL	290	1060	156	285	33	6	3	125	21	83	.269	.324	.320	.644	94	339	4	
5 Yrs			IND	70	267	58	77	16	6	1	41	15	25	.288	.358	.404	.763	113	108	4	
1 Yr			EWL	37	140	25	35	4	1	0	25	4	16	.250	.327	.357	.684	87	50	0	

20. The Negro Leagues All-Star Register

Newton "Newt" Allen

Postseason Batting

Year	Age	Tm	Lg	Series	Opp	Rslt	G	AB	R	H	2B	3B	HR	RBI	SB	BB	BA	OBP	SLG	OPS	HBP
1924 □	23	KCM	NNL	WS	HIL	W	10	39	8	11	7	0	0	2	1	2	.282	.333	.462	.779	1
1925	24	KCM	NNL	NNC	SLS	W	7	27	7	10	1	0	1	2	3	1	.370	.414	.519	.911	1
1925	24	KCM	NNL	WS	HIL	L	6	27	3	7	1	0	0	2	1	0	.259	.259	.296	.556	0
1926	25	KCM	NNL	NNC	CAG	L	8	30	2	5	0	0	0	1	0	1	.167	.219	.167	.360	1
1937 □	36	KCM	NAL	ALC	CAG	W	4	17	0	4	1	0	0	0	1	2	.235	.350	.294	.610	
1939 □	38	KCM	NAL	ALC	SLS	W	5	18	3	4	1	0	0	1	1	0	.222	.222	.278	.500	
1942	41	KCM	NAL	WS	HG	W	3	14	1	4	1	0	0	2	0	1	.286	.333	.357	.690	0
6 Yrs (7 Series)			NgL				43	172	24	45	12	0	1	10	7	7	.262	.306	.349	.639	4
2 Yrs				NNC			15	57	9	15	1	0	1	3	3	2	.263	.311	.333	.621	2
2 Yrs				ALC			9	35	3	8	2	0	0	1	2	2	.229	.289	.286	.556	1
3 Yrs				WS			19	80	12	22	9	0	0	6	2	3	.275	.310	.388	.689	1

All-Star Batting

Year	Age	Lg	Game	G	AB	R	H	2B	3B	HR	RBI	SB	BB	BA	OBP	SLG	OPS	HBP
1936	35	WES	EWA	2B	5	0	0	0	0	0	0	0	0	.000	.000	.000	.000	0
1937	36	WES	EWA	2B	4	0	0	0	0	0	0	0	0	.000	.000	.000	.000	0
1938	37	WES	EWA	2B	4	0	0	0	0	0	0	0	0	.000	.000	.000	.000	0
1941	40	WES	EWA	SS	2	0	0	0	0	0	0	0	0	.000	.000	.000	.000	0
1943	42	SAS	NSA	SS	1	0	0	0	0	0	0	0	0	.000	.000	.000	.000	0
5 Yrs (5 GP)		NgL		5	16	0	0	0	0	0	0	0	0	.000	.000	.000	.000	0

Sam Bankhead
Tied professional record for most positions started in All-Star Games (5)
Standard Batting

Year	Age	Tm	Lg	G	AB	R	H	2B	3B	HR	RBI	SB	BB	BA	OBP	SLG	OBP	OPS+	TB	HBP	Awards
1932	21	TOTAL	NSL	11	27	5	8	1	1	0	2	1	0	.296	.296	.407	.704	120	11	0	
1932	*21*	*BBB*	*NSL*	*3*	*7*	*1*	*1*	*0*	*0*	*0*	*1*	*0*	*0*	*.143*	*.143*	*.143*	*.286*	*-10*	*1*	*0*	
		LVB	*NSL*	*1*	*4*	*0*	*1*	*0*	*1*	*0*	*1*	*0*	*0*	*.250*	*.250*	*.250*	*.500*	*57*	*1*	*0*	
		NEG	*NSL*	*7*	*16*	*4*	*6*	*1*	*0*	*0*	*1*	*1*	*0*	*.375*	*.375*	*.563*	*.938*	*192*	*9*	*0*	
1933 *	22	NEG	NN2	37	143	26	42	5	2	0	18	5	13	.294	.353	.357	.709	96	51	0	EWA
1934 *	23	NEG	NN2	37	148	25	50	3	2	1	20	10	8	.338	.376	.405	.781	114	60	1	EWA
1935	24	PC	NN2	51	207	49	70	13	8	2	32	8	24	.338	.412	.507	.919	131	105	2	
1936 *	25	PC	NN2	63	231	37	77	16	4	1	39	6	20	.333	.386	.450	.837	114	104	0	EWA
1937	26	TOTAL	NN2+IND	11	42	6	9	2	0	0	1	0	4	.214	.283	.262	.545	50	11	0	
		PC	*NN2*	*8*	*33*	*5*	*9*	*2*	*0*	*0*	*0*	*0*	*2*	*.273*	*.314*	*.333*	*.648*	*71*	*11*	*0*	
		SDS	*IND*	*3*	*9*	*1*	*0*	*0*	*0*	*0*	*1*	*0*	*2*	*.000*	*.182*	*.000*	*.182*	*-29*	*0*	*0*	
1938 *	27	PC	NN2	32	128	23	29	5	0	2	16	6	13	.227	.298	.313	.610	76	40	0	EWA
1939	28	HG	NN2	33	133	28	42	5	2	2	20	8	15	.316	.385	.429	.814	119	57	1	
1940	29	CBM	MEX	93	384	80	122	19	11	8	74	32	43	.318	.388	.487	.875	126	187	1	
1941	30	CBM	MEX	101	405	74	142	21	12	8	85	19	59	.351	.433	.521	.954	139	211	0	
1942 *	31	HG	NN2	42	150	23	40	4	3	1	26	4	21	.267	.357	.353	.710	108	53	0	EWA
1943 *	32	HG	NN2	71	262	53	68	4	2	1	40	17	32	.260	.347	.302	.648	73	79	3	EWA, NSA
1944 *	33	HG	NN2	55	212	45	56	8	5	1	33	9	31	.264	.358	.363	.721	94	77	0	EWA
1945	34	TOTAL	NN2+NAL	33	124	14	40	6	1	0	19	2	11	.323	.378	.387	.765	115	48	0	
		HG	*NN2*	*32*	*120*	*14*	*39*	*6*	*1*	*0*	*19*	*2*	*11*	*.325*	*.382*	*.392*	*.773*	*117*	*47*	*0*	
		CBE	*NAL*	*1*	*4*	*0*	*1*	*0*	*0*	*0*	*0*	*0*	*0*	*.250*	*.250*	*.250*	*.500*	*48*	*1*	*0*	
1946 *	35	HG	NN2	50	197	28	54	4	1	3	26	4	13	.274	.319	.350	.669	86	69	0	EWA
1947	36	HG	NN2	60	218	19	51	9	2	1	24	13	21	.234	.304	.307	.612	69	67	1	
1948	37	HG	NN2	40	151	29	39	6	0	2	13	6	19	.258	.345	.351	.696	105	53	1	
1949	38	HG	NN2																		Played in unrecorded Black league
1950	39	HG	NN2																		Played in unrecorded Black league
1951	40	Farnham	PROV																		Played in minor leagues (Integration)
17 Yrs			NgL	820	3162	564	939	131	57	33	488	150	347	.297	.368	.406	.774	112	1283	9	
162 Game Avg.			Pro	162	625	111	186	26	11	7	96	69	69	.297	.232	.061	.252	112	7994	2	
8 Yrs		HG	NN2	383	1443	239	389	46	17	11	201	63	163	.270	.346	.348	.694	92	502	5	
2 Yrs		CBM	MEX	194	789	154	264	40	23	16	159	51	102	.335	.411	.504	.916	133	398	1	
5 Yrs		PC	NN2	154	599	114	185	36	12	5	88	20	59	.309	.373	.434	.807	136	260	2	
3 Yrs		NEG	NSL+NN2	81	307	55	98	9	5	1	39	16	21	.319	.365	.391	.756	110	120	1	
1 Yr		SDS	IND	3	9	1	0	0	0	0	0	0	0	.000	.182	.000	.182	-29	0	0	
1 Yr		BBB	NSL	3	7	1	1	0	0	0	1	0	0	.143	.143	.143	.286	-10	1	0	
1 Yr		LVB	NSL	1	4	0	1	0	1	0	0	0	0	.250	.250	.250	.500	57	1	0	
1 Yr		CBE	NAL	1	4	0	1	0	0	0	0	0	0	.250	.250	.250	.500	48	1	0	
14 Yrs		HG	NN2	611	2333	404	666	90	33	17	327	98	243	.285	.355	.374	.729	99	873	8	
2 Yrs		CBM	MEX	194	789	154	264	40	23	16	159	51	102	.335	.411	.504	.916	133	398	1	
1 Yr		NSL	NSL	11	27	5	8	1	1	0	2	1	0	.296	.296	.407	.704	11	11	0	
1 Yr		IND	IND	3	9	1	0	0	0	0	0	0	2	.000	.182	.000	.182	-29	0	0	
1 Yr		NAL	NAL	1	4	0	1	0	0	0	0	0	0	.250	.250	.250	.500	48	1	0	

Sam Bankhead

Postseason Batting

Year	Age	Tm	Lg	Series	Opp	Rslt	G	AB	R	H	2B	3B	HR	RBI	SB	BB	BA	OBP	SLG	OPS	HBP
1932 □	21	NEG	NSL	NSC	CAG	L	2	6	0	0	0	0	0	0	0	0	.000	.000	.000	.000	0
1935 □	24	PC	NN2	NLC	NYC	W	7	21	5	8	0	0	0	2	1	4	.381	.480	.381	.861	0
1939	28	HG	NN2	NLP	PS	W	2	6	1	0	0	0	0	0	0	2	.000	.250	.000	.250	
1939	28	HG	NN2	NLC	BEG	L	5	18	2	6	0	0	0	1	0	2	.333	.400	.333	.733	0
1942	31	HG	NN2	WS	KCM	L	2	7	1	2	0	0	0	0	0	0	.286	.286	.286	.571	0
1943	32	HG	NN2	WS	BBB	W	5	19	1	5	1	0	0	3	0	1	.263	.300	.316	.616	0
1944	33	HG	NN2	WS	BBB	W	5	20	6	7	0	0	0	0	1	2	.350	.435	.350	.759	1
1945	34	HG	NN2	WS	CBE	L	4	16	0	1	0	0	0	0	0	0	.063	.063	.063	.125	0
1948	37	HG	NN2	NLC	BEG	W	4	14	5	3	2	0	0	0	0	2	.214	.353	.357	.670	1
1948 □	37	HG	NN2	WS	BBB	W	1	4	0	0	0	0	0	0	0	0	.000	.000	.000	.000	
7 Yrs (9 Series)			NgL				37	131	21	32	3	0	0	6	2	13	.244	.322	.267	.580	2
1 Yr				NLP			2	6	1	0	0	0	0	0	0	0	.000	.000	.000	.000	0
1 Yr				NSC			2	6	0	0	0	0	0	0	0	0	.000	.000	.000	.000	
3 Yrs				NLC			16	53	12	17	2	0	0	3	1	8	.321	.419	.358	.768	1
5 Yrs				WS			17	66	8	15	1	0	0	3	1	3	.227	.271	.242	.503	1

All-Star Batting

Year	Age	Lg	Game	G	AB	R	H	2B	3B	HR	RBI	SB	BB	BA	OBP	SLG	OPS	HBP
1933	22	WES	EWA	RF	4	2	2	0	0	0	0	1	0	.500	.500	.500	1.000	0
1934	23	WES	EWA	RF	3	0	1	0	0	0	0	0	0	.333	.333	.333	.667	0
1936	25	EAS	EWA	LF	4	1	2	1	0	0	0	0	0	.500	.500	.750	1.250	0
1938	27	EAS	EWA	CF/CF	8	0	2	0	0	0	1	1	1	.250	.333	.250	.583	0
1942	31	EAS	EWA	2B/2B	7	3	4	1	0	0	2	0	0	.571	.571	.714	1.286	0
1943	32	EAS	EWA	2B/2B	3	0	0	0	0	0	0	0	0	.000	.000	.000	.000	0
1943	32	SAS	NSA	SS	4	0	2	1	0	0	2	0	0	.500	.500	.750	1.250	0
1944	33	EAS	EWA	2B	2	1	1	0	0	0	1	0	0	.500	.500	.500	1.000	0
1946	35	EAS	EWA	SS	2	0	0	0	0	0	0	0	0	.000	.000	.000	.000	0
8 Yrs (11 GP)		NgL			37	7	14	3	0	0	6	2	1	.378	.395	.459	.854	0

John Beckwith
Standard Batting

Year	Age	Tm	Lg	G	AB	R	H	2B	3B	HR	RBI	SB	BB	BA	OBP	SLG	OPS	OPS+	TB	HBP	Awards
1919	19	COG	WES	4	17	1	3	1	1	0	0	0	1	.176	.222	.235	.458	45	4	0	
1920	20	COG	NNL	36	137	16	39	7	1	2	22	1	8	.285	.324	.394	.718	117	54	0	
1921	21	COG	NNL	47	186	34	69	13	5	4	35	4	14	.371	.415	.559	.974	183	104	0	
1922	22	CAG	NNL	67	226	44	81	21	5	7	52	11	20	.358	.415	.588	1.004	186	133	2	
1923	23	CAG	NNL	72	270	36	82	21	9	8	77	5	19	.304	.349	.537	.887	140	145	0	
1924	24	BBS	ECL	33	124	33	46	6	1	7	31	6	13	.371	.431	.605	1.035	194	75	0	
1925	25	BBS	ECL	50	183	47	74	14	1	15	64	3	24	.404	.473	.738	1.211	217	135	0	
1926	26	BBS	ECL+IND	56	206	43	66	17	4	9	55	4	20	.320	.386	.573	.959	163	118	2	
1926	26	*TOTAL*	*ECL*	*54*	*199*	*42*	*66*	*17*	*4*	*9*	*54*	*4*	*19*	*.332*	*.393*	*.593*	*.986*	*170*	*118*	*1*	
		BBS	*ECL*	*28*	*90*	*19*	*30*	*11*	*1*	*4*	*24*	*1*	*8*	*.333*	*.394*	*.611*	*1.005*	*179*	*55*	*1*	
		HBG	*ECL*	*26*	*109*	*23*	*36*	*6*	*3*	*5*	*30*	*3*	*11*	*.330*	*.392*	*.578*	*.970*	*163*	*63*	*0*	
		HG	*IND*	*2*	*7*	*1*	*0*	*0*	*0*	*0*	*1*	*0*	*1*	*.000*	*.222*	*.000*	*.222*	*-44*	*0*	*1*	
1927	27	HBG	ECL	67	266	62	94	20	3	9	61	0	18	.353	.399	.553	.951	146	147	2	
1928	28	HG	EAS	19	72	8	22	2	2	1	10	0	2	.306	.333	.431	.764	106	31	1	
1929	29	HG	ANL	56	207	57	80	17	2	14	60	2	22	.386	.448	.691	1.139	175	143	1	
		TOTAL	*ANL*	*47*	*176*	*45*	*64*	*13*	*2*	*13*	*52*	*2*	*18*	*.364*	*.426*	*.682*	*1.107*	*170*	*120*	*1*	
		HG	*ANL*	*9*	*31*	*12*	*16*	*4*	*0*	*1*	*8*	*0*	*4*	*.516*	*.571*	*.742*	*1.313*	*205*	*23*	*0*	
		NLG	*ANL*																		
1930	30	NLG	EAS	23	74	25	36	7	3	6	33	4	8	.486	.537	.905	1.442	221	67	0	
1931	31	BBS	IND	33	112	26	38	4	1	12	35	0	10	.339	.393	.714	1.108	220	80	0	
1932	32	NWB	EWL	2	8	2	3	0	0	1	4	0	0	.375	.375	.875	1.250	240	7	0	
1933	33	NBY	IND	16	61	9	21	5	0	2	15	0	6	.344	.403	.525	.928	163	32	0	
1934	34	*TOTAL*	*NN2+IND*	14	29	6	7	3	1	0	4	0	2	.241	.290	.621	.911	13	18	0	
		ND	*NN2*	*1*	*3*	*0*	*0*	*0*	*0*	*0*	*0*	*0*	*0*	*.000*	*.000*	*.000*	*.000*	*0*	*0*	*0*	
		NBY	*IND*	*13*	*26*	*6*	*7*	*3*	*1*	*2*	*4*	*0*	*2*	*.269*	*.321*	*.692*	*1.014*	*199*	*18*	*0*	
1935	35	HG	NN2	6	15	5	2	1	0	0	1	0	2	.133	.235	.200	.435	13	3	0	
1936	36	BRG	IND	1	1	0	1	0	0	0	2	0	2	1.000	1.000	4.000	5.000	1208	4	0	
1937	37	BRG	IND	3	3	0	1	0	0	0	0	0	0	.333	.333	.333	.667	98	0	0	
18 Yrs (+1)			NgL	601	2180	449	762	159	38	100	561	44	188	.350	.403	.595	.998	158	1297	8	2
162 Game Avg.			Pro	162	588	121	205	43	10	27	151	12	51	.350	.403	.595	.998	158	350	2	
1 Yr			Pre-NgL	4	17	1	3	1	1	0	0	0	1	.176	.222	.235	.458	45	4	0	
19 Yrs			Pre-NgL+NgL	605	2197	450	765	160	38	100	561	44	189	.348	.402	.592	.994	157	1301	8	2
162 Game Avg.			Pre-NgL+Pro	162	588	120	205	43	10	27	150	12	51	.348	.402	.592	.994	157	348	2	
4 Yrs		BBS	ECL+IND	142	509	125	188	35	4	38	154	13	55	.369	.432	.678	1.110	205	345	4	1
2 Yrs		CAG	NNL	139	496	80	163	42	14	15	129	16	39	.329	.380	.560	.940	161	278	2	
2 Yrs		HBG	ECL	95	375	85	130	26	6	14	91	4	29	.347	.397	.560	.957	155	210	2	
2 Yrs		COG	NNL+WES	83	323	50	108	20	6	6	57	5	22	.334	.377	.489	.866	139	158	0	
2 Yrs		HG	EAS+IND	74	270	54	88	16	4	14	64	2	23	.326	.385	.570	.956	154	154	3	
2 Yrs		NLG	ANL+EAS	32	105	37	52	11	3	7	41	4	12	.495	.547	.857	1.404	216	90	0	
1 Yr		NBY	IND	29	87	15	28	8	1	4	19	0	0	.322	.379	.575	.954	199	50	0	
1 Yr		NWB	EWL	2	8	2	3	0	0	1	4	0	0	.375	.375	.875	1.250	240	7	0	
2 Yrs		BRG	IND	4	4	0	2	0	0	0	2	0	2	.500	.500	1.250	1.750	376	5	0	
1 Yr		ND	NN2	1	3	0	0	0	0	0	0	0	0	.000	.000	.000	.000	-100	0	0	
4 Yrs			NNL	222	819	130	271	62	20	21	186	21	61	.331	.379	.532	.911	159	436	2	
4 Yrs			ECL	204	772	184	280	57	9	40	210	17	74	.363	.420	.615	1.036	140	475	3	1
6 Yrs			IND	74	225	43	70	13	2	17	58	0	21	.311	.372	.613	.986	195	138	1	
1 Yr			ANL	56	207	57	80	17	2	14	60	2	22	.386	.448	.691	1.139	175	143	1	
2 Yrs			EAS	42	146	33	58	9	5	7	43	4	10	.397	.439	.671	1.111	164	98	1	
1 Yr			EWL	2	8	2	3	0	0	1	4	0	0	.375	.375	.875	1.250	240	7	0	
1 Yr			NN2	1	3	0	0	0	0	0	0	0	0	.000	.000	.000	.000	-100	0	0	

20. The Negro Leagues All-Star Register

James "Cool Papa" Bell
Holds NgL career records for games played, plate appearances (6438), at bats, runs scored, hits, total bases, bases on balls, and stolen bases

Standard Batting

Year	Age	Tm	Lg	G	AB	R	H	2B	3B	HR	RBI	SB	BB	BA	OBP	SLG	OPS	OPS+	TB	HBP	Awards
1922	19	SLS	NNL	18	40	6	15	3	1	1	5	0	0	.375	.405	.575	.980	153	23	2	
1923	20	SLS	NNL	49	108	24	26	5	1	2	17	1	7	.241	.287	.361	.648	58	39	0	
1924	21	SLS	NNL	65	242	52	73	12	3	1	33	12	20	.302	.355	.388	.743	88	94	0	
1925	22	SLS	NNL	87	380	94	132	33	6	10	58	30	30	.347	.395	.545	.940	133	207		
1926	23	SLS	NNL	91	386	107	129	27	7	12	58	36	48	.334	.413	.534	.947	124	206	4	
1927	24	SLS	NNL	97	419	90	131	23	5	5	39	21	31	.313	.360	.427	.787	112	179	0	
1928	25	SLS	NNL	79	338	81	112	21	6	6	41	19	32	.331	.391	.482	.873	127	163	1	
1929	26	SLS	NNL	97	391	98	125	26	5	3	40	49	49	.320	.397	.435	.832	117	170	1	
		TOTAL	NNL	93	374	95	122	26	5	3	39	49	48	.326	.404	.447	.851	122	167	1	
	—	SLS	NNL	4	17	3	3	0	0	0	1	0	1	.176	.222	.176	.399	5	3	0	
1930	27	SLS	NNL	79	342	104	121	19	5	6	56	11	35	.354	.417	.491	.908	140	168	2	
1931	28	SLS	NNL	33	132	46	38	7	2	1	18	16	24	.288	.397	.394	.791	103	52	0	
1932	29	TOTAL	EWL+IND	57	223	61	79	14	9	0	30	15	24	.354	.424	.498	.922	148	111	3	
		TOTAL	EWL	39	159	40	54	9	3	0	18	9	14	.340	.397	.434	.831	124	69	1	
		DW	EWL	29	119	28	38	6	2	0	13	8	11	.319	.382	.403	.785	111	48	1	
		HG	EWL	10	40	12	16	3	1	0	5	1	3	.400	.442	.525	.967	164	21	0	
		TOTAL	IND	18	64	21	25	5	6	0	12	6	10	.391	.487	.656	1.143	206	42	2	
		PC	IND	2	7	4	3	1	1	0	1	0	1	.429	.500	.857	1.357	260	6	0	
1932	29	KCM	IND	16	57	17	22	4	5	0	11	6	9	.386	.485	.632	1.117	199	36	2	EWA
1933 *	30	PC	NN2	73	295	62	89	12	4	2	28	16	28	.302	.364	.390	.754	107	115	1	EWA
1934 *	31	PC	NN2	69	272	52	89	10	3	1	28	14	34	.327	.404	.397	.801	127	108	1	EWA
1935 *	32	PC	NN2	49	197	68	68	14	6	2	30	12	31	.345	.434	.508	.942	137	100	0	EWA
1936 *	33	TOTAL	NN2+IND	44	178	43	53	5	2	1	22	7	19	.298	.365	.365	.731	92	65	0	
		PC	NN2	41	165	39	48	4	1	0	20	6	17	.291	.357	.358	.715	84	59	0	
1936	33	NAS	IND	3	13	4	5	1	1	1	2	1	2	.385	.467	.462	.928	187	6	0	
1937	34	TOTAL	NN2+IND	11	47	11	17	2	0	2	9	9	6	.362	.434	.532	.966	173	25	0	
		PC	NN2	8	36	9	13	2	0	2	7	1	3	.361	.410	.583	.994	158	21	0	
		SDS	IND	3	11	2	4	0	0	0	2	0	3	.364	.500	.364	.864	222	4	0	
1938	35													Played in unrecorded Mexican league							
1939	36													Played in unrecorded Mexican league							
1940	37	VEZ	MEX											No statistics available							
1941	38	ULT	MEX	89	382	119	167	29	15	12	79	28	45	.437	.496	.686	1.182	205	262	0	
1942 *	39	TOTAL	CBM	NAL-IND	100	421	85	132	21	15	4	48	14	65	.314	.407	.463	.870	118	195	1
		CAG	NAL	27	102	14	30	4	2	0	7	0	12	.294	.368	.373	.741	142	38		
	—	AAS	IND	26	98	14	29	4	2	0	7	0	12	.296	.373	.378	.750	136	37		
	—		IND	1	4	0	1	0	0	0	0	0	0	.250	.250	.250	.500	288	1		
1943 *	40	HG	NN2	64	259	63	92	11	5	0	30	12	35	.355	.432	.436	.868	131	113	0	EWA
1944 *	41	HG	NN2	52	211	43	68	8	3	1	24	4	36	.322	.421	.403	.824	122	85		EWA
1945	42	HG	NN2	44	164	34	48	6	1	1	19	10	31	.293	.405	.360	.765	116	59	0	
1946	43	HG	NN2	39	120	23	48	4	2	0	16	6	16	.400	.471	.467	.937	161	56	0	

James "Cool Papa" Bell
Standard Batting (continued)

Year	Age	Tm	Lg	G	AB	R	H	2B	3B	HR	RBI	SB	BB	BA	OBP	SLG	OPS	OPS+	TB	HBP	Awards
24 Yrs			NgL	1413	5649	1380	1882	316	108	73	735	334	658	.333	.404	.466	.870	127	2633	16	
162 Game Avg.			Pro	162	648	158	216	36	12	8	84	38	75	.333	.404	.466	.870	127	302	2	
10 Yrs		SLS	NNL	691	2761	699	899	176	41	47	364	195	275	.326	.389	.470	.859	119	1298	10	
6 Yrs		PC	NN2+IND	242	972	234	310	43	16	8	114	49	114	.319	.392	.421	.812	112	409	2	
5 Yrs		HG	EWL+NN2	209	794	175	272	32	12	2	94	33	121	.343	.430	.421	.850	132	334	0	
1 Yr		CBM	MEX	100	421	85	132	21	15	4	48	14	65	.314	.407	.463	.870	118	195	1	
1 Yr		ULT	MEX	89	382	119	167	29	15	12	79	28	45	.437	.496	.686	1.182	205	262	0	
2 Yrs		CAG	NNL+NAL	30	115	17	32	4	2	0	8	0	13	.278	.352	.348	.699	117	40	0	
1 Yr		DW	EWL	29	119	28	38	6	2	0	13	8	11	.319	.382	.403	.785	111	48	1	
1 Yr		KCM	IND	16	57	17	22	4	5	0	11	6	9	.386	.485	.632	1.117	199	36	2	
1 Yr		NAS	IND	3	13	4	5	1	0	0	2	1	2	.385	.467	.462	.928	187	6	0	
1 Yr		SDS	IND	3	11	2	4	0	0	0	2	0	3	.364	.500	.364	.864	222	4	0	
1 Yr		AAS	IND	1	4	0	1	0	0	0	0	0	0	.250	.250	.250	.500	288	1	0	
1 Yr		VEZ	MEX											No statistics available								
10 Yrs			NNL	695	2778	702	902	176	41	47	365	195	276	.325	.388	.468	.856	118	1301	10	
1 Yr			NAL	26	98	14	29	4	2	0	7	0	12	.296	.373	.378	.750	136	37	0	
1 Yr			EWL	39	159	40	54	9	3	0	18	9	14	.340	.397	.434	.831	124	69	1	
9 Yrs			NN2	439	1719	393	563	71	26	10	202	81	231	.328	.408	.417	.824	123	716	2	
2 Yrs			MEX	189	803	204	299	50	30	16	127	42	110	.372	.449	.569	1.018	159	457	1	
4 Yrs			IND	25	92	27	35	6	6	0	16	7	15	.380	.477	.576	1.053	209	53	2	

Postseason Batting

Year	Age	Tm	Lg	Series	Opp	Rslt	G	AB	R	H	2B	3B	HR	RBI	SB	BB	BA	OBP	SLG	OPS	HBP
1925	22	SLS	NNL	NNC	KCM	L	7	29	5	8	1	0	0	0	0	0	.276	.276	.310	.586	0
1928 □	25	SLS	NNL	NNC	CAG	W	7	27	7	11	0	1	0	5	4	4	.407	.484	.481	.965	0
1930 □	27	SLS	NNL	NNC	DS	W	6	24	5	7	3	0	1	3	3	1	.292	.370	.542	.912	0
1935 □	32	PC	NN2	NLC	NYC	W	7	23	2	3	0	0	0	1	0	3	.130	.231	.217	.448	0
1943 □	40	HG	NN2	WS	BBB	W	7	34	5	10	1	1	0	4	0	4	.294	.368	.382	.751	0
1944 □	41	HG	NN2	WS	BBB	W	5	24	1	6	0	0	0	3	2	0	.250	.250	.333	.583	0
1945	42	HG	NN2	WS	CBE	L	4	14	1	3	0	0	0	0	1	2	.214	.313	.286	.598	0
7 Yrs (7 Series)			NgL				43	175	26	48	6	4	1	16	10	16	.274	.335	.371	.707	0
3 Yrs			NNC				20	80	17	26	4	1	1	8	7	7	.325	.379	.438	.817	0
1 Yr			NLC				7	23	2	3	0	0	0	1	0	3	.130	.231	.217	.448	0
3 Yrs			WS				16	72	7	19	1	1	0	7	3	6	.264	.321	.347	.668	0

All-Star Batting

Year	Age	Lg	Game	Tm	G	AB	R	H	2B	3B	HR	RBI	SB	BB	BA	OBP	SLG	OPS	HBP
1933	30	EAS	EWA		CF	5	1	0	0	0	0	0	0	0	.000	.000	.000	.000	0
1934	31	EAS	EWA		CF	4	1	1	0	0	0	0	0	1	.250	.250	.250	.500	0
1935	32	WES	EWA		CF	4	2	1	1	0	0	1	0	2	.250	.500	.250	.750	0
1936	33	EAS	EWA		CF	3	1	3	3	0	0	1	0	0	1.000	1.000	1.333	2.333	0
1942	39	WES	EWA		RF/RF	6	0	2	0	0	0	0	0	0	.333	.333	.333	.667	0
1943	40	EAS	EWA		LF	4	0	0	0	0	0	0	0	0	.000	.250	.333	.583	0
1944	41	EAS	EWA		LF	5	0	0	0	0	0	0	0	0	.000	.000	.000	.000	0
7 Yrs (8 GP)		NgL			8	30	5	6	1	0	0	1	2	3	.200	.273	.233	.506	0

20. The Negro Leagues All-Star Register

Irvin "Chester" Brooks
Standard Batting

Year	Age	Tm	Lg	G	AB	R	H	2B	3B	HR	RBI	SB	BB	BA	OBP	SLG	OPS	OPS+	TB	HBP	Awards
1918	27	BRG	EAS	19	67	5	16	0	0	0	1	1	6	.239	.301	.239	.540	59	16	0	
1919	28	BRG	EAS	14	41	8	13	3	1	0	5	2	4	.317	.378	.439	.817	142	18	0	
1920	29	BRG	EAS	18	67	8	16	1	0	1	6	0	3	.239	.282	.299	.580	109	20	1	
1921	30	BRG	EAS	11	45	10	17	4	0	0	7	3	3	.378	.417	.467	.883	111	21	0	
1922	31	BRG	IND	7	30	7	13	3	3	1	10	1	2	.433	.469	.833	1.302	281	25	0	
1923	32	BRG	ECL	10	42	8	16	3	0	3	6	0	2	.381	.409	.667	1.076	208	28	0	
1924	33	BRG	ECL	36	136	16	41	4	1	2	19	2	12	.301	.358	.390	.748	119	53		
1925	34	BRG	ECL	34	119	24	41	2	0	6	32	1	12	.345	.405	.513	.917	139	61		
1926	35	BRG	ECL	26	88	9	25	5	1	1	16	3	12	.284	.370	.398	.768	122	35	0	
1927	36	BRG	ECL	33	124	21	35	6	3	4	25	0	15	.282	.364	.476	.840	123	59	1	
1928	37	BRG	EAS	9	35	5	10	2	0	1	7	0	2	.286	.342	.429	.771	113	15	1	
1929	38	BRG	IND	6	22	2	5	1	0	0	0	0	0	.227	.261	.273	.534	84	6	0	
1930	39	BRG	EAS	13	48	7	20	3	0	1	9	1	4	.417	.462	.542	1.003	141	26	0	
1931	40	BRG	IND	2	5	0	0	0	0	0	0	0	1	.000	.167	.000	.167	-44	0	0	
1933	42	BRG	IND	1	4	0	1	0	0	0	1	0	0	.250	.250	.250	.500	40	1	0	
13 Yrs (+2)			NgL	206	765	117	240	34	8	20	138	11	69	.314	.373	.458	.830	153	350	3	
162 Game Avg.				162	602	92	189	27	6	16	109	9	54	.314	.373	.458	.830	153	275	2	
2 Yrs			Pre-NgL	33	108	10	29	3	1	0	6	3	10	.269	.331	.315	.645	91	34	0	
15 Yrs			Pre-NgL+NgL	239	873	127	269	37	9	20	144	14	79	.308	.368	.440	.807	145	384	3	
162 Game Avg.			Pre-NgL+Pro	162	592	86	182	25	6	14	98	9	54	.308	.368	.440	.807	145	260	2	
13 Yrs		BRG	EAS+ECL+IND	206	765	117	240	34	8	20	138	11	69	.314	.373	.458	.830	153	350	3	
5 Yrs		ECL		139	509	78	158	20	5	16	98	6	53	.310	.377	.464	.840	146	236	1	
6 Yrs		EAS		51	195	30	63	10	0	3	29	4	12	.323	.368	.421	.789	168	116	2	
4 Yrs		IND		16	61	9	19	4	3	1	11	1	4	.311	.354	.525	.878	168	32	0	

Willard Brown
EXTENDED BATTING RECORD

Year	Age	Tm	Lg	G	AB	R	H	2B	3B	HR	RBI	SB	BB	BA	OBP	SLG	OPS	OPS+	TB	HBP	Awards
1935	20	KCM	IND	13	47	8	16	3	0	5	13	2	5	.340	.404	.723	1.127	202	34	0	
1936 *	21	KCM	IND	11	47	11	18	1	2	1	10	3	1	.383	.396	.553	.949	156	26	0	EWA
1937 *	22	KCM	NAL	53	200	47	76	10	10	10	57	10	17	**.380**	.431	**.680**	**1.111**	**212**	**136**	1	EWA
1938	23	KCM	NAL	**42**	160	32	55	13	4	6	43	19	10	.344	.382	.588	.970	173	**94**	0	
1939	24	KCM	NAL	44	174	37	64	15	7	3	42	8	9	**.368**	**.399**	**.586**	**.985**	**186**	**102**	0	
1940	25	KCM	NAL+MEX	72	301	49	104	18	4	8	61	13	10	.346	.367	.512	.878	127	154	0	
–	–	KCM	NAL	2	7	0	0	0	0	0	0	0	0	.000	.000	.000	.000	-100	0	0	
–	–	JNL	MEX	70	294	49	104	18	4	8	61	13	10	.354	.375	.524	.899	132	154	0	
1941	26	KCM	NAL	33	128	28	42	6	4	5	29	9	13	.328	.390	.555	.945	196	71	0	
–	–	VEZ	MEX											No statistics recorded							
1941-42		Humacao-Arecibo	PRWL	35	122	22	50	13	4	4	26	2	8	.410		.680			83		
1942 *	27	KCM	NAL	35	142	25	48	6	2	4	26	2	8	.338	.373	.493	.866	172	70	0	EWA
1943 *	28	KCM	NAL	53	197	33	67	13	2	7	31	4	16	**.340**	**.390**	**.533**	**.923**	**194**	**105**	0	EWA, NSA
1944	29	KCM	NAL	1	4	0	1	0	0	0	0	0	0	.250	.250	.250	.500	60	1	0	
1945	30										Did not play in major or minor leagues (Military Service)										
1946	31	KCM	NAL	36	137	27	44	10	5	3	25	3	7	.321	.354	.533	.887	163	73	0	
1946-47		Santurce	PRWL		254	44	99	25	4	9	50	9	12	.390		.626			159		
1947	32	TOTAL	NAL+AL	60	226	34	71	19	7	6	56	7	12	.314	.349	.540	.889	132	104	0	
–	–	KCM	NAL	39	159	30	59	16	7	5	50	2	12	**.371**	**.415**	**.654**	**1.069**	**187**	**104**	0	
–	–	SLB	AL	21	67	4	12	3	0	1	6	0	0	.179	.179	.269	.448	22			
1947-48		Santurce	PRWL		234	79	101	20	5	27	86		22	.432	.476	.906			212		
1948 *	33	KCM	NAL	44	166	40	67	22	2	6	53	7	22	**.404**		**.669**	**1.145**	**200**	**111**	1	EWA
1948-49		Santurce	PRWL		294	59	95	20	3	18	69			.323		.595			175		
1949	34	KCM	NAL											Did not play in unrecorded Black league							
1949-50		Santurce	PRWL		331	65	117	21	6	16	97	6		.353		.598			198		MVP-1
1950	35	Ottawa	BORD	30	128	1	45	7	1	1	1	1		.352		.445			57		
1950-51		Santurce	PRWL		305	57	99	19	3	14	76	3		.325		.544			166		
1951	36	TOTAL	MEX											Played in unrecorded Mexican league							
–	–	Jalisco	MEX											Played in unrecorded Mexican league							
–	–	Nuevo Laredo																				
1951-52		Santurce	PRWL		112	14	33	4	1	4	22	0	5	.295		.455			51		
1952-53		Santurce	PRWL	138	114	20	39	7	0	3	20	3	35	.342	.357	.482	.876		55		
1953	38	Dallas	TL		522	91	162	36	2	23	108			.310		.519			271	3	
1953-54		Santurce	PRWL		151	16	40	6	1	4	22	2		.265		.397			60		
1954	39	TOTAL	TL	144	**583**	**92**	**183**	**36**	**4**	**35**	**120**		**35**	.314	.353	.569	.922		**332**	**0**	
–	–	Dallas	TL	108																	
–	–	Houston	TL	36																	
1955	40	Houston	TL	149	544	73	164	34	4	19	104	3	39	.301	.348	.483	.832		263	0	
1956	41	TOTAL	TL+WL	127	**436**	**61**	**130**	**19**	**0**	**17**	**87**	2	**41**	.298	.360	.459	.819		**200**	1	
–	–	Austin	TL	22																	
–	–	San Antonio	TL	54																	
–	–	Tulsa	TL	28																	
–	–	Topeka	WL	23	85	11	25	2	0	3	14	0	5	.294	.333	.424	.757		36	0	
1956-57		Santurce	PRWL		23	2	6	0	0	2	5			.261		.522			12		
1957	42	Minot	MDAK											Played in unrecorded independent league							

Willard Brown
EXTENDED BATTING RECORD (continued)

Year Age	Tm	Lg	G	AB	R	H	2B	3B	HR	RBI	SB	BB	BA	OBP	SLG	OPS	OPS+	TB	HBP	Awards
PROFESSIONAL TOTALS			497	1929	371	673	136	49	64	446	89	130	.349	.391	.570	.960	172	1099	2	
12 yrs		NgL	476	1862	367	661	133	49	63	440	87	130	.355	.398	.581	.978	178	1081	2	
1 yr		AL	21	67	4	12	3	0	1	6	2	0	.179	.179	.269	.448	22	0	0	
162 Game Avg.		Pro	162	629	121	219	44	16	21	145	29	42	.349	.391	.570	.960	172	358	1	
10 Yrs		PRWL		1940	378	679	135	27	101	473			.350		.604	.954		1171		
MINOR LEAGUE TOTALS		4 yrs	439	1669	245	520	98	7	76	316	7	111	.312	.356	.515	.871		860	4	
3 yrs		TL	386	1456	233	450	89	6	72	301	7	106	.309	.358	.527	.884		767	4	
1 yr		BORD	30	128	1	45	7	1	1	1	0		.352		.445	.797		57		
1 yr		WL	23	85	11	25	2	0	3	14		5	.294	.333	.424	.757		36	0	
TOTALS AT ALL LEVELS OF PLAY			936	5538	994	1872	369	83	241	1235	96	241	.338	.366	.565	.931		3130	6	

Postseason Batting

Year	Age	Tm	Lg	Series	Opp	Rslt	G	AB	R	H	2B	3B	HR	RBI	SB	BB	BA	OBP	SLG	OPS	HBP
1937 □	22	KCM	NAL	ALC	CAG	W	4	16	4	6	1	0	0	2	2	0	.375	.375	.438	.813	0
1939 □	24	KCM	NAL	ALC	SLS	W	3	10	0	3		1	0	3	0	0	.300	.300	.600	.900	
1942 □	27	KCM	NAL	WS	HG	W	4	15	7	7			1	2	1	4	.467	.579	.867	1.446	0
1946	31	KCM	NAL	WS	NE	L	7	29	4	7		0	2	10	0	3	.241	.241	.483	.724	0
1948	33	KCM	NAL	ALC	BBB	L	7	28	4	10	3		0	5	0	1	.357	.379	.571	.951	0
1950		Santurce	PRWL	CS	Carta	L	7	23	3	8		0	0	3		0	.348	.348	.391	.739	
1951 □	36	Santurce	PRWL	CS	Vaega	W	5	20	4	5		0	1	3	0	0	.250	.250	.400	.650	
1953 □	38	Santurce	PRWL	CS		W	6	24	8	10	3	0	4	13	0	5	.417	.417	1.042	1.458	0
8 Yrs (8 Series)							43	165	34	56	11	2	9	41	8	5	.339	.359	.594	.953	0
3 Yrs			NgL	ALC			14	54	8	19	5	1	1	10	3	1	.352	.364	.537	.901	0
2 Yrs			NgL	WS			11	44	11	14		2	3	12	4	4	.318	.375	.614	.989	0
3 Yrs			PRWL	CS			18	67	15	23	4	0	5	19	1	0	.343	.343	.627	.970	

Roy Campanella
Standard Batting

Year	Age	Tm	Lg	G	AB	R	H	2B	3B	HR	RBI	SB	BB	BA	OBP	SLG	OPS	OPS+	TB	HBP	Awards
1937	15	WEG	NN2	6	18	2	3	1	0	0	0	0	1	.167	.211	.222	.433	12	4	0	
1938	16	BEG	NN2	9	30	4	6	0	0	0	2	0	1	.200	.226	.200	.426	30	6	0	
1939	17	BEG	NN2	16	42	6	8	1	0	0	4	0	3	.190	.244	.214	.459	25	9		
1940	18	BEG	NN2	32	107	15	28	4	1	5	21	1	2	.262	.275	.458	.733	83	49		
1941 *	19	BEG	NN2	27	87	17	30	8	3	4	26	2	11	.345	.418	.644	1.062	205	56		EWA
1942 *	20	BEG	NN2	41	146	24	43	5	3	1	34	1	14	.295	.356	.390	.747	114	57		EWA
1943	21	MON	MEX																		ASG
1944 *	22	TOTAL	NN2	32	134	28	52	13	2	3	30	4	5	.388	.410	.582	.992	169	78		EWA
		BEG	*NN2*	*31*	*129*	*26*	*51*	*13*	*2*	*3*	*30*	*3*	*5*	*.395*	*.418*	*.597*	*1.015*	*166*	*77*		
	–	*PS*	*NN2*	*1*	*5*	*2*	*1*	*0*	*0*	*0*	*0*	*1*	*0*	*.200*	*.200*	*.200*	*.400*	*3*	*1*		
1945 *	23	BEG	NN2	52	182	48	70	16	3	5	43	1	32	.385	.479	.588	1.067	192	107	1	EWA
1946	24	Nashua	NENL							Played in minor leagues (Integration)											MVP-1
1947	25	Montreal	IL							Played in minor leagues (Integration)											MVP-1
1948	26	BRO	NL	83	279	32	72	11	3	9	45	3	36	.258	.345	.416	.761	102	116	1	MVP-21
1949 *	27	BRO	NL	130	436	65	125	22	2	22	82	3	67	.287	.385	.498	.883	131	217	3	ASG,MVP-15
1950 *	28	BRO	NL	126	437	70	123	19	3	31	89	1	55	.281	.364	.551	.916	134	241	2	ASG,MVP-13
1951 *	29	BRO	NL	143	505	90	164	33	1	33	108	1	53	.325	.393	.590	.983	159	298	4	ASG,MVP-1
1952 *	30	BRO	NL	128	468	73	126	18	1	22	97	8	57	.269	.352	.453	.805	120	212	3	ASG,MVP-10
1953 *	31	BRO	NL	144	519	103	162	26	3	41	142	4	67	.312	.395	.611	1.006	154	317	4	ASG,MVP-1
1954 *	32	BRO	NL	111	397	43	82	14	3	19	51	1	42	.207	.285	.401	.686	74	159	2	ASG
1955 *	33	BRO	NL	123	446	81	142	20	1	32	107	2	56	.318	.395	.583	.978	152	260	6	ASG,MVP-1
1956 *	34	BRO	NL	124	388	39	85	6	1	20	73	1	66	.219	.333	.394	.727	88	153	1	ASG
1957	35	BRO	NL	103	330	31	80	9	0	13	62	1	34	.242	.316	.388	.703	82	128	4	
18 Yrs (+3)			Pro	**1430**	**4951**	**771**	**1401**	**226**	**30**	**260**	**1017**	**34**	**602**	**.283**	**.363**	**.498**	**.861**	**125**	**2467**	**31**	
8 Yrs			NgL	215	746	144	240	48	12	18	161	9	69	.322	.380	.491	.871	137	366	1	
10 Yrs			MLB	1215	4205	627	1161	178	18	242	856	25	533	.276	.362	.500	.860	123	2101	30	
162 Game Avg.			Pro	**162**	**561**	**87**	**159**	**26**	**3**	**29**	**115**	**4**	**68**	**.283**	**.363**	**.498**	**.861**	**125**	**279**	**4**	
10 Yrs		BRO	NL	1215	4205	627	1161	178	18	242	856	25	533	.276	.360	.500	.860	123	2101	30	
7 Yrs		BEG	NN2	208	723	140	236	47	12	18	160	8	68	.326	.385	.499	.884	141	361	1	
1 Yr		WEG	NN2	6	18	2	3	1	0	0	0	0	1	.167	.211	.222	.433	12	4	0	
1 Yr		PS	NN2	1	5	2	1	0	0	0	0	1	0	.200	.200	.200	.400	3	1		
10 Yrs			NL	1215	4205	627	1161	178	18	242	856	25	533	.276	.360	.500	.861	123	2101	30	
8 Yrs			NN2	215	746	144	240	48	12	18	161	9	69	.322	.372	.491	.862	137	366	1	

Roy Campanella

Postseason Batting

Year	Age	Tm	Lg	Series	Opp	Rslt	G	AB	R	H	2B	3B	HR	RBI	SB	BB	BA	OBP	SLG	OPS	HBP
1939	17	BEG	NN2	NLP		W	4	13	2	4	0	0	0	2	0	2	.308	.400	.308	.708	
1939 □	17	BEG	NN2	NLC	HG	W	5	17	3	6	1	0	1	6	0	0	.353	.353	.588	.941	0
1949	27	BRO	NL	WS	NYY	L	5	15	2	4	1	0	1	2	0	3	.267	.389	.533	.922	0
1952	30	BRO	NL	WS	NYY	L	7	28	0	6	0	0	0	1	0	1	.214	.241	.214	.456	0
1953	31	BRO	NL	WS	NYY	L	6	22	6	6	0	0	1	2	0	2	.273	.360	.409	.769	1
1955 □	33	BRO	NL	WS	NYY	W	7	27	4	7	3	0	2	4	0	3	.259	.333	.593	.926	0
1956	34	BRO	NL	WS	NYY	L	7	22	2	4	1	0	0	3	0	3	.182	.280	.227	.507	0
6 Yrs (7 Series)			**Pro**				**41**	**144**	**19**	**37**	**6**	**0**	**5**	**20**	**0**	**14**	**.257**	**.327**	**.403**	**.726**	**1**
1 Yr (2 Series)			NgL	NLP			9	30	5	10	1	0	1	8	0	2	.333	.375	.467	.842	0
1 Yr				NLP			4	13	3	4	0	0	0	2	0	2	.308	.400	.308	.708	0
1 Yr				NLC			5	17	3	6	1	0	1	6	0	0	.353	.353	.588	.941	0
5 Yrs (5 Series)			MLB	WS			32	114	14	27	5	0	4	12	0	12	.237	.315	.386	.695	1
5 Yrs (5 Series)				WS			32	114	14	27	5	0	4	12	0	12	.237	.315	.386	.695	1

All-Star Batting

Year	Age	Lg	Game	G	AB	R	H	2B	3B	HR	RBI	SB	BB	BA	OBP	SLG	OPS	HBP
1941	19	BEG	NN2	C	5	0	1	0	0	0	0	0	0	.200	.200	.200	.400	0
1942	20	BEG	NN2		DNP													
1944	22	BEG	NN2	3B	1	1	1	0	0	1	1	0	0	1.000	1.000	1.000	2.000	0
1945	23	BEG	NN2	C	5	5	1	2	0	0	0	0	0	.200	.200	.600	.800	0
1949	27	BRO	NL	C	2	0	0	0	0	0	0	0	1	.000	.333	.000	.333	0
1950	28	BRO	NL	C	6	0	0	0	0	0	0	0	0	.000	.000	.000	.000	0
1951	29	BRO	NL	C	4	0	0	0	0	0	0	0	0	.000	.000	.000	.000	0
1952	30	BRO	NL	C	1	0	0	0	0	0	0	0	0	.000	.000	.000	.000	0
1953	31	BRO	NL	C	4	1	1	0	0	0	0	0	1	.250	.500	.250	.500	0
1954	32	BRO	NL	C	3	0	1	0	0	0	0	0	0	.333	.500	.333	.833	0
1955	33	BRO	NL															
1956	34	BRO	NL		1	0	0	0	0	0	0	0	0					0
12 Yrs (10 GP)		**Pro**		**9**	**31**	**7**	**5**	**2**	**0**	**0**	**1**	**0**	**3**	**.161**	**.235**	**.226**	**.461**	**0**
4 Yrs (3 GP)		NgL		4	11	6	3	2	0	0	1	0	0	.273	.273	.455	.727	0
8 Yrs (7 GP)		MLB		5	20	1	2	0	0	0	0	0	3	.100	.217	.100	.317	0

Oscar Charleston

Holds NgL career record for extra-base hits; hit .300+ in 19 different seasons; holds professional record for hitting .300+ in all six professional leagues in which he played (broke Hugh Duffy's record of four professional leagues)

Standard Batting

Year	Age	Tm	Lg	G	AB	R	H	2B	3B	HR	RBI	SB	BB	BA	OBP	SLG	OPS	OPS+	TB	HBP	Awards
1915	18	ABC	WES	57	221	31	57	9	5	2	31	14	13	.258	.302	.371	.670	99	82	1	
1916	19	TOTAL	EAS+WES	33	122	25	39	1	3	0	13	7	14	.320	.390	.377	.767	122	46	0	
–	–	NLS	EAS	15	64	18	22	0	1	0	4	5	8	.344	.417	.375	.792	124	24	0	
–	–	ABC	WES	18	58	7	17	1	2	0	9	2	6	.293	.359	.379	.739	120	22	0	
1917	20	ABC	WES	48	178	26	52	6	4	1	19	3	14	.292	.354	.388	.731	146	69	3	
1918	21	ABC	WES	40	154	39	60	8	8	3	46	13	13	.390	.437	.604	1.041	196	93	0	
1919	22	TOTAL	WES	46	180	48	72	9	6	8	45	16	19	**.400**	.460	.650	1.107	235	117	1	
–	–	CAG	WES	41	164	44	67	7	6	8	42	13	17	.409	.467	.671	1.135	245	110	1	
–	–	DS	WES	5	16	4	5	2	0	0	3	3	2	.313	.389	.438	.826	134	7	0	
1920	23	ABC	NNL	92	346	80	122	20	11	5	59	20	37	.353	.418	.517	.932	176	179	2	
1921	24	SLG	NNL	77	284	104	123	17	12	**15**	91	32	41	**.433**	**.512**	**.736**	**1.241**	**250**	209	5	
1922	25	ABC	NNL	**101**	**401**	**105**	**150**	**25**	**18**	**19**	**102**	21	41	.374	.433	.668	1.100	193	**268**	1	
1923	26	ABC	NNL	84	308	68	112	25	6	11	94	**25**	48	.364	.453	.591	1.040	168	182	2	
1924	27	HBG	ECL	54	205	63	83	22	5	**15**	63	20	28	**.405**	**.476**	**.780**	**1.257**	**252**	160		
1925	28	HBG	ECL	71	255	97	109	23	3	**20**	97	17	**51**	.427	.523	.776	1.299	228	198		
1926	29	TOTAL	ECL+IND	50	177	45	56	12	1	11	46	25	35	.316	.442	.582	1.011	177	103	5	
–	–	HBG	ECL	48	169	43	52	12	1	11	43	**24**	34	.308	.438	.568	.992	174	96	5	
–	–	HG	IND	2	8	2	4	0	0	0	3	1	1	.500	.556	.875	1.431	245	7	0	
1927	30	HBG	ECL	69	248	68	99	20	7	**13**	74	21	**49**	.399	.502	.694	1.192	209	172	2	
1928	31	HIL	EAS	60	207	54	72	11	**6**	11	44	11	**40**	**.348**	**.453**	**.618**	**1.072**	**184**	**128**	0	
1929	32	TOTAL	ANL	**82**	291	71	106	**25**	7	7	64	8	**56**	.364	.471	.570	1.037	152	166	3	
–	–	HIL	ANL	78	278	69	100	**23**	7	7	62	8	54	.360	.469	.568	1.032	151	158	3	
–	–	HG	ANL	4	13	2	6	2	0	0	2	0	2	.462	.533	.615	1.149	183	8	0	
1930	33	HG	EAS	53	217	47	68	17	2	**12**	55	7	18	.313	.371	.576	.942	134	125	2	
1931	34	HG	IND	48	189	36	63	**14**	6	3	33	1	18	.333	.394	.519	.910	157	98	1	
1932	35	PC	IND	**67**	**244**	**45**	**78**	**16**	4	4	39	**16**	27	.320	.392	.467	.855	133	114	2	
1933 *	36	PC	NN2	69	257	**66**	86	**19**	**7**	**13**	66	7	24	.335	.396	.615	1.006	172	158	2	EWA
1934 *	37	PC	NN2	59	199	35	64	10	2	7	41	5	27	.322	.410	.497	.900	156	99	**3**	EWA
1935 *	38	PC	NN2	41	155	21	42	10	1	2	29	8	16	.271	.343	.387	.726	84	60	1	EWA
1936	39	TOTAL	NN2+IND	35	104	19	36	9	0	4	20	0	15	.346	.433	.548	.977	155	57	1	
–	–	PC	NN2	32	93	18	32	8	0	4	18	0	13	.344	.430	.559	.984	152	52	1	
–	–	NAS	IND	3	11	1	4	1	0	0	2	0	2	.364	.462	.455	.916	183	5	0	
1937	40	PC	NN2	15	41	4	9	2	0	0	6	0	2	.220	.273	.341	.597	61	14	1	
1938	41	PC	NN2	1	1	0	0	0	0	0	0	0	0	.000	.000	.000	.000	-100	0	0	
1939	42	TOTAL	NN2+NAL	14	46	9	13	0	0	1	4	0	7	.283	.391	.769	1.118		18		
–	–	TC	NN2	7	25	5	7	1	0	0	1	0	4	.280	.379	.320	.699	92	8		
–	–	TC	NAL	7	21	4	6	1	0	1	3	0	3	.286	.375	.476	.851	148	10		
1940	43	TIC	NAL	6	13	2	5	0	0	0	2	1	3	.385	.500	.385	.885	176	5		
1941	44	PS	NN2	1	1	1	0	0	0	0	0	0	2	.000	.667	.000	.667	100	0		

Oscar Charleston
Standard Batting (continued)

Year	Age	Tm	Lg	G	AB	R	H	2B	3B	HR	RBI	SB	BB	BA	OBP	SLG	OPS	OPS+	TB	HBP	Awards
22 Yrs (+5)			NgL	1149	4189	1040	1496	299	98	174	1029	245	585	.357	.440	.600	1.043	179	2513	33	
162 Game Avg.			Pro	162	591	147	211	42	14	25	145	35	82	.357	.440	.600	1.043	179	354	5	
5 Yrs			Pre-NgL	224	855	169	280	33	26	14	154	53	73	.327	.384	.476	.862	158	407	5	
27 Yrs			Pre-NgL+NgL	1373	5044	1209	1776	332	124	188	1183	298	658	.352	.431	.579	1.012	176	2920	38	
162 Game Avg.			Pre-NgL+Pro	162	595	143	210	39	15	22	140	35		.352	.431	.579	1.012	176			
8 yrs		PC	NN2+IND	285	991	190	311	65	14	31	199	36	111	.314	.388	.502	.894	139	497	10	
3 Yrs		ABC	NNL	277	1055	253	384	70	35	35	255	66	126	.364	.434	.596	1.032	180	629	5	
4 Yrs		HBG	ECL	242	877	271	343	77	16	58	277	82	162	.391	.489	.714	1.207	218	626	7	
2 Yrs		HIL	EAS	138	485	123	172	34	13	18	106	19	94	.355	.462	.590	1.054	165	286	3	
4 Yrs		HG	ANL+EAS+IND	107	427	87	141	33	8	16	93	9	39	.330	.390	.557	.950	148	238	3	
1 Yr		SLG	NNL	77	284	104	123	17	12	15	91	32	41	.433	.512	.736	1.256	250	209	5	
2 Yrs		TC	NN2+NAL	14	46	9	13	2	0	1	4	0	7	.283	.377	.391	.769	118	18		
1 Yr		TIC	NAL	6	13	2	5	5	0	0	2	1	3	.385	.500	.385	.885	415	5		
1 Yr		NAS	IND	3	11	1	4	1	0	0	2	0	2	.364	.462	.455	.916	183	5	0	
4 Yrs			NNL	354	1339	357	507	87	47	50	346	98	167	.379	.451	.626	1.080	195	838	10	
4 Yrs			ECL	242	877	271	343	77	16	58	277	82	162	.391	.489	.714	1.207	218	626	7	
8 Yrs			NN2	225	772	150	240	50	10	27	161	20	88	.311	.387	.506	.897	139	391	8	
4 Yrs			IND	120	452	84	149	31	10	8	77	18	48	.330	.398	.496	.896	146	224	3	
2 Yrs			EAS	113	424	101	140	28	8	23	99	18	58	.330	.413	.597	1.012	177	253	2	
1 Yr			ANL	82	291	71	106	25	7	7	64	8	56	.364	.471	.570	1.046	152	166	3	
2 Yrs			NAL	13	34	6	11	1	0	1	5	1	6	.324	.425	.441	.866	159	15		

Postseason Batting

Year	Age	Tm	Lg	Series	Opp	Rslt	G	AB	R	H	2B	3B	HR	RBI	SB	BB	BA	OBP	SLG	OPS	HBP
1935 □	38	PC	NN2	NLC	NYC	W	7	26	4	8	0	0	3	5	0	4	.308	.400	.654	1.054	0
1 Yr (1 Series)			NgL				7	26	4	8	0	0	3	5	0	4	.308	.400	.654	1.054	0
1 Yr				NLC			7	26	4	8	0	0	3	5	0	4	.308	.400	.654	1.054	0

All-Star Batting

Year	Age			Lg	Game		G	AB	R	H	2B	3B	HR	RBI	SB	BB	BA	OBP	SLG	OPS	HBP
1933	36			EAS	EWA		1	2	2	0	0	0	0	0	0	0	.000	.000	.000	.000	2
1934	37			EAS	EWA		1	4	2	0	0	0	0	0	0	0	.000	.000	.000	.000	0
1935	38			WES	EWA		1	3	-1	0	0	0	0	0	0	0	.000	.000	.000	.000	0
3 Years (3 GP)				NgL			3	9	3	0	0	0	0	0	1	0	.000	.182	.000	.182	2

Ray Dandridge
Standard Batting

Year	Age	Tm	Lg	G	AB	R	H	2B	3B	HR	RBI	SB	BB	BA	OBP	SLG	OPS	OPS+	TB	HBP	Awards
1933	19	TOTAL	NN2	16	57	3	10	0	2	0	5	0	2	.182	.196	.255	.451	22	14	1	
		ID	NN2	14	55	3	10	0	2	0	5	0	1	.182	.196	.255	.451	21	14	1	
		NEG	NN2	2	2	0	0	0	0	0	0	0	1	.000	.500	.000	.500	51	0	0	
1934	20	ND	NN2	35	118	20	51	12	4	0	29	0	7	.432	.464	.602	1.066	165	71	0	EWA
1935 *	21	ND	NN2	39	150	19	45	9	5	0	20	6	5	.300	.323	.427	.749	87	64	0	
1936	22	NE	NN2	32	125	22	38	6	0	1	17	6	7	.304	.341	.376	.717	84	47	0	EWA
1937 *	23	TOTAL	NN2	36	136	25	51	10	3	0	31	5	11	.375	.422	.515	.936	137	70	0	
		NE	NN2	32	120	23	45	10	3	0	28	4	11	.375	.427	.508	.936	137	61	0	
		HG	NN2	4	16	2	6	0	0	0	3	1	0	.375	.375	.563	.938	139	9	0	
1938 *	24	NE	NN2	27	103	24	38	9	2	1	19	0	8	.369	.414	.524	.939	140	54	0	EWA
1939	25		MEX														Played in unrecorded Mexican league				
1940	26	VEZ	MEX	27	127	27	44	8	3	1	27	6	5	.346	.371	.480	.852	120	61	0	
1941	27	VEZ	MEX	101	430	94	158	32	5	8	86	12	35	.367	.415	.521	.936	134	224	0	
1942	28	NE	NN2	30	105	12	19	2	1	0	8	0	14	.181	.277	.219	.496	45	23		
1943	29	VEZ	MEX														Played in unrecorded Mexican league				
1944 *	30	NE	NN2	30	123	18	42	7	2	1	19	3	6	.341	.372	.455	.827	122	56		EWA
1945	31	VEZ	MEX														Played in unrecorded Mexican league				
1946	32	VEZ	MEX														Played in unrecorded Mexican league				
1947	33	VEZ	MEX														Played in unrecorded Mexican league				
1948	34	VEZ	MEX														Played in unrecorded Mexican league				
1949	35	Minneapolis	AA														Played in minor leagues (Integration)				
1950	36	Minneapolis	AA														Played in minor leagues (Integration)				ROY-1
1951	37	Minneapolis	AA														Played in minor leagues (Integration)				MVP-1
1952	38	Minneapolis	AA														Played in minor leagues (Integration)				
1953	39	TOTAL	PCL														Played in minor leagues (Integration)				
		Sacramento	PCL																			
		Oakland	PCL																			
1555	41	Bismarck	NDAK														Played in unrecorded independent league				
10 Yrs (+12)			NgL	373	1474	264	496	95	27	13	261	38	100	.336	.379	.464	.843	115	684	1	
162 Game Avg.			Pro	162	640	115	215	41	12	6	113	17	43	.336	.379	.464	.843	115	297		
5 Yrs		NE	NN2	151	576	99	182	34	8	3	91	13	46	.316	.367	.418	.785	106	241		
2 Yrs		VEZ	MEX	128	557	121	202	40	8	9	113	18	40	.363	.405	.512	.917	131	285	0	
2 Yrs		ND	NN2	74	268	39	96	21	9	0	49	6	12	.358	.386	.504	.889	121	135	0	
1 Yr		ID	NN2	14	55	3	10	0	2	0	5	0	1	.182	.196	.255	.451	21	14	0	
1 Yr		HG	NN2	4	16	2	6	0	0	0	3	1	0	.375	.375	.563	.938	139	9	0	
1 Yr		NEG	NN2	2	2	0	0	0	0	0	0	0	1	.000	.500	.000	.500	51	0	1	
8 Yrs			NN2	245	917	143	294	55	19	4	148	20	60	.321	.363	.435	.798	106	399	1	
2 Yrs			MEX	128	557	121	202	40	8	9	113	18	40	.363	.405	.512	.917	131	285	0	

All-Star Batting

Year	Age	Lg	Game	G	AB	R	H	2B	3B	HR	RBI	SB	BB	BA	OBP	SLG	OPS	HBP
1935	21	EAS	EWA	2B	1	0	1	0	0	0	1	0	0	1.000	1.000	1.000	2.000	0
1937	23	EAS	EWA	3B	5	1	2	0	0	0	0	1	0	.400	.400	.400	.800	0
1938	24	EAS	EWA	3B	4	0	0	0	0	0	0	0	0	.000	.000	.000	.000	0
1944	30	EAS	EWA	3B	5	0	3	1	0	0	2	0	1	.600	.600	.800	1.400	0
4 Yrs (4 GP)		NgL		4	15	1	6	1	0	0	3	1	1	.400	.400	.467	.867	0

20. The Negro Leagues All-Star Register

Lorenzo "Piper" Davis
Standard Batting

Year	Age	Tm	Lg	G	AB	R	H	2B	3B	HR	RBI	SB	BB	BA	OBP	SLG	OPS	OPS+	TB	HBP	Awards
1942	24	BBB	NAL	1	2	0	0	0	0	0	0	0	0	.000	.000	.000	.000	-100	0		
1943	25	BBB	NAL	39	142	28	41	12	2	2	24	3	16	.289	.365	.444	.808	152	63	1	
1944	26	BBB	NAL	24	91	10	19	3	1	**2**	12	0	5	.209	.250	.330	.580	86	30		
1944	26	HG	NN2	1	3	1	0	0	0	0	0	1	0	.000	.250	.000	.250	-29	0		
1945	27	BBB	NAL	23	86	14	31	3	2	2	12	2	5	**.360**	.396	.512	.907	168	44	0	
1946 *	28	BBB	NAL	9	32	6	9	1	2	0	0	1	7	.281	.410	.438	.848	149	14	0	EWA
1947 *	29	BBB	NAL	13	54	13	19	3	3	1	10	0	5	.352	.407	.574	.981	164	31	0	EWA
1948 *	30	BBB	NAL	28	104	23	40	8	2	1	18	5	7	.385	.439	.529	.967	137	55	3	EWA
1949	31	Leones de Ponce	BSN																		Played in unrecorded Puerto Rican league
1950	32	Jalisco	MEX																		Played in unrecorded Mexican League
1951	33	TOTAL	IL+PCL																		Played in minor leagues (Integration) & unrecorded independent league
		Ottawa	IL																		Played in minor league (Integration)
		Oakland	PCL																		Played in unrecorded independent league
1952	34	Oakland	PCL																		Played in unrecorded independent league
1953	35	Oakland	PCL																		Played in unrecorded independent league
1954	36	Oakland	PCL																		Played in unrecorded independent league
1955	37	TOTAL	PCL																		Played in unrecorded independent league
		Oakland	PCL																		Played in unrecorded independent league
		Los Angeles	PCL																		Played in unrecorded independent league
1956	38	Los Angeles	PCL–AA																		Played in minor leagues (Integration) & unrecorded independent league
1957	39	TOTAL	PCL																		Played in minor league (Integration)
		Los Angeles	PCL																		Played in minor leagues (Integration)
		Fort Worth	AA																		Played in minor leagues (Integration)
1958	40	Fort Worth	AA																		Played in minor leagues (Integration)
8 yrs (+10)			NgL	138	514	95	159	30	12	8	76	13	46	.309	.371	.461	.832	139	237	4	
162 Game Avg.			Pro	162	603	112	187	35	14	9	89	15	54	.309	.371	.461	.832	139	711	5	
7 Yrs				137	511	94	159	30	12	8	76	12	45	.311	.371	.464	.835	140	237	4	
1 Yr			NN2	1	3	1	0	0	0	0	0	1	1	.000	.250	.000	.250	-29	0		
7 Yrs			NAL	137	511	94	159	30	12	8	76	12	45	.311	.371	.464	.835	140	237	4	
1 Yr			NN2	1	3	1	0	0	0	0	0	1	1	.000	.250	.000	.250	-29	0		

Postseason Batting

Year	Age	Tm	Lg	Series	Opp	Rslt	G	AB	R	H	2B	3B	HR	RBI	SB	BB	BA	OBP	SLG	OPS	HBP
1943	25	BBB	NAL	ALC	CAG	W	2	6	2	1	0	0	0	1	0	0	.167	.286	.167	.452	1
1944	26	BBB	NAL	WS	HG	L	7	30	1	8	1	0	0	3	0	2	.267	.313	.300	.613	0
1944	26	BBB	NAL	WS	HG	L	5	22	2	4	0	0	0	1	0	0	.182	.182	.182	.364	0
1948	30	BBB	NAL	ALC	KCM	W	7	29	4	11	3	0	1	4	0	2	.379	.419	.483	.902	0
1948	30	BBB	NAL	WS	HG	L	1	4	0	1	0	0	0	0	0	0	.250	.250	.500	.750	0
3 Yrs (5 Series)			NgL				22	91	8	25	2	0	1	9	0	4	.275	.313	.330	.635	1
2 Yrs				ALC			9	35	5	12	3	0	1	5	0	2	.343	.395	.429	.807	1
3 Yrs				WS			13	56	3	13	1	0	0	4	0	2	.232	.259	.268	.526	0

All-Star Batting

Year	Age	Lg	Game	G	AB	R	H	2B	3B	HR	RBI	SB	BB	BA	OBP	SLG	OPS	HBP
1946	28	WES	EWA	2B2B	7	2	3	0	0	0	2	0	1	.429	.500	.429	.929	0
1947	29	WES	EWA	2B2B	8	2	3	1	0	0	3	1	1	.375	.444	.500	.944	0
1948	30	WES	EWA	2B2B	7	1	1	1	0	0	0	1	1	.143	.250	.286	.536	0
3 Yrs (6 GP)					22	5	7	2	0	0	5	2	3	.318	.400	.409	.809	0

Elwood "Bingo" DeMoss
Standard Batting

Year	Age	Tm	Lg	G	AB	R	H	2B	3B	HR	RBI	SB	BB	BA	OBP	SLG	OPS	OPS+	TB	HBP	Awards
1910	20	TOTAL	WES	4	16	1	2	0	0	0	0		0	.125	.125	.125	.250	-17	2	0	
		KCG	WES	1	4	0	0	0	0	0	0		0	.000	.000	.000	.000	-100	0	0	
		OKM	WES	3	12	1	2	0	0	0	0		0	.167	.167	.167	.333	11	2	0	
1911	21	KCG	WES	20	70	9	19	6	0	0	1	6	4	.271	.311	.357	.668	81	25	0	
1912	22	TOTAL	WES	11	42	8	13	2	0	0	9	1	5	.310	.383	.357	.740	113	15	0	
		FLP	WES	9	36	6	11	1	0	0	8	1	3	.306	.359	.333	.692	101	12	0	
		WBS	WES	2	6	2	2	1	0	0	1	0	2	.333	.500	.500	1.000	188	3	0	
1913	23	TOTAL	WES	13	53	4	12	0	1	0	4	1	3	.226	.268	.264	.532	53	14	0	
		FLP	WES	4	18	0	2	0	0	0	1	0	1	.111	.158	.111	.269	-24	2	0	
		COG	WES	3	13	1	2	1	0	0	1	1	1	.154	.214	.308	.522	55	4	0	
		CAG	WES	3	10	1	3	0	0	0	0	0	0	.300	.300	.300	.600	76	3	0	
		SLG	WES	3	12	2	5	0	1	0	3	0	1	.417	.462	.417	.878	146	5	0	
1914	24	TOTAL	WES	11	46	7	8	1	0	0	0	2	4	.174	.255	.196	.451	31	9	1	
		WBS	WES	2	8	3	1	0	0	0	0	1	0	.125	.222	.125	.347	-4	1	1	
		FLP	WES	6	24	2	5	1	0	0	0	1	2	.208	.269	.250	.519	60	6	0	
		CAG	WES	3	14	2	2	0	0	0	0	0	2	.143	.250	.143	.393	19	2	0	
1915	25	ABC	WES	59	201	47	43	7	1	1	14	26	41	.214	.365	.274	.639	90	55	7	
1916	26	TOTAL	WES	27	90	14	21	3	3	0	10	9	9	.233	.317	.333	.650	95	30	2	
		IBA	WES	5	18	1	3	1	0	0	2	4	1	.167	.250	.222	.472	49	4	1	
		ABC	WES	22	72	13	18	2	3	0	8	5	8	.250	.333	.361	.694	107	26	1	
1917	27	CAG	WES	58	215	33	43	4	1	0	12	17	24	.200	.280	.219	.499	73	47	0	
1918	28	CAG	WES	26	98	16	19	2	1	0	8	7	13	.194	.295	.235	.529	60	23	1	
1919	29	CAG	WES	42	162	42	37	8	2	0	13	7	27	.228	.346	.302	.648	98	49	2	
1920	30	CAG	NNL	67	236	65	74	14	2	0	36	11	34	.314	.409	.390	.799	149	92	4	
1921	31	CAG	NNL	84	312	66	83	13	1	0	24	16	35	.266	.342	.324	.666	99	101	1	
1922	32	CAG	NNL	65	215	46	49	10	0	2	24	18	31	.228	.352	.251	.603	75	54	6	
1923	33	CAG	NNL	76	278	56	71	7	1	1	31	12	31	.255	.337	.309	.646	78	86	3	
1924	34	CAG	NNL	67	226	43	50	8	0	1	21	12	26	.221	.313	.279	.591	76	63	3	
1925	35	CAG	NNL	60	194	34	42	6	0	0	17	6	28	.216	.315	.247	.563	61	48	4	
1926	36	ABC	NNL	81	314	37	81	10	3	0	36	24	22	.258	.317	.309	.626	60	97	5	
1927	37	DS	NNL	40	144	23	33	5	3	0	14	0	6	.229	.260	.306	.566	53	44	0	
1928	38	DS	NNL	40	120	14	19	4	1	0	10	0	8	.158	.223	.208	.431	18	25	2	
1929	39	DS	NNL	13	51	5	16	1	0	0	8	4	2	.314	.340	.333	.673	76	17	0	
1930	40	DS	NNL	15	54	7	15	2	0	0	3	0	2	.278	.304	.315	.618	68	17	0	
11 Yrs (+10)			NgL	608	2144	396	533	74	14	3	224	103	229	.249	.328	.300	.629	115	644	25	
162 Game Avg.			Pro	162	571	106	142	20	4	1	60	27	61	.249	.328	.300	.629	115	172	7	
10 Yrs			Pre-NgL	271	993	181	217	33	8	2	75	76	130	.219	.317	.271	.588	79	269	13	
21 Yrs			Pre-NgL+NgL	879	3137	577	750	107	22	4	299	179	359	.239	.325	.291	.616	104	913	38	
11 Yrs		CAG	NNL+WES	551	1960	404	473	66	10	3	186	106	255	.241	.335	.290	.625	87	568	21	
3 Yrs		ABC	NNL+WES	162	587	97	142	19	7	1	58	55	71	.242	.337	.303	.640	76	178	13	
4 Yrs		DS	NNL	108	369	49	83	12	4	0	35	4	18	.225	.265	.279	.544	47	103	2	
2 Yrs		KCG	WES	21	74	9	19	6	0	0	9	6	4	.257	.295	.338	.633	71	25	0	
3 Yrs		FLP	WES	19	78	8	18	2	0	0	9	2	6	.231	.286	.256	.542	60	20	0	
1 Yr		IBA	WES	5	18	1	3	1	0	0	2	4	1	.167	.250	.222	.472	49	4	1	
2 Yrs		WBS	WES	4	14	5	3	1	0	0	1	1	2	.214	.353	.286	.639	78	4	1	
1 Yr		COG	WES	3	13	1	2	1	0	0	1	1	1	.154	.214	.308	.522	55	4	0	
1 Yr		SLG	WES	3	12	2	5	0	1	0	3	0	1	.417	.462	.417	.878	146	5	0	
1 Yr		OKM	WES	3	12	1	2	0	0	0	0	0	0	.167	.167	.167	.333	11	2	0	
11 yrs			NNL	608	2144	396	533	74	14	3	224	103	229	.249	.328	.300	.629	79	644	25	
10 yrs			WES	271	993	181	217	33	8	1	75	76	130	.219	.317	.271	.588	79	269	13	

Martin Dihigo
Standard Batting

Year	Age	Tm	Lg	G	AB	R	H	2B	3B	HR	RBI	SB	BB	BA	OBP	SLG	OPS	OPS+	TB	HBP	Awards
1923	18	CSE	ECL	34	120	15	25	3	3	0	15	1	6	.208	.246	.283	.529	55	34	0	
1924	19	CSE	ECL	47	180	30	47	7	4	2	27	3	11	.261	.304	.378	.681	100	68		
1925	20	CSE	ECL	42	160	21	49	8	2	3	22	3	19	.306	.380	.438	.817	118	70		
1926	21	CSE	ECL	43	152	42	57	9	2	14	44	8	29	.375	.475	.737	1.212	237	112	0	
1927	22	CSE	TOTAL	56	219	45	69	9	2	13	48	10	16	.315	.367	.553	.920	141	121	2	
		CSE	ECL+IND	55	215	44	68	9	2	13	48	9	16	.316	.369	.558	.927	143	120	2	
		HG	ECL	1	4	1	1	0	0	0	0	1	0	.250	.250	.250	.500	10	1	0	
1928	23	HG	IND	19	67	13	21	1	1	4	14	0	9	.313	.395	.537	.932	151	36	0	
1929	24	HIL	EAS	78	271	68	90	14	4	18	79	8	56	.332	.448	.613	1.061	156	166	1	
1930	25	HIL	ANL	17	69	15	26	3	2	6	23	0	5	.377	.427	.739	1.166	174	51	1	
		TOTAL	EAS	1	4	0	2	0	0	0	1	0	0	.500	.500	.500	1.000	143	2	0	
		HIL	EAS	16	65	15	24	3	2	6	22	0	5	.369	.423	.754	1.176	176	49	1	
1931	26	SC2	EAS	49	166	39	56	8	5	7	35	1	23	.337	.424	.572	.996	178	95	2	
		TOTAL	IND	43	141	35	44	6	3	7	32	1	23	.312	.416	.546	.962	166	77	2	
		HIL	IND	6	25	4	12	2	2	0	3	0	0	.480	.480	.720	1.200	248	18	0	
		BBS	IND																		
1932	27													Played in unrecorded Cuban league							
1933	28													Played in unrecorded Cuban league							
1934	29													Played in unrecorded Cuban league							
1935 *	30	NYC	NN2	42	144	30	47	12	1	7	34	7	18	.326	.409	.569	.978	145	82	2	EWA
1936	31	NYC	NN2	39	127	31	38	8	1	9	33	7	22	.299	.407	.591	.997	145	75	1	
1937	32	VEZ	MEX											Played in unrecorded Mexican league							
1938	33	VEZ	MEX											Played in unrecorded Mexican league							
1939	34	VEZ	MEX											Played in unrecorded Mexican league							
1940	35	VEZ	MEX	78	302	60	110	17	6	9	73	9	17	.364	.402	.550	.952	145	166	2	
1941	36	ULT	MEX	92	329	74	102	25	4	12	59	7	57	.310	.412	.520	.932	133	171	0	
1942	37	ULT	MEX											Played in unrecorded Mexican league							
1943	38	ULT	MEX											Played in unrecorded Mexican league							
1944	39	JN2	MEX											Played in unrecorded Mexican league							
1945 *	40	NYC	NN2	18	50	9	15	1	0	2	7	1	7	.300	.386	.440	.826	137	22	0	EWA
14 Yrs (+9)			NgL	654	2356	492	752	125	37	106	513	65	295	.319	.397	.539	.936	143	1269	**11**	
162 Game Avg.			Pro	162	584	122	186	31	9	26	127	16	73	.319	.397	.539	.936	143	208	3	
5 Yrs		CSE	ECL	221	827	152	246	36	13	32	156	24	81	.297	.362	.489	.850	133	404	2	
3 Yrs		HIL	ANL+EAS+IND	122	416	103	136	20	7	25	112	9	79	.327	.438	.589	1.027	159	245	3	
3 Yrs		NYC	NN2	99	321	70	100	21	2	18	74	15	47	.312	.404	.558	.962	144	179	3	
1 Yr		ULT	MEX	92	329	74	102	25	4	12	59	7	57	.310	.412	.520	.932	133	171	0	
1 Yr		VEZ	MEX	78	302	60	110	17	6	9	73	9	17	.364	.402	.550	.952	145	166	2	
2 Yrs		HG	EAS+IND	20	71	14	22	1	1	4	14	1	9	.310	.388	.521	.909	143	37	0	
1 Yr		SC2	EAS	16	65	15	24	3	2	6	22	0	5	.369	.423	.754	1.176	176	49	1	
1 Yr		BBS	IND	6	25	4	12	2	2	0	3	0	0	.480	.480	.720	1.200	248	18	0	
5 Yrs			ECL	221	827	152	246	36	13	32	156	24	81	.297	.362	.489	.850	133	404	2	
2 Yrs			MEX	170	631	134	212	42	10	21	132	16	74	.336	.407	.534	.941	139	337	2	
3 Yrs			NN2	99	321	70	100	21	2	18	74	15	47	.312	.404	.558	.962	144	179	3	
1 Yr			ANL	78	271	68	90	14	4	18	79	8	56	.332	.448	.613	1.061	156	166	1	
3 Yrs			IND	50	170	40	57	8	5	7	35	2	23	.335	.421	.565	.985	174	96	2	
2 Yrs			EAS	36	136	28	47	4	3	10	37	0	14	.346	.411	.640	1.050	163	87	1	

Martin Dihigo
Postseason Batting

Year	Age	Tm	Lg	Series	Opp	Rslt	G	AB	R	H	2B	3B	HR	RBI	SB	BB	BA	OBP	SLG	OPS	HBP
1935	30	NYC	NN2	NLC	PC	L	7	26	2	5	0	0	0	1	0	2	.192	.250	.192	.442	0
1 Yr (1 Series)				NLC			7	26	2	5	0	0	0	2	0	2	.192	.250	.192	.442	0
1 Yr							7	26	2	5	0	0	0	2	0	2	.192	.250	.192	.442	0

All-Star Batting

Year	Age	Tm	Lg	Game	Opp	G	AB	R	H	2B	3B	HR	RBI	SB	BB	BA	OBP	SLG	OPS	HBP
1935	30		EAS	EWA		P	5	1	1	0	0	0	1	1	1	.200	.333	.200	.533	0
1945	40		EAS	EWA		P	1	0	0	0	0	0	0	0	0	.000	.000	.000	.000	0
2 Yrs (2 GP)			NgL			2	6	1	1	0	0	0	1	1	1	.167	.286	.167	.452	0

Larry Doby
Standard Batting

Year	Age	Tm	Lg	G	AB	R	H	2B	3B	HR	RBI	SB	BB	BA	OBP	SLG	OPS	OPS+	TB	HBP	Awards
1942	18	NE	NN2	23	81	18	25	3	2	1	14	3	7	.309	.364	.432	.796	132	35	1	
1943	19	NE	NN2	28	103	18	31	8	3	4	22	5	20	.301	.419	.553	.973	153	57		
1944	20	NE	NN2	1	5	0	1	0	0	0	0	0	1	.200	.333	.200	.533	46	1		
1945	21								Did not play in major or minor leagues (Military Service)												
1946 *	22	NE	NN2	59	232	59	85	12	10	7	52	5	30	.366	.441	.595	1.036	184	138	1	EWA
1947	23	TOTAL	NN2+AL	59	145	28	45	11	5	8	43	3	18	.310	.387	.621	1.007	172	90	0	
–	–	NE	NN2	30	113	25	40	10	5	8	41	3	17	.354	.438	.743	1.182	220	84	0	
–	–	CLE	AL	29	32	3	5	1	0	0	2	0	1	.156	.182	.188	.369	4	6	0	
1948	24	CLE	AL	121	439	83	132	23	9	14	66	9	54	.301	.384	.490	.873	134	215	5	MVP-29
1949 *	25	CLE	AL	147	547	106	153	25	3	24	85	10	91	.280	.389	.468	.857	128	256	7	ASG
1950 *	26	CLE	AL	142	503	110	164	25	5	25	102	8	98	.326	.442	.545	.986	156	274	6	ASG, MVP-8
1951 *	27	CLE	AL	134	447	84	132	27	5	20	69	4	101	.295	.428	.512	.941	160	229	3	ASG
1952 *	28	CLE	AL	140	519	104	143	26	8	32	104	5	90	.276	.383	.541	.924	163	281	0	ASG, MVP-12
1953 *	29	CLE	AL	149	513	92	135	18	5	29	102	3	96	.263	.385	.487	.873	137	250	6	ASG
1954 *	30	CLE	AL	153	577	94	157	18	4	32	126	2	85	.272	.368	.484	.852	129	279	3	ASG, MVP-2
1955 *	31	CLE	AL	131	491	91	143	17	5	26	75	2	61	.291	.372	.505	.877	130	248	2	ASG
1956	32	CHW	AL	140	504	89	135	22	3	24	102	0	102	.268	.395	.466	.861	126	235	4	
1957	33	CHW	AL	119	416	57	120	27	2	14	79	2	56	.288	.376	.464	.839	127	193	2	
1958	34	CLE	AL	89	247	41	70	10	1	13	45	0	26	.283	.352	.490	.842	129	121	0	
1959	35	TOTAL	AL	39	113	6	26	4	2	0	13	1	10	.230	.293	.301	.594	61	34	0	
–	–	DET	AL	18	55	5	12	3	1	0	4	0	8	.218	.317	.309	.627	68	17	0	
–	–	CHW	AL	21	58	1	14	1	1	0	9	1	2	.241	.267	.293	.560	55	17	0	
1962	38	Nagoya	JAP																		Played in unrecorded Japanese league

Larry Doby

Standard Batting (continued)

Year	Age	Tm	Lg	G	AB	R	H	2B	3B	HR	RBI	SB	BB	BA	OBP	SLG	OPS	OPS+	TB	HBP	Awards
17 Yrs (+2)			Pro	1733	6027	1108	1742	287	77	281	1142	66	964	.289	.389	.502	.893	127	3026	40	
13 Yrs			MLB	1533	5348	960	1515	243	52	253	970	47	871	.283	.388	.490	.878	125	2655	38	
5 Yrs			NgL	200	679	148	227	44	25	28	172	19	93	.334	.416	.596	1.014	139	405	2	
162 Game Avg.			Pro	162	563	104	163	27	7	26	107	6	90	.289	.391	.502	.893	127	283	4	
10 Yrs		CLE	AL	1235	4315	808	1234	190	45	215	776	44	703	.286	.389	.500	.889	140	2159	32	
3 Yrs		CHW	AL	280	978	147	269	50	6	38	190	3	160	.275	.378	.455	.833	122	445	6	
5 Yrs		NE	NN2	200	679	148	227	44	25	28	172	19	93	.334	.416	.596	.986	139	405	2	
1 Yr		DET	AL	18	55	5	12	3	1	0	4	0	8	.218	.313	.309	.622	68	17	0	
5 Yrs			NN2	200	679	148	227	44	25	28	172	19	93	.334	.416	.596	.986	139	405	2	
13 Yrs			AL	1533	5348	960	1515	243	52	253	970	47	871	.283	.388	.490	.878	125	2655	38	

Postseason Batting

Year	Age	Tm	Lg	Series	Opp	Rslt	G	AB	R	H	2B	3B	HR	RBI	SB	BB	BA	OBP	SLG	OPS	HBP
1946 □	22	NE	NN2	WS	HG	W	7	22	7	5	2	1	1	5	1	3	.227	.452	.500	.952	0
1948 □	24	CLE	AL	WS	BOS	W	6	22	1	7	1	1	0	2	0	2	.318	.375	.500	.875	0
1954	30	CLE	AL	WS	CLE	L	4	16	0	2	0	0	0	0	0	2	.125	.222	.125	.347	0
3 Yrs (3 Series)			Pro				17	60	8	14	3	2	1	7	1	7	.233	.370	.400	.770	0
1 Yr (1 Series)			NgL				7	22	7	5	2	1	1	5	1	3	.227	.452	.500	.952	0
1 Yr				WS			7	22	7	5	2	1	1	5	1	3	.227	.452	.500	.952	0
2 Yrs (2 Series)			MLB				10	38	1	9	1	1	0	2	0	4	.237	.310	.342	.652	0
2 Yrs				WS			10	38	1	9	1	1	0	2	0	4	.237	.310	.342	.652	0

All-Star Batting

Year	Age		Lg	Game	G	AB	R	H	2B	3B	HR	RBI	SB	BB	BA	OBP	SLG	OPS	HBP
1946	22		NN2	EWA	2B	4	2	2	0	0	0	0	0	0	.500	.500	.500	1.000	0
1946	22		NN2	EWA	2B	3	0	1	0	0	0	1	0	0	.333	.333	.333	.667	0
1949	25		AL	ASG	1	1	0	0	0	0	0	0	0	0	.000	.000	.000	.000	0
1950	26		AL	ASG	CF	6	1	2	0	0	1	2	0	0	.333	.333	.500	.833	0
1951	27		AL	ASG	1	1	0	0	0	0	0	0	0	0	.000	.000	.000	.000	0
1952	28		AL	ASG	1	0	0	0	0	0	0	0	0	0					0
1953	29		AL	ASG	1	1	0	0	0	0	0	0	0	0	.000	.000	.000	.000	0
1954	30		AL	ASG	1	1	1	1	0	0	0	1	0	1	1.000	1.000	4.000	5.000	0
1955	31		AL	ASG	1														
8 Yrs (8 GP)			Pro		8	17	4	6	1	0	1	2	0	2	.353	.421	.588	1.009	0
1 Yr (2 GP)			NgL		2	7	2	3	0	0	0	1	0	1	.429	.500	.429	.929	0
7 Yrs (6 GP)			MLB		6	10	2	3	1	0	1	1	0	1	.300	.364	.700	1.064	0

Luscious "Big Luke" Easter
EXTENDED BATTING RECORD

Year	Age	Tm	Lg	G	AB	R	H	2B	3B	HR	RBI	SB	BB	BA	OBP	SLG	OPS	OPS+	TB	HBP	Awards
1935	19	STL	(without AB)	1		1	1			1	1										
1936	20	STL	(without AB)	1		2	3			1	4										
1937	21	STL	(without AB)	1																	
		STL	(with AB)	11	4									.750		1.500	2.250				
1938	22	STL	(with AB)		102	26	28	1		2	2		1	.275							
		East	Argus EWA	6	1	1	0						1	.000	.500	.000	.500				Argus EWA
1939 *	23	STL	(with AB)	8	59	6	27	1		2	1	1		.458							
		East	Argus EWA	1	4	3	2	1			4			.500		.750		.500			Argus EWA
1940 *	23	STL	(without AB)	4	15	2	8	2		2	2			.533		1.200					
		East	Argus EWA	2	4	3	1	2	1	2	2		2	.250	.500	.250	.750				Argus EWA
1941	25	STL	Ind											No statistics available							
1942	26										Did not play in major or minor leagues (Military Service)									
1943	27										Did not play in major or minor leagues (Military Service)									
1944	28										Did not play in major or minor leagues (Military Service)									
1945	29										Did not play in major or minor leagues (Military Service)									
1946	30	CIN Crescents	HFL+Ind	22		23	34	3	1	74	152	4	1	.415					261	0	
			HFL TOTALS	19		21	29	2	1	12	25	3	1						69		
			Partial HFL record	12	50	16	24	2	2	7	20	3	1	.480		.980	1.460				
		CIN Crescents	Other HFL games	7		5	5	1	0	5	5								49		
			Ind. with AB	3	10	2	5	1	1	1	3	1		.500		.900	1.400			20		
			Ind. without AB	9				0	2	61	124	1								250	1	
1947	31	TOTAL	NN2+Ind	161	218	61	63	0	2	48	72	2	24	.271	.351	.445	.796	119	269	3	
			NN2	61		77	102	11	6	5	34			.382					97		
		HG	Ind. games	100		34	59	11	6	43	43			.341					172		
1947-48		Patriotas	VPBL	27		43	43	5	1	8	18					.681	1.022		45	1	EWA, EWA
1948 *	32	TOTAL	NN2+Ind	44	138	8	14	2	4	64	94	3	28	.304	.418	.514	.933	173	317	1	
			NN2	39		93	108	9	3	5	32	2	26	.416					71		
		HG	Ind. games			30	42	8		58	58								232		
			NN2 CS	4	15	5	7	0	1	1	4	1	2	.467	.529	.800	1.329	297	12	0	
			NgL WS	1	4	0	1	1	0	0	0	0	0	.250	.250	.500	.750	125	2	0	
		East	EWA	2	4	0	0	0	0	0	0	0	1	.000	.200	.000	.200	-21	0	0	
1948-4		Indios de Mayaguez	PRWL	80	249	81	100	27	9	14	80	15		.402	.441	.751	1.153		187		
			Caribbean Series	6	25		10	2	1	0	7	1		.400		.560	.960		14		MVP-1
1949	33	TOTAL	PCL+AL	115	367	77	130	32	3	29	106	1	53	.354		.695	1.136		255	4	
		San Diego	Exhibition	14	49	15	21	6	3	4	12			.429		.918	1.347		45		
			PCL	80	273	56	99	23	0	25	92	1	45	.363	.460	.722	1.181		197	4	
		Cleveland	AL	21	45	6	10	3	0	0	2	0	8	.222	.340	.289	.629	68	13	0	

Luscious "Big Luke" Easter
EXTENDED BATTING RECORD (continued)

Year	Age	Tm	Lg	G	AB	R	H	2B	3B	HR	RBI	SB	BB	BA	OBP	SLG	OPS	OPS+	TB	HBP	Awards
1950	34	Cleveland	AL	141	540	96	151	20	4	28	107	0	70	.280	.373	.487	.860	122	263	10	
—	—	LE's All-Stars	(with AB)	2	7	1	4	1	0	0	1			.571		.714	1.286		5		
—	—		(without AB)	7		4				3	4								15	1	
1951	35	Cleveland	AL	128	486	65	131	12	5	27	103	0	37	.270	.333	.481	.814	124	234	9	TSN AL POY
—	—	JR All-Stars	(without AB)	5		3				2	4								21		
1952	26	TOTAL	AL+AA	141	487	76	132	3	3	37	109	2	54	.271	.344	.536	.880		261	5	
—	—	Cleveland	AL	127	437	63	115	10	3	31	97	1	44	.263	.337	.513	.850	141	224	5	
—	—	Indianapolis	AA	14	50	13	17	2	0	6	12	1	10	.340	.450	.740	1.190		37	0	
1953	37	Cleveland	AL	68	211	26	64	9	0	7	31	0	15	.303	.361	.445	.806	119	94	4	
—	—	JR All-Stars	(with AB)	2	7		4	1						.571		.714	1.286		5		
—	—		(without AB)	31		21	26	5	1	20	25								93		
1954	38	TOTAL	AL+AAA-Level	129	434	93	138	18	1	29	91	2	69	.318	.416	.565	.981		245	4	
—	—	Cleveland	AL	6	6	0	1	0	0	0	0	0	0	.167	.167	.167	.333	-9	1	0	
—	—	Cleveland	Exhibition	1		1	2	0	0	1	1								5		
—	—	Ottawa	IL	66	230	49	80	10	0	15	48	1	42	.348	.453	.587	1.040		135	2	
—	—	San Diego	PCL	56	198	43	55	8	1	13	42	1	27	.278	.370	.525	.895		104	2	
1954-5		Culiacán Hermosillo	Mexican PCL	28	224	20	83			20	60			.371		.638	1.286		143		MVP-1
1955	39	Charleston	AA	144	477	78	135	25	5	30	102	1	101	.283	.411	.545	.956		260	3	
1955-56		TOTAL	PRWL		191	31	56	7	1	17	40	1		.293		.607	.901		116		
—	—	San Juan	PRWL		121		33			7	17			.273		.446	.719				
—	—	Ponce	PRWL		70		23			10	23			.329		.757	1.086				
1956	40	Buffalo	IL	145	483	75	148	20	3	35	106	0	105	.306	.434	.578	1.012		279	4	
1956-57		Caguas	PRPBL	18	145	20	37	5	1	7	25		100	.255	.396	.448	.703		65		
1957 a	41		IL	154	534	87	149	27	2	40	128	0	1	.279	.273	.562	.957		300	3	ASG, MVP-1
—	—	Buffalo	IL 1st Round	6	21	6	5	1	0	3	4		1	.238		.714	.987		15		
—	—		IL Semifinals	5	19	0	2	1	0	0	2		0	.105	.150	.158	.308		3		
—	—		IL Finals	5	18	2	2	0	0	0	1		0	.111	.111	.278	.389		5		
1958	42	Buffalo	IL	148	502	89	154	33	0	38	109	1	89	.307	.417	.600	1.017		301	6	
1959	43	Buffalo / Rochester	IL	143	478	68	125	32	2	22	76	0	84	.262	.379	.475	.853		227	6	
1960	44	Rochester	IL	115	275	36	83	12	1	14	57	0	30	.302	.375	.505	.880		139	2	
1961	45	Rochester	IL	82	203	24	59	13	1	10	51	0	19	.291	.360	.512	.872		104	3	
1962	46	Rochester	IL	93	249	39	70	11	1	15	60	0	33	.281	.381	.514	.895		128	7	
1963	47	Rochester	IL	77	188	20	51	8	1	6	35	0	23	.271	.357	.420	.777		79	2	
1964	48	Rochester	IL	10	10	0	2	0	0	0	1	0	0	.200	.200	.200	.400		2	0	

Luscious "Big Luke" Easter
EXTENDED BATTING RECORD (continued)

Year	Age	Tm	Lg	G	AB	R	H	2B	3B	HR	RBI	SB	BB	BA	OBP	SLG	OPS	OPS+	TB	HBP	Awards
PROFESSIONAL TOTALS																					
NgL totals				591	2081	320	573	73	21	103	406	5	224	.275	.355	.479	.834	128	997	32	
AL totals				100	356	64	101	19	9	10	66	4	50	.284	.378	.472	.850	140	168	4	
				491	1725	256	472	54	12	93	340	1	174	.274	.350	.481	.830	125	829	28	
162 Game Avg.				162	570	88	157	20	6	28	111	1	61	.275	.355	.479	.834	128	2455	9	
FOREIGN LEAGUE TOTALS				98	585	132	193	39	11	38	145	16		.330		.629	.959		368		
PRWL totals				80	440	112	156	34	10	31	120	16		.355		.689	1.043		303		
PRPBL totals				18	145	20	37	5	1	7	25			.255		.448	.703		65		
PLAYOFF, MINOR LEAGUE, INDEPENDENT & EXHIBITION TOTALS				1442	4792	785	1464	245	24	311	1045	13	718	.306	.401	.561	.962		2690	44	
IL totals				1033	3152	487	921	166	11	195	671	2	525	.292	.399	.537	.936		1694	35	
AA totals				158	527	91	152	27	5	36	114	2	111	.288	.415	.564	.979		297	3	
PCL totals				136	471	99	154	31	1	38	134	2	72	.327	.423	.639	1.062		301	6	
Mexican PCL totals				28	224	20	83			20	60			.371		.638	1.009		143		
IL playoff totals				16	58	8	9	2	0	4	7		2	.155	.183	.397	.580		23		
Exhibition totals (with at-bats)				14	49	15	21	6	3	4	12			.429		.918	1.347		45		
HFL totals				12	50	16	24	2	1	7	20	3	1	.480		.980	1.460		49		
Titanium Giants totals (with at-bats)				22	180	37	66	4	1	5	10	1	0	.367	.370	.483	.853		87		
Caribbean Series totals				6	25		10	2	1	0	7	1	0	.400		.560	.960		14		
NgL playoff totals				5	19	5	8	1	1	1	4	1	0	.421	.476	.737	1.213		14	0	
CIN Crescents (with at-bats)				3	10	2	5	1	0	0	3		0	.500	.500	.900	1.400		9		
All-Star Game totals				5	13	4	3	1	0	0	2		4	.231	.412	.308	.719		4		
Luke Easter's All-Stars (with at-bats)				2	7	1	4	1	0	0	0	0	0	.571		.714	1.286		5		
Jackie Robinson's All-Stars (with at-bats)				2	7	0	4	1	0	0	0	0	0	.571	.571	.714	1.286		5		
ADDITIONAL NUMBERS (AT-BATS UNAVAILABLE)																					
Independent NgL totals (without at-bats)				119		171	195		2	164	231	2							691	1	
Jackie Robinson's All-Stars (without at-bats)				36		24	36	8	2	22	29								114		
Venezuelan League totals				27		8	14	5	1	8	18			.341					45		
Luke Easter's All-Stars (without at-bats)				7		4	5	1		3	4								15	1	
Titanium Giants totals (without at-bats)				12		6	14	1		5	2										
Cleveland exhibition totals (without at-bats)				1		1	2			1	1										
TOTALS (with at-bats)				2131	7458	1237	2230	357	56	452	1596	34	942	.299	.383	.544	.927	128	4055	76	
162 Game Avg.				162	567	94	170	27	4	34	121	3	72	.299	.383	.544	.927	128	308	6	
Additional totals without at-bats				202		214	266	17	5	203	290	2	0						902	2	
MINIMUM TOTALS FOR CAREER				2333		1451	2496	374	61	655	1886								5265		

20. The Negro Leagues All-Star Register

Josh Gibson

Holds professional records for highest batting average, highest slugging average, most home run titles (13), most consecutive home run titles (8), most RBI titles (9), most consecutive RBI titles (7), most titles in total bases (8), and most Triple Crowns (5); holds NgL records for most home runs, most extra bases on long hits (1053), highest batting average, highest on-base percentage, highest slugging average, highest OPS, highest OPS+, highest isolated power (.3371), highest secondary average (.5019), and fewest at bats per home run (13.41); hit .300+ in all five professional leagues in which he played

Standard Batting

Year	Age	Tm	Lg	G	AB	R	H	2B	3B	HR	RBI	SB	BB	BA	OBP	SLG	OPS	OPS+	TB	HBP	Awards
1930	18	MRS	NNL	1	4	0	2	0	0	0	0	0	0	.500	.500	.500	1.000	171	2	0	
1930	18	HG	EAS	32	107	20	40	3	2	9	37	0	8	.374	.422	.692	1.109	174	74	1	
1931	19	HG	IND	48	183	39	57	14	4	8	42	0	13	.311	.360	.563	.920	158	103	1	
1932	20	PC	IND	63	237	44	76	13	6	8	44	1	25	.321	.388	.527	.913	136	125	1	
1933 *	21	PC	NN2	68	238	61	94	15	7	18	74	4	20	.395	.442	.744	1.186	218	177	0	EWA
1934 *	22	TOTAL	NN2+IND	66	242	56	77	19	4	15	60	4	30	.318	.396	.616	1.009	183	149	1	EWA
–	–	PC	NN2	65	240	56	76	19	4	15	59	4	30	.317	.395	.617	1.009	183	148	1	
–	–	HG	IND	1	2	0	1	0	0	0	1	0	0	.500	.500	.500	1.000	204	1	0	
1935 *	23	PC	NN2	44	168	48	62	11	4	10	57	10	24	.369	.448	.661	1.109	176	111	0	EWA
1936 *	24	PC	NN2	50	175	51	68	7	4	18	66	6	30	.389	.478	.783	1.261	218	137	0	EWA
1937	25	HG	NN2	39	156	60	65	13	7	20	73	2	25	.417	.500	.974	1.472	272	152	1	
1938 *	26	HG	NN2	46	165	53	61	11	4	13	54	2	29	.370	.467	.721	1.185	212	119	0	EWA
1939 *	27	HG	NN2	27	102	34	41	4	3	11	46	4	18	.402	.492	.824	1.315	248	84	0	EWA
1940	28	TOTAL	NN2+MEX	23	94	33	43	7	4	11	38	3	18	.457	.545	.968	1.513	287	91	0	
–	–	HG	NN2	1	2	1	0	0	0	0	0	0	2	.000	.500	.000	.500	41	0	0	
–	–	VEZ	MEX	22	92	32	43	7	4	11	38	3	16	.467	.546	.989	1.535	292	91	0	
1941	29	VEZ	MEX	94	358	100	134	31	3	33	124	7	75	.374	.484	.754	1.237	208	270	1	
1942 *	30	HG	NN2	48	162	44	53	7	2	10	52	1	35	.327	.447	.580	1.027	200	94	0	EWA
1943 *	31	HG	NN2	69	249	93	116	22	9	20	109	4	52	.466	.560	.867	1.426	276	216	1	EWA, NSA
1944 *	32	HG	NN2	49	177	39	59	6	6	9	48	3	20	.333	.401	.588	.989	164	104	0	EWA
1945	33	HG	NN2	43	148	36	55	6	5	8	39	1	28	.372	.472	.642	1.113	211	95	0	
1946 *	34	HG	NN2	47	169	34	54	12	3	13	52	1	15	.320	.375	.657	1.032	184	111	0	EWA
17 Yrs			NgL	857	3134	845	1157	201	77	234	1015	53	465	.369	.452	.706	1.159	205	2214	8	
162 Game Avg.			Pro	162	592	160	219	38	15	44	192	10	88	.369	.452	.706	1.159	205	419	2	
12 Yrs		HG	EAS+NN2+IND	450	1622	453	602	98	45	121	553	18	245	.371	.455	.711	1.167	212	1153	5	
5 Yrs		PC	NN2+IND	290	1058	260	376	65	25	69	300	25	129	.355	.426	.660	1.087	185	698	2	
2 Yrs		VEZ	MEX	116	450	132	177	38	7	44	162	10	91	.393	.496	.802	1.299	225	361	1	
1 Yr		MRS	NNL	1	4	0	2	0	0	0	0	0	0	.500	.500	.500	1.000	171	2	0	
11 Yrs			NN2	596	2151	610	804	133	58	165	729	42	328	.374	.458	.720	1.178	213	928	4	
2 Yrs			MEX	116	450	132	177	38	7	44	162	10	91	.393	.496	.802	1.299	225	361	1	
3 Yrs			IND	112	422	83	134	27	10	16	87	1	38	.318	.377	.543	.921	498	229	2	
1 Yr			EAS	32	107	20	40	3	2	9	37	0	8	.374	.422	.692	1.118	174	74	1	
1 Yr			NNL	1	4	0	2	0	0	0	0	0	0	.500	.500	.500	1.000	171	2	0	

Josh Gibson

Postseason Batting

Year	Age	Tm	Lg	Series	Opp	Rslt	G	AB	R	H	2B	3B	HR	RBI	SB	BB	BA	OBP	SLG	OPS	HBP
1935 ¤	23	PC	NN2	NLC	NYC	W	7	31	5	11	0	0	1	5	0	0	.355	.355	.516	.871	0
1939	27	HG	NN2	NLP	PS	W	2	6	1	1	0	0	1	2	0	2	.167	.375	.667	1.042	0
1939	27	HG	NN2	NLC	BEG	L	5	17	3	6	0	0	2	4	0	4	.353	.476	.706	1.182	0
1942	30	HG	NN2	WS	KCM	L	4	13	2	1	0	0	0	0	1	2	.077	.200	.077	.277	0
1943 ¤	31	HG	NN2	WS	BBB	W	7	26	8	5	1	0	0	2	1	6	.192	.344	.231	.575	0
1944 ¤	32	HG	NN2	WS	BBB	W	5	15	3	6	0	0	1	2	0	7	.400	.591	.600	1.191	0
1945	33	HG	NN2	WS	CBE	L	4	14	0	2	1	0	0	1	0	2	.143	.250	.214	.464	0
6 Yrs (7 Series)			NgL				34	122	22	32	2	0	5	16	2	23	.262	.379	.418	.797	0
1 Yr				NLP			2	6	1	1	0	0	1	2	0	2	.167	.375	.667	1.042	0
2 Yrs				NLC			12	48	8	17	0	0	3	9	0	4	.354	.404	.583	.987	0
4 Yrs				WS			20	68	13	14	2	0	1	5	2	17	.206	.365	.279	.644	0

All-Star Batting

Year	Age	Lg	Game	Opp	Rslt	G	AB	R	H	2B	3B	HR	RBI	SB	BB	BA	OBP	SLG	OPS	HBP
1933	21	EAS	EWA			C	2	0	1	0	0	0	0	0	0	.500	.500	.500	1.000	0
1934	22	EAS	EWA			C	4	0	2	1	0	0	0	0	0	.500	.500	.750	1.250	0
1935	23	WES	EWA			C	5	3	4	2	0	0	1	0	1	.800	.833	1.200	2.033	0
1936	24	EAS	EWA			C	3	2	2	0	0	0	1	1	0	.667	.667	.667	1.333	0
1938	26	EAS	EWA			C	1	0	0	0	0	0	0	0	0	.000	.000	.000	.000	0
1939	27	EAS	EWA			C/C	5	1	1	0	1	0	4	0	3	.200	.444	.600	1.044	0
1942	30	EAS	EWA			C/C	7	1	3	0	0	0	2	0	4	.429	.636	.429	1.065	0
1943	31	SAS	NSA			C	3	0	2	0	0	0	1	0	1	.667	.750	.667	1.417	0
1943	31	EAS	EWA			C	3	1	1	0	0	0	0	0	0	.333	.500	.333	.833	0
1944	32	EAS	EWA			C	3	1	2	1	0	0	0	0	1	.667	.750	1.000	1.750	0
1946	34	EAS	EWA			C/C	5	0	1	0	0	0	0	0	1	.200	.333	.200	.533	0
10 Yrs (11 GP)		NgL				14	41	8	19	4	1	0	9	1	12	.463	.585	.610	1.195	0

Ulysses "Frank" Grant
Standard Batting

Year	Age	Tm	Lg	G	AB	R	H	2B	3B	HR	RBI	SB	BB	BA	OBP	SLG	OPS	OPS+	TB	HBP	Awards
1885	19		IND											Played in unrecorded independent league							
1886	20	TOTAL	IL+EL											Played in minor leagues (Integration)							
–	–	Meriden	EL											Played in minor leagues (Integration)							
–	–	Buffalo	IL																		
1887	21	Buffalo	INTA											Played in minor leagues (Integration)							
1888	22	Buffalo	INTA											Played in minor leagues (Integration)							
1889	23	Trenton	MIDS											Played in minor leagues (Integration)							
1890	24	TOTAL	EISL+ATLA											Played in minor leagues (Integration)							
–	–	Harrisburg	EISL																		
–	–	Harrisburg	ATLA											Played in minor leagues (Integration)							
1891	25	TOTAL	IND+CTST	7	33	12	13	3	0	1	12	3	4	.394	.459	.576	1.035	168	19	0	
–	–	CBG	IND	3	14	5	6	1	0	0	5	1	3	.429	.529	.500	1.029	171	7	0	
–	–	GOR	IND	4	19	7	7	2	0	1	7	2	1	.368	.400	.632	1.032	165	12	0	
–	–	Ansonia	CTST											Played in minor leagues (Integration)							
1892	26	CBG	IND											No statistics available							
1893	27	CBG	IND											No statistics available							
1894	28	CBG	IND	1	2	4	2	0	1	0	2		3	1.000	1.000	2.000	3.000	492	4	0	
1895	29	CBG	IND											No statistics available							
1896	30	CBG	IND											No statistics available							
1897	31	CBG	IND	4	18	5	8	2	1	0	8		1	.444	.474	.667	1.140	168	12	0	
1898	32	CXG	IND	4	16	3	7	1	0	0	3			.438	.471	.500	.971	190	8	0	
1899	33	CXG	IND	6	26	4	7	1	2	0	1		1	.269	.296	.462	.758	94	12	0	
1900	34	TOTAL	IND	4	12	3	1	1	0	0	0		4	.083	.353	.167	.520	45	2	1	
–	–	CBG	IND	2	5	2	1	1	0	0	0		3	.200	.556	.400	.956	192	2	1	
–	–	CCG	IND	2	7	1	0	0	0	0	0		1	.000	.125	.000	.125	-60	0	0	
1901	35		IND											No statistics available							
1902	36		IND											No statistics available							
1903	37	PG	EAS	7	24	2	6	0	0	0	1		3	.250	.333	.333	.583	144	6	0	
1904	38		IND											No statistics available							
1905	39		IND											No statistics available							
1906	40	NCO	EAS	1	4	1	3	1	0	0	1		0	.750	.750	1.000	1.750	433	4	0	
1907	41	BRG	NAC	1	2	0	0	0	0	0	0		0	.000	.333	.000	.333	12	0	1	
9 Yrs (+14)			Pre-NgL	35	137	34	47	9	4	1	28	3	17	.343	.423	.489	.912	152	67	2	
162 Game Avg.			Pre-NgL	162	634	157	218	42	19	5	130	14	79	.343	.423	.489	.912	152	310	9	

James "Joe" Greene

Standard Batting

Year	Age	Tm	Lg	G	AB	R	H	2B	3B	HR	RBI	SB	BB	BA	OBP	SLG	OPS	OPS+	TB	HBP	Awards
1932	20	BCA	NSL	10	33	2	4	0	0	0	1	1	3	.121	.194	.121	.316	0	4	0	
1933	21													No statistics available							
1934	22													No statistics available							
1935	23													No statistics available							
1936	24	TOTAL		2	4	0	1	0	0	0	1	0	0	.250	.250	.250	.500	28	1	0	
–	–	CAG	IND	1	3	0	0	0	0	0	0	0	0	.000	.000	.000	.000	-100	0	0	
–	–	HG	NN2	1	1	0	1	0	0	0	1	0	0	1.000	1.000	1.000	2.000	412	1	0	
1937	25	BCA	IND	9	31	2	7	2	0	0	3	0	1	.226	.250	.290	.540	68	9	0	
1938	26	BCA	NAL	28	87	15	26	4	4	0	10	0	12	.299	.396	.437	.833	137	38	0	
1939	27	KCM	NAL	32	106	11	24	4	2	2	10	0	10	.226	.293	.349	.642	87	37	2	
1940 *	28	KCM	NAL	20	62	19	20	5	3	1	12	3	15	.323	.455	.548	1.003	215	34	0	EWA
1941	29	KCM	NAL	26	83	15	21	5	3	0	20	0	10	.253	.333	.458	.791	148	38	0	
1942 *	30	KCM	NAL	24	84	17	19	5	1	4	18	1	12	.226	.323	.452	.775	143	38	0	EWA
1943	31	KCM	NAL	2	8	0	1	0	1	0	0	0	0	.125	.125	.375	.500	58	3	0	
1944														Did not play in major or minor leagues (Military Service)							
1945														Did not play in major or minor leagues (Military Service)							
1946	34	KCM	NAL	24	63	13	16	1	0	2	11	1	22	.254	.447	.365	.812	142	23	0	
1947	35	KCM	NAL	37	97	22	28	4	1	2	17	2	25	.289	.444	.412	.856	132	40	2	
1948	36	CBE	NAL	11	30	6	5	0	0	2	5	3	7	.167	.324	.367	.691	82	11	0	
12 Yrs (+5)			NgL	225	688	122	172	27	19	13	108	9	117	.250	.362	.401	.763	125	276	4	
162 Game Avg.			Pro	162	495	88	124	19	14	9	78	6	84	.250	.362	.401	.763	125	199	3	
7 Yrs		KCM	NAL	165	503	97	129	21	15	11	88	8	94	.256	.376	.423	.799	137	213	2	
3 Yrs		BCA	NSL–NAL+IND	47	151	19	37	6	4	0	14	1	16	.245	.325	.338	.663	93	51	2	
1 Yr		CBE	NAL	11	30	6	5	0	0	2	5	3	7	.167	.324	.367	.691	82	11	0	
1 Yr		CAG	IND	1	3	0	0	0	0	0	0	0	0	.000	.000	.000	.000	-100	0	0	
1 Yr		HG	NN2	1	1	0	1	0	0	0	1	0	0	1.000	1.000	1.000	2.000	412	1	0	
9 Yrs		KCM	NAL	204	620	118	160	25	19	13	103	8	113	.258	.376	.423	.798	135	262	4	
2 Yrs		BCA	IND	10	34	2	7	2	0	0	3	0	1	.206	.229	.265	.493	53	9	0	
1 Yr		CBE	NSL	10	33	4	4	0	0	0	1	0	3	.121	.194	.121	.316	0	4	0	
1 Yr		HG	NN2	1	1	0	1	0	0	0	1	0	0	1.000	1.000	1.000	2.000	412	1	0	

Postseason Batting

Year	Age	Tm	Lg	Series	Opp	Rslt	G	AB	R	H	2B	3B	HR	RBI	SB	BB	BA	OBP	SLG	OPS	HBP
1938	26	BCA	NSL	ALC	MRS	L	2	6	0	0	0	0	0	0	0	0	.000	.000	.000	.000	0
1939 □	27	KCM	NAL	ALC	SLS	W	5	17	3	4	2	0	0	2	0	1	.235	.278	.353	.631	0
1942 □	30	KCM	NAL	WS	HG	W	4	16	6	8	0	0	2	5	0	3	.500	.579	.813	1.391	0
1946	34	KCM	NAL	WS	NE	L	1	4	1	1	0	0	0	0	0	0	.250	.250	.250	.500	0
4 Yrs (4 Series)			NgL				12	43	10	13	4	0	2	6	0	4	.302	.362	.465	.827	0
2 Yrs			ALC				7	23	3	4	2	0	0	2	0	1	.235	.278	.353	.631	0
2 Yrs			WS				5	20	7	9	0	0	2	6	0	3	.750	.829	1.063	1.891	0

All-Star Batting

Year	Age	Tm	Lg	Game	G	AB	R	H	2B	3B	HR	RBI	SB	BB	BA	OBP	SLG	OPS	HBP
1940	28	KCM	WES	EWA	C	2	0	0	0	0	0	0	0	1	.000	.333	.000	.333	0
1942	30	KCM	WES	EWA	C/C	6	0	0	0	0	0	1	0	1	.000	.143	.000	.143	0
2 Yrs (3 GP)			NgL		3	8	0	0	0	0	0	1	0	2	.000	.200	.000	.200	0

20. The Negro Leagues All-Star Register

Pete Hill
Standard Batting

Year	Age	Tm	Lg	G	AB	R	H	2B	3B	HR	RBI	SB	BB	BA	OBP	SLG	OPS	OPS+	TB	HBP	Awards
1904	21	PG	IND	8	31	3	10	0	0	0	4	3	1	.323	.344	.323	.666	110	10	0	
1905	22	PG	EAS	11	48	12	29	6	2	1	17	9	1	.604	.612	.875	1.487	313	42	1	
1906	23	PG	EAS	29	113	25	42	2	5	0	12	11	13	.372	.441	.478	.919	179	54	0	
1907	24	PG	NAC	15	60	8	19	1	0	2	7	3	4	.317	.359	.433	.793	171	26	0	
1908	25	LEL	WES	20	79	22	31	10	2	1			11	.392	.467	.608	1.074	175	48	0	
1909	26	LEL	WES	25	96	21	34	7	1	**2**	**24**	2	**13**	**.354**	.431	.510	.942	**199**	**49**	0	
1910	27	LEL	WES	22	94	28	48	10	4	4	18	1	6	**.511**	**.540**	**.830**	**1.370**	**312**	78	0	
1911	28	CAG	WES	30	113	25	41	9	1	1	27	1	8	.363	.405	.487	.892	173	55	0	
1912	29	CAG	WES	40	158	41	63	10	4	2	23	0	14	.399	.448	.551	.998	201	87	1	
1913	30	CAG	WES	44	173	35	59	9	0	2	34	1	19	.341	.409	.428	.837	145	74	1	
1914	31	CAG	WES	44	172	35	53	9	2	2	22	2	14	.308	.367	.459	.826	147	79	2	
1915	32	CAG	WES	54	204	40	52	13	4	6	29	2	24	.255	.333	.426	.760	158	87	2	
1916	33	CAG	WES	56	184	41	56	7	2	2	33	8	27	**.304**	.399	.397	.796	153	73	0	
1917	34	CAG	WES	58	193	29	47	8	3	0	23	9	**41**	.244	.381	.316	.697	142	61	2	
1918	35	CAG	WES	25	86	22	24	4	2	0	14	5	10	.279	.361	.372	.733	121	32	2	
1919	36	DS	WES	38	139	40	55	9	6	**16**	**52**	6	23	**.396**	**.488**	**.892**	**1.380**	**288**	**124**	1	
1920	37	DS	NNL	45	135	25	38	7	1	3	22	5	**38**	.281	.443	.415	.857	144	56	1	
1921	38	DS	NNL	61	205	33	69	9	6	3	44	4	29	.337	.433	.483	.916	156	99	6	
1922	39	PRS	IND	5	9	5	4	2	0	0	2	0	3	.444	.444	.667	1.282	263	6	1	
1923	40	MB	NNL	26	81	8	24	4	0	0	8	1	9	.296	.374	.346	.719	92	28		
1924	41	BBS	ECL	20	69	13	18	2	1	0	7	1	8	.261	.338	.319	.657	89	22		
1925	42	BBS	ECL	7	18	2	5	0	0	1	3	0	0	.278	.278	.444	.722	89	8		
6 Yrs (+16)			NgL	164	517	86	158	24	8	7	86	11	87	.306	.414	.424	.838	133	219	**9**	
162 Game Avg.			NgL	162	511	85	156	24	8	7	85	11	86	.306	.414	.424	.838	133	216	**9**	
16 Yrs			Pre-NgL	500	1864	412	624	111	36	40	343	51	227	.335	.410	.497	.907	188	927	11	
22 Yrs			Pre-NgL+NgL	664	2381	498	782	135	44	47	429	62	314	**.328**	**.411**	**.481**	**.892**	176	1146	**20**	
162 Game Avg.			Pre-NgL+Pro	162	581	122	191	33	11	11	105	15	77	**.328**	**.411**	**.481**	**.892**	176	280	5	
2 Yrs		DS	NNL+WES	106	340	58	107	16	7	6	66	9	67	.315	.437	.456	.893	151	155	7	
2 Yrs		BBS	ECL	27	87	15	23	2	1	1	10	1	8	.264	.326	.345	.671	89	30	1	
1 Yr		MB	NNL	26	81	8	24	4	0	0	8	1	9	.296	.374	.346	.719	92	28	1	
1 Yr		PRS	IND	5	9	5	4	2	0	0	2	0	3	.444	.615	.667	1.282	263	6	1	
3 Yrs			NNL	132	421	66	131	20	7	6	74	10	76	.311	.426	.435	.860	140	183	8	
2 Yrs			ECL	27	87	15	23	2	1	1	10	1	8	.264	.326	.345	.671	89	30		
1 Yr			IND	5	9	5	4	2	0	0	2	0	3	.444	.615	.667	1.282	263	6	1	

Sammy T. Hughes
Standard Batting

Year	Age	Tm	Lg	G	AB	R	H	2B	3B	HR	RBI	SB	BB	BA	OBP	SLG	OPS	OPS+	TB	HBP	Awards
1930	19	LVB	NNL	18	62	7	16	2	1	1	7	2	3	.258	.292	.371	.663	78	23	0	
1931	20	LOW	NNL	24	83	13	28	9	1	1	14	0	7	.337	.389	.506	.895	150	42	0	
1932	21	WAP	EWL	36	114	22	40	3	3	1	15	2	14	.351	.426	.456	.882	149	52	1	EWA
1933	22	NEG	NN2	24	90	12	30	4	1	0	14	1	10	.333	.400	.400	.800	122	36	0	
1934 *	23	NEG	NN2	37	135	26	43	7	0	1	21	5	12	.319	.374	.393	.767	111	53	0	EWA
1935 *	24	CEG	NN2	27	119	31	38	10	2	0	17	0	15	.319	.396	.437	.832	105	52	0	EWA
1936 *	25	WEG	NN2	32	119	29	38	2	5	3	22	1	16	.319	.404	.496	.900	133	59	1	EWA
1937	26	TOTAL	NN2+IND	27	99	23	32	7	3	2	13	1	9	.323	.385	.515	.900	132	51	1	
	-	WEG	NN2	26	95	23	31	7	3	2	13	0	9	.326	.390	.526	.917	134	50	1	
	-	NAS	IND	1	4	0	1	0	0	0	0	1	0	.250	.250	.250	.500	85	1	0	
1938 *	27	BEG	NN2	26	105	24	38	7	4	2	22	3	10	.362	.422	.562	.984	134	59	1	EWA
1939 *	28	BEG	NN2	22	90	20	34	7	2	0	12	0	10	.378	.440	.500	.940	153	45		EWA
1940	29	BEG	NN2	53	206	47	55	13	3	6	36	4	26	.267	.349	.447	.796	108	92		
1941	30	ULT	MEX	82	340	67	110	23	6	3	34	14	38	.324	.392	.453	.844	111	154		
1942	31	BEG	NN2	50	199	39	55	12	1	2	30		17	.276	.333	.377	.710	104	75		
1943											Did not play in major or minor leagues (Military Service)										
1944											Did not play in major or minor leagues (Military Service)										
1945											Did not play in major or minor leagues (Military Service)										
1946	35	BEG	NN2	42	127	26	34	3	1	2	17	2	28	.268	.408	.354	.762	107	45	2	
13 Yrs (+3)			NgL	500	1888	386	591	109	33	24	274	36	215	.313	.385	.444	.829	119	838	6	
162 Game Avg.			Pro	162	612	125	191	35	11	8	89	12	70	.313	.385	.444	.829	119	272	2	
5 Yrs		BEG	NN2	193	727	156	216	42	11	12	117	10	91	.297	.378	.435	.812	116	316	3	
1 Yr		ULT	MEX	82	340	67	110	23	6	3	34	14	38	.324	.392	.453	.844	111	154		
2 Yrs		NEG	NN2	61	225	38	73	11	1	1	35	6	22	.324	.385	.396	.780	115	89	0	
2 Yrs		WEG	NN2	58	214	52	69	9	8	5	35	1	25	.322	.398	.509	.908	133	109	2	
1 Yr		WAP	EWL	36	114	22	40	3	3	1	15	2	14	.351	.426	.456	.882	149	52	1	
1 Yr		CEG	NN2	27	119	31	38	10	2	0	17	0	15	.319	.396	.437	.832	105	52	0	
1 Yr		LOW	NNL	24	83	13	28	9	1	1	14	0	7	.337	.389	.506	.895	150	42	0	
1 Yr		LVB	NN2	18	62	7	16	2	1	1	7	2	3	.258	.292	.371	.663	78	23	0	
1 Yr		NAS	IND	1	4	0	1	0	0	0	0	1	0	.250	.250	.250	.500	85	1	0	
10 Yrs		NN2		339	1285	277	396	72	22	18	204	17	153	.308	.384	.440	.824	118	566	5	
1 Yr		MEX		82	340	67	110	23	6	3	34	14	38	.324	.392	.453	.844	111	154		
2 Yrs		NNL		42	145	20	44	11	2	2	21	2	10	.303	.348	.448	.797	119	65	0	
1 Yr		EWL		36	114	22	40	3	3	1	15	2	14	.351	.426	.456	.882	149	52	1	
1 Yr		IND		1	4	0	1	0	0	0	0	1	0	.250	.250	.250	.500	85	1	0	

20. The Negro Leagues All-Star Register

Sammy T. Hughes

Postseason Batting

Year	Age	Tm	Lg	Series	Opp	Rslt	G	AB	R	H	2B	3B	HR	RBI	SB	BB	BA	OBP	SLG	OPS	HBP
1939	28	BEG	NN2	NLP	NE	W	4	15	6	7	2	0	1	5	1	2	.467	1	.800	1.329	
1939 α	28	BEG	NN2	NLC	HG	W	4	11	1	3	1	0	0	1	0	4	.273	0	.364	.830	
1 Yr (2 Series)			NgL				8	26	7	10	3	0	1	6	1	6	.385	1	.615	1.115	
1 Yr				NLP			4	15	6	7	2	0	1	5	1	2	.467	1	.800	1.329	
1 Yr				NLC			4	11	1	3	1	0	0	1	0	4	.273	0	.364	.830	

All-Star Batting

Year	Age	Tm	Lg	Lg	G	AB	R	H	2B	3B	HR	RBI	SB	BB	BA	OBP	SLG	OPS	HBP
1934	23			EWA	2B										.000	.000	.000	.000	0
1935	24			EWA	2B	4	0	1	0	0	0	0	0	0	.250	.250	.250	.500	0
1936	25			EWA	2B	5	2	1	0	0	0	0	0	1	.200	.333	.400	.733	0
1938	27			EWA	2B	5	1	2	1	0	0	1	0	0	.400	.400	.600	1.000	0
1939	28			EWA	2B2B	5	1	1	0	0	0	2	0	2	.200	.429	.200	.629	0
5 Yrs (6 GP)			NgL			21	4	5	2	0	0	3	0	3	.238	.333	.333	.667	0

Monte Irvin

Standard Batting

Year	Age	Tm	Lg	G	AB	R	H	2B	3B	HR	RBI	SB	BB	BA	OBP	SLG	OPS	OPS+	TB	HBP	Awards
1938	19	NE	NN2	1	1	0	0	0	0	0	0	0	8	.000	.000	.000	.000	-100	0	0	
1939	20	NE	NN2	27	97	15	25	3	1	3	18	1	8	.258	.314	.402	.716	89	39		
1940	21	NE	NN2	38	143	30	53	9	4	4	39	2	15	.371	.430	.573	1.004	157	82		
1941 *	22	NE	NN2	41	152	34	60	12	1	8	48	8	13	.395	.442	.645	1.087	211	98		EWA
1942	23	NE	NN2	4	18	7	11	3	0	1	11	0	0	.611	.611	1.056	1.667	383	19		
1942	23	VCZ	MEX																		Played in unrecorded Mexican league
1943	24	NE	NN2	1	4	1	1	0	0	0	0	0	0	.250	.250	.250	.500	31	1	0	MVP-1
1944																						Did not play in major or minor leagues (Military Service)
1945	26	NE	NN2	2	9	0	1	0	0	0	0	0	0	.111	.111	.111	.222	-39	1	0	
1946 *	27	NE	NN2	57	217	52	80	17	2	6	54	2	28	.369	.443	.548	.989	173	119	1	EWAx2
1947 *	28	NE	NN2	57	204	41	62	6	1	11	47	6	32	.304	.401	.505	.903	147	103	1	EWAx2
1948 *	29	NE	NN2	44	156	26	42	4	2	6	29	2	20	.269	.356	.436	.788	129	68	1	EWA
1949	30	NYG	NL	36	76	7	17	3	2	0	7	0	17	.224	.366	.316	.681	84	24	2	
1950	31	NYG	NL	110	374	61	112	19	5	15	66	3	52	.299	.392	.497	.882	131	186	5	
1951	32	NYG	NL	151	558	94	174	19	11	24	121	12	89	.312	.415	.514	.921	147	287	9	MVP-3
1952 *	33	NYG	NL	46	126	10	39	2	1	4	21	0	10	.310	.365	.437	.797	120	55	1	ASG, MVP-31
1953	34	NYG	NL	124	444	72	146	21	5	21	97	2	55	.329	.406	.541	.943	141	240	3	
1954	35	NYG	NL	135	432	62	113	13	3	19	64	7	70	.262	.363	.438	.801	108	189	2	
1955	36	NYG	NL	51	150	16	38	7	1	1	17	3	17	.253	.337	.333	.671	79	50	3	MVP-15
1956	37	CHC	NL	111	339	44	92	13	3	15	50	1	41	.271	.346	.460	.807	116	156	0	
18 Yrs (+2)			Pro	1036	3500	572	1066	151	43	138	689	52	467	.305	.390	.491	.883	135	1717	28	
10 Yrs			NgL	272	1001	206	335	54	12	39	246	24	116	.335	.405	.529	.936	159	530	3	
8 Yrs			MLB	764	2499	366	731	97	31	99	443	28	351	.293	.384	.475	.862	125	1187	25	
162 Game Avg.			Pro	162	547	89	167	24	7	22	108	8	73	.305	.390	.491	.883	135	268	4	
10 Yrs		NE	NN2	272	1001	206	335	54	12	39	246	24	116	.335	.405	.529	.936	159	530	3	
7 Yrs		NYG	NL	653	2160	322	639	84	28	84	393	27	310	.296	.389	.477	.871	145	1031	25	
1 Yr		CHC	NL	111	339	44	92	13	3	15	50	1	41	.271	.346	.460	.807	116	156	0	
10 Yrs			NN2	272	1001	206	335	54	12	39	246	24	116	.335	.405	.529	.936	159	530	3	
8 Yrs			NL	764	2499	366	731	97	31	99	443	28	351	.293	.384	.475	.862	125	1187	25	

Monte Irvin
Postseason Batting

Year	Age	Tm	Lg	Series	Opp	Rslt	G	AB	R	H	2B	3B	HR	RBI	SB	BB	BA	OBP	SLG	OPS	HBP
1939 □	20	NE	NN2	NLP	BEG	L	4	12	0	3	0	0	0	0	0	3	.250	.400	.250	.650	0
1946 □	27	NE	NN2	WS	KCM	W	7	26	10	12	2	0	3	8	1	4	.462	.533	.885	1.418	0
1951	32	NYG	NL	WS	NYY	L	6	24	3	11	0	1	0	2	2	2	.458	.500	.542	1.042	0
1954 □	35	NYG	NL	WS	CLE	W	4	9	1	2	1	0	0	0	0	0	.222	.222	.333	.556	0
4 Yrs (4 Series)			Pro				21	71	14	28	3	1	3	13	3	9	.394	.463	.592	1.054	0
2 Yrs (2 Series)			NgL	NLP			11	38	10	15	2	0	3	9	1	7	.395	.489	.684	1.173	0
1 Yr				WS			4	12	0	3	0	0	0	1	0	3	.250	.400	.250	.650	0
1 Yr							7	26	10	12	2	0	3	8	1	4	.462	.533	.885	1.418	0
2 Yrs (2 Series)			MLB	WS			10	33	4	13	1	1	0	4	2	2	.394	.429	.485	.913	0
2 Yrs							10	33	4	13	1	1	0	4	2	2	.394	.429	.485	.913	0

All-Star Batting

Year	Age	Tm	Game	G	AB	R	H	2B	3B	HR	RBI	SB	BB	BA	OBP	SLG	OPS	HBP
1941	22	NN2	EWA	3B	5	0	2	1	0	0	0	1	0	.400	.400	.600	1.000	0
1946	27	NN2	EWA	LF/LF	8	1	2	0	0	0	1	1	0	.250	.250	.250	.500	0
1947	28	NN2	EWA	LF/LF	6	2	1	0	0	0	0	0	2	.167	.444	.167	.542	1
1948	29	NN2	EWA	RF	2	0	0	0	0	0	0	0	0	.000	.000	.000	.000	0
1952	33	NL	ASG	DNP														
5 Yrs (6 GP)		Pro		6	21	3	5	1	0	0	1	2	2	.238	.333	.286	.590	1
4 Yrs (6 GP)		NgL		6	21	3	5	1	0	0	1	2	2	.238	.333	.286	.590	1
1 Yr (0 GP)		MLB		0														

Sam "The Jet" Jethroe

Standard Batting

Year	Age	Tm	Lg	G	AB	R	H	2B	3B	HR	RBI	SB	BB	BA	OBP	SLG	OPS	OPS+	TB	HBP	Awards
1938	21	AB3	NAL	1	3	0	1	1	0	0	0	0	0	.333	.333	.667	1.000	183	2	0	
1941	24	STL	East									Played in unrecorded independent league									
1942 *	25	CCB	NAL	31	118	19	36	10	1	1	18	7	6	.305	.339	.432	.771	137	51	0	EWA
1943	26	CBE	NAL	36	142	28	44	12	4	1	14	5	5	.310	.339	.472	.805	153	67	0	
1944 *	27	CBE	NAL	17	65	15	25	4	0	1	10	1	7	.385	.444	.492	.937	194	32	0	EWA
1945	28	CBE	NAL	20	76	14	25	5	5	1	19	5	8	.329	.407	.566	.973	185	43	2	
1946 *	29	CBE	NAL	16	63	14	16	5	2	1	10	3	5	.254	.319	.365	.684	104	23	1	EWA
1947 *	30	CBE	NAL	16	62	20	22	5	2	2	6	10	8	.355	.429	.597	1.025	177	37	0	EWA
1948	31	CBE	NAL	9	35	10	10	4	1	1	6	5	4	.286	.405	.543	.948	149	19	3	
1948	31	Montreal	IL									Played in minor leagues (Integration)									
1949	32	Montreal	IL									Played in minor leagues (Integration)									
1950	33	BSN	NL	141	582	100	159	28	8	18	58	35	52	.273	.338	.442	.780	109	257	5	ROY-1
1951	34	BSN	NL	148	572	101	160	29	10	18	65	35	57	.280	.356	.460	.816	125	263	11	
1952	35	BSN	NL	151	608	79	141	23	7	13	58	28	68	.232	.318	.357	.675	89	217	9	
1953	36	Toledo	AA									Played in minor leagues (Integration)									
1954	37	PIT	NL	2	1	0	0	0	0	0	0	0	0	.000	.000	.000	.000	-100	0	0	
1955	38	Toronto	IL									Played in minor leagues (Integration)									
1956	39	Toronto	IL									Played in minor leagues (Integration)									
1957	40	Toronto	IL									Played in minor leagues (Integration)									
1958	41	Toronto	IL									Played in minor leagues (Integration)									
12 Yrs (+6)			Pro	588	2327	400	639	123	39	57	264	134	220	.275	.345	.434	.780	119	1011	31	
8 Yrs			NgL	146	564	120	179	43	14	8	83	36	43	.317	.372	.486	.858	156	274	6	
4 Yrs			MLB	442	1763	280	460	80	25	49	181	98	177	.261	.337	.418	.755	107	737	25	
162 Game Avg.			Pro	162	641	110	176	34	11	16	73	37	61	.275	.345	.434	.780	119	279	9	
3 Yrs			NL	440	1762	280	460	80	25	49	181	98	177	.261	.337	.418	.755	107	737	25	
6 Yrs			NAL	114	443	101	142	32	13	7	65	29	37	.321	.381	.499	.880	161	221	6	
1 Yr			NAL	31	118	19	36	10	1	1	18	7	6	.305	.339	.432	.771	137	51	0	
1 Yr			NL	2	1	0	0	0	0	0	0	0	0	.000	.000	.000	.000	-100	0	0	
1 Yr			NAL	1	3	0	1	1	0	0	0	0	0	.333	.333	.667	1.000	183	2	0	
4 Yrs			NL	442	1763	280	460	80	25	49	181	98	177	.261	.337	.418	.755	107	737	25	
8 Yrs			NAL	146	564	120	179	43	14	8	83	36	43	.317	.372	.486	.858	156	274	6	

Postseason Batting

Year	Age	Tm	Lg	Series	Opp	Rslt	G	AB	R	H	2B	3B	HR	RBI	SB	BB	BA	OBP	SLG	OPS	HBP
1945 □	28	CBE	NAL	WS	HG	W	4	15	1	4	0	0	0	2	1	2	.267	.353	.400	.753	0
1947	30	CBE	NAL	WS	NYC	L	5	19	4	6	2	0	0	1	0	4	.316	.435	.421	.856	0
2 Yrs (2 Series)			NgL				9	34	5	10	2	0	0	3	1	6	.294	.400	.412	.812	0
2 Yrs				WS			9	34	5	10	2	0	0	3	1	6	.294	.400	.412	.812	0

All-Star Batting

Year	Age	Tm	Lg	Game		G	AB	R	H	2B	3B	HR	RBI	SB	BB	BA	OBP	SLG	OPS	HBP
1942	25			EWA	CF/CF	6	1	0	0	0	0	0	0	0	.167	.167	.167	.333	0	
1944	27			EWA	CF	3	0	0	0	0	0	0	0	0	.000	.000	.000	.000	0	
1946	29			EWA	CF/CF	7	2	2	0	0	0	0	0	1	0	.000	.125	.000	.125	1	
1947	30			EWA	CF/CF	8	2	0	4	2	0	0	4	2	0	.500	.556	1.000	1.500	1	
4 Yrs (7 GP)			NgL			7	24	5	5	0	0	0	4	3	0	.208	.269	.375	.583	2	

Grant "Home Run" Johnson
Standard Batting

Year	Age	Tm	Lg	G	AB	R	H	2B	3B	HR	RBI	SB	BB	BA	OBP	SLG	OPS	OPS+	TB	HBP	Awards
1893	20			Played in unrecorded semi-professional league																	
1894	21			Played in unrecorded semi-professional league																	
1895	22	PFG	IND											No statistics available							
1896	23	PFG	IND											No statistics available							
1897	24	PFG	IND	1	5		1	0	0	0	0		0	.200	.200	.200	.400	-4	1	0	
1898	25	PFG	IND											No statistics available							
1899	26	CCG	IND	4	17	4	9	1	0	2	7		0	.529	.529	.941	1.471	274	16	0	
1900	27	CU	IND	3	12	1	3	0	1	0	2		1	.250	.308	.417	.724	118	5	0	
1901	28	CCG	IND	1	4	1	2	1	0	0	0	1	1	.500	.600	.750	1.350	320	3	0	
1902	29	CCG	WES	3	12	4	2	0	0	0	0		2	.167	.286	.167	.452	30	2	0	
1903	30	CXG	EAS	7	27	2	8	1	0	0	3		2	.296	.345	.333	.678	149	9	0	
1904	31	CXG	IND	8	31	8	12	2	0	1	7	2	4	.387	.472	.548	1.021	236	17	1	
1905	32	PG	EAS	11	46	11	17	4	0	1	8	5	4	.370	.431	.522	.953	166	24	1	
1906	33	BRG	EAS	24	94	21	34	10	2	3	22	3	9	.362	.459	.606	1.066	223	57	8	
1907	34	BRG	NAC	22	82	11	24	3	3	0	5		5	.293	.348	.402	.751	150	33	2	
1908	35	BRG	NAC	23	93	15	29	6	1	0	19	4	6	.312	.354	.398	.751	137	37	0	
1909	36	BRG	INT	5	22	2	4	0	0	0	1	2	0	.182	.182	.182	.364	7	4	0	
1910	37	LEL	WES	21	89	19	29	9	0	1	14		5	.326	.368	.461	.829	151	41	1	
1911	38	TOTAL	WES+EAS	26	93	16	27	5	0	0	8	2	12	.290	.383	.344	.727	118	32	2	
–	–	PG	EAS	17	61	9	20	4	0	0	4	2	7	.328	.414	.393	.808	133	24	2	
–	–	COG	WES	9	32	7	7	1	0	0	4	0	5	.219	.324	.250	.574	89	8	0	
1912	39	BRG	EAS	10	36	6	11	3	1	0	7	1	3	.306	.419	.444	.863	149	16	4	
1913	40	BRG	EAS	16	62	12	28	3	0	0	10	1	3	.452	.500	.500	1.000	219	31	3	
1914	41	NLG	EAS	7	27	7	12	2	0	0	5	2	4	.444	.531	.519	1.050	192	14	1	
17 Yrs (+5)			Pre-NgL	192	752	141	252	50	8	8	118	23	61	.335	.402	.455	.857	161	342	23	
162 Game Avg.			Pre-NgL	162	635	119	213	42	7	7	100	19	51	.335	.402	.455	.857	161	289	19	

William "Judy" Johnson
Standard Batting

Year	Age	Tm	Lg	G	AB	R	H	2B	3B	HR	RBI	SB	BB	BA	OBP	SLG	OPS	OPS+	TB	HBP	Awards
1918	18	TOTAL	EAS	3	8	0	3	1	0	0	0	0	1	.375	.444	.500	.944	155	4	0	
—	—	AC	EAS	1	4	0	1	0	0	0	0	0	0	.250	.250	.250	.500	42	1	0	
—	—	HIL	EAS	2	4	0	2	1	0	0	0	0	1	.500	.600	.750	1.350	267	3	0	
1919	19											Played in unrecorded semi-professional league									
1920	20											Played in unrecorded semi-professional league									
1921	21	HIL	EAS	29	97	12	26	2	5	2	14	1	7	.268	.317	.454	.771	94	44	0	
1922	22	HIL	IND	39	125	18	35	3	3	0	15	3	11	.280	.338	.320	.658	93	40	0	
1923	23	HIL	ECL	61	212	32	58	9	1	2	30	5	14	.274	.319	.354	.672	88	75	0	
1924	24	HIL	ECL	68	256	50	86	21	5	4	47	10	20	.336	.384	.504	.888	150	129		
1925	25	HIL	ECL	70	262	61	102	15	8	6	66	6	19	.389	.431	.576	1.007	155	151		
1926	26	HIL	ECL	87	335	63	109	19	6	2	63	16	23	.325	.374	.436	.805	116	146	3	
1927	27	HIL	ECL	77	279	32	70	12	5	1	37	1	19	.251	.301	.358	.657	71	100	1	
1928	28	TOTAL	EAS	62	219	23	53	11	5	0	36	2	15	.242	.300	.352	.645	73	77	2	
—	—	HIL	EAS	60	213	22	51	11	5	0	36	2	15	.239	.296	.352	.642	72	75	2	
—	—	CAS	EAS	2	6	1	2	0	0	0	0	0	1	.333	.429	.333	.762	95	2		
1929	29	TOTAL	ANL+IND	84	342	81	125	21	5	7	72	14	21	.365	.404	.518	.920	124	177	1	
—	—	DMS	IND	2	7	2	2	0	0	1	3	0	0	.286	.286	.714	1.000	208	5	0	
—	—	TOTAL	ANL	82	335	79	123	21	5	6	69	14	21	.367	.406	.513	.918	122	172	1	
—	—	HIL	ANL	78	319	78	119	21	5	6	69	14	21	.373	.413	.527	.938	127	168	1	
—	—	HG	ANL	4	16	1	4	0	0	0	0	0	0	.250	.250	.250	.500	24	4	0	
1930	30	HG	EAS	55	217	46	62	8	5	3	32	5	24	.286	.360	.410	.767	93	89	1	
1931	31	HIL	IND	49	175	21	43	6	4	2	25	5	8	.246	.279	.360	.639	77	63	0	
1932	32	TOTAL	EWL+IND	63	229	47	76	5	5	2	32	5	21	.332	.388	.410	.798	116	94	0	
—	—	HIL	EWL	25	87	16	31	3	3	1	12	2	9	.356	.417	.414	.830	128	36	0	
—	—	PC	IND	38	142	31	45	2	2	1	20	3	12	.317	.370	.408	.779	109	58	0	
1933 *	33	PC	NN2	70	270	40	68	17	2	0	43	9	17	.252	.296	.330	.626	71	89	0	EWA
1934	34	PC	NN2	69	256	34	68	14	3	1	40	5	16	.266	.309	.355	.664	87	91	0	
1935	35	PC	NN2	46	178	34	50	11	2	2	30	3	7	.281	.308	.399	.707	77	71	0	
1936 *	36	TOTAL	NN2	54	193	26	44	10	1	2	20	5	20	.228	.304	.290	.591	53	56	1	EWA
—	—	PC	NN2	53	188	25	43	10	1	2	20	5	20	.229	.306	.293	.595	54	55	1	
—	—	NYC	NN2	1	5	1	1	0	0	0	0	0	0	.200	.200	.200	.400	0	1	0	
17 Yrs (+3)			NgL	983	3645	620	1075	184	61	37	602	93	263	.295	.344	.409	.753	99	1492	9	
162 Game Avg.			Pro	162	601	102	177	30	10	6	99	15	43	.295	.344	.409	.753	99	246	1	
1 Yr			Pre-NgL	3	8	0	3	1	0	0	0	0	1	.375	.444	.500	.944	155	4	0	
18 Yrs			Pre-NgL+NgL	986	3653	620	1078	185	61	37	602	93	264	.295	.344	.410	.754	99	1496	9	
162 Game Avg.			Pre-NgL+Pro	162	600	102	177	30	10	6	99	15	43	.295	.344	.410	.754	99	246	1	
8 Yrs			ECL+ANL+EWL+E AS+IND	643	2360	405	730	122	47	27	414	64	166	.309	.356	.435	.792	109	1027	7	
5 Yrs		HIL	PC	276	1034	164	274	54	9	6	153	24	72	.265	.313	.352	.665	78	364	1	
2 Yrs		PC	HG	59	233	47	66	8	5	3	32	5	28	.283	.353	.399	.752	88	93	1	
1 Yr		HG	DMS	2	7	2	2	0	0	1	3	0	0	.286	.286	.714	1.000	208	5	0	
1 Yr		DMS	EAS	2	6	1	2	0	0	0	0	0	0	.333	.429	.333	.762	95	2	0	
1 Yr		CAS	NYC	1	5	1	1	0	0	0	0	0	0	.200	.200	.200	.400	0	1	0	
5 Yrs			ECL	363	1344	238	425	76	26	16	243	38	95	.316	.363	.447	.810	116	601	4	
4 Yrs			NN2	239	897	134	230	52	8	3	133	22	60	.256	.304	.342	.646	73	307	1	
3 Yrs			EAS	146	533	81	141	21	15	6	82	8	47	.265	.328	.394	.722	85	210	3	
4 Yrs			IND	128	449	72	125	11	6	6	63	10	31	.278	.325	.370	.695	94	166	0	
1 Yr			ANL	82	335	79	123	21	5	6	69	14	21	.367	.406	.513	.920	122	172	1	
1 Yr			EWL	25	87	16	31	3	3	1	12	2	9	.356	.417	.414	.830	128	36	0	

William "Judy" Johnson
Postseason Batting

Year	Age	Tm	Lg	Series	Opp	Rslt	G	AB	R	H	2B	3B	HR	RBI	SB	BB	BA	OBP	SLG	OPS	HBP
1924	24	HIL	ECL	WS	KCM	L	10	44	7	15	5	1	1	7	0	2	.341	.370	.568	.938	0
1925 a	25	HIL	ECL	WS	KCM	W	6	24	1	6	1	0	0	1	1	0	.250	.240	.292	.532	0
1935 a	35	PC	NN2	NLC	NYC	W	4	11	0	1	0	0	0	1	0	0	.091	.091	.091	.182	0
3 Yrs (3 Series)			NgL				20	79	8	22	6	1	1	9	1	2	.278	.296	.418	.714	0
1 Yr			NLC				4	11	0	1	0	0	0	1	0	0	.091	.091	.091	.182	0
2 Yrs			WS				16	68	8	21	6	1	1	8	1	2	.309	.329	.471	.799	0

All-Star Batting

Year	Age	Lg	Game	G	AB	R	H	2B	3B	HR	RBI	SB	BB	BA	OBP	SLG	OPS	HBP
1933	33	EAS	EWA	3B	1	0	1	0	0	0	0	0	0	1.000	1.000	1.000	2.000	0
1936	36	EAS	EWA	3B	2	0	1	0	0	0	1	0	0	.500	.500	.500	1.000	0
2 Yrs (2 GP)		NgL			3	0	2	0	0	0	1	0	0	.667	.667	.667	1.333	0

Walter "Buck" Leonard
Standard Batting

Year	Age	Tm	Lg	G	AB	R	H	2B	3B	HR	RBI	SB	BB	BA	OBP	SLG	OPS	OPS+	TB	HBP	Awards
1933	25	BRG	IND	1	4	1	1	0	0	0	0	0	0	.250	.250	.250	.500	40	1	0	
1934	26	HG	IND	20	78	12	26	3	0	3	17	0	6	.333	.381	.487	.868	162	38	0	
1935 *	27	HG	NN2	40	157	30	61	18	3	4	36	5	17	.389	.451	.618	1.069	172	97	1	EWA
1936	28	HG	NN2	35	124	35	43	3	4	6	34	2	29	.347	.471	.581	1.051	167	72	0	
1937 *	29	HG	NN2	42	170	54	64	15	3	13	55	2	25	.376	.462	.729	1.191	203	124	2	EWA
1938 *	30	HG	NN2	42	150	41	63	11	5	9	53	1	24	.420	.500	.740	1.240	217	111	0	EWA
1939 *	31	HG	NN2	30	109	35	42	10	0	11	48	2	21	.385	.485	.780	1.264	235	85		EWA
1940 *	32	HG	NN2	49	168	44	62	12	3	8	48	2	34	.369	.475	.619	1.094	185	104		EWA
1941 *	33	HG	NN2	47	161	54	56	9	6	11	40	6	38	.348	.472	.683	1.156	231	110		EWA
1942	34	HG	NN2	30	100	16	22	5	0	0	12	3	19	.220	.345	.270	.615	81	27		
1943 *	35	HG	NN2	67	254	71	84	16	8	4	63	2	47	.331	.439	.504	.943	150	128	2	EWA, NSA
1944 *	36	HG	NN2	49	179	47	60	14	6	7	43	1	29	.335	.428	.598	1.026	174	107		EWA
1945 *	37	HG	NN2	36	138	30	47	5	3	5	30	0	20	.341	.431	.529	.960	169	73	2	EWA
1946 *	38	HG	NN2	49	166	37	56	6	4	7	44	3	38	.337	.461	.548	1.009	181	91	0	EWA
1947	39	HG	NN2	32	102	17	31	5	1	6	23	2	22	.304	.432	.549	.981	167	56	1	
1948 *	40	HG	NN2	35	113	20	30	7	0	4	17	1	27	.265	.415	.434	.849	149	49	2	EWA
16 Yrs			NgL	604	2173	544	748	139	46	98	563	32	396	.344	.447	.586	1.033	178	1273	10	
162 Game Avg.			NgL	162	583	146	201	37	12	26	151	9	106	.344	.447	.586	1.033	178	341	3	
15 Yrs			NN2+IND	603	2169	543	747	139	46	98	563	32	396	.344	.448	.586	1.034	178	1272	10	
1 Yr		HG	IND	1	4	1	1	0	0	0	0	0	0	.250	.250	.250	.500	40	1		
13 Yrs			NN2	583	2091	531	721	136	46	95	546	32	390	.345	.450	.590	1.040	178	1234	10	
2 Yrs		BRG	IND	21	82	13	27	3	0	3	17	0	6	.329	.375	.476	.851	156	39		

20. The Negro Leagues All-Star Register

Walter "Buck" Leonard

Postseason Batting

Year	Age	Tm	Lg	Series	Opp	Rslt	G	AB	R	H	2B	3B	HR	RBI	SB	BB	BA	OBP	SLG	OPS	HBP
1939	31	HG	NN2	NLP	PS	W	2	7	2	3	0	0	0	1	0	0	.429	.429	1.000	1.429	
1939	31	HG	NN2	NLC	BEG	L	5	13	1	6	0	0	0	2	1	4	.462	.588	.462	1.050	1
1942	34	HG	NN2	WS	KCM	L	4	16	3	4	0	0	0	1	0	1	.250	.333	.250	.583	0
1943 □	35	HG	NN2	WS	BBB	W	7	27	7	8	3	1	0	4	1	6	.296	.424	.481	.906	0
1944 □	36	HG	NN2	WS	BBB	W	5	16	5	8	1	0	1	2	1	5	.500	.636	.750	1.386	1
1945	37	HG	NN2	WS	CBE	L	4	15	1	3	0	0	0	0	0	1	.200	.250	.200	.450	0
1948	40	HG	NN2	NLC	BEG	W	4	14	0	5	1	0	0	3	0	3	.357	.471	.429	.899	0
1948 □	40	HG	NN2	WS	BBB	W	1	4	0	0	0	0	0	0	0	0	.000	.000	.000	.000	0
6 Yrs (8 Series)			NgL				32	112	19	37	6	1	2	13	3	20	.330	.440	.455	.887	2
1 Yr				NLP			2	7	2	3	1	0	0	1	0	0	.429	.429	1.000	1.429	0
2 Yrs				NLC			9	27	1	11	1	0	0	5	1	7	.407	.529	.444	.974	1
5 Yrs				WS			21	78	16	23	4	1	2	7	2	13	.295	.409	.410	.806	2

All-Star Batting

Year	Age	Lg	Game	G	AB	R	H	2B	3B	HR	RBI	SB	BB	BA	OBP	SLG	OPS	HBP
1935	27	WES	EWA	1B	2	0	0	0	0	0	1	0	0	.000	.000	.000	.000	0
1937	29	EAS	EWA	1B	4	2	2	0	0	1	2	0	1	.500	.600	1.250	1.850	0
1938	30	EAS	EWA	1B	3	0	1	0	0	0	0	0	0	.333	.333	.333	.667	0
1939	31	EAS	EWA	1B/1B	7	2	2	0	0	0	1	0	2	.286	.444	.286	.730	0
1940	32	EAS	EWA	1B	4	2	3	0	0	0	3	2	2	.750	.833	.750	1.583	0
1941	33	EAS	EWA	1B	5	1	2	0	0	1	3	0	0	.400	.400	1.000	1.400	0
1943	35	EAS	EWA	1B	4	1	1	0	0	1	1	0	0	.250	.250	1.000	1.250	0
1943	35	SAS	NSA	1B	3	2	0	0	0	0	0	0	2	.000	.400	.000	.400	0
1944	36	EAS	EWA	1B	3	1	1	0	1	0	0	0	1	.333	.500	1.000	1.500	0
1945	37	EAS	EWA	1B	3	1	1	0	0	0	0	0	2	.333	.600	.333	.933	0
1946	38	EAS	EWA	1B/1B	7	0	1	0	0	0	2	0	0	.143	.143	.143	.286	0
1948	40	EAS	EWA	1B	4	0	1	1	0	0	0	0	0	.250	.250	.500	.750	0
11 Yrs (14 GP)		NgL			49	12	15	1	1	3	14	2	10	.306	.424	.551	.975	0

John Henry "Pop" Lloyd
Hit 300+ in four different professional leagues
Standard Batting

Year	Age	Tm	Lg	G	AB	R	H	2B	3B	HR	RBI	SB	BB	BA	OBP	SLG	OPS	OPS+	TB	HBP	Awards
1906	22	CXG	EAS	11	35	4	8	0	1	0	3	3	6	.229	.357	.286	.643	99	10	1	1
1907	23	PG	NAC	15	57	9	14	1	0	1	5	2	4	.246	.306	.316	.622	113	18	1	
1908	24	PG	NAC	30	124	31	53	7	4	1	25	4	8	**.427**	**.462**	**.573**	**1.035**	222	**71**	0	
1909	25	PG	INT	18	78	17	35	9	2	2	17	0	6	**.449**	**.488**	**.692**	**1.180**	272	**54**	0	
1910	26	LEL	WES	21	89	12	33	9	1	2	23	3	6	.371	.385	.562	.946	185	50	0	
1911	27	NLG	EAS	15	60	12	25	2	2	1	16	2	5	**.417**	**.462**	.567	1.028	174	34	0	
1912	28	NLG	EAS	21	82	13	29	4	1	1	11	6	3	.354	.384	.463	.847	121	**38**	1	
1913	29	NLG	EAS	16	61	13	23	1	2	0	10	3	5	.377	.424	.459	.883	182	28	0	
1914	30	CAG	WES	48	188	36	57	12	5	0	30	7	19	.303	.367	.420	.787	136	79	0	
1915	31	TOTAL	EAS+WES	51	206	35	76	14	3	1	42	10	12	.369	.404	.481	.884	171	99	0	
		NLS	EAS	33	136	21	54	11	3	0	26	**10**	7	**.397**	**.427**	**.522**	**.949**	178	**71**	0	
		CAG	WES	18	70	14	22	3	0	1	16	0	5	.314	.360	.400	.760	158	28	0	
1916	32	CAG	WES	62	223	38	75	9	2	1	34	6	20	.336	.396	.408	.804	156	91	2	
1917	33	CAG	WES	57	206	26	62	12	7	1	39	6	15	**.301**	.348	**.442**	**.790**	175	**91**	0	
1918	34	BRG	EAS	21	86	15	31	6	4	0	16	1	6	.360	.402	.453	.856	152	39	0	
1919	35	TOTAL	EAS	24	86	8	32	6	3	0	16	**5**	8	**.372**	.426	**.512**	**.937**	184	44	0	
		BRG	EAS	5	15	1	3	0	1	0	2	0	2	.200	.294	.333	.627	86	5	0	
		AC	EAS	19	71	7	29	6	2	0	14	5	6	.408	.455	.549	1.004	205	39	0	
1920	36	BRG	EAS	22	82	8	25	3	2	0	9	4	9	.305	.374	.390	.764	176	32	0	
1921	37	COB	NNL	90	362	65	126	20	8	0	54	24	25	.348	.392	.448	.839	137	162	1	
1922	38	NYB	IND	65	266	45	79	17	0	2	37	9	12	.297	.330	.383	.713	110	102	1	
1923	39	HIL	ECL	41	150	34	55	13	1	1	23	5	9	.367	.403	.507	.909	153	76	0	
1924	40	AC	ECL	58	216	37	79	12	3	1	47	7	18	.366	.415	.463	.877	150	100	0	
1925	41	AC	ECL	71	254	43	84	8	5	3	57	13	32	.331	.406	.437	.843	120	111	0	
1926	42	NLG	ECL	49	184	27	60	6	3	1	32	4	16	.326	.386	.408	.794	102	75	2	
1927	43	NLG	ECL	29	111	17	34	8	1	1	18	0	4	.306	.330	.423	.754	84	47	0	
1928	44	NLG	ECL	36	133	31	51	4	1	5	23	4	10	.383	.431	.541	.972	134	72	1	
1929	45	NLG	ANL	59	219	43	80	16	5	3	54	19	9	.365	.416	.525	.941	119	115	0	
1930	46	NLG	EAS	44	155	29	59	8	2	1	31	3	13	.381	.429	.477	.906	106	74	0	
1931	47	HAR	IND	17	59	4	15	2	0	0	6	0	4	.254	.302	.288	.590	75	17	0	
1932	48	PBG	IND	4	15	4	5	1	0	0	3	1	0	.333	.333	.600	.933	147	9	0	
13 Yrs (+14)			NgL	585	2206	387	752	118	31	20	394	76	171	.341	.390	.450	.839	124	992	5	
162 Game Avg.			Pro	162	611	107	208	33	9	6	109	21	47	.341	.390	.450	.839	124	275	1	
14 Yrs			Pre-NgL	410	1581	269	553	90	35	11	287	58	119	.350	.397	.472	.869	169	746	5	
27 Yrs			Pre-NgL+NgL	995	3787	656	1305	208	66	31	681	134	290	**.345**	**.393**	**.459**	**.852**	143	1738	10	
162 Game Avg.			Pre-NgL_Pro	162	617	107	212	34	11	5	111	22	47	**.345**	**.393**	**.459**	**.852**	143	283	2	
5 Yrs		NLG	ECL-ANL+EAS	217	802	147	284	42	12	11	158	13	62	.354	.403	.478	.880	110	383	3	
2 Yrs		AC	ECL+EAS	129	470	80	163	20	8	4	104	20	50	.347	.410	.449	.859	134	211	0	
1 Yr		COB	NNL	90	362	65	126	20	8	0	54	24	25	.348	.392	.448	.839	137	162	1	
1 Yr		NYB	IND	65	266	45	79	17	0	2	37	9	12	.297	.330	.383	.713	110	102	1	
1 Yr		HIL	ECL	41	150	34	55	13	1	1	23	5	9	.367	.403	.507	.909	153	76	0	
1 Yr		BRG	IND	22	82	8	25	3	2	0	9	4	9	.305	.374	.390	.764	175	32	0	
1 Yr		HAR	IND	17	59	4	15	2	0	0	6	0	4	.254	.302	.288	.590	75	17	0	
1 Yr		PBG	IND	4	15	4	5	1	0	0	3	1	0	.333	.333	.600	.933	147	9	0	
6 Yrs		ECL		284	1048	189	363	51	14	13	200	33	89	.346	.399	.459	.858	126	481	3	
1 Yr		NNL		90	362	65	126	20	8	0	54	24	25	.348	.392	.448	.839	137	162	1	
3 Yrs		IND		86	340	53	99	20	0	3	46	10	16	.291	.325	.376	.701	106	128	1	
2 Yrs		EAS		66	237	37	84	11	4	1	40	7	22	.354	.409	.447	.857	130	106	0	
1 Yr		ANL		59	219	43	80	16	5	3	54	19	19	.365	.416	.525	.941	119	115	0	

20. The Negro Leagues All-Star Register

Dick Lundy

Tied Chuck Klein and Junior Wells's professional record by leading his league in home runs and steals in the same year (1920)

Standard Batting

Year	Age	Tm	Lg	G	AB	R	H	2B	3B	HR	RBI	SB	BB	BA	OBP	SLG	OPS	OPS+	TB	HBP	Awards
1916	17	TOTAL	EAS	2	8	0	0	0	0	0	0	0	0	.000	.000	.000	.000	-100	0	0	
		BRG	*EAS*	*1*	*4*	*0*	*0*	*0*	*0*	*0*	*0*	*0*	*0*	*.000*	*.000*	*.000*	*.000*	*-100*	*0*	*0*	
		AC	*EAS*	*1*	*4*	*0*	*0*	*0*	*0*	*0*	*0*	*0*	*0*	*.000*	*.000*	*.000*	*.000*	*-100*	*0*	*0*	
1917	18	AC	EAS	13	49	6	18	3	0	0	3	0	5	.367	.426	.429	.854	135	21	0	
1918	19	TOTAL	EAS	16	60	8	21	4	3	0	11	1	4	.350	.391	.517	.907	150	31	0	
		HIL	*EAS*	*11*	*40*	*6*	*14*	*3*	*3*	*0*	*9*	*0*	*4*	*.350*	*.409*	*.575*	*.984*	*168*	*23*	*0*	
		AC	*EAS*	*5*	*20*	*2*	*7*	*1*	*0*	*0*	*2*	*1*	*0*	*.350*	*.350*	*.400*	*.750*	*113*	*8*	*0*	
1919	20	HIL	EAS	19	69	11	24	2	3	0	6	2	6	.348	.408	.464	.872	180	32	1	
1920	21	AC	EAS	34	125	22	43	2	3	2	18	6	11	.344	.406	.496	.902	210	62	2	
1921	22	AC	EAS	44	164	32	56	7	7	3	33	9	10	.341	.386	.524	.911	136	86	2	
1922	23	TOTAL	IND	20	68	11	16	3	2	0	11	7	9	.235	.325	.338	.663	91	23	0	
		OBG	*IND*	*17*	*57*	*7*	*12*	*2*	*1*	*0*	*7*	*4*	*9*	*.211*	*.308*	*.281*	*.588*	*68*	*16*	*0*	
		NTB	*IND*	*3*	*11*	*4*	*4*	*1*	*1*	*0*	*4*	*3*	*1*	*.364*	*.417*	*.636*	*1.053*	*208*	*7*	*0*	
1923	24	AC	ECL	50	185	41	59	7	3	3	34	4	11	.319	.364	.438	.801	127	81	1	
1924	25	AC	ECL	63	242	55	79	8	4	8	52	13	23	.326	.385	.492	.877	149	119	0	
1925	26	AC	ECL	71	259	53	71	12	2	5	48	6	36	.274	.363	.394	.757	97	102		
1926	27	AC	ECL	54	198	41	70	17	4	2	43	3	22	.354	.421	.510	.931	153	101	1	
1927	28	AC	ECL	86	332	60	111	20	6	9	76	9	34	.334	.403	.512	.915	138	170	4	
1928	29	TOTAL	ECL+EAS	56	208	34	69	17	3	4	54	8	20	.332	.393	.500	.893	128	104	1	
		AC	*ECL*	*54*	*201*	*33*	*68*	*17*	*3*	*3*	*50*	*8*	*20*	*.338*	*.401*	*.498*	*.898*	*130*	*100*	*1*	
		ELS	*EAS*	*2*	*7*	*1*	*1*	*0*	*0*	*1*	*4*	*0*	*0*	*.143*	*.143*	*.571*	*.714*	*73*	*4*	*0*	
1929	30	BBS	ANL	70	261	53	92	16	6	4	59	9	21	.352	.403	.506	.909	121	132	1	
1930	31	BBS	EAS	41	145	29	51	10	0	4	34	3	12	.352	.401	.503	.905	116	73	0	
1931	32	BBS	IND	54	196	23	52	6	3	2	23	6	13	.265	.311	.357	.668	96	70	0	
1932	33	BBS	EWL	46	160	27	61	15	0	1	31	9	11	.381	.431	.494	.925	152	79	3	EWA
1933 *	34	TOTAL	IND+NN2	30	106	15	22	3	1	1	17	1	10	.208	.288	.283	.571	66	30	2	
		PS	*IND*	*29*	*101*	*15*	*22*	*3*	*1*	*1*	*17*	*1*	*10*	*.218*	*.301*	*.297*	*.598*	*74*	*30*	*2*	
		PC	*NN2*	*1*	*5*	*0*	*0*	*0*	*0*	*0*	*0*	*0*	*0*	*.000*	*.000*	*.000*	*.000*	*-100*	*0*	*0*	
1934 *	35	ND	NN2	15	42	5	12	2	1	0	7	1	4	.286	.362	.381	.743	86	16	1	EWA
1935	36	TOTAL	NN2+IND	26	96	17	30	8	1	1	16	0	9	.313	.371	.448	.819	107	43	0	
		TOTAL	*NN2*	*25*	*92*	*16*	*29*	*7*	*1*	*1*	*16*	*0*	*8*	*.315*	*.370*	*.446*	*.816*	*106*	*41*	*0*	
		ND	*NN2*	*2*	*7*	*2*	*2*	*1*	*0*	*0*	*1*	*0*	*0*	*.286*	*.286*	*.429*	*.714*	*77*	*3*	*0*	
		NYC	*NN2*	*23*	*85*	*14*	*27*	*6*	*1*	*1*	*15*	*0*	*8*	*.318*	*.376*	*.447*	*.823*	*108*	*38*	*0*	
		NBY	*IND*	*1*	*4*	*1*	*1*	*1*	*0*	*0*	*0*	*0*	*1*	*.250*	*.400*	*.500*	*.900*	*143*	*2*	*0*	
1937	38	TOTAL	NgL	15	47	14	17	3	3	0	7	2	9	.362	.464	.553	1.017	165	26	0	
		BRG	*IND*	*2*	*8*	*2*	*2*	*1*	*2*	*0*	*1*	*1*	*2*	*.250*	*.400*	*.625*	*1.025*	*200*	*5*	*0*	
		NE	*NN2*	*13*	*39*	*12*	*15*	*2*	*1*	*0*	*6*	*1*	*7*	*.385*	*.478*	*.538*	*1.017*	*158*	*21*	*0*	

Dick Lundy
Standard Batting (continued)

Year	Age	Tm	Lg	G	AB	R	H	2B	3B	HR	RBI	SB	BB	BA	OBP	SLG	OPS	OPS+	TB	HBP	Awards
17 Yrs (+4)			NgL	775	2834	532	911	161	49	49	563	96	265	.321	.383	.465	.848	129	1317	19	
162 Game Avg.				162	592	111	190	34	10	10	118	20	55	.321	.383	.465	.848	129	360	4	
4 Yrs			Pre-NgL	50	186	25	63	9	6	0	20	3	15	.339	.391	.452	.843	146	84	1	
21 Yrs			Pre-NgL+NgL	825	3020	557	974	170	55	49	583	99	280	.323	.384	.464	.848	130	1401	20	
162 Game Avg.			Pre-NgL+Pro	162	593	109	191	33	11	10	114	19	55	.323	.384	.464	.848	130	275	4	
8 Yrs		AC	ECL+EAS	456	1706	337	557	95	32	35	354	58	167	.326	.390	.481	.872	138	821	12	
4 Yrs		BBS	ANL+EWL+EAS+ND	211	762	132	256	47	9	11	147	27	57	.336	.385	.465	.850	120	354	4	
1 Yr		PS	IND	29	101	15	22	3	1	1	17	1	10	.218	.301	.297	.598	74	30	2	
1 Yr		NYC	NN2	23	85	14	27	6	1	1	15	0	8	.318	.376	.447	.823	108	38	0	
1 Yr		OBG	IND	17	57	7	12	2	1	0	7	4	8	.211	.308	.281	.588	68	16	0	
2 Yrs		ND	IND	17	49	7	14	3	1	0	8	1	4	.286	.352	.388	.740	85	19	1	
1 Yr		NE	NN2	13	39	12	15	2	2	0	6	1	7	.385	.478	.538	1.017	158	21	0	
1 Yr		NYB	IND	3	11	4	4	1	1	0	4	3	1	.364	.417	.636	1.053	208	7	0	
1 Yr		BRG	IND	2	8	2	2	1	0	0	1	1	2	.250	.400	.625	1.025	150	5	0	
1 Yr		ELS	EAS	2	7	1	1	0	0	0	4	0	0	.143	.143	.571	.714	73	4	0	
1 Yr		NBY	IND	1	4	1	1	1	0	0	0	0	1	.250	.400	.500	.900	143	2	0	
1 Yr		PC	NN2	1	5	0	0	0	0	0	0	0	0	.000	.000	.000	.000	-100	0	0	
6 Yrs			ECL	378	1417	283	458	81	22	30	303	43	146	.323	.390	.475	.865	132	673	8	
4 Yrs			EAS	121	441	84	151	24	10	10	89	18	33	.342	.393	.510	.904	149	225	4	
5 Yrs			IND	106	377	52	93	14	7	3	52	15	35	.247	.314	.345	.659	92	130	2	
1 Yr			ANL	70	261	53	92	16	6	4	59	9	21	.352	.403	.506	.909	121	132	1	
3 Yrs			NN2	54	178	33	56	11	4	1	29	2	19	.315	.384	.438	.822	119	78	1	
1 Yr			EWL	46	160	27	61	15	0	1	31	9	11	.381	.431	.494	.925	152	79	3	

Postseason Batting

Year	Age	Tm	Lg	Series	Opp	Rslt	G	AB	R	H	2B	3B	HR	RBI	SB	BB	BA	OBP	SLG	OPS	HBP
1926	27	AC	ECL	WS	CAG	L	11	40	4	12	1	1	0	6	4	7	.300	.404	.375	.779	0
1927	28	AC	ECL	WS	CAG	L	9	36	3	8	0	0	0	7	0	1	.222	.243	.250	.493	0
2 Yrs (2 Series)							20	76	7	20	1	1	0	7	4	8	.263	.333	.316	.649	0
2 Yrs			NgL	WS			20	76	7	20	1	1	0	7	4	8	.263	.333	.316	.649	0

All-Star Batting

Year	Age	Tm	Lg	Game	Opp	Rslt	G	AB	R	H	2B	3B	HR	RBI	SB	BB	BA	OBP	SLG	OPS	HBP
1933	34		EAS	EWA			SS	3	0	0	0	0	0	0	0	0	.000	.250	.000	.250	0
1934	35		EAS	EWA			SS	4	0	0	0	0	0	0	0	1	.000	.000	.000	.000	0
2 Yrs			NgL				2	7	0	0	0	0	0	0	0	1	.000	.125	.000	.125	0

20. The Negro Leagues All-Star Register

James "Biz" Mackey
Standard Batting

Year	Age	Tm	Lg	G	AB	R	H	2B	3B	HR	RBI	SB	BB	BA	OBP	SLG	OPS	OPS+	TB	HBP	Awards
1920	22	ABC	NNL	48	173	23	54	6	3	1	21	1	13	.312	.360	.399	.759	124	69	0	
1921	23	ABC	NNL	94	355	58	117	14	11	8	70	5	22	.330	.377	.499	.867	147	177	5	
1922	24	ABC	NNL	90	328	59	121	16	17	8	83	5	30	.369	.423	.595	1.016	171	195	1	
1923	25	HIL	ECL	51	182	32	77	11	2	5	44	6	10	**.423**	**.456**	**.588**	**1.041**	**190**	107	1	
1924	26	HIL	ECL	**68**	**273**	50	**90**	19	3	4	42	8	14	.330	.362	.465	.828	133	127		
1925	27	HIL	ECL	62	210	49	73	17	5	6	54	12	29	.348	.427	.562	.989	151	118		
1926	28	HIL	ECL	85	312	59	**102**	**25**	3	10	76	13	34	.327	.400	.522	.915	145	**163**	4	
1927	29	TOTAL	ECL+IND	31	104	26	37	4	4	1	25	1	13	.356	.442	.500	.932	143	52	2	
		HIL	ECL	30	101	25	36	4	3	1	24	1	13	*.356*	*.440*	*.485*	*.915*	*141*	*49*	*2*	
		HG	IND	1	3	1	1	0	1	0	1	0	1	*.333*	*.500*	*1.000*	*1.500*	*224*	*3*	*0*	
1928	30	TOTAL	NgL	56	209	46	71	17	6	4	43	6	23	.340	.408	.536	.941	150	112	1	
		HIL	EAS	54	203	44	69	16	5	4	41	6	22	*.340*	*.407*	*.527*	*.932*	*148*	*107*	*1*	
		BBS	ECL	2	6	2	2	1	1	0	2	0	1	*.333*	*.429*	*.833*	*1.262*	*207*	*5*	*0*	
1929	31	HIL	ANL	52	186	35	67	12	3	2	38	6	30	.360	.449	.489	.938	128	91	0	
1930	32	TOTAL	EAS	37	133	32	55	10	3	5	36	2	11	.414	.462	.647	1.105	165	86	1	
		HIL	EAS	30	108	26	48	10	3	4	34	2	10	*.444*	*.496*	*.704*	*1.195*	*187*	*76*	*1*	
		BBS	EAS	7	25	6	7	0	0	1	2	0	1	*.280*	*.308*	*.400*	*.708*	*69*	*10*	*0*	
1931	33	HIL	IND	44	152	28	55	6	2	3	33	0	17	.362	.426	.487	.913	154	74	0	
1932	34											Did not play in major or minor leagues (holdout)									
1933 *	35	TOTAL	IND+NN2	27	95	10	27	5	0	0	14	1	12	.775	.965	.830	1.783	100	32	**2**	EWA
		PS	IND	26	91	10	25	5	0	0	14	1	11	*.275*	*.365*	*.330*	*.683*	*95*	*30*	*2*	
		PC	NN2	1	4	0	2	0	0	0	0	0	1	*.500*	*.600*	*.500*	*1.100*	*205*	*2*	*0*	
1934	36	PS	NN2	24	64	2	16	5	0	1	12	0	3	.250	.284	.375	.659	84	24	0	
1935 *	37	PS	NN2	46	148	20	43	10	1	1	20	1	14	.291	.356	.392	.744	87	58	1	EWA
1936 *	38	WEG	NN2	43	170	20	49	8	3	1	30	0	11	.288	.335	.371	.702	83	63	1	EWA
1937	39	TOTAL	NN2+IND	23	70	8	19	4	0	1	9	0	8	.271	.346	.371	.718	96	26	0	
		WEG	NN2	21	62	8	16	3	0	1	8	0	8	*.258*	*.343*	*.355*	*.698*	*80*	*22*	*0*	
		NAS	IND	2	8	0	3	1	0	0	1	0	0	*.375*	*.375*	*.500*	*.875*	*221*	*4*	*0*	
1938 *	40	BEG	NN2	32	104	17	32	5	0	1	16	1	18	.308	.410	.385	.794	109	40	0	
1939	41	TOTAL	NN2	24	68	7	21	1	0	1	11	1	5	.309	.356	.368	.724	95	25	0	
		BEG	NN2	13	39	4	10	1	0	0	9	1	4	*.256*	*.326*	*.359*	*.685*	*85*	*14*	*0*	
		NE	NN2	11	29	3	11	0	0	1	2	0	1	*.379*	*.400*	*.379*	*.779*	*108*	*11*	*0*	
1940	42	NE	NN2	37	123	17	38	4	0	1	25	0	15	.309	.384	.366	.750	94	45	0	
1941	43	NE	NN2	26	69	7	17	2	1	0	10	0	9	.246	.333	.304	.638	85	21	0	
1942	44		IND									Played in unrecorded independent league									
1943	45		IND									Played in unrecorded independent league									
1944	46		IND									Played in unrecorded independent league									
1945	47	NE	NN2	18	55	5	15	1	1	1	8	0	8	.273	.365	.382	.747	103	21	0	
1946	48	NE	NN2	10	10	0	2	0	0	0	1	0	1	.200	.273	.200	.473	31	2	0	
1947 *	49	NE	NN2	30	69	2	18	0	0	0	9	0	8	.261	.338	.261	.599	64	18	0	EWA

James "Biz" Mackey

Standard Batting (continued)

Year	Age	Tm	Lg	G	AB	R	H	2B	3B	HR	RBI	SB	BB	BA	OBP	SLG	OPS	OPS+	TB	HBP	Awards
24 Yrs (+3)			NgL	1058	3662	612	1216	202	68	64	730	70	359	.332	.395	.4768	.868	133	1746	19	
162 Game Avg.			Pro	162	561	94	186	31	10	10	112	11	55	.332	.395	.477	.868	133	267	3	
9 Yrs		HIL	ECL+EAS	476	1727	348	617	120	29	39	386	55	179	.357	.420	.528	.946	150	912	9	
3 Yrs		ABC	NNL	232	856	140	292	36	31	17	174	11	65	.341	.392	.515	.903	152	441	6	
6 Yrs		NE	NN2	132	355	34	101	7	2	2	55	1	42	.285	.360	.332	.693	87	118		
3 Yrs		PS	NN2+IND	96	303	32	84	20	1	2	46	2	28	.277	.344	.370	.708	89	112	3	
2 Yrs		WEG	NN2	64	232	28	65	11	3	1	38		19	.280	.337	.366	.701	82	85	1	
2 Yrs		BEG	NN2	45	143	21	42	6	0	2	25	1	22	.294	.388	.378	.766	102	54	0	
2 Yrs		BBS	EAS	9	31	8	9	1	1	1	4	0	2	.290	.333	.484	.817	96	15	0	
1 Yr		NAS	IND	2	8	0	3	0	0	0	1	0	0	.375	.375	.500	.875	221	4	0	
1 Yr		PC	NN2	1	4	0	2	0	0	0	0	0	1	.500	.600	.500	1.100	205	2	0	
1 Yr		HG	IND	1	3	1	1	0	1	0	1	0	0	.333	.500	1.000	1.500	224	3	0	
10 Yrs			NN2	312	946	105	269	39	6	7	150	3	101	.284	.355	.360	.714	89	341	2	
6 Yrs			ECL	298	1084	217	380	77	17	26	242	40	101	.351	.409	.525	.931	151	569	7	
3 Yrs			NNL	232	856	140	292	36	31	17	174	11	65	.341	.392	.515	.903	152	441	6	
2 Yrs			EAS	91	336	76	124	26	8	9	77	8	33	.369	.429	.574	1.000	155	193	2	
4 Yrs			IND	73	254	39	84	12	3	3	49	2	29	.331	.404	.437	.836	136	111	2	
1 Yr			ANL	52	186	35	67	12	3	2	38	6	30	.360	.449	.489	.938	128	91	0	

Postseason Batting

Year	Age	Tm	Lg	Series	Opp	Rslt	G	AB	R	H	2B	3B	HR	RBI	SB	BB	BA	OBP	SLG	OPS	HBP
1924	26	HIL	ECL	WS	KCM	L	10	41	7	10	0	1	0	0	0	6	.244	.340	.293	.633	0
1925 □	27	HIL	ECL	WS	KCM	W	6	25	4	9	3	1	1	3	1	3	.360	.429	.680	1.109	0
1934 □	36	PS	NN2	NLC	CAG	W	6	19	2	7	2	0	0	2	0	2	.368	.429	.632	1.060	0
1939	41	NE	NN2	NLP	BEG	L	3	12	2	6	0	0	0	1	0	0	.500	.500	.500	1.000	
1946 □	48	NE	NN2	WS	KCM	W	1	1	0	0	0	0	0	0	0	0	.000	.000	.000	.000	0
5 Yrs (5 Series)			NgL				26	98	15	32	5	2	1	7	1	11	.327	.394	.480	.874	0
1 Yr			NLP				3	12	2	6	0	0	0	1	0	0	.500	.500	.500	1.000	0
1 Yr			NLC				6	19	2	7	2	0	0	2	0	2	.368	.429	.632	1.060	0
3 Yrs			WS				17	67	11	19	3	2	1	4	1	9	.284	.368	.433	.801	0

All-Star Batting

Year	Age	Tm	Lg	Game	G	AB	R	H	2B	3B	HR	RBI	SB	BB	BA	OBP	SLG	OPS	HBP
1933	35		EAS	EWA	C	3	0	1	0	0	0	0	0	0	.333	.333	.333	.667	0
1935	37		EAS	EWA	C	5	1	0	0	0	0	0	0	1	.000	.167	.000	.167	0
1936	38		EAS	EWA	C	2	0	2	1	0	0	2	0	0	1.000	1.000	1.500	2.500	0
1938	40		EAS	EWA	C	4	0	0	0	0	0	0	0	0	.000	.000	.000	.000	0
1947	49		EAS	EWA		1	0	0	0	0	0	0	0	1	.000	1.000	.000	1.000	0
5 Yrs (5 GP)			NgL		5	14	1	3	1	0	0	2	0	2	.214	.313	.286	.598	0

Oliver "Ghost" Marcell
Standard Batting

Year	Age	Tm	Lg	G	AB	R	H	2B	3B	HR	RBI	SB	BB	BA	OBP	SLG	OPS	OPS+	TB	HBP	Awards
1918	23	TOTAL	EAS	22	88	16	23	0	0	0	4	4	8	.261	.323	.261	.584	72	23	0	
		AC	EAS	1	4	0	1	0	0	0	0	0	0	.250	.250	.250	.500	42	1	0	
		BRG	EAS	21	84	16	22	0	0	0	4	4	8	.262	.326	.262	.588	73	22	0	
1919	24	TOTAL	EAS	16	62	9	18	2	0	0	2	4	6	.290	.353	.323	.676	99	20	0	
		BRG	EAS	15	58	9	18	2	0	0	2	4	6	.310	.375	.345	.720	113	20	0	
		HIL	EAS	1	4	0	0	0	0	0	0	0	0	.000	.000	.000	.000	-100	0	0	
1920	25	AC	EAS	36	132	21	34	7	4	0	13	2	14	.258	.333	.371	.705	142	49	1	
1921	26	AC	EAS	66	253	48	83	11	3	1	40	7	22	.328	.384	.407	.791	108	103	1	
1922	27	NYB	IND	62	244	43	68	11	2	1	29	4	18	.279	.336	.352	.688	103	86	3	
1923	28	NLG	ECL	27	101	18	34	2	1	1	14	4	16	.337	.432	.406	.838	121	41	1	
1924	29	NLG	ECL	54	210	49	63	12	3	2	38	8	26	.300	.380	.414	.794	106	87	0	
1925	30	TOTAL	ECL	68	236	43	73	6	3	5	33	5	23	.309	.371	.424	.794	106	100	1	
		NLG	ECL	6	23	3	4	0	0	0	0	1	3	.174	.269	.174	.443	12	4	0	
		AC	ECL	62	213	40	69	6	3	5	33	4	20	.324	.382	.451	.833	116	96	1	
1926	31	AC	ECL	52	179	39	50	9	1	2	31	2	29	.279	.383	.374	.757	107	67	1	
1927	32	AC	ECL	86	313	47	100	11	6	2	56	8	33	.319	.390	.412	.802	110	129	3	
1928	33	TOTAL	ECL+EAS	40	155	27	46	5	2	2	22	2	7	.297	.331	.394	.725	86	61	1	
		AC	ECL	38	147	25	43	4	2	2	20	2	7	.293	.329	.388	.717	84	57	1	
		ELS	EAS	2	8	2	3	1	0	0	2	0	0	.375	.375	.500	.875	120	4	0	
1929	34	BBS	ANL	74	266	37	79	11	3	0	39	4	25	.297	.362	.361	.723	77	96	2	
1930	35	BRG	EAS	13	46	2	13	1	0	0	2	0	3	.283	.327	.304	.631	53	14	0	
11 Yrs (+2)			NgL	578	2135	374	643	86	28	16	318	46	216	.301	.369	.390	.759	103	833	14	
162 Game Avg.			NgL	162	598	105	180	24	8	4	89	13	61	.301	.369	.390	.759	103	233	4	
2 Yrs			Pre-NgL	38	150	25	41	2	0	0	6	8	14	.273	.335	.287	.622	83	43	0	
13 Yrs			Pre-NgL+NgL	616	2285	399	684	88	28	16	324	54	230	.299	.367	.383	.750	102	876	14	
162 Game Avg.			Pre-NgL+Pro	162	601	105	180	23	7	4	85	14	60	.299	.367	.383	.750	102	230	4	
6 Yrs		AC	ECL+EAS	340	1237	220	379	48	19	12	193	25	125	.306	.373	.405	.778	111	501	7	
3 Yrs		NLG	ECL	87	334	70	101	14	4	3	52	13	45	.302	.388	.395	.784	104	132	2	
1 Yr		BBS	ANL	74	266	37	79	11	3	0	39	4	25	.297	.362	.361	.723	77	96	2	
1 Yr		NYB	IND	62	244	43	68	11	2	1	29	4	18	.279	.336	.352	.688	103	86	3	
1 Yr		BRG	EAS	13	46	2	13	1	0	0	2	0	3	.283	.327	.304	.631	53	14	0	
1 Yr		ELS	EAS	2	8	2	3	1	0	0	2	0	0	.375	.375	.500	.875	120	4	0	
6 Yrs		AC	ECL	325	1186	221	363	44	16	14	192	29	134	.306	.380	.406	.785	106	481	7	
4 Yrs		EAS	EAS	117	439	73	133	20	7	1	58	9	39	.303	.363	.387	.750	113	170	2	
1 Yr			ANL	74	266	37	79	11	3	0	39	4	25	.297	.362	.361	.723	77	96	2	
1 Yr			IND	62	244	43	68	11	2	1	29	4	18	.279	.336	.352	.688	103	86	3	

Postseason Batting

Year	Age	Tm	Lg	Series	Opp	Rslt	G	AB	R	H	2B	3B	HR	RBI	SB	BB	BA	OBP	SLG	OPS	HBP
1926	31	AC	ECL	WS	CAG	L	11	42	5	13	2	0	0	5	1	5	.310	.408	.357	.765	2
1927	32	AC	ECL	WS	CAG	L	9	34	2	8	1	3	0	2	0	3	.235	.297	.265	.562	0
2 Yrs (2 Series)			NgL				20	76	7	21	3	3	0	7	1	8	.276	.360	.316	.661	2
2 Yrs				WS			20	76	7	21	3	3	0	7	1	8	.276	.360	.316	.661	2

Willie Mays
Standard Batting

Year	Age	Tm	Lg	G	AB	R	H	2B	3B	HR	RBI	SB	BB	BA	OBP	SLG	OPS	OPS+	TB	HBP	Awards
1948	17	**BBB**	NAL	13	43	6	10	2	1	0	6		4	.233	.313	.326	.638	70	14	1	
1949	18	BBB	NAL																		Played in unrecorded Black league
1950	19	BBB	NAL																		Played in unrecorded Black league
		Trenton	ISLG																		Played in minor leagues (Integration)
		Minneapolis	AA																		Played in minor leagues (Integration)
1951	20	NYG	NL	121	464	59	127	22	5	20	68	7	57	.274	.356	.472	.828	120	219	2	ROY-1
1952	21	NYG	NL	34	127	17	30	2	4	4	23	4	16	.236	.326	.409	.736	102	52	1	
1953																					Did not play in major or minor leagues (Military Service)
1954 *	23	**NYG**	NL	151	565	119	195	33	13	41	110	8	66	**.345**	.411	**.667**	**1.078**	**175**	377	2	ASG, MVP-1
1955 *	24	NYG	NL	152	580	123	185	18	13	**51**	127	24	79	.319	.400	**.659**	**1.059**	**174**	**382**	4	ASG, MVP-4
1956 *	25	NYG	NL	152	578	101	171	27	8	36	84	**40**	68	.296	.369	.557	.926	146	322	1	ASG, MVP-17
1957 *	26	NYG	NL	152	585	112	195	26	**20**	35	97	**38**	76	.333	.407	**.626**	1.033	**173**	366	1	ASG, GG, MVP-4
1958 *	27	SFG	NL	152	600	**121**	208	33	11	29	96	**31**	78	.347	.419	.583	**1.002**	**165**	350	1	ASG, GG, MVP-2
1959 *	28	SFG	NL	151	575	125	180	43	5	34	104	**27**	65	.313	.381	.583	.964	156	335	2	ASGx2, GG, MVP-6
1960 *	29	SFG	NL	153	595	107	**190**	29	12	29	103	25	61	.319	.381	.555	.936	160	330	4	ASGx2, GG, MVP-3
1961 *	30	SFG	NL	154	572	**129**	176	32	3	40	123	18	81	.308	.393	.584	.977	160	334	2	ASGx2, GG, MVP-6
1962 *	31	SFG	NL	162	621	130	189	36	5	**49**	141	18	78	.304	.384	.615	.999	165	**382**	4	ASGx2, GG, MVP-2
1963 *	32	SFG	NL	157	596	115	187	32	7	38	103	8	66	.314	.380	.582	.962	175	347	2	ASG, GG, MVP-5
1964 *	33	SFG	NL	157	578	121	171	21	9	**47**	111	19	82	.296	.383	**.607**	**.990**	**172**	351	1	ASG, GG, MVP-6
1965 *	34	SFG	NL	157	558	118	177	21	3	**52**	112	9	76	.317	**.398**	**.645**	**1.043**	**185**	**360**	0	ASG, GG, MVP-1
1966 *	35	SFG	NL	152	552	99	159	29	4	37	103	5	70	.288	.368	.556	.924	149	307	2	ASG, GG, MVP-3
1967 *	36	SFG	NL	141	486	83	128	22	2	22	70	6	51	.263	.334	.453	.787	124	220	2	ASG, GG
1968 *	37	SFG	NL	148	498	84	144	20	5	23	79	12	67	.289	.372	.488	.860	156	243	2	ASG, GG, MVP-13
1969 *	38	SFG	NL	117	403	64	114	17	3	13	58	6	49	.283	.362	.437	.798	124	176	3	ASG
1970 *	39	SFG	NL	139	478	94	139	15	2	28	83	5	79	.291	.390	.506	.897	140	242	3	ASG
1971 *	40	SFG	NL	136	417	82	113	24	5	18	61	23	**112**	.271	**.425**	.482	.907	158	201	3	ASG, MVP-19
1972 *	41	TOTAL	NL	88	244	35	61	11	1	8	22	4	60	.250	.400	.402	.802	132	98	1	ASG
1972	41	SFG	NL	19	49	8	9	2	0	0	3	3	17	.184	.394	.224	.618	79	11	0	
		NYM	NL	69	195	27	52	9	1	8	19	1	43	.267	.402	.446	.848	145	87	1	
1973 *	42	NYM	NL	66	209	24	44	10	0	6	25	1	27	.211	.303	.344	.647	81	72	1	ASG

20. The Negro Leagues All-Star Register 223

Willie Mays
Standard Batting (continued)

Year	Age	Tm	Lg	G	AB	R	H	2B	3B	HR	RBI	SB	BB	BA	OBP	SLG	OPS	OPS+	TB	HBP	Awards
23 Yrs (+4)			Pro	3005	10924	2068	3293	525	141	660	1909	338	1468	.301	.384	.557	.941	155	6080	45	
22 Yrs			MLB	2992	10881	2062	3283	523	140	660	1903	338	1464	.302	.384	.557	.941	155	6066	44	
1 Yr			NgL	13	43	6	10	2	1	0	6	0	4	.233	.313	.326	.638	70	14	1	
162 Game Avg.			Pro	162	589	111	178	28	8	36	103	18	**79**	.301	.384	.557	.940	155	328	2	
14 Yrs		SFG	NL	2095	7578	1480	2284	376	76	459	1350	215	1032	.301	.387	.553	.940	157	4189	31	
6 Yrs		NYG	NL	762	2899	531	903	128	63	187	509	121	362	.311	.390	.593	.983	157	1718	11	
2 Yrs		NYM	NL	135	404	51	96	19	1	14	44	2	70	.238	.353	.394	.747	112	159	2	
1 Yr		BBB	NAL	13	43	6	10	2	1	0	6	0	4	.233	.313	.326	.638	70	14	1	
22 Yrs			NL	2992	10881	2062	3283	523	140	660	1903	338	1464	.302	.387	.557	.944	155	6080	44	
1 Yr			NAL	13	43	6	10	2	1	0	6	0	4	.233	.313	.326	.638	70	14	1	

Postseason Batting

Year	Age	Tm	Lg	Series	Opp	Rslt	G	AB	R	H	2B	3B	HR	RBI	SB	BB	BA	OBP	SLG	OPS	HBP
1948	17	BBB	NAL	ALC	KCM	W	7	25	4	7	0	0	0	5	0	0	.280	.438	.320	.758	1
1948	17	BBB	NAL	WS	HG	L	1	3	1	0	0	0	0	0	0	1	.000	.250	.000	.250	0
1951	20	NYG	NL	WS	NYY	L	6	22	1	4	0	0	0	1	0	2	.182	.250	.182	.432	0
1954 a	23	NYG	NL	WS	CLE	W	4	14	4	4	1	0	0	3	0	4	.286	.444	.357	.802	0
1962	31	SFG	NL	WS	NYY	L	7	28	3	7	2	0	1	1	0	1	.250	.276	.321	.597	0
1971	40	SFG	NL	NLCS	PIT	L	4	15	2	4	2	0	1	3	0	3	.267	.389	.600	.989	0
1973	42	NYM	NL	NLCS	CIN	W	1	3	1	1	0	0	0	1	0	0	.333	.333	.333	.667	0
1973	42	NYM	NL	WS	OAK	L	3	7	1	2	0	0	0	1	0	0	.286	.286	.286	.571	0
5 Yrs (6 Series)			Pro				33	117	17	29	6	0	2	15	0	11	.248	.348	.325	.668	1
1 Yr (2 Series)			NgL		ALC		8	28	5	7	0	0	0	5	0	1	.250	.417	.286	.686	1
1 Yr					ALC		7	25	4	7	0	0	0	5	0	0	.280	.438	.320	.739	1
1 Yr					WS		1	3	1	0	0	0	0	0	0	1	.000	.250	.000	.250	0
5 Yrs (6 Series)			MLB				25	89	12	22	5	0	1	10	0	10	.247	.323	.337	.660	0
2 Yrs				NLCS			5	18	3	5	2	0	1	4	0	3	.278	.381	.556	.937	0
4 Yrs				WS			20	71	9	17	3	0	0	6	0	7	.239	.308	.282	.589	0

Orestes "Minnie" Miñoso

Holds MLB record (10) and professional record (14) for most times leading league in hit by pitch - Tied Alejandro Oms's professional record by playing in 36 seasons

EXTENDED BATTING RECORD

Year	Age	Tm	Lg	G	AB	R	H	2B	3B	HR	RBI	SB	BB	BA	OBP	SLG	OPS	OPS+	TB	HBP	Awards
1945-46	19/20	Marinao	CWL	37	143	14	42	7	2	0	13	5		.294		.371	.664		53		
1946	20	TOTAL	NN2+Exh	40	159	25	37	5	2	4	15	2	13	.233	.299	.365	.664		58	2	
		NYC	NN2	37	146	22	33	5	2	4	14	1	13	.226	.298	.370	.668	86	54	2	
		NYC	Exh	3	13	3	4				1	1		.308			.615		4		
1946-47	20/21	Marinao	CWL	64	253	36	63	9	5	0	20	7		.249		.324	.573		82		
1947 *	21	TOTAL	NN2+Exh	43	194	42	71	14	4	2	27	6	13	.366	.411	.510	.922		99	2	EW, EW
		NYC	NN2	40	177	42	63	13	4	2	25	5	13	.356	.406	.508	.915	153	90	2	
			Exh	3	17		8	1			2	1		.471			1.000		9		
1947-48	21/22	Marinao	CWL	70	270	43	77	15	13	1	36	7		.285		.448	.733		121		
1948 *	22	Total	NN2+Exh+A	47	196	41	76	20	7	4	35	12	8	.388	.415	.622	1.037		89	1	EW, EW
		NYC	NN2	35	151	26	52	11	6	3	27	5	8	.344	.381	.556	.938	176	84	1	
			Exh	1	5	1	3	2	1			1		.600		1.000	1.667		5		
		Dayton	A	11	40	14	21	7		1	8	6		.525		.825	1.350		33		
1948/49	22/23	Marinao	CWL	69	260	42	69	8	5	4	27	9		.265		.381	.646		99		
1949	23	TOTAL	AL+PCL	146	548	101	161	19	7	23	76	13	53	.294	.371	.480	.851		263	14	
		CLE	AL	9	16	2	3	0	0	1	1	0	2	.188	.350	.375	.725	93	6	2	
		San Diego	PCL	137	532	99	158	19	7	22	75	13	51	.297	.371	.483	.855		257	12	
1950	24	San Diego	PCL	169	599	130	203	40	10	20	115	30	58	.339	.405	.539	.945		323	9	
1950/51	24/25	Marinao	CWL	66	252	54	81	12	6	4	41	10		.321		.464	.786		117		
1951 *	25	TOTAL	AL	146	530	112	173	34	14	10	76	31	72	.326	.422	.500	.922	151	265	16	ASG, MVP-4, RoY-2
		CLE	AL	8	14	3	6	2	0	0	2	0	1	.429	.529	.571	1.101	205	8	2	
		CHW	AL	138	516	109	167	32	14	10	74	31	71	.324	.419	.498	.917	149	257	14	
1951/52	25/26	Marinao	CWL	42	144	19	39	6	1	2	10	1		.271		.368	.639		53		
1952 *	26	CHW	AL	147	569	96	160	24	9	13	61	22	71	.281	.375	.424	.798	121	241	14	ASG
1952/53	26/27	Marinao	CWL	71	266	67	87	9	5	13	42	13		.327		.545	.872		145		
1953 *	27	CHW	AL	151	556	104	174	24	8	15	104	25	74	.313	.410	.466	.875	133	259	17	ASG, MVP-4
1953/54	27/28	Marinao	CWL	47	176	35	52	9	3	9	36	2		.295		.534	.830		94		
1954 *	28	CHW	AL	153	568	119	182	29	18	19	116	18	77	.320	.411	.535	.946	154	304	16	ASG, MVP-4
1955	29	CHW	AL	139	517	79	149	26	7	10	70	19	76	.288	.387	.424	.811	117	219	10	

20. The Negro Leagues All-Star Register

Orestes "Minnie" Miñoso
EXTENDED BATTING RECORD (continued)

Year	Age	Tm	Lg	G	AB	R	H	2B	3B	HR	RBI	SB	BB	BA	OBP	SLG	OPS	OPS+	TB	HBP	Awards
1955/56	29/30	Marinao	CWL	64	252	47	70	10	3	8	36	9		.278		.437	.714		110		
1956	30	CHW	AL	151	545	106	172	29	11	21	88	12	86	.316	.425	.525	.950	149	286	23	MVP-27
1956/57	30/31	Marinao	CWL	50	218	40	68	13	3	7	38			.312		.495	.840		108	11	
1957 *	31	CHW	AL	153	568	96	176	36	5	12	103	18	79	.310	.408	.454	.862	135	258	21	ASG, GG, MVP-8
1957/58	31/32	Marinao	CWL	58	238	37	60	9	1	8	34	3		.252		.399	.696		95	15	
1958	32	CLE	AL	149	556	94	168	25	2	24	80	14	59	.302	.383	.484	.867	139	269	15	MVP-18
1958/59	32/33	Marinao	CWL	55	228	33	60	8	1	5	25	8		.263		.373	.667		85	10	
1959 *	33	CLE	AL	148	570	92	172	32	0	21	92	8	54	.302	.377	.468	.846	134	267	17	ASGx2, GG, MVP-12
1959/60	33/34	Marinao	CWL	45	169	25	39	3	2	4	23	4		.231		.343	.574		58		
1960 *	34	CHW	AL	154	591	89	184	32	4	20	105	17	52	.311	.374	.481	.855	130	284	13	ASGx2, GG, MVP-4
1960/61	34/35	Marinao	CWL	35	128	12	32	7	1	1	12	1		.250		.344	.648		44	10	
1961	35	CHW	AL	152	540	91	151	28	3	14	82	9	67	.280	.369	.420	.789	113	227	16	
1962	36	STL	NL	39	97	14	19	5	0	1	10	4	7	.196	.271	.278	.549	42	27	3	
1963	37	WSA	AL	109	315	38	72	12	2	4	30	8	33	.229	.315	.317	.632	78	100	8	
1963/64	37/38	Escogito	DWL	14																	
1964	38	TOTAL	AL-PCL	82	209	26	54	11	0	5	31	6	17	.258	.335	.383	.718	92	80	7	
		CHW	AL	30	31	4	7	0	0	1	5	0	5	.226	.351	.323	.674	92	10	1	
		Indianapolis	PCL	52	178	22	47	11	0	4	26	6	12	.264	.332	.393	.725		70	6	
1965	39	Jalisco	MEX	134	469	106	169	35	10	14	82	7		.360		.567	.928		266		
1966	40	Jalisco	MEX	107	376	70	131	18	1	6	45	6		.348		.449	.798				
1966/67	40/41	Hermosillo	MEXSEL	84	302	38	104	13	0	9	36			.344		.477	.821				
1967 □	41	TOTAL	MEXSEL-MEX	49	137	25	44	8	5	5	22	1		.321		.562	.883		77		
		Jalisco	MEX	13	37	5	9	1	2	2	3			.243		.378	.622		14		
		Orizaba	MEXSEL	36	100	20	35	7	3	3	19	1		.350		.630	.980		63		
1968	42	TOTAL	MEXSEL-MEX	78	199	39	69	22	3	6	36	1		.347		.578	.925				ASG
		Jalisco	MEX AAA	22	54	9	16	5	1	2	13	1		.296		.537	.833		29		
		Puerto Mexico	MEXSEL	56	145	30	53	17	2	4	23	0		.366		.593	.959				
1969	43	TOTAL	MEXSEL-MEX	110	296	51	91	13	3	4	46	0		.307		.412	.720		44		ASG
		Jalisco	MEX	36	103	18	33	3	1	2	14			.320		.427	.748				
		Puerto Ponasco	MEXSEL	74	193	33	58	10	2	2	32			.301		.404	.705				
1969/70	43/44	Mazatlan	MEXSEL	59	220	30	79	12	3	5	35			.359		.509	.868				
1970	44	Union Laguna	MEX	40	47	6	22	6	0	3	17	0	0	.468		.723	1.191		34		ASG
1971	45	Union Laguna	MEX	112	336	37	106	15	2	6	57	5	0	.315		.426	.741		143		
1972	46	Union Laguna	MEX	121	425	48	121	24	1	12	63	5	0	.285		.431	.715		183		
1973	47	Union Laguna	MEX	120	407	50	108	15	1	12	83	10	0	.265		.396	.661		161		
1976	50	CHW	AL	3	8	0	1	0	0	0	0	0	0	.125	.125	.125	.250	-27	1	0	
1980	54	CHW	AL	2	2	0	0	0	0	0	0	0	0	.000	.000	.000	.000	-100	0	0	
1993	67	St. Paul	NORL	1	1	0	0	0	0	0	0	0	0	.000	.000	.000	.000		0	0	
2003	67	St. Paul	NORL	1	0	0	0	0	0	0	0	0	1	.000	1.000	.000	1.000		0	0	

Orestes "Minnie" Miñoso
EXTENDED BATTING RECORD (continued)

Year	Age	Tm	Lg	G	AB	R	H	2B	3B	HR	RBI	SB	BB	BA	OBP	SLG	OPS	OPS+	TB	HBP	Awards
PROFESSIONAL TOTALS				1947	7053	1226	2111	365	95	195	1089	216	848	.299	.387	.461	.848	131	3251	197	
MLB totals				1835	6579	1136	1963	336	83	186	1023	205	814	.298	.391	.459	.851	130	3023	192	9xAS, 3xGG
NgL totals				112	474	90	148	29	12	9	66	11	34	.312	.365	.481	.846	140	228	5	4xEW
162 Game Avg.				162	587	102	176	30	8	16	91	18	71	.299	.387	.461	.848	131	270	16	
FOREIGN LEAGUE TOTALS				1787	6211	1004	1883	306	80	147	915	114		.303	.308	.449	.757		2790	46	3xAS
CWL totals				773	2997	504	839	125	51	66	393	79		.280	.291	.422	.713		1264	46	
MEX AAA totals				705	2254	349	715	122	19	56	377	35		.317		.463	.780		1043		
MEX A totals				309	960	151	329	59	10	25	145			.343		.503	.846		483		
PCL totals				358	1309	251	408	70	17	46	216	49	121	.312	.382	.497	.878		650	27	
A totals				11	40		21	7	1	1				.525	.525	.825	1.350		33		
Exhibition totals				7	35	4	15	3	0	0	3	3		.429		.514	.943		18	0	
NORL totals				2	1	0	0	0	0	0	0	0	1	.000	.500	.000	.500		0		
DWL totals				14																	
TOTALS AT ALL LEVELS OF PLAY				4126	14649	2485	4438	751	193	389	2223	382	970	.303	.356	.460	.816		6742	270	
162 Game Avg.				162	575	98	174	29	8	15	87	15	38	.303	.357	.460	.818		265	11	

Postseason Batting

Year	Age	Tm	Lg	Series	Opp	Rslt	G	AB	R	H	2B	3B	HR	RBI	SB	BB	BA	OBP	SLG	OPS	HBP
1947□	21	NYC	NN2	WS	CLE	W	5	21	4	7	1	0	0	0	0	4	.333	.440	.381	.821	0
1957	31	Marinaro	CWL	WS			6	23	5	9	3	0	0	7	1		.391		.391	.783	0
1958	32	Marinaro	CWL	WS			6	22	3	7	0	0	0	2	0		.318		.318	.636	0
3 Yrs (3 Series)							17	66	12	23	1	0	0	9	1	4	.348	.386	.364	.749	0
2 Yrs			CWL	WS			12	45	8	16	3	0	0	9	1		.356		.356		0
1 Yr			NN2	WS			5	21	4	7	1	0	0	0	0	4	.333	.440	.381	.821	0

All-Star Batting

Year	Age	Lg	Game	G	AB	R	H	2B	3B	HR	RBI	SB	BB	BA	OBP	SLG	OPS	HBP
1947	21	EAS	EWA	3B3B	7	0	1	0	0	0	0	0	0	.143	.143	.143	.286	0
1948	22	EAS	EWA	3B3B	6	1	3	2	0	0	4	0	2	.500	.625	.833	1.458	0
1951	25	AL	ASG		1	0	0	0	0	0	0	0	0	.000	.000	.000	.000	0
1952	26	AL	ASG		2	1	0	0	0	0	0	0	0	.000	.000	.000	.000	0
1953	27	AL	ASG		1	0	1	0	1	0	0	0	0	1.000	1.000	2.000	3.000	0
1954	28	AL	ASG	LF	4	1	2	2	0	0	1	0	0	.500	.600	1.000	2.000 1.100	0
1957	31	AL	ASG			DNP												
1959	33	AL	ASG	LF	5	0	0	0	0	0	0	0	0	1.000	1.000	2.000	3.000	0
1959	33	AL	ASG											.000	.000	.000	.000	0
1960	34	AL	ASG	LF	3	0	0	0	0	0	0	0	0	.000	.000	.000	.000	0
1960	34	AL	ASG	LF	2	1	0	0	0	0	0	0	1	.000	.333	.000	.333	0
1968	42	MxAAA	ASG		1	0	0	0	0	0	0	0	0	.000	.000	.000	.000	0
1970	44	MxAAA	ASG		1	0	1	0	0	0	0	0	0	.250	.250	.250	.500	0
1971	45	Mex AA	ASG		2	0	1	0	0	0	0	0	0	.500	.500	.500	1.000	0
11 Yrs (12 GP)					16	41	4	12	4	0	2	4	0	4	.293	.356	.390	.746	0
9 Yrs			MLB		8	20	2	6	2	0	0	2	0	2	.300	.364	.400	.764	0
4 Yrs			NgL		4	13	1	4	2	0	2	2	0	2	.308	.400	.462	.862	0
3 Yrs			MEX		3	8	1	2	0	0	0	0	0	0	.250		.250		0

Walter "Dobie" Moore

Standard Batting

Year	Age	Tm	Lg	G	AB	R	H	2B	3B	HR	RBI	SB	BB	BA	OBP	SLG	OPS	OPS+	TB	HBP	Awards
1916	20									Did not play in major or minor leagues (Military Service)											
1917	21									Did not play in major or minor leagues (Military Service)											
1918	22									Did not play in major or minor leagues (Military Service)											
1919	23									Did not play in major or minor leagues (Military Service)											
1920	24	KCM	NNL	48	190	37	63	10	4	2	31	4	13	.332	.380	.458	.838	148	87	2	
1921	25	KCM	NNL	64	244	46	79	21	7	8	56	8	11	.324	.355	.566	.921	161	138	1	
1922	26	KCM	NNL	77	329	69	127	24	3	7	63	16	16	.386	.414	.541	.956	154	178	0	
1923	27	KCM	NNL	94	378	70	138	22	9	8	79	10	21	.365	.407	.534	.942	145	202	6	
1924	28	KCM	NNL	75	299	64	106	20	11	5	62	2	26	.355	.415	.545	.960	172	163	5	
1925	29	KCM	NNL	78	321	71	100	17	12	4	77	12	15	.312	.342	.477	.819	125	153		
1926	30	KCM	NNL	17	60	14	24	4	3	0	18	7	11	.400	.500	.567	1.067	183	34	1	
7 Yrs (+4)			NgL	**453**	**1821**	**371**	**637**	**118**	**49**	**34**	**386**	**59**	**113**	**.350**	**.393**	**.524**	**.917**	**151**	**955**	**15**	
162 Game Avg.			Pro	**162**	**651**	**133**	**228**	**42**	**18**	**12**	**138**	**21**	**40**	**.350**	**.393**	**.524**	**.917**	**151**	**342**	**5**	
7 Yrs		KCM	NNL	453	1821	371	637	118	49	34	386	59	113	.350	.393	.524	.917	151	955	15	
7 Yrs			NNL	453	1821	371	637	118	49	34	386	59	113	.350	.393	.524	.917	151	955	15	

Postseason Batting

Year	Age	Tm	Lg	Series	Opp	Rslt	G	AB	R	H	2B	3B	HR	RBI	SB	BB	BA	OBP	SLG	OPS	HBP
1924 □	28	KCM	NNL	WS	HIL	W	10	40	7	12	0	0	0	4	2	1	.300	.317	.300	.617	0
1925	29	KCM	NNL	NNC	SLS	W	7	27	4	4	4	2	1	4	0	3	.148	.233	.407	.641	1
1925	29	KCM	NNL	WS	HIL	L	6	22	0	8	3	1	0	4	1	2	.364	.440	.591	1.031	
2 Yrs (3 Series)			NgL				**23**	**89**	**11**	**24**	**3**	**3**	**1**	**12**	**3**	**6**	**.270**	**.330**	**.404**	**.720**	**2**
1 Yr				NNC			7	27	4	4	4	2	1	4	0	3	.148	.258	.407	.641	1
2 Yrs				WS			16	62	7	20	3	1	0	8	3	3	.323	.364	.403	.757	1

John "Buck" O'Neil
Standard Batting

Year	Age	Tm	Lg	G	AB	R	H	2B	3B	HR	RBI	SB	BB	BA	OBP	SLG	OPS	OPS+	TB	HBP	Awards
1933	21	Tampa Black	Ind	Played in unrecorded Black league																	
1934	22	Miami Giants	Ind	Played in unrecorded Black league																	
1935	23	NY Tigers	Ind	Played in unrecorded Black league																	
1936	24	Acme Giants	Ind	Played in unrecorded Black league																	
1937	25	MRS	NAL	9	34	5	10	1	4	0	4	0	0	.294	.294	.559	.853	142	19	0	
1938	26	KCM	NAL	40	132	27	34	7	3	3	19	11	17	.258	.342	.424	.767	125	56	0	
1939	27	KCM	NAL	46	155	19	28	5	4	1	22	3	14	.181	.249	.284	.532	55	44		
1940	28	KCM	NAL	31	114	19	35	7	3	1	30	5	6	.307	.342	.447	.789	148	51		
1941	29	KCM	NAL	32	129	18	30	5	3	0	11	6	7	.233	.272	.302	.574	80	39		
1942 *	30	KCM	NAL	36	143	20	40	7	1	1	23	2	5	.280	.304	.364	.668	110	52		EWA
1943 *	31	KCM	NAL	41	151	21	43	4	0	1	17	4	9	.285	.329	.331	.660	111	50	1	EWA
1944				Did not play in major or minor leagues (Military Service)																	
1945				Did not play in major or minor leagues (Military Service)																	
1946	34	KCM	NAL	37	124	18	35	3	3	0	11	1	23	.282	.395	.355	.749	123	44	0	
1947	35	KCM	NAL	51	177	41	47	12	3	2	27	9	21	.266	.347	.401	.748	102	71	1	
1948	36	KCM	NAL	24	84	8	19	1	0	0	11	2	7	.226	.286	.238	.524	39	20	0	
1949	37	KCM	NAL	Played in unrecorded Black league																	
1950	38	KCM	NAL	Played in unrecorded Black league																	
1951	39	KCM	NAL	Played in unrecorded Black league																	
1952	40	KCM	NAL	Played in unrecorded Black league																	
1953	41	KCM	NAL	Played in unrecorded Black league																	
1954	42	KCM	NAL	Played in unrecorded Black league																	
1955	43	KCM	NAL	Played in unrecorded Black league																	
10 Yrs (+13)			NgL	347	1243	196	321	52	23	9	175	43	109	.258	.319	.359	.678	101	446	2	
162 Game Avg.			NgL	162	580	92	150	24	11	4	82	20	51	.258	.318	.359	.677	101	208	1	
9 Yrs		KCM	NAL	338	1209	191	311	51	19	9	171	43	109	.257	.320	.353	.673	100	427	2	
1 Yr		MRS	NAL	9	34	5	10	1	4	0	4	0	0	.294	.294	.559	.853	142	19	0	
10 Yrs			NAL	347	1243	196	321	52	23	9	175	43	109	.258	.319	.359	.678	101	446	2	

Postseason Batting

Year	Age	Tm	Lg	Series	Opp	Rslt	G	AB	R	H	2B	3B	HR	RBI	SB	BB	BA	OBP	SLG	OPS	HBP
1939 □	27	KCM	NAL	ALC	SLS	W	5	16	4	8	1	0	0	0	0	1	.500	.529	.688	1.217	0
1942 □	30	KCM	NAL	WS	HG	W	4	16	3	6	0	0	0	2	1	0	.375	.375	.500	.875	0
1946 □	34	KCM	NAL	WS	CAG	W	7	27	4	9	0	0	2	5	2	2	.333	.379	.630	1.009	0
1948	36	KCM	NAL	ALC	BBB	L	6	20	0	4	0	0	0	1	0	0	.200	.200	.250	.450	0
4 Yrs (4 Series)			NgL				22	79	11	27	1	0	2	9	3	3	.342	.366	.519	.885	0
2 Yrs				ALC			11	36	4	12	1	0	0	1	0	1	.333	.351	.444	.796	0
2 Yrs				WS			11	43	7	15	0	0	2	7	3	2	.349	.378	.581	.959	0

All-Star Batting

Year	Age	Tm	Lg	Game	G	AB	R	H	2B	3B	HR	RBI	SB	BB	BA	OBP	SLG	OPS	HBP
1942	30	KCM	WES	EWA		8	0	0	0	0	0	0	0	0	.000	.000	.000	.000	0
1943	31	KCM	WES	EWA		2	0	0	0	0	0	1	0	0	.000	.000	.000	.000	0
2 Yrs (3 GP)			NgL			10	0	0	0	0	0	1	0	0	.000	.000	.000	.000	0

Alejandro Oms

Tied Minnie Miñoso's professional record by playing in 36 seasons - Hit .300+ in four different professional leagues

Standard Batting

Year	Age	Tm	Lg	G	AB	R	H	2B	3B	HR	RBI	SB	BB	BA	OBP	SLG	OPS	OPS+	TB	HBP	Awards
1910	14											Played in unrecorded semi-professional league									
1911	15											Played in unrecorded semi-professional league									
1912	16											Played in unrecorded semi-professional league									
1913	17											Played in unrecorded semi-professional league									
1914	18											Played in unrecorded semi-professional league									
1915	19	El Tosca										Played in unrecorded Cuban league									
1916	20	El Tosca										Played in unrecorded Cuban league									
1917	*21*	*CSE*	*EAS*	*26*	*97*	*15*	*23*	*1*	*1*	*0*	*11*	*0*	*11*	*.237*	*.315*	*.268*	*.583*	*63*	*26*	*0*	
—	—	El Tosca										Played in unrecorded Cuban league									
1918	22	El Tosca										Played in unrecorded Cuban league									
1919	23	El Tosca										Played in unrecorded Cuban league									
1920	24	El Tosca										Played in unrecorded Cuban league									
1921	25	CSE	EAS	12	58	20	29	4	4	4	20	2	2	.500	.517	.810	1.327	216	47	0	
1922	26	CSE	IND	17	72	11	28	6	1	0	13	4	5	.389	.436	.500	.936	159	36	1	
1923	27	CSE	ECL	31	128	27	47	5	3	3	26	10	11	.367	.417	.523	.941	174	67	0	
1924	28	CSE	ECL	32	120	22	39	6	3	2	25	2	15	.325	.400	.475	.875	156	57		
1925	29	CSE	ECL	45	167	35	52	13	1	7	37	4	29	.311	.413	.527	.940	150	88		
1926	30	CSE	ECL	42	149	22	40	10	2	4	30	3	22	.268	.363	.443	.806	125	66	0	
1927	31	CSE	ECL	54	194	43	65	14	3	7	44	9	25	.335	.414	.546	.960	153	106	1	
1928	32	CSE	ECL	30	119	28	38	9	1	5	24	3	12	.319	.391	.538	.929	140	64	2	
1929	33	SC2	IND	3	11	0	3	0	1	0	1	0	2	.273	.385	.455	.839	192	5	0	
1930	34	SC2	EAS	16	59	13	19	4	2	2	11	1	7	.322	.394	.525	.919	119	31	0	
1931	35	SC2	IND	11	46	3	9	2	1	1	6	0	2	.196	.229	.348	.577	67	16	0	
1932	36	CS2	IND	4	14	6	6	3	0	0	3	0	5	.429	.579	.643	1.222	230	9	0	
1933	37	CS2	IND	5	20	3	7	0	0	1	3	0	2	.350	.435	.500	.935	160	10	1	
1934	38		VBPL									Played in unrecorded Venezuelan league									
1935 *	39	NYC	NN2	41	159	29	60	12	5	3	30	1	14	.377	.428	.572	1.000	151	91	0	EWA
1936	40	Santa Marta	VBPL									Played in unrecorded Venezuelan league									
1937	41	Maracaibo	VBPL									Played in unrecorded Venezuelan league									
1938	42	Maracaibo	VBPL									Played in unrecorded Venezuelan league									
1939	43	Vargas	VBPL									Played in unrecorded Venezuelan league									
1940	44											Played in unrecorded Cuban league									
1941	45											Played in unrecorded Cuban league									
1942	46	Estrellas	VBPL									Played in unrecorded Venezuelan league									
1943	47		VBPL									Played in unrecorded Venezuelan league									
1944	48		VBPL									Played in unrecorded Venezuelan league									
1945	49		VBPL									Played in unrecorded Venezuelan league									

Alejandro Oms

Standard Batting (continued)

Year	Age	Tm	Lg	G	AB	R	H	2B	3B	HR	RBI	SB	BB	BA	OBP	SLG	OPS	OPS+	TB	HBP	Awards
14 yrs (+22)			NgL	343	1316	262	442	88	23	39	273	40	153	.336	.407	.527	.934	155	693	5	
162 Game Avg.			Pro	162	622	124	209	42	11	18	129	19	72	.336	.407	.527	.934	155	327	2	
1 Yr			Pre-NgL	26	97	15	23	1	1	0	11	0	11	.237	.315	.268	.583	63	26	0	
15 Yrs			Pre-NgL+NgL	369	1413	277	465	89	24	39	284	40	164	.329	.401	.509	.910	149	719	5	
162 Game Avg.			Pre-NgL+Pro	162	620	122	204	39	11	17	125	18	72	.329	.401	.509	.910	149	316	2	
8 Yrs		CSE	ECL+EAS	263	1007	208	338	67	15	32	219	37	121	.336	.409	.527	.936	154	531	4	
1 Yr		NYC	NN2	41	159	29	60	12	5	3	30	1	14	.377	.428	.572	1.000	151	91	0	
3 Yrs		SC2	EAS+IND	30	116	16	31	6	3	3	18	2	11	.267	.331	.448	.779	105	52	0	
2 Yrs		CS2	IND	9	34	9	13	3	0	1	6	0	7	.382	.500	.559	1.059	189	19	1	
6 Yrs		ECL		234	877	177	281	57	13	28	186	31	114	.320	.400	.511	.911	149	448	3	
1 Yr		NN2		41	159	29	60	12	5	3	30	1	14	.377	.428	.572	1.000	151	91	0	
5 Yrs		IND		40	163	23	53	11	3	2	26	5	16	.325	.392	.466	.859	141	76	2	
2 Yrs		EAS		28	117	33	48	8	2	6	31	3	9	.410	.452	.667	1.119	219	78	0	

Postseason Batting

Year	Age	Tm	Lg	Series	Opp	Rslt	G	AB	R	H	2B	3B	HR	RBI	SB	BB	BA	OBP	SLG	OPS	HBP
1935	39	NYC	NN2	NLC	PC	L	6	18	4	4	1	0	0	2	0	2	.222	.300	.278	.578	0
1 Yr (1 Series)				NLC			6	18	4	4	1	0	0	2	0	2	.222	.300	.278	.578	0
1 Yr			NgL				6	18	4	4	1	0	0	2	0	2	.222	.300	.278	.578	0

All-Star Batting

Year	Age	Tm	Lg	G	AB	R	H	2B	3B	HR	RBI	SB	BB	BA	OBP	SLG	OPS	HBP
1935	39	EAS	EWA	1	4	1	2	0	0	0	1	0	1	.500	.600	.500	1.100	0
1 Yr (1 GP)			NgL	1	4	1	2	0	0	0	1	0	1	.500	.600	.500	1.100	0

Spottswood "Spot" Poles
Standard Batting

Year	Age	Tm	Lg	G	AB	R	H	2B	3B	HR	RBI	SB	BB	BA	OBP	SLG	OPS	OPS+	TB	HBP	Awards
1909	21	PG	INT	17	63	11	15	2	1	0	6	3	7	.238	.314	.302	.616	96	19	0	
1910	22	PG	EAS	19	77	13	15	4	0	1	5	1	7	.195	.271	.286	.556	65	22	1	
1911	23	NLG	EAS	15	62	12	19	1	1	0	6	10	7	.306	.394	.355	.749	101	22	2	
1912	24	TOTAL	EAS	17	72	10	27	0	0	0	10	5	0	.375	.392	.375	.767	103	27	2	
	—	NLG	EAS	16	67	8	25	0	0	0	9	3	0	.373	.391	.373	.764	101	25	2	
	—	BRG	EAS	1	5	2	2	0	0	0	1	2	0	.400	.400	.400	.800	131	2	0	
1913	25	NLG	EAS	17	65	17	19	4	0	0	6	6	11	.292	.403	.354	.756	141	23	1	
1914	26	TOTAL	EAS	29	124	31	52	8	1	0	15	12	14	.419	.486	.500	.986	173	62	2	
	—	NLS	EAS	1	3	1	2	0	0	0	1	2	2	.667	.800	.667	1.467	291	2	0	
	—	NLG	EAS	28	121	30	50	8	1	0	14	10	12	.413	.474	.496	.970	170	60	2	
1915	27	NLS	EAS	38	157	29	41	8	2	0	14	9	16	.261	.337	.338	.675	98	53	2	
1916	28	NLG	EAS	18	73	16	22	1	0	0	5	2	10	.301	.386	.356	.742	94	26	0	
1917	29	TOTAL	EAS	22	79	21	28	6	0	0	9	3	12	.354	.463	.430	.894	131	34	4	
	—	NLG	EAS	15	53	15	21	5	0	0	8	3	10	.396	.522	.491	1.013	162	26	4	
	—	HIL	EAS	6	23	6	6	1	0	0	1	0	2	.261	.320	.304	.624	64	7	0	
	—	PAS	EAS	1	3	0	1	0	0	0	0	0	0	.333	.333	.333	.667	91	1	0	
1918	30													Did not play in major or minor leagues (Military Service)							
1919	31	TOTAL	EAS	16	68	12	20	3	2	0	5	1	6	.294	.351	.397	.748	129	27	0	
	—	HIL	EAS	5	21	2	4	1	0	0	1	0	1	.190	.227	.238	.465	50	5	0	
	—	AC	EAS	11	47	10	16	2	2	0	4	1	5	.340	.404	.468	.872	165	22	0	
1920	32	NLG	EAS	12	47	8	15	3	0	0	4	4	6	.319	.396	.383	.779	167	18	0	
1921	33	NLG	EAS	13	54	17	21	6	1	2	7	4	6	.389	.459	.648	1.107	149	35	1	
1922	34	NLG	IND	15	57	11	21	4	0	0	4	4	4	.368	.419	.439	.858	129	25	1	
1923	35	NLG	ECL	33	109	18	31	3	1	0	11	2	14	.284	.371	.330	.701	86	36	1	
4 Yrs (+11)			NgL	73	267	54	88	16	2	2	26	11	30	.330	.403	.427	.830	122	114	3	
162 Game Avg.			Pro	162	593	120	195	36	4	4	58	24	67	.330	.403	.427	.830	122	253	7	
10 Yrs			Pre-NgL	208	840	172	258	37	7	2	81	52	90	.307	.383	.375	.758	115	315	14	
14 Yrs			Pre-NgL+NgL	281	1107	226	346	53	9	4	107	63	120	.313	.388	.388	.776	117	429	17	
162 Game Avg.			Pre-NgL+Pro	162	638	130	199	31	5	2	62	36	69	.313	.388	.388	.776	117	247	10	
4 Yrs			ECL+EAS+IND	73	267	54	88	16	2	2	26	11	30	.330	.403	.427	.830	122	114	3	
2 Yrs		NLG	EAS	25	101	25	36	9	1	2	11	5	12	.356	.430	.525	.955	157	53	1	
1 Yr			ECL	33	109	18	31	3	1	0	11	2	14	.284	.371	.330	.701	86	36	1	
1 Yr			IND	15	57	11	21	4	0	0	4	4	4	.368	.419	.439	.858	129	25	1	

Cumberland "Cum" Posey
Standard Batting

Year	Age	Tm	Lg	G	AB	R	H	2B	3B	HR	RBI	SB	BB	BA	OBP	SLG	OPS	OPS+	TB	HBP	Awards
1911	21	HG												Played in unrecorded Black league							
1912	22	HG												Played in unrecorded Black league							
1913	23	HG												Played in unrecorded Black league							
1914	24	HG												Played in unrecorded Black league							
1915	25	HG												Played in unrecorded Black league							
1916	26	HG												Played in unrecorded Black league							
1917	27	HG												Played in unrecorded Black league							
1918	28	HG	WES	2	7	1	1	0	0	0	0	0	1	.143	.250	.143	.393	17	1	0	
1919	29	HG												Played in unrecorded Black league							
1920	30	HG												Played in unrecorded Black league							
1921	31	HG	WES	2	6	0	0	0	0	0	0	0	2	.000	.250	.000	.250	-28	0	0	
1922	32	HG	IND	1	2	0	1	0	0	0	1	0	0	.500	.500	.500	1.000	184	1	0	
1923	33	HG	IND											Played in unrecorded Black league							
1924	34	HG	IND											Played in unrecorded Black league							
1925	35	HG	IND											Played in unrecorded Black league							
1926	36	HG	IND											Played in unrecorded Black league							
1927	37	HG	IND											Played in unrecorded Black league							
1928	38	HG	EAS											Played in unrecorded Black league							
1929	39	HG	ANL											Played in unrecorded Black league							
2 Yrs (+17)			NgL	3	8	0	1	0	0	0	0	0	2	.125	.300	.125	.425	40	1	0	
1 Yr			Pre-NgL	2	7	1	1	0	0	0	0	0	1	.143	.250	.143	.393	17	1	0	
2 Yrs			Pre-NgL+NgL	5	15	1	2	0	0	0	1	0	3	.133	.278	.133	.411	156	2	0	
2 Yrs		HG	WES+IND	3	8	0	1	0	0	0	0	0	2	.125	.300	.125	.425	40	1	0	
1 Yr			WES	2	6	0	0	0	0	0	0	0	2	.000	.250	.000	.250	-28	0	0	
1 Yr			IND	1	2	0	1	0	0	0	1	0	0	.500	.500	.500	1.000	184	1	0	

Managerial Record

Year	Age	Tm	Lg	W	L	W-L%	T	G	Finish
1921	31	HG	WES	3	4	.429	1	8	2
1922	32	HG	IND	4	3	.571	0	7	1
1923	33	HG	IND			No records available			
1924	34	HG	IND	4	4	.500	0	8	1
1925	35	HG	IND	2	1	.667	0	3	1
1926	36	HG	IND			No records available			
1927	37	HG	IND	6	1	.857	0	7	1
1928	38	HG	EAS	11	9	.550	0	20	2
1929	39	HG	ANL	32	34	.485	3	69	4
1930	40	HG	EAS	45	15	.750	1	61	2
1931	41	HG	IND	34	21	.618	1	56	2
1932	42	HG	EWL	20	11	.645	0	31	2
1933	43	HG	NN2	15	14	.517	3	32	3
1934	44	HG	IND	16	13	.552	1	30	1
1935	45	HG	NN2	26	36	.419	2	64	7
13 yrs		HG		218	166	.568	12	396	
13 yrs			NgL	218	166	.568	12	396	

Jackie Robinson
Standard Batting

Year	Age	Tm	Lg	G	AB	R	H	2B	3B	HR	RBI	SB	BB	BA	OBP	SLG	OPS	OPS+	TB	HBP	Awards
1942	23			Did not play in major or minor leagues (Military Service)																	
1943	24			Did not play in major or minor leagues (Military Service)																	
1944	25			Did not play in major or minor leagues (Military Service)																	
1945 *	26	KCM	NAL	34	120	25	45	13	1	4	27	3	16	.375	.449	.600	1.049	212	72	0	EWA
1946	27	Montreal	IL																		MVP-1
1947	28	BRO	NL	151	590	125	175	31	5	12	48	29	74	.297	.383	.427	.810	112	252	9	RoY-1, MVP-5
1948	29	BRO	NL	147	574	108	170	38	8	12	85	22	57	.296	.367	.453	.820	117	260	7	MVP-15
1949 *	30	BRO	NL	156	593	122	203	38	12	16	124	37	86	.342	.432	.528	.960	152	313	8	ASG, MVP-1
1950 *	31	BRO	NL	144	518	99	170	39	4	14	81	12	80	.328	.423	.500	.923	139	259	5	ASG, MVP-15
1951 *	32	BRO	NL	153	548	106	185	33	7	19	88	25	79	.338	.429	.527	.957	154	289	9	ASG, MVP-6
1952 *	33	BRO	NL	149	510	104	157	17	3	19	75	24	106	.308	.440	.465	.904	149	237	14	ASG, MVP-7
1953 *	34	BRO	NL	136	484	109	159	34	7	12	95	17	74	.329	.425	.502	.927	137	243	7	ASG, MVP-12
1954 *	35	BRO	NL	124	386	62	120	22	4	15	59	7	63	.311	.417	.505	.922	135	195	7	ASG
1955	36	BRO	NL	105	317	51	81	6	2	8	36	12	61	.256	.381	.363	.743	95	115	3	
1956	37	BRO	NL	117	357	61	98	15	2	10	43	12	60	.275	.383	.412	.795	106	147	3	MVP-16
11 Yrs (+4)			Pro	1416	4997	972	1563	286	55	141	761	200	756	.313	.410	.477	.887	134	2382	72	
10 Yrs			NL	1382	4877	947	1518	273	54	137	734	197	740	.311	.410	.474	.883	132	2310	72	
1 Yr			NAL	34	120	25	45	13	1	4	27	3	16	.375	.449	.600	1.049	212	72	0	
162 Game Avg.			Pro	162	572	111	179	33	6	16	87	23	86	.313	.410	.477	.887	134	273	8	
10 Yrs		BRO	NL	1382	4877	947	1518	273	54	137	734	197	740	.311	.410	.474	.883	132	2310	72	
1 Yr		KCM	NAL	34	120	25	45	13	1	4	27	3	16	.375	.449	.600	1.049	212	72	0	

Postseason Batting

Year	Age	Tm	Lg	Series	Opp	Rslt	G	AB	R	H	2B	3B	HR	RBI	SB	BB	BA	OBP	SLG	OPS	TB	HBP
1947	28	BRO	NL	WS	NYY	L	7	27	3	7	2	0	0	3	2	2	.259	.310	.333	.644	9	0
1949	30	BRO	NL	WS	NYY	L	5	16	2	3	1	0	0	2	0	4	.188	.350	.250	.600	4	0
1952	33	BRO	NL	WS	NYY	L	7	23	4	4	0	0	1	2	2	7	.174	.367	.304	.671	7	0
1953	34	BRO	NL	WS	NYY	L	6	25	3	8	2	0	0	2	1	1	.320	.346	.400	.746	10	0
1955 □	36	BRO	NL	WS	NYY	W	6	22	5	4	1	1	0	1	0	2	.182	.250	.318	.568	7	0
1956	37	BRO	NL	WS	NYY	L	7	24	5	6	1	0	0	2	0	5	.250	.379	.417	.796	10	0
6 Yrs (6 Series)							38	137	22	32	7	1	1	12	6	21	.234	.335	.343	.679	47	0
6 Yrs			MLB	WS			38	137	22	32	7	1	1	12	6	21	.234	.335	.343	.679	47	0

Jackie Robinson
All-Star Batting

Year	Age	Lg	Game	G	AB	R	H	2B	3B	HR	RBI	BB	SB	BA	OBP	SLG	OPS	TB	HBP
1945	26	WES	EWA	SS	5	0	0	0	0	0	0	0	0	.000	.000	.000	.000	0	0
1949	30	NL	ASG	2B	4	3	1	1	0	0	0	1	0	.250	.400	.500	.900	2	0
1950	31	NL	ASG	2B	4	1	1	0	0	0	0	0	0	.250	.250	.250	.500	1	0
1951	32	NL	ASG	2B	4	1	2	0	0	0	1	1	0	.500	.600	.500	1.100	2	0
1952	33	NL	ASG	2B	3	1	1	1	0	0	1	0	0	.333	.333	1.333	1.667	4	0
1953	34	NL	ASG	1	1	0	0	0	0	0	0	0	0	.000	.000	.000	.000	0	0
1954	35	NL	ASG	LF	2	1	1	0	0	1	2	0	0	.500	.500	1.000	1.500	2	0
7 Yrs (7 GP)		Pro		7	23	7	6	2	0	1	4	2	0	.261	.320	.478	.798	11	0
6 Yrs		MLB		6	18	7	6	2	0	1	4	2	0	.333	.400	.611	1.011	11	0
1 Yr		NgL		1	5	0	0	0	0	0	0	0	0	.000	.000	.000	.000	0	0

Charles "Bullet" Rogan
Standard Batting

Year	Age	Tm	Lg	G	AB	R	H	2B	3B	HR	RBI	SB	BB	BA	OBP	SLG	OPS	OPS+	TB	HBP	Awards
1920	26	KCM	NNL	48	186	20	55	6	8	1	19	9	10	.296	.335	.430	.765	126	80	1	
1921	27	KCM	NNL	83	259	48	79	12	8	6	47	19	30	.305	.384	.483	.866	147	125	3	
1922	28	KCM	NNL	74	241	58	89	11	7	15	55	16	35	.369	.453	.660	1.113	195	159	2	
1923	29	KCM	NNL	68	207	38	75	12	3	7	44	5	19	.362	.416	.551	.967	151	114	0	
1924	30	KCM	NNL	49	149	31	59	8	7	5	33	5	12	.396	.444	.617	1.062	200	92	1	
1925	31	KCM	NNL	50	125	24	45	7	8	2	40	6	14	.360	.424	.592	1.016	180	74		
1926	32	KCM	NNL	53	136	30	39	7	3	1	18	7	23	.287	.405	.404	.809	115	55	4	
1927	33	KCM	NNL	59	124	21	41	4	3	2	22	1	16	.331	.435	.460	.895	142	57	0	
1928	34	KCM	NNL	64	201	40	70	14	5	3	41	5	23	.348	.405	.512	.917	157	103	3	
1929	35	KCM	NNL	72	259	65	93	16	9	7	69	26	41	.359	.449	.571	1.020	164	148	1	
1930	36	KCM	NNL	30	108	26	32	6	0	1	20	5	18	.296	.397	.380	.776	111	41	0	
1932	38	Jamestown ND	IND										Played for unrecorded independent team								
1933	39	KCM	IND	5	14	3	5	0	0	0	5	1	0	.357	.357	.571	.929	175	8	0	
1934	40	KCM	IND	7	28	2	3	1	0	0	1	0	0	.107	.107	.143	.250	-22	4	0	
1935	41	KCM	IND	7	21	1	3	1	0	0	2	0	1	.143	.182	.190	.372	3	4	0	
1936 *	42	KCM	IND	2	3	2	2	0	0	0	2	0	2	.667	.800	.667	1.467	301	2	0	EWA
1937 *	43	KCM	NAL	17	28	7	10	2	1	0	8	1	4	.357	.455	.500	.955	171	14	1	NSA
1938	44	KCM	NAL	13	28	5	6	2	1	0	3	3	3	.214	.290	.250	.540	58	7	0	
17 Yrs (+1)			NgL	701	2117	421	706	108	60	51	429	107	251	.333	.408	.513	.922	151	1087	16	
162 Game Avg.			Pro	162	489	97	163	25	14	12	99	25	58	.333	.408	.513	.922	151	251	4	
17 Yrs		KCM	NNL+NAL+IND	701	2117	421	706	108	60	51	429	107	251	.333	.408	.513	.922	151	1087	16	
11 Yrs			NNL	650	1995	401	677	103	59	50	408	104	241	.339	.414	.525	.940	156	1048	15	
2 Yrs			NAL	30	56	12	16	3	1	0	11	2	7	.286	.375	.375	.750	115	21	1	
4 Yrs			IND	21	66	8	13	2	0	0	10	1	3	.197	.232	.273	.505	42	18	0	

Charles "Bullet" Rogan
Postseason Batting

Year	Age	Tm	Lg	Series	Opp	Rslt	G	AB	R	H	2B	3B	HR	RBI	SB	BB	BA	OBP	SLG	OPS	HBP
1924 □	30	KCM	NNL	HC	WS	W	10	40	4	14	1	0	0	6	3	3	.350	.395	.375	.770	0
1925 □	31	KCM	NNL	SLS	NNC	W	7	20	3	9	0	0	0	2	1	1	.450	.500	.450	.926	1
1926	32	KCM	NNL	CAG	NNC	L	6	12	1	7	1	0	0	2	0	2	.583	.643	.667	1.310	0
1937 □	43	KCM	NAL	CAG	ALC	W	1	6	0	0	0	0	0	0	0	0	.000	.000	.000	.000	0
4 Yrs (4 Series)			**NgL**				**24**	**78**	**8**	**30**	**2**	**0**	**0**	**10**	**4**	**6**	**.385**	**.435**	**.410**	**.839**	**1**
2 Yrs				NNC			13	32	4	16	1	0	0	4	1	3	.500	.556	.531	1.074	1
1 Yr				ALC			1	6	0	0	0	0	0	0	0	0	.000	.000	.000	.000	0
1 Yr				WS			10	40	4	14	1	0	0	6	3	3	.350	.395	.375	.770	0

All-Star Batting

Year	Age	Lg	Game	G	AB	R	H	2B	3B	HR	RBI	SB	BB	BA	OBP	SLG	OPS	HBP
1936	42	WES	EWA	LF	1	0	0	0	0	0	0	0	0	.000	.000	.000	.000	0
1937	43	SAS	NSA	RF	4	2	3	1	0	0	2	0	0	.750	.750	1.000	1.750	0
2 Yrs (2 GPs)		**NgL**		**2**	**5**	**2**	**3**	**1**	**0**	**0**	**2**	**0**	**0**	**.600**	**.600**	**.800**	**1.400**	**0**

Louis Santop

Standard Batting

Year	Age	Tm	Lg	G	AB	R	H	2B	3B	HR	RBI	SB	BB	BA	OBP	SLG	OPS	OPS+	TB	HBP	Awards
1910 (+10)	21	OKM	WES	1	4	0	0	0	0	0	0	0	0	.000	.000	.000	.000	-100	0	0	
1911	22	TOTAL	EAS	31	116	20	37	5	2	4	25	7	8	.319	.363	.500	.863	275	58	0	
–	–	PG	EAS	16	63	9	20	2	1	4	12	3	4	.317	.358	.571	.930	166	36	0	
–	–	NLG	EAS	15	53	11	17	3	1	0	13	4	4	.321	.368	.415	.784	109	22	0	
1912	23	NLG	EAS	14	50	7	14	0	1	0	5	1	3	.280	.294	.320	.614	61	16	0	
1913	24	NLG	EAS	13	55	6	21	3	0	0	14	1	3	.382	.414	.436	.850	171	24	0	
1914	25	NLG	EAS	29	120	17	45	4	2	1	24	5	11	.375	.427	.467	.894	149	56	0	
1915	26	NLS	EAS	36	139	20	43	9	1	2	32	0	8	.309	.347	.432	.779	128	60	0	
1916	27	TOTAL	EAS	36	136	31	51	12	7	0	33	6	23	.375	.469	.566	1.035	186	77	1	
–	–	NLS	EAS	26	97	18	34	9	4	0	23	3	19	.351	.462	.526	.987	179	51	1	
–	–	BRG	EAS	10	39	13	17	3	3	0	10	3	4	.436	.488	.667	1.155	204	26	0	
1917	28	BRG	EAS	24	89	24	35	8	1	1	24	9	11	.393	.460	.539	.999	174	48	0	
1918	29	TOTAL	EAS	17	68	11	28	6	2	1	18	3	7	.412	.474	.603	1.077	200	41	1	
–	–	HIL	EAS	11	43	9	19	3	2	1	14	1	5	.442	.510	.674	1.185	222	29	1	
–	–	BRG	EAS	6	25	2	9	3	0	0	4	2	2	.360	.407	.480	.887	161	12	0	
1919	30	TOTAL	EAS	10	38	5	11	1	1	1	6	1	3	.289	.341	.447	.789	136	17	0	
–	–	BRG	EAS	8	31	5	10	1	1	1	6	1	2	.323	.364	.516	.880	161	16	0	
–	–	HIL	EAS	2	7	0	1	0	0	0	0	0	1	.143	.250	.143	.393	26	1	0	
1920	31	HIL	EAS	19	64	13	20	5	1	0	7	0	7	.313	.397	.422	.819	186	27	2	
1921	32	HIL	EAS	37	115	29	42	12	2	5	35	4	11	.365	.425	.635	1.060	166	73	1	
1922	33	HIL	IND	37	101	20	40	8	4	2	23	3	17	.396	.487	.614	1.101	221	62	1	
1923	34	HIL	ECL	34	113	17	33	4	3	2	21	1	9	.292	.355	.434	.788	119	49	1	
1924	35	HIL	ECL	48	178	28	63	10	2	5	29	4	10	.354	.385	.517	.902	154	92	0	
1925	36	HIL	ECL	21	32	2	6	1	0	0	8	1	3	.188	.257	.219	.476	23	7	0	
1926	37	HIL	ECL	12	27	5	9	1	1	0	7	0	2	.333	.379	.370	.750	100	10	0	
7 Yrs (+10)			NgL	208	630	114	213	41	12	14	130	14	59	.338	.399	.508	.907	170	320	5	
162 Game Avg.			Pro	162	491	89	166	32	9	11	101	11	46	.338	.399	.508	.907	170	249	4	
10 Yrs			Pre-NgL	211	815	141	285	48	17	10	181	33	75	.350	.406	.487	.893	171	397	2	
17 Yrs			Pre-NgL+NgL	419	1445	255	498	89	29	24	311	47	134	.345	.403	.496	.899	171	717	7	
162 Game Avg.			Pre-NgL+NgL	162	559	99	193	34	11	9	120	18	52	.345	.403	.496	.899	171	277	3	
7 Yrs		HIL	ECL+EAS+IND	208	630	114	213	41	12	14	130	14	59	.338	.399	.508	.907	170	320	5	
4 Yrs			ECL	115	350	52	111	16	5	7	65	9	24	.317	.363	.451	.814	127	158	1	
2 Yrs			EAS	56	179	42	62	17	3	5	42	4	18	.346	.415	.559	.974	173	100	3	
1 Yr			IND	37	101	20	40	8	4	2	23	1	17	.396	.487	.614	1.101	221	62	1	

Postseason Batting

Year	Age	Tm	Lg	Series	Opp	Rslt	G	AB	R	H	2B	3B	HR	RBI	SB	BB	BA	OBP	SLG	OPS	HBP
1924	35	HIL	ECL	WS	KCM	L	9	24	2	8	0	0	0	2	0	4	.333	.429	.333	.762	0
1925 □	36	HIL	ECL	WS	KCL	W	2	2	0	0	0	0	0	0	0	0	.000	.000	.000	.000	0
2 Yrs (2 Series)							11	26	2	8	0	0	0	2	0	4	.308	.400	.308	.708	0
2 Yrs			NgL	WS			11	26	2	8	0	0	0	2	0	4	.308	.400	.308	.708	0

Charlie "Chino" Smith
Standard Batting

Year	Age	Tm	Lg	G	AB	R	H	2B	3B	HR	RBI	SB	BB	BA	OBP	SLG	OPS	OPS+	TB	HBP	Awards
1925	23	BRG	ECL	35	133	29	42	7	0	5	28	3	12	.316	.372	.481	.854	122	64		
1926	24	BRG	ECL	28	102	21	37	4	2	2	17	5	11	.363	.435	.500	.935	170	51	2	
1927	25	BRG	ECL	33	127	24	58	11	4	3	34	5	18	.457	.534	.677	1.211	222	86	3	
1928	26	BRG	EAS	9	35	9	13	2	3	1	7	0	0	.371	.389	.686	1.075	193	24	1	
1929	27	NLG	ANL	66	246	86	111	29	4	22	81	16	48	.451	.551	.870	1.421	228	214	7	
1930	28	NLG	EAS	51	175	60	73	16	7	8	56	1	38	.417	.534	.726	1.260	184	127	6	
1931	29	BRG	IND	2	7	1	1	0	0	0	0	0	0	.143	.143	.143	.286	-11	1	0	
7 Yrs			NgL	224	825	230	335	69	20	41	223	30	127	.406	.495	.687	1.183	190	567	19	
162 Game Avg.			Pro	162	597	166	242	50	14	30	161	22	92	.406	.495	.687	1.183	190	410	14	
2 Yrs		NLG	ANL+EAS	117	421	146	184	45	11	30	137	17	86	.437	.544	.810	1.354	412	341	13	
5 Yrs		BRG	ECL+EAS+IND	107	404	84	151	24	9	11	86	13	41	.374	.439	.559	.998	696	226	6	
3 Yrs			ECL	96	362	74	137	22	6	10	79	13	41	.378	.449	.555	1.004	514	201	5	
1 Yr			ANL	66	246	86	111	29	4	22	81	16	48	.451	.551	.870	1.421	228	214	7	
2 Yrs			EAS	60	210	69	86	18	10	9	63	1	38	.410	.514	.719	1.233	377	151	7	
1 Yr			IND	2	7	1	1	0	0	0	0	0	0	.143	.143	.143	.286	-11	1	0	

Norman "Turkey" Stearnes

Holds NgL career record for triples; tied Sam Crawford's professional record for most times leading league in triples (6).

Standard Batting

Year	Age	Tm	Lg	G	AB	R	H	2B	3B	HR	RBI	SB	BB	BA	OBP	SLG	OPS	OPS+	TB	HBP	Awards
1923	22	DS	NNL	69	279	70	101	18	14	17	85	2	17	.362	.401	.710	1.110	181	198	1	
1924	23	DS	NNL	61	248	57	84	9	12	9	44	2	17	.339	.386	.581	.966	169	144	2	
1925	24	DS	NNL	94	367	93	136	24	14	19	126	11	45	.371	.439	.668	1.107	187	245		
1926	25	DS	NNL	93	342	94	131	33	9	21	103	21	41	.383	.458	.716	1.174	185	245	6	
1927	26	DS	NNL	91	340	79	119	25	12	19	114	13	46	.350	.429	.662	1.091	191	225	1	
1928	27	DS	NNL	80	315	80	101	16	7	24	78	5	29	.321	.387	.644	1.031	175	203	5	
1929	28	DS	NNL	68	259	64	101	17	4	16	91	12	38	.390	.468	.672	1.140	194	174	0	
1930	29	DS	NNL+EAS	54	202	57	73	18	12	8	71	13	26	.361	.434	.688	1.122	177	139	0	
–	–	DS	NNL	35	129	26	42	9	8	2	38	6	14	.326	.392	.566	.957	157	73	0	
–	–	NLG	EAS	19	73	31	31	9	4	6	33	7	12	.425	.506	.904	1.410	213	66	0	
1931	30	DS	NNL_IND	54	190	35	57	12	0	8	40	8	22	.300	.381	.511	.892	143	97	3	
1931	30	DS	NNL	38	133	29	50	10	0	2	33	6	20	.376	.465	.632	1.096	200	84	2	
1931	30	KCM	IND	16	57	6	7	2	0	6	7	2	2	.123	.167	.228	.395	11	13	1	
1932 *	31	CAG	NSL	44	168	43	49	9	2	4	25	11	21	.292	.374	.440	.814	155	74	1	EWA
1933 *	32	CAG	NN2	41	175	46	62	12	5	7	30	5	18	.354	.418	.600	1.018	176	105	2	EWA
1934 *	33	CAG	NN2	39	154	42	53	7	7	6	28	6	14	.344	.402	.597	1.000	190	92	1	EWA
1935 *	34	CAG	NN2	47	170	43	66	10	6	6	52	9	23	.388	.469	.624	1.093	183	106	3	
1936	35	PS	NN2	52	210	45	74	8	5	10	43	1	19	.352	.411	.581	.992	150	122	2	
1937 *	36	KCM	NAL	19	66	13	23	4	1	2	11	2	8	.348	.434	.530	.965	175	35	2	EWA
–	–	DTS	NAL	15	52	11	19	3	1	1	9	1	7	.365	.441	.519	.960	171	27	0	
–	–	CAG	NAL	4	14	2	4	1	0	1	2	1	1	.286	.412	.571	.983	188	8	2	
1938	37	KCM	NAL	32	120	20	31	4	4	4	23	10	14	.258	.341	.408	.749	115	49	1	
–	–	CAG	NAL	19	69	14	18	2	1	2	10	5	7	.261	.338	.406	.743	121	28	1	
–	–	KCM	NAL	13	51	6	13	2	3	0	13	5	7	.255	.345	.412	.757	107	21	0	
1939 *	38	KCM	NAL	49	185	42	61	9	1	7	39	12	17	.330	.386	.503	.889	159	93		EWA
1940	39	KCM	NAL	29	99	15	26	3	1	4	25	3	16	.263	.365	.434	.800	151	43		

Norman "Turkey" Stearnes
Standard Batting (continued)

Year	Age	Tm	Lg	G	AB	R	H	2B	3B	HR	RBI	SB	BB	BA	OBP	SLG	OPS	OPS+	TB	HBP	Awards
18 Yrs			NgL	1016	3889	938	1348	238	118	189	1028	141	431	.347	.416	.614	1.030	174	2389	29	
162 Game Avg.			Pro	162	620	150	215	38	19	30	164	22	69	.347	.416	.614	1.030	174	381	5	
9 Yrs		DS	NNL	629	2412	592	865	161	80	135	712	78	267	.359	.426	.660	1.086	183	1591	17	
6 Yrs		CAG	NSL+NN2+NAL	194	750	190	252	41	21	26	147	32	84	.336	.409	.551	.960	171	413	9	
4 Yrs		KCM	NAL+IND	107	392	69	107	16	7	11	84	22	42	.273	.345	.434	.779	129	34	1	
1 Yr		PS	NN2	52	210	45	74	8	5	10	43	1	19	.352	.411	.581	.992	150	122	2	
1 Yr		NLG	EAS	19	73	31	31	9	4	6	33	7	12	.425	.506	.904	1.410	213	66	0	
1 Yr		DTS	NAL	15	52	11	19	3	1	1	9	1	7	.365	.441	.519	.960	171	27	0	
9 Yrs			NNL	629	2412	592	865	161	80	135	712	78	267	.359	.426	.660	1.086	183	1591	17	
4 Yrs			NN2	179	709	176	255	37	23	29	153	17	74	.360	.425	.599	1.025	173	425	7	
4 Yrs			NAL	129	470	90	141	20	7	15	98	26	55	.300	.377	.468	.845	148	84	3	
1 Yr			NSL	44	168	43	49	9	2	4	25	11	21	.292	.374	.440	.814	155	74	1	
1 Yr			EAS	19	73	31	31	9	4	6	33	7	12	.425	.506	.904	1.410	213	66	0	
1 Yr			IND	16	57	6	7	2	2	0	7	2	2	.123	.167	.228	.395	11	13	1	

Postseason Batting

Year	Age	Tm	Lg	Series	Opp	Rslt	G	AB	R	H	2B	3B	HR	RBI	SB	BB	BA	OBP	SLG	OPS	HBP
1930	29	DS	NNL	NNC	SLS	L	7	30	9	14	4	1	3	11	1	1	.467	.484	.967	1.451	0
1932 a	31	CAG	NSL	NSC	NEG	W	2	10	6	7	0	1	2	5	0	0	.700	.700	1.500	2.200	0
1934	33	CAG	NN2	NLC	PS	L	6	24	4	11	1	1	1	4	4	0	.458	.480	.708	1.167	1
1937	36	CAG	NAL	ALC	KCM	L	4	19	2	5	1	0	0	1	0	1	.263	.300	.316	.616	0
1939 a	38	KCM	NAL	ALC	SLS	W	5	13	3	3	1	0	1	5	0	3	.231	.375	.538	.913	0
5 Yrs (5 Series)			NgL				24	96	24	40	7	3	7	26	5	5	.417	.451	.771	1.216	1
2 Yrs			ALC				9	32	5	8	2	0	1	6	0	4	.250	.333	.406	.740	0
1 Yr			NNC				7	30	9	14	4	1	3	11	1	1	.467	.484	.967	1.451	0
1 Yr			NSC				2	10	6	7	0	1	2	5	0	0	.700	.700	1.500	2.200	0
1 Yr			NLC				6	24	4	11	1	1	1	4	4	0	.458	.480	.708	1.167	1

All-Star Batting

Year	Age	Tm	Lg	Game	Opp	G	AB	R	H	2B	3B	HR	RBI	SB	BB	BA	OBP	SLG	OPS	HBP
1933	32		WES	EWA		CF	5	1	2	1	0	0	0	0	0	.400	.400	.600	1.000	0
1934	33		WES	EWA		CF	4	0	0	0	0	0	0	0	0	.000	.000	.000	.000	0
1935	34		WES	EWA		RF	3	0	1	0	0	0	0	0	0	.333	.333	.333	.667	1
1937	36		WES	EWA		CF	4	0	0	0	0	0	0	0	0	.000	.000	.000	.000	0
1939	38		WES	EWA		RF	3	0	1	0	0	0	1	0	1	.333	.500	.333	.833	0
5 Yrs (5 GP)			NgL			5	19	1	4	1	0	0	2	0	1	.211	.250	.263	.513	0

Ted "T.R." Strong

Standard Batting

Year	Age	Tm	Lg	G	AB	R	H	2B	3B	HR	RBI	SB	BB	BA	OBP	SLG	OPS	OPS+	TB	HBP	Awards
1936	19	CAG	IND	13	42	5	7	2	1	1	8	4	3	.167	.222	.333	.556	59	14	0	
1937 *	20	TOTAL	NAL	25	96	22	31	11	2	1	18	4	16	.323	.435	.510	.945	161	49	3	EWA, NSA
—	—	LA	NAL	19	73	16	23	8	1	0	13	3	15	.315	.432	.452	.884	140	33	0	
—	—	KCM	NAL	2	8	1	2	2	0	0	1	0	0	.250	.250	.500	.750	109	4	0	
—	—	CAG	NAL	4	15	5	6	1	1	1	4	1	1	.400	.526	.800	1.326	288	12	3	
1938 *	21	TOTAL	NAL	20	72	20	28	5	4	3	20	7	5	.389	.436	.694	1.130	229	50	1	EWA
—	—	AB3	NAL	17	59	14	23	4	2	2	14	7	4	.390	.429	.627	1.056	203	37	1	
—	—	KCM	NAL	3	13	6	5	1	2	1	6	0	2	.385	.467	1.000	1.467	349	13	0	
1939 *	22	KCM	NAL	46	159	33	50	8	2	3	29	14	22	.314	.398	.447	.844	147	71	3	EWA
1940	23	JNL	MEX	71	277	57	92	14	14	11	57	7	28	.332	.399	.603	1.002	157	167	0	
1941 *	24	TOTAL	MEX+NAL	49	174	46	57	7	6	8	41	2	34	.328	.438	.575	1.012	191	100	3	EWA
—	—	VCZ	MEX	19	76	19	25	2	5	2	14	1	8	.329	.393	.539	.932	132	41	0	
—	—	KCM	NAL	30	98	27	32	5	1	6	27	1	26	.327	.468	.602	1.070	236	59	3	
1942 *	25	KCM	NAL	34	132	31	48	8	0	6	32	14	14	.364	.425	.561	.985	209	74	0	EWA
1943	26									Did not play in major or minor leagues (Military Service)											
1944	27									Did not play in major or minor leagues (Military Service)											
1945	28									Did not play in major or minor leagues (Military Service)											
1946	29	KCM	NAL	33	106	29	38	2	2	3	23	2	19	.358	.465	.500	.965	187	53	2	
1947	30	KCM	NAL	37	100	9	21	4	0	1	12	0	20	.210	.352	.280	.632	72	28	2	
1948	31	IC	NAL	12	36	5	14	1	0	0	10	0	7	.389	.500	.417	.917	150	15	1	
1949	32									Played in unrecorded Black league											
1950	33									Played in unrecorded independent league											
1951	34									Played in unrecorded Black league											
10 Yrs			NgL	340	1194	257	386	62	31	37	250	37	168	.323	.412	.520	.932	163	621	12	
162 Game Avg.			Pro	162	569	122	184	30	15	18	119	18	80	.323	.412	.520	.932	163	3144	6	
7 Yrs		KCM	NAL	185	616	136	196	30	8	20	130	18	103	.318	.419	.490	.909	173	302	4	
1 Yr		JNL	MEX	71	277	57	92	14	14	11	57	7	28	.332	.399	.603	1.002	157	167	3	
1 Yr		LA	NAL	19	73	16	23	8	1	0	13	3	15	.315	.432	.452	.884	140	33	0	
1 Yr		VCZ	MEX	19	76	19	25	2	5	2	14	1	8	.329	.393	.539	.932	132	41	0	
2 Yrs		CAG	NAL+IND	17	57	10	13	3	2	2	12	0	4	.228	.313	.456	.769	119	26	3	
1 Yr		AB3	NAL	17	59	14	23	4	2	2	14	7	3	.390	.429	.627	1.056	203	37	1	
1 Yr		IC	NAL	12	36	5	14	1	0	0	10	0	7	.389	.500	.417	.917	150	15	1	
8 Yrs			NAL	237	799	176	262	44	12	23	171	29	129	.328	.427	.499	.926	173	399	9	
2 Yrs			MEX	90	353	76	117	16	18	13	71	8	36	.331	.398	.589	.987	152	208	3	
1 Yr			IND	13	42	5	7	2	1	1	8	0	3	.167	.222	.333	.556	59	14	0	

Postseason Batting

Year	Age	Tm	Lg	Series	Opp	Rslt	G	AB	R	H	2B	3B	HR	RBI	SB	BB	BA	OBP	SLG	OPS	HBP
1937 □	20	KCM	NAL	ALC	CAG	W	4	15	3	6	1	1	0	3	0	3	.400	.500	.467	.967	0
1939 □	22	KCM	NAL	ALC	SLS	W	5	19	1	5	1	0	0	0	1	0	.263	.263	.316	.579	
1942 □	25	KCM	NAL	WS	HG	W	4	18	6	6	2	1	0	4	1	1	.333	.400	.556	.924	1
1946	29	KCM	NAL	WS	NE	L	4	15	2	2	2	0	0	2	0	0	.133	.188	.333	.521	
4 Yrs (4 Series)			NgL				17	67	12	19	3	2	0	10	2	5	.284	.342	.418	.751	1
2 Yrs				ALC			9	34	4	11	2	1	0	4	1	3	.324	.378	.382	.761	0
2 Yrs				WS			8	33	8	8	1	1	0	6	1	2	.242	.306	.455	.740	1

Ted "T.R." Strong
All-Star Batting

Year	Age	Lg	Game	G	AB	R	H	2B	3B	HR	RBI	SB	BB	BA	OBP	SLG	OPS	HBP
1937	20	WES	EWA	1B	4	1	2	0	0	0	2	0	0	.500	.500	1.250	1.750	0
1937	20	NOS	NSA	SS	6	3	4	0	1	1	3	0	0	.667	.667	1.500	2.167	0
1938	21	WES	EWA	1B	3	1	0	0	0	0	0	0	1	.000	.250	.000	.250	0
1939	22	WES	EWA	1B/1B	6	0	1	0	0	0	0	0	2	.167	.375	.167	.542	0
1941	24	WES	EWA	RF	4	0	2	0	0	1	1	0	0	.500	.500	1.250	1.750	0
1942	25	WES	EWA	RF/RF	6	0	3	1	0	0	0	0	2	.500	.625	.500	1.125	0
6 Yrs (8 GP)		NgL			29	5	12	1	2	2	6	0	5	.414	.500	.793	1.293	0

George "Mule" Suttles
Standard Batting

Year	Age	Tm	Lg	G	AB	R	H	2B	3B	HR	RBI	SB	BB	BA	OBP	SLG	OPS	OPS+	TB	HBP	Awards
1923	22	BBB	IND	37	138	23	40	6	3	1	16	6	6	.290	.319	.399	.718	131	55	0	
1924	23	BBB	NNL	79	274	43	87	21	3	3	49	3	15	.318	.362	.449	.811	130	123	4	
1925	24	BBB	NNL	68	242	45	80	6	5	10	59	5	30	.331	.404	.521	.925	154	126		
1926	25	SLS	NNL	89	358	90	152	28	19	32	130	15	31	.425	.472	.877	1.349	215	314	1	
1927	26	SLS	NNL	36	98	31	44	9	4	9	37	1	18	.449	.534	.898	1.432	281	88	0	
1928	27	SLS	NNL	76	301	73	108	17	12	21	75	6	22	.359	.404	.704	1.109	188	212	1	
1929	28	TOTAL	NNL	99	372	82	127	31	7	18	110	10	37	.341	.401	.608	1.009	160	226	0	
		SLS	NNL	95	359	80	124	29	7	18	108	10	34	.345	.402	.616	1.018	162	221	0	
		CAG	NNL	4	13	2	3	2	0	0	2	0	3	.231	.375	.385	.760	99	5	0	
1930	29	TOTAL	NNL+EAS	59	210	70	84	19	7	17	79	13	34	.400	.492	.800	1.292	230	168	4	
		SLS	NNL	46	164	58	67	14	7	13	64	12	31	.409	.508	.817	1.325	246	134	2	
		BBS	EAS	13	46	12	17	5	0	4	15	1	3	.370	.431	.739	1.171	175	34	2	
1931	30	SLS	NNL	34	121	35	36	11	4	7	36	4	23	.298	.418	.628	1.046	167	76	2	
1932	31	TOTAL	EWL	55	187	31	58	22	3	4	48	5	30	.310	.411	.524	.935	158	98	2	
		DW	EWL	27	97	13	28	11	0	1	22	0	15	.289	.384	.433	.817	120	42	0	
		WAP	EWL	28	90	18	30	11	3	3	26	5	15	.333	.439	.622	1.061	198	56	2	
1933 *	32	CAG	NN2	41	157	29	39	8	1	7	34	5	16	.248	.318	.446	.764	108	70	0	EWA
1934 *	33	CAG	NN2	39	147	20	45	4	3	4	30	2	13	.306	.363	.456	.818	139	67	0	EWA
1935 *	34	CAG	NN2	43	142	29	40	9	0	9	37	5	24	.282	.386	.535	.921	138	76	0	EWA
1936	35	NE	NN2	28	99	29	40	7	0	12	36	3	10	.404	.464	.838	1.302	229	83	1	
1937 *	36	NE	NN2	30	107	24	34	4	3	7	32	0	14	.318	.397	.607	1.004	152	65	0	EWA
1938 *	37	NE	NN2	27	86	18	25	0	0	6	22	0	10	.291	.365	.535	.899	162	46	0	EWA
1939 *	38	NE	NN2	31	114	31	40	6	0	7	25	3	13	.351	.417	.588	1.005	165	67	0	EWA
1940	39	NE	NN2	37	125	29	36	10	0	5	32	3	23	.288	.399	.488	.887	128	61		
1941	40	NBY	NN2	20	63	8	16	1	0	1	7	1	7	.254	.299	.317	.616	84	20	1	
1942	41	NE	NN2	7	12	2	5	1	0	1	3	0	1	.417	.417	.750	1.167	238	9		
1943	42	NE	NN2	8	13	3	4	2	0	1	5	0	2	.308	.400	.692	1.092	183	9	0	
1944	43	NE	NN2	13	27	7	5	0	0	2	6	0	5	.185	.313	.481	.794	112	13		

George "Mule" Suttles
Standard Batting (continued)

Year	Age	Tm	Lg	G	AB	R	H	2B	3B	HR	RBI	SB	BB	BA	OBP	SLG	OPS	OPS+	TB	HBP	Awards
22 Yrs			NgL	956	3393	752	1145	225	75	184	908	91	380	.337	.407	.611	1.017	167	2072	15	
162 Game Avg.			Pro	162	575	127	194	38	13	31	154	15	64	.337	.407	.611	1.017	167	351	3	
5 Yrs		SLS	NNL	389	1447	379	548	113	53	104	465	49	162	.379	.444	.746	1.190	193	1079	8	
3 Yrs		BBB	NNL+IND	184	654	111	207	33	11	14	124	14	51	.317	.370	.465	.834	139	304	4	
8 Yrs		NE	NN2	181	583	143	189	33	4	41	161	10	77	.324	.404	.605	1.009	165	353	1	
4 Yrs		CAG	NNL+NN2	127	459	80	127	23	4	20	103	12	56	.277	.355	.475	.830	127	218	0	
1 Yr		WAP	EWL	28	90	18	30	11	3	3	26	5	15	.333	.439	.622	1.061	198	56	2	
1 Yr		DW	EWL	27	97	13	28	11	0	1	22	0	15	.289	.384	.433	.817	120	42	0	
1 Yr		NBY	NN2	20	63	8	16	1	0	1	7	1	4	.254	.299	.317	.616	84	20		
1 Yr		BBS	EAS	13	46	12	17	5	0	4	15	1	3	.370	.431	.739	1.171	175	34	2	
8 Yrs			NNL	540	1976	469	718	142	61	117	575	57	210	.363	.428	.675	1.102	179	1333	12	
12 Yrs			NN2	324	1092	229	329	55	8	62	269	23	134	.301	.378	.537	.915	145	586	1	
1 Yr			EWL	55	187	31	58	22	3	4	48	5	30	.310	.411	.524	.935	158	98	2	
1 Yr			IND	37	138	23	40	6	3	1	16	6	6	.290	.319	.399	.718	131	55	0	
1 Yr			EAS	13	46	12	17	5	0	4	15	1	3	.370	.431	.739	1.171	175	34	2	

Postseason Batting

Year	Age	Tm	Lg	Series	Opp	Rslt	G	AB	R	H	2B	3B	HR	RBI	SB	BB	BA	OBP	SLG	OPS	HBP
1928 □	27	SLS	NNL	NNC	CAG	W	7	27	3	9	2	1	0	8	0	2	.333	.379	.481	.861	0
1930 □	29	SLS	NNL	NNC	DS	W	7	23	5	7	0	1	2	5	0	7	.304	.467	.652	1.119	0
1934	33	CAG	NN2	NLC	PS	L	6	18	0	5	0	0	1	1	1	3	.278	.381	.333	.714	0
1939	38	NE	NN2	NLP	BEG	L	4	15	3	4	1	0	3	5	0	0	.267	.267	.933	1.200	0
4 Yrs (4 Series)			NgL				24	83	11	25	4	2	5	19	1	12	.301	.389	.578	.968	0
1 Yr			NLP				4	15	3	4	1	0	3	5	0	0	.267	.267	.933	1.200	
3 Yrs			NLC				17	56	8	16	2	2	2	11	1	10	.286	.394	.625	1.019	

All-Star Batting

Year	Age	Tm	Lg	Game	G	AB	R	H	2B	3B	HR	RBI	SB	BB	BA	OBP	SLG	OPS	HBP
1933	32		WES	EWA	1B	4	2	2	1	0	1	3	0	0	.500	.500	1.500	2.000	0
1934	33		WES	EWA	1B	4	0	3	0	0	0	1	0	0	.750	.750	1.250	2.000	0
1935	34		WES	EWA	LF	2	3	1	0	0	1	3	0	4	.500	.833	2.000	2.833	0
1937	36		EAS	EWA	LF	3	0	1	0	0	0	0	0	2	.333	.600	.333	.933	0
1938	37		EAS	EWA	1B	4	0	0	0	0	0	0	0	0	.000	.000	.000	.000	0
1939	38		EAS	EWA	RF	4	0	0	0	0	0	0	0	0	.000	.000	.000	.000	0
6 Yrs (6 GP)			NgL			21	5	7	1	0	2	6	0	6	.333	.481	.762	1.243	0

Ben Taylor
Standard Batting

Year	Age	Tm	Lg	G	AB	R	H	2B	3B	HR	RBI	SB	BB	BA	OBP	SLG	OPS	OPS+	TB	HBP	Awards
1909	20	BG	WES	1	1	1	1	0	0	0	0	0	0	1.000	1.000	1.000	2.000	532	1	0	
1910	21	WBS	WES	6	23	0	6	1	1	0	0	0	0	.261	.261	.391	.652	103	9	0	
1911	22	WBS	WES	14	34	5	12	3	0	0	5	0	2	.353	.389	.441	.830	130	15	0	
1912	23	SLG	WES	8	19	0	9	3	0	0	0	0	0	.474	.474	.632	1.105	197	12	0	
		TOTAL	WES+EAS																		
–	–	WBS	WES	3	11	0	3	1	0	0	2	0	0	.273	.273	.364	.636	82	4	0	
–	–	NLG	EAS	5	8	0	6	2	0	0	2	0	0	.750	.750	1.000	1.750	354	8	0	
1913	24		TOTAL	25	103	18	34	4	2	1	16	1	8	.330	.378	.437	.815	132	45	0	
–	–	WBS	WES	8	33	5	10	0	1	0	5	1	4	.303	.378	.364	.742	101	12	0	
–	–	C4G	WES	17	70	13	24	4	1	1	11	0	4	.343	.378	.471	.850	147	33	0	
1914	25	ABC	WES	60	216	50	79	23	8	4	53	27	33	.366	.452	.602	1.054	178	130	1	
1915	26	ABC	WES	60	215	35	63	18	5	1	47	14	28	.293	.385	.437	.822	143	94	4	
1916	27	ABC	WES	41	150	23	47	9	3	0	28	6	10	.313	.360	.347	.707	111	52	1	
1917	28	ABC	WES	57	218	27	64	9	4	0	39	5	18	.294	.350	.372	.722	140	81	1	
1918	29	ABC	WES	41	157	30	48	5	6	2	37	5	12	.306	.363	.452	.815	132	71	2	
1919	30		TOTAL	WES+EAS	21	79	11	24	4	3	0	12	4	10	.304	.382	.430	.812	143	34	0	
–	–	JBC	WES	2	8	2	3	1	0	0	2	1	2	.375	.500	.500	1.000	174	4	0	
–	–	AC	EAS	19	71	9	21	3	3	0	10	3	8	.296	.367	.423	.790	140	30	0	
1920	31	ABC	NNL	93	343	57	110	20	5	4	64	13	31	.321	.379	.443	.822	143	152	1	
1921	32	ABC	NNL	106	408	84	160	25	9	3	89	9	36	.392	.448	.520	.967	173	212	5	
1922	33	ABC	NNL	92	365	75	136	34	4	2	70	3	29	.373	.420	.515	.935	150	188	1	
1923	34		TOTAL	IND+ECL	26	91	14	33	4	1	1	19	0	15	.363	.453	.495	.947	206	45	0	
–	–	WP	IND	24	85	14	32	4	1	1	18	0	15	.376	.470	.518	.988	221	44	0	
–	–	BBS	ECL	2	6	0	1	0	0	0	1	0	0	.167	.167	.167	.333	-3	1	0	
1924	35	WP	ECL	50	201	33	62	6	2	3	39	3	21	.308	.374	.403	.777	126	81		
1925	36	HBG	ECL	70	268	40	87	14	4	5	65	0	26	.325	.384	.463	.847	116	124		
1926	37	BBS	ECL	53	167	16	50	7	3	1	23	4	28	.299	.403	.395	.798	123	66	1	
1927	38	BBS	ECL	65	236	35	79	9	5	2	43	1	26	.335	.401	.441	.841	123	104	0	
1928	39	BBS	ECL	57	220	26	70	14	3	2	38	2	12	.318	.356	.436	.793	96	96	1	
1929	40	AC	ANL	39	115	12	31	6	0	4	17	1	14	.270	.354	.426	.780	93	49	1	
10 Yrs (+8)			NgL	651	2414	392	818	139	38	28	467	36	238	.339	.400	.463	.863	137	1117	10	
162 Game Avg.				162	601	98	204	35	9	7	116	9	59	.339	.400	.463	.863	137	278	2	
8 Yrs			Pro	334	1215	200	387	73	30	8	241	62	121	.319	.384	.448	.832	142	544	9	
18 Yrs			Pre-NgL+NgL	985	3629	592	1205	212	68	36	708	98	359	.332	.395	.458	.853	139	1661	19	
162 Game Avg.			Pre-NgL+Pro	162	597	97	198	35	11	6	116	16	59	.332	.395	.458	.853	139	273	3	
3 Yrs		ABC	NNL+WES	291	1116	216	406	79	20	9	223	25	96	.364	.418	.495	.912	156	552	7	
4 Yrs		BBS	ECL	177	629	77	200	30	11	5	105	7	66	.318	.385	.424	.809	112	267	2	
2 Yrs		WP	ECL+IND	74	286	47	94	10	3	5	57	3	36	.329	.404	.437	.841	70	125	0	
1 Yr		HBG	ECL	70	268	40	87	14	4	5	65	0	26	.325	.384	.463	.847	116	124	0	
1 Yr		AC	ANL	39	115	12	31	6	0	4	17	1	14	.270	.354	.426	.780	93	49	1	
6 Yrs			ECL	297	1098	150	349	50	17	13	209	10	113	.318	.383	.430	.812	116	472	2	
3 Yrs			NNL	291	1116	216	406	79	20	9	223	25	96	.364	.418	.495	.912	156	552	7	
1 Yr			ANL	39	115	12	31	6	0	4	17	1	14	.270	.354	.426	.780	93	49	1	
1 Yr			IND	24	85	14	32	4	1	1	18	0	15	.376	.470	.518	.988	221	44	0	

20. The Negro Leagues All-Star Register 243

Cristóbal Torriente
Standard Batting

Year	Age	Tm	Lg	G	AB	R	H	2B	3B	HR	RBI	SB	BB	BA	OBP	SLG	OPS	OPS+	TB	HBP	Awards
1913	19	CSH	WES	25	100	15	38	9	6	2	26	8	4	.380	.410	.650	1.060	192	65	1	
1914	20	CSH	WES	33	117	28	46	10	4	2	22	6	21	.393	.486	.598	1.084	207	70	1	
1915	21	CSH	WES	52	196	35	68	12	3	2	32	12	18	.347	.405	.469	.874	181	92	0	
1916	22	CSH	WES	58	205	37	71	12	3	2	43	7	28	.346	.427	.454	.881	181	93	1	
TOTAL			WES	51	183	30	60	10	2	2	38	7	22	.328	.403	.437	.840	171	80	1	
1916	22	CSW	WES	7	22	7	11	2	0	0	5	0	6	.500	.607	.591	1.198	266	13	0	
1917	23	ALL	WES	57	218	27	64	9	4	0	39	6	8	.294	.319	.372	.690	127	81	0	
1918	24	CSW	WES	36	133	31	48	5	9	1	27	3	16	.361	.430	.556	.986	210	74	0	
1919	25	CAG	WES	42	146	32	48	10	3	3	36	7	32	.329	.464	.500	.964	194	73	5	
1920	26	CAG	NNL	66	231	53	95	21	9	2	58	8	30	.411	.479	.606	1.085	238	140	0	
1921	27	CAG	NNL	84	290	74	102	8	13	12	74	19	36	.352	.430	.593	1.023	203	172	4	
1922	28	CAG	NNL	55	190	46	55	9	1	8	36	12	29	.289	.384	.474	.857	145	90	0	
1923	29	CAG	NNL	74	261	69	101	22	5	4	63	5	44	.387	.481	.556	1.036	183	145	3	
1924	30	CAG	NNL	74	255	59	93	27	6	8	81	12	46	.365	.467	.612	1.079	204	156	3	
1925	31	CAG	NNL	89	296	53	78	11	7	9	66	5	55	.264	.379	.439	.818	130	130		
1926	32	KCM	NNL	77	276	58	97	17	6	5	65	18	37	.351	.446	.511	.957	153	141	10	
1927	33	DS	NNL	88	323	45	101	17	2	6	62	5	41	.313	.390	.433	.824	123	140	0	
1928	34	DS	NNL	37	111	14	36	8	3	1	25	2	5	.324	.353	.477	.831	124	53	0	
1929	35													Played in unrecorded league							
1930	36													Played in unrecorded league							
1931	37													Played in unrecorded league							
1932	38	TOTAL	NgL		47	2	12	1	2	0	6	4	2	.255	.286	.362	.647	78	17	0	
1932	38	FCC	IND	11	45	2	11	1	1	0	6	4	2	.244	.277	.311	.588	59	14	0	
1932	38	LVB	NSL	2	2	0	1	0	0	0	0	0	0	.500	.500	1.500	2.000	516	3	0	
10 Yrs (+10)			NgL	644	2280	473	770	141	54	55	536	97	325	.338	.425	.519	.944	166	1184	20	
162 Game Avg.				162	574	119	194	35	14	14	135	24	82	.338	.425	.519	.944	166	298	5	
7 Yrs			Pre-NgL	303	1115	205	383	67	31	12	225	49	127	.343	.414	.491	.906	179	548	8	
17 Yrs			Pre-NgL+NgL	947	3395	678	1153	208	85	67	761	146	452	.340	.421	.510	.932	171	1732	28	
162 Game Avg.			Pre-NgL+Pro	162	581	116	197	36	15	11	130	25	77	.340	.421	.510	.932	171	296	5	
7 Yrs		CAG	NNL	442	1523	354	524	98	41	43	378	68	240	.344	.437	.547	.983	184	833	10	
2 Yrs		DS	NNL	125	434	59	137	25	5	7	87	7	46	.316	.381	.445	.826	123	193	0	
1 Yr		KCM	NNL	77	276	58	97	17	2	6	65	18	37	.351	.446	.511	.957	153	141	10	
1 Yr		FCC	IND	11	45	2	11	1	1	0	6	4	2	.244	.277	.311	.588	59	14	0	
1 Yr		LVB	NSL	2	2	0	1	0	0	0	0	0	0	.500	.500	1.500	2.000	516	3	0	
9 Yrs			NNL	644	2233	471	758	140	52	55	530	93	323	.339	.427	.523	.950	168	1167	20	
1 Yr			IND	11	45	2	11	1	1	0	6	4	2	.244	.277	.311	.588	59	14	0	
1 Yr			NSL	2	2	0	1	0	0	0	0	0	0	.500	.500	1.500	2.000	516	3	0	

Postseason Batting

Year	Age	Tm	Lg	Series	Opp	Rslt	G	AB	R	H	2B	3B	HR	RBI	SB	BB	BA	OBP	SLG	OPS	HBP
1926	32	KCM	NNL	NNC	CAG	L	8	31	4	11	2	0	0	5	0	1	.355	.375	.419	.794	0
1 Yr (1 Series)			NgL	NNC			8	31	4	11	2	0	0	5	0	1	.355	.375	.419	.794	0
1 Yr							8	31	4	11	2	0	0	5	0	1	.355	.375	.419	.794	0

Quincy Trouppe
Standard Batting

Year	Age	Tm	Lg	G	AB	R	H	2B	3B	HR	RBI	SB	BB	BA	OBP	SLG	OPS	OPS+	TB	HBP	Awards
1930	17	SLS	NNL	1	2	0	0	0	0	0	0	0	0	.000	.000	.000	.000	-100	0	0	
1931	18	SLS	NNL	20	56	7	11	3	0	1	10	0	8	.196	.308	.375	.672	75	21	1	
1932	19	TOTAL	EWL-IND	55	198	26	55	8	2	1	29	5	12	.278	.325	.328	.647	76	65	2	
–	–	TOTAL	EWL	39	139	20	33	4	1	0	15	2	7	.237	.274	.281	.555	140	39	0	
–	–	DW	EWL	29	105	14	22	2	2	0	9	2	7	.210	.259	.229	.488	32	24	0	
–	–	HG	EWL	10	34	6	11	2	1	0	6	0	0	.324	.324	.441	.765	108	15	0	
–	–	KCM	IND	16	59	6	22	4	0	0	14	3	5	.373	.439	.441	.863	137	26	2	
1933	20	CAG	NN2	15	45	11	13	1	2	1	10	0	5	.289	.360	.467	.827	126	21	0	
1934	21		IND											Played in unrecorded independent league							
1935	22	TOTAL	IND	7	22	2	5	0	0	1	3	1	2	.227	.292	.364	.655	204	8	0	
–	–	KCM	IND	2	6	2	2	0	0	1	2	1	2	.333	.500	.833	1.333	258	5	0	
–	–	BIS	IND	5	16	0	3	0	0	0	1	0	0	.188	.188	.188	.375	5	3	0	
1936	23	KCM	IND	7	19	4	6	0	0	0	3	1	5	.316	.458	.316	.774	113	6	0	
1938 *	25	AB3	NAL	17	52	18	19	5	2	2	10	0	9	.365	.476	.654	1.113	239	34	2	EWA
1939	26	SL3	NAL	5	20	7	9	2	1	0	6	1	3	.450	.522	.650	1.172	240	13	0	
1940	27	CBM	MEX	76	276	67	93	25	2	6	67	9	48	.337	.437	.543	.979	154	150	1	
1941	28	CBM	MEX	98	363	73	111	25	4	9	67	9	66	.306	.413	.471	.884	121	171	0	
1942	29													Did not play in major or minor leagues (War Service)							
1943	30													Did not play in major or minor leagues (War Service)							
1944	31													Did not play in major or minor leagues (War Service)							
1945 *	32	CBE	NAL	13	38	6	7	0	0	1	4	1	8	.184	.326	.263	.589	75	10	0	EWA
1946 *	33	CBE	NAL	15	42	4	8	3	1	1	7	0	9	.190	.333	.381	.714	117	16	0	EWA
1947 *	34	CBE	NAL	12	23	4	7	1	0	0	1	1	6	.304	.448	.348	.796	117	8	0	EWA
1948 *	35	CAG	NAL	8	30	5	12	4	0	0	6	0	5	.400	.486	.533	1.019	173	16	0	EWA
14 Yrs			NgL	349	1186	236	356	77	20	22	223	29	186	.300	.398	.454	.850	132	539	6	
162 Game Avg.			Pro	162	551	110	165	36	9	10	104	13	86	.300	.398	.454	.850	132	3638	3	
2 Yrs		CBM	MEX	174	639	140	204	50	6	15	134	18	114	.319	.423	.502	.925	275	321	1	
3 Yrs		CBE	NAL	40	103	16	22	4	1	2	12	2	23	.214	.357	.330	.687	124	34	0	
1 Yr		DW	EWL	29	105	14	22	2	2	0	9	2	7	.210	.259	.229	.488	32	24	0	
3 Yrs		KCM	IND	25	84	12	30	4	0	1	19	5	12	.357	.449	.440	.878	140	31	2	
2 Yrs		CAG	NN2+NAL	23	75	16	25	5	2	1	16	0	10	.333	.412	.493	.905	145	37	0	
2 Yrs		SLS	NNL	21	58	7	11	3	0	2	10	0	8	.190	.299	.362	.650	69	21	1	
1 Yr		AB3	NAL	17	52	18	19	5	2	2	10	0	9	.365	.476	.654	1.113	239	34	2	
1 Yr		HG	EWL	10	34	6	11	2	1	0	6	0	0	.324	.324	.441	.765	108	15	0	
1 Yr		SL3	NAL	5	20	7	9	2	1	0	6	1	3	.450	.522	.650	1.172	240	13	0	
1 Yr		BIS	IND	5	16	0	3	0	0	0	1	0	0	.188	.188	.188	.375	5	3	0	
6 Yrs			MEX	174	639	140	204	50	6	15	134	18	114	.319	.422	.502	.925	275	321	2	
6 Yrs			NAL	70	205	46	62	15	4	4	34	4	40	.302	.421	.473	.889	160	97	2	
3 Yrs			EWL	39	139	20	33	4	1	0	15	2	7	.237	.274	.281	.555	51	39	0	
3 Yrs			IND	30	100	12	33	4	0	1	20	5	12	.330	.412	.400	.802	204	34	2	
2 Yrs			NNL	21	58	7	11	3	0	2	10	0	8	.190	.299	.362	.650	69	21	1	
1 Yr			NN2	15	45	11	13	1	2	1	10	0	5	.289	.360	.467	.827	126	21	0	

20. The Negro Leagues All-Star Register

Quincy Trouppe

Postseason Batting

Year	Age	Tm	Lg	Series	Opp	Rslt	G	AB	R	H	2B	3B	HR	RBI	SB	BB	BA	OBP	SLG	OPS	HBP
1945 □	32	CBE	NAL	WS	CLE	W	4	15	2	6	1	1	0	0	0	1	.400	.438	.600	1.038	0
1947	34	CBE	NAL	WS	NYC	L	5	19	3	2	1	0	0	0	0	1	.105	.150	.158	.308	0
2 Yrs (2 Series)			NgL				9	34	5	8	2	1	0	0	0	2	.235	.235	.353	.588	0
2 Yrs				WS			9	34	5	8	2	1	0	0	0	2	.235	.235	.353	.588	0

All-Star Batting

Year	Age	Lg	Game	G	AB	R	H	2B	3B	HR	RBI	SB	BB	BA	OBP	SLG	OPS	HBP
1938	25	WES	EWA	LF	4	0	0	0	0	0	0	0	0	.000	.000	.000	.000	0
1945	32	WES	EWA	C	1	2	1	0	0	0	0	0	3	1.000	1.000	1.000	2.000	0
1946	33	WES	EWA	C/C	2	0	0	0	0	0	0	0	3	.000	.600	.000	.600	0
1947	34	WES	EWA	C/C	4	2	2	0	1	0	1	0	0	.500	.600	1.000	1.600	0
1948	35	WES	EWA	C/C	4	0	0	0	0	0	0	0	1	.000	.200	.000	.200	0
5 Yrs (8 GP)		NgL		8	15	4	3	0	1	0	1	0	8	.200	.478	.333	.812	0

Willie "El Diablo" Wells

Holds NgL career records for doubles; tied Chuck Klein and Dick Lundy's professional record by leading his league in home runs and steals in the same season (1930)

Standard Batting

Year	Age	Tm	Lg	G	AB	R	H	2B	3B	HR	RBI	SB	BB	BA	OBP	SLG	OPS	OPS+	TB	HBP	Awards
1924	18	TOTAL	IND+NNL	49	186	30	55	13	4	1	37	2	13	.296	.348	.425	.773	98	79	2	
		SLG	*IND*	*4*	*16*	*1*	*4*	*1*	*0*	*0*	*0*	*0*	*1*	*.250*	*.294*	*.313*	*.607*	*64*	*5*	*0*	
		SLS	*NNL*	*45*	*170*	*29*	*51*	*12*	*4*	*1*	*37*	*2*	*12*	*.300*	*.353*	*.435*	*.789*	*101*	*74*	*2*	
1925	19	SLS	NNL	87	338	83	98	19	7	8	53	18	53	.290	.386	.459	.845	111	155		
1926	20	SLS	NNL	84	279	66	104	12	4	13	64	16	50	.373	.470	.584	1.054	150	163	1	
1927	21	SLS	NNL	96	361	90	131	21	5	29	108	9	56	.363	.450	.690	1.140	204	249	1	
1928	22	SLS	NNL	78	315	82	113	28	5	22	81	13	25	.359	.414	.689	1.103	182	217	5	
1929	23	TOTAL	NNL	99	377	109	137	24	6	26	128	31	53	.363	.444	.666	1.110	186	251	2	
		SLS	*NNL*	*95*	*361*	*105*	*129*	*22*	*5*	*26*	*124*	*30*	*53*	*.357*	*.442*	*.662*	*1.104*	*184*	*239*	*2*	
		CAG	*NNL*	*4*	*16*	*4*	*8*	*2*	*1*	*0*	*4*	*1*	*0*	*.500*	*.500*	*.750*	*1.250*	*222*	*12*	*0*	
1930	24	SLS	NNL	90	336	112	138	34	3	17	114	18	52	**.411**	.492	.682	1.174	208	**229**	2	
1931	25	SLS	NNL	34	122	35	39	12	3	3	27	9	24	.320	.439	.541	.980	151	66	2	
1932	26	TOTAL	EWL+IND	55	208	40	57	16	6	2	41	4	19	.274	.346	.438	.784	111	91	4	
		TOTAL	*EWL*	*39*	*151*	*25*	*42*	*14*	*3*	*2*	*29*	*3*	*11*	*.278*	*.335*	*.450*	*.786*	*112*	*68*	*2*	
		DW	*EWL*	*29*	*113*	*20*	*32*	*13*	*2*	*2*	*20*	*3*	*9*	*.283*	*.341*	*.434*	*.775*	*108*	*49*	*1*	
		HG	*EWL*	*10*	*38*	*5*	*10*	*1*	*1*	*0*	*9*	*0*	*2*	*.263*	*.317*	*.500*	*.817*	*122*	*19*	*1*	
		KCM	*IND*	*16*	*57*	*15*	*15*	*2*	*3*	*0*	*12*	*1*	*8*	*.263*	*.373*	*.404*	*.777*	*109*	*23*	*2*	
1933 *	27	CAG	NN2	36	156	30	41	7	3	0	23	8	7	.263	.307	.346	.653	84	54	3	EWA
1934 *	28	CAG	NN2	38	144	23	30	7	4	0	13	4	17	.208	.292	.313	.604	77	45	0	EWA
1935 *	29	CAG	NN2	47	183	53	65	14	5	5	36	14	25	.355	.435	.568	1.004	160	104	1	EWA
1936	30	NE	NN2	29	111	24	35	6	1	2	12	0	12	.315	.387	.441	.829	113	49	0	
1937 *	31	TOTAL	NN2	32	120	32	39	9	5	3	27	2	12	.325	.386	.558	.945	138	67	0	EWA
		NE	*NN2*	*28*	*103*	*28*	*38*	*9*	*5*	*3*	*27*	*2*	*10*	*.369*	*.425*	*.641*	*1.066*	*167*	*66*	*0*	
		HG	*NN2*	*4*	*17*	*4*	*1*	*0*	*0*	*0*	*0*	*0*	*2*	*.059*	*.158*	*.059*	*.217*	*-41*	*1*	*0*	
1938 *	32	NE	NN2	27	90	22	29	7	2	2	15	3	13	.322	.419	.511	.930	163	46	2	EWA
1939 *	33	NE	NN2	31	126	27	34	12	0	3	19	3	13	.270	.338	.357	.695	85	45		EWA
1940	34	VEZ	MEX	84	339	95	117	30	2	3	57	17	35	.345	.411	.472	.883	129	160	3	
1941	35	VEZ	MEX	100	403	102	140	29	6	9	77	14	57	.347	.430	.516	.946	136	208	1	
1942 *	36	NE	NN2	47	181	48	62	8	0	3	34	3	19	.343	.405	.436	.841	145	79		EWA
1943	37		MEX											Played in unrecorded Mexican league							
1944	38		MEX											Played in unrecorded Mexican league							
1945 *	39	TOTAL	NN2	26	95	12	23	6	0	0	9	1	9	.242	.321	.305	.626	78	29	2	EWA
		NE	*NN2*	*8*	*26*	*5*	*2*	*0*	*0*	*0*	*1*	*0*	*3*	*.077*	*.200*	*.077*	*.277*	*-16*	*2*	*1*	
		NBY	*NN2*	*18*	*69*	*7*	*21*	*6*	*0*	*0*	*8*	*1*	*6*	*.304*	*.368*	*.391*	*.760*	*114*	*27*	*1*	
1946	40	TOTAL	NN2	61	226	21	66	13	0	1	37	2	20	.292	.352	.389	.742	102	88	1	
		NBY	*NN2*	*9*	*32*	*3*	*8*	*0*	*0*	*0*	*2*	*1*	*3*	*.250*	*.333*	*.250*	*.583*	*66*	*8*	*1*	
		BEG	*NN2*	*52*	*194*	*18*	*58*	*13*	*0*	*1*	*35*	*1*	*17*	*.299*	*.355*	*.412*	*.768*	*108*	*80*	*0*	
1947	41	CIC	NAL	5	18	2	6	0	1	0	3	0	1	.333	.368	.444	.813	129	8	0	
1948	42	MRS	NAL	6	17	6	8	2	1	0	3	1	2	.471	.526	.706	1.232	222	12	0	

20. The Negro Leagues All-Star Register

Willie "El Diablo" Wells

Standard Batting (continued)

Year	Age	Tm	Lg	G	AB	R	H	2B	3B	HR	RBI	SB	BB	BA	OBP	SLG	OPS	OPS+	TB	HBP	Awards
23 Yrs			NgL	1241	4731	1144	1567	319	76	152	1018	192	587	.331	.409	.527	.9359	144	2494	33	
162 Game Avg.			Pro	162	618	149	205	42	10	20	133	25	77	.331	.409	.527	.936	144	1393	4	
8 Yrs		SLS	NNL	609	2282	602	803	160	36	119	608	115	325	.352	.436	.610	1.046	168	1392	15	
2 Yrs		VEZ	MEX	184	742	197	257	59	8	12	134	31	92	.346	.421	.496	.917	133	368	4	
6 Yrs		NE	NN2	170	637	154	200	32	8	13	108	11	70	.314	.385	.451	.836	127	287	4	
4 Yrs		CAG	NNL+NN2	125	499	110	144	30	13	5	76	27	49	.289	.357	.431	.788	114	215	4	
1 Yr		BEG	NN2	52	194	18	58	13	3	1	35	1	17	.299	.355	.412	.768	108	80	0	
1 Yr		DW	EWL	29	113	20	32	13	2	0	20	3	9	.283	.341	.434	.775	108	49	1	
2 Yrs		NBY	NN2	27	101	10	29	6	0	0	10	2	9	.287	.357	.347	.704	99	35	2	
1 Yr		KCM	IND	16	57	15	15	2	3	0	12	2	8	.263	.373	.404	.777	109	23	2	
2 Yrs		HG	EWL+NN2	14	55	9	11	1	1	2	9	0	4	.200	.267	.364	.630	72	20	1	
1 Yr		CIC	NAL	5	18	2	6	0	1	0	3	0	1	.333	.368	.444	.813	129	8	0	
1 Yr		MRS	NAL	6	17	6	8	2	1	0	6	1	2	.471	.526	.706	1.232	222	12	0	
1 Yr		SLG	IND	4	16	1	4	0	1	0	0	0	1	.250	.294	.313	.607	64	5	0	
8 Yrs			NNL	613	2298	606	811	162	37	119	612	116	325	.353	.436	.611	1.047	168	1404	15	
10 Yrs			NN2	374	1432	292	424	79	23	19	225	40	147	.296	.366	.423	.789	115	606	10	
2 Yrs			MEX	184	742	197	257	59	8	12	134	31	92	.346	.421	.496	.917	133	368	4	
1 Yr			EWL	39	151	25	42	14	3	2	29	3	11	.278	.335	.450	.786	112	68	2	
1 Yr			IND	20	73	16	19	3	3	0	12	1	9	.260	.357	.384	.741	109	28	2	
2 Yrs			NAL	11	35	8	14	2	2	0	6	1	3	.400	.447	.571	1.019	174	20	0	

Postseason Batting

Year	Age	Tm	Lg	Series	Opp	Rslt	G	AB	R	H	2B	3B	HR	RBI	SB	BB	BA	OBP	SLG	OPS	HBP
1925	19	SLS	NNL	NNC	KCM	L	7	24	4	5	1	1	0	1	0	3	.208	.296	.375	.671	0
1928 □	22	SLS	NNL	NNC	CAG	W	7	26	7	8	1	0	3	9	0	4	.308	.419	.769	1.169	1
1930 □	24	SLS	NNL	NNC	DS	W	7	31	6	13	0	0	2	9	0	1	.419	.438	.677	1.115	0
1934	28	CAG	NN2	NLC	PS	L	6	23	2	5	1	1	0	0	0	1	.217	.280	.261	.511	0
1939	33	NE	NN2	NLP	BEG	L	4	14	1	1	0	1	0	2	0	4	.071	.278	.071	.349	1
5 Yrs (5 Series)			NgL				31	118	20	32	5	3	5	19	0	13	.271	.353	.483	.827	2
1 Yr			NLP				4	14	1	1	0	1	0	2	0	4	.071	.278	.071	.349	1
3 Yrs			NNC				21	81	17	26	2	1	5	19	0	8	.321	.389	.617	.999	1
1 Yr			NLC				6	23	2	5	1	1	0	0	0	1	.217	.280	.261	.511	0

All-Star Batting

Year	Age	Tm	Lg	Game	Opp	G	AB	R	H	2B	3B	HR	RBI	SB	BB	BA	OBP	SLG	OPS	HBP
1933	27		WES	EWA		SS	3	2	2	1	0	0	0	0	0	.667	.667	1.000	1.667	0
1934	28		WES	EWA		SS	3	0	1	0	0	0	0	0	1	.333	.500	.667	1.167	0
1935	29		WES	EWA		SS	3	0	0	0	0	0	0	0	0	.000	.000	.000	.000	0
1937	31		EAS	EWA		SS	5	1	1	0	0	0	0	0	0	.200	.200	.200	.400	0
1938	32		EAS	EWA		SS/SS	7	2	3	1	0	1	2	0	0	.429	.500	.857	1.357	0
1939	33		EAS	EWA		SS/SS	7	2	2	0	0	0	2	0	0	.286	.444	.429	.804	1
1942	36		EAS	EWA		SS/SS	10	1	4	0	0	0	2	1	0	.400	.455	.500	.900	1
1945	39		EAS	EWA		2B	5	0	1	0	0	0	0	2	0	.200	.200	.400	.600	0
8 Yrs (11 GP)			NgL			11	43	8	14	6	1	0	7	1	3	.326	#REF!	.512	.881	2

Sol White
Standard Batting

Year	Age	Tm	Lg	G	AB	R	H	2B	3B	HR	RBI	SB	BB	BA	OBP	SLG	OPS	OPS+	TB	HBP	Awards
1886	18		IND									Played in unrecorded independent league									
1887	19	PKS	NCL	7	32	6	9	4	0	0	5	0	3	.281	.343	.406	.749	102	13	0	
1888	20	PKS										Played in unrecorded semi-professional league									
1889	21	GOR										Played in unrecorded Black league									
1890	22	CBG										Played in unrecorded Black league									
1891	23	TOTAL	IND	7	36	17	15	0	1	3	12	2	1	.417	.432	.722	1.155	195	26	0	
–	–	CBG	IND	3	16	6	8	0	0	0	5	2	1	.500	.529	.625	1.154	201	10	0	
–	–	GOR	IND	4	20	11	7	0	1	3	7	0	0	.350	.350	.800	1.150	191	16	0	
1892	*24*	*PKS*										*Played in unrecorded Black league*									
1893	*25*	*CBG*																			
1894	26	CBG	IND	1	3	2	1	1	0	0	1		1	.333	.500	.667	1.167	136	2	0	
1895	27	PFG										Played in unrecorded semi-professional league									
1896	28	CXG	IND	2	10	4	2	1	0	0	3	1		.200	.273	.300	.573	45	3	0	
1897	29	CXG	IND	5	19	6	6	1	1	2	8	3		.316	.409	.789	1.199	177	15	0	
1898	30	CXG	IND	5	24	4	8	0	0	0	5	0	0	.333	.333	.667	100	8	0	
1899	31	CXG	IND	6	26	6	11	2	0	0	4	0	2	.423	.464	.500	.964	151	13	0	
1900	32	CCG	IND	4	16	0	5	3	0	0	2	0	0	.313	.353	.500	.853	156	8	1	
1901	33											Played in unrecorded Black league									
1902	34	PG										Played in unrecorded Black league									
1903	35	PG	EAS	7	25	4	9	1	0	0	1	1	1	.360	.385	.400	.785	230	10	0	
1904	36	PG	IND	8	33	6	12	2	0	0	4	3	2	.364	.400	.424	.824	160	14	0	
1905	37	PG	EAS	5	20	2	3	1	0	0	0	0	0	.150	.190	.200	.390	9	4	1	
1906	38	PG	EAS	9	22	0	2	1	0	0	0	1	0	.091	.136	.136	.227	-31	3	0	
1907	39	PG	NAC	5	16	0	1	0	0	0	1	0	0	.063	.118	.063	.180	-38	1	0	
1908	40	PG										Played in unrecorded Black league									
1909	41	PG										Played in unrecorded Black league									
1910	42											Played in unrecorded Black league									
1911	43											Played in unrecorded Black league									
12 Yrs (+13)			Pre-NgL	71	282	57	84	17	2	5	49	7	15	.298	.338	.426	.763	106	120	2	
162 Game Avg.			Pre-NgL	162	643	130	192	39	5	11	112	16	34	.298	.338	.426	.763	106	274	5	

Artie Wilson
Standard Batting

Year	Age	Tm	Lg	G	AB	R	H	2B	3B	HR	RBI	SB	BB	BA	OBP	SLG	OPS	OPS+	TB	HBP	Awards
1944 *	23	BBB	NAL	22	95	17	40	4	4	0	15	1	6	.421	.455	.547	1.003	222	52	1	EWA
1945	24	BBB	NAL	25	101	14	32	6	0	0	10	2	8	.317	.373	.376	.749	119	38	1	
1946 *	25	BBB	NAL	9	37	7	12	0	0	0	0	3	5	.324	.405	.324	.729	100	12	0	EWA
1947 *	26	BBB	NAL	14	54	10	17	1	1	0	3	3	11	.315	.431	.370	.801	117	20	0	EWA
1948 *	27	BBB	NAL	29	119	31	52	7	7	0	18	6	15	.437	.507	.613	1.121	198	73	2	EWA
1949	28	TOTAL	PCL																		
		San Diego	PCL									Played in minor leagues (Integration)								
		Oakland	PCL									Played in minor leagues (Integration)								
1950	29	Oakland	PCL									Played in minor leagues (Integration)								
1951	30	NYG	NL	19	22	2	4	0	0	0	1	2	2	.182	.250	.182	.432	18	4	0	
1951	30	TOTAL	PCL+AA+IL									Played in minor leagues (Integration)								
		Oakland	AA									Played in minor leagues (Integration)								
		Minneapolis	IL									Played in minor leagues (Integration)								
		Ottowa																			
1952	31	Seattle	PCL									Played in minor leagues (Integration)								
1953	32	Seattle	PCL									Played in minor leagues (Integration)								
1954	33	Seattle	PCL									Played in minor leagues (Integration)								
1955	34	Portland	PCL									Played in minor leagues (Integration)								
1956	35	TOTAL	PCL									Played in minor leagues (Integration)								
		Portland	PCL									Played in minor leagues (Integration)								
		Sacramento	PCL									Played in minor leagues (Integration)								
1957	36	Sacramento	PCL									Played in minor leagues (Integration)								
1962	41	TOTAL	AAA+B									Played in minor leagues (Integration)								
		Portland	AAA									Played in minor leagues (Integration)								
		Tri-City	B									Played in minor leagues (Integration)								
6 Yrs			Pro	118	428	81	157	18	12	0	47	16	47	.367	.433	.465	.898	157	199	3	
5 Yrs			NgL	99	406	79	153	18	12	0	46	14	45	.377	.443	.480	.923	164	195	3	
1 Yr			MLB	19	22	2	4	0	0	0	1	2	2	.182	.250	.182	.432	18	4	0	
162 Game Avg.			Pro	162	588	111	216	25	16	0	65	22	65	.367	.433	.465	.898	157	273	4	
5 Yrs		BBB	NAL	99	406	79	153	18	12	0	46	14	45	.377	.443	.480	.923	164		3	
1 Yr		NYG	NL	19	22	2	4	0	0	0	1	2	2	.182	.250	.182	.432	18		0	
5 Yrs			NAL	99	406	79	153	18	12	0	46	14	45	.377	.443	.480	.923	164		3	
1 Yr			NL	19	22	2	4	0	0	0	1	2	2	.182	.250	.182	.432	18		0	

Artie Wilson
Postseason Batting

Year	Age	Tm	Lg	Series	Opp	Rslt	G	AB	R	H	2B	3B	HR	RBI	SB	BB	BA	OBP	SLG	OPS	HBP
1944	23	BBB	NAL	WS	HG	L	5	20	1	5	0	0	0	0	1	2	.250	.348	.250	.568	1
1948	27	BBB	NAL	ALC	KCM	W	7	30	6	12	1	1	0	0	0	3	.400	.455	.500	.955	0
1948	27	BBB	NAL	WS	HG	L	1	4	0	2	0	0	0	0	0	0	.500	.500	.500	1.000	0
2 Yrs (3 Series)			NgL				13	54	7	19	1	1	0	0	1	5	.352	.417	.407	.814	1
1 Yr				ALC			7	30	6	12	1	1	0	0	0	3	.400	.455	.500	.955	0
2 Yrs				WS			6	24	1	7	0	0	0	0	1	2	.292	.370	.292	.638	1

All-Star Batting

Year	Age	Tm	Game	G	AB	R	H	2B	3B	HR	RBI	SB	BB	BA	OBP	SLG	OPS	HBP
1944	23	WES	EWA	SS	5	1	2	0	0	0	0	0	0	.400	.400	.400	.800	0
1946	25	WES	EWA	SS/SS	7	2	2	0	0	0	0	1	0	.286	.286	.286	.571	0
1947	26	WES	EWA	SS/SS	8	4	4	0	0	0	1	2	2	.500	.600	.500	1.100	0
1948	27	WES	EWA	SS/SS	7	0	3	0	0	0	1	0	1	.429	.500	.429	.929	0
4 Yrs (7 GP)			NgL		7	27	7	11	0	0	0	2	3	3	.407	.467	.407	.874	0

20. The Negro Leagues All-Star Register

Ernest "Jud" Wilson
Holds NgL career record for times hit by pitch
Standard Batting

Year	Age	Tm	Lg	G	AB	R	H	2B	3B	HR	RBI	SB	BB	BA	OBP	SLG	OPS	OPS+	TB	HBP	Awards
1922	26	BBS	IND	32	115	20	39	8	2	1	20	10	7	.339	.382	.470	.852	147	54	1	
1923	27	BBS	ECL	53	195	32	66	9	4	7	44	4	23	.338	.408	.533	.942	172	104	0	
1924	28	BBS	ECL	51	195	37	75	9	1	4	53	5	16	.385	.431	.503	.934	167	98		
1925	29	BBS	ECL	61	227	45	84	16	4	8	53	12	20	.370	.421	.581	1.003	163	132		
1926	30	BBS	ECL	48	161	46	60	17	2	3	36	24	29	.373	.487	.559	1.046	192	90	7	
1927	31	BBS	ECL	67	249	65	105	30	6	9	65	20	30	.422	.493	.699	1.192	213	174	5	
		TOTAL																			
		BBS	ECL	66	245	64	104	30	6	9	65	20	30	.424	.496	.706	1.203	216	173	5	
		NLG	ECL	1	4	1	1	0	0	0	0	0	0	.250	.250	.250	.500	23	1	0	
1928	32	BBS	ECL	42	158	41	63	18	2	6	45	10	25	.399	.492	.652	1.144	182	103	4	
1929	33	BBS	ANL	76	280	77	113	23	4	10	75	21	44	.404	.492	.621	1.114	170	174	5	
1930	34	BBS	EAS	40	150	36	65	13	4	2	27	0	11	.433	.472	.613	1.085	158	92	0	
1931	35	HG	IND	42	164	52	68	10	4	10	44	3	19	.415	.484	.707	1.191	234	116	3	
1932	36	TOTAL	EWL+IND	48	184	34	64	9	2	4	37	2	18	.348	.415	.484	.898	142	89	3	
		HG	EWL	18	67	10	25	3	0	0	12	0	8	.373	.447	.418	.865	137	28	1	
		PC	IND	30	117	24	39	6	2	4	25	2	10	.333	.395	.521	.917	145	61	2	
1933 *	37	TOTAL	IND+NN2	27	98	24	36	9	0	2	23	1	14	.367	.446	.520	.967	163	51	0	EWA
		PS	IND	26	93	24	35	9	0	2	23	1	14	.376	.458	.538	.996	171	50	0	
		PC	NN2	1	5	0	1	0	0	0	0	0	0	.200	.200	.200	.400	10	1	0	
1934 *	38	PS	NN2	61	218	41	78	10	4	4	39	3	29	.358	.435	.495	.931	160	108	1	EWA
1935 *	39	PS	NN2	51	193	38	68	14	5	9	52	4	15	.352	.402	.617	1.018	151	119	1	EWA
1936	40	TOTAL	NN2	49	180	35	60	3	4	8	40	1	22	.333	.412	.528	.940	137	95	2	
		PS	NN2	48	175	35	59	3	3	8	39	1	22	.337	.417	.526	.943	138	92	2	
		NYC	NN2	1	5	0	1	0	1	0	1	0	0	.200	.200	.600	.800	92	3	0	
1937	41	TOTAL	NN2+IND	25	91	10	29	6	2	0	14	1	4	.319	.347	.429	.776	101	39	0	
		PS	NN2	23	82	10	26	6	2	0	13	1	4	.317	.349	.439	.788	96	36	0	
		NAS	IND	2	9	0	3	0	0	0	1	0	0	.333	.333	.333	.667	146	3	0	
1938	42	PS	NN2	36	94	18	28	4	1	3	24	0	18	.298	.431	.457	.888	126	43	4	
1939	43	PS	NN2	42	113	18	33	4	1	2	24	0	23	.292	.412	.398	.810	114	45		
1940	44	HG	NN2	36	96	17	25	4	0	0	20	0	22	.260	.398	.302	.700	86	29		
1941	45	HG	NN2	30	94	22	40	10	2	1	26	0	13	.426	.495	.606	1.102	217	57		
1942	46	HG	NN2	42	109	26	27	5	1	2	26	0	28	.248	.401	.367	.768	126	40		
1943	47	HG	NN2	63	213	29	65	11	6	0	56	0	31	.305	.393	.413	.807	114	88	0	
1944	48	HG	NN2	24	58	4	12	2	1	0	10	0	9	.207	.313	.276	.589	59	16	0	
1945	49	HG	NN2	26	62	7	19	4	0	1	11	0	6	.306	.403	.419	.822	131	26	4	

Ernest "Jud" Wilson
Standard Batting (continued)

Year	Age	Tm	Lg	G	AB	R	H	2B	3B	HR	RBI	SB	BB	BA	OBP	SLG	OPS	OPS+	TB	HBP	Awards
24 Yrs			NgL	1072	3697	774	1322	248	62	96	864	121	476	.358	.436	.536	.972	158	1982	40	
162 Game Avg.			Pro	162	559	117	200	37	9	15	131	18	72	.358	.436	.536	.972	158	300	6	
9 Yrs		BBS	ECL+ANL+EAS+ND	469	1726	398	669	143	29	50	418	106	205	.388	.459	.591	1.050	176	1020	22	
7 Yrs		PS	NN2/+ND	287	968	184	327	50	16	28	214	9	125	.338	.418	.509	.927	141	493	8	
8 Yrs		HG	EWL+NN2+IND	281	863	167	281	49	14	14	205	3	136	.326	.422	.463	.886	146	400	8	
1 Yr		PC	IND+NN2	31	122	24	40	6	2	4	25	2	10	.328	.388	.508	.896	139	62	2	
1 Yr		NAS	IND	2	9	0	3	0	0	0	0	1	0	.333	.333	.333	.667	146	3	0	
1 Yr		NLG	ECL	1	4	1	1	0	0	0	1	0	0	.250	.250	.250	.500	23	1	0	
1 Yr		NYC	NN2	1	5	0	1	0	1	0	0	0	0	.200	.200	.600	.800	92	3	0	
12 Yrs			NN2	484	1517	265	482	77	27	30	341	8	220	.318	.408	.463	.872	132	703	12	
6 Yrs			ECL	322	1185	266	453	99	19	37	296	75	143	.382	.455	.592	1.047	182	701	16	
5 Yrs			IND	132	498	120	184	33	8	17	113	17	50	.369	.433	.570	1.003	180	335	6	
1 Yr			ANL	76	280	77	113	23	4	10	75	21	44	.404	.492	.621	1.114	170	174	5	
1 Yr			EAS	40	150	36	65	13	4	2	27	0	11	.433	.472	.613	1.085	158	92	0	
1 Yr			EWL	18	67	10	25	3	0	0	12	0	8	.373	.447	.418	.865	137	28	1	

Postseason Batting

Year	Age	Tm	Lg	Series	Opp	Rslt	G	AB	R	H	2B	3B	HR	RBI	SB	BB	BA	OBP	SLG	OPS	HBP
1934 □	38	PS	NN2	NLC	CAG	W	6	20	2	6	1	0	0	1	0	1	.300	.417	.450	.783	3
1939	43	PS	NN2	NLP	HG	L	2	4	1	0	0	0	0	0	0	4	.000	.500	.000	.500	
1942	46	HG	NN2	WS	KCM	L	4	7	1	2	1	0	0	1	0	3	.286	.429	.429	.929	0
1943 □	47	HG	NN2	WS	BBB	W	7	29	2	5	0	0	0	3	0	3	.172	.273	.207	.457	1
1944 □	48	HG	NN2	WS	BBB	W	2	2	0	1	0	0	0	2	0	0	.500	.667	.500	1.167	0
1945	49	HG	NN2	WS	CLE	L	4	6	0	2	0	0	0	1	0	1	.333	.429	.333	.667	1
6 Yrs (6 Series)			NgL				25	68	6	16	3	0	0	8	0	12	.235	.388	.309	.659	5
1 Yr				NLP			2	4	1	0	0	0	0	0	0	4	.000	.500	.000	.500	
1 Yr				NLC			6	20	2	6	1	0	0	1	0	1	.300	.417	.450	.783	3
4 Yrs				WS			17	44	3	10	2	0	0	7	0	7	.227	.358	.273	.606	2

All-Star Batting

Year	Age	Tm	Lg	Game	Opp	G	AB	R	H	2B	3B	HR	RBI	SB	BB	BA	OBP	SLG	OPS	HBP
1933	37		EAS	EWA		3B	3	1	2	0	0	0	3	0	0	.667	.667	.667	1.333	0
1934	38		EAS	EWA		3B	3	0	1	0	0	0	1	0	1	.333	.500	.333	.833	0
1935	39		EAS	EWA		3B	5	1	2	0	0	0	1	0	1	.400	.500	.400	.900	0
3 Yrs (3 GP)			NgL			3	11	2	5	0	0	0	5	0	2	.455	.538	.455	.993	0

"Wild" Bill Wright
Standard Batting

Year	Age	Tm	Lg	G	AB	R	H	2B	3B	HR	RBI	SB	BB	BA	OBP	SLG	OPS	OPS+	TB	HBP	Awards
1932	18	NEG	NSL	26	78	12	20	2	1	0	5	3	6	.256	.310	.308	.617	94	24	0	
1933	19	NEG	NN2	36	137	18	44	6	4	1	18	3	2	.321	.340	.445	.786	115	61	2	
1934	20	NEG	NN2	38	135	22	34	6	2	2	15	6	10	.252	.313	.370	.683	87	50	2	
1935 *	21	CEG	NN2	31	122	17	38	5	5	3	21	5	12	.311	.378	.508	.886	116	62	1	EWA
1936 *	22	TOTAL	NN2+IND	40	155	38	52	8	6	2	30	5	15	.335	.398	.503	.901	135	78	1	EWA
		WEG	*NN2*	*37*	*141*	*37*	*49*	*8*	*5*	*2*	*27*	*4*	*15*	*.348*	*.414*	*.518*	*.932*	*141*	*73*	*1*	
		NAS	*IND*	*3*	*14*	*1*	*3*	*0*	*1*	*0*	*3*	*1*	*0*	*.214*	*.214*	*.357*	*.571*	*74*	*5*	*0*	
1937 *	23	TOTAL	NN2+IND	39	154	26	57	8	11	7	38	0	7	.370	.398	.701	1.099	180	108	0	EWA
		WEG	*NN2*	*37*	*147*	*26*	*56*	*8*	*11*	*7*	*38*	*0*	*6*	*.381*	*.405*	*.728*	*1.133*	*186*	*107*	*0*	
		NAS	*IND*	*2*	*7*	*0*	*1*	*0*	*0*	*0*	*0*	*0*	*1*	*.143*	*.250*	*.143*	*.393*	*48*	*1*	*0*	
1938 *	24	BEG	NN2	33	130	22	39	8	2	4	31	5	10	.300	.359	.485	.844	116	63	2	EWA
1939 *	25	BEG	NN2	25	96	23	35	4	1	1	24	4	7	.365	.408	.458	.866	134	44	0	EWA
1940	26	SRC	MEX											No statistics available							
1940	26	ROM	MEX	87	350	94	126	30	10	8	67	29	47	.360	.437	.571	1.009	160	200	1	EWA
1941	27	ROM	MEX	100	387	98	151	25	9	17	85	26	72	.390	.487	.633	1.120	179	245	1	
1942 *	28	BEG	NN2	50	197	43	71	14	4	5	37	6	13	.360	.403	.548	.951	135	108	1	EWA
1943	29		MEX											Played in unrecorded Mexican league							
1944	30		MEX											Played in unrecorded Mexican league							
1945 *	31	BEG	NN2	48	190	40	69	12	5	3	34	5	12	.363	.401	.526	.927	158	100	0	
1946	32		MEX											Played in unrecorded Mexican league							
1947	33		MEX											Played in unrecorded Mexican league							
1948	34		MEX											Played in unrecorded Mexican league							
1949	35		MEX											Played in unrecorded Mexican league							
1950	36		MEX											Played in unrecorded Mexican league							
1951	37		MEX											Played in unrecorded Mexican league							
13 Yrs			NgL	553	2131	453	736	128	60	53	405	97	213	.345	.408	.536	.944	144	1143	11	
162 Game Avg.			Pro	162	624	133	216	37	18	16	119	28	62	.345	.408	.536	.944	144	335	3	
2 Yrs		ROM	MEX	187	737	192	277	55	19	25	152	55	119	.376	.464	.604	1.068	170	445	2	
4 Yrs		BEG	NN2	156	613	128	214	38	12	13	126	20	42	.349	.394	.514	.907	138	315	3	
3 Yrs		NEG	NSL+NN2	100	350	52	98	14	7	3	38	12	18	.280	.323	.386	.708	100	135	4	
2 Yrs		WEG	NN2	74	288	63	105	16	16	9	65	4	21	.365	.410	.625	1.035	164	180	1	
1 Yr		CEG	NN2	31	122	17	38	5	5	3	21	5	12	.311	.378	.508	.886	116	62	1	
2 Yrs		NAS	IND	5	21	1	4	0	1	0	3	1	1	.190	.227	.286	.513	65	6	0	
9 Yrs			NN2	335	1295	248	435	71	39	28	245	38	87	.336	.382	.516	.898	134	668	9	
2 Yrs			MEX	187	737	192	277	55	19	25	152	55	119	.376	.464	.604	1.068	170	445	2	
1 Yr			NSL	26	78	12	20	2	1	0	5	3	6	.256	.310	.308	.617	94	24	0	
2 Yrs			IND	5	21	1	4	0	1	0	3	1	1	.190	.227	.286	.513	65	6	0	

"Wild" Bill Wright

Postseason Batting

Year	Age	Tm	Lg	Series	Opp	Rslt	G	AB	R	H	2B	3B	HR	RBI	SB	BB	BA	OBP	SLG	OPS	HBP
1939	25	BEG	NN2	NLP	NE	W	4	16	4	6	1	0	0	2	0	1	.375	.412	.438	.849	
1939 a	25	BEG	NN2	NLC	HG	W	5	17	4	7	3	0	0	3	0	3	.412	.500	.588	1.088	
1 Yr (2 Series)			NgL				9	33	8	13	4	0	0	5	0	4	.394	.459	.515	.975	
1 Yr				NLP			4	16	4	6	1	0	0	2	0	1	.375	.412	.438	.849	
1 Yr				NLC			5	17	4	7	3	0	0	3	0	3	.412	.500	.588	1.088	

All-Star Batting

Year	Age	Lg	Game	G	AB	R	H	2B	3B	HR	RBI	SB	BB	BA	OBP	SLG	OPS	HBP
1935	21	WES	EWA	PH	1	0	0	0	0	0	0	0	0	.000	.000	.000	.000	0
1936	22	EAS	EWA	CF	2	0	0	0	0	0	0	0	0	.000	.000	.000	.000	0
1937	23	EAS	EWA	CF	5	2	2	0	1	0	0	1	0	.400	.400	.600	1.000	0
1938	24	EAS	EWA	RF/RF	9	2	3	1	0	0	1	0	0	.333	.333	.444	.778	0
1939	25	EAS	EWA	CF/CF	9	2	4	2	0	0	2	0	0	.444	.444	.667	1.111	0
1942	28	EAS	EWA	RF/RF	9	1	4	1	0	0	3	0	0	.444	.444	.556	1.000	0
1945	31	EAS	EWA	RF	1	0	0	0	0	0	0	0	0	.000	.000	.000	.000	0
7 Yrs (10 GP)		NgL			36	7	13	5	0	0	6	1	0	.361	.361	.500	.861	0

Dave Brown

Holds NgL records for highest win-loss precentage and fewest hits per 9 innings

Standard Pitching

Year	Age	Tm	Lg	W	L	W-L%	ERA	G	CG	SHO	IP	H	R	ER	HR	BB	SO	ERA+	WHIP	BA	H9	HR9	BB9	SO9	SO/W
1919	24	CAG	WES	1	2	.333	4.40	4	0	0	14.1	17	10	7	0	9	6	68	1.814	.375	10.7	0.0	5.7	3.8	0.67
1920	25	CAG	NNL	13	3	.813	1.82	20	13	2	148.2	84	42	30	0	51	101	165	.908	.165	5.1	0.0	3.1	6.1	1.98
1921	26	CAG	NNL	17	2	.895	2.50	26	15	5	180.1	136	62	50	2	45	126	135	1.004	.204	6.8	0.1	2.2	6.3	2.80
1922	27	CAG	NNL	13	3	.813	2.90	28	8	3	155.0	136	63	50	2	55	103	121	1.232	.232	7.9	0.1	3.2	6.0	1.87
1923	28	NLG	ECL	5	6	.455	3.28	13	6	0	74.0	86	37	27	2	23	47	137	1.473	.305	10.5	0.2	2.8	5.7	2.04
1924	29	NLG	ECL	13	8	.619	2.00	27	16	1	179.2	146	64	40	2	41	107	241	1.041	.218	7.3	0.1	2.1	5.4	2.61
1925	30	NLG	ECL	1	0	1.000	1.00	1	1	0	9.0	7	1	1	0	1	8	576	1.556		7.0	0.0	7.0	8.0	1.14
6 Yrs (+1)			NgL	62	22	.738	2.39	115	59	11	746.2	595	269	198	6	222	492	169	1.094		7.2	0.1	2.7	5.9	2.22
162 Game Avg.			NgL	24	9	.738	2.39	45	23	4	292.1	233	105	77	2	87	193	169	1.094		7.2	0.1	2.7	5.9	2.22
Pre-NgL				1	2	.333	4.40	4	0	0	14.1	17	10	7	0	9	6	68	1.814		10.7	0.0	5.7	3.8	0.67
Pre-NgL + NgL				63	24	.724	2.42	119	59	11	761.0	612	279	205	6	231	498	167	1.108		7.2	0.1	2.7	5.9	2.16
162 Game Avg.				24	9	.724	2.42	45	22	4	287.2	231	106	78	2	87	188	167	1.108		7.2	0.1	2.7	5.9	2.16
3 Yrs		CAG	NNL	43	8	.843	2.42	74	36	10	484.0	356	167	130	4	151	330	140	1.048		6.6	0.1	2.8	6.1	2.19
3 Yrs		NLG	ECL	19	14	.576	2.33	41	23	1	262.2	239	102	68	2	71	162	223	1.180		8.2	0.1	2.4	5.6	2.28
3 Yrs			NNL	43	8	.843	2.42	74	36	10	484.0	356	167	130	4	151	330	140	1.048		6.6	0.1	2.8	6.1	2.19
3 Yrs			ECL	19	14	.576	2.33	41	23	1	262.2	239	102	68	2	71	162	223	1.180		8.2	0.1	2.4	5.6	2.28

20. The Negro Leagues All-Star Register 255

Ray Brown

Holds professional single-season record for highest win-loss percentage (1938); tied Warren Spahn for professional record for most seasons leading league in wins (8)

Standard Pitching

Year	Age	Tm	Lg	W	L	W-L%	ERA	G	CG	SHO	IP	H	R	ER	HR	BB	SO	ERA+	WHIP	H9	HR9	BB9	SO9	SO/W
1931	23	TOTAL	NNL-IND	7	6	.538	2.73	19	12	1	122.0	99	55	37	2	36	81		1.115	7.3	0.1	2.8	6.0	2.19
		AB2	NNL	7	6	.538	2.83	16	12	1	117.2	97	55	37	2	36	79	149	1.130	7.4	0.2	2.8	6.0	2.19
		KCM	IND	0	0		0.00	3	0	0	4.1	2	0	0	0	0	2		0.692	4.2	0.0	2.1	4.2	2.00
1932	24	TOTAL	EWL	7	7	.500	3.67	16	11	0	115.1	119	61	47	5	38	51	118	1.361	9.3	0.4	3.0	4.0	1.34
1933	25		HG	NN2	6	2	.750	2.60	9	6	0	69.1	67	33	20	2	16	41	175	1.197	8.7	0.3	2.1	5.3	2.56
1934	26	HG	IND	1	2	.333	5.96	3	2	0	22.2	29	16	15	0	6	13	60	1.544	11.5	0.0	2.4	5.2	2.17
1935 *	27	HG	NN2	8	5	.615	3.26	17	10	1	105.0	99	51	38	4	48	48	162	1.333	8.5	0.3	4.1	4.1	1.17
1936	28	HG	NN2	6	3	.667	3.74	13	7	0	86.2	77	46	36	4	26	39	133	1.188	8.0	0.4	2.7	4.1	1.50
1937	29	HG	NN2	11	3	.786	3.21	21	12	0	126.0	109	54	45	4	37	74	155	1.159	7.8	0.3	2.6	5.3	2.00
1938*	30	HG	NN2	14	0	1.000	1.88	20	11	4	129.0	106	32	27	3	26	70	258	1.023	7.4	0.2	1.8	4.9	2.69
1939	31	HG	NN2	6	2	.750	4.06	8	7	0	71.0	81	43	32	0	19	22	120	1.408	10.3	0.0	2.4	2.8	1.16
1940*	32	HG	NN2	16	2	.889	1.88	19	17	3	153.0	124	41	32	0	34	67	262	1.033	7.3	0.0	2.0	3.9	1.97
1941	33	HG	NN2	11	6	.647	2.92	20	14	1	138.2	141	63	45	0	32	53	136	1.248	9.2	0.0	2.1	3.4	1.66
1942	34	HG	NN2	10	5	.667	3.30	18	11	1	122.2	124	54	45	0	37	51	115	1.313	9.1	0.0	2.7	3.7	1.38
1943	35	HG	NN2	6	1	.857	4.10	14	6	2	74.2	75	37	34	1	25	29	114	1.339	9.0	0.1	3.0	3.5	1.16
1944	36	HG	NN2	11	1	.917	2.71	19	12	3	136.0	137	52	41		18	52	147	1.140	9.1	0.0	1.2	3.4	2.89
1945	37	HG	NN2	3	2	.600	3.31	5	3	0	32.2	32	21	12		6	12	90	1.163	8.8	0.0	1.7	3.4	2.00
16 Yrs			NgL	123	47	.724	3.03	221	141	18	1504.2	1419	659	506	25	398	703	159	1.208	8.5	0.1	2.4	4.2	1.77
162 Game Avg.			NgL	25	10	.724	3.03	45	29	4	306.1	289	134	103	5	81	143	159	1.208	8.5	0.1	2.4	4.2	1.77
14 Yrs		HG	EWL+NN2+IND	114	38	.750	3.03	197	125	16	1340.2	1274	583	452	23	342	601	162	1.205	8.6	0.2	2.3	4.0	1.76
1 Yr		AB2	NNL	7	6	.538	2.83	16	12	1	117.2	97	55	37	2	36	79	149	1.130	7.4	0.2	2.8	6.0	2.19
1 Yr		DW	EWL	2	3	.400	3.64	5	4	1	42.0	46	21	17	0	19	21	117	1.548	9.9	0.0	4.1	4.5	1.11
1 Yr		KCM	IND	0	0		0.00	3	0	0	4.1	2	0	0	0	0	2		0.692	4.2	0.0	2.1	4.2	2.00
12 Yrs		HG	NN2	108	32	.771	2.94	183	116	16	1244.2	1172	527	407	18	317	558	166	1.196	8.5	0.1	2.3	4.0	1.76
1 Yr		HG	NNL	7	6	.538	2.83	16	12	1	117.2	97	55	37	2	36	79	149	1.130	7.4	0.2	2.8	6.0	2.19
1 Yr		HG	EWL	7	7	.500	3.67	16	11	1	115.1	119	61	47	5	38	51	118	1.361	9.3	0.4	3.0	4.0	1.34
2 Yrs		HG	IND	1	2	.333	5.00	6	2	0	27.0	31	16	15	0	7	15		1.407	10.3	0.0	2.3	5.0	2.14

Postseason Pitching

Year	Age	Tm	Lg	Ser	Opp	Rslt	W	L	W-L%	ERA	G	GS	CG	SHO	IP	H	R	ER	HR	BB	SO	WHIP	H9	HR9	BB9	SO9	SO/W
1939	31	HG	NN2	NLP	PS	W	1	0	1.000	0.00	1			0	0	9.0	4	0	0	0	2	6	1.000	7.0	0.0	2.0	6.0	3.00
1942	34	HG	NN2	WS	KCM	L	0	1	.000	6.00	3			1	0	9.0	16	9	6	2	2	7	2.000	16.0	2.0	2.0	7.0	3.50
1943 □	35	HG	NN2	WS	BBB	W	2	0	1.000	0.00	3			1	1	11.2	5	1	0	0	5	6	0.857	3.9	0.0	3.9	4.6	1.20
1944 □	36	HG	NN2	WS	BBB	W	1	0	1.000	0.00	1			1	1	9.0	3	0	0	0	1	5	0.444	3.0	0.0	1.0	5.0	1.67
1945	37	HG	NN2	WS	CBE	L	0	1	.000	1.00	1			0	0	9.0	9	5	1	0	2	1	1.222	9.0	0.0	2.0	1.0	0.50
5 Yrs (5 Series)			NgL				4	2	.667	1.32	7			4	2	47.2	38	15	7	2	14	25	1.091	7.2	0.2	2.6	4.7	1.79
4 Yrs				WS			3	2	.600	1.63	6			3	2	38.2	31	15	7	2	12	19	1.112	7.2	0.2	2.8	4.4	1.58
1 Yr				NLP			1	0	1.000	0.00	1			1	0	9.0	4	0	0	0	2	6	1.000	7.0	0.0	2.0	6.0	3.00

All-Star Pitching

Year	Age	Tm	Lg	W	L	W-L%	ERA	G	GS	CG	SHO	IP	H	R	ER	HR	BB	SO	WHIP	H9	HR9	BB9	SO9	SO/W
1935	27	WES	EWA	0	0		4.50	1		0	0	4.0	6	2	2	0	0	1	1.500	13.5	0.0	0.0	2.3	∞
1938	30	EAS	EWA	0	0		0.00	1		0	0	3.0	2	0	0	0	2	6	1.333	6.0	0.0	6.0	18.0	3.00
1940	32	EAS	EWA	0	0		0.00	1		0	0	3.0	2	0	0	0	0	3	0.667	6.0	0.0	0.0	9.0	∞
3 Yrs (3 GP)				0	0		1.80	3		0	0	10.0	10	2	2	0	2	10	1.200	9.0	0.0	1.8	9.0	5.00

Leon Day

Holds NgL record for most East-West Game appearances as pitcher (7)

Standard Pitching

Year	Age	Tm	Lg	W	L	W-L%	ERA	G	CG	SHO	IP	H	R	ER	HR	BB	SO	ERA+	WHIP	H9	HR9	BB9	SO9	SO/W
1934	17	BBS	NN2	0	0		33.00	2	0	0	3.0	11	12	11	0	2	2	13	4.333	33.0	0.0	6.0	6.0	1.00
1935 *	18	BE	NN2	7	4	.636	4.34	17	8	1	103.2	103	59	50	5	41	62	115	1.389	8.9	0.4	3.6	5.4	1.51
1936	19	NE	NN2	5	5	.500	3.30	12	6	1	76.1	69	39	28	3	39	54	150	1.415	8.1	0.4	4.6	6.4	1.38
1937 *	20	TOTAL	NN2	3	0	1.000	5.56	6	2	1	34.0	35	23	21	4	12	25	119	1.382	9.3	1.1	3.2	6.6	2.08
1938	21	NE	NN2	1	1	.500	2.79	3	1	1	9.2	6	3	3	2	2	3	177	0.828	5.6	1.9	1.9	2.8	1.50
1939 *	22	NE	NN2	7	3	.700	3.41	13	7	1	87.0	79	46	33		25	30	142	1.195	8.2	0.0	2.6	3.1	1.20
1940	23	VEZ	MEX	6	0	1.000	3.22	9	4	0	67.0	61	27	24		26	29	146	1.299	8.2	0.0	3.5	3.9	1.12
1941	24	NE	NN2	2	2	.500	3.95	4	2	0	27.1	30	18	12		14	13	101	1.610	9.9	0.0	4.6	4.3	0.93
1942 *	25	NE	NN2	8	2	.800	1.73	10	9	2	83.1	49	18	16	2	27	86	232	0.912	5.3	0.0	2.9	9.3	3.19
1943 *		TOTAL	NN2+IND	4	3	.571	3.94	11	3	0	61.2	56	32	27		26	47	238	1.330	8.2	0.0	3.8	6.9	1.81
1944	27										Did not play (Military Service)													
1945	28										Did not play (Military Service)													
1946	29	NE	NN2	13	2	.867	2.39	15	14	2	132.0	98	42	35	3	51	109	184	1.129	6.7	0.2	3.5	7.4	2.14
1947 *	30										Played in unrecorded Mexican league													
1948	31										Played in unrecorded Mexican league													
12 Yrs (+4)			NgL	64	24	.727	3.63	111	65	10	685.0	646	337	276	17	292	546	164	1.369	8.5	0.2	3.8	7.2	1.87
162 Game Avg.			NgL	26	10	.727	3.63	45	26	4	278	262	137	112	7	118	221	164	1.369	8.5	0.2	3.8	7.2	1.87
8 Yrs		NE	NN2	46	17	.730	2.85	70	49	10	488.2	401	197	155	9	195	387	161	1.220	7.4	0.2	3.6	7.1	1.98
1 Yr		BE	NN2	7	4	.636	4.34	17	8	1	103.2	103	59	50	5	41	62	115	1.389	8.9	0.4	3.6	5.4	1.51
1 Yr		VEZ	MEX	6	0	1.000	3.22	9	4	0	67.0	61	27	24	0	26	29	146	1.299	8.2	0.0	3.5	3.9	1.12
2 Yrs		HG	NN2	1	0	1.000	5.93	2	1	0	13.2	14	10	9	3	2	19	262	1.171	9.2	2.0	1.3	12.5	9.50
1 Yr		BBS	NN2	0	0		33.00	2	0	0	3.0	11	12	11	0	2	2	13	4.333	33.0	0.0	6.0	6.0	1.00
1 Yr		NAS	IND	0	1	.000	1.00	1	1	0	9.0	6	2	1	0	6	8	936	1.333	6.0	0.0	6.0	8.0	1.33
11 Yrs			NN2	58	23	.716	3.71	101	60	10	609.0	579	308	251	18	260	509	155	1.378	8.6	0.3	3.8	7.5	1.96
1 Yr			MEX	6	0	1.000	3.22	9	4	0	67.0	61	27	24	0	26	29	146	1.299	8.2	0.0	3.5	3.9	1.12
1 Yr			IND	0	1	.000	1.00	1	1	0	9.0	6	2	1	0	6	8	936	1.333	6.0	0.0	8.0	8.0	1.33

Postseason Pitching

Year	Age	Tm	Lg	Ser	Rslt	Opp	W	L	W-L%	ERA	G	GF	CG	SHO	IP	H	R	ER	BB	SO	WHIP	H9	BB9	SO9	SO/W
1939 □	22	NE		NLP	L	BEG	0	1	.000	7.50	1		0	0	6.0	10	9	5	5	5	1.833	9.0	7.5	1.5	0.20
1946 □	29	NE		WS	W	NCM	1	0	1.000	4.50	2		0	0	6.0	7	6	3	4	6	1.667	9.0	9.0	9.0	1.50
2 Yrs (2 Series)			NgL				1	1	.500	6.00	3		0	0	12.0	17	15	8	9	7	2.167	12.8	6.8	5.3	0.78
1 Yr				NLP			0	1	.000	7.50	1		0	0	6.0	10	9	5	5	5	1.833	15.0	7.5	1.5	0.20
1 Yr				WS			1	0	1.000	4.50	2		0	0	6.0	7	6	3	4	6	1.667	10.5	6.0	9.0	1.50

All-Star Pitching

Year	Tm	Lg	W	L	W-L%	ERA	GF	CG	SHO	IP	H	R	ER	BB	SO	WHIP	H9	HR9	BB9	SO9	SO/W
1935	EAS	EWA	0	0		6.75		0	0	4.0	6	3	3	2	3	2.000	13.5	9.0	4.5	6.8	1.50
1937	EAS	EWA	0	0		0.00		0	0	3.0	1	0	0	0	4	0.333	3.0	0.0	0.0	12.0	∞
1939	EAS	EWA (x2)	0	0		0.00		0	0	6.0	0	0	0	3	4	0.500	0.0	0.0	4.5	6.0	1.33
1942	EAS	EWA	1	0	1.000	0.00		0	0	4.1	3	0	0	2	10	1.154	6.2	4.5	4.2	20.8	5.00
1943	EAS	EWA	0	0		0.00		0	0	2.0	1	0	0	1	0	1.000	4.5	0.0	4.5	0.0	0.00
1946	EAS	EWA	0	0		0.00		0	0	2.0	2	0	0	0	1	1.000	9.0	0.0	0.0	4.5	∞
6 Yrs (7 GP)			1	0	1.000	1.27		0	0	0.0	13	3	3	8	22	0.984	5.5	3.4	9.3	2.75	

20. The Negro Leagues All-Star Register

Martin Dihigo

Standard Pitching

Year	Age	Tm	Lg	W	L	W-L%	ERA	G	CG	SHO	IP	H	R	ER	HR	BB	SO	ERA+	WHIP	H9	HR9	BB9	SO9	SO/W
1923	18	CSE	ECL	2	2	.500	4.05	5	2	0	33.1	35	17	15	2	8	11	104	1.290	9.5	0.5	2.2	3.0	1.38
1924	19	CSE	ECL	3	3	.500	2.39	9	3	0	49.0	43	17	13		11	24	195	1.102	7.9	0.0	2.0	4.4	2.18
1925	20	CSE	ECL	4	4	.500	3.70	10	7	0	73.0	75	33	30		28	31	140	1.411	9.2	0.0	3.5	3.8	1.11
1926	21	CSE	ECL	3	1	.750	3.86	5	4	0	35.0	36	17	15	0	13	28	115	1.400	9.3	0.0	3.3	7.2	2.15
1927	22	CSE	ECL	2	0	1.000	2.50	2	2	0	18.0	20	6	5	0	8	17	188	1.556	10.0	0.0	4.0	8.5	2.13
1928	23	HG	EAS	1	1	.500	6.35	2	2	0	17.0	27	14	12	4	4	14	64	1.824	14.3	2.1	2.1	7.4	3.50
1929	24	HIL	ANL	4	3	.571	2.63	8	5	0	51.1	43	23	15	2	12	29	199	1.071	7.5	0.4	2.1	5.1	2.42
1930	25	SC2	EAS	0	1	.000	0.00	1	1	0	6.0	3	0	0	0	3	4		1.000	4.5	0.0	4.5	6.0	1.33
1931	26	HIL	IND	1	1	.500	3.50	2	2	0	18.0	19	9	7	1	6	9	94	1.389	9.5	0.5	3.0	4.5	1.50
1932	27										Played in unrecorded Cuban league													
1933	28										Played in unrecorded Cuban league													
1934	29										Played in unrecorded Cuban league													
1935	30	NYC	NN2	3	1	.750	2.70	8	3	0	43.1	37	18	13	1	16	38	185	1.223	7.7	0.2	3.3	7.9	2.38
1936	31	NYC	NN2	6	2	.750	3.69	10	6	0	75.2	73	38	31	7	17	56	124	1.189	8.7	0.8	2.0	6.7	3.29
1937	32										Played in unrecorded Mexican league													
1938	33										Played in unrecorded Mexican league													
1939	34										Played in unrecorded Mexican league													
1940	35	VEZ	MEX	8	6	.571	3.54	17	8	2	109.1	106	48	43	2	48	65	133	1.409	8.7	0.0	4.0	5.4	1.35
1941	36	ULI	MEX	9	10	.474	4.01	23	9	1	157.0	177	82	70		43	93	119	1.401	10.1	0.0	2.5	5.3	2.16
1942	37	ULI	MEX								Played in unrecorded Mexican league													
1943	38	ULI	MEX								Played in unrecorded Mexican league													
1944	39	JN2	MEX								Played in unrecorded Mexican league													
1945	40	NYC	NN2	0	3	.000	3.86	3	2	2	23.1	24	15	10	6	6	12	91	1.286	9.3	0.0	2.3	4.6	2.00
14 Yrs (+9)				46	35	.568	3.53	102	54	4	686.0	694	323	269	17	217	419	138	1.328	9.1	0.2	2.8	5.5	1.93
162 Game Avg.				20	15	.568	3.53	45	24	2	302.6	306	143	119	8	96	185	138	1.328	9.1	0.2	2.8	5.5	1.93
5 Yrs		CSE	ECL	14	10	.583	3.37	31	18	1	208.1	209	90	78	2	68	111	147	1.330	9.0	0.1	2.9	4.8	1.63
1 Yr		ULT	MEX	9	10	.474	4.01	23	9	1	157.0	177	82	70		43	93	119	1.401	10.1	0.0	2.5	5.3	2.16
3 Yrs		NYC	NN2	9	6	.600	3.41	21	11	2	142.1	134	67	54	8	39	106	137	1.215	8.5	0.5	2.5	6.7	2.72
1 Yr		VEZ	MEX	8	6	.571	3.54	17	8	2	109.1	106	48	43	2	48	65	133	1.409	8.7	0.0	4.0	5.4	1.35
2 Yrs		HIL	ANL-IND	5	4	.556	2.86	10	7	0	69.1	62	32	22	3	18	38	172	1.154	8.0	0.4	2.3	4.9	2.11
1 Yr		HG	EAS	1	1	.500	6.35	2	2	0	17.0	27	14	12	4	4	14	64	1.824	14.3	2.1	2.1	7.4	3.50
1 Yr		SC2	EAS	0	1	.000	0.00	1	1	0	6.0	3	0	0	0	3	4		1.000	4.5	0.0	4.5	6.0	1.33
2 Yrs			MEX	17	16	.515	3.82	40	17	4	266.1	283	130	113		91	158	125	1.404	9.6	0.0	3.1	5.3	1.74
5 Yrs			ECL	14	10	.583	3.37	31	18	1	208.1	209	90	78	2	68	111	147	1.330	9.0	0.1	2.9	4.8	1.63
3 Yrs			NN2	9	6	.600	3.41	21	11	2	142.1	134	67	54	8	39	106	137	1.215	8.5	0.5	2.5	6.7	2.72
1 Yr			ANL	4	3	.571	2.63	8	5	0	51.1	43	23	15	2	12	29	199	1.071	7.5	0.4	2.1	5.1	2.42
2 Yrs			EAS	1	2	.333	4.70	3	3	0	23.0	30	14	12	4	7	18	64	1.609	11.7	1.6	2.7	7.0	2.57
1 Yr			IND	1	1	.500	3.50	2	2	0	18.0	19	9	7	1	6	9	94	1.389	9.5	0.5	3.0	4.5	1.50

Postseason Pitching

Year	Age	Tm	Lg	Ser	Rslt	Opp	W	L	W-L%	ERA	G	CG	SHO	IP	H	R	ER	BB	SO	WHIP	H9	BB9	SO9	SO/W
1935	30	NYC	NN2	NLCL		PC	1	1	.500	18.00	2	1	0	11.1	12		4	2	6	7.000	54.0	9.0	27.0	3.00
1 Yr (1 Series)			NgL				1	1	.500	18.00	2	1	0	11.1	12		4	2	6	7.000	54.0	9.0	27.0	3.00
1 Yr			NLC				1	1	.500	18.00	2	1	0	11.1	12		4	2	6	7.000	54.0	9.0	27.0	3.00

All-Star Pitching

Year	Tm	Lg	W	L	W-L%	ERA	G	CG	SHO	IP	H	R	ER	BB	SO	WHIP	H9	BB9	SO9	SO/W
1935	EAS	EWA	0	1		16.20	1	0	0	1.2	3	4	3	2	1	3.000	16.2	10.8	5.4	0.50
1945	EAS	EWA	0	0		2.70	1	0	0	3.1	2	1	1	0	0	0.600	5.4	0.0	0.0	∞
2 Yrs (2 GP)			0	1	.000	7.20	2	0	0	0.0	5	5	4	2	1	1.400	9.0	3.6	1.8	0.50

John Donaldson
Standard Pitching

Year	Age	Tm	Lg	W	L	W-L%	ERA	G	CG	SHO	IP	H	R	ER	HR	BB	SO	ERA+	WHIP	H9	HR9	BB9	SO9	SO/W
1911	20	TN Minstrels									Played in unrecorded Black league													
1912	21	ALL									Played in unrecorded Black league													
1913	22	ALL									Played in unrecorded Black league													
1914	23	ALL									Played in unrecorded Black league													
1915	24	ALL									Played in unrecorded Black league													
1916	25	ALL	WES	2	0	1.000	3.60	2	2	0	15.0	12	7	6	0	6	19	92	1.200	7.2	0.0	3.6	11.4	3.17
1917	26	ALL	WES	3	4	.429	1.95	8	7	0	60.0	41	20	13	0	13	45	134	0.900	6.2	0.0	2.0	6.8	3.46
1918	27	TOTAL	WES+EAS	7	6	.538	2.13	15	11	3	114.1	112	38	27	0	32	57	166	1.259	8.8	0.0	2.5	4.5	1.78
1919	28	DS	WES	5	5	.500	2.33	11	9	2	85.0	68	31	22	0	29	38	143	1.141	7.2	0.0	3.1	4.0	1.31
1920	29	KCM	NNL	6	6	.500	3.78	14	8	1	95.1	100	50	40	0	25	54	91	1.311	9.4	0.0	2.4	5.1	2.16
1921	30	KCM	NNL	0	3	.000	4.97	8	1	0	41.2	41	27	23	0	11	15	74	1.248	8.9	0.0	2.4	3.2	1.36
1922	31	TOTAL	NNL-IND								No pitching statistics recorded													
1923	32	TOTAL	NNL-IND								No pitching statistics recorded													
1924	33	TOTAL	NNL-IND								No pitching statistics recorded													
1925	34	Bertha MN	IND								Played for unrecorded independent team													
1926	35	TOTAL	IND								Played for unrecorded independent team													
1927	36	Bertha MN	IND								Played for unrecorded independent team													
1928	37	Melrose MN	IND								Played for unrecorded independent team													
1929	38	TOTAL	IND								Played for unrecorded independent team													
1930	39	St. Cloud MN	IND								Played for unrecorded independent team													
1931	40	TOTAL	IND								Played for unrecorded independent team													
1932	41	DAS	IND	0	1	.000	4.50	1	1	0	8.0	9	6	4	0	1	5	106	1.250	10.1	0.0	1.1	5.6	5.00
1933	42	Ind. team(s)									Played for unrecorded barnstorming team(s)													
1934	43	Ind. team(s)									Played for unrecorded barnstorming team(s)													
1935	44	Ind. team(s)									Played for unrecorded barnstorming team(s)													
1936	45	Ind. team(s)									Played for unrecorded barnstorming team(s)													
1937	46	Ind. team(s)									Played for unrecorded barnstorming team(s)													
1938	47	Ind. team(s)									Played for unrecorded barnstorming team(s)													
1939	48	TOTAL	IND								Played for unrecorded barnstorming team(s)													
1940	49	Ind. team(s)	IND								Played for unrecorded barnstorming team(s)													
3 Yrs (+28)			NgL	6	10	.375	4.16	23	10	1	145.0	150	83	67	0	37	74	87	1.290	9.3	0.0	2.3	4.6	2.00
162 Game Avg.			NgL	1	2	.375	4.16	45	2	0	29.2	31	17	14	0	8	15	87	1.290	9.3	0.0	2.3	4.6	2.00
Pre-NgL				17	15	.531	2.23	36	29	5	274.1	233	96	68	0	80	159	148	1.141	7.6	0.0	2.6	5.2	1.99
Pre-NgL + NgL				23	25	.479	2.90	59	39	6	419.1	383	179	135	0	117	233	127	1.192	8.2	0.0	2.5	5.0	1.99
162 Game Avg.				18	19	.479	2.90	45	30	5	319.2	292	137	103	0	89	178	97	1.192	8.2	0.0	2.5	5.0	1.99
2 Yrs		KCM	NNL	6	9	.400	4.14	22	9	1	137.0	141	77	63	0	36	69	86	1.292	9.3	0.0	2.4	4.5	1.92
1 Yr		DAS	IND	0	1	.000	4.50	1	1	0	8.0	9	6	4	0	1	5	106	1.250	10.1	0.0	1.1	5.6	5.00
2 Yrs			NNL	6	9	.400	4.14	22	9	1	137.0	141	77	63	0	36	69	86	1.292	9.3	0.0	2.4	4.5	1.92
1 Yr			IND	0	1	.000	4.50	1	1	0	8.0	9	6	4	0	1	5	106	1.250	10.1	0.0	1.1	5.6	5.00

20. The Negro Leagues All-Star Register

Andrew "Rube" Foster
Standard Pitching

Year	Age	Tm	Lg	W	L	W-L%	ERA	G	CG	SHO	IP	H	R	ER	HR	BB	SO	ERA+	WHIP	H9	HR9	BB9	SO9	SO/W
1902	22	CUG	WES	1	2	.500	2.50	2	2	1	18.0	15	7	5	0	1	15	215	1.222	7.5	0.5	3.5	7.5	2.14
1903	23	CXG	EAS	4	0	1.000	0.75	4	4	1	36.0	19	6	3	0	7	19	192	0.722	4.8	0.0	1.8	4.8	2.71
1904	24	PG	IND	2	0	1.000	1.50	4	4	1	36.0	21	10	6	3	9	41	147	0.833	5.3	0.8	2.3	10.3	4.56
1905	25	PG	EAS	2	0	1.000	1.13	3	3	0	32.0	21	9	4	1	3	21	194	0.750	5.9	0.3	0.8	5.9	7.00
1906	26	PG	EAS	4	2	.667	2.00	10	7	1	72.0	62	28	16	0	21	39	155	1.153	7.8	0.0	2.6	4.9	1.86
1907	27	LEL		1	0	1.000	0.00	1	1	1	9.0	7	1	0	0	1	4		0.889	7.0	0.0	1.0	4.0	4.00
1908	28	LEL	WES	5	1	.833	2.00	6	6	0	54.0	46	21	12	1	18	26	162	1.185	7.7	0.2	3.0	4.3	1.44
1909	29	LEL	WES	2	0	1.000	0.00	2	2	0	18.0	11	0	0	0	4	11		0.833	5.5	0.0	2.0	5.5	2.75
1910	30	LEL	WES	3	0	1.000	1.13	4	4	2	40.0	29	8	5	0	5	20	204	0.850	6.5	0.0	1.1	4.5	4.00
1911	31	CAG	WES	4	1	.800	2.06	8	6	0	56.2	46	18	13	1	12	33	158	1.024	7.3	0.2	1.9	5.2	2.75
1912	32	CAG	WES	6	2	.750	2.06	10	7	0	74.1	66	31	17	2	21	31	131	1.117	8.0	0.0	2.1	3.8	1.82
1913	33	CAG	WES	4	3	.571	4.69	8	5	1	63.1	75	42	33	2	21	38	66	1.516	10.7	0.3	3.0	5.4	1.81
1914	34	CAG	WES	5	4	.556	2.48	10	7	2	72.2	57	29	20	2	25	32	116	1.128	7.1	0.2	3.1	4.0	1.28
1915	35	CAG	WES	5	5	.500	4.05	7	4	0	53.1	48	30	24	0	13	20	58	1.144	8.1	0.0	2.2	3.4	1.54
1916	36	CAG	WES	1	1	.500	1.00	2	2	0	18.0	17	2	2	0	9	8	242	1.444	8.5	0.0	4.5	4.0	0.89
1917	37	CAG	WES	2	1	.667	3.33	3	2	0	27.0	21	11	10	0	11	11	54	1.185	7.0	0.0	3.7	3.7	1.00
15 Yrs		Pre-NgL		50	18	.735	2.25	84	64	7	680.1	561	257	170	12	183	369	139	1.094	7.4	0.2	2.4	4.9	2.02
162 Game Avg		Pre-NgL		30	11	.735	2.25	51	39	4	413.2	341	156	103	7	111	224	139	1.094	7.4	0.2	2.4	4.9	2.02

Willie Foster
Standard Pitching

Year	Age	Tm	Lg	W	L	W-L%	ERA	G	CG	SHO	IP	H	R	ER	HR	BB	SO	ERA+	WHIP	H9	HR9	BB9	SO9	SO/W
1923	19	TOTAL	IND+NNL	6	2	.750	2.19	12	6	1	70.0	49	28	17	0	16	50	160	0.929	6.3	0.1	2.8	5.7	3.13
–	–	MRS	IND	6	2	.750	1.74	9	6	1	62.0	43	21	12	0	12	46	172	0.887	6.2	0.0	1.7	6.7	3.83
–	–	CAG	NNL	0	0		5.63	3	0	0	8.0	6	7	5	0	4	4	68	1.250	6.8	1.1	4.5	4.5	1.00
1924	20	TOTAL	NNL	7	1	.875	2.16	12	5	3	66.2	47	23	16	0	24	53		1.065	6.3	0.0	3.2	7.2	2.21
1925	21	TOTAL	NNL	6	0	1.000	1.62	12	5	2	78.0	57	20	14	4	21	49		1.000	6.6	0.0	2.4	5.7	2.33
1926	22	CAG	NNL	13	4	.765	1.80	27	12	6	174.2	115	42	35		56	111	199	0.979	5.9	0.2	2.9	5.7	1.98
1927	23	CAG	NNL	21	5	.808	2.03	31	21	6	217.0	187	70	49		65	119	145	1.161	7.8	0.0	2.7	4.9	1.83
1928	24	CAG	NNL	13	8	.619	2.82	27	19	3	195.0	184	72	61	8	61	119	110	1.256	8.5	0.4	2.8	5.5	1.95
1929	25	CAG	NNL	9	7	.563	2.70	23	13	1	133.1	123	63	40		46	82	114	1.268	8.3	0.0	3.1	5.5	1.78
1930	26	CAG	NNL	11	8	.579	3.73	26	13	1	161.2	151	75	67		57	133	100	1.287	8.4	0.0	3.2	7.4	2.33
1931	27	TOTAL	IND	10	2	.833	2.27	13	11	2	103.0	79	36	26	1	34	88	165	1.097	6.9	0.1	3.0	7.7	2.59
1932	28	CAG	NSL	8	5	.615	2.09	17	13	1	116.1	101	39	27	2	24	76	128	1.074	7.8	0.0	1.9	5.9	3.17
1933	29	CAG	NN2	6	4	.600	2.47	13	7	1	83.2	63	34	23	2	17	61	175	0.956	6.8	0.2	1.8	6.6	3.59
1934	30	CAG	NN2	3	2	.600	2.88	11	5	2	56.1	52	22	18	0	22	17	126	1.314	8.3	0.0	3.5	2.7	0.77
1935	31	CAG	NN2	4	3	.571	2.84	8	6	2	82.1	73	36	26	2	32	31	163	1.275	8.0	0.2	3.5	3.4	0.97
1936	32	PC	NN2	4	3	.571	4.30	8	5	0	46.0	45	27	22	4	18	21	113	1.370	8.8	0.8	3.5	4.1	1.17
1937	33	CAG	NAL	4	5	.444	3.90	16	4	2	80.2	77	44	35	4	30	46	108	1.326	8.6	0.4	3.3	5.1	1.53
15 Yrs		NgL		126	60	.677	2.57	260	144	34	1664.2	1403	631	476	26	523	1056	143	1.157	7.6	0.1	2.8	5.7	2.02
162 Game Avg.		NgL		22	10	.677	2.57	45	25	6	288.1	243	109	82	5	91	183	143	1.157	7.6	0.1	2.8	5.7	2.02
13 Yrs			NNL+NN2+NAL+NSL	104	53	.662	2.61	228	120	28	1435.2	1234	547	416	21	453	883	141	1.175	7.7	0.1	2.8	5.5	1.95
1 Yr		CAG	NN2	4	5	.444	3.90	16	3	2	80.2	77	44	35	1	30	46	113	1.326	8.6	0.4	3.3	5.1	1.53
1 Yr		PC	IND	9	2	.818	2.34	12	10	2	96.0	63	34	25		35	76	157	1.094	7.1	0.1	2.7	7.1	2.62
2 Yrs		HG	IND	7	2	.778	1.52	10	7	2	71.0	44	21	12	0	15	60		0.831	5.6	0.0	1.9	7.6	4.00
1 Yr		MRS	NNL	1	0	1.000	0.00	1	1	0	9.0	3	1	0	0	3	4		0.444	1.0	0.0	3.0	4.0	1.33
1 Yr		BBB	IND	1	0	1.000	1.29	1	1	0	7.0	3	1	1	0	5	12	268	1.143	3.9	0.0	6.4	15.4	2.40
8 Yrs		KCM	NNL	80	33	.708	2.50	162	88	22	1034.1	870	372	287	13	334	670	142	1.164	7.6	0.1	2.9	5.8	2.01
4 Yrs			NN2	18	13	.581	2.99	43	23	3	268.1	233	119	89	8	89	130	150	1.200	7.8	0.3	3.0	4.4	1.46
2 Yrs			IND	16	4	.800	2.07	22	17	2	165.0	122	57	38	1	46	134	167	1.018	6.7	0.1	2.5	7.3	2.91
1 Yr			NSL	8	5	.615	2.09	17	13	2	116.1	101	39	27	2	24	76	128	1.074	7.8	0.2	1.9	5.9	3.17
1 Yr			NAL	4	5	.444	3.90	16	3	2	80.2	77	44	35	4	30	46	108	1.326	8.6	0.4	3.3	5.1	1.53

Willie Foster

Postseason Pitching

Year	Age	Tm	Lg	Ser	Rslt	Opp	W	L	W-L%	ERA	G	GS	CG	SHO	IP	H	R	ER	BB	SO	WHIP	H9	HR9	BB9	SO9	SO/W
1926	22	CAG	NNL	NNC	W	KCM	1	2	.333	2.38	4		2	1	22.2	20	12	6	8	10	1.235	7.9		3.2	4.0	1.25
1926 □	22	CAG	NNL	WS	W	AC	2	0	1.000	1.27	4		3	1	28.1	26	8	4	13	19	1.376	8.3		4.1	6.0	1.46
1927	23	CAG	NNL	NNC	W	BBB	2	0	1.000	2.00	3		2	1	18	13	4	4	3	12	0.889	6.5		1.5	6.0	4.00
1927 □	23	CAG	NNL	WS	W	AC	2	2	.500	3.00	4		2	0	24	27	9	8	10	13	1.542	10.1		3.8	4.9	1.30
1928	24	CAG	NNL	NNC	L	SLS	2	2	.500	4.89	4		4	0	35	34	20	19	12	20	1.314	8.7		3.1	5.1	1.67
1932	28	CAG	NSL	NSC	W	NEG	2	0	1.000	1.50	2		2	0	18	17	7	3	3	20	1.111	8.5		1.5	10.0	6.67
1934	30	CAG	NN2	NLC	L	PS	1	1	.500	1.50	3		2	0	18	14	4	3	9	20	1.278	7.0		4.5	10.0	2.22
1937	33	CAG	NAL	ALC	L	KCM	0	0		1.42	1		0	0	6.1	5	2	1	1	2	0.947	7.1		1.4	2.8	2.00
6 Yrs (8 series)			NgL				12	7	.632	2.54	25		17	3	170.1	156	66	48	59	116	1.262	8.2		3.1	6.1	1.97
6 yrs			CAG				12	7	.632	2.54	25		17	3	170.1	156	66	48	59	116	1.262	8.2		3.1	6.1	1.97
3 yrs			NNC				5	4	.556	3.45	11		8	2	75.2	67	36	29	23	42	1.189	8.0		2.7	5.0	1.83
2 yrs			WS				4	2	.667	2.06	8		5	1	52.1	53	17	12	23	32	1.452	9.1		4.0	5.5	1.39
1 yr			NLC				1	1	.500	1.50	3		2	0	18.0	14	4	3	9	20	1.278	7.0		4.5	10.0	2.22
1 yr			NSC				2	0	1.000	1.50	2		2	0	18.0	17	7	3	3	20	1.111	8.5		1.5	10.0	6.67
1 yr			ALC				0	0		1.42	1		0	0	6.1	5	2	1	1	2	0.947	7.1		1.4	2.8	2.00

All-Star Pitching

Year	Age	Tm	Lg	W	L	W-L%	ERA	GS	CG	SHO	IP	H	R	BB	SO	WHIP	H9	BB9	SO9	SO/W
1933	29	WES	EWA	1	0	1.000	5.14	1		0	9.0	7	7	1	4	1.429	9.0	3.9	5.1	1.33
1934	30	WES	EWA	0	1	.000	2.25	0		0	3.0	4	1	1	2	1.250	9.0	2.3	4.5	2.00
1937	33	NOS	NSA	1	0	1.000	2.00	1		1	9.0	9	5	0	13	1.000	9.0	0.0	13.0	∞
3 Yrs (3 GP)			NgL	2	1	.667	3.15	2		1	21.0	20	13	2	19	1.200	9.0	1.8	8.6	4.75

Stuart "Slim" Jones

Standard Pitching

Year	Age	Tm	Lg	W	L	W-L%	ERA	G	GS	CG	SHO	IP	H	R	ER	BB	SO	ERA+	WHIP	H9	HR9	BB9	SO9	SO/W
1932	19	BBS	EWL	0	3	.000	3.96	4		1	0	25.0	27	14	11	8	14	104	1.480	9.7	0.0	3.6	5.0	1.40
1933	20	SOX	NN2	5	3	.625	4.23	12		4	0	66.0	52	40	31	13	51	100	1.197	7.1	0.4	3.7	7.0	1.89
1934 *	21	PS	NN2	20	4	.833	1.24	30		20	6	203.0	141	44	28	6	164	313	0.926	6.3	0.3	2.1	7.3	3.49
1935 *	22	PS	NN2	4	5	.444	5.88	16		4	0	67.1	86	51	44	6	36	86	1.545	11.5	0.8	2.4	4.8	2.00
1936	23	PS	NN2	2	4	.333	6.96	14		1	0	42.2	48	42	33	5	21	22	70	1.617	10.1	1.1	4.4	4.6	1.05
1937	24	PS	NN2	1	0	1.000	5.06	1		0	0	5.1	6	3	3	0	5	3	102	1.688	10.1	0.0	5.1	1.7	0.33
1938	25	PS	NN2	0	0		1.42	7		0	0	12.2	13	6	2	4	7	342	1.342	9.2	1.4	2.8	5.0	1.75
7 Yrs			NgL	32	21	.604	3.24	84		30	6	422.0	373	198	152	22	130	295	229	1.192	8.0	0.5	2.8	6.3	2.27
162 Game Avg.			NgL	17	11	.604	3.24	45		16	3	226.1	200	106	81	12	70	158	229	1.192	8.0	0.5	2.8	6.3	2.27
5 Yrs			PS	27	15	.643	2.99	68		25	6	331.0	294	144	110	19	93	230	233	1.169	8.0	0.5	2.5	6.3	2.47
1 Yr			SOX	5	3	.625	4.23	12		4	0	66.0	52	40	31	3	27	51	100	1.197	7.1	0.4	3.7	7.0	1.89
1 Yr			BBS	0	3	.000	3.96	4		3	0	25.0	27	14	11	0	10	14	104	1.480	9.7	0.0	3.6	5.0	1.40
6 Yrs			NN2	32	18	.640	3.20	80		29	6	397.0	346	184	141	22	120	281	237	1.174	7.8	0.5	2.7	6.4	2.34
1 Yr			EWL	0	3	.000	3.96	4		1	0	25.0	27	14	11	0	10	14	104	1.480	9.7	0.0	3.6	5.0	1.40

Postseason Pitching

Year	Age	Tm	Lg	Ser	Rslt	Opp	W	L	W-L%	ERA	G	GS	CG	SHO	IP	H	R	ER	BB	SO	WHIP	H9	HR9	BB9	SO9	SO/W
1934 □	21	PS	NN2	NLC	W	CAG	1	2	.333	1.45	3		2	1	18.2	14	4	3	1	17	0.804	6.8		0.5	8.2	17.00
1 Yr (1 WS)			Pro				1	2	.333	1.45	3		2	1	18.2	14	4	3	1	17	0.804	6.8		0.5	8.2	17.00

All-Star Pitching

Year	Age	Tm	Lg	W	L	W-L%	ERA	GS	CG	SHO	IP	H	R	ER	BB	SO	WHIP	H9	HR9	BB9	SO9	SO/W
1934	21	EAS	EWA	0	0		0.00	1		0	3.0	1	0	0	0	4	0.667	3.0	3.0	3.0	12.0	4.00
1935	22	EAS	EWA	0	0		0.00	1		0	3.0	2	1	0	3	1	1.000	6.0		6.0	3.0	0.50
2 Yrs (2 GP)				0	0		0.00	2		0	0	6.0	3	1	0	3	5	0.833	3.0		4.5	7.5	1.67

20. The Negro Leagues All-Star Register

Don "Newk" Newcombe

Standard Pitching

Year	Age	Tm	Lg	W	L	W-L%	ERA	G	CG	SHO	IP	H	R	ER	HR	BB	SO	ERA+	WHIP	H9	HR9	BB9	SO9	SO/W
1944	18	NE	NN2	1	3	.250	3.83	9	3	0	42.1	42	22	18		24	21	118	1.559	8.9	0.0	5.1	4.5	0.88
1945	19	NE	NN2	3	3	.500	2.60	7	6	0	55.1	43	23	16	1	16	33	159	1.066	7.0	0.2	2.6	5.4	2.06
1946	20	Nashua	NENL								Played in minor leagues (Integration)													
1947	21	Nashua	NENL								Played in minor leagues (Integration)													
1948	22	Montreal	IL								Played in minor leagues (Integration)													
1949 *	23	BRO	NL	17	8	.680	3.17	38	19	5	244.1	223	89	86	17	73	149	130	1.211	8.2	0.6	2.7	5.5	2.04
1950 *	24	BRO	NL	19	11	.633	3.70	40	20	4	267.1	258	120	110	22	75	130	111	1.246	8.7	0.7	2.5	4.4	1.73
1951 *	25	BRO	NL	20	9	.690	3.28	40	18	3	272.0	235	115	99	19	91	164	120	1.199	7.8	0.6	3.0	5.4	1.80
1952	26										Did not play in major or minor leagues (Military Service)													
1953	27										Did not play in major or minor leagues (Military Service)													
1954	28	BRO	NL	9	8	.529	4.55	29	6	1	144.1	158	81	73	24	49	82	91	1.434	9.9	1.5	3.1	5.1	1.67
1955 *	29	BRO	NL	20	5	.800	3.20	34	17	1	233.2	222	103	83	35	38	143	128	1.113	8.6	1.5	1.5	5.5	3.76
1956	30	BRO	NL	27	7	.794	3.06	38	18	5	268.0	219	101	91	33	46	139	131	0.989	7.4	1.1	1.5	4.7	3.02
1957	31	BRO	NL	11	12	.478	3.49	28	12	0	198.2	199	86	77	28	33	90	118	1.168	9.0	1.3	1.5	4.1	2.73
1958	32	TOTAL	NL	7	13	.350	4.67	31	8	0	167.2	212	98	87	31	36	69	98	1.479	11.4	1.7	1.9	3.7	1.92
1959	33	CIN	NL	13	8	.619	3.16	30	17	2	222.0	216	87	78	25	27	100	129	1.095	8.8	1.0	1.1	4.1	3.70
1960	34	TOTAL	NL+AL	6	9	.400	4.48	36	1	0	136.2	160	76	68	22	22	63	85	1.332	10.5	1.2	1.4	4.1	2.86
12 Yrs (+5)		TOTAL	Pro	153	96	.608	3.54	360	145	24	2252.1	2187	1001	886	253	530	1183	118	1.206	8.7	1.0	2.1	4.7	2.23
2 Yrs			*NgL*	*4*	*6*	*.400*	*3.13*	*16*	*9*	*1*	*97.2*	*85*	*45*	*34*	*1*	*40*	*54*	*141*	*1.280*	*7.8*	*0.1*	*3.7*	*5.0*	*1.35*
10 Yrs			*MLB*	*149*	*90*	*.623*	*3.56*	*344*	*136*	*24*	*2154.2*	*2102*	*956*	*852*	*252*	*490*	*1129*	*117*	*1.203*	*8.8*	*1.1*	*2.0*	*4.7*	*2.30*
162 Game Avg.				19	11	.623	3.56	45	17	3	269.1	263	120	107	32	61	141	15	1.203	8.8	1.1	2.0	4.7	2.30
8 Yrs		BRO/LAD	NL	123	66	.651	3.51	258	111	22	1662.2	1567	732	649	189	413	913	119	1.191	8.5	1.0	2.2	4.9	2.21
3 Yrs		CIN	NL	24	21	.533	3.64	66	25	2	438.0	474	196	177	57	69	189	114	1.240	9.7	1.2	1.4	3.9	2.74
1 Yr		CLE	AL	2	3	.400	4.33	20	0	0	54.0	61	28	26	6	8	27	87	1.278	10.2	1.0	1.3	4.5	3.38
2 Yrs		NE	NN2	4	6	.400	3.13	16	9	0	97.2	85	45	34		40	54	141	1.280	7.8	0.0	3.7	5.0	1.35
9 Yrs			NL	147	87	.628	3.54	324	136	24	2100.2	2041	928	826	246	482	1102	118	1.201	8.7	1.1	2.1	4.7	2.29
1 Yr			AL	2	3	.400	4.33	20	0	0	54.0	61	28	26	6	8	27	87	1.278	10.2	1.0	1.3	4.5	3.38
2 Yrs			NN2	4	6	.400	3.13	16	9	0	97.2	85	45	34		40	54	141	1.280	7.8	0.0	3.7	5.0	1.35

Postseason Pitching

Year	Age	Tm	Lg	Ser	Rslt	Opp	W	L	W-L%	ERA	G	GS	CG	SHO	IP	H	R	ER	BB	SO	WHIP	H9	BB9	SO9	SO/W
1949	23	BRO	NL	WS	L	NYY	0	2	.000	3.09	2	2	1	0	11.2	10	4	4	3	11	1.114	7.7	2.3	8.5	3.67
1955 □	29	BRO	NL	WS	W	NYY	0	1	.000	9.53	1	1	0	0	5.2	8	6	6	2	4	1.765	12.7	3.2	6.4	2
1956	30	BRO	NL	WS	L	NYY	0	1	.000	21.21	2	2	0	0	4.2	11	11	11	0	3		21.2	5.8	7.7	1.33
3 Yrs (3 Series)		BRO	MLB				0	4	.000	8.59	5	5	1	0	22.0	29	21	21	8	19	1.682	11.9	3.3	7.8	2.38
3 Yrs				WS			0	4	.000	8.59	5	5	1	0	22.0	29	21	21	8	19	1.682	11.9	3.3	7.8	2.38

All-Star Pitching

Year	Age	Tm	Lg	W	L	W-L%	ERA	G	CG	SHO	IP	H	R	ER	BB	SO	WHIP	H9	BB9	SO9	SO/W
1949	23	BRO	NL	0	1	.000	6.75	1	0	0	2.2	3	2	2	1	0	1.500	10.1	3.4	0.0	0.0
1950	24	BRO	NL	0	0		9.00	1	0	0	2.0	2	3	2	1	0	2.000	13.5	4.5	0.0	0
1951	25	BRO	NL	0	0		0.00	1	0	0	3.0	2	0	0	0	3	0.667	6.0	0.0	9.0	∞
1955	29	BRO	NL	0	0		0.00	1	0	0	1.0	1	0	0	0	1	1.000	9.0	0.0	9.0	
4 Yrs (4 GP)			MLB	0	1	.000	4.15	4	0	0	8.2	8	5	4	2	4	1.269	9.3	2.1	5.2	2.50

Satchel Paige

Holds NgL records for most strikeouts, lowest ERA, lowest WHIP, most strikeouts per 9 innings, and highest strikeout-to-walk ratio

EXTENDED PITCHING RECORD

Year	Age	Tm	Lg	W	L	W-L%	ERA	G	CG	SHO	IP	H	R	ER	HR	BB	SO	ERA+	WHIP	H9	HR9	BB9	SO9	SO/W
1927	21	BBB	NNL	7	2	.778	2.39	20	5	3	98.0	79	37	26	1	27	93	150	1.082	7.3	0.1	2.5	8.5	3.44
1928	22	BBB	NNL	11	4	.733	2.32	25	10	1	132.0	113	47	34	2	25	121	171	1.045	7.7	0.1	1.7	8.3	4.84
1929	23	BBB	NNL	11	9	.550	3.68	29	14	0	185.2	188	104	76		43	189	118	1.244	9.1		2.1	9.2	4.40
1929/30		Santa Clara CA	CL	6	5	.545		15	8		72.0													
1930	24	TOTALS	NNL+EAS	3	1	.750	0.88	4	3	1	102.2	31	12	10	2	10	22	162	0.399	2.7		0.9	1.9	2.20
1931	25	TOTALS	NNL+IND	4	2	.667	1.76	9	5	1	46.0	43	14	9	2	13	42	308	1.217	8.4	0.4	2.5	8.2	3.23
1931/32		PHI Giants	CWL	6	0	1.000		6	6		58.0						70						10.9	
1932	26	TOTALS	TOTAL	10	6	.625	2.21	23	13	3	138.1	106	50	34	1	50	141	205	1.128	6.9	0.1	3.3	9.2	2.82
		PC	IND	*9*	*6*	*.600*	*2.28*	*22*	*12*	*3*	*130.1*	*100*	*48*	*33*	*1*	*44*	*126*	*188*	*1.105*	*6.9*	*0.1*	*3.0*	*8.7*	*2.86*
			Vs. MLB	1	0	1.000	1.13	1	1	0	8.0	6	2	1	0	6	15	483	1.500	6.8	0.0	6.8	16.9	2.50
1932/33		BEG (Tom Wilson's Elite Giants)		7	0	1.000	0.00	7			63.0						91						13.0	
1933 *	27	TOTALS	TOTAL	10	5	.667	1.61	*19*	15	*0*	150.2	*49*	*33*	*27*		35	188	213	0.826	5.6	0.2	2.1	11.2	5.37
		PC	NN2	*4*	*5*	*.444*	*1.94*	*12*	*8*	*0*	*78.2*	*49*	*23*	*17*	*2*	*16*	*77*					*1.8*	*8.8*	*4.81*
		Bismarck	Ind. Semi-Pro	6	0	1.000	1.25	7	7		72.0		10	10	*2*	19	111					2.4	13.9	5.84
1933/34		BEG (Tom Wilson's Elite Giants)	CWL	16	2	.889	1.62	20	18	7	172.0			31		27	244						12.8	9.04
1934 *	28	PC	NN2	13	3	.813	1.54	19	15	5	145.2	97	36	25	2	30	152	262	0.872	6.0	0.1	1.9	9.4	5.07
1934/35		BEG (Tom Wilson's Elite Giants)	CWL	8	0	1.000		*8*	7		69.0					20	104						13.6	5.20
1935	29	TOTALS	TOTAL	34	2	.944	1.57	41	25	5	298.2	22	56	52	0	22	432	169	0.147	0.7	0.3	0.7	13.0	19.64
		TOTAL	IND	*2*	*0*	*1.000*	*0.22*	*6*	*4*	*3*	*41.0*	*22*	*4*	*1*	*0*	*2*	*67*	*134*	*1.326*	*8.4*	*0.6*	*3.5*	*14.7*	*11.17*
		Bismarck	Ind. Semi-Pro	29	2	.935	1.96	31	18		229.2		50	50		16	321	315	0.706	4.2	0.0	2.1	12.7	6.00
		House of David	Post Tourn	3	0	1.000	0.32	4	3	2	28.0	2		1			44					1.4	13.8	20.06
1935/36		BEG (Tom Wilson's Elite Giants)	CWL	13	0	1.000		13	6		94.0					28	113						10.8	4.04
1936 *	30	TOTALS	TOTAL	13	2	.867	3.86	19	8	2	88.2	75	43	38	5	38	156	87	1.274	7.6	0.5	3.9	15.8	4.11
		PC	NN2	*8*	*2*	*.800*	*3.64*	*11*	*7*	*2*	*71.2*	*67*	*33*	*29*	*5*	*28*	*72*		*1.326*	*8.4*	*0.6*	*3.5*	*9.0*	*2.57*
			Vs. MLB	1	0	1.000	1.06	3	1	0	17.0	8	3	2	0	4	24			4.2	0.0	2.1	12.7	6.00
		Bismarck	Post Tourn.	4	0	1.000	1.62	5			39.0		7	7		6	60					1.4	13.8	10.00
1937	31	TOTALS	TOTAL	*2*	*3*	*.750*	*3.15*	*13*	*2*	*0*	*20.0*	*23*	*9*	*7*	*2*	*4*	*18*	87	*1.350*	10.4	0.9	1.8	8.1	4.50
		SDS	IND	2	1	.500		3	2	0	20.0	23	9	7	2	4	18							
		Ciudad Trujillo	Dom. Lg.	8	2	.800		10																
		Santo Domingo Stars	Post Tourn.							0	19.1	28				12	7	Denver Post Tournament – no statistics recorded						
1939	33	Agrario de México	MEX	1	1	.500		3	0	0						Played in unrecorded barnstorming games								
1939-40		Guayama	PRWL	19	3	.864	1.93	22			205.0		44	44		44	208					1.9	9.1	4.73
1940	34	Guayama	PRWL								81.0					Played in unrecorded barnstorming games								
1940-41		TOTALS	NN2+NAL	4	5	.444	3.89	9	3	0	55.0	39	16	14		5	70	181	0.800	6.4		0.8	7.7	9.40
1941 *	35	KCM	NAL	6	0	1.000	2.29	10	5	0	72.1	62	23	14		11	47	179	1.009	7.7		1.4	7.0	5.09
1942 *	36	TOTALS	NAL	2	5	.286	2.12	11	3	0	123.2	109	52	40	2	31	56		1.132	7.9		2.3	7.4	3.29
1943 *	37	KCM	CWL	10	8	.556	2.91	28	1		36.0					10	102					2.5	9.8	3.90
1943/44		BEG	NAL	3	1	.750	0.72	4	1	3	87.2	53	13	7	5	18	39							
1944 *	38	KCM	NAL	6	4	.667		14	5	*1*	65.0	*33*	*19*	*15*	*5*	22	85	447	0.810	5.4		1.8	8.7	4.72
1945	39	TOTALS	NAL-CWL	4	4	.500	3.55	*10*	2	*1*	38.0	33	19	15	0	18	68		1.132	7.8		3.0	9.4	3.09
1945	39	KCM	NaL	3	1	.500		8	1		27.0					10	41	108				2.4	9.7	4.10
1945	39	KC Royals	CWL	1	3	.500		2	1	0	11.0		15	13	1	12	27					4.0	9.0	2.25
1946	40	TOTALS	TOTAL	4	4	.500	2.66	*13*	1	0	59.0	40	15	13	*1*	17	61	236	1.136	8.2	0.2	2.0	8.2	3.59
1946	40	KCM	NaL	*3*	*0*	*1.000*	*1.67*	*6*	*1*	0	*27.0*	*21*	*5*	*5*	*0*	*4*	*24*		*0.926*	*7.0*	*0.0*	*1.3*	*8.0*	*6.00*
1946	40		Vs. MLB	1	2	.333	4.24	5	0	0	17.0	19	10	8	1	7	16		1.471	10.1	0.5	4.2	8.5	2.67
1947	41	KC Royals	CWL	0	2	.000		2	0		15.0					6	21					3.2		3.00
		TOTALS	NAL-CWL	2	3	.400		*7*	*2*		52.0	*13*	*3*	*2*	*0*	15	78						12.6	5.20
1947-48		Santurce	PRWL	0	3	.000	2.91	*3*			34.0		11	11		13	26					3.4	6.9	2.00

Satchel Paige
EXTENDED PITCHING RECORD (continued)

Year	Age	Tm	Lg	W	L	W-L%	ERA	G	CG	SHO	IP	H	R	ER	HR	BB	SO	ERA+	WHIP	H9	HR9	BB9	SO9	SO/W
1948	43	CLE	AL	6	1	.857	2.48	21	3	2	72.2	61	21	20	2	22	43	165	1.142	7.6	0.2	2.7	5.3	1.95
1949	43	CLE	AL	4	7	.364	3.04	31	1	0	83.0	70	29	28	4	33	54	132	1.241	7.6	0.4	3.6	5.9	1.64
1950	44										Played in unrecorded barnstorming games													
1951	45	SLB	AL	3	4	.429	4.79	23	0	0	62.0	67	39	33	6	29	48	93	1.548	9.7	0.9	4.2	7.0	1.66
1952*	46	SLB	AL	12	10	.545	3.07	46	3	2	138.0	116	51	47	5	57	91	127	1.254	7.6	0.3	3.7	5.9	1.60
1953*	47	SLB	AL	3	9	.250	3.53	57	0	0	117.1	114	51	46	12	39	51	119	1.304	8.7	0.9	3.0	3.9	1.31
1954	48										Played in unrecorded barnstorming games													
1955	49										Played in unrecorded barnstorming games													
1956	50	PHI-min	AAA	11	4	.733	1.86	37	2	2	111.0	101	29	23	4	28	79		1.162	8.2	0.3	2.3	6.4	2.82
1957	51	PHI-min	AAA	10	8	.556	2.42	40	5	1	119.0	98	35	32	15	11	76		0.916	7.4	1.1	0.8	5.7	6.91
1958	52	PHI-min	AAA	10	10	.500	2.95	28	7	1	110.0	94	44	36	8	15	40		0.991	7.7	0.7	1.2	3.3	2.67
1959	53										Played in unrecorded Cuban league													
1960	54										Played in unrecorded semi-pro league													
1961	55	STL-min	AAA	0	0		2.88	5	0	0	25.0	28	12	8	1	5			1.320	10.1	0.4	1.8	0.0	0.00
1965	59	KCA	AL	0	0		0.00	1	0	0	3.0	1	0	0	0	0	1		0.333	3.0	0.0	0.0	3.0	∞
1966	60	CIN-min	A	0	0		9.00	1	0	0	2.0	5	2	2	0	0	0		2.500	22.5	0.0	0.0	0.0	∞
1967	61	AZ Earthquakes	IC								Played in unrecorded semi-pro league													
24 Yrs (+8)			Pro	131	87	.601	2.50	420	111	27	1948.1	1571	689	541	50	506	191		1.066	7.3	0.3	2.3	7.6	3.24
18 Yrs			NgL	103	56	.648	2.24	241	104	23	1472.1	1142	498	367	21	326	212		0.997	7.0	0.2	2.0	8.3	4.15
6 Yrs			MLB	28	31	.475	3.29	179	7	4	476.0	429	191	174	29	180	288		1.279	8.1	0.5	3.4	5.4	1.60
162 Game Avg.			Pro	14	9	.601	2.50	45	12	3	208.2	168	74	58	5	54	21		1.066	7.3	0.3	2.3	7.6	3.24
Minor, Foreign, Winter & Semi-Pro Leagues				167	50	.770	2.28	285	97	6	1820.2	354	304	282	28	313	1640		0.495	8.2	0.1	1.6	9.3	5.79
4 Yrs			AAA	31	22	.585	2.44	110	14		365.0	321	120	99	28	59	1352		1.041	7.9		1.5	4.8	3.31
9 Yrs			CWL	56	7	.889		65	47		571.0					118	288		0.116			1.9	12.1	6.52
4 Yrs			Ind. Semi-Pro	35	2	.946	1.72	38	25		301.2		31	60		35	769					1.0	12.9	12.34
3 Yrs			PRWL	23	11	.676	2.53	34	8		320.0		60	90		83	432		0.259			2.3	8.6	3.66
1 Yr			CL	6	5	.545		15			72.0						304							
3 Yrs			Dom Rep	8	2	.800		10	3	2	67.0	28				6	104		2.069	13.0		5.6	3.3	0.58
1 Yr			Denver Post Tournament	2	1	1.000	.000	2			19.1	5	2	2		12	7		2.500	22.5		0.0	0.0	
1 Yr			MEX	1	1	.500	9.00	3	0	0	2.0	2			0	1	0					0.0	0.0	
3 Yrs			Vs. MLB	0	0		2.36	9	0	0	42.0	33	15	11	1	16	55		0.943	0.0	0.2	2.0	11.8	3.44
TOTALS IN ALL REGULAR-SEASON PLAY				301	139	.684	2.37	714	210	33	3811.0	1958	1008	834	79	835	3506	369	0.646	7.4	0.2	1.9	8.7	4.56
162 Game Avg.				19	9	.684	2.37	45	13	2	240.1	123	64	53	5	53	221							

Postseason Pitching

Year	Age	Tm	Lg	Ser	Rslt	Opp	W	L	W-L%	ERA	G	CG	SHO	IP	H	R	ER	BB	SO	WHIP	H9	HR9	BB9	SO9	SO/W
1927	21	BBB	NNL	NNC L		CAG	0	0		4.35	2		0	10.1	9	6	5	2	7	1.065	7.8	1.7	1.7	6.1	3.50
1942 □	36	KCM	NAL	WS W		HG	2	0	1.000	2.20	4	0	0	16.1	10	6	4	4	18	0.857	5.5	2.2	2.2	9.9	4.50
1946	40	KCM	NAL	WS L		NE	1	1	.500	4.50	3	0	0	10.0	16	7	5	1	13	1.700	14.4	0.9	0.9	11.7	13.00
1948 □	42	CLE	AL	WS W		BSN	0	0		0.00	1	0	0	0.2	0	0	0	0	0	0.000	0.0	0.0	0.0	0.0	∞
4 Yrs (4 Series)			Pro				3	1	.750	3.38	10	0	0	37.1	35	19	14	7	38	1.125	8.4	1.7	1.7	9.2	5.43
3 Yrs (3 Series)			NgL				3	1	.750	3.44	9	0	0	36.2	35	19	14	7	38	1.145	8.6	1.7	1.7	9.3	5.43
1 NNC			NgL				0	0		4.35	2	0	0	10.1	9	6	5	2	7	1.065	7.8	1.7	1.7	6.1	3.50
2 WS			NgL				3	1	.750	3.08	7	0	0	26.1	26	13	9	5	31	1.177	8.9	1.7	1.7	10.6	6.20
1 Yr (1 Series)			MLB				0	0		0.00	1	0	0	0.2	0	0	0	0	0	0.000	0.0	0.0	0.0	0.0	∞
1 WS			MLB				0	0		0.00	1	0	0	0.2	0	0	0	0	0	0.000	0.0	0.0	0.0	0.0	∞

Satchel Paige
All-Star Pitching

Year	Age	Tm	Lg	W	L	W-L%	ERA	GS	IP	CG	SHO	H	R	ER	BB	SO	WHIP	H9	HR9	BB9	SO9	SO/W
1933	27	PC	EAS					DNP														
1934	28	PC	EAS	1	0	1.000	0.00	0	4.0	0	0	3	0	0	0	5	0.750	6.8	0.0	0.0	11.3	∞
1936	30	PC	EAS	0	0		0.00	0	3.0	0	0	2	1	0	0	4	0.667	6.0	0.0	0.0	12.0	∞
1941	35	KCM	WES	0	0		0.00	0	2.0	0	0	1	0	0	1	2	1.000	4.5	0.0	4.5	9.0	2.0
1942	36	KCM	WES	0	1	.000	3.00	0	3.0	0	0	5	3	1	2	2	2.333	15.0	0.0	6.0	6.0	1.0
1943	37	MRS	SAS	1	0	1.000	1.50	1	6.0	0	0	8	1	1	0	5	1.333	12.0	0.0	0.0	7.5	∞
1943	37	KCM	WES	1	0	1.000	0.00	0	3.0	0	0	0	0	0	1	4	0.333	0.0	0.0	3.0	12.0	4.0
1944	38	KCM	WES					DNP														
1952	46	SLB	AL					DNP														
1953	47	SLB	AL	0	0		18.00	0	1.0	0	0	3	2	2	1	0	4.000	27.0	9.0	9.0	0.0	0.0
10 Yrs (7 GP)				**3**	**1**	**.750**	**1.64**	**2**	**22.0**	**0**	**0**	**22**	**7**	**4**	**5**	**22**	**1.227**	**9.0**	**2.0**	**2.0**	**9.0**	**4.4**
8 Yrs (8 GP)			NgL	3	1	.750	0.86	2	21.0	0	0	19	5	2	4	22	1.095	8.1	1.7	1.7	9.4	5.5
2 Yrs (1 GP)			MLB	0	0		18.00	0	1.0	0	0	3	2	2	1	0	4.000	27.0	9.0	9.0	0.0	0.0

Eustaquio Pedroso
Pitched 11-inning no-hitter vs. AL-champion Detroit Tigers in Cuban-American Major League Clubs Series, November 18, 1909

Standard Pitching

Year	Age	Tm	Lg	W	L	W-L%	ERA	G	CG	SHO	IP	H	R	ER	HR	BB	SO	ERA+	WHIP	H9	HR9	BB9	SO9	SO/W
1907	20		CUB								Played in unrecorded Cuban league													
1908	21		CUB								Played in unrecorded Cuban league													
1909	22		CUB								Played in unrecorded Cuban league													
1910	23	CSH	EAS	6	2	.750	1.82	9	7	0	69.1	49	29	14		26	39	218	1.082	6.4	0.0	3.4	5.1	1.50
1911	24	AC2	WES	1	7	.125	4.43	8	8	0	67.0	70	49	33	4	27	44	93	1.448	9.4	0.5	3.6	5.9	1.63
1912	25	CSH	WES	3	3	.500	2.64	10	6	2	64.2	48	29	19	0	19	40	135	1.036	6.7	0.0	2.6	5.6	2.11
1913	26	CSH	WES	5	4	.556	3.81	11	7	0	80.1	90	45	34	1	14	26	98	1.295	10.1	0.1	1.6	2.9	1.86
1914	27	CSH	WES	3	6	.333	3.36	9	9	0	75.0	75	39	30	0	29	42	116	1.295	8.4	0.0	3.2	4.7	1.45
1915	28	CSH	WES	9	7	.563	3.31	21	13	2	138.2	131	75	51	4	61	98	108	1.385	8.5	0.3	4.0	6.4	1.61
1916	29	CSW	WES	6	9	.400	3.91	21	13	1	149.2	155	83	65	4	52	79	81	1.383	9.3	0.2	3.1	4.8	1.52
1917	30	CSW	WES	2	3	.400	3.25	7	4	0	44.1	55	19	16	1	15	17	83	1.579	11.2	0.2	3.0	3.5	1.13
1921	34	ALC	EAS	0	1	.000	9.00	1	0	0	4.0	5	4	4	0	4	0	56	2.250	11.3	0.0	9.0	0.0	0.00
1922	35	CSW	NNL	4	9	.308	6.75	16	10	0	109.1	141	96	82	12	36	53	77	1.619	11.6	1.0	3.0	4.4	1.47
1923	36	CSW	NNL	5	4	.556	4.84	13	7	0	89.1	105	61	48	3	23	28	102	1.433	10.6	0.3	2.3	2.8	1.22
1924	37	CSW	NNL	3	7	.300	6.36	16	8	0	99.0	139	84	70	11	21	36	78	1.616	12.6	1.0	1.9	3.3	1.71
1926	39	CSE	ECL	3	1	.750	2.96	7	4	0	45.2	40	17	15	5	14	10	151	1.182	7.9	1.0	2.8	2.0	0.71
5 Yrs (+11)			**NgL**	**15**	**22**	**.405**	**5.67**	**53**	**29**	**1**	**347.1**	**430**	**263**	**219**	**31**	**98**	**127**	**93**	**1.520**	**11.1**	**0.8**	**2.5**	**3.3**	**1.30**
162 Game Avg.			NgL	13	19	.405	5.67	45	25	1	294.2	365	223	186	26	83	108	79	1.520	11.1	0.8	2.5	3.3	1.30
Pre-NgL				35	41	.461	3.40	96	67	5	694.1	673	368	262	14	243	385	112	1.319	8.7	0.2	3.1	5.0	1.58
Pre-NgL + NgL				**50**	**63**	**.442**	**4.16**	**149**	**96**	**6**	**1041.2**	**1103**	**631**	**481**	**45**	**341**	**512**	**106**	**1.386**	**9.5**	**0.4**	**2.9**	**4.4**	**1.50**
162 Game Avg.				**15**	**19**	**.442**	**4.16**	**45**	**29**	**2**	**314.2**	**333**	**191**	**145**	**14**	**103**	**155**	**106**	**1.386**	**9.5**	**0.4**	**2.9**	**4.4**	**1.50**
3 Yrs		CSW	NNL	12	20	.375	6.05	45	25	1	297.2	385	241	200	26	80	117	85	1.562	11.6	0.8	2.4	3.5	1.46
1 Yr		CSE	ECL	3	1	.750	2.96	7	4	0	45.2	40	17	15	5	14	10	151	1.182	7.9	1.0	2.8	2.0	0.71
1 Yr		ALC	EAS	0	1	.000	9.00	1	0	0	4.0	5	4	4	0	4	0	56	2.250	11.3	0.0	9.0	0.0	0.00
3 Yrs			NNL	12	20	.375	6.05	45	25	1	297.2	385	241	200	26	80	117	85	1.562	11.6	0.8	2.4	3.5	1.46
1 Yr			ECL	3	1	.750	2.96	7	4	0	45.2	40	17	15	5	14	10	151	1.182	7.9	1.0	2.8	2.0	0.71
1 Yr			EAS	0	1	.000	9.00	1	0	0	4.0	5	4	4	0	4	0	56	2.250	11.3	0.0	9.0	0.0	0.00

20. The Negro Leagues All-Star Register

"Cannonball" Dick Redding
Standard Pitching

Year	Age	Tm	Lg	W	L	W-L%	ERA	G	CG	SHO	IP	H	R	ER	HR	BB	SO	ERA+	WHIP	H9	HR9	BB9	SO9	SO/W
1911	21	TOTAL	EAS	8	5	.615	3.58	16	13	0	125.2	115	70	50	3	50	89	118	1.313	8.2	0.2	3.6	6.4	1.78
1912	22	NLG	EAS	5	5	.500	2.20	10	9	1	82	68	28	20	2	17	73	181	1.037	7.5	0.2	1.9	8.0	4.29
1913	23	NLG	EAS	1	0	1.000	4.91	2	1	0	14.2	14	11	8	4	3	2	58	1.159	8.6	2.5	1.8	1.2	0.67
1914	24	NLG	EAS	7	4	.636	4.18	14	9	1	103.1	100	73	48	2	39	62	93	1.345	8.7	0.2	3.4	5.4	1.59
1915	25	TOTAL	EAS	8	4	.667	1.06	19	11	1	119.0	81	31	14	0	33	93	313	0.958	6.1	0.0	2.5	7.0	2.82
1916	26	NLG	EAS	8	2	.800	2.68	10	8	2	80.2	73	36	24	1	23	50	174	1.190	8.1	0.1	2.6	5.6	2.17
1917	27	CAG	WES	14	3	.824	0.70	22	15	5	153.2	87	19	12	0	44	111	258	0.852	5.1	0.0	2.6	6.5	2.52
1918	28	NLG	EAS	4	0	1.000	0.00	4	1	0	18.2	16	3	0	0	4	11		1.071	7.7	0.0	1.9	5.3	2.75
1919	29	TOTAL	EAS	7	4	.636	1.31	12	7	1	96.1	62	21	14	1	23	55	226	0.913	5.8	0.1	2.4	5.1	2.12
1920	30	AC	EAS	16	6	.538	2.72	15	12	3	112.2	100	47	34	2	26	72	83	1.145	8.0	0.2	2.3	5.8	2.48
1921	31	AC	EAS	16	11	.593	3.17	31	22	3	224.1	224	99	79	9	62	130	140	1.275	9.0	0.4	2.5	5.2	2.10
1922	32	NYB	IND	10	8	.556	3.61	23	15	0	154.2	183	75	62	6	42	75	128	1.455	10.6	0.3	2.4	4.4	1.79
1923	33	BRG	ECL	2	4	.333	4.33	9	4	0	68.2	86	42	33	6	15	35	97	1.471	11.3	0.4	2.0	4.6	2.33
1924	34	BRG	ECL	2	4	.333	5.12	6	6	0	51	61	32	29	3	17	24	90	1.529	10.8	0.0	3.0	4.2	1.41
1925	35	BRG	ECL	3	4	.429	4.57	8	4	0	43.1	58	25	22		9	25	116	1.546	12.0	0.0	1.9	5.2	2.78
1926	36	BRG	ECL	1	5	.167	2.98	7	4	0	42.1	35	18	14	1	14	10	145	1.157	7.4	0.2	3.0	2.1	0.71
1927	37	BRG	ECL	1	4	.200	5.10	7	4	0	42.1	50	33	24	3	11	13	95	1.441	10.6	0.6	2.3	2.8	1.18
1928	38	BRG	EAS	1	0	1.000	3.00	1	1	0	9	15	4	3	0	3	5	145	2.000	15.0	0.0	3.0	5.0	1.67
1929	39	BRG	IND	1	0	1.000	0.00	1	1	0	9	3		0	0	2	6		0.556	3.0	0.0	2.0	6.0	3.00
1930	40	BRG	EAS	1	1	.500	3.50	2	2	0	18	20	11	7	1	5	4	191	1.389	10.0	0.5	2.5	2.0	0.80
1931	41	BRG	IND	0	1	.000	13.50	1	0	0	4	7	7	6	2	1	0	25	2.000	15.8	4.5	2.3	0.0	0.00
1933	43										Served as manager													
1936	46	BRG	IND	0	0		54.00	1	0	0	0.1	2	3	2	0	0	0	12	9.000	54.0	0.0	27.0	0.0	0.00
13 Yrs (+9)			NgL	45	48	.484	3.64	112	75	5	779.2	844	396	315	27	211	399	119	1.353	9.7	0.3	2.4	4.6	1.89
162 Game Avg.			NgL	18	19	.484	3.64	45	30	2	313.1	339	159	127	11	85	160	119	1.353	9.7	0.3	2.4	4.6	1.89
Pre-NgL				62	27	.697	2.15	109	74	12	794.0	616	292	190	13	239	546	127	1.077	7.0	0.1	2.7	6.2	2.28
Pre-NgL + NgL				107	75	.588	2.89	221	149	17	1573.2	1460	688	505	40	450	945	158	1.214	8.3	0.2	2.6	5.4	2.10
162 Game Avg.				22	15	.588	2.89	45	30	3	320.1	297	140	103	8	92	192	158	1.214	8.3	0.2	2.6	5.4	2.10
2 Yrs			EAS	23	17	.575	3.02	46	34	5	337.0	324	146	113	11	91	202	121	1.231	8.7	0.3	2.4	5.4	2.22
10 Yrs			ECL+EAS+IND	12	23	.343	4.38	43	26	0	288.0	337	175	140	10	78	122	112	1.441	10.5	0.3	2.4	3.8	1.56
1 Yr			IND	10	8	.556	3.61	23	15	0	154.2	183	75	62	6	42	75	128	1.455	10.6	0.3	2.4	4.4	1.79
4 Yrs			EAS	25	18	.581	3.04	49	37	5	364.0	359	161	123	12	99	211	125	1.258	8.9	0.3	2.4	5.2	2.13
5 Yrs			ECL	9	21	.300	4.43	37	22	0	247.2	290	150	122	7	66	107	107	1.437	10.5	0.3	2.4	3.9	1.62
4 Yrs			IND	11	9	.550	3.75	26	16	0	168.0	195	85	70	8	46	81	125	1.435	10.4	0.4	2.5	4.3	1.76

Charles "Bullet" Rogan

Holds all-time NgL record for wild pitches

Standard Pitching

Year	Age	Tm	Lg	W	L	W-L%	ERA	G	CG	SHO	IP	H	R	ER	HR	BB	SO	ERA+	WHIP	H9	HR9	BB9	SO9	SO/W
1920	26	KCM	NNL	7	5	.583	3.12	14	12	0	121.0	111	55	42	2	43	89	111	1.273	8.3	0.1	3.2	6.6	2.07
1921	27	KCM	NNL	16	8	.667	1.72	26	22	3	204.0	168	74	39	4	71	124	214	1.172	7.4	0.2	3.1	5.5	1.75
1922	28	KCM	NNL	14	8	.636	2.83	26	20	2	193.2	165	87	61	3	45	118	157	1.084	7.7	0.1	2.1	5.5	2.62
1923	29	KCM	NNL	**16**	11	.593	2.94	34	**20**	4	**248.1**	212	111	81	4	77	**151**	137	1.164	7.7	0.1	2.8	5.5	1.96
1924	30	KCM	NNL	**16**	5	.762	3.14	23	17	1	175.0	155	85	61	2	57	101	123	1.211	8.0	0.1	2.9	5.2	1.77
1925	31	KCM	NNL	15	2	**.882**	**1.74**	22	**15**	4	155.1	126	36	30		31	96	278	**1.011**	7.3	0.0	1.8	**5.6**	**3.10**
1926	32	KCM	NNL	12	3	.800	2.86	19	10	0	122.2	119	55	39	3	33	68	144	1.239	8.7	0.2	2.4	5.0	2.06
1927	33	KCM	NNL	14	7	.667	2.32	29	12	4	155.1	142	52	40		33	109	143	1.127	8.2	0.1	1.9	**6.3**	**3.30**
1928	34	KCM	NNL	10	2	.833	3.24	17	8	0	114.0	122	47	41	4	14	54	117	1.193	9.6	0.3	1.1	4.3	3.86
1929	35	KCM	NNL	0	0		0.00	1	0	0	3.0	2	0	0	0	0	3		0.667	6.0	0.0	0.0	9.0	∞
1930	36	KCM	IND										No pitching statistics recorded												
1932	38	Jamestown ND											Played for unrecorded independent team												
1933	39	KCM	IND	0	0		13.50	1	0	0	1.1	4	3	2	0	0	0	18	3.000	27.0	0.0	0.0	0.0	∞
1934	40	KCM	IND										No pitching statistics recorded												
1935	41	KCM	IND	1	0	1.000	4.76	1	0	0	5.2	6	5	3	3	1	1	79	1.235	9.5	4.8	1.6	1.6	1.00
1936	42	KCM	IND	1	0	1.000	0.00	1	0	0	6.0	3	0	0	0	0	3		0.500	4.5	0.0	0.0	4.5	∞
1937	43	KCM	NAL	0	1	.000	13.50	2	0	0	5.1	7	9	8	0	1	5	31	1.500	11.8	0.0	1.7	8.4	5.00
1938	44	KCM	NAL	0	0		0.00	1	0	0	2.0	1	0	0	0	0	0		0.500	4.5	0.0	0.0	0.0	∞
17 Yrs (+I)				122	52	.701	**2.66**	217	136	18	1512.2	1343	619	447	25	406	922	160	1.156	**8.0**	**0.1**	2.4	**5.5**	2.27
162 Game Avg.				25	11	.701	**2.66**	45	28	4	313.2	279	128	93	5	84	191	33	1.156	**8.0**	**0.1**	2.4	**5.5**	2.27
17 Yrs		KCM	NNL+NAL+IND	122	52	.701	2.66	217	136	18	1512.2	1343	619	447	25	406	922	160	1.156	8.0	0.1	2.4	5.5	2.27
11 Yrs			NNL	120	51	.702	2.62	211	136	18	1492.1	1322	602	434	22	404	913	161	1.157	8.0	0.1	2.4	5.5	2.26
4 Yrs			IND	2	0	1.000	3.46	3	0	0	13.0	13	8	5	3	1	4	67	1.077	9.0	2.1	0.7	2.8	4.00
2 Yrs			NAL	0	1	.000	9.82	3	0	0	7.1	8	9	8	0	1	5	31	1.227	9.8	0.0	1.2	6.1	5.00

Postseason Pitching

Year	Age	Tm	Lg	Ser	Rslt	Opp	W	L	W-L%	ERA	G	CG	SHO	IP	H	R	ER	HR	BB	SO	WHIP	H9	HR9	BB9	SO9	SO/W
1924 □	30	KCM	NNL	WS	W	HC	2	1	.667	2.89	4	3	0	28	25	9	9	0	9	13	1.214	8.0	0.0	2.9	4.2	1.44
1925 □	31	KCM	NNL	NNC	W	SLS	3	0	1.000	2.42	3	3	1	26	23	10	7	2	2	17	0.962	8.0	0.7	0.7	5.9	8.50
1926 □	32	KCM	NNL	NNC	L	CAG	3	1	.750	2.84	4	2	0	25.1	21	8	8	3	10	14	1.224	7.5	1.1	3.6	5.0	1.40
1937 □	43	KCM	NAL	ALC	W	CAG										No pitching statistics recorded										
4 Yrs (3 Series)			NgL				8	2	.800	2.72	11	8	1	79.1	69	27	24	5	21	44	1.134	7.8	0.6	2.4	5.0	2.10
2 Yrs				NNC			6	1	.857	2.63	7	5	1	51.1	44	18	15	5	12	31	1.091	7.7	0.9	2.1	5.4	2.58
1 Yr				WS			2	1	.667	2.89	4	3	0	28	25	9	9	0	9	13	1.214	8.0	0.0	2.9	4.2	

20. The Negro Leagues All-Star Register

Elvis "Hilton" Smith

Standard Pitching

Year	Age	Tm	Lg	W	L	W-L%	ERA	G	CG	SHO	IP	H	R	ER	BB	HR	BB	SO	ERA+	WHIP	H9	HR9	BB9	SO9	SO/W
1932	25	MRM	NSL	0	0		4.76	1	0	0	5.2	6		3	0			2	66	1.059	9.5	0.0	0.0	3.2	∞
1933	26	MRM	IND								Played in unrecorded Black league														
1934	27	MRM	IND								Played in unrecorded Black league														
1935	28	BIS	IND	0	1	.000	4.50	1	0	0	2.0	3	3	1	1	0	1	2	82	2.000	13.5	0.0	4.5	9.0	2.00
1936	29	KCM	IND	0	0		9.00	1	0	0	2.0	5	3	2	0	3	3	2	56	4.000	22.5	0.0	13.5	9.0	0.67
1937 *	30	KCM	NAL	11	4	.733	1.59	21	9	3	130.1	85	32	23	27	2	27	99		0.859	5.9	0.1	1.9	6.8	3.67
1938 *	31	KCM	NAL	7	2	.778	1.88	17	6	1	100.2	89	32	21	11	3	11	79	197	0.993	8.0	0.3	1.0	7.1	7.18
1939 *	32	KCM	NAL	6	5	.545	2.43	20	6	1	111.1	87	44	30	21		21	85	151	0.970	7.0	0.0	1.7	6.9	4.05
1940 *	33	KCM	NAL	8	8	.500	4.76	26	7	1	132.1	140	82	70	38		38	102	92	1.345	9.5	0.0	2.6	6.9	2.68
		TOTAL	MEX+NAL	5	3	.625	5.09	14	2		86.2	95	55	49	27		27	60	95	1.408	9.9	0.0	2.8	6.2	2.22
		ULT	MEX								No statistics recorded														
		JNL	NAL	3	5	.375	4.14	12	3	0	45.2	45	27	21	11		11	42	85	1.226	8.9	0.0	2.2	8.3	3.82
1941 *	34	KCM	NAL	13	5	.722	2.58	25	9	2	139.1	103	46	40	36		36	88	176	0.998	6.7	0.0	2.3	5.7	2.44
		TOTAL	MEX+NAL	3	5	.375	3.88	12	3		62.2	49	32	27	28		28	35	123	1.229	7.0	0.0	4.0	5.0	1.25
		ULT	MEX	10	0	1.000	1.53	13	6	2	76.2	54	46	13	8		8	53	220	0.809	6.3	0.0	0.9	6.2	6.63
1942 *	35	KCM	NAL	5	4	.556	4.69	11	4	0	71.0	79	46	37	15		15	42	81	1.324	10.0	0.0	1.9	5.3	2.80
1943	36	KCM	NAL	3	2	.600	2.70	9	3		50.0	42	15	15	9		9	24	137	1.020	7.6	0.0	1.6	4.3	2.67
1944	37	KCM	NAL	2	1	.667	0.79	5	1		22.2	11	4	2	3		3	8	405	0.618	4.4	0.0	1.2	3.2	2.67
1945	38	KCM	NAL	6	4	.600	3.27	11	6	0	77.0	76	37	28	19	2	19	42	117	1.234	8.9	0.2	2.2	4.9	2.21
1946	39	KCM	NAL	4	2	.667	1.70	7	3	0	47.2	39	14	9	10	2	10	15	231	1.028	7.4	0.2	1.9	2.8	1.50
1947	40	KCM	NAL	7	4	.636	5.47	15	6	0	75.2	104	54	46	13	2	13	25	78	1.546	12.4	0.2	1.5	3.0	1.92
1948	41	KCM	NAL	4	2	.667	3.96	11	4		63.2	72	39	28	22	2	22	39	113	1.476	10.2	0.3	3.1	5.5	1.77
15 Yrs (+2)				**76**	**44**	**.633**	**3.10**	**179**	**67**	**8**	**1031.1**	**941**	**455**	**355**	**228**	**12**	**228**	**654**	**157**	**1.133**	**8.2**	**0.1**	**2.0**	**5.7**	**2.87**
162 Game Avg.				**19**	**11**	**.633**	**3.10**	**45**	**17**	**2**	**259.1**	**237**	**114**	**89**	**57**	**3**	**57**	**164**	**40**	**1.133**	**8.2**	**0.1**	**2.0**	**5.7**	**2.87**
13 Yrs		KCM	NAL-IND	68	35	.660	2.82	149	58	7	870.1	782	359	273	169	12	169	551	167	1.093	8.1	0.1	1.7	5.7	3.26
2 Yrs		ULT	MEX	8	8	.500	4.58	26	9		149.1	144	87	76	55	0	55	95	107	1.333	8.7	0.0	3.3	5.7	1.73
1 Yr		MRM	NSL	0	0		4.76	1	0	0	5.2	6		3	0			2	66	1.059	9.5	0.0	0.0	3.2	∞
1 Yr		BIS	IND	0	1		4.50	1	0	0	2.0	3	3	1	1	0	1	2	82	2.000	13.5	0.0	4.5	9.0	2.00
1 Yr		CAG	IND	0	0		0.00	1	0	0	2.0	1	0	0	0	0	0	2		0.500	4.5	0.0	0.0	9.0	∞
12 Yrs		KCM	NAL	68	35	.660	2.82	150	58	7	872.1	783	359	273	169	12	169	553	167	1.091	8.1	0.1	1.7	5.7	3.27
2 Yrs		KCM	MEX	8	8	.500	4.58	26	9		149.1	144	87	76	55	0	55	95	107	1.333	8.7	0.0	3.3	5.7	1.73
1 Yr		KCM	NSL	0	0		4.76	1	0	0	5.2	6	4	3	0		0	2	66	1.059	9.5	0.0	0.0	3.2	∞
2 Yrs		KCM	IND	0	1		6.75	2	0	0	4.0	8	5	3	4		4	4	69	3.000	18.0	0.0	9.0	9.0	1.00

Postseason Pitching

Year	Age	Tm	Lg	W	L	W-L%	ERA	G	CG	SHO	IP	H	R	ER	BB	H	R	ER	BB	SO	WHIP	H9	HR9	BB9	SO9	SO/W
1937 □	30	KCM	NAL	0	0		2.40	3	0	0	15.0			4		19	4	4	1	17	1.533	11.4		2.4	10.2	4.25
1939 □	32	KCM	NAL	0	1	.000	1.26	3	1	0	14.1	14		2		14	2	2	1	19	1.186	8.8		1.9	11.9	6.33
1942 □	35	KCM	NAL	1	0	1.000	0.00	1	0	0	5.0	5		0		5	0	0	2	2	1.400	9.0		3.6	3.6	1.00
1946	39	KCM	NAL	0	1	.000	1.29	2	1		14.0	15		2		15	2	2	1	7	1.286	9.6		1.9	4.5	2.33
4 Yrs (4 Series)		NgL		**1**	**3**	**.250**	**1.49**	**9**	**2**	**0**	**48.1**			**8**		**48**	**8**	**8**	**12**	**45**	**1.243**	**9.0**		**2.2**	**8.4**	**3.75**
2 Yrs			ALC	0	2	.000	1.84	6	1	0	29.1			6		29	6	6	7	36	1.231	8.9		2.1	11.0	5.14
2 Yrs			WS	1	1	.500	0.95	3	1	0	19.0			2		19	2	2	5	9	1.263	9.0		2.4	4.3	1.80

Postseason Pitching (Series)

Year	Age	Tm	Lg	Ser	Rslt	Opp	W	L	W-L%	ERA
1937 □	30	KCM	NAL	ALC	W	CAG	0	0		∞
1939 □	32	KCM	NAL	ALC	W	SLS	1	0	1.000	2.25
1942 □	35	KCM	NAL	WS	W	HG	0	0		6.00
1946	39	KCM	NAL	WS	L	NE	0	1	.000	6.00

All-Star Pitching

Year	Age	Tm	Lg	W	L	W-L%	ERA	G	GS	CG	SHO	IP	H	R	ER	BB	SO	WHIP	H9	HR9	BB9	SO9	SO/W
1937	30	WES	EWA	0	0		∞	1	0	0	0	0	0	2		1	0	∞	∞		∞	0.0	0.00
1938	31	WES	EWA	1	0	1.000	2.25	1		1	0	4	3	1	1	1	3	1.000	6.8		2.3	6.8	3.00
1939	32	WES	EWA x2	0	0		0.00	2		0	0	6	4	0	0	1	4	0.833	6.0		1.5	6.0	4.00
1940	33	WES	EWA	0	0		6.00	1		0	0	3	4	2	2	1	3	1.333	12.0		3.0	9.0	∞
1941	34	WES	EWA	0	1	.000	3.00	1		1	0	3	2	1	1	2	2	1.333	6.0		6.0	9.0	∞
1942	35	WES	EWA	0	0		∞	1		0	0	0	2	0	0	1	0	∞	∞		∞	0.0	∞
6 Yrs (7 GP)				**1**	**1**	**.500**	**4.26**	**7**		**2**	**0**	**19.0**	**18**		**9**	**4**	**16**	**1.158**	**8.5**		**1.9**	**7.6**	**4.00**

"Cyclone" Joe Williams
Standard Pitching

Year	Age	Tm	Lg	W	L	W-L%	ERA	G	CG	SHO	IP	H	R	ER	HR	BB	SO	ERA+	WHIP	H9	HR9	BB9	SO9	SO/W
1907	21	SBB	SOU	2	0	1.000	2.00	2	2	0	18	13	7	4	1	2	11	122	0.833	6.5	0.5	1.0	5.5	5.50
1908	22	SBB	SOU	1	2	.333	0.33	3	3	0	27	9	3	1	0	3	27	103	0.444	3.0	0.0	1.0	9.0	9.00
1909	23	SBB	WES	0	1	.000	3.38	1	1	0	8	8	4	3	0	0	8	95	1.250	9.0	0.0	2.3	9.0	4.00
1910	24	COG	WES	5	2	.714	1.89	8	5	0	57	44	20	12	0	8	45	146	0.912	6.9	0.0	1.3	7.1	5.63
1911	25	COG	WES	3	5	.375	4.10	10	6	2	68	74	37	31	2	25	52	81	1.456	9.8	0.3	3.3	6.9	2.08
1912	26	NLG	EAS	7	2	.778	2.18	11	9	0	86.2	76	29	21	1	15	61	182	1.050	7.9	0.1	1.6	6.3	4.07
1913	27	NLG	EAS	9	2	.818	1.87	14	11	3	101.1	111	34	21	1	25	70	153	1.342	9.9	0.1	2.2	6.2	2.80
1914	28	NLG	EAS	5	3	.625	2.36	10	5	1	68.2	68	33	18	0	21	43	166	**1.296**	8.9	0.1	2.8	5.6	2.05
1915	29	NLG	EAS	6	1	.857	2.10	7	5	0	55.2	49	24	13	0	17	34	152	1.060	7.9	0.1	1.6	5.5	**3.40**
1916	30	NLG	EAS	5	2	.714	1.56	9	6	0	63.1	70	21	11	0	17	37	299	1.374	9.9	0.1	2.4	5.3	2.18
1917	31	NLG	EAS	**10**	0	**1.000**	1.69	12	9	0	101	88	30	19	0	31	70	263	1.178	7.8	0.0	2.8	6.2	2.26
1918	32	NLG	EAS	**10**	6	.625	1.07	16	**14**	0	**134.2**	**128**	43	16	1	**32**	**93**	297	**1.188**	8.6	0.1	**2.1**	**6.2**	**2.91**
1919	33	NLG	EAS	9	3	.750	2.63	13	**11**	**2**	102.2	93	48	**30**	1	21	**86**	124	1.120	8.2	0.1	1.9	**7.5**	**3.91**
1920	34	NLG	EAS	2	3	.400	1.84	5	5	1	44	42	18	9	0	7	26	129	1.114	8.6	0.0	1.4	5.3	3.71
1921	35	NLG	EAS	3	1	.750	3.05	5	2	0	20.2	17	9	7	1	4	16	184	1.016	7.4	0.4	1.7	7.0	4.00
1922	36	NLG	IND	4	3	.571	1.91	8	6	0	56.2	51	18	12	0	12	40	251	1.112	8.1	0.0	1.9	6.4	3.33
1923	37	NLG	IND	3	3	.500	4.80	15	4	0	54.1	66	44	29	2	6	33	93	1.325	10.9	0.3	1.0	5.5	5.50
1924	38	BRG	ECL	3	8	.273	3.74	15	8	0	96.1	107	54	40	0	13	55	124	1.246	10.0	0.0	1.2	5.1	**4.23**
1925	39	BRG	ECL	2	0	1.000	2.25	2	2	0	16	10	4	4	2	4	22	100	0.875	5.6	1.1	2.3	12.4	5.50
1926	40	HG	IND	0	0		4.00	1	1	0	9	11	4	4	0	0	7	81	1.222	11.0	0.0	0.0	7.0	∞
1927	41	HG	IND	2	0	1.000	1.13	2	1	0	16	9	2	2	0	1	16	224	0.625	5.1	0.0	0.6	9.0	16.00
1928	42	HG	IND	3	1	.750	4.50	4	2	0	28	32	16	14	2	5	16	91	1.321	10.3	0.6	1.6	5.1	3.20
1929	43	HG	EAS	5	7	.417	3.26	18	13	0	129.2	134	65	47	7	28	85	165	1.249	9.3	0.5	1.9	5.9	3.04
1930	44	HG	ANL	**11**	5	.688	2.60	17	**13**	**1**	131.1	104	49	38	6	22	**116**	205	0.959	7.1	0.4	**1.5**	7.9	**5.27**
1931	45	HG	IND	6	2	.750	2.41	11	7	0	78.1	59	26	21	1	25	54	152	1.072	6.8	0.1	2.9	6.2	2.16
1932	46	TOTAL	EWL	5	1	.833	2.72	12	7	0	76.0	77	32	23	0	19	28	163	1.263	9.1	0.0	2.3	3.3	1.47
13 Yrs (+13)				49	34	.590	2.97	108	68	4	756.1	719	341	250	21	146	514	161	1.144	8.6	0.25	1.7	6.1	3.52
162 Game Avg.				735	510	.590	2.97	1620	1020	60	11345.0	10785	5115	3750	315	2190	7710	161	1.144	8.6	0.25	1.7	6.1	3.52
Pre-NgL				72	29	.713	2.02	116	87	11	892.0	831	333	200	9	213	637	189	1.170	8.4	0.09	2.1	6.4	2.99
Pre-NgL + NgL				121	63	.658	2.46	224	155	15	1648.1	1550	674	450	30	359	1151	176	1.158	8.5	0.16	2.0	6.3	3.21
162 Game Avg.				605	315	.658	2.46	1120	775	75	8241.2	7750	3370	2250	150	1795	5755	176	1.158	8.5	0.16	2.0	6.3	3.21
8 Yrs		HG	EAS+ANL+EWL+IND	33	16	.673	2.81	63	42	2	457.1	407	185	143	18	99	333	170	1.106	8.0	0.35	1.9	6.6	3.36
4 Yrs		NLG	EAS	12	10	.545	2.92	26	17	1	175.2	176	89	57	3	29	115	164	1.167	9.0	0.15	1.5	5.9	3.97
1 Yr		BRG	ECL	3	8	.273	3.74	15	8	0	96.1	107	54	40	0	13	55	124	1.246	10.0	0.00	1.2	5.1	4.23
1 Yr		DW	EWL	1	0	1.000	3.33	4	1	0	27.0	29	13	10	0	5	11	127	1.259	9.7	0.00	1.7	3.7	2.20
4 Yrs			EAS	19	10	.655	2.73	31	22	1	224.0	195	92	68	9	38	174	174	1.040	7.8	0.36	1.5	7.0	4.58
5 Yrs			IND	14	5	.737	2.20	24	18	1	176.0	140	54	43	3	42	139	182	1.034	7.2	0.15	2.1	7.1	3.31
2 Yrs			ECL	6	11	.353	4.12	23	12	0	150.2	173	98	69	2	19	88	113	1.274	10.3	0.12	1.1	5.3	4.63
1 Yr			ANL	5	7	.417	3.26	18	13	1	129.2	134	65	47	7	28	85	165	1.249	9.3	0.49	1.9	5.9	3.04
1 Yr			EWL	5	1	.833	2.72	12	3	0	76.0	77	32	23	0	19	28	163	1.263	9.1	0.00	2.3	3.3	1.47

21

A Proposed Major Leagues Organizational Chart

Here's a chart of the leagues I assert should be recognized as Major Leagues. A number of other, non–Major leagues, marked in *italics*, are included for purposes of historical illustration.

My definition of Negro Leagues as Major Leagues, which I urge MLB and Baseball Reference to adopt, differs from theirs in two key respects. First, my system includes inter-league play by independent teams affiliated with established NgL structures (detailed in the next section); second, I include the Mexican Leagues for two years only, 1940 and 1941.

Drawn by outrageous salary offers from owners determined to establish the MEX as North America's top Black league, NgL players—whose pay was far from commensurate with their Major League brethren—flocked south by the score, including Sam Bankhead, Cool Papa Bell, Willard Brown, Ray Dandridge, Martin Dihigo, Josh Gibson, Sammy Hughes, Ted Strong, Quincy Trouppe, Willie Wells, Wild Bill Wright, and many others. The quality of MEX play obviously soared (can you name a league that *wouldn't* be improved by Josh Gibson?); they probably had more great Black players in those two years than either the NN2 or NAL. (This wasn't the Mexican League's only attempt to establish itself as a top-level league: the original version of the 1946 MacPhail Report complains about "the Mexican raids on our players.")[1]

(See charts on the following pages.)

A Proposed Major Leagues Organizational Chart

(Leagues whose names are printed in italics are not considered Major Leagues; they are included here for illustrative purposes)

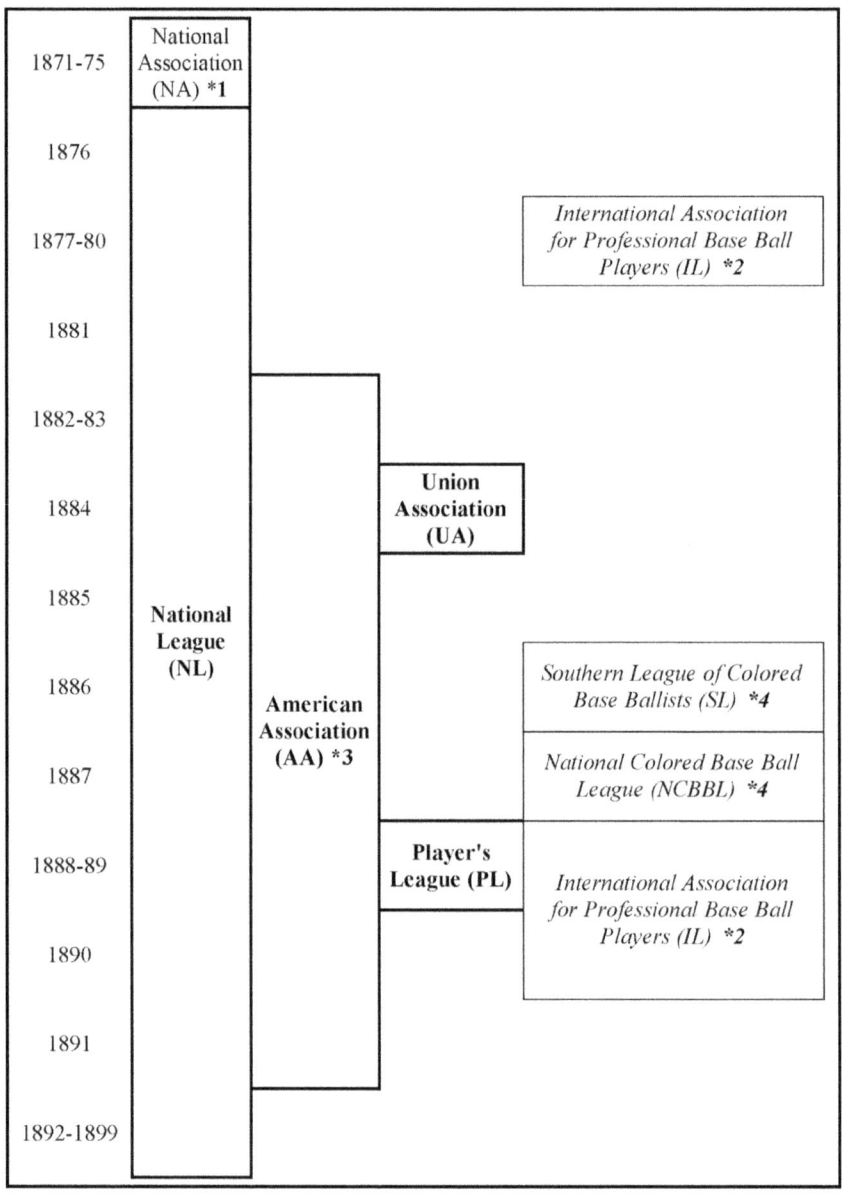

21. A Proposed Major Leagues Organizational Chart

Years	NL	AL	FL/NNL	Other
1900		*American Baseball League*		
1901-05				
1906				International League of Independent Professional Base Ball Clubs (INL) *4
1907-10				National Association of Colored Baseball Clubs of the United States & Cuba (NAC) *4
1911				
1912				United States Baseball League (USBL) *2
1913	**National League (NL)**	**American League (AL)**	*Federal League (FL)*	
1914-15			**Federal League (FL)**	
1916-19				
1920-22			**Negro National League (NNL) *5**	Independent Black teams (IND)
1923-28				Eastern Colored League (ECL)
1929				American Negro League (ANL)
1930-31				Independent Black teams (EAS/IND)

1932			Negro Southern League (NSL)	East-West League (EWL)	
1933-36			Independent Black teams (IND)		
1937-38					
1939					*Negro American Association (NAA) *4*
1940-41				Negro National League (NN2) *6	Mexican League (MEX)
1942-44			Negro American League (NAL)		
1945-46	National League (NL)	American League (AL)			*United States League (USL) *4*
1947					
1948					*Negro American Association (NAA) *4*
1949					
1950-51			NAL *7	(NN2 absorbed by NAL)	
1952-62					
1963-					

*1. The National Association's status as a Major League is disputed; Retrosheet and SABR consider its numbers valid, MLB and the Hall of Fame do not.
*2. The IL (which existed in two incarnations from 1877–80 and from 1888–90) and the USBL were established as intended rivals to the existing professional leagues, but are generally not accorded the status of top-level pro leagues.
*3. Not to be confused with the minor-league American Association, which operated from 1902–62 and 1969–97.
*4. The SL, the NCBBL, the INL, the NAC, the NAA and the USL are generally not accorded the status of top-level pro leagues; the NCL, the USL, and the first (1939) incarnation of the NAA were in fact formed specifically as Black minor leagues. They are listed here as an acknowledgment of the multiple attempts by owners of Black independent teams to form economically sustainable organized leagues.
*5. The 1920 season marks the beginning of general recognition of the Negro Leagues, including affiliated independent teams, as top-level pro leagues.
*6. The NN2 was also known as the East-West League for 1934–35.
*7. Post-1948 Black leagues are generally not accorded the status of top-level professional leagues.

22

A Proposed Negro Leagues Team Roster

This chart lists every NgL team that should, in my view, be considered Major League, together with their league affiliations. Years in which teams competed as independent entities, currently excluded from Baseball Reference, are printed in **bold**. (The Mexican Leagues for 1940 and 1941, which I believe should be included in their entirety within the Major League record, are not included in the chart, for the sake of maintaining a semblance of clarity in an already complex illustration.)

Some top-level NgL squads never associated themselves with established leagues, playing instead as wholly independent teams; others, like the Homestead Grays, cycled in and out of league affiliations as suited their financial situation. For three years, 1925–27, the Grays, one of the strongest and certainly the most iconic of all NgL teams, achieved that rarest of Negro Leagues trifecta: they maintained their independence from league structures, stayed afloat financially, and engaged in regular competition with league-affiliated teams.

Oscar Charleston played for the Grays in 1926; Martin Dihigo and Biz Mackey were on the roster in 1927; Cyclone Williams pitched for the Grays all three years. Did these Hall of Fame giants lack big league skills just for the years they played with the independent Grays?

In 1929 the Grays were affiliated with the ANL; in 1930, with Eastern independent clubs; in 1931 they were a wholly independent franchise; in 1932 they were with the EWL; in 1933, with the NN2. The independent Grays squad of 1931, which featured Gibson, Charleston, Jud Wilson and Cyclone Williams, is sometimes cited as the greatest professional team of all time, in any league—but Baseball Reference omits its statistics entirely.

Did the Grays somehow shed their top-level status in 1930 and 1931, only to regain it arbitrarily in 1932? Isn't the proposition self-evidently ridiculous?

The weakest claim to Major League status among NgL independent clubs listed by Seamheads is probably held by the 1935 Bismarck Club. It's true that 10 of the club's 18 players made no appearance in NgL play other than with this one team. But this was no pickup squad: the roster also included NgL All-Stars Barney Morris, Satchel Paige, Ted "Double Duty" Radcliffe, Hilton Smith and Quincy Trouppe, and the team succeeded in winning or drawing exactly half of its eight games against established NgL clubs.

John Donaldson's All-Stars, which played only the 1932 season, also had two

The 1931 Homestead Grays. Can a team with seven Hall of Famers (five pictured here) be other than Major League? Back row, from left: Cum Posey, Bill Evans, Jasper Washington, Ambrose Reid, Cyclone Joe Williams, Josh Gibson, George Scales, Oscar Charleston, Charlie Williams. Front row, from left: George Britt, Charles Henry Williams, Jud Wilson, Vic Harris, Double Duty Radcliffe, Tex Burnett, and Ted Page (courtesy of Heritage Auctions, HA.com).

players who appeared in NgL ranks only for this one team—but the other nine players on the squad were all established Major Leaguers.

Beyond these two teams, every independent squad listed by Seamheads has what I regard as solid big league credentials. Expanding the Major League database to encompass them is no different in substance than including the records of the 73 MLB teams that failed to see the dawn of the 20th century.

It's as necessary to include NgL-affiliated independent teams and the 1940–41 Mexican League in Major League records as it is to include the 1890 Players' League, and for the same reason: to eliminate irrational gaps in the records of countless worthy players, whose careers are otherwise truncated by the economic instability that forced teams to form and break league affiliations each and every year. For the sake of fairness and equity in the process of statistical integration, these teams simply must be included.

As for the chart itself: Like any illustration that would attempt to tackle this thorny issue, this is an oversimplification of a fantastically complex business and financial situation. I've done my best to get it right. The stories of these teams involve not only sudden team collapse and equally sudden regeneration, but also endless swapping between major league, minor league, and independent status, all while jumping in and out of league affiliations.

22. A Proposed Negro Leagues Team Roster

I present the chart for two reasons: first, to illustrate which independent clubs I believe should be included in the MLB database, and second, in the hope that it might help the reader to untangle the ever-shifting cacophony of NgL team names and league affiliations.

(See charts on the following eight pages.)

A Proposed Negro League Team Roster

	1920	1921	1922	1923	1924	1925	1926	1927	1928	1929	1930	1931
Akron Grays (aka Akron Black Tyrites)												
Cleveland Giants												
Columbus Blue Birds												
All Cubans		IND										
Atlanta Black Crackers (1)												
Indianapolis ABCs (4)												
Atlanta Black Crackers (2)												
Atlantic City Bacharach Giants	IND				ECL	ECL	ECL	ECL	ECL	ANL		
New York Bacharach Giants			IND									
Original Bacharach Giants			IND									
Baltimore Black Sox (1)	IND	IND	IND		ECL	ECL	ECL	ECL	ANL	IND	IND	
Baltimore Sox												
Baltimore Black Sox (2)												
Nashville Elite Giants										IND	NNL	
Cleveland Cubs (aka Foster Memorial Giants)											NNL	
Columbus Elite Giants												
Washington Elite Giants												
Baltimore Elite Giants												
Birmingham Black Barons				IND	NNL	NNL		NNL	NNL	NNL	NNL	
Bismarck Club												
Brooklyn Royal Giants	IND	IND	IND		ECL	ECL	ECL	ECL	IND	IND	IND	IND
Chicago American Giants	NNL	NNL	NNL	NNL	NNL	NNL	NNL	NNL	NNL	NNL	NNL	
Chicago Columbia Giants												NNL
Chicago Giants	NNL	NNL										
Cincinnati Tigers												
Cleveland Browns					NNL							

22. A Proposed Negro Leagues Team Roster

1932	1933	1934	1935	1936	1937	1938	1939	1940	1941	1942	1943	1944	1945	1946	1947	1948
	NN2															
NSL					IND	NAL	NAL									
											IND	IND				
EWL																
	NN2															
		NN2														
NSL	NN2	NN2														
				NN2												
					NN2	NN2										
							NN2	NN2	NN2	NN2	NN2	NN2	NN2	NN2	NN2	NN2
NSL					NAL	NAL		NAL	NAL	NAL	NAL	NAL	NAL	NAL	NAL	NAL
			IND													
	IND				IND	IND										
NSL	NN2	NN2	NN2	IND	NAL	NAL	NAL	NAL	NAL	NAL	NAL	NAL	NAL	NAL	NAL	NAL
				IND	NAL											

| 1932 | 1933 | 1934 | 1935 | 1936 | 1937 | 1938 | 1939 | 1940 | 1941 | 1942 | 1943 | 1944 | 1945 | 1946 | 1947 | 1948 |

	1920	1921	1922	1923	1924	1925	1926	1927	1928	1929	1930	1931
Cincinnati-Cleveland Buckeyes												
Cleveland Buckeyes												
Cleveland Elites							NNL					
Cleveland Hornets								NNL				
Cleveland Tigers									NNL			
Cleveland Red Sox												
Cleveland Stars												
Cleveland Tate Stars		IND	NNL	IND								
Colored All Stars									IND			
Columbus Buckeyes		NNL										
Cuban House of David												IND
Cuban Stars East (1)	IND	IND	IND		ECL	ECL	ECL	ECL	ECL	ANL		
Cuban Stars East (2)												
Cuban Stars West	NNL		NNL	NNL	NNL	NNL	NNL	NNL	NNL	NNL	NNL	NNL
Cincinnati Cuban Stars		NNL										
Danny McClellan's All Stars										IND		
Dayton Marcos	NNL							NNL				
Detroit Stars (1)	NNL	NNL	NNL	NNL	NNL	NNL	NNL	NNL	NNL	NNL	NNL	NNL
Detroit Stars (3)												
Detroit Wolves												
Donaldson's All Stars												
Eastern League Stars										IND		
Harrisburg Giants			IND	IND	ECL	ECL	ECL	ECL				
Hilldale Club (aka Hilldale Daisies, Darby Daisies)	IND	IND	IND		ECL	ECL	ECL	ECL	IND	ANL	IND	IND
Homestead Grays		IND	IND		IND	IND	IND	IND	IND	ANL	IND	IND
Indianapolis ABCs (1)	NNL	NNL	NNL	NNL	NNL	NNL	NNL					
Indianapolis ABCs (2) *Detroit Stars (2)*												NNL
Indianapolis Athletics												
	1920	1921	1922	1923	1924	1925	1926	1927	1928	1929	1930	1931

1932	1933	1934	1935	1936	1937	1938	1939	1940	1941	1942	1943	1944	1945	1946	1947	1948
										NAL						
											NAL	NAL	NAL	NAL	NAL	NAL
		NN2														
EWL																
IND	IND	IND	IND	IND	IND											
					NAL											
EWL																
IND																
EWL																
EWL	NN2	IND	NN2	NN2	NN2	NN2	NN2	NN2	NN2	NN2	NN2	NN2	NN2	NN2	NN2	NN2
NSL	NN2															
					NAL											
1932	1933	1934	1935	1936	1937	1938	1939	1940	1941	1942	1943	1944	1945	1946	1947	1948

Team	1920	1921	1922	1923	1924	1925	1926	1927	1928	1929	1930	1931
Cincinnati Clowns												
Cincinnati-Indianapolis Clowns												
Indianapolis Clowns												
Jacksonville Red Caps												
Cleveland Bears												
Kansas City Monarchs	NNL	NNL	NNL	NNL	NNL	NNL	NNL	NNL	NNL	NNL	NNL	IND
Little Rock Grays												
Louisville Black Caps											NNL	
Columbus Turf Club (aka Columbus Turfs)												
Louisville White Sox												NNL
Memphis Red Sox			IND	NNL	NNL			NNL	NNL	NNL	NNL	
Milwaukee Bears				NNL								
Monroe Monarchs												
Montgomery Grey Sox												
NAL All Stars												
Harlem Stars (aka New York All Stars)												IND
New York Black Yankees												
New York Cubans												
New York Lincoln Giants	IND	IND	IND		ECL	ECL	ECL	ECL	ECL	ANL	IND	
Newark Browns												
Newark Dodgers												
Brooklyn Eagles												
Newark Eagles												
Newark Stars							ECL					
NNL All Stars										IND		
Pennsylvania Red Caps (of New York)	IND											
Philadelphia Bacharach Giants												
Philadelphia Royal Stars			IND									

22. A Proposed Negro Leagues Team Roster

	1932	1933	1934	1935	1936	1937	1938	1939	1940	1941	1942	1943	1944	1945	1946	1947	1948
												NAL					
													NAL	NAL	NAL	NAL	
																	NAL
					IND	NAL			NAL	NAL		IND					
							NAL	NAL									
	IND	IND	IND	IND	IND	NAL	NAL	NAL	NAL	NAL	NAL	NAL	NAL	NAL	NAL	NAL	NAL
	NSL																
	NSL																
						NAL	NAL	NAL	NAL	NAL	NAL	NAL	NAL	NAL	NAL	NAL	NAL
	NSL																
	NSL																
									IND								
	IND	IND	IND	IND	NN2	NN2	NN2	NN2	NN2	NN2	NN2	NN2	NN2	NN2	NN2	NN2	NN2
				NN2	NN2			NN2	NN2	NN2	NN2	NN2	NN2	NN2	NN2	NN2	NN2
	EWL																
			NN2	NN2													
				NN2													
					NN2	NN2	NN2	NN2	NN2	NN2	NN2	NN2	NN2	NN2	NN2	NN2	NN2
					IND	IND					IND						
	IND	IND	NN2		IND												
	1932	1933	1934	1935	1936	1937	1938	1939	1940	1941	1942	1943	1944	1945	1946	1947	1948

	1920	1921	1922	1923	1924	1925	1926	1927	1928	1929	1930	1931
Philadelphia Stars												
Philadelphia Tigers									ECL			
Pittsburgh Crawford Giants (aka Crawford Colored Giants)												IND
Pittsburgh Crawfords												
Toledo Crawfords												
Toledo-Indianapolis Crawfords (aka Indianapolis Crawfords)												
Pittsburgh Keystones		IND	NNL									
Pollock's Cuban Stars												
Richmond Giants			IND									
Santo Domingo Stars (aka Ciudad Trujillo)												
St. Louis Giants (2)					IND							
St. Louis Giants (1)	NNL	NNL										
St. Louis Stars (1)			NNL	NNL	NNL	NNL	NNL	NNL	NNL	NNL	NNL	NNL
St. Louis Stars (2)												
Indianapolis ABCs (3)												
St. Louis Stars (3)												
St. Louis-New Orleans Stars (aka New Orleans-St. Louis Stars)												
Harrisburg Stars (aka Harrisburg-St. Louis Stars)												
Stars of Cuba										IND	IND	IND
Toledo Tigers				NNL								
Washington Black Senators												
Washintgon Pilots												
Washington Potomacs				IND	ECL							
Wilmington Potomacs						ECL						
	1920	1921	1922	1923	1924	1925	1926	1927	1928	1929	1930	1931

22. A Proposed Negro Leagues Team Roster

1932	1933	1934	1935	1936	1937	1938	1939	1940	1941	1942	1943	1944	1945	1946	1947	1948
	IND	NN2	NN2	NN2	NN2	NN2	NN2	NN2	NN2	NN2	NN2	NN2	NN2	NN2	NN2	NN2

IND	NN2	NN2	NN2	NN2	NN2	NN2

NN2/NAL

NAL

| EWL | IND |

IND (1936)

NAL (1937)

NAL (1938)

NAL (1939)

NAL (1940) NAL (1941)

NN2 (1943)

NN2 (1938)

EWL (1932)

| 1932 | 1933 | 1934 | 1935 | 1936 | 1937 | 1938 | 1939 | 1940 | 1941 | 1942 | 1943 | 1944 | 1945 | 1946 | 1947 | 1948 |

23

Negro Leagues and Early MLB Team Failures

Here's a series of charts outlining the constant team failures and shifts in league affiliation in the Negro Leagues and the early Major Leagues.

This isn't a complete history of such events—merely a demonstration of one of the many similarities between the NgL and early MLB. It's important to note that independent NgL teams aren't listed here.

Team names given in these charts are those most associated with those teams at the time. Wherever two or more team names are grouped together, this means either that the team changed its name, or that it absorbed part or all of a previous team's structure and players.

(See charts on the following 12 pages.)

League Affiliations of NgL Teams with

Year:	20	21	22	23	24	25	26	27	28	29	30
Chicago American Giants	NNL	NNL	NNL	NNL	NNL	NNL	NNL	NNL	NNL	NNL	
Chicago Columbia Giants											NNL
Cole's American Giants											
Cuban Stars (West)	NNL		NNL	NNL	NNL	NNL	NNL	NNL	NNL	NNL	NNL
Detroit Stars (I)	NNL	NNL	NNL	NNL	NNL	NNL	NNL	NNL	NNL	NNL	NNL
Indianapolis ABCs (I)	NNL	NNL	NNL	NNL	NNL	NNL	NNL	NNL			
Kansas City Monarchs	NNL	NNL	NNL	NNL	NNL	NNL	NNL	NNL	NNL	NNL	NNL
St. Louis Giants	NNL	NNL									
St. Louis Stars			NNL	NNL	NNL	NNL	NNL	NNL	NNL	NNL	NNL
Atlantic City Bacharach Giants				ECL	ECL	ECL	ECL	ECL	ECL	ANL	
Baltimore Black Sox (I)				ECL	ECL	ECL	ECL	ECL	ECL	ANL	
Brooklyn Royal Giants				ECL	ECL	ECL	ECL	ECL	ECL		
Cubans Stars (East)				ECL	ECL	ECL	ECL	ECL	ECL	ANL	
Hilldale Club				ECL	ECL	ECL	ECL	ECL	ECL	ANL	
New York Lincoln Giants				ECL	ECL	ECL	ECL	ECL	ECL	ANL	
Birmingham Black Barons					NNL	NNL		NNL	NNL	NNL	NNL
Memphis Red Sox					NNL	NNL		NNL	NNL	NNL	NNL
Harrisburg Giants					ECL	ECL	ECL	ECL			
Homestead Grays										ANL	
Washington Homestead Grays											
Nashville Elite Giants											NNL
Columbus Elite Giants											
Washington Elite Giants											
Baltimore Elite Giants											
Pittsburgh Crawfords											
Toledo Crawfords											
Indianapolis Crawfords											
Philadelphia Stars											
Newark Dodgers											
Newark Eagles											
New York Cubans											
New York Black Yankees											
Indianapolis ABCs (III)											
St. Louis Stars (III)											
New Orleans-St. Louis Stars											
Cincinnatti Buckeyes											
Cleveland Buckeyes											
Cincinnatti Clowns											
Cincinnatti-Indianapolis Clowns											
Indianapolis Clowns											
Year:	20	21	22	23	24	25	26	27	28	29	30

4+ Years' Franchise Continuity

31	32	33	34	35	36	37	38	39	40	41	42	43	44	45	46	47	48
NNL						NAL	NAL	NAL	NAL	NAL	NAL	NAL	NAL	NAL	NAL	NAL	NAL
		NN2	NN2	NN2													
NNL	EWL																
NNL		NN2															
NNL						NAL	NAL	NAL	NAL	NAL	NAL	NAL	NAL	NAL	NAL	NAL	NAL
NNL		NN2															
	EWL	NN2															
		NN2	NN2														
	EWL																
	NSL					NAL	NAL	NAL	NAL	NAL	NAL	NAL	NAL	NAL	NAL	NAL	NAL
	NSL					NAL	NAL	NAL	NAL	NAL	NAL	NAL	NAL	NAL	NAL	NAL	NAL
		EWL	NN2	NN2	NN2	NN2	NN2	NN2									
								NN2	NN2	NN2	NN2	NN2	NN2	NN2	NN2	NN2	NN2
		NSL	NN2	NN2													
				NN2													
						NN2	NN2										
								NN2	NN2	NN2	NN2	NN2	NN2	NN2	NN2	NN2	NN2
			NN2	NN2	NN2	NN2	NN2	NN2									
							NAL										
								NAL									
				NN2	NN2	NN2	NN2	NN2	NN2	NN2	NN2	NN2	NN2	NN2	NN2	NN2	NN2
				NN2	NN2												
						NN2	NN2	NN2	NN2	NN2	NN2	NN2	NN2	NN2	NN2	NN2	NN2
				NN2	NN2			NN2	NN2	NN2	NN2	NN2	NN2	NN2	NN2	NN2	NN2
						NN2	NN2	NN2	NN2	NN2	NN2	NN2	NN2	NN2	NN2	NN2	NN2
						NAL											
							NAL										
								NAL	NAL								
										NAL							
											NAL	NAL	NAL	NAL	NAL	NAL	NAL
										NAL							
											NAL						
														NAL	NAL	NAL	NAL
31	32	33	34	35	36	37	38	39	40	41	42	43	44	45	46	47	48

League Affiliations of Short-Lived NgL Teams

	Year:	20	21	22	23	24	25	26	27	28	29	30
Chicago Giants		NNL	NNL									
Dayton Marcos		NNL						NNL				
Cincinnatti Cubans			NNL									
Columbus Buckeyes			NNL									
Cleveland Tate Stars				NNL	NNL							
Pittsburgh Keystones			NNL									
Milwaukee Bears					NNL							
Toledo Tigers					NNL							
Washington Potomacs						ECL						
Wilmington Potomacs							ECL					
Cleveland Browns						NNL						
Cleveland Elites								NNL				
Cleveland Hornets									NNL			
Cleveland Tigers										NNL		
Cleveland Cubs												
Indianapolis ABCs (II)												
Louisville White Sox												
Cleveland Stars												
Detroit Wolves												
Newark Browns												
Washington Pilots												
Atlanta Black Crackers												
Indianapolis ABCs (IV)												
Knoxville Giants												
Louisville Black Caps												
Monroe Monarchs												
Montgomery Grey Sox												
Columbus Blue Birds												
Akron Black Tyrites												
Cleveland Giants												
Baltimore Black Sox (II)												
Cleveland Red Sox												
Philadelphia Bacharach Giants												
Brooklyn Eagles												
Cincinnatti Tigers												
Detroit Stars (III)												
Indianapolis Athletics												
St. Louis Stars (II)												
Washington Black Senators												
	Year:	20	21	22	23	24	25	26	27	28	29	30

	31	32	33	34	35	36	37	38	39	40	41	42	43	44	45	46	47	48
	NNL																	
	NNL																	
	NNL																	
		EWL																
		EWL																
		EWL																
		EWL																
		NSL							NAL									
									NAL									
		NSL																
		NSL																
		NSL																
		NSL																
			NN2															
			NN2															
			NN2															
				NN2														
				NN2														
				NN2														
					NN2													
						NAL												
						NAL												
						NAL												
						NAL												
							NN2											
	31	32	33	34	35	36	37	38	39	40	41	42	43	44	45	46	47	48

League Affiliations of Early MLB Teams

Year:	71	72	73	74	75	76	77	78	79	80	81	82
Boston Red Stockings[1]	NA	NA	NA	NA	NA	NL	NL	NL	NL	NL	NL	NL
Boston Beaneaters												
Chicago White Stockings[2]	NA		NA	NA	NL	NL	NL	NL	NL	NL	NL	NL
Chicago Pirates												
Philadelphia Athletics (NA)	NA	NA	NA	NA	NA							
Athletic Club of Philadelphia						NL						
New York Mutuals	NA	NA	NA	NA	NA							
Brooklyn Atlantics		NA	NA	NA	NA							
Cincinnatti Red Stockings (NL)						NL	NL	NL	NL	NL		
Providence Grays									NL	NL	NL	NL	NL
Indianapolis Blues								NL				
Milwaukee Grays								NL				
Troy Trojans									NL	NL	NL	NL
New York Gothams												
New York Giants (NL)												
New York Giants (PL)												
Buffalo Bisons									NL	NL	NL	NL
Cleveland Blues									NL	NL	NL	NL
Cincinnatti Red Stockings (AA)											AA	AA
Cincinnatti Reds												
Detroit Wolverines											NL	NL
Pittsburgh Alleghenys												AA
Pittsburgh Burghers												
Pittsburgh Pirates												
Year:	71	72	73	74	75	76	77	78	79	80	81	82

1. *The oldest continuously operating baseball franchise in the world; today they play in Atlanta, but I decline to print their current name.*
2. *Known today as the Chicago Cubs.*

with 4+ Years' Franchise Continuity

	83	84	85	86	87	88	89	90	91	92	93	94	95	96	97	98	99	00
	NL	NL	NL	NL	NL	NL	NL	NL	NL	NL	NL	NL	NL	NL	NL	NL	NL	NL
	NL	NL	NL	NL	NL	NL	NL	NL	NL	NL	NL	NL	NL	NL	NL	NL	NL	NL
								PL										
	NL	NL	NL															
	NL	NL																
			NL	NL	NL	NL	NL	NL	NL	NL	NL	NL	NL	NL	NL	NL	NL	NL
								PL										
	NL	NL	NL															
	NL	NL																
	AA	AA	AA	AA	AA	AA	AA											
								NL	NL	NL	NL	NL	NL	NL	NL	NL	NL
	NL	NL	NL	NL	NL	NL												
	AA	AA	AA	AA	NL	NL	NL	NL										
								PL										
									NL	NL	NL	NL	NL	NL	NL	NL	NL
	83	84	85	86	87	88	89	90	91	92	93	94	95	96	97	98	99	00

Year:	71	72	73	74	75	76	77	78	79	80	81	82
St. Louis Brown Stockings (AA)												AA
St. Louis Browns[5]												
Baltimore Orioles[4]												AA
Louisville Eclipse												AA
Louisville Colonels (2)												
Philadelphia Athletics (AA)												AA
Philadelphia Quakers												
Philadelphias												
Philadelphia Phillies												
New York Metropolitans												
Brooklyn Grays												
Brooklyn Ward's Wonders												
Brooklyn Superbas[3]												
St Louis Maroons												
Indianapolis Hoosiers												
Washington Nationals (NL)												
Cleveland Blues												
Cleveland Spiders												
Washington Statesmen												
Washington Senators[6]												
Year:	71	72	73	74	75	76	77	78	79	80	81	82

3. *Known today as the Los Angeles Dodgers.*
4. *Not to be confused with today's Orioles, this team was forced out of the NL in 1899 by league contraction.*
5. *Known today as the St. Louis Cardinals*
6. *Not to be confused with the later AL franchise.*

23. Negro Leagues and Early MLB Team Failures

	83	84	85	86	87	88	89	90	91	92	93	94	95	96	97	98	99	00
	AA	AA	AA	AA	AA	AA	AA	AA	AA	NL	NL	NL	NL	NL	NL	NL	NL	NL
	AA	AA	AA	AA	AA	AA	AA	AA	AA	NL	NL	NL	NL	NL	NL	NL	NL	
	AA	AA																
			AA	AA	AA	AA	AA	AA	AA	NL	NL	NL	NL	NL	NL	NL	NL	
	AA	AA	AA	AA	AA	AA	AA	AA										
	NL																	
		NL	NL	NL	NL	NL	NL											
								NL	NL	NL	NL	NL	NL	NL	NL	NL	NL	NL
	AA	AA	AA	AA	AA													
		AA	AA	AA	AA	AA	AA	NL	NL	NL	NL	NL	NL	NL	NL	NL		
								PL										
																NL	NL	
		UA	NL	NL														
					NL	NL	NL											
				NL	NL	NL	NL											
					AA	AA												
							NL	NL	NL	NL	NL	NL	NL	NL	NL	NL	NL	
								AA										
									NL	NL	NL	NL	NL	NL	NL	NL	NL	
	83	84	85	86	87	88	89	90	91	92	93	94	95	96	97	98	99	00

League Affiliations of Short-Lived Early MLB Teams

Year:	71	72	73	74	75	76	77	78	79	80	81	82
Washington Olympics	NA	NA			NA							
Troy Haymakers	NA	NA										
Cleveland Forest Citys	NA	NA										
Fort Wayne Kekiongas	NA											
Rockford Forest Citys	NA											
Baltimore Canaries		NA	NA	NA								
Washington Nationals (NA)		NA			NA							
Washington Blue Legs			NA									
Brooklyn Eckfords		NA										
Middletown Mansfields		NA										
Philadelphia White Stockings			NA	NA	NA							
Baltimore Marylands			NA									
Elizabeth Resolutes			NA									
Hartford Dark Blues				NA	NA							
St. Louis Brown Stockings (NA/NL)					NA	NL	NL					
Philadelphia Centennials					NA							
New Haven Elm Citys					NA							
Keokuk Westerns					NA							
Louisville Colonels (1)						NL	NL					
Hartford Dark Blues						NL						
Brooklyn Hartfords							NL					
Mutual Club of New York						NL						
Syracuse Stars (NL)										NL		
Worcester Ruby Legs											NL	NL	NL
Cincinnati Stars										NL		
Columbus Buckeyes												
Indianapolis Hoosiers												
Richmond Virginians												
Toledo Blue Stockings												
Washington Nationals (AA)												

	83	84	85	86	87	88	89	90	91	92	93	94	95	96	97	98	99	00
	AA	AA																
		AA																
		AA																
		AA																
		AA																

Year:	71	72	73	74	75	76	77	78	79	80	81	82
Altoona Mountain Citys												
Baltimore Monumentals												
Boston Reds												
Chicago Browns												
Pittsbugh Stogies												
Cincinnatti Outlaw Reds												
Kansas City Cowboys (UA)												
Milwaukee Brewers (UA)[7]												
Philadelphia Keystones												
St. Louis Maroons												
St. Paul Saints												
Washington Nationals (UA)												
Wilmongton Quicksteps												
Kansas City Cowboys (NL)												
Kansas City Cowboys (AA)												
Columbus Solons												
Boston Reds												
Philadelphia Athletics												
Buffalo Bisons												
Cleveland Infants												
Brooklyn Gladiators												
Rochester Broncos												
Syracuse Stars (AA)												
Toledo Maumees												
Cincinnatti Kelly's Killers												
Milwaukee Brewers (AA)[7]												
Year:	71	72	73	74	75	76	77	78	79	80	81	82

7. *Neither the UA nor the AA team should be confused with the later AL franchise.*

	83	84	85	86	87	88	89	90	91	92	93	94	95	96	97	98	99	00
		UA																
		UA																
		UA																
		UA																
		UA																
		UA																
		UA																
		UA																
		UA																
		UA																
		UA																
		UA																
			NL															
						AA	AA											
							AA	AA	AA									
								PL	AA									
								PL	AA									
								PL										
								PL										
								AA										
								AA										
								AA										
								AA										
									AA									
									AA									
	83	84	85	86	87	88	89	90	91	92	93	94	95	96	97	98	99	00

24

Negro Leaguers Who Played in the Majors

Here's a roster of the 85 pioneers who played in both the Negro Leagues and the Majors. All deserve a place in this book in honor of their skills and courage.

This chart gives each player's name, the MLB awards they earned, the last NgL team for which they played, the year of their admittance to the Majors, and the MLB team that signed them. Names of the 41 men who also played in the NgL prior to the end of the 1948 season are marked with an asterisk.

As they never played in the Negro Leagues, the chart doesn't include pioneers **Saturnina "Nino" Escalera** and **Chuck Harmon**, who integrated the Cincinnati Reds on April 17, 1954; **Ozzie Virgil, Sr.**, who integrated the Detroit Tigers on June 6, 1958; and **Elijah "Pumpsie" Green**, who completed the integration of the Major Leagues when he became the first Black player for the Boston Red Sox on July 21, 1959, 12 years, three months and six days after Jackie Robinson first broke the Major League color barrier. (No ex–Negro Leaguer ever played for the Red Sox.)

Nothing better illustrates the molasses-drip pace of integration than the gap between Branch Rickey's bold experiment and Boston's grudging acceptance of reality. It's worth repeating that six years into the so-called post-integration era, only six of 16 Major League teams had given a Black player any form of trial. Not until 1953 was real movement seen—and still it took the Red Sox another seven years to catch up with the rest of the civilized world.

Perhaps it's more than coincidental that the Red Sox were the last MLB team to integrate. In his 1948 autobiography, Satchel Paige wrote that he'd pitched in "every state in the United States except Maine and Boston." On May 1, 2017, a Red Sox fan was removed from Fenway Park for throwing peanuts at Baltimore Orioles outfielder Adam Jones. "I was called the n-word a handful of times tonight," said Jones after the game. "Thanks. Pretty awesome." Pitcher C.C. Sabathia immediately confirmed to ESPN that "when you go to Boston, [Black players] expect it," saying he'd "never been called the n-word" in any other city. Former outfielder Torii Hunter revealed in June 2020 that "I've been called the n-word in Boston 100 times…. It happened all the time. From little kids. And grownups right next to them didn't say anything…. I had a no-trade clause to Boston in every contract I've ever had. And I always wanted to play for them, and it sucks."[1]

In recounting these facts, I'm not judging Boston as a city; I've been there, I love the place; but truths must be told, and the Red Sox have some fan educating to do.

The Kansas City Monarchs were raided most heavily by far, losing 20 players to the Majors; the next-most raided team was the Indianapolis Clowns, who affirmed their professional worth by sending 10 players to the Big Show.

Cleveland's numerous signings of Negro Leaguers—14 players from 1948 to 1957—show that Hank Greenberg was as much a progressive on civil rights as Branch Rickey and Bill Veeck. In his *New Historical Abstract* Bill James justly criticizes Greenberg for his handling of the Cleveland franchise as general manager. Greenberg's evaluation of Negro Leaguers recommended to him by Larry Doby tends to confirm James's scathing assessment: "Our guys checked 'em out and their reports were not good. They said that Aaron has a hitch in his swing and will never hit good pitching. [Ernie] Banks is too slow and didn't have enough range, and Mays can't hit a curveball."[2] Imagine Cleveland in the '40s and '50s with those three on board...

But whatever his failings in other areas, on the most important issue of his time, Hank Greenberg placed himself squarely on the right side of history. Perhaps the prejudice shown to him years before as the Majors' first-ever Jewish superstar rendered him especially sensitive to injustice meted out to others. "My [Beaumont] teammate Jo-Jo White, when he saw me, he couldn't understand," Greenberg remembered, "because he was always told that Jews had horns. And here I was, I looked like a normal human being, and he just couldn't figure it out."

This tallies with Larry Doby's recollections of first entering MLB: "I think the toughest thing for some of my teammates when I first got to Major League baseball was the fact that they had not had the opportunity to associate with Afro-American people.... When some of the stories would go around where Afro-Americans had tails, when I'd go and take a shower, they didn't see the tail. So that gave them some kind of an education." But as Greenberg's son Stephen emphasized: "My dad said, many times, that he didn't know what hazing was until he saw what Jackie Robinson went through in 1947."[3]

A representative story about Greenberg from ex–Negro Leaguer Al "Fuzzy" Smith:

> At that time, wasn't only but two Afro-American players [on Cleveland's roster], Larry Raines and myself.... When we got to the Lord Baltimore Hotel, I got off the bus and I was standin' on the side, because all the white players was goin' in, and we didn't stay at that hotel.... I'm pretty sure Hank just didn't realize, at that particular time, because when he come up to me and he said, "Al," he said, "what're you standin' here for?" I said, "Hank, we don't stay here at this hotel. The Afro-American players don't stay here." And here's the very words he said: "This will cease this year." And he calls [Harold] "Spud" Goldstein, who was the travelin' secretary. He says, "I want you to write letters to every hotel that we got contracts with, that if the Afro-American players can't stay along with the white players, that we will cease stayin' at that hotel." And the next year, we stayed at the Lord Baltimore Hotel.[4]

As Jackie himself wrote for *Ebony* in July 1948: "The man had class. He reeked with it, that Hank Greenberg did."

	Player	MLB Awards and Honors	Final NgL team	ML debut	Team
1.	Jackie Robinson •	ROY, 6×AS, MVP, HOF	KC Monarchs (1st)	April 15, 1947	NL—**BRO Dodgers (1st)**
2.	Larry Doby •	7×AS, HOF	NE×W Eagles (1st)	July 5, 1947	AL—**CLE (1st)**
3.	Hank Thompson •		KC Monarchs (2nd)	July 17, 1947	AL—**STL Browns (1st)**
4.	Willard Brown •	HOF	KC Monarchs (3rd)	July 19, 1947	AL—STL Browns (2nd)
5.	Dan Bankhead •		MEM Red Sox (1st)	August 26, 1947	NL—BRO Dodgers (2nd)

In addition to integrating the NL, Jackie Robinson integrated the triple-A International League on April 18, 1946.

In addition to integrating the AL, Larry Doby integrated the American Basketball League on January 3, 1948.

Hank Thompson holds several unique distinctions: he not only integrated the St Louis Browns, but also, in his second stint in the Majors, co-integrated the New York Giants on July 8, 1949, being called up the same day as Monte Irvin. He was also the first Black player to play in both the NL and AL.

6.	Roy Campanella •	8×AS, 3×MVP, HOF	BAL Elite Giants (1st)	April 20, 1948	NL—BRO Dodgers (3rd)
7.	Satchel Paige •	2×AS, HOF	KC Monarchs (4th)	July 9, 1948	AL—CLE (2nd)

Roy Campanella integrated the class-B New England League on May 8, 1946, and the triple-A American Association on May 22, 1948. He became the first Black man to (temporarily) manage white players in organized baseball when he took the helm of the Nashua Dodgers, replacing the ejected Walter Alston, on June 15, 1946.

8.	Minnie Miñoso •	9×AS, 3×GG	NY Cubans (1st)	April 19, 1949	AL—CLE (3rd)
9.	Don Newcombe •	ROY, 4×AS, CYA, MVP	NEW Eagles (2nd)	May 20, 1949	NL—BRO Dodgers (4th)
10.	Monte Irvin •	AS, HOF	NEW Eagles (3rd)	July 8, 1949	NL—**NYG Giants (1st)**
11.	Luke Easter •		HOM Grays (1st)	August 11, 1949	AL—CLE (4th)

Minnie Miñoso, Cleveland's third Black player, went on to integrate the Chicago White Sox on May 1, 1951.

12.	Sam "The Jet" Jethroe •	ROY	CLE Buckeyes (1st)	April 18, 1950	NL—**BOS (1st)**

For the whole of the 1950 season, Larry Doby and Luke Easter were the only Black players in the American League.

13.	Luis Marquez •		HOM Grays (2nd)	April 18, 1951	NL—BOS (2nd)
14.	Ray Noble •		NY Cubans (2nd)	April 18, 1951	NL—NYG Giants (2nd-t)

24. Negro Leaguers Who Played in the Majors

	Player	MLB Awards and Honors	Final NgL team	ML debut	Team
15.	Artie Wilson •		BBB Black Barons (1st)	April 18, 1951	NL—NYG Giants (2nd-t)
16.	Harry "Suitcase" Simpson •	AS	PHI Stars (1st)	April 21, 1951	AL—CLE (5th)
17.	Willie Mays •	ROY, 24×AS, 12×GG, 2×MVP, HOF	BBB Black Barons (2nd)	May 25, 1951	NL—NYG Giants (4th)
18.	Sam Hairston •		IND Clowns (1st)	July 21, 1951	AL—**CHW White Sox (1st)**
19.	Bob Boyd •		MEM Red Sox (2nd)	September 8, 1951	AL—CHW White Sox (2nd)
20.	Sam "Toothpick" Jones •	2×AS	CLE Buckeyes (2nd)	September 22, 1951	AL—CLE (6th)

Willie Mays integrated the class–B Inter-State League on June 24, 1950.

	Player		Final NgL team	ML debut	Team
21.	Hector Rodriguez •		NY Cubans (3rd)	April 15, 1952	AL—CHW White Sox (3rd)
22.	George Crowe •	AS	NY Black Yankees (1st)	April 16, 1952	NL—BOS (3rd)
23.	James "Bus" Clarkson •		PHI Stars (2nd)	April 30, 1952	NL—BOS (4th)
24.	Quincy Trouppe •		CLE Buckeyes (3rd)	April 30, 1952	AL—CLE (7th)
25.	Joe Black •	ROY	BAL Elite Giants (2nd)	May 1, 1952	NL—BRO Dodgers (5th)
26.	Dave Pope •		HOM Grays (3rd)	July 1, 1952	AL—CLE (8th)
27.	Sandy Amoros •		NY Cubans (4th)	August 22, 1952	NL—BRO Dodgers (6th)
28.	Bill Bruton •		PHI Stars (3rd)	April 13, 1953	NL—**MIL (1st)**
29.	Jim "Junior" Gilliam •	ROY, 2×AS	BAL Elite Giants (3rd)	April 14, 1953	NL—BRO Dodgers (7th)
30.	Connie Johnson •		KC Monarchs (5th)	April 17, 1953	AL—CHW White Sox (4th)
31.	Jim Pendleton •		CHI Am. Giants (1st)	April 17, 1953	NL—MIL (2nd)
32.	Dave Hoskins •		LOU Buckeyes (1st)	April 18, 1953	AL—CLE (9th)
33.	Al Smith •	3×AS	CLE Buckeyes (4th)	July 10, 1953	AL—CLE (10th)
34.	Bob Trice •		HOM Grays (4th)	September 13, 1953	AL—**PHI Athletics (1st)**
35.	Ernie Banks •	13×AS, GG, 2×MVP, HOF	KC Monarchs (6th)	September 17, 1953	NL—**CHC Cubs (1st)**

	Player	MLB Awards and Honors	Final NgL team	ML debut	Team
36.	Gene Baker •	AS	KC Monarchs (7th)	September 20, 1953	NL—CHC Cubs (2nd)

Dave Hoskins integrated the class–A Central League on August 1, 1948, and the double-A Texas League on April 14, 1952.

Ernie Banks became the second (temporary) Black manager in MLB when he took the helm from ejected Chicago Cubs manager Whitey Lockman on May 8, 1973.

Gene Baker integrated the class–A Western League on May 16, 1950. He became the second Black manager in organized baseball, taking over the class–D Batavia Pirates on June 20, 1961, and was the first (temporary) Black manager in MLB, taking the helm of the Pittsburgh Pirates for the ejected Danny Murtaugh on September 21, 1963. (Ex-Negro Leaguer Sam Bankhead was the first Black manager in organized baseball, serving as player-manager of the class–C Farnham Pirates for the 1951 season.)

	Player	MLB Awards and Honors	Final NgL team	ML debut	Team
37.	Hank Aaron	25×AS, 3×GG, MVP, HOF	IND Clowns (2nd)	April 13, 1954	NL—MIL (3rd)
38.	Tom Alston		GRE Red Wings (1st)	April 13, 1954	NL—**STL Cardinals (1st)**
39.	Curt Roberts		KC Monarchs (8th)	April 13, 1954	NL—PIT Pirates (1st)
40.	José Santiago •		NY Cubans (5th)	April 17, 1954	AL—CLE (11th)
41.	Charlie White		PHI Stars (4th)	April 18, 1954	NL—MIL (4th)
42.	Jehosie "Jay" Heard •		NO Eagles (1st)	April 24, 1954	AL—**BAL Orioles (1st)**
43.	Bill Greason •		BBB Black Barons (3rd)	May 31, 1954	NL—STL Cardinals (2nd)
45.	Joe "Cephus" Taylor		CHI Am. Giants (2nd)	August 26, 1954	AL—PHI Athletics (2nd)
44.	Carlos Paula		HAV Cuban Giants (1st)	September 6, 1954	AL—**WAS Senators (1st)**
46.	Joe Durham		CHI AM. Giants (3rd)	September 10, 1954	AL—BAL Orioles (2nd)

Hank Aaron co-integrated the class–A Southern Atlantic (Sally) League, together with Horace Garner, Albert Isreal, Felix Mantilla, and Fleming "Junior" Reedy, on April 14, 1953.

Curt Roberts was the first Negro Leaguer to play for the Pirates, but Carlos Bernier integrated the team on April 22, 1953.

	Player	MLB Awards and Honors	Final NgL team	ML debut	Team
47.	Elston Howard •	12×AS, 2×GG, MVP, World Series MVP	KC Monarchs (9th)	April 14, 1955	AL—**NY Yankees (1st)**
48.	Bob Thurman •		KC Monarchs (10th)	April 14, 1955	NL—CIN Reds (1st)
49.	Roberto Vargas •		CHI Am. Giants (4th)	April 17, 1955	NL—MIL (5th)

24. Negro Leaguers Who Played in the Majors

	Player	MLB Awards and Honors	Final NgL team	ML debut	Team
50.	Lino Donoso •		NY Cubans (6th)	June 18, 1955	NL—PIT Pirates (2nd)
51.	Milt Smith		PHI Stars (5th)	July 21, 1955	NL—CIN Reds (2nd)
52.	Billy Harrell		BBB Black Barons (4th)	September 2, 1955	AL—CLE (12th)
53.	Vibert "Webbo" Clarke •		MEM Red Sox (3rd)	September 4, 1955	AL—WAS Senators (2nd)

Bob Thurman was the first ex–Negro Leaguer to play for the Reds, but Chuck Harmon and Nino Escalera integrated the team on April 17, 1954.

	Player	MLB Awards and Honors	Final NgL team	ML debut	Team
54.	Charlie Neal	3×AS, GG	ATL Black Crackers (1st)	April 17, 1956	NL—BRO Dodgers (8th)
55.	Pat Scantlebury		NY Cubans (7th)	April 19, 1956	NL—CIN Reds (3rd)
56.	Charlie Peete		IND Clowns (3rd)	July 17, 1956	NL—STL Cardinals (3rd)
57.	Joe Caffie		CLE Buckeyes (5th)	September 13, 1956	AL—CLE (13th)
58.	Larry Raines		CHI Am. Giants (5th)	April 16, 1957	AL—CLE (14th)
59.	John Kennedy		BBB Black Barons (5th)	April 22, 1957	NL—PHI Phillies (1st)
60.	Frank Barnes		KC Monarchs (11th)	September 22, 1957	NL—STL Cardinals (4th)
61.	Juan "Pancho" Herrera		KC Monarchs (12th)	April 15, 1958	NL—PHI Phillies (2nd)
62.	Bob Wilson •		NEW Eagles (4th)	May 17, 1958	NL—LA Dodgers (9th)
63.	Hank Mason		KC Monarchs (13th)	September 12, 1958	NL—PHI Phillies (3rd)
64.	George Altman	3×AS	KC Monarchs (14th)	April 11, 1959	NL—CHC Cubs (3rd)
65.	Maury Wills	7×AS, 2×GG, MVP	RAL Tigers (1st)	June 6, 1959	NL—LA Dodgers (10th)
66.	Marshall Bridges		MEM Red Sox (4th)	June 17, 1959	NL—STL Cardinals (4th)
67.	Jim Proctor		IND Clowns (4th)	September 14, 1959	AL—DET Tigers (1st)

Jim Proctor was the first ex–Negro Leaguer to play for the Tigers, but Ozzie Virgil, Sr., integrated the team on June 6, 1958.

	Player	MLB Awards and Honors	Final NgL team	ML debut	Team
68.	Lou Johnson		KC Monarchs (15th)	April 17, 1960	NL—CHC Cubs (4th)
69.	Walt Bond		KC Monarchs (16th)	April 19, 1960	AL—CLE (15th)
70.	Clarence "Choo-Choo" Coleman		IND Clowns (5th)	April 16, 1961	NL—PHI Phillies (4th)
71.	Hal Jones		KC Monarchs (17th)	April 25, 1961	AL—CLE (16th)
72.	Bobby Prescott		JAC Eagles (1st)	June 17, 1961	AL—**KC Athletics (1st)**
73.	John Wyatt	AS	IND Clowns (5th)	September 8, 1961	AL—KC Athletics (2nd)
74.	Donn Clendenon	World Series MVP	KC Monarchs (18th)	September 22, 1961	NL—PIT Pirates (2nd)
75.	J.C. Hartman		KC Monarchs (19th)	July 21, 1962	**NL—HOU Colt .45s (1st)**

1962 was the Colt .45s' inaugural season.

	Player	MLB Awards and Honors	Final NgL team	ML debut	Team
76.	Charlie Dees		LOU Clippers (1st)	May 26, 1963	NL—LA Angels (1st)
77.	Willie Smith		BBB Black Barons (7th)	June 18, 1963	AL—DET Tigers (2nd)
78.	George Smith		IND Clowns (6th)	August 4, 1963	AL—DET Tigers (3rd)
79.	John "Blue Moon" Odom	2×AS	RAL Tigers (2nd)	September 5, 1964	AL—KC Athletics (3rd)
80.	George Spriggs		DET Stars (1st)	September 15, 1965	NL—PIT Pirates (3rd)
81.	Paul Casanova	AS	IND Clowns (7th)	September 18, 1965	AL—WAS Senators (3rd)
82.	Hal King		IND Clowns (8th)	September 6, 1967	NL—HOU Astros (2nd)
83.	Ike Brown		KC Monarchs (20th)	June 17, 1969	AL—DET Tigers (4th)
84.	Billy Parker		IND Clowns (9th)	September 9, 1971	AL—CAL Angels (2nd)
85.	Harry Chappas		IND Clowns (10th)	September 7, 1978	AL—CHW White Sox (5th)

Harry Chappas was born to Greek parents, and thus represents an oddity of ethnicity in this list; nonetheless he did play for the Indianapolis Clowns, a thoroughly integrated outfit by 1978 and the last Negro League club to close up shop, finally disbanding in 1989.

25

Short Notes on Diverse Subjects

Thoughts I wanted to convey, but which didn't seem to fit into the core arguments of the book...

- *A note on my treatment of other writers' work:*

I quote a lot of writers in these pages. Sometimes I disagree with or criticize them. But by selecting the Negro Leagues as their topic, they've already earned my respect. I couldn't have written this book without them. The mistakes, of course, are mine; if you catch one, please let me know via my publisher.

- *A note on my use and capitalization of the adjective "Black":*

As an outsider to the Black experience, I deemed it sensible to allow Black voices to determine how I reference Black people in my text.

I agree with the logic advanced by social commentator and former NFL linebacker Emmanuel Acho:

> Do I call Black people Black, or African American? The most simple and safe answer is calling Black people Black, because it's accurate. There are Jamaicans in America, there are Cubans in America; they're not African. And some Black people don't identify as African because that heritage got stripped from them during slavery.[1]

I also agree with the position pioneered by Temple University professor Lori L. Tharps:

> In the mid–1920s, W.E.B. Du Bois began a letter-writing campaign, demanding that book publishers, newspaper editors and magazines capitalize the N in Negro when referring to Black people.... Du Bois wanted that word to confer respect on the page as well as in daily life.... In the late 1980s, Jesse Jackson pushed "African-American" into common usage, offering a new term that wasn't tainted by a racist history—and conferred the respect of indisputable capital letters.... By 2000, Black Americans had a choice of what to call themselves on the census: "Black, African Am., or Negro" (because some older people preferred it).... If we've traded Negro for Black, why was that first letter demoted back to lowercase, when the argument had already been won?... Black should always be written with a capital B.[2]

I've shaped my practice accordingly.

- *A note on my tone of moral certitude, which may strike some as arrogant:*

In his booklet *Eastern Colored League*, David Lawrence writes:

> In America, we have, up until very recently, kept Black and white people almost entirely separate from one another. This creates the illusion, based on a purely visual impression of skin tones, that these are two different sets of people.... By keeping people separate, we're using cultural, social and legal artifice to construct a situation that doesn't actually occur in nature.[3]

Well, exactly.

Now try replacing the word "people" in Lawrence's powerful prose with "players":

> In America, we have, up until very recently, kept Black and white *players* almost entirely separate from one another. This creates the illusion, based on a purely visual impression of skin tones, that these are two different sets of *players*.... By keeping *players* separate, we're using cultural, social and legal artifice to construct a situation that doesn't actually occur in nature.

There's my moral certitude in a nutshell.

- *A note on my use of traditional Triple Crown slash lines in a brave new sabermetric world:*

I quote a lot of Triple Crown slash lines in this book. Please know that I'm aware of Steven Goldman's admonition: "For many, the bare-boned presentation of the triple crown statistics still says all they need to know, but given the sheer amount of descriptive information now available, limiting oneself to these numbers is a lot like saying you don't need to see a highfalutin' movie because we have hieroglyphics."[4]

For the record, "the bare-boned presentation of the triple crown statistics" does *not* say all I need to know. Important evaluative tools like OPS+ and WAR are now readily applicable to NgL play, thanks once again to the crew at Seamheads. But the old reliable slash line can often serve to illustrate a basic point.

For example, Willard Brown's 1953–55 slash lines show that long after the Majors pronounced him worthless, the man could rake. No deeper analysis is required to illustrate the folly of the all-white ownership and managerial structure that treated the potential second coming of Joe DiMaggio with such ignorant disdain.

- *A note on the everyday tribulations faced by Negro League players:*

I regard the fantastic pace of life in the NgL, playing endless rounds of scheduled and un-scheduled games, including up to three games on Sundays, as a major point in the NgL's favor as a Major League. I can't cite it as a proof of professionalism; there's no statistic or number I can assign to it that demonstrates anything definitively; but it does, I think, merit a mention within these covers.

William "Judy" Johnson remembered: "Every two hours you had to average a hundred miles. With nine men in the car!" "The schedule," agreed Roy Campanella, "was a rugged one. Rarely were we in the same city two nights in a row. Mostly we played by day and travelled by night; sometimes we played by day and by night and usually in two different cities.... Many's the time we never even bothered to take off our uniforms going from one place to another.... The bus was our home, dressing room, dining room, and hotel."[5]

The playoffs were even more extreme. "In 1946," remembered Larry Doby, "when the Newark Eagles won the Negro World Series … they would have the game, one game in Newark, they'd have another game in New York, they'd have another game in Philadelphia, and they'd have another game in Washington. By going around different cities they would draw more people."[6]

There was no such thing as a disabled list in Black baseball. "You didn't get hurt when you played in the Negro Leagues," asserted Campanella. "You played no matter what happened to you because if you didn't play, you didn't get paid."[7]

To me it's incredible that these men were able to accomplish what they did—especially against Major Leaguers—while working in a state of what must have been near-perpetual exhaustion. Major League baseball is a trial to be sure, 162 games a year, plus spring training, plus the playoffs—but what Negro Leaguers experienced was on another level entirely.

For an excellent first-person perspective on this glorious grind, see Jackie Robinson's piece "What's Wrong with Negro Baseball?" in the June 1948 issue of *Ebony*.

- *A note on the theory that Cap Anson's racist actions may have been inspired by the actions of another player:*

In "The Momentous Drawing of the Sport's 19th-Century 'Color Line' is Still Tripping Up History Writers," Howard W. Rosenberg writes that "future Chicago second baseball [Fred] Pfeffer had been in an incident with [Fleet] Walker in [August] 1881.… Alternative inspiration speculation can be that other incidents such as the 1881 one provided a model or that, within baseball, Pfeffer was seen as Anson's instigator."[8]

I respect Mr. Rosenberg's research; it was he who discovered, and first printed, much of the accepted evidence regarding Anson and the color line. However, I cannot endorse his "alternative inspiration speculation" about Pfeffer. First, Pfeffer's actions were reported locally, in Louisville; Anson's were reported nationally. Second, no national agitation or violence was initiated by Pfeffer's action; indeed, the Louisville press noted how unpopular his stance was with local fans. Third, Pfeffer didn't possess anywhere near the national stature and popularity that Anson enjoyed. Fourth, Pfeffer committed an overt racist act once that we know of; Anson did so multiple times. Fifth, there's no evidence for the proposition that Pfeffer influenced *anyone*—whereas we have contemporary, first-hand accounts from Pat Powers and George W. Howe testifying to Anson's pervasive influence in barring Black players, and to his willingness to intervene personally to prevent their advancement.

I think the weight of the evidence shows pretty clearly that Cap Anson was who he was: a great player and not-so-great human being who didn't need outside influence to formulate his damaging views on Black Americans.

- *A note on Bill Veeck's charge that Judge Landis prevented him from buying the Philadelphia Phillies in 1942:*

Some readers may wonder why, in my section on Kenesaw Landis and his opposition to integration, I didn't mention a damning claim by Bill Veeck, that Landis sabotaged Veeck's intended purchase of the Philadelphia Phillies in 1942 to prevent

Veeck from stocking the team with Black players. Veeck's claim is a source of tremendous controversy among historians.

Stories about Veeck's intention to purchase the Phillies can be traced back to the October 8, 1942, *Milwaukee Journal*, in which Sam Levy reports that Veeck "spent three days in New York denying silly rumors that he intended to buy the Philadelphia Phils"—exactly what one might have expected him to do if he intended to stealthily stock the team with Black players. There's plenty of other contemporary evidence too, marshalled by Veeck biographer Paul Dickson, that his interest in making the purchase was genuine.

So the first part of the debate is easy: it can't be seriously doubted that Veeck did in fact make inquiries about buying the Phillies in 1942. But there are three further elements to the question, crucial to determining the truth of the matter:

- Why did Veeck want to buy the Phillies?
- What—or who—deterred him from making the purchase?
- Apart from the man's own words, is there contemporary confirmation of Veeck's plan?

Veeck's first publicly mentioned rationale for why he *wanted to buy the team* came in the October 18, 1942, *Milwaukee Journal*: "The Phils have many potential stars among their younger players, who belong in the [minor league] American Association at least for one season. Those players would win a pennant for us and then would be ready for the majors."[9]

Veeck's statement may well have been a veil for his true intentions. There's little doubt that any mention by Veeck of Black players in the Majors in 1942 would have been met with howls of disapproval (at least privately, where their power could be flexed out of public view) by MLB's executive and ownership structure. Nonetheless, it's a matter of historical record that neither Black players nor Kenesaw Landis figured in Veeck's explanation.

The first public explanation of why Veeck *decided not to make the purchase* came in the February 10, 1943, *Milwaukee Sentinel*. Veeck confirmed that the money was available, but said that he loved Milwaukee, where he already owned the triple-A Brewers franchise, and didn't want to leave: "There were some rather sizeable figures, like $500,000, in the way of backing if we indicated we wanted to take over but, both [Brewers manager] Charles ["Jolly Cholly" Grimm] and I insist again, we are most happy here, and intend to stay here."

Again, it's possible that Veeck had no wish to air his true reasons in public; and again, the fact of the matter is that neither Black ballplayers nor the Judge were mentioned.

Branch Rickey announced Jackie Robinson's minor league contract on October 23, 1945; Jackie made his exhibition debut for Montreal on March 17, 1946, his regular-season debut on April 18. On June 25, with Jackie's future success in the Majors far from certain, Veeck expanded on his reasons for not buying the Phillies in an interview with Walter "Red" Smith in the *New York Herald Tribune*.

Despite Rickey's contractual rupture of the minor-league color barrier eight months earlier and Jackie's on-field breach three months before, there's no mention of Black ballplayers in the interview. In fact, Smith's article contradicts the notion of interference with Veeck's plans by Landis or any other baseball executive: "[Veeck] had the financial backing and an inside track, but at the last moment he decided the risk was too great to take with his friends' money."

The sole obstacle Veeck mentions to Smith is finance, not systemic racism. Rick Swaine's contention that this article supports Veeck's claim because June 1946 was "well before there were kudos to bestow for anti-segregationist activities" therefore cannot obtain.[10]

Potential evidence *against* Veeck's contention was provided by Veeck himself on July 20, 1946. With Jackie well on his way to winning the international League MVP, Veeck told the Black-owned *Call and Post* for that "none of the present crop of Negro players measure up to big league standards." That doesn't sound like the voice of an owner willing to field an all–Black team.

The first public mention of Veeck's *intention to field an all–Black team* was reported by Vernon Gibson in the July 25, 1947, *St. Petersburg Times*: "Bill Veeck ... revealed recently that he tried to buy the Philadelphia Phillies during the war with an eye to making them an all–Negro club."

Note the timing. By now Jackie had been in the Major Leagues for three and a half months, hitting .302 with 78 runs scored and a league-leading 16 steals en route to the Rookie of the Year award. Already he rivalled Eddie Stanky, Joe Gordon and Bobby Doerr as MLB's top second baseman. The writing was on the wall: Black players were in the Majors to stay. There were, in fact, "kudos to bestow" within the progressive community by July 25, 1947.

Veeck gave two detailed post–1947 accounts of his purported scheme. Per the September 1948 *Baseball Digest*:

> [Veeck] made arrangements with the nation's leading promoter of Negro baseball to assemble an all-star colored team and take them into training off the beaten path the next spring. ["The nation's leading promoter of Negro baseball" refers to Abe Saperstein, founder of the Harlem Globetrotters and owner, at various times, of three different NgL teams; Veeck later hired Saperstein as his personal scout for Black baseball talent.] Without mentioning a word of his idea to any one, Veeck then planned to have his regular squad go through spring training at the club's regular spa, but at noon of Opening Day [April 14, 1943], release enough surplus rookies to enable him to sign a dozen or so Negro players to National league contracts and then send an entire Negro team out on the field as his starting lineup.... "What could they have done?" Veeck posed later. "They would either have had to play my team or forfeit the game."

Veeck's 1961 autobiography conveys more particulars:

> I tried to buy the Philadelphia Phillies and stock it with Negro players well before I went into the service.... The players were going to be assembled for me by Abe Saperstein and Doc Young [sic], the sports editor of the *Chicago Defender*, two of the most knowledgeable men in the country on the subject of Negro baseball. With Satchel Paige, Roy Campanella, Luke Easter, Monte Irvin, and countless others in action and available, I had not the slightest doubt that in 1944 [sic], a war year, the Phils would have leaped from seventh place to the pennant.[11]

In the latter account, Veeck conflated the names of Black sportswriters A.S. "Doc"

Young and Fay Young—an unfortunate mistake, as Doc Young referred to Veeck's scheme in 1953 as an "unsubstantiated story."[12]

But Fay Young, the man Veeck intended to name, *did* comment on the plan, though tangentially, in reporting on a speech by Veeck to the Chicago Urban League in the February 26, 1949, *Chicago Defender*—and thereby provided the first *contemporary proof* of Veeck's intent:

> "We didn't win [the AL pennant] by any six games [Young quotes Veeck as saying]. If any one of those six victories turned in by Paige had been a defeat, we wouldn't have played in the world series, we wouldn't have been American League champions—and you wouldn't have invited me here.
>
> "When I was in Milwaukee, a gentleman, now sitting at my right out there, and I talked for several hours about integrating Negroes in major league baseball. At that time I was planning to buy the Philadelphia Nationals [*sic*]."
>
> Few know that the "gentleman" Veeck referred to was none other than your columnist.

Young doesn't confirm Veeck's story in literal terms—but there's a strong inference to be drawn that Veeck's claim to have wished to stock the "Nationals" with top Black talent was true.

As I've not seen them reproduced elsewhere, Veeck's further words to the League, as quoted by Fay Young, merit a place in the history of the man and his times:

> "I have a friend who is an architect. He is a great one but he and I differ on some things. I tell him if I were in his place, instead of building projects such as homes or apartments in spots, I would build them without any thought to renting or selling to any particular group or race. It seems to me that we CAN live together the same as my players can play together.
>
> "I have all races on my ball club—some are even from the south. But they play together as one team. That's real democracy. Now why can't my architect friend build places where a family isn't barred because of its race. Maybe it would be a sacrifice, but I want to see Negro families live in districts heretofore barred to them and thus acquaint the other races with them. Both groups would then get to know each other better.
>
> "I had some players—two or three of them—who objected to playing with Doby. Needless to say it now, they aren't with the [Cleveland] ball club. The spirit of unity prevails. The spirit of brotherhood and democracy and teamwork carried us to the American League pennant and to a world championship. That spirit should be the spirit of all Americans."
>
> A thunderous applause greeted Veeck when he finished. His hearers stood up and continued it for fully five minutes.... The trouble is we haven't enough 100 per cent white Americans like Bill Veeck.[13]

The second contemporary proof of Veeck's intentions is a strong one indeed. Abe Saperstein himself verified Veeck's story unambiguously in the August 14, 1954, *Philadelphia Independent*:

> In 1942 the Phillies were for sale and Veeck attempted to buy them. But Bill Cox got more money and got the club. Do you know what Veeck planned to do? He was going to take the Phils to spring training and then—on the day the season opened—dispose of the entire team. Meanwhile, with a team composed entirely of Negroes, who would have trained separately, he could have opened the 1943 season. I don't think there was a team in either league, back in 1943, that could have stopped the team he was going to assemble.[14]

In my opinion, analysis of this question has heretofore underestimated the significance of Saperstein's words: a man whom Veeck credited as being personally involved in the plan, confirming not just the substance, but the particulars of Veeck's story, seven years before Veeck published his autobiography.

A final piece of potential supporting evidence for Veeck's claim comes from the January 6, 1986, *Chicago Tribune*, in which sportswriter John Carmichael said Veeck told him at the time: "I'm going to buy the Phillies. And do you know what I'm going to do? I'm going to put a whole Black team on the field."

Carmichael gave his account 43 years after the fact, by which time Veeck's version had been in circulation for 41—and gave it in the context of Veeck's obituary, which, in the *Tribune*, comprised quotes from his contemporaries, assembled by Jerome Holtzman as a demonstration of Veeck's humanity. Carmichael prefaced his account by noting that "my memory isn't as good as it used to be," and stated that Veeck said these words "before he got into baseball," which is incorrect whether the incident in question happened or not. One must ask why a prominent newspaper columnist, whose ability to feed his family was dependent upon his ability to produce stories like this, would fail to mention it for decades—particularly given the national prominence accorded to stories on baseball integration at the time Veeck went public with his version of events.

It's at least possible that Veeck's long-accepted and oft-reported version of events—or, perhaps, a desire to present his friend Veeck, who called Carmichael "one of the all-time greats," as a good and moral person—may have misted a long-ago memory. Paul Dickson was right to include the story in his excellent biography of Veeck, but I believe he erred in presenting it as established fact.[15]

Young and Saperstein's accounts, though, are a different order of proof. Jules Tygiel writes that "the only voice telling the story is Veeck's"—but Saperstein's recounting, especially, is as clear as can be.[16]

Barring the discovery of new documents in MLB's archives, I suspect a definitive answer is unattainable at this distance in time. Also, as Mr. Tygiel observes, it's impossible to prove a negative.[17]

Personally, though, I believe Veeck's story. For me, Saperstein's point-by-point confirmation tilts the argument heavily, perhaps decisively, in Veeck's favor.

Such a plan would have been in Veeck's liberalistic and showman-like nature. As owner of the Cleveland franchise, I'd argue that Veeck was second only to Brach Rickey as a proponent of integration in the critical period 1947–49, signing Larry Doby to break the AL color barrier and following him with Satchel Paige, Minnie Miñoso and Luke Easter. Irrespective of the merits of this specific claim, Veeck deserves to be remembered as one of the Good Guys. As Larry Doby remembered, "I always had complete faith in Bill. I didn't question his integrity."[18]

Evidence that Kenesaw Landis was involved in deterring Veeck, however, is completely absent. As Veeck himself told Jules Tygiel, "I have no proof of that. I can only surmise." My own surmise is that—on this one occasion only—Landis *didn't* do something creepy to postpone the integration of baseball.[19]

That's my view. The debate continues.

- *A note on Veeck's oft-quoted story about Larry Doby and Joe Gordon:*

Often, as seen in the quotes above, Bill Veeck got small details wrong in his recountings—and sometimes, like fellow showman P.T. Barnum, he just plain made stuff up.

It was Cleveland's All-Star second-sacker Joe Gordon who eventually persuaded Eddie Robinson to loan Larry Doby his first baseman's glove on July 6, 1947. Gordon consistently emerges as an admirable figure in this tumultuous period. However, an oft-reprinted story told about Gordon by Veeck is demonstrably false.

According to Veeck, in one of Doby's earliest games, he struck out swinging on three straight pitches, stalked to the end of the dugout bench and sat with his head cradled in his hands. Gordon, next up to the plate, flailed ineffectively at the first three pitches he saw, sat down next to Doby and cradled his own head in *his* hands. "I never asked Gordon then," said Veeck, "and I wouldn't ask him today, if he struck out deliberately. After that, every time that Doby went out on the field, he would pick up Gordon's glove and throw it to him. It's as nice a thing as I ever saw or heard of in sports."[20]

This cannot be true. Doby and Gordon appeared together in 27 games in 1947, in only two of which—July 6 (second game) and July 26—did Gordon bat after Doby, and in neither of those games did Gordon strike out.

Bill Veeck wanted to be remembered as having been on the side of the angels. The irony, of course, is that he was; he didn't need extra credit. Demonstrable distortions in small matters like this have served only to call into question Veeck's veracity on other issues—and that's a shame.

- *A note on Ford Frick:*

In the story of baseball's segregation and integration, some whites come off as good guys in spite of any flaws they may have possessed (Branch Rickey, Bill Veeck); others come off as villains no matter what their other qualities (Cap Anson, Larry MacPhail). But for one white authority figure, Ford Frick, I feel an almost hopeless sense of ambiguity.

On the downside of the coin, Frick co-signed the MacPhail Report—and at a 1969 meeting of the Hall of Fame governing board, "suggested that a special wing be set up for the Negro League players." The first Jim Crow inductee was to have been Satchel Paige; as Bowie Kuhn observed at the time, "Technically, you'd have to say he's not in the Hall of Fame." "If it were me under those conditions," remarked Jackie Robinson bitterly, "I'd prefer not to be in it." Larry Doby concurred: "With another wing, whatever good they've done, they've torn it down. How do I explain this to the kids?"[21]

The idea of a separate (but equal?) wing was ultimately scuttled by Paige himself, who declared, "I was just as good as the white boys. I ain't going in the back door of the Hall of Fame."[22]

On the upside:

In the May 9, 1947, *New York Herald Tribune*, sports editor Stanley Woodward reported that Frick had warned potential anti–Jackie Robinson strikers on the St. Louis Cardinals that they would be suspended. This story (repeated as true in countless books and articles) was amended by Woodward in the next day's *Tribune*, where he confirmed that a strike by Cardinals players had indeed been in the making, and clarified that Frick had not spoken to the players personally, but had asked Cardinals owner Sam Breadon to "relay" a written statement to potential strikers. We don't know for certain that Breadon relayed the message to the recalcitrant players, though Frick said he had—but it's a matter of record that there was no strike.[23]

Frick's written statement (itself often misquoted) came into the possession of Woodward, who printed it verbatim:

> If you do this you will be suspended from the league. You will find that the friends you think you have in the press box will not support you, that you will be outcasts. I do not care if half the league strikes. All will be suspended and I don't care if it wrecks the National League for five years. This is the United States of America and one citizen has as much right to play as another.
>
> The National League will go down the line with Robinson whatever the consequences. You will find if you go through with your intention that you have been guilty of complete madness.

This bold pronouncement, couched in the strongest possible terms and issued at a moment decisive not only for the history of baseball but of the United States itself, redounds strongly to Frick's credit. Woodward himself believed it to be "the most noble statement ever made by a baseball man."[24]

Like many of his time and place, Frick seems to have drifted with the tides of history. He endorsed a covert racist policy in 1946, then warned off potential racist strikers in 1947, before reverting to a retrogressive stance by 1969. In the final analysis, among the movers and shapers of baseball's policies on segregation and integration, I think his statement to potential strikers tilts the scales, and we have to give Mr. Frick a (qualified) thumbs up.

- *A note on the notion that Major League Baseball deliberately ruined the Negro Leagues:*

Economists Dr. Rodney Fort and Dr. Joel Maxcy posit that "the demise of AAB [African American baseball] is another episode in the history of the relentless drive by MLB to be the only major league." I cannot agree.[25]

Prior to 1947 there's no record of any form of hostile action by MLB against the NgL. MLB owners profited by renting major- and minor-league stadiums to NgL teams (though they wouldn't let the teams use their locker rooms or shower facilities). This income source was cited in the original MacPhail Report as a reason to *maintain* separate leagues.

Unlike past rival leagues, NgL teams couldn't have raided MLB for talent if they'd wanted to. Apart from a handful of light-skinned Latin players, there was zero player movement between the two leagues. The moment the veil of segregation was lifted, though, MLB and the NgL became direct competitors for talent—a competition the NgL was guaranteed to lose. With pockets far deeper than their NgL counterparts, white owners took advantage of an enormous pool of professional players bound by unenforceable contracts. The NgL was destroyed not by MLB hostility, but by a leakage of players—and, crucially, of paying spectators—to the Majors.

MLB didn't need to "wrestle viable team locations away from AAB," as Fort and Maxcy assert. MLB franchises were concentrated in the same 10 cities for half a century, 1903–1953, a time frame which encompasses the entire professional history of the Negro Leagues. In all that time, MLB never made a move to expand either to cities where NgL franchises operated, or indeed to anywhere else in the country. In 1946, the final year of full segregation, NgL and MLB teams co-existed successfully in six of those 10 cities: Chicago, Cincinnati, Cleveland, New York, Philadelphia, and Pittsburgh (host to the Homestead Grays). If MLB had chosen to establish a new franchise in a city with an NgL team, not only would the local team not have protested, they likely would have celebrated the building of a new Major League stadium they could rent.[26]

Ford and Maxcy's study, which does contain valuable data, undermines itself with statements like, "It could be that MLB fans as a whole were the beneficiaries of integration" *(gee, you think?)*, "There is limited evidence that the 'first family' of AAB stars had much impact on the enjoyment of MLB fans," and "The impact on MLB was negligible in terms of the product on the field." I leave it to the reader to decide whether players like Jackie Robinson, Roy Campanella, Satchel Paige and Willie Mays had "negligible" impact on "the product on the field."[27]

26

A Long Note

Major League Baseball vs. the Truth

I don't believe the following story has been told before now…

The MacPhail Report was issued secretly to MLB owners on August 27, 1946. Branch Rickey publicly revealed the existence of the Report on February 17, 1948:

> After I had signed Robinson, but before he had played a game, a joint major league meeting adopted unanimously a report prepared by a joint committee which stated that however well-intentioned, the use of Negro players would hazard all the physical properties of baseball.
>
> You can't find a copy of that report anywhere, but I was at the meeting where it was adopted. I sat silently while the other 15 clubs approved it. I've tried to get a copy, but league officials tell me all were destroyed.
>
> But *let them deny they adopted such a report, if they dare. I'd like to see the color of the man's eyes who would deny it.*
>
> President Ford Frick passed out copies at the National League meeting. Each copy bore the name of the man to whom it was handed.
>
> After we read them, they were collected. Frick checked off the names to see that he had all the copies. Then in the joint meeting the report was read, and adopted. [Emphasis mine.][1]

MLB executives and team owners rushed en masse to the nearest microphone, either to evade Rickey's charges or to lie outright:

- Pittsburgh owner Bill Benswanger: "[The 'Negro question'] never was raised."
- Cleveland co-owner Alva Bradley: "Major League owners would never be unwise enough to do a thing like that…. The meeting was solely to pick a new commissioner. Mr. Rickey is liable to say anything."
- St. Louis owner Sam Breadon: "[I don't care to] comment either way."
- NL president Ford Frick: "I remember the meeting and recall that we were dealing with changes in player contracts, but I don't remember anything about that Negro phase or phrase."
- Cincinnati president and GM Warren Giles: "I recall nothing of the sort."
- Senators co-owner Clark Griffith: "I don't remember that we passed any such resolution."
- Philadelphia executive Roy Mack: "Never heard of it at all."
- Chicago president Phil Wrigley: "No such vote was ever taken. If the question

ever was presented in such a form as Rickey claims, I—or any representative of the Cubs—never would have voted for it."[2]

Larry MacPhail cemented the historical distortion in a blistering 1,500-word written statement provided to the United Press on February 21:

> 1—Rickey was lying if and when he said that the committee recommended that Negro players be banned from major league baseball.
> 2—Rickey was lying if and when he said that all 15 major league clubs (all except Brooklyn) took action of any kind to prevent Rickey or any other club owner from signing Negro players....
> 3—Rickey was lying if and when he said that copies of the committee's report were collected to destroy evidence having to do with the participation of Negroes in the major leagues. The printed reports were collected at the request of the commissioner because they contained a criticism of the commissioner.

(This was a lie: the Report contained no such criticism of Chandler, by name or by title.)

> The committee agreed to delete certain paragraphs. As it was impossible to reprint the report, it was agreed that all copies be collected so that *the report, as revised, would be the only signed copy. That report as originally written, and as revised, is and has always been in my possession.* [Emphasis mine.]

(MacPhail felt free to tell these lies because he believed, incorrectly, that all copies of the Report other than his had been destroyed.)

> False and inflammatory statements made by a baseball executive in an attempt to glorify himself, do not help any. [Winston] Churchill must have had Rickey in mind when he said, "There, but for the grace of God, goes God."[3]

For the rest of his life, Rickey refused to speak to MacPhail.

"The best proof," Rickey had said the day he revealed the Report's existence, "is the production of the document." To the horror of its authors, the full Report was published in the October 15, 1951, *Congressional Record* by a subcommittee on monopoly power. The subcommittee's mandate was to study the potential abuse of MLB's monopoly status, not the "Race Question"; but the production of key documents dragged the enduring shame of Larry MacPhail and Major League Baseball into the light—and uncovered a sustained effort by MLB's legal team to deny, misrepresent, censor, and otherwise conceal the truth about the Report.[4]

At the subcommittee's hearings, MLB lawyer Paul Porter and NL lawyer Louis Carroll sought to befog what should have been a crystal-clear issue by producing not one, but two documents: MacPhail's un-doctored Report (hereafter referred to as the "original Report"), and a purported "final version" from which numerous damaging items—including the ultra-racist language—had been stripped (hereafter the "censored Report").

Baseball historians have accepted that the document the owners voted on was the *censored* Report. For example (and I'm not picking on him, he's an excellent writer and researcher, and his conclusions on the issue are typical), William J. Marshall writes:

26. A Long Note

> The 1946 report drafted by Larry MacPhail ... contained a recommendation against integration. The draft, however, was too explicit according to baseball's attorneys.... *A diluted version, mentioning nothing about baseball's monopolistic tendencies or racial issues, was pieced together* and distributed to all the owners. *It was the vote on this revised report that Rickey initially referred to* when he claimed that the owners voted fifteen to one against Robinson's entrance into the game. Not long after, he identified the meeting and report to which he had referred and *retracted his claim*. [Emphasis mine.][5]

I'll let the actors themselves tell the story. Congressional hearings are very boring, and the substance of these (very boring) hearings would fill a book larger than this one; besides which, this isn't a textbook. So rather than tax you with an interminable series of ellipses, I've elided a tremendous amount of text—but nothing relevant to the basic story. In their attempt to hide the original Report in plain sight, Porter and Carroll sought, quite deliberately, to make the proceedings as confusing as possible; I've therefore added clarifying interjections, and italicized key passages for emphasis.[6]

Our Cast of Characters

For the Prosecution:
Emanuel Celler (D–NY), Chairman
Patrick J. Hillings (R–CA), member
Kenneth B. Keating (R–NY), member
Thomas J. Lane (D–MA) member
Edwin E. Willis (D–LA), member
E. Ernest Goldstein, General Counsel
John Paul Stevens, Associate Counsel
Peter S. Craig, Special Assistant

For the Defense:
Paul Porter, Counsel for Major League Baseball
Louis Carroll, Counsel for the National League
Leland "Larry" MacPhail, Yankees president and general manager

In Absentia:
Ben Fiery, Counsel for the American League

The Scene:
The U.S. House of Representatives, October 15, 1951

GOLDSTEIN: I would like to submit for the record a document entitled "Report for Submission to National and American Leagues on August 27, 1946."
THE CHAIRMAN: Was this document received from organized baseball?
GOLDSTEIN: It was not. Early in the month of August [1951] information came to the staff that there was a document entitled "Report." On August 10 you wrote to the counsel for organized baseball [Porter] and requested that all reports, minutes, and relevant documents relating to the period beginning January 1945 be made available to the subcommittee.

On September 21, Mr. Paul Porter called me [and said] that they were unable to provide the material we requested.

Mr. Carroll had informed us that a document had been prepared and brought to Chicago on August 26 by Mr. L.S. MacPhail; that Mr. MacPhail's [original] document was, in the opinion of counsel for baseball, not an accurate report of the steering committee; and that *they had mutilated the document by cutting it*; and not having had sufficient time to rewrite the document, they submitted their [censored] report as *a cut-up document*, deleting certain paragraphs and other material. Mr. Carroll went on to explain that in their view all of the mutilated [censored] documents had been recaptured [i.e., confiscated] and had subsequently been destroyed on his recommendation.

I made a further attempt to obtain the document, and I was shown a copy of a document bound in a gray cover [the original Report, not the censored version], a mimeographed document of some 25 pages, which was unsigned. The person who had the document requested that his confidence be kept. He asked that it not be Photostatted because he had already written certain comments on the margin.

Three copies of the original Report are known to have escaped Carroll's shredder. MacPhail's copy was eventually submitted to Goldstein by Carroll. Contradicting his claim of February 21, 1948, MacPhail's copy was *not* signed by meeting attendees. A second copy, which survives today, had been issued to MLB commissioner Happy Chandler. In view of Goldstein's statement that the source himself annotated the margins, and as Chandler's copy bears no marginalia, Goldstein's copy was probably provided to him by the possessor of the final copy known to have survived, AL president Will Harridge.

> **GOLDSTEIN:** On [Friday,] October 12, Mr. Porter came to our office [this happened around 3:00 p.m.; the relevance of the timing will become apparent as we proceed], and we showed him a copy [of the original Report], and he requested that he be allowed to take it with him. I pointed out that we had not finished collating the corrections we wished to make on a rehearing of the transcription.

Was Porter trying to "borrow" Goldstein's copy of the original Report to make it disappear? Goldstein implies that the copy Porter asked for was the only one in the subcommittee's possession; we know that the source asked that it not be duplicated. The question is, did Porter know, or guess, that Goldstein had no other copy? Given the events testified to in these hearings, I judge it not improbable that Mr. Porter was attempting a Nixonian ploy to make the bad words go away forever. (Tricky Dick was a lawyer too.)

> **GOLDSTEIN:** On the morning of Saturday, October 13, Mr. Craig informed me that Mr. Porter had called him and said that they believed they had found the document in question. This morning [October 15], Mr. Porter, Mr. Carroll, and Mr. Fiery showed us a Photostat of a *non-mutilated* final report [the censored Report], as well as a document in gray covers [the original Report], which was identical with the one which I was able to copy originally.

Goldstein immediately puts his finger on the first of many contradictions in the lawyers' testimony: the censored "final report" shown to him by Porter was not "mutilated" or "cut up," as Carroll had claimed. Numerous small discrepancies between the two documents show that the censored version was completely re-typed—contradicting MacPhail's claim of February 21, 1948, that "it was impossible to reprint the report."

> **REP. KEATING:** I think the first thing that we would be interested in hearing would be an

26. A Long Note 319

explanation of the failure to produce the report when requested, and some explanation of how it happened to turn up the day after they learned we had a copy.

Keating raises a key question—but MLB's lawyers produced their documents the *same* day they discovered Goldstein had a copy of the original, not the next day.

> **PORTER:** I do not think there is any great mystery about this document. The simple facts are that this document was not available in either the National League files, the American League files, or in the files of the commissioner's office. *I had no knowledge as to the contents of it* [possibly true, but Porter's actions say otherwise]. I searched my own files and confirmed my recollection that I had removed that file following the meetings in August 1946. When we had the meeting with the staff in September—
>
> **REP. KEATING:** Let me interrupt there; maybe it is your phraseology that troubles me. You say that you had removed the file. What do you mean?
>
> **CARROLL:** I had destroyed the file.
>
> **REP. KEATING:** Destroyed it?
>
> **CARROLL:** [I destroyed it] after the culmination of the committee's work in 1946. I got in touch with Mr. MacPhail, and he told me that he thought he had a copy in his files, and he would make a search. He subsequently called me and said he had been unable to locate it. So [we] called the Yankee office. On Friday [October 12] they called and said they had found a file that contained the report of this joint steering committee of August 27, 1946.
>
> **GOLDSTEIN:** When did you tell Mr. Porter that you had found the documents?
>
> **CARROLL:** I think it was late Friday afternoon.
>
> **PORTER:** It was *late Friday*, Mr. Goldstein; it was not until *after 5:30 or 6 o'clock*.

Having been asked to produce relevant documents in early August, MLB's lawyers failed to produce a thing—until they discovered that Goldstein already had a copy of the original Report; then, as if by magic, both a copy of the original *and* a censored version were "discovered" in a matter of hours.

> **REP. KEATING:** Was that the day after it had been disclosed to you that the subcommittee had a copy?

Carroll now subtly launches the first salvo in the lawyers' attempt to sell the original Report as an un-submitted "draft":

> **CARROLL:** Oh no; this was in September that it was disclosed that they had this *draft*, and—
>
> **GOLDSTEIN:** [naively accepting Carroll's characterization of the original report] The first day that the *draft* was shown to any of the counsel for organized baseball was the same day that the document was found; that is Mr. Keating's question.
>
> **REP. KEATING:** That is my question.
>
> **CARROLL:** [ducking and weaving] I am not familiar with the timing of that.

Blatant perjury. Together with Porter and Fiery, Carroll personally delivered both the original and censored Reports to Goldstein.

> **REP. KEATING:** But you saw it Friday morning, and the document was found Friday afternoon?
>
> **GOLDSTEIN:** It was shown [to Porter] on *Friday afternoon, about 3 o'clock*.

So, by the lawyers' own admission, the gap between their learning that Goldstein had a copy of the original Report, and their supposed discovery of documents they'd been claiming they couldn't find for over two months, was three hours *at most*.

> REP. KEATING: But your testimony is that *it was a pure coincidence that those things happened at the same time?*
> CARROLL: *Oh yes, it is.* At that time, August 26, Mr. MacPhail came to Chicago with his draft of the report [i.e., the original], which no member of the committee and counsel had seen. The report contained a good deal of material that was objectionable to members of the committee [and] to counsel. At the August 26 meeting the committee refused to sign the report in that form, and certain deletions were made. Following the meeting, realizing that there was material in that report that represented discussion and controversy, I collected the National League's copies [of the censored Report], and they were destroyed. So far as I know, at the time this request came out those deleted [censored] copies were not available.

Unlike the original Report, which Carroll was now peddling as a "draft," the censored Report contained no section titled "Race Question." No other copy of the censored Report has been seen from that day to this.

> CARROLL: Now counsel felt that there was no occasion to leave copies of that around for the press or for public consumption, and that is the reason, and the only reason that I know, why we recommended or caused those copies to be destroyed. We did not find the deleted [censored] copy, have not found it yet, but we are still searching, and have not found it yet except in the form in which I have delivered it to you.
> THE CHAIRMAN: Not all copies were destroyed.
> CARROLL: Apparently not.
> THE CHAIRMAN: Because I secured a copy.

What Chairman Celler has is the *original* Report obtained via back channels by Goldstein, not the censored version Carroll is attempting to foist on the subcommittee—but Celler fails to notice the difference. The Chairman was holding a royal flush, but Carroll persuaded him that all he held was a pair of twos.

> GOLDSTEIN: With reference to Mr. Carroll's technical distinction between the report as it finally came out [the censored Report], and what he claims was Mr. MacPhail's report [the original], we knew of only one document being in existence.

Goldstein's right: clearly there was only one document—until Porter and Carroll got their hands on it.

> REP. HILLINGS: Did every major league team or some representative thereof receive a copy of this particular [original] report?
> CARROLL: No, not in this form.

How, then, did Happy Chandler and Will Harridge end up with copies?

> REP. HILLINGS: And what was the distribution of this particular report confined to?
> CARROLL: It was confined to a display of it, as far as I know. Apparently I do not know all about it, because as far as I know all the copies were in Mr. MacPhail's possession. This original draft was produced by him at Chicago on August 26, and *the copies that were distributed to the clubs on the 27th had the material objected to by the committee deleted.*

An obvious falsehood, escaping classification as definite perjury only because Carroll hedges his bets with that "apparently I do not know all about it" disclaimer.

26. A Long Note

The "draft" containing the Race Question section *was* distributed beyond Larry MacPhail's hands, to Chandler and Harridge at minimum. Also, how could committee members "object to" material they'd never read? And again: The one and only copy of the censored Report ever seen was presented to the subcommittee by MLB's lawyers, as against at least three surviving copies of the original Report.

> GOLDSTEIN: I was shown the gray-covered [original] document on the condition that I would dictate the contents and then subsequently transcribe it. The document which I submitted for the record is a transcript of the gray-covered document. But at no time has anyone produced any signed document, either the one that Mr. Carroll gave us this morning, or any other one.

Goldstein makes a crucial point here: Why couldn't MLB's lawyers produce "the only *signed* copy" of the censored version, which MacPhail had claimed, in his written statement of February 21, 1948, "is and always has been in my possession"?

> REP. WILLIS: Was the disputed document we are talking about [the censored Report] ever signed?
> CARROLL: [evading the question] *Mr. MacPhail's draft* was never signed. I am quite sure of that. I am certain of that.
> REP. WILLIS: [pressing the point] Was it ever signed by anyone?
> CARROLL: Whether the deleted one that was submitted as the official report [the censored Report] was signed, I could not state.
> REP. KEATING: You mean that none of those [signed copies of the censored Report] is in existence?
> CARROLL: We are trying to locate copies in the American League office. Those that were distributed in the National League I collected following the meeting.
> REP. KEATING: After those so-called deletions were made, and there was something agreed upon in the way of a document, you collected [the censored Report] on behalf of the National League and destroyed them?
> CARROLL: Yes. We just decided that before some of them turned up in the hands of outsiders—these were confidential matters, and it has been our experience in baseball that if these documents are allowed to float around, they turn up in hands where the confidence is violated. This is apparently what happened to the gray document [the original report], and that is the very thing we wanted to avoid.

Carroll fails to explain the contradiction between his earlier testimony that the original Report was never distributed, and the fact that multiple copies of the original were "floating around." He also fails to explain why the owners would want every copy of a document they'd agreed to minutes before to disappear forever.

> THE CHAIRMAN: As far as you know, that is the only copy extant of this [censored] report?
> CARROLL: We are still searching.

The lawyers' putative "search" produced nothing—but the subcommittee never followed up.

> REP. LANE: I do not think that you quite answered Congressman Willis's question. He asked you whether or not these representatives signed the [censored] MacPhail Report.
> PORTER: [evading the issue of why the lawyers can't produce a signed copy of the censored Report by changing the subject] None of them signed *this* [the original

> Report]. Of that I am sure, because I was present at the meeting of the committee at which this report was considered and amended. Mr. MacPhail's draft was not acceptable, and it was here amended, and nobody signed it in the form in which Mr. Goldstein has introduced it in the record. I am positive of that. [Porter tries again to dismiss the three-hour "coincidence"...] There was certainly no relationship in my mind as to the production of this or any other document, and a disclosure by Mr. Goldstein that he had had it.
>
> **REP. KEATING:** And after Mr. Goldstein disclosed to you that the subcommittee had a copy, at 3:00 or 3:30 this Friday afternoon, you did not then communicate in any way with Mr. Carroll?
>
> **PORTER:** No. Mr. Carroll called me and said, "We have discovered a copy." *There was absolutely no relationship between these two events. It is pure coincidence.*

Amazingly, no one on the subcommittee, including the perceptive Mr. Goldstein, realized the potentially seismic import of what they held in their hands; nor did they pursue Carroll and Porter's obvious perjury and falsification of documents. Their task was to look at monopoly power, and that's what they stuck to.

On October 24, Larry MacPhail delivered himself into the subcommittee's hands. For 29 excruciating pages of transcript the subcommittee asked him about everything *but* baseball segregation. Obviously MacPhail wasn't going to volunteer the topic, which by October 1951 had the potential to do tremendous damage to MLB in general and Larry MacPhail in particular.

Goldstein and his Associate Counsel, future Supreme Court Justice John Paul Stevens, did grill MacPhail briefly on the deletions from the original Report:

> **GOLDSTEIN:** Now, could you tell us how it came about that there were deletions made in the report?
>
> **MACPHAIL:** There were not any deletions made in the recommendations to the Committee. The deletions were made in the paragraphs which were argumentative.

Bald-faced perjury. Of seven major deleted sections, one lays out word-for-word changes to the reserve clause "so as to remove the grounds on which the option could be attacked successfully"; another recommends that MLB "should assume responsibility for seeing that baseball has adequate, intelligent, and timely activities in the public-relations field" to hide MLB's antagonism towards a proposed players' union; a third specifies exact dollar amounts for minimum pricing of MLB tickets; a fourth recommends that teams encourage their players to form club-specific representative groups rather than unionize. Goldstein's failure to recommend perjury charges indicates that like the rest of the subcommittee, he didn't appreciate the true significance of the deletions. The subcommittee had both versions at its fingertips, but never performed even a cursory comparison to determine whether MacPhail was telling the truth.

> **GOLDSTEIN:** We will take up specific deletions, but I wondered just what procedures were gone through. You say counsel objected to some and other members of the [steering] committee objected to some?
>
> **MACPHAIL:** No. The commissioner objected to two or three paragraphs which were critical of the commissioner, and we took those out.
>
> **GOLDSTEIN:** Was he present at some of the meetings, too?
>
> **MACPHAIL:** No; I do not think the commissioner knew anything about the report or

the recommendations until I read the report to him in the Blackstone Hotel the day before it was presented to the major leagues [August 25, 1946]. There were two or three paragraphs critical of the conduct of the commissioner's office, and he objected to their inclusion in the report. I reported that to the committee, and the committee thought we should strike them out.

Repeating his lie of February 21, 1948. No text critical of Chandler or his office can be found in the original Report, and the deleted sections comprise vastly more than "two or three paragraphs."

> GOLDSTEIN: And, in addition to the commissioner's criticism, I take it that your counsel and your fellow members of the committee also thought that certain paragraphs were not reflective necessarily of the facts.
> MACPHAIL: I don't think there were too many deletions.

More perjury. The deleted sections comprised almost half of the original Report.

> STEVENS: After [the deletions] did you have the document mimeographed again?
> MACPHAIL: No; we just took the shears and cut out a few paragraphs. Here is the document as originally prepared. It has got a 1, a 2, and a 3 [numbered sections] there, and the 3 must have been eliminated.
> REP. BRYSON: It must have been a very short paragraph, just two or three lines.
> MACPHAIL: I think that is all it was, sir.

It's incredible that the subcommittee, with both the original and censored Reports ready to hand, didn't check to see if the deleted section was "just two or three lines." The major subdivisions of the Report were lettered, not numbered, and the sections allowed to survive in the censored Report were *re-lettered* to disguise the deletions.

...And just like that, MacPhail and MLB were off the hook. A few members asked questions about specific deletions, all related to baseball's business practices, and that was all. Porter, Carroll, and MacPhail's deception was so successful that in the final report on the hearings, Chairman Celler wrote: "Organized baseball undoubtedly owes much of its public support to its unquestioned integrity."[7]

* * *

Any notion that the owners insisted on changes to MacPhail's original Report out of some principled disagreement with its terms is rendered nonsensical by a look at what MLB's lawyers chose to delete. In terms of protecting baseball from charges of dubious and often illegal business practices, the sections deleted from the "final report" presented to counsellor Goldstein were dead on-target[8]:

- The first major block of deleted text dealt with baseball's monopoly status: "This partnership, and the agreement among the partners to cooperate in the business of baseball, constitutes a monopoly.... Baseball faces the most critical period in all its history. It is under attack as an illegal monopoly.... The character of American baseball for many years to come will be determined in large measure by its ability to withstand the pressures of today."
- The second round of deletions hid the lawyers' unvarnished opinion, intended for owners' eyes only, that the reserve clause—which prevented

players from changing teams except by owner-initiated trade, and which Curt Flood challenged all the way to the Supreme Court in 1972—was legally unsound: "In the well-considered opinion of counsel for both major leagues, the present reserve clause could not be enforced in an equity court."

- The third round dealt with MLB's so far successful attempts to deter players from forming a union: "Your committee felt that attempts to organize players represented our most pressing problem…. The concrete evidence that we were willing to meet with the players on a friendly basis and consider our mutual problems … has already been effective in preventing the spread of guild sentiment…. If it were not for this, we believe guild representation and collective bargaining would now be in effect at Pittsburgh." The Major League Baseball Players Association wasn't recognized by MLB as a legitimate union until Marvin Miller's April 11, 1966, election by player vote—20 years after this sub-rosa discussion on how to discourage players from unionizing.
- The fourth major deletion excised MLB's plan to obscure baseball's antagonism towards unionization by creating a public-relations arm and re-shaping public opinion: "Baseball was completely ineffectual in putting its side of the story before the public in connection with [Yankees pitcher Johnny] Murphy's one-man campaign to organize the players…. It is a contradictory state of affairs that baseball, which has practically lived off sports page advertising for years, should practically handcuff itself in matters of this nature."
- The fifth deletion was the Race Question section—and this one stands out like a sore thumb. Of all the carefully targeted excisions made by Porter and Carroll, this is the only one that had nothing to do with baseball's bad business practices. Sure, the rental income derived from NgL teams is mentioned—but only as another in a series of excuses not to integrate. The clear intent behind this deletion was to hide MLB's scathing opinions about the talent and professionalism of Black players.
- The sixth round of deletions, which returned to economic themes, hid owners' monopolistic agreement to raise ticket prices across MLB.
- The seventh and final round again concerned the subject of union-busting, hiding the recommendation that "players on all major league clubs be encouraged to elect representatives to represent the players in discussion and conference with club management" on a team-by-team basis. It's unstated, but obvious, that if players can be organized by team, they'll be less likely to organize across the league.

If Porter and Carroll's shifty testimony, MacPhail's blatant perjury, and the laser-focused nature of the lawyers' deletions still don't convince you, here's more proof: Branch Rickey said on February 17, 1948, that the version of the Report agreed to by owners stated that "however well-intentioned, the use of Negro players would hazard all the physical properties of baseball." As he emphasized, Rickey couldn't obtain a copy from which to quote directly—but that's not a bad recollection at a distance of one and a half years; the uncensored Report does indeed state that that "if

Negroes participate in major-league games ... the preponderance of Negro attendance in parks ... could conceivably threaten the value of the major league franchises owned by these clubs." How could he possibly have known this if, as Carroll insisted, he'd never seen the original Report?

Rickey affirmed that "I was at the meeting where it was adopted. I sat silently while the other 15 clubs approved it." Is there any reason to doubt it?[9]

Rickey later elaborated on the dissemination of the original Report to Roger Kahn:

> Frick passed out a report on integration prepared under the direction of MacPhail and Phil Wrigley.... MacPhail was angry. He stood up and glared at me. Robinson was then playing for Montreal. Did I realize, MacPhail said, that when Montreal played in Baltimore and Newark more than half the fans in attendance were Negroes? And did I further realize that all those Negroes were going to drive away our white fans?
>
> He was raging. I made no answer. We read a report that essentially said the time was not right for bringing Negroes into the major leagues. I hoped someone would challenge the report. No one did. Then Frick asked all of us to return our copies to him. After that was done the MacPhail–Wrigley report against Negroes simply vanished from the face of the earth.[10]

As for the supposed retraction of Rickey's charges referenced by William Marshall and other historians, the AP, which carried Rickey's initial scoop on the Report's existence, reported him as saying two days later (February 19, 1948): "In light of further information since my address at Wilberforce, I understand fully that there were *other reasons* than the so-called Negro reference for removing the report from publicity. I had believed that the *major reason* for suppression [of the Report] was the reference to Negro employment. I am told that many members of the leagues who were present do not remember the reference to this matter." (Emphasis mine.) It's easy to imagine what the "further information" obtained by Rickey pertained to; he was no doubt hastily acquainted with the fact that if the uncensored Report was released, various owners and executives could face federal charges for labor and anti-trust violations.[11]

As Rickey stated, the *major* reason for suppression of the Report was the disastrous series of revelations pertaining to MLB's corrupt business practices, which could (and probably should) have led to prosecution of the authors. But at no point does Rickey retract his core contention that the Report, as agreed to by club owners, recommended the indefinite continuance of segregation. As for the other owners not remembering "the reference to this matter," that's nothing more than self-interest: after all, they voted to a man to approve the Report.

In reply to MacPhail's mendacious written statement of February 21, Rickey was even more direct: "No statement in the Wilberforce address ... has been denied in whole or in part by these typically MacPhailian distortions, untruths and inventions. They are unworthy of further comment."[12]

Happy Chandler wasn't present at the meeting where the Report was adopted. In April 1945, immediately after his election as the new Commissioner of Baseball, he told the *Pittsburgh Courier*'s Eric "Ric" Roberts: "I'm for [Franklin D. Roosevelt's] Four Freedoms. If a Black boy can make it in Okinawa and Guadalcanal, hell, he can make it in baseball. Once I tell something, brother, I never change. You can count on me." Owners clearly saw the Report as a means of undermining Chandler's ability to further the cause of MLB integration.[13]

Though Ben Fiery was part of the team that presented the sham MacPhail Report to Goldstein, he wasn't present at the 1951 hearings, and therefore uttered no falsehoods; his culpability can't be proven. But as for Louis Carroll and Paul Porter, there's no doubt whatsoever. Carroll was secretary of the meeting that agreed to the original Report, and Porter backed up his perjury under oath.

And remember: These aren't MLB *bosses*, they're MLB *lawyers*. The odds that they did any of this on their own initiative are vanishingly small.

Major League Baseball did its level best to hide in plain sight the evidence of its owners' collusion against Black players—and succeeded, too, for three quarters of a century.

Acknowledgments

I'm pleased to record my debt of gratitude to the staff at **Seamheads**, without whose research this book—in fact, the idea itself—would have been an impossibility, and to the staff at **Baseball Reference** for taking the time to answer my often obscure questions—and, existentially, for agreeing with the premise that Negro Leaguers are Major Leaguers, and taking concrete action to integrate NgL and MLB statistics.

I'm particularly indebted to Seamheads co-founder **Kevin Johnson**, who corresponded with me extensively, wrote an original essay on Negro Leagues ballparks, and provided me with key unpublished NgL data to assist me in tackling Mr. James's 23 tests. His peer review of the manuscript was instrumental in crafting a stronger and sounder book.

Authors **Tom Van Hyning** and **Jorge Colón-Delgado** were very helpful to me, providing specialized information on Willard Brown, Luke Easter and Satchel Paige, and on Latin baseball in general. They're also stunningly nice people.

Kudos to **Howard W. Rosenberg** for helpful email exchanges. I told Mr. Rosenberg candidly at the beginning of our conversations that he'd likely disagree with certain of my conclusions, but that didn't deter him from maintaining a lengthy and collegial correspondence.

My thanks to **Sean Gibson** for his generosity in providing an excellent image of his great-grandfather; to **Bill James** for taking the time to answer questions via email; and to Professor **Lori L. Tharps** for sharing with me her thoughts on capitalization of the adjective "Black."

Thanks to **Adele Heagney** at the St. Louis Central Library: the best, most diligent, and most thorough librarian I worked with in over two years of research. Thanks also to **Ronda Cornelius** at the Kansas City Library and **Greg Guderian** at the Newark Public Library for going Above and Beyond the Call.

Special thanks to SABR Editorial Director **Jacob Pomrenke** for helping me with numerous questions large and small. I trust that SABR understands what a valuable asset they have in Jacob.

For assistance with newspaper clippings, image identification and releases, and other specialized queries, thanks to **Sarah Applegate** at the Los Angeles Museum of Art; **Stefani Baldivia** at California State University, Chico, Meriam Library Special Collections; **John Boutet** at the Buffalo Bisons Hall of Fame; **Kelly Burdick** at the *Watertown Daily Times* (NY); **Julie Burns** at The People's Archive, Washington, D.C. Public Library; **Carla Cantagallo** at the University of Kentucky; **Brandon Costa** at

Sports Video Group; Negro Leagues Baseball Museum Vice President and Curator **Ray Doswell**; **Kelly Dunnagan** at the Louisville Free Public Library; **Rylan Edwards** at Bill James Online; **Robert Fleck III** at Oak Knoll Books (DE); **Natalie Hamilton** at *Smithsonian* magazine; author **John R. Husman**; **Cathy Jock** at the official website for Ogdensburg NY; **Alec E. Johnson** at the *Watertown Daily Times* (NY); **Isaac Johnson** at the Buffalo & Erie County (NY) Public Library; **Stacy Joosse** for the Alaska Goldpanners; **Thom Karmik** at Baseball History Daily; **Troy R. Kinunen** at MEARS Online Auctions; **Thomas A. Lamb III** at Carleton College (MN); **Mark Langill** for the Los Angeles Dodgers; author and Negro Leagues expert **Larry Lester**; **Glenn Longacre** at the National Archives at Chicago; Broome County (NY) Historian **Roger Luther**; **John Murphy** at the online Baseball Hall of Merit; **Steve Lansdale** at Heritage Auctions (Dallas TX); **Suzanna Mitchell** for the San Francisco Giants Photography team; **A.J. Muhammad** and **Auburn Nelson** at the Schomburg Center for Research in Black Culture; **Angelique Nelson** at Real Times Media; **Doug Remley** at the National Museum of African American History and Culture; **Carla Rezcek** at the Detroit Public Library; SABR member **Chuck Rosciam**; **John Sheppard** at the Great Lakes Naval Station (IL) Public Affairs Office; **Melissa Shriver** at the Milwaukee Public Library; **Katie Starmer** for Major League Baseball Legal & Business Affairs; Archivist **Jennifer Steinhardt** at the National Museum of the American Sailor; **Tom Steman** at St. Cloud State University (MN); **Jason D. Stratman** at the Missouri Historical Society Library and Research Center; **Gary Sykes** at UK Press Online; SABR Publications Editor **Cecelia Tan**; **Mariam Touba** at the Patricia D. Klingenstein Library, New York Historical Society; **Heather Winter** at Hake's Auctions (York PA); and **Savannah Wood** at The Afro-American Newspapers.

Heartfelt thanks to **Gary Mitchem**, my editor at McFarland, for taking a chance on a neophyte author and walking him step by step through the world of publishing.

A shout-out to the late **Ursula K. Le Guin**, whose words guide my pen (she's better at it than me, obviously, but I do my best): "A sentence or paragraph is like a chord or harmonic sequence in music: its meaning may be more clearly understood by the attentive ear, even though it is read in silence, than by the attentive intellect."[1]

Last and far from least, my thanks to **David Hagen**, my favorite baseball artist, for vital encouragement and helpful comments on draft chapters—and for suggesting the title.

In writing this book I've followed in the footsteps of numerous dedicated pioneers in the field of Negro Leagues research, including **Sol White**, **John Holway**, **Robert Peterson**, **Donn Rogosin**, and many others. My envy of researchers like Holway and Rogosin is complete: they met and interviewed the giants I know only through their numbers.

The only Negro Leaguers I've had the privilege to meet are **Larry Doby**, **John "Buck" O'Neil**, and **Alfred "Slick" Surratt**. I cherish the brief moments I spent with them, and I thank them for their patience with, and kindness to, the skinny kid who stuttered and stared in awe at these living symbols of the triumph of the human spirit.

An Open Letter to Atlanta's Ownership and Management

A number of stories in this book revolve around Cleveland's professional baseball team. Like many others, I found Cleveland's previous team moniker offensive; Atlanta's current one too, which in the time frame encompassed by this book was used by Milwaukee. At no point (except in the Bibliography and Index, where I had no alternative) have I used these monikers in the book.

But rather than carp about the issue, I'd like to propose a simple, constructive solution:

Dear Atlanta Ownership and Management,

Why don't you re-brand your team as the Grays, or the Americans? The first name symbolically honors the greatness of the Negro Leagues; the second pays homage to the people you have till now so casually demeaned.

Love,
Philip Lee

Chapter Notes

I agree with Scott Simkus that "scholarly techniques yield books which are footnoted, with innovative source material, and they are 90 percent accurate. And sadly, many of these books are nearly impossible to enjoy. The footnotes and commitment to scholarly standards sometimes sucks the soul out of the material. They become textbooks, and nobody buys textbooks unless they're required to."

I too find the intrusion of constant inter-textual numbering a barrier to enjoyable reading. That's no judgment on the writers from whose work I drew, many of whom employ footnotes and endnotes galore; that's just me. My endnotes are always sited (*and cited*) at the ends of paragraphs, to minimize interruption of the reading flow; these notes often contain multiple citations, and I've tried to state clearly which citation relates to which quote or idea.

In sum, I've done my best to craft prose that's historically accurate, bears little or no resemblance to a textbook, and retains some semblance, however fleeting, of a soul.

In consulting references for this book, I attempted in all cases to obtain the original, primary source. In reading other writers' bibliographies, I'd often notice that a chain had formed: one writer would cite the sources of a second writer, who would cite a third, and so on. Wherever possible I've returned to the primary sources. Occasionally I found strange errors in transcription or attribution—errors that have crept through book after book, decade after decade, in a self-perpetuating cycle.

In all but a handful of cases (noted below), I succeeded in tracking down the primary source. In a few cases, institutions that I know hold the relevant information wouldn't acknowledge repeated attempts at contact; in others, I declined to do business with institutions that charge either outrageous or open-ended fees (the effect is the same in practical terms), despite the fact that I could provide the author, the edition, the date, the page, and sometimes even the column that holds the pertinent information. I won't name and shame the offending institutions—but I will observe that charging more than a nominal fee for information is a hindrance to research, and thus an obstacle to a true and complete understanding of our collective history.

My sincere thanks to the dedicated librarians, archivists, authors and historians throughout the United States and Canada who helped me obtain the vast majority of the information I sought.

Introduction

1. John Thorn and Pete Palmer, *The Hidden Game of Baseball*, rev. ed. (New York: Doubleday, 1985), p. 4.

2. William Brashler, *Josh Gibson: A Life in the Negro Leagues,* paperback ed. (Chicago: Ivan R. Dee, 2000), pp. xii–xiii.

3. Eric Enders, "Negro Leagues: Measuring the Quality of Competition," Hall of Miller and Eric (website), May 10, 2017, Homemlb.wordpress.com/2017/05/10/negro-leagues-measuring-the-quality-of-competition/.

4. Howard Bryant, "MLB Can Add Negro Leagues to Official Records but Can Never Change What It Did to Black Players," ESPN, December 18, 2020. espn.com/mlb/story/_/id/30540089/mlb-add-negro-leagues-official-records-never-change-did-black-players.

5. Cory Franklin, "There Is a Better Way to Honor the Negro Leagues," Inside Sources, January 12, 2021. insidesources.com/there-is-a-better-way-to-honor-the-negro-leagues/.

6. Owen Poindexter, "MLB's Move to 'Elevate' the Negro Leagues Risks Diminishing Them," Slate, December 23, 2020. slate.com/culture/2020

/12/negro-leagues-major-league-baseball-record-books-complications.html.

7. Lawrence Ritter and Donald Honig, *The 100 Greatest Ballplayers of All Time* (New York: Crown, 1981), p. ii.

8. Thorn and Palmer, *Hidden Game*, p. 248, note 1.

9. Rob Neyer, "March Archives," ESPN, March 3, 2000, espn.go.com/mlb/s/2000/0307/406215.html.

10. Bill James, *The New Bill James Historical Baseball Abstract*, updated ed. (New York: Free Press, 2001), p. 194.

11. Holway is quoted from *Voices from the Great Black Baseball Leagues*, rev. ed. (New York: Da Capo, 1992), p. xix.

12. Eric Garcia McKinley, "The Color of Baseball Statistics," Baseball Prospectus, February 3, 2016, baseballprospectus.com/news/article/28355/prospectus-feature-the-color-of-baseball-statistics/#_ftn11.

13. Neyer, "March Archives."

14. Neyer, "March Archives."

15. The Rickey quote is from "Goodby to Some Old Baseball Ideas," *Life*, August 2, 1954, p. 78.

Chapter 1

1. Peterson, *Only the Ball Was White: A History of Legendary Black Players and All-Black Professional Teams*, expanded paperback ed. (New York: Oxford University Press, 1992), p. 30.

2. The original source for these quotes is *The Ball Players' Chronicle*, December 19, 1867. For a definitive account of these events, see Ryan A. Swanson's *When Baseball Went White: Reconstruction, Reconciliation, and Dreams of a National Pastime* (Lincoln: University of Nebraska Press, 2014), ch. 4.

3. *DeWitt Base Ball Guide for 1868*, p. 85, as quoted in Swanson, *When Baseball Went White*, p. 101.

4. Roger Brooke Taney and the Supreme Court of the United States, *U.S. Reports: Dred Scott v. Sandford* (1856), PDF, pp. 407–415.

5. *Louisville Courier-Journal*, August 22, 1881.

6. This text is excerpted from an obituary of Walker from an unknown newspaper, hand-dated "13 May [19]24" (viewable at digitalshoebox.org/digital/collection/books/id/59339/). I was unable to determine the original source newspaper, which has ramifications for when, exactly, Walker faced this discrimination. The article mentions "the Syracuse (N.Y.) Stars, the Cleveland Whites; also the Oberlin and Ann Arbor teams," which would seem to encompass the whole of his baseball career. It's the reference to the Whites that led me to place the quote where I did chronologically; others may interpret the reference differently.

7. The Husman quote is from "Cap Anson vs. Fleet Walker," part of *Jackie Robinson 75: Baseball's Re-Integration*, an online exhibit at the SABR website, https://sabr.org/jackie75/segregation/.

8. *Toledo Daily Blade*, August 11, 1883, p. 3.

9. Brown is quoted in Rosenberg, *Cap Anson 4: Bigger than Babe Ruth: Captain Anson of Chicago* (Arlington, VA: Tile Books, 2003–2006), p. 424.

10. For Rosenberg's speculation on Anson's role, see "Cap Anson and the Color Line: Did He Truly Influence Baseball's 'Gentlemen's Agreement'?" Black Athlete, June 15, 2008.

11. *Toledo Daily Blade*, May 5, 1884, p. 3.

12. Quoted in numerous modern publications, probably appearing first in Petersen, *Only the Ball Was White*, p. 23. It's reprinted with many small differences in wording and punctuation—but that's hardly surprising, as *Sporting Life*, the *Cincinnati Enquirer*, and probably other papers introduced small variations within days of its first appearance in the press. I've reproduced the earliest known printing of the text, which, in the absence of the letter itself, must be considered the *prima facie* version; this appeared in the *Toledo Evening Bee*, September 18, 1884, p. 4.

13. White, *Sol White's History*, p. 76.

14. Malloy, "Sol White," p. lviii.

15. In his 1995 introduction to *Sol White's History of Colored Base Ball*, Jerry Malloy misattributed this quote to the *Newark Journal* for the next day, April 9, 1887. In an earlier article ("Out at Home," written in 1983), Malloy misattributed the quote to *Sol White's History of Colored Base Ball*, an error that many writers, including official MLB historian John Thorn, have passed on over the years.

16. Richard White, "Baseball's John Fowler: The 1887 Season in Binghamton, New York," *Afro Americans in New York Life and History* 16, no. 1 (January 31, 1992): 7.

17. The "watermelons at home plate" and "simmerian visitors" quotations are from the *Binghamton Daily Leader* for June 10, 1887, p. 4.

18. The Browns players' letter is quoted in numerous publications, probably appearing first in Peterson's *Only the Ball Was White*, p. 31; as it's the earliest version I could locate, I've accepted Peterson's wording.

19. Stovey's 1887 NEL wins total is sometimes reported as 33 or 35.

20. This account is composited from two 1888 accounts: the May 24 *Toronto Daily Mail*, p. 2, and the June 6 *Sporting Life*, June 6, p. 9. A curious postscript: The November 24 *Daily Mail* reported (p. 4) that "if any ill-feeling had existed between Manager C.H. Cushman, of Toronto, and Catcher Walker over the trouble they had in Toronto during a game last season, it was entirely blotted out at the banquet last evening. Mr. Cushman proposed a toast to the health of the colored players of the association, and after Walker had responded with a witty little speech, both gentlemen explained the affair at Toronto. The whole affair arose through a misunderstanding and was caused by a crowd of 'hoodlums,' it was said." Make of this what you will.

21. Not even local newspapers necessarily mentioned Anson's refusal to play if Walker took the

field; the September 28 *Syracuse Daily Standard* covers the game at length (p. 7) but makes no mention of Anson's action.

22. The Blackistone quote is from "It's Time for Baseball to Acknowledge Cap Anson's Role in Erecting Its Color Barrier," *Washington Post*, December 2, 2015. washingtonpost.com/sports/nationals/its-time-for-baseball-to-acknowledge-cap-ansons-role-in-erecting-a-color-barrier/2015/12/02/b9b97eb8-9916-11e5-94f0-9eeaf-f906ef3_story.html.

23. Roosevelt's first known use of the phrase "race suicide" came in an October 18, 1902, letter, marked "Private" but subsequently widely distributed: "What is fundamentally infinitely more important than any other question in this country … is, the question of race suicide, complete or partial, which must follow from the attitude of our people [*sic*] as a whole toward wifehood, motherhood, and fatherhood…. The man or woman who deliberately avoids marriage and has a heart so cold as to know no passion and a brain so shallow and selfish as to dislike having children, is in effect a criminal against the race." Compare with Joseph Goebbels: "We are not willing to stand aside and watch the collapse of our national life and the destruction of the blood we have inherited…. Families with many children are given particular attention, since we want to rescue the nation from decline." Compare also with Tucker Carlson: "The Democratic Party is trying to replace the current electorate, the voters now casting ballots, with new people, more obedient voters from the Third World…. Our civilization is superior, and we need to defend it." This is not merely a problem of the past. (The Roosevelt quote is from his letter to Bessie Van Voorst, October 18, 1902, Theodore Roosevelt Center at Dickinson State University, theodorerooseveltcenter.org/Research/Digital-Library/Record/ImageViewer?libID=o183324&imageNo=1., pp. 1–2; the Goebbels quote is from a speech given on March 18, 1933, retrieved at research.calvin.edu/german-propaganda-archive/goeb55.htm; the Carlson quote is compounded from *Tucker Carlson Tonight* for April 9, 2021, and July 10, 2017.)

24. Numerous papers across the US ran the "race suicide" story, including the April 5 *Baltimore Sun*. The wire service quote is universally misattributed to the March 18 *Chicago Daily Tribune*—an odd error, considering that the election wasn't held until April 4 and the article is written in the past tense.

25. Anson, *A Ball Player's Career: Being the Personal Experiences and Reminiscences of Adrian C. Anson* (Chicago: Era, 1900), pp. 148–150.

26. White, *Sol White's History*, pp. 76–77.

Chapter 2

1. Many of the events cited in the first half of this chapter are chronologized in James Charlton's *Baseball Chronology: The Complete History of the Most Important Events in the Game of Baseball* (New York: Macmillan, 1991) or documented in Bruce Nash and Allen Zullo's *The Baseball Hall of Shame* (Washington, DC: Lyons Press).

2. The description of Anson's "bat" is from the *Boston Sunday Globe*, June 30, 1889, p. 4.

3. The Gerlach quote is from "Umpire Honor Rolls," *Baseball Research Journal* 8 (1979), research.sabr.org/journals/umpire-honor-rolls.

4. Bill James addresses this issue in detail in *The New Bill James Historical Baseball Abstract* (New York: Free Press, 2001), which, if you don't own it, go correct that situation right away. There are some great baseball books out there—*The Boys of Summer* and *Ty Cobb: A Terrible Beauty* spring immediately to mind—but for my money, the *New Historical Abstract* is still the best of them all.

5. "Was The Federal League Really a Major League?," National Pastime Museum, accessed September 10, 2022, https://www.thenationalpastimemuseum.com/article/was-federal-league-really-major-league/.

Chapter 3

1. David A. Kaiser, "A Troubling Myth About Jackie Robinson Endures," *Time,* April 15, 2006, time.com/4294175/jackie-robinson-burns-landis-myth/; David Pietrusza, *Judge and Jury: The Life and Times of Judge Kenesaw Mountain Landis* (South Bend, IN: Diamond, 1998), p. xv.

2. Macht is quoted from "Does Baseball Deserve This Black Eye? A Dissent from the Universal Casting of Blame on Kenesaw Mountain Landis for Baseball's Failure to Sign Black Players Before 1946," *Baseball Research Journal* 38, no. 1 (summer 2009): 26–30.

3. The Cuban Giants are quoted in the *Washington Post*, November 2, 1921, p. 17.

4. Rule 691 is quoted in "World's Champions May Not Go Barnstorming Anymore," *St. Louis Post-Dispatch*, November 8, 1911, p. 24.

5. Michael M. Oleksak and Mary Adams Oleksak, *Beisbol: Latin Americans and the Grand Old Game* (Grand Rapids, MI: Masters Press, 1991), pp. 20–22.

6. Durocher's progressive attitudes on race are well documented. "Hank [Thompson] and I were the first players of color the [New York] Giants ever had," wrote Monte Irvin, "and when we arrived Leo Durocher called a clubhouse meeting. 'Hey, men, listen up here,' Durocher said. 'We've got two new members, Hank and Monte, and I think they can help us. Let me say this: the only thing I'm going to say about color is if you can play baseball and help us win and make some money, I don't give a damn if you're green, you can play on this team.' Leo was sincere about that, and he showed it in many ways. We had a lot of southerners on the team … but we never had any problems with race, and I attribute a lot of that to Leo." (Monte Irvin and Phil Pepe,

Few and Chosen: Defining Negro Leagues Greatness [Chicago: Triumph, 2007], ch. 5, n.p.).

7. The Durocher quote was originally given to a reporter for the *Daily Worker*, July 17, 1942, and was subsequently quoted in numerous papers the same day, including in "'Big Time' Ball Knows No Color Line," *Lincoln* (NE) *Star*; Landis's phone call to Cummiskey is in "Landis Steps to Bat for Negro Ball Players"; Landis's INS statement is quoted in numerous papers, including the *Fresno* (CA) *Bee*, July 17, 1942, p. 10; Landis's press conference was reported in numerous papers, including the *Capitol Times* (Madison WI), July 18, 1942, p. 8.

8. Moffi is quoted from *The Conscience of the Game: Baseball's Commissioners from Landis to Selig* (Lincoln: University of Nebraska Press, 2006), p. 42.

9. Sengstacke is paraphrasing President Roosevelt's Executive Order 8802 of June 25, 1941, which prohibited "discrimination in the employment of workers in defense industries or government because of race, creed, color, or national origin."

10. "Joint Meeting of the National League of Professional Base Ball Clubs and the American League of Professional Base Ball Clubs," pp. 9–87.

11. Occasional lapses in spelling and grammar, typical of the telegram age, are amended here for readability. The original telegrams can be found in the Baseball Hall of Fame Online Collection: American Youth for Democracy, Accession Number BL-287-2016-75; College Station Post Office Employees, Accession Number BL-287-2016-49; Hotel and Club Union, Accession Number BL-287-2016-47; International Workers Order, Accession Number BL-287-2016-50; United Office and Professional Workers of America (two telegrams), Accession Numbers BL-287-2016-74 and BL-287-2016-53.

12. Brewer is quoted in Tygiel, *Extra Bases: Reflections on Jackie Robinson, Race, and Baseball History* (Lincoln: University of Nebraska Press, 2002), p. 69.

13. Heydler is quoted in the *Indianapolis Recorder*, March 4, 1933, p. 2. The late Robert W. Peterson doesn't provide an exact date for the Griffith quote, which is cited by Scott Simkus, Julies Tygiel and others, but always with Peterson as the source. I couldn't find any reference to the quote within the limited 1938 Google News Archive collection of Lacy's paper, the Black-owned *Washington Tribune*, and Lacy makes no mention of the interview in his autobiography. I pass along the Griffith quote with the qualification that I was unable to confirm it independently.

14. Durocher is quoted in Cummiskey, "Landis Steps to Bat for Negro Ball Players," unknown newspaper, July 17, 1942, at the National Baseball Hall of Fame, collection.baseballhall.org/PASTIME/landis-steps-bat-negro-ball-players-article-1942-july-17.

15. The July 28 *Evening News* interview is misattributed by Moore to the issue for July 30.

16. MacPhail, "Statement of Opinion on 'The Negro in Baseball,'" submitted by MacPhail to the New York City Mayor's Committee on Unity, ca. September–October 1945, pp. 3–4. Accessible at nlbm.mlblogs.com/mcphail-letter-shows-staunch-objection-to-integrate-baseball-c293bab9676. The original document, which was my textual source for this book, is un-dated—but the October 4, 1945, *Sporting News* refers to it as if it had just been submitted to the Committee (p. 14), so MacPhail presumably handed it over in late September or early October 1945. Much of its language was subsequently recycled for the "Race Question" section of the MacPhail Report—proving, if proof is needed, the weight of the man's hand on the racist tone of that document.

17. See Rick Swaine's *The Integration of Major League Baseball: A Team by Team History* (Jefferson, NC: McFarland, 2009) for a look at the appalling comments *The Sporting News* continued to make on race issues as late as 1961.

18. "Report of Major League Steering Committee for Submission to the National and American Leagues at Their Meetings in Chicago," August 27, 1946, pp. 483–485, in *Study of Monopoly Power: Hearings Before the Subcommittee on Study of Monopoly Power of the Committee of the Judiciary, Serial No. 1, Part 6: Organized Baseball*. Government Printing Office, 1952. babel.hathitrust.org/cgi/pt?id=umn.31951d03669259b&view=1up&seq=809.

19. Light, *The Cultural Encyclopedia of Baseball*, 2nd ed. (Jefferson, NC: McFarland, 2005), p. 487.

20. Some of you may argue for Willard Brown over Irvin or Doby in the starting squad—and you may be correct—but Monte and Larry both produced at All-Star levels in the Majors, while Brown, as we'll see later, wasn't given a proper chance. For the purposes of this exercise we'll go with demonstrated MLB ability. It should be noted, though, that the availability of a .349 career hitter who *isn't* selected for the starting squad speaks volumes about the depth of talent in the first wave of Negro Leaguers to reach the Majors.

21. Murray is quoted by numerous sources, including Schoenfeld, "Ten Reasons Willie Mays is Greatest Ever," ESPN, May 6, 2011, espn.com/blog/sweetspot/post/_/id/10260/ten-reasons-willie-mays-is-greatest-ever.

22. Rickey's quote is often mangled by historians in the re-telling—but that's probably a reflection on contemporary reporting; the *Pittsburgh Courier*, for instance, misquoted him just three days after the appearance of the original article. Rickey was equally cold-blooded about Southern players who might strike against Jackie: "Even if some players quit," he said, "they'll be back after a year or two in a cotton mill." (*Knoxville* [IN] *News-Sentinel*, October 24, 1945, p. 12.)

23. Barnhill is quoted in Holway, *Black Diamonds: Life in the Negro Leagues from the Men Who Lived It* (Westport, CT: Meckler, 1989), p. 142; Manley is quoted in Thorn, "Black Ball, Part

5," *Our Game* (blog), March 20, 2015. ourgame.mlblogs.com/black-ball-part-5-79ae6fe4012f.

24. The Atlanta Crackers quote is in Swaine, *Integration of Major League Baseball*, p. 97. See Steve Jacobsen's *Carrying Jackie's Torch: The Players Who Integrated Baseball—and America* (Chicago: Lawrence Hall, 2007), and especially the chapter on Eddie Murray's brother Charlie, for a harrowing account of the Black minor league experience from the 1940s all the way through the 1970s.

25. Bates, "Baseball's Failed 1978 Donald Sterling Moment," SBNation. sbnation.com/mlb/2014/5/1/5672616/donald-sterling-baseball-racist-owners-calvin-griffith-bowie-kuhn.

26. Koppel, ABC News *Nightline*, April 6, 1987.

27. Quoted by numerous sources, including the *New York Times*, "Baseball's Very Big Problem."

Chapter 4

1. Morgan is quoted in Craggs, "Say-It-Ain't-So Joe," SF Weekly, July 6, 2005, sfweekly.com/news/say-it-aint-so-joe/.

2. Schoenfield, "Generation OPS: How Powerful Young All-Stars are Re-Defining the Game." ESPN, July 9, 2019, espn.co.uk/mlb/story/_/id/27148938/generation-ops-how-powerful-young-all-stars-redefining-game.

3. This and the following lists are based on NgL inter-league play only, and exclude all other forms of competition, including exhibition, playoff, and All-Star games.

4. Bradford Doolittle and David Schoenfield, "What the Stats in an 82-Game Season Could Look Like," ESPN, May 27, 2020. espn.co.uk/mlb/story/_/id/29207026/will-anyone-hit-400-post-112-era-82-game-2020-mlb-leaderboard-look-like.

Chapter 5

1. James's tests can be found in *The New Bill James Historical Abstract*: the structural tests on p. 31, the statistical tests on p. 876, and the prevalence of teenaged 20-game winners on pp. 864–865.

2. Stahl, "The Secret History of Black Baseball Players in Canada's Great White North," Salon, April 30, 2017, salon.com/2017/04/30/the-secret-history-of-black-baseball-players-in-canadas-great-white-north_partner/.

3. Irvin, *Nice Guys Finish First*, p. 63.

4. See "NgL and Early MLB League Structure" for a breakdown of early league instabilities.

5. Doby, April 13, 2000, interview with Fay Vincent and Claire Smith, SABR Oral History Collection, oralhistory.sabr.org/interviews/doby-larry-1994/.

6. The Thorn quote is from "1860s–1900s: Lumber and Crossed Fingers," This Great Game. thisgreatgame.com/ballparks-eras-1860s-1900s.html.

7. O'Neil quote from "Inning 5: Shadow Ball," undated interview at the PBS companion site for *Baseball: A Film by Ken Burns*, PBS, aired September 22, 1994, web.archive.org/web/20210227041054/http://www.pbs.org/kenburns/baseball/shadowball/oneil.html.

8. Doby, interview with Vincent and Smith.

9. Paige is quoted in Larry Tye, *Satchel: The Life and Times of an American Legend* (New York: Random House, 2009), p. 25.

10. Two James quotes are compounded here: the first is from *The New Bill James Historical Abstract*, p. 170, and the second is quoted in Simkus, as an epigraph preceding the Introduction to *Outsider Baseball*. Simkus cites the quote as originating from "billjamesonline.com, April 2012." I couldn't find the original source among James's posts for April 2012, so I emailed him to ensure the quote was authentically his. His reply: "It sounds like something I would say, and it is true; a lot of the minor league organizations of that era made PHENOMENAL mistakes in judging talent. But I don't have any idea when I said this or where I said it....I answer questions from readers in a section of Bill James Online called 'Hey, Bill'....The quote may have come from a 'Hey, Bill' answer." (James, personal correspondence with the author, 2021.)

11. Data set parameters and limitations for this and the following fielding studies: NgL data for 1940–48 includes MEX data for 1940–41 only. No fielding data for ECL, 1924–25; NNL, 1925, 1927, 1929–30; NSL, 1932; NN2 or NAL, 1939–42, 1944. No HBP data for IND, 1929; NN2 or NAL, 1939–42, 1944. No SF data for any NgL season.

12. James, personal correspondence with the author, 2020.

13. For this study, league OPS is weighted by plate appearances per player.

14. James, *New Bill James*, pp. 864-65.

Chapter 6

1. White, *Sol White's History*, p. 65.

2. John Badham, *The Bingo Long Traveling All-Stars & Motor Kings* (Detroit: Motown Productions, 1976), starting at 29 min., 48 sec.

3. Borges, "Baseball's Dirty Secret," The National, April 11, 2009. thenational.ae/sport/baseball-s-dirty-secret-1.495096. In April 2000, Larry Doby gave a withering assessment of *Bingo Long* to Fay Vincent and Claire Smith: "If kids look at that and they don't know the history of Afro-American baseball, that's what they'll focus on.... If you think about that era, particularly from an Afro-American standpoint, you think about a Stepin Fetchit, or Amos and Andy, and a lot of people judge Afro-Americans like that kind of a person.... If you show baseball in its true form as far as the Negro Leagues are concerned, you'll see baseball players as good as any player in the American League or the National League.... That, to me, was a bad image, not just on Negro baseball—on

baseball, period." (Doby interview with Vincent and Smith, author's transcription.)

4. Posnanski, "The Baseball 100: No. 76, Willie McCovey," Athletic, January 11, 2020, theathletic.co.uk/1516206/2020/01/11/the-baseball-100-no-76-willie-mccovey/.

5. Jacobsen, *Carrying Jackie's Torch*, p. 8.

6. Paige is quoted in Lew Freedman, *African American Pioneers of Baseball: A Biographical Encyclopedia* (Westport, CT: Greenwood, 2007), p. 126.

7. Alan Schwartz, "Numbers Are Cast in Bronze, but Are Not Set in Stone," *New York Times*, July 31, 2005, nytimes.com/2005/07/31/sports/baseball/numbers-are-cast-in-bronze-but-are-not-set-in-stone.html.

8. Neyer, "Two More Walks for Williams," ESPN, May 29, 2002, espn.go.com/mlb/columns/neyer_rob/1388300.html.

9. Beer is quoted from "How Would Oscar Have Fared in MLB?," Oscar Charleston.com, February 2, 2019, oscarcharleston.com/2019/02/02/how-would-oscar-have-fared-in-mlb/.

10. Costas on the April 27, 2019, episode of *Real Time with Bill Maher* (author's transcription); Costas's comments begin at 18 min, 39sec.

11. The "legend" quote is found in *The Man Who Shot Liberty Valance* (Hollywood, CA: Paramount, 1962) at 119 min., 47 sec.

Chapter 7

1. Hubbell is quoted in Wendell Smith, "'Negroes Will Never Crash Majors,' Says Bill Terry; Carl Hubbell Lauds Colored Players," *Pittsburgh Courier*, July 22, 1939, p. S1.

2. Kuhn is quoted in Wells Twombly, "Crumbs for the Outcasts," *Sporting News*, February 20, 1971, 41.

3. Robinson is quoted in Ben Bradlee, Jr., *The Kid: The Immortal Life of Ted Williams* (New York: Little, Brown, 2013), p. 510.

Chapter 8

1. James's essay on the subject can be found in *The Bill James Historical Baseball Abstract*, p. 221.

2. The words shouted by Japanese soldiers are cited by numerous sources, including Robert Elias, *The Empire Strikes Out: How Baseball Sold U.S. Foreign Policy and Promoted the American Way Abroad* (New York: New Press, 2010), p. 159.

3. The first Julia Ruth Stevens quote is in "Babe Ruth's Effect on American Culture," Babe Ruth Central, baberuthcentral.com/hero-and-icon/babe-ruths-effect-on-american-culture; the second is in Kerasotis, "Home, at the Other House That Ruth Built," *New York Times*, March 10, 2014, nytimes.com/2014/03/11/sports/baseball/yankees-home-at-the-other-house-that-ruth-built.html?ref=sports&_r=1.

Chapter 9

1. James, *New Bill James*, p. 664.

2. Irvin is quoted in Freedman, *African American Pioneers*, p. 138; Manley is quoted in numerous sources, including the National Baseball Hall of Fame website, "Monte Irvin," baseballhall.org/hall-of-famers/irvin-monte.

3. Three Irvin quotes are compounded here: the first is in Golenbock, *In the Country of Brooklyn: Inspiration to the World* (New York: HarperCollins, 2008), p. 149; the second is from *Nice Guys Finish First*, pp. 102–103; the third is in Posnanski, "Remembering Monte Irvin," The Greatness That Was and the Legend That Could've Been." NBC Sportsworld, undated. sportsworld.nbcsports.com/monte-irvin-legend/.

4. Posnanski, "Remembering Monte Irvin."

Chapter 10

1. I wanted to use, but cannot verify, a purported quote by Dan Daniel from *The Sporting News* for July 16, the day before Brown and Thompson joined the Browns: "In St. Louis they say that the fans would never stand for Negroes on the Cardinals or the Browns." This quote is frequently included in histories of the time. Jules Tygiel reproduces the quote on page 219 of *Baseball's Great Experiment: Jackie Robinson and His Legacy* (New York: Oxford University Press, 1983), attributing it to "*Sporting News*, July 16, 1947" (p. 365, n. 31); the quote is reprinted by Swaine, who cites Tygiel as his source, in *The Integration of Major League Baseball*; others, in turn, cite Swaine. Daniel has two articles in the July 16 issue, but neither contains the quote; in fact, I couldn't find this or any similar quote by Daniel or any other writer, in any issue of *The Sporting News* from 1942 through 1948, despite using a wide variety of search combinations. The closest match I found was a somewhat similar quote from page 16 of the very issue cited by Tygiel, attributed to "a big league All-Star": "I know we are going to have Negroes on all clubs, with the possible exception of the Senators, Cardinals and Browns."

2. The shoe story is as told to George Stanford by Browns infielder Billy Hitchcock; see Stanford, "Willard Brown / Hank Thompson," Baseball Fever, January 28, 2006.

3. Etkin, *Innings Ago: Recollections by Kansas City Ballplayers of their Days in the Game* (Marceline, MO: Normandy Square, 1987), pp. 101–102.

4. Etkin, *Innings Ago*, pp. 101–102.

5. Etkin, *Innings Ago*, pp. 101–102.

6. DeWitt is quoted in Cobbledick, "Premature Shower in Final Game of '47 Proved Washout for Heath as a Brownie," *Sporting News*, December 17, 1947, 7.

7. Robinson is quoted in Jacobsen, *Carrying Jackie's Torch*, pp. 142–143.

8. DeWitt and Thompson are quoted in Robert

Kuhn McGregor, *A Calculus of Color: The Integration of Baseball's American League* (Jefferson, NC: McFarland, 2015), p. 115. Contradicting his earlier assessments, Hank Thompson shared a much more charitable recollection of Heath and other white teammates in the December 1965 issue of *Sport* magazine: "Muddy Ruel treated me fair. So did the fans. I can't say the same for all the players. They never said anything directly to me or to Willard. But some reacted in ways that were just as clear.... John Berardino, Jeff Heath, Bob Dillinger, Walt Judnich and Vern Stephens went out of their way to make life easier for me and Brown. If they'd see us snubbed, they'd sit down and begin signing with us. Stephens in particular would chat with me and Brown, tell us about the other pitchers in the league, talk to me about how he made the double play, so we'd mesh smoothly." The great majority of histories that cover the Browns of these years recount a less rosy version of events. Only Vern Stephens emerges unscathed by the verdict of history.

9. The absence of 1949 NgL records for walks and hit by pitch prevents calculation of OPS and OPS+. Thanks to Kevin Johnson for providing me with post–1948 NgL statistics (such as they exist).

Chapter 11

1. The smaller comparison set indicated by the phrase "live-ball catchers" is sometimes necessitated by missing data—and in the case of 19th century catcher Deacon White, by the completely different nature of the game when he was active. White caught without protective equipment and bare-handed the incoming pitches; can you imagine how he would've coped with the likes of Sandy Koufax or Randy Johnson?

2. Chalek, "A Reductive View of Catcher Defense," Hall of Merit discussion board, January 19, 2006, post 25 (username "Dr. Chaleeko"), baseballthinkfactory.org/hall_of_merit/discussion/yogi_berra. My thanks to the good Doctor for permission to quote him at length.

3. Rizzuto quote in William F. McNeil, *Backstop: A History of the Catcher and a Sabermetric Ranking of 50 All-Time Greats* (Jefferson, NC: McFarland, 2006), p. 75.

4. Meany, *The Artful Dodgers* (New York: Grosset & Dunlap, 1954), p 101.

5. Two Cochrane quotes are compounded here: the first is in Lacy, "Mickey Cochrane Envisions Campy as 'Great' Catcher," *Washington Afro-American,* May 4, 1950, 19; the second is in McNeil, *Backstop,* p. 75. The Dickey quote, which appears in Lacy's column in the *Washington Afro-American* for April 18, 1950, p. 18, is misattributed by Lanctot to the *Baltimore Afro-American* for April 22.

6. Wargo's summary is found at the Hall of Merit discussion board, post 20 (username "ronw"), baseballthinkfactory.org/hall_of_merit/discussion/election_results_hom_voters_think_gibson_bench_berra_and_carter_are_the_fin.

7. Erskine is quoted in "Bill James on Fielding, Part 7," Fox Sports, January 29, 2015. foxsports.com/stories/other/bill-james-on-fielding-part-7.

8. "Bill James on Fielding, Part 7."

9. Two Cobb quotes are compounded here: the first is quoted verbatim in McGowen, "Campy Caught 100 Contests in Nine Straight Campaigns," *Sporting News,* February 5, 1958, p. 11, and paraphrased in numerous early 1958 newspaper articles printed after Campy's career-ending automobile accident (post–1958 reprintings have generally copied the paraphrasings); the second is in McNeil, *Backstop,* p. 223; the Speaker quote is likewise from McNeil, *Backstop,* p. 223; the Campanella quote is from *It's Good to Be Alive* (Lincoln: University of Nebraska Press, 1995), p. 178.

10. Campanella is generally cited as co-integrating the New England League with Don Newcombe. Campy joined the NENL on May 8, 1946; Newcombe joined on May 16.

11. See Campanella, *Good to Be Alive,* pp. 96–98.

12. The first Benswanger quote is in Peterson, *Only the Ball,* p. 177, and is often mistakenly said to be from 1940; Rodney is quoted in Irwin Silber, *Press Box Red: The Story of Lester Rodney, the Communist Who Helped Break the Color Line in American Sports* (Philadelphia: Temple University Press, 2003), p. 69; the second Benswanger quote is from the *Philadelphia Tribune,* August 1, 1942, p. 13.

13. Both James quotes are from *The New Bill James Historical Baseball Abstract,* pp. 181 and 372.

14. O'Malley is quoted in Frommer, *Rickey and Robinson,* p. 115; two Sukeforth quotes are compounded here: the first is in Tygiel's introduction to *It's Good to Be Alive,* p. xi; the second is in the National Baseball Hall of Fame website's "Roy Campanella," baseballhall.org/hall-of-famers/campanella-roy.

15. The first Campanella quote is in Frommer, *Rickey and Robinson,* p. 111; the second is in Young, "Inside Sports," *Jet,* p. 59.

16. Golenbock, *Bums,* p. 216.

17. Bavasi is quoted in Fimrite, "Triumph of the Spirit"; Alston is quoted in Watson, "Forgotten Stories of Courage and Inspiration."

18. The Posnanski quote is from "No. 66: Roy Campanella," *Joe Blogs,* January 4, 2015, web.archive.org/web/20150316203132/http://joeposnanski.com/no-66-roy-campanella/.

19. Campanella is quoted in Lanctot, *Campy: The Two Lives of Roy Campanella* (New York: Simon & Schuster, 2011), p. 308.

20. The Soderholm-Difatte quote is from *The Golden Era of Major League Baseball: A Time of Transition and Integration* (Lanham, MD: Rowman & Littlefield, 2015), p. 73; King is quoted in numerous sources, including Lipsyte, "Playing the Game They Loved," *New York Times,* August 7, 1983. nytimes.com/1983/08/07/books/playing-the-game-they-loved.html.

Chapter 12

1. Bugliosi, *Outrage*, p. 289 (slightly abridged here).

2. The Murphy quote is from "Luke Easter," Negro Leagues Baseball Museum website, nlbemuseum.com/history/players/easter.html.

3. It's possible that "'Fireball' Blocker" (recorded by Seamheads as "Blocker," Detroit Stars, 1931), "E. Smith" (recorded by Seamheads as Eugene Smith, NgL 1940–42 and 1946–48) and George Glass (recorded by Seamheads as "Glass," Newark Eagles 1942) also played for both the Giants and recognized Negro League teams, but biographical and newspaper information are too incomplete to be certain that these are the same men.

4. Posnanski, "Invisible Man," NBC Sportsworld, undated, sportsworld.nbcsports.com/invisible-man/.

5. The James quote is from *The New Bill James Historical Abstract*, p. 245.

6. A number of sources cite Easter as hitting 74 home runs in 1946. However, it's unfortunately not true, as claimed by Alex Painter, that this number was "widely reported in multiple contemporary accounts" (Painter, "A Legend of Halberstamian Proportions," *Negro Leagues Up Close* (blog), May 27, 2020. homeplatedontmove.wordpress.com/2020/05/27/luke-easter-a-legend-of-halberstamian-proportions/). In fact, no concrete documentation exists for the specific total of 74—but we can get very close indeed. It can be verified that Easter hit 12 home runs in Hawaiian Fall League play ("Luke Easter Is Top Hitter of Cincinnati Crescents," *Honolulu Star-Crescent*, Oct. 16). As the Honolulu press was simultaneously tracking his independent home runs and these 12 were separately reported, this leaves 62 homers to account for via independent play. Such play was almost never documented in newspapers, and an exact independent total of 62 can't be confirmed—but it *is* possible to document his 40th, 41st, 42nd, 43rd, 49th, 50th, 52nd, 57th, 58th, and 60th independent home runs via contemporary reporting, primarily through the *Honolulu Star-Bulletin* and sometimes confirmed by papers in the continental United States. The highly reliable *Oakland Tribune* is the medium of reportage for number 60 (October 22, 1946, p. 17). This is as close to absolute verification as it's possible to get for virtually any independent-league feat of the time. The contemporary press also spoke of Easter potentially breaking Joe Hauser's organized-ball record of 63, set in International League play in 1930, but this feat was never celebrated, which fixes Easter's final independent-ball tally between 60 and 62. There seems to me no logical rationale to deny Easter the final two un-documentable homers with which he is universally credited.

7. Easter's independent-league total is cited in Manning, "They're Gonna Like Big Luke," *Collier's Weekly*, August 5, 1950, p. 70. Another source, Cy Kritzer's "Luke 'Loves Buffalo'" (*Buffalo Evening News*, July 13, 1957, 5), pegs Easter's 1947 totals at 60 home runs with a .320 average. Kritzer's article is the only source that claims these numbers, against multiple sources that confirm 43 homers; also, Manning was writing three years after the season in question, Kritzer was writing a decade later.

8. Manning, "Big Luke." The Grays team itself confirmed these numbers to multiple reporters, including Kritzer, "Luke 'Loves Buffalo.'"

9. Finch, "Easter, Padre Negro from St. Louis, Playing the Blues with Bat on Coast," *St. Louis Sporting News*, March 30, 1949, 2.

10. *Cleveland Plain Dealer*, November 18, 1953, p. 27.

11. The Manning quote is from "They're Gonna Like Big Luke," p. 70.

12. Easter is quoted in Bump, "Luke Easter: Better Than Ruth?," *Rochester (NY) Democrat and Chronicle*, December 27, 1972, 37.

13. The un-named Cleveland player is quoted in the *Cleveland Plain Dealer*, May 5, 1950, p. 24; Easter is quoted in Grayson, "Easter's Return Takes Half of World Off Doby's Shoulders," *Ogdensburg. (NY) Journal*, July 7, 1953, 6.

14. Doby's allegation against Lopez is reported in Branson, *Greatness in the Shadows: Larry Doby and the Integration of the American League* (Lincoln: University of Nebraska Press, 2016), p. 195. Singletary (p. 250, n. 37) cites the primary source as "Joseph Thomas Moore, personal notes of comments by Doby, 18 Dec. 1980."

15. Moffi, *Conscience of the Game*, p. 38.

16. Easter is quoted in Samuelson, "About a Man Named Easter," *Metropolitan Pasadena (CA) Star-News*, June 7, 1949, p. 20.

17. Cited by numerous sources including Swaine, *The Black Stars Who Made Baseball Whole* (Jefferson, NC: McFarland, 2006), p. 85. The quote is not "gettin' my oil changed," as some sources have it; the imposition of a patois on the articulate Easter is a common feature of white reporting on Black baseball stars of the time irrespective of whether or not it figured in their speech, and there's no reason to allow that practice to continue to stain the record.

18. The Grayson quote is from "Luke Easter Is a Shot in the Arm to Lagging Indians," *Defiance (OH) Crescent News*, July 7, 1953, p. 7; Bock is quoted in Lebovitz, *The Best of Hal Lebovitz: Great Sportswriting from Six Decades in Cleveland* (Cleveland OH: Gray, 2004), p. 67.

19. "Indians Manager Al Lopez Is About Concerned Tribe's Out," *Somerset (PA) Daily American*, August 15, 1953.

20. Easter is quoted in Cattau, "Easter: The First Black Major Leaguer from St. Louis," *St. Louis Post-Dispatch*, April 5, 1992, p. 11.

21. The Keltner list, today ubiquitous in baseball analysis, originated in James, *The Politics of Glory: How Baseball's Hall of Fame Really Works* (New York: Macmillan, 1994), p. 275.

22. Cattau, "So, Maybe There Is Such a Thing

as 'The Natural,'" *Smithsonian,* August 1991, Gale Document Number GALE|CGSXXX576519146, p. 127.

23. James, *The Bill James Baseball Abstract 1981* (n.p.: self-published, 1981), p. 2.

24. Kritzer, "Luke 'Loves' Buffalo."

25. Murphy, "Luke Easter," SABR Biography Project, sabr.org/bioproj/person/f29a4070. Murphy cites the primary source, which I was unable to verify personally, as "Luke Easter—King of Swat?" by James Goodrich, printed in the *Negro Digest,* August 1950, pp. 3–8.

26. Gaylon H. White, *Singles and Smiles: How Artie Wilson Broke Baseball's Color Barrier* (Lanham, MD: Rowman & Littlefield, 2018), p. 65.

27. Holway, *Black Diamonds,* p. 33.

28. Van Hyning, "Luke Easter, Larger Than Life Figure: Mexico, Puerto Rico, and Minors: Caribbean, Minors, and American League. Part 1." Béisbol 101, April 2020. beisbol101.com/2020/04/luke-easter-larger-than-life-figure-caribbean-minors-and-american-league-part-i/."

29. Pollock, *Barnstorming to Heaven: Syd Pollock and His Great Black Teams* (Tuscaloosa: University of Alabama Press, 2006), p. 123.

30. Posnanski, "Invisible Man."

31. Holway, *Black Diamonds,* p. 173.

32. Finch, "Easter, Padre Negro from St. Louis."

33. Grayson is quoted from "Lean, Hungry Indians Are as Strong as Brace on Easter's Knee," *Ogdenburg (NY) Journal,* April 17, 1952, p. 14, and the previously cited "Luke Easter is a Shot in the Arm to Lagging Indians."

34. Two Greenberg quotes are compounded here: the first is in "Big Luke Easter Is Counted on to Pace Tribe's Hitting," AP story, as printed in the *Arizona Daily Star,* Nov. 24, 1949, p. 13; the second is in Manning, "They're Gonna Like Big Luke," p. 70.

35. Tygiel, *Baseball's Great Experiment: Jackie Robinson and His Legacy* (New York: Oxford University Press, 1983), p. 247. Tygiel cites the primary source as an un-dated clipping held by the National Baseball Hall of Fame.

36. Van Hyning, "Luke Easter, Larger than Life Figure."

37. Lebovitz, *Best of Hal Lebovitz,* p. 67.

38. *Sandusky (OH) Register,* July 21, 1951, p. 6.

39. Pitoniak, "The Legend of Luke: On Easter Sunday, a Hero Is Remembered," *Rochester (NY) Democrat and Chronicle,* April 12, 1998, p. D1.

40. Pitoniak, "Legend of Luke."

41. Posnanski, "Invisible Man."

42. The Overfield quote is from "Easter's Charisma, Remarkable Slugging Captivated Fans, Saved Buffalo Franchise in Mid-1950s." *Baseball Research Journal* 13 (1984), sabr.org/journal/article/easters-charisma-remarkable-slugging-captivated-fans-saved-buffalo-franchise-in-mid-1950s/; the house-owner quote is in "Events & Discoveries," *Sports Illustrated,* July 15, 1957, 22.

43. Ward, "In the Wake of the News," *Chicago Tribune,* May 24, 1949, p. 39.

44. White, *Singles and Smiles,* p. 65.

45. Cattau, "So, Maybe There Really Is Such a Thing as 'The Natural,'" p. 123.

46. Schlemmer, "Easter's Long Homer Benches Nelson," *Akron (OH) Beacon Journal,* April 5, 1954, p. 18.

47. Van Hyning, "Luke Easter, Larger than Life Figure."

48. "Negro Stars on the Horizon," unknown author and publication, April 1956, p. 46. Photocopy held by the National Hall of Fame, Accession Number BL-287-2016-378.

49. Swaine, *Black Stars,* p. 79.

50. Smith, "Wendell Smith's Sports Beat," *Pittsburgh Courier,* April 2, 1949, p. 22.

51. Manning, p. 70.

52. Talbot, "Sports Roundup."

53. Cattau, "Easter: The First Black Major Leaguer from St. Louis," p. 9.

54. Manning, "They're Gonna Like 'Big Luke,'" p. 70.

55. Tygiel, *Baseball's Great Experiment,* p. 246. Tygiel cites his original source as *The Sporting News,* March 23, 1949, but despite using numerous combinations of Boolean search terms, I was unable to locate the quote in this or any other issue. Tygiel's citations are highly reliable in my experience, and I'm assuming the quote is genuine and he got his source note wrong.

56. Cattau, "So, Maybe There Really Is Such a Thing as 'The Natural,'" p. 127.

57. Manning, "They're Gonna Like 'Big Luke,'" p. 20.

58. Manning, "They're Gonna Like 'Big Luke,'" p. 20.

59. "Easter's 2 Homers Help Tribe Beat Cubs, 13–12," *Janesville (WI) Daily Gazette,* April 3, 1950, p. 12.

60. *Harrisburg (PA) Telegraph,* July 22, 1946, p. 17.

61. "New Orleans Black Pels Meet," *Montgomery Advertiser,* July 14, 1946, p. 8.

62. Cattau, "So, Maybe There Really Is Such a Thing as 'The Natural,'" p. 123.

63. *The Sporting News,* April 20, 1949, p. 33.

64. UPI article, San Mateo (CA) Times, May 18, 1949, p. 14.

Chapter 13

1. Anyone holding box scores or other information on either Larry Doby at Great Lakes NAS, or Woody Petersen in any phase of his baseball career, is cordially invited to correspond with the author via his publisher.

2. Tygiel, *Baseball's Great Experiment,"* p. 213.

3. Veeck is quoted in the July 12, 1947, *Pittsburgh Courier,* p. 14. Wendell Smith wrote that Veeck had spoken with Nunn "last winter," i.e., the winter of 1946.

4. The Veeck quote is as remembered by Doby in his oral interview with Tom Harris, February 18,

1994, SABR Oral History Collection, oralhistory.sabr.org/interviews/doby-larry-1994/.; Brissie is quoted in Berkow, "Larry Doby: He Crossed Color Barrier, Only, He Was Second," *New York Times*, February 23, 1997, archive.nytimes.com/www.nytimes.com/specials/baseball/robinson-dolby-0223.html; the Doby quote is from his oral interview with Fay Vincent and Claire Smith, April 13, 2000. SABR Oral History Collection. oralhistory.sabr.org/interviews/doby-larry-2000/.

5. The first Doby quote is in "The Black Athlete," *Sports Illustrated*, July 22, 1968, archive.org/stream/Sports-Illustrated-1968-07-22/Sports-Illustrated-1968-07-22_djvu.txt; the second is in Anderson, "As Baseball Honors Robinson, Has It Forgotten Larry Doby?," *New York Times*, March 29, 1987, sec. 5, 3; Izenberg's reporting is found in "Hall Selection Caps Hard Journey," *Newark (NJ) Star Ledger*, March 4, 1998, as quoted in *The Congressional Record*, "Congratulations to Larry Doby on His Introduction to the Baseball Hall of Fame," S2001.

6. Berkow, "Larry Doby."

7. As with his stats for Great Lakes, if any reader has information pertaining to Doby's ABL appearances, please do correspond with the author via his publisher.

8. The Hollis quote is from "Lombardi's Drive Tops Them All," *Ogdensburg (NY) Journal*, May 16, 1952, 6.

9. Anderson, "Larry Doby Understands Handshakes," *New York Times*, April 20, 1995, B15.

10. Carpenter, "Larry Doby: The Jackie Robinson of the Indians' Last World Series Champions," *Guardian*, October 26, 2016. theguardian.com/sport/2016/oct/26/larry-doby-cleveland-indians-world-series-first-black-player-jackie-robinson.

11. Gromek is quoted in Freedman, *African American Pioneers*, p. 114.

12. Lopez is quoted in King, "He's Learned to Laugh," in *Baseball Stars of 1955*, ed. Bruce Jacobs. (New York: Lion Books, 1955), p. 40.

13. The Hano quote is from *A Day in the Bleachers* (New York: Bantam Books, 1955), p. 119.

14. Both Dean and Houtteman are quoted in Moore, *Larry Doby: The Struggle of the American League's First Black Player* (Mineola, NY: Dover, 2011), p. 103.

15. No less than six Doby quotes are compounded here; I hope the reader will forgive me for taking the liberty of constructing a coherent statement from the reticent Doby, who rarely spoke at length about his travails, from multiple sources. The first quote is in "Larry Doby Enters Major Leagues," JRank. sports.jrank.org/pages/1209/Doby-Larry-Enters-Major-Leagues.html.; the second is in Dickson, *Bill Veeck: Baseball's Greatest Maverick* (New York: Walker, 2012), p. 129; the third is from "Larry Doby Doesn't Mind Being 'Second Black' Again," *Jet*, July 20, 1978, p. 58; the fourth is in Crowe, *Just as Good: How Larry Doby Changed America's Game* (Somerville, MA: Candlewick, 2012), no page numbers; the fifth is in "The Legacy of Larry Doby," WBUR-FM, June 20, 2003. wbur.org/onlyagame/2003/06/20/the-legacy-of-larry-doby.; the sixth is in Bechtel, "After Jackie Robinson, Doby Blazed a Trail of His Own," *Sports Illustrated*, June 30, 2003. si.com/vault/2003/06/30/345718/the-next-one-larry-doby1923-2003-after-jackie-robinson-doby-blazed-a-trail-of-his-own.

Chapter 14

1. Professor Lisa Doris Alexander offers the following defense of Barry Bonds' extracurricular activities: "Many sportswriters point to Lance Williams and Mark Fainaru-Wada's *Game of Shadows* as gospel for the steroid era though the authors included sealed grand jury testimony in their work, ... An overwhelming majority of sportswriters and sports reporters are white.... By focusing on Bonds, sportswriters diverted attention from any unethical/illegal practices their fellow journalists employed to get the story." Rather than addressing the overwhelming, uncontroverted evidence of Bonds' steroid abuse itemized in *Game of Shadows*, Alexander attacks the reporters ad hominem on the basis of their race. By similar logic, Carl Bernstein, who happens to be Jewish and who also used sealed grand jury testimony in documenting criminal activity, would still be a local beat reporter in Washington, DC, and Richard "The Jews Are Born Spies" Nixon would be President for Life. (Alexander is quoted from "I'm the King of the World," In *From Jack Johnson to LeBron James: Sports, Media, and the Color Line*, ed. Chris Lamb (Lincoln: University of Nebraska Press, 2016), 522–533; Nixon is quoted from his clandestine Oval Office recording of July 5, 1971, which can be accessed at millercenter.org/the-presidency/educational-resources/nixon-the-jews-are-born-spies.)

2. Tinker is quoted in Ribowsky, *Josh Gibson: The Power and the Darkness* (Urbana: University of Illinois Press, 2004), p. 33.

3. The Aaron quote is from *I Had a Hammer: The Hank Aaron Story* (New York: HarperCollins, 1991), p. 104; Mays is quoted in "Stan 'The Man' Musial Dies at 92," ESPN, January 9, 2013, espn.com/mlb/story/_/id/8860690/st-louis-cardinals-hall-famer-stan-musial-dies-age-92.

4. Both the Reilly and Kent quotes are in Reilly, "He Loves Himself Barry Much," *Sports Illustrated*, August 21, 2001, web.archive.org/web/20011007193444/http://sportsillustrated.cnn.com/inside_game/magazine/life_of_reilly/news/2001/08/21/life_of_reilly/.

5. Martin is quoted in multiple sources including Achenbach, "Beatle Juice," *Miami Herald*, February 4, 2014. miamiherald.com/news/local/community/miami-dade/article1959850.html.

6. Miles is quoted in Tye, *Satchel: The Life and Times of an American Legend* (New York: Random House, 2009), pp. 148–149.

7. Dalkowski's high school coach is quoted in

Eisenberg, "Lost Phenom Find His Way," *Baltimore Sun*, February 16, 2003, web.archive.org/web/20200507034318/https://www.baltimoresun.com/news/bs-xpm-2003-02-16-0302160411-story.html; the Ripken Sr. quote is from *The Ripken Way: A Manual for Baseball and Life* (New York: Diversion, 1999), no page numbers given.

8. Dean is quoted in the *Chicago Defender*, September 24, 1938, p. 9; the Hubbell quote, which is passed on with caveats, is cited in many publications as originating in the *Los Angeles Times*, July 17, 1942, but while the issue does mention Hubbell ("Hubbell Bumps Pirates, 3-1," p. 20), I couldn't find the famous quote about Paige in this or any issue between 1937 and 1945; Leonard is quoted in Resnick, "Satchel Paige: One of Life's Gool Ol' Boys," *Munster (IN) Times*, June 9, 1982, 11; the Radcliffe quote is as told to Bob Motley in Tye *Satchel*, p. 97; Johnson is quoted in Resnick, "Satchel Paige."

9. Feller is quoted in Daley, A., "Ol' Satch Looks Back and Gains," *New York Times*, February 10, 1971, p. 52; Cochrane is quoted in Hawkins, "Win, Lose or Draw," *Washington (DC) Evening Star*, July 26, 1947, p. A11; the first DiMaggio quote is from the *Daily Worker*, September 13, 1937, p. 8; the second DiMaggio quote is from the *New York Daily News*, February 25, 1936, p. 41; Bessick's telegram is quoted in Tye, *Satchel*, 97. DiMaggio sang Satchel's praises on many occasions: "Joe DiMaggio says Paige is the greatest pitcher he has ever batted against" (*Life*, June 2, 1942, p. 91); "Paige is the best pitcher I ever faced" (*Honolulu Advertiser*, July 27, 1943, p. 6).

10. Irvin, *Few and Chosen*, p. 129.

11. Bell is quoted in Kelly, "A Legendary Talent That's Hard to Fathom," MLB.com, mlb.com/history/negro-leagues/players/satchel-paige; Courtenay is quoted in Kirschenbaum, "A Most Unnatural Natural," *Sports Illustrated*, June 21, 1982, vault.si.com/vault/1982/06/21/scorecard. Google "New York Yankees Ichiro Suzuki Astounding Throw 4 Bats" to see Ichiro, possessor of possibly the most accurate outfield throwing arm of all time, perform Satchel's soda-bottle trick with baseball bats standing on end at home plate.

12. Paige's record against Dean in the 1934–35 barnstorming tour is cited by Murray, "A Tribute to Satchel," *Oakland Tribune*, June 24, 1964, p. 39; Wasdell is quoted in Povich, "This Morning with Shirley Povich," *Washington Post*, April 7, 1939, sec. III, 21.

13. Doby is quoted from his 2000 oral interview with Vincent and Smith; Paige is quoted in Leonard with Riley, *Buck Leonard: The Black Lou Gehrig* (New York: Carroll & Graf, 1995), p. 187; the Hawkins quote is from "Win, Lose or Draw."

Chapter 15

1. Bates, "All Done with All-Time Teams," Baseball Prospectus, April 18, 2012. baseballprospectus.com/news/article/16513/the-platoon-advantage-all-done-with-all-time-teams/.

Chapter 21

1. *Report of the Subcommittee on Study of Monopoly Power of the Committee on the Judiciary Pursuant to H. Res. 95.* May 27, 1952. Government Printing Office, 1952, p. 483, books.google.co.uk/books?id=BKfD49GILIIC&pg=PP5&#v=onepage&q&f=false.

Chapter 24

1. The Paige quote is from *Pitchin' Man; Satchel Paige's Own Story* (Cleveland, OH: Gray, 1948; New York: Ishi, 2015), p. 41 (citation to 2015 edition); Jones is quoted in Nightengale, "Orioles' Adam Jones Berated by Racist Taunts at Fenway Park," *USA Today*, May 1, 2017. usatoday.com/story/sports/mlb/2017/05/01/orioles-adam-jones-berated-racist-taunts-fenway-park-peanuts/101187172/; Sabathia is quoted in Rivera, "CC Sabathia: 'I've Never Been Called the N-Word' Anywhere but in Boston," ESPN, May 2, 2017. espn.com/mlb/story/_/id/19296595/new-york-yankees-pitcher-cc-sabathia-says-black-players-expect-racism-boston; the Hunter quote is from "Torii Hunter on Speaking Out and Why He Asked for a No-Trade Clause to the Red Sox." From *Golic and Wingo*, June 4, 2000. youtube.com/watch?v=pHc3FsXvcuM.

2. Schneider, *The Cleveland Indians Encyclopedia*. 3rd ed. (Champaign, IL: Sports Publishing, 2004), p. 7.

3. Doby is quoted from his oral interview with Fay Vincent and Claire Smith, April 13, 2000; Hank and Stephen Greenberg are quoted in Kempner, dir., *The Life and Times of Hank Greenberg* DVD (Hank's quote starts at 9:13, Stephen's at 1:20:31).

4. Interview with Al "Fuzzy" Smith, special feature on the *Life and Times of Hank Greenberg* DVD.

Chapter 25

1. Acho, interview with Stephen Colbert, *The Late Show with Stephen Colbert*, YouTube, June 9, 2020, youtube.com/watch?v=U4oQNOAUkb0.

2. Tharps, "The Case for Black with a Capital B," *New York Times*, November 18, 2014. nytimes.com/2014/11/19/opinion/the-case-for-black-with-a-capital-b.html.

3. Lawrence and Denaro, *Eastern Colored League* (San Francisco: AJ Publishing, 2003), p. 66.

4. Goldman, "Introduction: Beyond the Back of the Baseball Card: Baseball 101," in *Extra Innings: More Baseball Between the Numbers from the Team at Baseball Prospectus*, ed. Steven Goldman (New York: Basic Books, 2012), p. 4.

5. Johnson is quoted in Robert Peterson, *Only the Ball*, p. 145; the Campanella quote is from *It's Good to Be Alive*, pp. 65–66.

6. Doby, oral interview with Fay and Smith, 2000.

7. Campanella is quoted in Thomas, "Roy Campanella, 71, Dies; Was Dodger Hall of Famer," *New York Times*, June 28, 1993, B8.

8. Rosenberg, "The Momentous Drawing of the Sport's 19th-Century 'Color Line' is Still Tripping Up History Writers," Atavist, June 14, 2016. howardwrosenberg.atavist.com/racism-bbhistory.

9. Misattributed by Dickson in *Bill Veeck* to the issue of October 18, 1943.

10. Swaine is quoted from *Integration of Major League Baseball*, p. 49.

11. In "A Baseball Myth Exploded," Larry Gerlach *et. al.* cast aspersions on Veeck's account by noting that "Easter ... would not even begin his professional career until 1946." But as we've seen, Easter was known as a monster power hitter within a limited circle as early as 1935—a circle that may well have included Saperstein, who regularly criss-crossed the nation in search of Black talent for his baseball and basketball teams.

12. Young discussed the rumor in *Great Negro Baseball Stars and How They Made the Major Leagues* (New York: A.S. Barnes, 1953), p. 52.

13. Larry Doby provided confirmation of one part of Veeck's remarks: "The day I joined the [Cleveland team] in Chicago, Lou Boudreau lined up all the players. One by one, Lou introduced me to each player, 'This is Joe Gordon,' and Gordon put his hand out. 'This is Bob Lemon,' and Lemon put his hand out. 'This is Jim Hegan,' and Hegan put his hand out. All the guys put their hands out, all but three. As soon as he could, Bill Veeck got rid of those three." (Dave Anderson, "As Baseball Honors Robinson, Has It Forgotten Larry Doby?," New York: Times, March 29, 1987, sec. 5, 3.)

14. Saperstein is quoted in Tygiel, "Revisiting Bill Veeck and the 1943 Phillies," *Baseball Research Journal 35* (2006): p. 113, from an Associated Negro Press article in the August 14, 1954, *Philadelphia Independent*. I was unable to confirm the article independently; Tygiel cites his original source as a March 23, 2005, email from author Christopher Hauser to SABR-L (*ibid.*, note 33).

15. Veeck is quoted in the *Chicago Daily Herald*, October 13, 1960, p. 173.

16. The Tygiel quote is from "Revisiting Bill Veeck," p. 114.

17. Tygiel makes his point in "Revisiting Bill Veeck," p. 112.

18. "Man Who Helped Blacks Make Baseball History Dies at 71," *Jet*, January 20, 1986, p. 46.

19. Veeck is quoted in Tygiel, *Baseball's Great Experiment*, p. 41. Tygiel cites his source as "Interview with Bill Veeck" (ch. 3, n. 28).

20. "Scorecard," *Sports Illustrated*, December 4, 1961.

21. Frick's suggestion is reported in multiple newspapers including the *Gettysburg (PA) Times*, June 17, 1982, p. 12; Kuhn is quoted in Durso, "Paige Is First Star of Old Negro Leagues to Be Selected for Hall of Fame," *New York Times*, February 10, 1971, p. 52.; Robinson is quoted in Gross, "Robinson Speaks Out," *New York Post*, February 4, 1971, as cited by Luke, p. 116; Doby is quoted in Gross, "Paige Belongs in Hall of Fame, Not in Dusty Old Museum Corner," *Virgin Islands Daily News,* February 20, 1971, 15.

22. Paige is quoted in James, *The Politics of Glory*, p. 187.

23. In "The 'Strike' Against Jackie Robinson: Truth or Myth?" (*Baseball Research Journal 46*, no. 1 [spring 2017]: 88–94), Warren Corbett raises legitimate questions about whether Cardinals players had in fact threatened a strike. What's known for certain is that Sam Breadon heard rumors of an intended strike; that he shared his fears with sportswriter Rutherford "Rud" Rennie, who passed the information to Stanley Woodward; and that Woodward received corroboration of the story, together with the famous written statement, from Ford Frick. Cardinals center fielder Terry Moore confirmed to the press that there had indeed been discussions of a strike—and though he dismissed them as "some high-sounding strike talk that meant nothing," how were Breadon or Frick to have known that? It's also known that Fred "Dixie" Walker circulated a petition against Jackie among his Dodgers teammates—demonstrating that a concerted players' movement against baseball integration was not outside the realm of possibility. Cardinals manager Eddie Dyer immediately denied Woodward's story—but what manager, then or now, would admit publicly that he'd lost control of his players? Corbett writes that "besides [Terry] Moore, [Marty] Marion, and possibly [Stan] Musial, no Cardinal had the clout to organize a strike," but that's post-facto speculation which, even if true, proves only that the abortive strike lacked the backing of the only players with enough influence to make it stick. I think the evidence is clear that there *was* strike talk among the Cardinals, and that Frick *did* deliver his written statement to the players—though not, as most histories have it, in person, but through Breadon's intermediacy. (Moore is quoted in Broeg, "Cardinal Players Deny They Planned Protest Strike Against Robinson," *St. Louis Post-Dispatch*, May 9, 1947, p. 9C; see also the *Brooklyn Daily Eagle*, May 9, 1947, p. 17.)

24. *New York Herald Tribune*, May 10, 1947, p. 15.

25. Fort and Maxcy are quoted from "The Demise of African American Baseball," *Journal of Sports Economics 2*, no. 1 (February 2001): p. 36.

26. Fort and Maxcy, "Demise of African American Baseball," p. 41.

27. Fort and Maxcy, "Demise of African American Baseball," pp. 46–47.

Chapter 26

1. Quoted in an AP story printed in numerous papers, including "Rickey Tells Attempt to Keep

Robinson Out of National League," *Centralia* (IL) *Evening Sentinel*.

2. The Benswanger, Bradley, Breadon, Giles, Griffith, and Mack quotes are from the *New York Daily News*, February 18, 1948, pp. 69 and 71; the Frick quote was carried by numerous AP subscribers, including the *Masillion* (OH) *Evening Independent*, February 17, 1948, p. 10; the Wrigley quote was also carried by numerous AP subscribers, including the *Eau Claire* (WI) *Leader-Telegram*, February 19, 1948, p. 13.

3. MacPhail's statement was carried by numerous newspapers, including the *New York Times*, February 21, 1948, p. 16.

4. Rickey is quoted in the *New York Daily News*, February 18, 1948, pp. 69 and 71.

5. Marshall, "Happy Chandler and Baseball's Pivotal Era," *Register of the Kentucky Historical Society* 99, No. 2 (Spring 2001), pp. 117–118.

6. The following excerpts are from *Study of Monopoly Power: Hearings Before the Subcommittee on Study of Monopoly Power of the Committee of the Judiciary, Serial No. 1, Part 6: Organized Baseball*, (Government Printing Office, 1952), pp. 472–516 and 1066–1067. babel.hathitrust.org/cgi/pt?id=umn.31951d03669259b&view=1up&seq=809.

7. *Report of the Subcommittee on Study of Monopoly Power of the Committee on the Judiciary Pursuant to H. Res. 95*, May 27, 1952 (Government Printing Office, 1952), p. 10, via Google Books. books.google.co.uk/books?id=BKfD49GILIIC&pg=PP5&#v=onepage&q&f=false.

8. The original, uncensored Report is found in *Study of Monopoly Power*, pp. 474–488.

9. Rickey is quoted in "Rickey Tells Attempt to Keep Robinson Out of National League," *Centralia (IL) Evening Sentinel*, February 17, 1948, 4.

10. Kahn, *Rickey & Robinson: The True, Untold Story of Baseball Integration* (New York: Rodale, 2014), p. 115.

11. Carried in numerous newspapers, including the *St. Louis Post-Dispatch*, February 19, 1948, p. 20.

12. *New York Times*, February 21, 1948, p. 16.

13. The Chandler quote, as remembered by Roberts, is in Holway, *Voices from the Great Black Baseball Leagues*, p. 14. Roberts stressed what he regarded as the historical importance of this famous quote to Holway: "The (Pittsburgh) *Courier* headlined that! Rickey couldn't have made a move but for that. The moment Rickey read that in the *Courier*, he began to move." In 1984, Chandler confirmed the substance of the quote to Peter Golenbock (*Bums*, p. 141), adding that "when Branch Rickey saw my quote, he began making plans." Neither Roberts nor Chandler's memory is accurate; I have no doubt that Chandler said what Roberts reported he said—but the quote was first seen by the public when Holway published Roberts's version in 1975. The earliest press mention of the quote I could find is in the *Lexington Herald-Sun* for July 26, 1981 (p. 24). What Chandler and Roberts seem to be referring to is a May 5, 1948, *Courier* article titled "Chandler's Views on Player Ban Sought" (p. 6), in which Roberts quotes Chandler as *evading* the question of baseball integration: "If it's discrimination you are afraid of, you have nothing to fear from me. Look at my record in Kentucky as Governor and you will discover that I have always tried to be fair with and considerate of colored people.... Negroes are active in most of the major sports in this country, aren't they? ... The colored people in Kentucky think well of me, I am sure; ask some of them and see." At the time, Roberts himself expressed a healthy skepticism towards Chandler's self-proclaimed "friend of the Blacks" credentials: "A check of his record in the Senate reveals that he was traditionally Southern in both his views and convictions" ("Chandler's Views on Player Ban Sought"). Rose-colored glasses seem to have misted many memories of these turbulent times.

Acknowledgments

1. Le Guin, 1976 Introduction to *The Left Hand of Darkness* (New York: Penguin, 2016), p. xxvii.

Bibliography

By far the most indispensable sources used to compile and analyze statistical information for this book were the Seamheads Negro Leagues Database, https://www.seamheads.com/NegroLgs/, and Baseball Reference, https://www.baseball-reference.com.

The Negro Leagues statistical base that underlies all charts, analyses, and player records in this book was researched and compiled for Seamheads by **Gary Ashwill**, **Larry Lester**, **Patrick Rock**, **Scott Simkus**, and **Wayne Stivers**, and is reproduced herein by kind permission of **Gary Ashwill**.

Additionally, key unpublished Negro Leagues data was generously provided by Seamheads co-founder **Kevin Johnson**.

Other resources I consulted include books, magazines, newspapers, Web postings, and personal correspondence.

Unpublished Sources

Chalek, Eric. Personal correspondence with the author, 2020–21.

Cobb, Chris. Personal correspondence with the author, 2021.

Delgado, Jorge Colón. Personal correspondence with the author, 2019–21.

James, Bill. Personal correspondence with the author, 2019–21.

Johnson, Kevin. Personal correspondence with the author, 2019–21.

Johnson, Kevin. Unpublished data on the Negro Leagues, provided 2019–20.

Rosenberg, Howard W. Personal correspondence with the author, 2021.

Tharps, Lori L. Personal correspondence with the author, 2020.

Van Hyning, Thomas E. Personal correspondence with the author, 2019–21.

Books and Articles

Aaron, Henry. Hall of Fame induction speech, August 1, 1982. National Baseball Hall of Fame and Museum, video, 7:00. youtube.com/watch?v=jy5t4BdSM0U.

Aaron, Henry, with Lonnie Wheeler. *I Had a Hammer: The Hank Aaron Story*. New York: HarperCollins, 1991.

Achenbach, Joel. "Beatle Juice." *Miami Herald*, February 4, 2014. miamiherald.com/news/local/community/miami-dade/article1959850.html.

Acho, Emmanuel. Interview by Stephen Colbert. *The Late Show with Stephen Colbert*, June 9, 2020, video, 6:21. youtube.com/watch?v=U4oQNOAUkb0.

Alexander, Lisa Doris. "I'm the King of the World: Barry Bonds and the Race for the Record." In *From Jack Johnson to LeBron James: Sports, Media, and the Color Line*, edited by Chris Lamb, 522–533. Lincoln: University of Nebraska Press, 2016.

Anderson, Dave. "As Baseball Honors Robinson, Has It Forgotten Larry Doby?" *New York Times*, March 29, 1987, sec. 5, 3.

———. "Larry Doby Understands Handshakes." *New York Times*, April 20, 1995, B15.

Anson, Adrian "Cap." *A Ball Player's Career: Being the Personal Experiences and Reminiscences of Adrian C. Anson*. Chicago: Era, 1900.

"Babe Ruth's Effect on American Culture." Babe Ruth Central. baberuthcentral.com/hero-and-icon/babe-ruths-effect-on-american-culture.

Badham, John, director. *The Bingo Long Traveling All-Stars & Motor Kings*. Written by William Brashler, Hal Barwood and Matthew Robbins, based on the novel by William Brashler. Detroit: Motown Productions, 1976. DVD, 110 min.

Barthel, Thomas. *Baseball Barnstorming and Exhibition Games, 1901–1962: A History of Off-Season Major League Play*. Jefferson, NC: McFarland, 2007.

Bates, Michael. "All Done with All-Time Teams." Baseball Prospectus, April 18, 2012. baseballprospectus.com/news/article/16513/the-platoon-advantage-all-done-with-all-time-teams/.

_____. "Baseball's Failed 1978 Donald Sterling Moment." SBNation. sbnation.com/mlb/2014/5/1/5672616/donald-sterling-baseball-racist-owners-calvin-griffith-bowie-kuhn.

Bechtel, Mark. "After Jackie Robinson, Doby Blazed a Trail of His Own." *Sports Illustrated*, June 30, 2003. si.com/vault/2003/06/30/345718/the-next-one-larry-doby1923–2003-after-jackie-robinson-doby-blazed-a-trail-of-his-own.

Beer, Jeremy. "How Would Oscar Have Fared in MLB?" OscarCharleston.com, February 2, 2019. oscarcharleston.com/2019/02/02/how-would-oscar-have-fared-in-mlb/.

"Bench5" [pseud.]. "Negro Leagues vs. Major Leagues." Baseball Fever, February 1, 2006. baseball-fever.com/forum/general-baseball/the-negro-leagues/2910-negro-leagues-vs-major-leagues#post2910.

Berkin, Carol, Christopher Miller, Robert Cherny, and James Gormly. *Making America: A History of the United States*, 7th ed. Stamford, CT: Stamgage Learning, 2015.

Berkow, Ira. "Larry Doby: He Crossed Color Barrier, Only, He Was Second." *New York Times*, February 23, 1997. archive.nytimes.com/www.nytimes.com/specials/baseball/robinson-dolby-0223.html.

"Big Luke Easter is Counted on to Pace Tribe's Hitting." *Arizona Daily Star*. (Tucson, AZ), November 24, 1949, 13.

"Big Man from Nicetown." *Time*, August 8, 1955, 50–55. Retrieved at time.com/vault/issue/1955-08-08/page/1/.

"'Big Time' Ball Knows No Color Line: 'Negroes Not Barred,' So Says Judge Landis." *Lincoln (NE) Star*, July 17, 1942, 10.

"Bill James on Fielding, Part 7." Fox Sports, January 29, 2015. foxsports.com/stories/other/bill-james-on-fielding-part-7.

Bjarkman, Peter C. *Baseball with a Latin Beat: A History of the Latin American Game*. Jefferson, NC: McFarland, 1994.

Black, Martha Jo, and Chuck Schoffner. *Joe Black: More Than a Dodger*. Chicago: Academy Chicago, 2015.

"The Black Athlete," *Sports Illustrated*, July 22, 1968, beginning on 28. no inter-textual page numbers provided. archive.org/stream/Sports-Illustrated-1968-07-22/Sports-Illustrated-1968-07-22_djvu.txt.

Blackistone, Kevin B. "It's Time for Baseball to Acknowledge Cap Anson's Role in Erecting Its Color Barrier." *Washington Post*, December 2, 2015. washingtonpost.com/sports/nationals/its-time-for-baseball-to-acknowledge-cap-ansons-role-in-erecting-a-color-barrier/2015/12/02/b9b97eb8-9916-11e5-94f0-9eeaff906ef3_story.html.

Borges, Ron. "Baseball's Dirty Secret." The National, April 11, 2009. thenational.ae/sport/baseball-s-dirty-secret-1.495096.

Bradlee, Ben, Jr. *The Kid: The Immortal Life of Ted Williams*. New York: Little, Brown, 2013.

Branson, Douglas M. *Greatness in the Shadows: Larry Doby and the Integration of the American League*. Lincoln: University of Nebraska Press, 2016.

Brashler, William. *Josh Gibson: A Life in the Negro Leagues*, paperback ed. Chicago: Ivan R. Dee, 2000.

Broeg, Bob. "Cardinal Players Deny They Planned Protest Strike Against Robinson." *St. Louis Post-Dispatch*, May 9, 1947, 9C.

"Brown, Willard 1911(?)—1996." Encyclopedia.com. encyclopedia.com/education/news-wires-white-papers-and-books/brown-willard-1911-1996.

Bruns, Roger. *Negro League Baseball*. Santa Barbara, CA: Greenwood, 2012.

Bryant, Howard. "MLB Can Add Negro Leagues to Official Records But Can Never Change What It Did to Black Players." ESPN, December 18, 2020. espn.com/mlb/story/_/id/30540089/mlb-add-negro-leagues-official-records-never-change-did-black-players.

Bucek, Jeanine, et al., eds. *The Baseball Encyclopedia*, 10th ed. New York: Macmillan, 1996.

Bugliosi, Vincent. *Outrage*, updated ed. New York: Dell 1996.

Bump, Larry. "Luke Easter: Better than Ruth?" *Rochester (NY) Democrat and Chronicle*, December 27, 1972, 37.

Burns, Ken. Interview: Buck O'Neil. PBS.org, undated. Companion site for *Baseball: A Film by Ken Burns*, PBS, aired September 22, 1994. web.archive.org/web/20210227041054/http://www.pbs.org/kenburns/baseball/shadowball/oneil.html.

Campanella, Roy. *It's Good to Be Alive*. Lincoln: University of Nebraska Press, 1995.

"Campy Swings, Dodgers Win." *Life*, June 6, 1953, 136–140.

"Cap's Great Shame—Racial Intolerance." Cap Chronicled. https://web.archive.org/web/20210128163318/capanson.com/chapter4.html.

Carpenter, Les. "Jarry Doby: The Jackie Robinson of the Indians' Last World Champions." *Guardian*, October 26, 2016. theguardian.com/sport/2016/oct/26/larry-doby-cleveland-indians-world-series-first-black-*player*-jackie-robinson.

Cattau, Daniel. "Easter: The First Black Major Leaguer from St. Louis." *St. Louis Post-Dispatch*, April 5, 1992, 8–12.

Cattau, Daniel. "So, Maybe There Really Is Such a Thing as 'The Natural.'" *Smithsonian*, August 1991, 117+, Gale Document Number GALE|CGSXXX576519146.

Chalek, Eric. "A Reductive View of Catcher Defense." Hall of Merit discussion board, January 19, 2006, post 25 (username "Dr. Chaleeko"). baseballthinkfactory.org/hall_of_merit/discussion/yogi_berra.

"Chandler's Views on Player Ban Sought," *Pittsburgh Courier*, May 5, 1948, 6.

Charlton, James, ed. *The Baseball Chronology: The Complete History of the Most Important Events in the Game of Baseball*. New York: Macmillan, 1991.

Chass, Murray. "Ex-A's Employee Cites Schott Racial Remarks." *New York Times,* November 26, 1992. nytimes.com/1992/11/26/sports/baseball-ex-a-s-employee-cites-schott-racial-remarks.html.

"Chronological History of the Major League Baseball Players Association." MLBPA. mlbplayers.com/history.

Clark, Dick, and Larry Lester, eds. *The Negro Leagues Book.* Cleveland: Society for American Baseball Research, 1994.

Cobbledick, Gordon. "Premature Shower in Final Game of '47 Proved Washout for Heath as a Brownie." *Sporting News,* December 17, 1947, 7.

"Congratulations to Larry Doby on His Introduction to the Baseball Hall of Fame." *Congressional Record,* Volume 144, Number 28. March 16, 1998, S2001–S2002.

Corbett, Warren. "The 'Strike' Against Jackie Robinson: Truth or Myth?" *Baseball Research Journal* 46, no. 1 (spring 2017): 88–94.

Costas, Bob. Interview by Bill Maher. *Real Time with Bill Maher,* season 16, episode 19, May 28, 2021.

Costello, Rory. "Willard Brown." SABR Biography Project. sabr.org/bioproj/person/49784799.

Craggs, Tommy. "Say-It-Ain't-So Joe." SF Weekly, July 6, 2005. sfweekly.com/news/say-it-aint-so-joe/.

Crowe, Chris. *Just as Good: How Larry Doby Changed America's Game.* Somerville, MA: Candlewick, 2012.

Cummiskey, Joe. "Landis Steps to Bat for Negro Ball Players." Unknown newspaper, July 17, 1942. National Baseball Hall of Fame. collection.baseballhall.org/PASTIME/landis-steps-bat-negro-ball-players-article-1942-july-17.

Daley, Arthur. "Ol' Satch Looks Back and Gains." *New York Times,* February 10, 1971, 52.

Daley, David. "The Jewish Babe Ruth." *Hartford Courant,* March 25, 2000.

Delaney, John R. "The 1887 Binghamton Bingos." *Baseball Research Journal* 11 (1982). research.sabr.org/journals/1887-binghamton-bingos.

Delgado, Jorge Colón. "Larry Doby tam- bién contribuyó en crear conciencia de la moronidad de la barrera racial." Beisbol 101. beisbol101.com/2019/04/larry-doby-tambien-contribuyo-en-crear-conciencia-de-la-moronidad-de-la-barrera-racial.

———. "Luscious Easter." Beisbol 101. beisbol101.com/luscious-easter/.

———. "Satchel Paige." Beisbol 101. beisbol101.com/leroy-satchel-paige/.

———. "Willard Brown." Beisbol 101 beisbol101.com/willard-brown-2/.

Dexter, Charles. *Larry Doby: Baseball Hero.* New York: Fawcett, 1950.

Dickson, Paul. *Bill Veeck: Baseball's Greatest Maverick.* New York: Walker, 2012.

———. *The Dickson Baseball Dictionary,* 3rd ed. New York: W.W. Norton, 2009.

———. *Leo Durocher: Baseball's Prodigal Son.* New York: Bloomsbury, 2017.

Doby, Larry. Interview by Fay Vincent and Claire Smith, April 13, 2000. SABR Oral History Collection. oralhistory.sabr.org/interviews/doby-larry-2000/.

———. Interview by Tom Harris, February 18, 1994. SABR Oral History Collection. oralhistory.sabr.org/interviews/doby-larry-1994/.

Dockterman, Ellen. "They Sent Babe Ruth to the Hospital." *Time,* July 4, 2013. newsfeed.time.com/2013/07/04/7-things-youd-rather-not-know-about-hot-dogs/slide/they-sent-babe-ruth-to-the-hospital.

Dolgan, Bob. "A Racial Milestone." *Cleveland Plain Dealer,* April 26, 1998, 18.

Doolittle, Bradford, and David Schoenfield. "What the Stats in an 82-Game Season Could Look Like." ESPN, May 27, 2020. espn.co.uk/mlb/story/_/id/29207026/will-anyone-hit-400-post-112-era-82-game-2020-mlb-leaderboard-look-like.

Durso, Joseph. "Paige is First Star of Old Negro Leagues to Be Selected for Hall of Fame." *New York Times,* February 10, 1971, 52.

Dyer, Thomas G. *Theodore Roosevelt and the Idea of Race.* Baton Rouge: Louisiana State University Press, 1980.

"Easter's 2 Homers Help Tribe Beat Cubs, 13–12." *Janesville (WI) Daily Gazette,* April 3, 1950, 12.

Eisenberg, John. "Lost Phenom Finds His Way." *Baltimore Sun,* February 16, 2003. web.archive.org/web/20200507034318/https://www.baltimoresun.com/news/bs-xpm-2003-02-16-0302160411-story.html.

"Election Results: HoM Voters Think Gibson, Bench, Berra and Carter are the Finest Among Backstops!" Hall of Merit. May 12, 2008. baseballthinkfactory.org/hall_of_merit/discussion/election_results_hom_voters_think_gibson_bench_berra_and_carter_are_the_fin/.

Elias, Robert. *The Empire Strikes Out: How Baseball Sold U.S. Foreign Policy and Promoted the American Way Abroad.* New York: New Press, 2010.

Enders, Eric. "The Last .400 Hitter." ericenders.com, September 2000. web.archive.org/web/20080518053806/http://www.ericenders.com:80/artiewilson.htm.

———. "Negro Leagues: Measuring the Quality of Competition." The Hall of Miller and Eric, May 10, 2017. Homemlb.wordpress.com/2017/05/10/negro-leagues-measuring-the-quality-of-competition/.

Essington, Amy. *The Integration of the Pacific Coast League: Race and Baseball on the West Coast.* Lincoln: University of Nebraska Press, 2018.

Etkin, Jack. *Innings Ago: Recollections by Kansas City Ballplayers of their Days in the Game.* Marceline, MO: Normandy Square, 1987.

"Events & Discoveries." *Sports Illustrated,* July 15, 1957, 22. vault.si.com/vault/1957/07/15/42659.

Evers, John J. "Johnny," and Hugh S. Fullerton. "Touching Second: Inside Plays in Big League Baseball—A Real Story of the National Pastime for Real Fans," ch. XIV, part 2. *Pittsburgh Press,* May 4, 1910, 6.

Faber, Charles F. "Carlos Bernier." SABR Biography Project. sabr.org/bioproj/person/a54d927b.

Ferkovich, Scott. "Bennett Park. Detroit." SABR Biography Project. sabr.org/bioproj/park/336604.

Fetter, Henry D. "The Party Line and the Color Line: The American Communist Party, the *Daily Worker*, and Jackie Robinson." *Journal of Sport History* 28, no. 3 (Fall 2001): 375–402.

Figueredo, Jorge S. *Who's Who in Cuban Baseball, 1878–1961*. Jefferson, NC: McFarland, 2003.

Fimrite, Ron. "Triumph of the Spirit." *Sports Illustrated*, September 4, 1990. vault.si.com/vault/1990/09/24/triumph-of-the-spirit-three-decades-after-his-crippling-accident-roy-campanella-is-still-getting-the-most-out-of-life.

Finch, Frank. "Easter, Padre Negro from St. Louis, Playing the Blues with Bat from Coast." *St. Louis Sporting News*, March 30, 1949, 2.

Fleitz, David L. *Cap Anson: The Grand Old Man of Baseball*. Jefferson, NC: McFarland, 2005.

Ford, John, director. *The Man Who Shot Liberty Valance*. Paramount Pictures, screenplay by James Warner Bellah and Willis Goldbeck, April 22, 1962.

Fort, Rodney, and Joel Maxcy. "The Demise of African American Baseball: A Rival League Explanation." *Journal of Sports Economics* 2, no. 1, February 2001, 35–49.

Franklin, Cory. "There Is a Better Way to Honor the Negro Leagues." Inside Sources, January 12, 2021. insidesources.com/there-is-a-better-way-to-honor-the-negro-leagues/.

Freedman, Lew. *African American Pioneers of Baseball: A Biographical Encyclopedia*. Westport, CT: Greenwood, 2007.

Friend, Harold. "Jackie Robinson and Branch Rickey's Explosive Revelation." Bleacher Report. bleacherreport.com/articles/361528-jackie-robinson-and-branch-rickeys-explosive-revelation.

Frommer, Harvey. *Rickey and Robinson: The Men Who Broke Baseball's Color Barrier*. Lanham, MD: Taylor Trade, 1982.

Gay, Timothy M. *Satch, Dizzy and Rapid Robert—The Wild Saga of Interracial Baseball Before Jackie Robinson*. New York: Simon & Schuster, 2010.

Gerlach, Larry R. "Umpire Honor Rolls." *Baseball Research Journal* 8 (1979). research.sabr.org/journals/umpire-honor-rolls.

Goldman, Steven. "Introduction: Beyond the Back of the Baseball Card: Baseball 101." In *Extra Innings*, 1–52.

Goldman, Steven, ed. *Extra Innings: More Baseball Between the Numbers from the Team at Baseball Prospectus*. New York: Basic Books, 2012.

Goldstein, Richard. "Steve Gromek, 82, a Pitcher Who Is Best Known for a Picture." *New York Times*, via The Deadball Era. thedeadballera.com/Obits/Obits_G/Gromek.Steve.Obit.html.

Golenbock, Peter. *Bums: An Oral History of the Brooklyn Dodgers*. New York: Putnam, 1984.

———. *In the Country of Brooklyn: Inspiration to the World*. New York: HarperCollins, 2008.

Grayson, Harry. "Easter's Return Takes Half of World Off Doby's Shoulders." *Ogdensburg. (NY) Journal*, July 7, 1953, 6.

———. "Lean, Hungry Indians Are as Strong as Brace on Easter's Knee." *Ogdenburg (NY) Journal*, April 17, 1952, 14.

———. "Luke Easter is a Shot in the Arm to Lagging Indians." *Defiance (OH) Crescent News*, July 7, 1953, 7.

Gross, Milton. "Paige Belongs in Hall of Fame, Not in Dusty Old Museum Corner." *Virgin Islands Daily News*, February 20, 1971, 15.

———. "Robinson Speaks Out." *New York Post*, February 4, 1971.

Hano, Arnold. *A Day in the Bleachers*. New York: Bantam Books, 1955.

Hawkins, Burton. "Win, Lose or Draw." *Washington (DC) Evening Star*, July 26, 1947, A11.

Heaphy, Leslie. *The Negro Leagues, 1869–1960*. Softcover reissue. Jefferson NC: McFarland, 2013.

Hodges, Jeremy, and Bill Nowlin. eds. *Base Ball's 19th Century "Winter Meetings," 1857–1900*. Phoenix: Society for American Baseball Research, 2018.

Hogan, Lawrence D. "Monte Irvin." SABR Biography Project. sabr.org/bioproj/person/883c3dad.

———. *Shades of Glory: The Negro Leagues and the Story of African American Baseball*. Washington, D.C.: National Geographic, 2006.

Hollis, John. "Lombardi's Drive Tops Them All." *Ogdensburg (NY) Journal*, May 16, 1952, 6.

Holtzman, Jerome. "Veeck's Friends Remember Humanity 1st, Baseball 2nd." *Chicago Tribune*, January 5, 1986, sec. 3, 2.

Holway, John B. *Black Diamonds: Life in the Negro Leagues from the Men Who Lived It*. Westport, CT: Meckler, 1989.

———. *Blackball Stars: Negro League Pioneers*. New York: Carroll & Graf, 1992.

———. *The Complete Book of Baseball's Negro Leagues*. Fern Park, FL: Hastings House, 2001.

———. *Voices from the Great Black Baseball Leagues*. Revised ed. New York: Da Capo, 1992.

Hosansky, David. "Why Did a Historic Home Run Lead to a Smashed Bat?" Hardball Times, April 12, 2017. tht.fangraphs.com/why-did-a-historic-home-run-lead-to-a-smashed-bat.

Hunter, Torii. Interview by Mike Golic, Sr., Mike Golic, Jr., and Trey Wingo. "Torii Hunter on Speaking Out and Why He Asked for a No-Trade Clause to the Red Sox." From *Golic and Wingo*, June 4, 2000. youtube.com/watch?v=pHc3FsXvcuM.

Husman, John R. "May 1, 1884: Fleet Walker's Major-League Debut." SABR Games Project. sabr.org/gamesproj/game/may-1-1884-fleet-walkers-major-league-debut/.

———. "Moses Fleetwood Walker." SABR Biography Project. sabr.org/bioproj/person/9fc5f867.

"Indians Manager Al Lopez Is About Concerned Tribe's Out." *Somerset (PA) Daily American*, August 15, 1953.

Irvin, Monte, with James A. Riley. *Nice Guys Finish First: The Autobiography of Monte Irvin.* New York: Carroll & Graf, 1996.

Irvin, Monte, with Phil Pepe. *Few and Chosen: Defining Negro Leagues Greatness.* Chicago: Triumph, 2007.

Izenberg, Jerry. "Hall Selection Caps Doby's Hard Journey." *Newark (NJ) Star Ledger,* March 4, 1998, as quoted in *The Congressional Record,* "Congratulations to Larry Doby on His Introduction to the Baseball Hall of Fame," S2001.

Jacobsen, Steve. *Carrying Jackie's Torch: The Players Who Integrated Baseball—and America.* Chicago: Lawrence Hall, 2007.

James, Bill. *The Bill James Baseball Abstract 1981.* Self-published, 1981.

———. *The Bill James Historical Baseball Abstract.* New York: Villard Books, 1985.

———. *The New Bill James Historical Baseball Abstract,* updated ed. New York: Free Press, 2001.

———. *The Politics of Glory: How Baseball's Hall of Fame Really Works.* New York: Macmillan, 1994.

———. "The Short Career Guys Group IV—The Joe DiMaggio Group." Bill James Online, April 7, 2010. billjamesonline.com/article1362/.

James, Bill, John Dewan, Don Zminda, Jim Callis, and Neil Munro. eds. *Stats Inc. All-Time Major League Handbook.* 2d ed. Morton Grove, IL: STATS, 2000.

Jessamy, Ken. "Judge Landis Gives 'Green Light' to Negro Ball Players." *Carolina Times* (Durham, NC), August 1, 1942, ed. 1, 1.

Johnson, Bill. "Josh Gibson." SABR Biography Project. sabr.org/bioproj/person/df02083c.

"Joint Meeting of the National League of Professional Base Ball Clubs and the American League of Professional Base Ball Clubs." New York: State Law Reporting Company, December 3, 1943, via the National Baseball Hall of Fame, baseballhall.org/discover-more/digital-collection/1389.

Jordan, David M., Larry R. Gerlach, and John Rossi. "A Baseball Myth Exploded." *National Pastime* 18 (1998): 3–13.

Kahn, Roger. *The Boys of Summer.* New York: Harper & Row, 1972.

———. *Rickey & Robinson: The True, Untold Story of Baseball Integration.* New York: Rodale, 2014.

Kaiser, David. "A Troubling Myth About Jackie Robinson Endures." *Time,* April 15, 2006. time.com/4294175/jackie-robinson-burns-landis-myth/.

Kashatus, William C. *Jackie and Campy: The Untold Story of Their Rocky Relationship and the Breaking of Baseball's Color Line.* Lincoln: University of Nebraska Press, 2014.

Kayser, Tom, and David King. *The Texas League Baseball Almanac.* Charleston, SC: History Press, 2014.

Kelley, Brent. *Voices from the Negro Leagues: Conversations with 52 Baseball Standouts of the Period 1924–1960.* Jefferson, NC: McFarland, 1998.

Kelly, Matt. "A Legendary Talent That's Hard to Fathom." MLB.com. mlb.com/history/negro-leagues/players/satchel-paige.

Kempner, Aviva, director. *The Life and Times of Hank Greenberg.* Documentary film, 1h35m., Cowboy Pictures, 1998.

Kentucky Historical Society 99, no. 2. (Spring 2001): 99–121.

Kerasotis, Peter. "Home, at the Other House That Ruth Built." *New York Times,* March 10, 2014. nytimes.com/2014/03/11/sports/baseball/yankees-home-at-the-other-house-that-ruth-built.html?ref=sports&_r=1.

King, Art. "He's Learned to Laugh." In *Baseball Stars of 1955.* Edited by Bruce Jacobs. New York: Lion Books, 1955.

Kirshenbaum, Jerry. "A Most Unnatural Natural." *Sports Illustrated,* June 21, 1982. vault.si.com/vault/1982/06/21/scorecard.

Klein, Christopher. "10 Things You May Not Know About the Harlem Globetrotters." History.com, May 5, 2021. history.com/news/10-things-you-may-not-know-about-the-harlem-globetrotters.

Knopp, Japheth. "Negro League Baseball, Black Community, and the Socio-Economic Impact of Integration." *Baseball Research Journal* 45, no. 1 (spring 2016): 66–75.

Knorr, Ted. "The Top Ten Reasons Why the Negro Leagues Should Be Declared a Major League." In *The Negro Leagues Were Major Leagues: Historians Reappraise Black Baseball,* edited by Todd Peterson, 98–108. Jefferson, NC: McFarland, 2020.

Koppel, Ted. Interview with Al Campanis and Roger Kahn. *Nightline,* April 6, 1987, 20m43s. youtube.com/watch?v=DFb5kEnWnKk.

Krabbenhoft, Herm. "The Accurate RBI Record of Babe Ruth." *Baseball Research Journal* 42, no. 1 (spring 2013): 37–44.

———. "How Many Hits Did Ty Cobb Make in His Major League Career? What Is His Lifetime Batting Average?" *Baseball Research Journal* 48, no. 1 (spring 2019): 92–98.

Kritzer, Cy. "Luke 'Loves Buffalo, Youngsters Especially'—and the Feeling's Mutual." *Buffalo Evening News,* July 13, 1957, 5.

Lacy, Sam. "Mickey Cochrane Envisions Campy as 'Great' Catcher." *Washington Afro-American,* May 4, 1950, 19.

Lacy, Sam, with Moses J. Newsom. *Fighting for Fairness: The Life Story of Hall of Fame Sportswriter Sam Lacy.* Centreville, MD: Tidewater, 1998.

Lahman, Sean. "Index of Online Baseball Guides." SeanLahman.com, August 20, 2014. seanlahman.com/2014/08/20/index-of-online-baseball-guides/.

Laing, Jeffrey Michael. *Bud Fowler: Baseball's First Black Professional.* Jefferson, NC: McFarland, 2013.

Lamb, Chris. *Blackout: The Untold Story of Jackie Robinson's First Spring Training.* Lincoln: University of Nebraska Press, 2004.

———. *Conspiracy of Silence: Sportswriters and the*

Long Campaign to Desegregate Baseball. Lincoln: University of Nebraska Press, 2012.

Lanctot, Neil. *Campy: The Two Lives of Roy Campanella.* New York: Simon & Schuster, 2011.

Landers, Chris. "10 Bizarre Baseball Rules You Won't Believe Actually Existed." Cut4, May 22, 2015. mlb.com/cut4/10-bizarre-rules-from-baseballs-past/c-124363454.

Lane, F.C. "Eventually There Will Be a Third Big League—Why Not Now?" *Baseball Magazine,* April 1915. digital.la84.org/digital/collection/p17103coll2/id/3908/rec/1.

_____. "Why Not Recognize the Federal League?" *Baseball Magazine,* March 1915. digital.la84.org/digital/collection/p17103coll2/id/3889/rec/1.

"Larry Doby Doesn't Mind Being 'Second Black' Again." *Jet,* July 20, 1978, 52–53.

"Larry Doby Enters Major Leagues." JRank. sports.jrank.org/pages/1209/Doby-Larry-Enters-Major-Leagues.html.

Lawrence, David, and Dom Denaro. *Eastern Colored League.* San Francisco: AJ Publishing, 2003.

Lebovitz, Hal. *The Best of Hal Lebovitz: Great Sportswriting from Six Decades in Cleveland.* Cleveland OH: Gray, 2004.

Lee, Philip. "Re-Thinking Roy Campanella." https://www.baseballthinkfactory.org/hall_of_merit/discussion/re_thinking_roy_campanella, December 26, 2018. Quoted by kind permission of Joe Dimino, representing the Hall of Merit.

Leehrsen, Charles. *Ty Cobb: A Terrible Beauty.* New York: Simon & Schuster, 2015.

"The Legacy of Larry Doby." WBUR-FM, June 20, 2003. wbur.org/onlyagame/2003/06/20/the-legacy-of-larry-doby.

Le Guin, Ursula K. Introduction to *The Left Hand of Darkness.* New York: Penguin, 2016.

Leonard, Buck, with James A. Riley. *Buck Leonard: The Black Lou Gehrig.* New York: Carroll & Graf, 1995.

Lester, Larry. *Black Baseball's National Showcase: The East-West All-Star Game, 1933–1953.* Lincoln: University of Nebraska Press, 2001.

_____. "Can You Read, Judge Landis?" *Black Ball: A Negro Leagues Journal* 1, no. 2 (fall 2008): 57–82.

Lewis, Ethan M. *"A Structure to Last Forever": The Players' League and the Brotherhood of 1890.* ethanlewis.org/pl/ch1.html.

Light, Jonathan Fraser. *The Cultural Encyclopedia of Baseball,* 2nd ed. Jefferson, NC: McFarland, 2005.

Lipsyte, Robert. "Playing the Game They Loved." *New York Times,* August 7, 1983. nytimes.com/1983/08/07/books/playing-the-game-they-loved.html.

Lowenfish, Lee. *Branch Rickey: Baseball's Ferocious Gentleman.* Lincoln: University of Nebraska Press, 2007.

Luke, Bob. *Willie Wells: "El Diablo" of the Negro Leagues.* Austin TX: University of Austin Press, 2007.

"Luke Easter." Negro Leagues Baseball Museum website. nlbemuseum.com/history/players/easter.html.

"Luke Easter Is Top Hitter of Cincinnati Crescents." *Honolulu Star-Crescent,* Oct. 16, 1946, 14.

Macht, Norman L. "Does Baseball Deserve This Black Eye? A Dissent from the Universal Casting of Blame on Kenesaw Mountain Landis for Baseball's Failure to Sign Black Players Before 1946." *Baseball Research Journal* 38, no. 1. (summer 2009): 26–30.

MacPhail, Leland S. "Larry." "Statement of Opinion on 'The Negro in Baseball.'" Submitted by MacPhail to the New York City Mayor's Committee on Unity, ca. September—October 1945. nlbm.mlblogs.com/mcphail-letter-shows-staunch-objection-to-integrate-baseball-c293bab9676.

Malloy, Jerry. "Out at Home." In *SABR 50 at 50: The Society for American Baseball Research's Fifty Most Essential Contributions to the Game,* edited by Bill Nowlin, 50–76. Lincoln: University of Nebraska Press, 2020.

_____. "Sol White and the Origins of African American Baseball." In *Sol White's History of Colored Base Ball, with Other Documents on the Early Black Game, 1886–1936.* Lincoln: University of Nebraska Press, 1995, xiii–lxiv.

"Man Behind the Plate." *Time,* February 10, 1958. content.time.com/time/subscriber/article/0,33009,868262,00.html.

"Man Who Helped Blacks Make Baseball History Dies at 71." *Jet,* January 20, 1986, 46.

Mancuso, Peter. "July 14, 1887: The Color Line Is Drawn." In *Inventing Baseball: The 100 Greatest Games of the 19th Century,* edited by Bill Felber, 189–191. Cleveland OH: Society for American Baseball Research, 2013.

Manning, Gordon. "They're Gonna Like Big Luke." *Collier's Weekly,* August 5, 1950.

Marshall, William. *Baseball's Pivotal Era, 1945–1951.* Lexington: University Press of Kentucky, 1999.

_____. "Happy Chandler and Baseball's Pivotal Era." *Register of the Kentucky Historical Society* 99, No. 2 (Spring 2001), 99–121.

Mathewson, Alfred Dennis. "Major League Baseball's Monopoly Power and the Negro Leagues." *American Business Law Journal* 291 (1987). digitalrepository.unm.edu/law_faculty scholarship/395.

McGowen, Roscoe. "Campy Caught 100 Contests in Nine Straight Campaigns." *Sporting News,* February 5, 1958, 11.

McGregor, Robert Kuhn. *A Calculus of Color: The Integration of Baseball's American League.* Jefferson, NC: McFarland, 2015.

McKenna, Brian. "Bud Fowler." SABR Biography Project. sabr.org/bioproj/person/200e2bbd.

_____. "George Stovey." SABR Biography Project. sabr.org/bioproj/person/8ff10f5c.

McKinley, Eric Garcia. "The Color of Baseball Statistics." Baseball Prospectus, February 3, 2016. baseballprospectus.com/news/

article/28355/prospectus-feature-the-color-of-baseball-statistics/#_ftn11.

McNeil, William F. *Backstop: A History of the Catcher and a Sabermetric Ranking of 50 All-Time Greats.* Jefferson, NC: McFarland, 2006.

___. *Baseball's Other All-Stars: The Greatest Players from the Negro Leagues, the Japanese Leagues, the Mexican Leagues, and the Pre-1960 Winter Leagues in Cuba, Puerto Rico and the Dominican Republic.* Jefferson, NC: McFarland, 2000.

___. *Black Baseball Out of Season: Pay for Play Outside of the Negro Leagues.* Jefferson, NC: McFarland, 2007.

___. *Cool Papas and Double Duties: The All-Time Greats of the Negro Leagues.* Jefferson, NC: McFarland, 2001.

Mead, Alden. "Figuring Probability Fluctuations in Baseball." *Baseball Research Journal* 13 (1984): 20–23.

Meany, Tom. *The Artful Dodgers.* New York: Grosset & Dunlap, 1954.

Mercurio, John A. *Babe Ruth's Incredible Records and the 44 Players Who Broke Them.* New York: S.P.I., 1993.

Miklich, Eric. "Evolution of 19th Century Baseball Rules." 19c Baseball. 19cbaseball.com/rules.html.

Moffi, Larry. *The Conscience of the Game: Baseball's Commissioners from Landis to Selig.* Lincoln: University of Nebraska Press, 2006.

Moffi, Larry, and Jonathan Kronstadt. *Crossing the Line: Black Major Leaguers, 1947–1959.* Jefferson NC: McFarland, 1994.

"Monte Irvin." National Baseball Hall of Fame website. baseballhall.org/hall-of-famers/irvin-monte.

Moore, Joseph Thomas. *Larry Doby: The Struggle of the American League's First Black Player.* Mineola NY: Dover, 2011.

"Moses Fleetwood Walker: Baseball's First African-American." JockBio. jockbio.com/Classic/Walker/Walker_bio.html.

Murphy, Justin. "Luke Easter." SABR Biography Project. sabr.org/bioproj/person/f29a4070.

Murray, Jim. "A Tribute to Satchel." *Oakland Tribune*, June 24, 1964, 39.

Nash, Bruce, and Allan Zullo. *The Baseball Hall of Shame.* Washington, D.C.: Lyons Press, 2012.

"Negro Stars on the Horizon." Unknown author and publication, April 1956. Photocopy held by the National Hall of Fame, Accession Number BL-287-2016-378.

"New Orleans Black Pels Meet." *Montgomery Advertiser*, July 14, 1946, 8.

"New York Yankees Ichiro Suzuki Astounding Throw '4 Bats.'" Video, 38s. youtube.com/watch?v=Xv_FtXOPYqk.

Neyer, Rob. "March Archives." ESPN, March 3, 2000. espn.go.com/mlb/s/2000/0307/406215.html.

___. *Rob Neyer's Big Book of Baseball Legends: The Truth, the Lies, and Everything Else.* New York: Simon & Schuster, 2008.

___. "Two More Walks for Williams." ESPN, May 29, 2002. espn.go.com/mlb/columns/neyer_rob/1388300.html.

___. "Was the Federal League Really a Major League?" National Pastime Museum, November 28, 2012. Accessed January 4, 2020. thenationalpastimemuseum.com/article/was-federal-league-really-major-league.

Nightengale, Bob. "Orioles' Adam Jones Berated by Racist Taunts at Fenway Park." *USA Today*, May 1, 2017. usatoday.com/story/sports/mlb/2017/05/01/orioles-adam-jones-berated-racist-taunts-fenway-park-peanuts/101187172/.

"1974 BBWAA Career Excellence Award Winner John Carmichael." National Baseball Hall of Fame website. baseballhall.org/discover-more/awards/spink/john-carmichael.

Odenkirk, James E. *Of Tribes and Tribulations: The Early Decades of the Cleveland Indians.* Jefferson, NC: McFarland, 2015.

Oleksak, Michael M., and Mary Adams Oleksak. *Beisbol: Latin Americans and the Grand Old Game.* Grand Rapids, MI: Masters Press, 1991.

O'Neil, Buck. "Negro League All Stars." Undated list. National Baseball Hall of Fame website. collection.baseballhall.org/PASTIME/list-negro-league-all-stars-buck-oneil-undated.

Overfield, Joseph. "Luke Easter's Charisma, Remarkable Slugging Captivated Fans, Saved Buffalo Franchise in Mid–1950s." *Baseball Research Journal* 13 (1984). sabr.org/journal/article/easters-charisma-remarkable-slugging-captivated-fans-saved-buffalo-franchise-in-mid–1950s/.

Paige, Satchel, with Hal Lebovitz. *Pitchin' Man.* Cleveland OH: Gray, 1948. Reprinted with introduction by Ken Thomas. New York: Ishi, 2015. Page references to the 2015 edition.

Painter, Alex. *Folk Hero Forever: The Eclectic, Enthralling Baseball Life of Luke Easter.* Self-published, 2018.

___. "A Legend of Halberstamian Proportions." *Negro Leagues Up Close* (blog), May 27, 2020. homeplatedontmove.wordpress.com/2020/05/27/luke-easter-a-legend-of-halberstamian-proportions/.

Peterson, Robert. *Only the Ball Was White: A History of Legendary Black Players and All-Black Professional Teams.* Expanded paperback ed. New York: Oxford University Press, 1992.

Peterson, Todd. "May the Best Man Win: The Black Ball Championships, 1866–1923." *Baseball Research Journal* 41, no. 1 (spring 2013): 7–24.

___, ed. *The Negro Leagues Were Major Leagues: Historians Reappraise Black Baseball.* Jefferson, NC: McFarland, 2020.

Pietrusza, David. *Judge and Jury: The Life and Times of Judge Kenesaw Mountain Landis.* South Bend IN: Diamond, 1998.

Pitoniak, Scott. "The Legend of Luke: On Easter Sunday, a Hero Is Remembered." *Rochester (NY) Democrat and Chronicle*, April 12, 1998, D1 and D5.

Poindexter, Owen. "MLB's Move to 'Elevate' the Negro Leagues Risks Diminishing Them." *Slate*, December 23, 2020. slate.com/culture/2020/12/negro-leagues-major-league-baseball-record-books-complications.html.

Pollock, Allan J. *Barnstorming to Heaven: Syd Pollock and His Great Black Teams*. Tuscaloosa: University of Alabama Press, 2006.

Posnanski, Joe. "The Baseball 100: No. 66, Roy Campanella." *Joe Blogs*, January 4, 2015. web.archive.org/web/20150316203132/http://joeposnanski.com/no-66-roy-campanella/.

_____. "The Baseball 100: No. 76, Willie McCovey." Athletic, January 11, 2020. theathletic.co.uk/1516206/2020/01/11/the-baseball-100-no-76-willie-mccovey/.

_____. "Happy (Luke) Easter." *Joe Blogs*, April 16, 2017. medium.com/joeblogs/happy-luke-easter-83e89adc228b.

_____. "Invisible Man." NBC Sportsworld, undated. sportsworld.nbcsports.com/invisible-man/.

_____. "Remembering Monte Irvin: The Greatness That Was and the Legend That Could've Been." NBC Sportsworld, undated. sportsworld.nbcsports.com/monte-irvin-legend/.

Povich, Shirley. "This Morning with Shirley Povich," *Washington Post*, April 7, 1939, sec. III, 21. In *From Timbuktu to Katrina: Sources in African-American History*, edited by Quintard Taylor. Boston MA: Thomson Wadsworth, 2008.

"Ranking the Hall of Merit Catchers—Discussion." Hall of Merit. baseballthinkfactory.org/hall_of_merit/discussion/ranking_the_hall_of_merit_catchers_discussion/.

"Ray Dandridge." National Baseball Hall of Fame website. baseballhall.org/hall-of-famers/dandridge-ray.

Reilly, Rick. "He Loves Himself Barry Much." *Sports Illustrated*, August 21, 2001. Web.archive.org/web/20011007193444/http://sportsillustrated.cnn.com/inside_game/magazine/life_of_reilly/news/2001/08/21/life_of_reilly/.

Reisler, Jim. *Black Writers / Black Baseball: An Anthology of Articles from Black Sportswriters Who Covered the Negro Leagues*. Jefferson, NC: McFarland, 2007.

"Report of Major League Steering Committee for Submission to the National and American Leagues at Their Meetings in Chicago," August 27, 1946. In *Study of Monopoly Power: Hearings Before the Subcommittee on Study of Monopoly Power of the Committee of the Judiciary, Serial No. 1, Part 6: Organized Baseball*. Government Printing Office, 1952. babel.hathitrust.org/cgi/pt?id=umn.31951d03669259b&view=1up&seq=809.

Report of the Subcommittee on Study of Monopoly Power of the Committee on the Judiciary Pursuant to H. Res. 95. May 27, 1952. Government Printing Office, 1952, via Google Books. books.google.co.uk/books?id=BKfD49GILIIC&pg=PP5&#v=onepage&q&f=false.

Resnick, Joe. "Satchel Paige: One of Life's Gool Ol' Boys." *Munster (IN) Times*, June 9, 1982, 11.

Revel, Layton. *Integration of Major League Baseball*. Center for Negro Leagues Research and Negro Southern League Museum, 2018. cnlbr.org/Portals/0/RL/Integration%20of%20Major%20League%20Baseball%202018-04.pdf.

Revel, Layton, and Luis Munoz. *Forgotten Heroes: Orestes "Minnie" Miñoso*. Carrollton, TX: Center for Negro League Baseball Research, undated. Retrieved at cnlbr.org/Portals/0/Hero/Orestes-Minoso.pdf.

Ribowsky, Mark. *A Complete History of the Negro Leagues, 1884–1955*. New York: Birch Lane, 1995.

_____. *Josh Gibson: The Power and the Darkness*. Urbana: University of Illinois Press, 2004.

Rickey, Branch. "Goodbye to Some Old Baseball Ideas." *Life*, August 2, 1954, 78–89.

"Rickey Tells Attempt to Keep Robinson Out of National League." *Centralia (IL) Evening Sentinel*, February 17, 1948, 4.

Riley, James A. *The Biographical Encyclopedia of the Negro Baseball Leagues*. New York: Carroll & Graf, 1994.

Ripken, Cal, Sr., with Larry Burke. *The Ripken Way: A Manual for Baseball and Life*. New York: Diversion Books, 1999.

Ritter, Lawrence, and Donald Honig. *The 100 Greatest Ballplayers of All Time*. New York: Crown, 1981.

Rivera, Marly, et. al. "CC Sabathia: 'I've Never Been Called the N-Word' Anywhere but in Boston." ESPN, May 2, 2017. espn.com/mlb/story/_/id/19296595/new-york-yankees-pitcher-cc-sabathia-says-black-players-expect-racism-boston.

Robinson, Jackie. "Jackie Tells How He Laughed at Scout When Asked to Try Out for Big Leagues." *Ebony*, June 1948, 20–24.

_____. "What's Wrong with Negro Baseball?" *Ebony*, June 1948, 16–18.

Rodney, Lester. "Time for Stalling is Over, Judge Landis." *Daily Worker*, May 23, 1942, 8.

Rogosin, Donn. *Invisible Men: Life in Baseball's Negro Leagues*. New York: Atheneum, 1983.

Roosevelt, Franklin D. Executive Order 8802, June 25, 1941. Franklin D. Roosevelt Presidential Library and Museum. docs.fdrlibrary.marist.edu/od8802t.html.

Roosevelt, Theodore, Jr., Letter to Bessie Van Voorst, October 18, 1902. Theodore Roosevelt Center at Dickinson State University. theodorerooseveltcenter.org/Research/Digital-Library/Record/ImageViewer?libID=o183324&imageNo=1.

Rosciam, Chuck. "Iron Man Catchers." *Encyclopedia of Baseball Catchers*. bb_catchers.tripod.com/catchers/ironmen.htm.

Rosenberg, Howard R. *Cap Anson*, 4 vols. Arlington, VA: Tile Books, 2003–2006.

_____. "Cap Anson and the Color Line: Did He Truly Influence Baseball's 'Gentleman's Agreement'?" Black Athlete, June 15, 2008. web.archive.org/web/20160406205835/http://

blackathletenet/2008/06/cap-anson-and-the-color-line/.

———. "The Momentous Drawing of the Sport's 19th-Century 'Color Line' Is Still Tripping Up History Writers." Atavist, June 14, 2016. howard-wrosenberg.atavist.com/racism-bbhistory.

Rossi, John. *Baseball and American Culture: A History.* Lanham, MD: Rowman & Littlefield, 2018.

Rothenberg, Matt. "Fast Feet, Cool Shoes." National Baseball Hall of Fame website. baseballhall.org/discover-more/stories/short-stops/fast-feet-cool-shoes.

———. "Fighting for Equality on the Baseball Grounds." National Baseball Hall of Fame website. Baseballhall.Org/discover/octavius-catto-philadelphia-black-baseball.

"Roy Campanella." National Baseball Hall of Fame website. Baseballhall.Org/hall-of-famers/campanella-roy.

Rutkoff, Peter, ed. *The Cooperstown Symposium on Baseball and American Culture, 1997 (Jackie Robinson).* Jefferson, NC: McFarland, 2000.

Ruzzo, Bob. "Fate and the Federal League: Were the Federals Incompetent, Outmaneuvered, or Just Unlucky?" *Baseball Research Journal* 42, no. 2 (2013): 30–41.

Rymer, Zachary D. "The Evolution of the Baseball from the Dead-Ball Era Through Today." Bleacher Report. bleacherreport.com/articles/1676509-the-evolution-of-the-baseball-from-the-dead-ball-era-through-today.

Sackman, Jeff. "How Competitive Was the 1914 Federal League?" Hardball Times, August 5, 2010. tht.fangraphs.com/how-competitive-was-the-1914-federal-league/.

Samuelson, R.C. "Rube." "About a Man Named Easter." *Metropolitan Pasadena (CA) Star-News,* June 7, 1949, 20.

Schlemmer, Jim. "Easter's Long Home Run Benches Nelson." *Akron (OH) Beacon Journal,* April 5, 1954, 18.

Schneider, Russell. *The Cleveland Indians Encyclopedia.* 3rd ed. Champaign, IL: Sports Publishing, 2004.

Schoenfield, David. "Generation OPS: How Powerful Young All-Stars Are Re-Defining the Game." ESPN, July 9, 2019. espn.co.uk/mlb/story/_/id/27148938/generation-ops-how-powerful-young-all-stars-redefining-game.

———. "Ten Reasons Why Willie Mays Is Greatest Ever." ESPN, May 6, 2011. espn.com/blog/sweetspot/post/_/id/10260/ten-reasons-willie-mays-is-greatest-ever.

Schudel, Matt. "Steve Dalkowski, Hard-Throwing Pitcher and Baseball's Greatest What-If Story, Dies of Coronavirus." *Washington Post,* April 24, 2020. washingtonpost.com/local/obituaries/steve-dalkowski-hard-throwing-pitcher-and-baseballs-greatest-what-if-story-dies-at-80/2020/04/24/aadf2e8c-8661-11ea-a3eb-e9fc93160703_story.html.

Schwartz, Alan. "Numbers Are Cast in Bronze, but Are Not Set in Stone." *New York Times,* July 31, 2005. nytimes.com/2005/07/31/sports/baseball/numbers-are-cast-in-bronze-but-are-not-set-in-stone.html.

"Scorecard." *Sports Illustrated,* December 4, 1961, 17.

Selter, Ronald M. *Ballparks of the Deadball Era: A Comprehensive Study of Their Dimensions, Configurations and Effects on Batting, 1901–1919.* Jefferson, NC: McFarland, 2008.

Seymour, Harold, and Dorothy Z. Seymour. *Baseball: The Golden Age.* New York: Oxford University Press, 1971.

Shea, Stuart, with George Castle. *Wrigley Field: The Unauthorized Biography.* Washington, D.C.: Potomac, 2004.

Sherman, Rodger. "Great College Teams Can't Even Beat the Harlem Globetrotters." SBNation, March 27, 2015. sbnation.com/college-basketball/2015/3/27/8300661/could-kentucky-beat-the-harlem-globetrotters-nope-syracuse.

Silber, Irwin. *Press Box Red: The Story of Lester Rodney, the Communist Who Helped Break the Color Line in American Sports.* Philadelphia: Temple University Press, 2003.

Simkus, Scott. *Outsider Baseball: The Weird World of Hardball on the Fringe, 1876–1950.* Chicago: Chicago Review Press, 2014.

Singletary, Wes. *Al Lopez: The Life of Baseball's El Señor.* Jefferson, NC: McFarland, 1999.

Smith, Wendell. "'Negroes Will Never Crash Majors,' Says Bill Terry; Carl Hubbell Lauds Colored Players." *Pittsburgh Courier,* July 22, 1939, 1 and S1.

———. "Wendell Smith's Sports Beat." *Pittsburgh Courier,* April 2, 1949, 22.

Snyder, Matt. "Remembering Ty Cobb and the 1910 AL Batting Title." CBS Sports, June 16, 2014. cbssports.com/mlb/news/remembering-ty-cobb-and-the-1910-al-batting-title/.

Soderholm-Difatte, Bryan. *America's Game: A History of Major League Baseball Through World War II.* Lanham, MD: Rowman & Littlefield, 2018.

———. *The Golden Era of Major League Baseball: A Time of Transition and Integration.* Lanham, MD: Rowman & Littlefield, 2015.

Spink, A.G Taylor. "No Good from Raising Race Issue." *Sporting News,* August 6, 1942, 4.

Stahl, Michael. "The Secret History of Black Baseball Players in Canada's Great White North." Salon, April 30, 2017. salon.com/2017/04/30/the-secret-history-of-black-baseball-players-in-canadas-great-white-north_partner/.

"Stan 'The Man' Musial Dies at 92." ESPN, January 9, 2013. espn.com/mlb/story/_/id/8860690/st-louis-cardinals-hall-famer-stan-musial-dies-age-92.

Stanford, George. "Willard Brown / Hank Thompson." Baseball Fever, January 28, 2006. A post at an online forum by Stanford (as "1947 Browns"). baseball-fever.com/forum/the-teams-of-yesteryear/st-louis-browns/37318-willard-brown-hank-thompson?p=1030136#post1030136.

Stezano, Martin. "After Jackie: The Guys of '47." History.com. history.com/news/after-jackie-the-guys-of-47.

Stilley, Aaron. "Q&A with Scott Simkus, Author of *Outside Baseball.*" *Royal Heritage* (blog), March 3, 2014. kcbbh.blogspot.com/2014/03/q-with-scott-simkus-author-of-outsider.html.

Sullivan, Dean A, ed. *Late Innings: A Documentary History of Baseball.* Lincoln: University of Nebraska Press, 2002.

Swaine, Rick. *The Black Stars Who Made Baseball Whole.* Jefferson, NC: McFarland, 2006.

———. *The Integration of Major League Baseball: A Team by Team History.* Jefferson NC: McFarland, 2009.

Swanson, Ryan A. *When Baseball Went White: Reconstruction, Reconciliation, and Dreams of a National Pastime.* Lincoln: University of Nebraska Press, 2014.

Talbot, Gayle. "Sports Roundup." *Ogdensburg (NY) Daily Journal,* March 17, 1953, 6.

Taney, Roger Brooke, and the Supreme Court of the United States. *U.S. Reports: Dred Scott v. Sandford,* 60 U.S. 19 How. 393, 1856, PDF. loc.gov/item/usrep060393a/.

Tharps, Lori L. "The Case for Black with a Capital B." *New York Times,* November 18, 2014. nytimes.com/2014/11/19/opinion/the-case-for-black-with-a-capital-b.html.

Thomas, Robert McG., Jr. "Roy Campanella, 71, Dies; Was Dodger Hall of Famer." *New York Times,* June 28, 1993, B8.

Thompson, Hank, with Arnold Hano. "How I Wrecked My Life—How I Hope to Save It." *Sport,* December 1965.

Thorn, John. *Baseball in the Garden of Eden.* New York: Simon & Schuster, 2011.

———. "Black Ball, Part 5." *Our Game* (blog), March 20, 2015. ourgame.mlblogs.com/black-ball-part-5-79ae6fe4012f.

———. "The Drawing of the Color Line." *Our Game* (blog), November 12, 2012. ourgame.mlblogs.com/the-drawing-of-the-color-line-1867-3ebec9782bb0.

———. "1860s–1900s: Lumber and Crossed Fingers." This Great Game. thisgreatgame.com/ballparks-eras-1860s-1900s.html.

———. "George Stovey." *Our Game* (blog), October 31, 2017. ourgame.mlblogs.com/george-stovey-899c332d3e18.

———. "Philadelphia Pythians of 1867: Another View." *Our Game* (blog), March 20, 2017. ourgame.mlblogs.com/philadelphia-pythians-of-1867-another-view-2fd3e58953da.

———. "Why Is the National Association Not a Major League … and Other Records Issues." *Our Game* (blog), May 4, 2015. ourgame.mlblogs.com/why-is-the-national-association-not-a-major-league-and-other-records-issues-7507e1683b66.

Thorn, John, and Pete Palmer. *The Hidden Game of Baseball,* rev. ed. New York: Doubleday, 1985.

Thorn, John, Pete Palmer, Michael Gershman, and David Pietruzka, eds. *Total Baseball,* 6th ed. New York: Total Sports, 1999.

Tourtelotte, Shane. "A Federal Case: Measuring the Federal League Against the Other Majors." Hardball Times, April 27, 2017. tht.fangraphs.com/a-federal-case-measuring-the-federal-league-against-the-other-majors.

Turnquist, Ryan. "Musial Passes Speaker on All-Time Hits List." National Baseball Hall of Fame website. baseballhall.org/discover-more/stories/inside-pitch/musial-passes-speaker-on-all-time-hits-list.

Twombly, Wells. "Crumbs for the Outcasts." *Sporting News,* February 20, 1971, 41.

Tye, Larry. *Satchel: The Life and Times of an American Legend.* New York: Random House, 2009.

———. "Sunday Forum: Satchel Paige and Pittsburgh, PA." *Pittsburgh Post-Gazette.* August 2, 2009. post-gazette.com/Op-Ed/2009/08/02/Sunday-Forum-Satchel-Paige-and-Pittsburgh-Pa/stories/200908020171.

Tygiel, Jules. *Baseball's Great Experiment: Jackie Robinson and His Legacy.* New York: Oxford University Press, 1983.

———. "Black Ball." In *Total Baseball,* 6th ed., edited by John Thorn et al. New York: Total Sports, 1999.

———. *Extra Bases: Reflections on Jackie Robinson, Race, and Baseball History.* Lincoln: University of Nebraska Press, 2002.

———. Introduction to Roy Campanella, *It's Good to Be Alive,* Bison Book ed. Lincoln NE: University of Nebraska Press, 1995.

———. "Revisiting Bill Veeck and the 1943 Phillies." *Baseball Research Journal* 35 (2006): 109–114.

———. "Those Who Came After." *Sports Illustrated,* June 27, 1983. web.archive.org/web/20140218221238/http://sportsillustrated.cnn.com/vault/article/magazine/MAG1120987/4/index.htm.

Unger, Norman O. "Original Globetrotter 'Kid' Oliver Buried in Chicago." *Jet,* January 23, 1984.

Van Hyning, Thomas E. "Luke Easter, Larger Than Life Figure: Caribbean, Minors, and American League. Part 1." Béisbol 101, April 2020. beisbol101.com/2020/04/luke-easter-larger-than-life-figure-caribbean-minors-and-american-league-part-i/.

———. "Luke Easter, Larger than Life Figure: Mexico, Puerto Rico, and Minors. Part 2." Béisbol 101, May 3, 2021. beisbol101.com/luke-easter-larger-than-life-figure-mexico-puerto-rico-and-minors-part-ii/.

———. "Monte Irvin: From Alabama to Newark, San Juan, Veracruz, Havana and Coopestown." Béisbol 101, May 28, 2021. beisbol101.com/monte-irvin-from-alabama-to-newark-san-juan-veracruz-havana-and-cooperstown/.

———. *Puerto Rico's Winter League: A History of Major League Baseball's Launching Pad.* Jefferson, NC: McFarland, 1995).

Vascellaro, Charlie. *Hank Aaron: A Biography.* Westport, CT: Greenwood, 2005.

"Vertical File Materials—Local History

Collection—Moses Fleetwood Walker." digitalshoebox.org/digital/collection/books/id/59339/.
Wancho, Joseph, ed. *Pitching to the Pennant: The 1954 Cleveland Indians.* Lincoln: University of Nebraska Press, 2014.
Ward, Arch. "In the Wake of the News." *Chicago Tribune,* May 24, 1949, 39.
Watkins, John J. "Gene Baker." SABR Biography Project. sabr.org/bioproj/person/ec0df53d.
Watson, Leroy, Jr. "Forgotten Stories of Courage and Inspiration: Roy Campanella." Bleacher Report. bleacherreport.com/articles/166177-forgotten-stories-of-courage-and-inspiration-roy-campanella.
Whalen, Thomas J. *When the Red Sox Ruled: Baseball's First Dynasty, 1912–1918.* Lanham, MD: Rowman & Littlefield, 2011.
White, Gaylon H. *Singles and Smiles: How Artie Wilson Broke Baseball's Color Barrier.* Lanham, MD: Rowman & Littlefield, 2018.
White, Richard. "Baseball's John Fowler: The 1887 Season in Binghamton, New York." In *Afro Americans in New York Life and History* 16, no. 1 (January 31, 1992): 7.
White, Sol. *Sol White's History of Colored Base Ball, with Other Documents on the Early Black Game, 1886–1936.* Lincoln: University of Nebraska Press, 1995.
Wilson, Doug. "Luke Easter: The Gold Rush of 1949 and What Might Have Been." Doug Wilson's Baseball Bookshelf, July 14, 2018. web.archive.org/web/20200501154256/dougwilsonbaseball.blogspot.com/2018/07/luke-easter-gold-rush-of-1949-and-what.html.
"World's Champions May Not Go Barnstorming Anymore." *St. Louis Post-Dispatch,* January 8, 1911, 24.
Yang, Avery. "Black History Month: Remembering Satchel Paige, Maybe the Best Pitcher to Ever Live." *Sports Illustrated,* February 2, 2002. si.com/mlb/2020/02/02/black-history-month-remembering-satchel-paige.
Young, A.S. "Doc." *Great Negro Baseball Stars and How They Made the Major Leagues.* New York: A.S. Barnes, 1953.
———. "Inside Sports." *Jet,* May 29, 1952, 59.
———. "Jackie Opens the Door—Wide!" *Ebony,* December 1968, 126–141.
———. "An 'Old Man' Makes Baseball History." *Ebony,* March 1969, 122–132.
Young, Fay. "Meet Bill Veeck." *Chicago Defender,* February 26, 1949, 14.
Zang, David W. *Fleet Walker's Divided Heart: The Life of Baseball's First Black Major Leaguer.* Lincoln: University of Nebraska Press, 1995.
Zimmerman, Jeff. "1960 Salina Blue Jays: The Year Satchel Paige Came to Town." FanGraphs, January 17, 2003. blogs.fangraphs.com/1960-salina-blue-jays-the-year-satchel-paige-came-to-town.
Zinn, John G. "June 21, 1890: No Hits—but No Win for Silver King." In *Inventing Baseball: The 100 Greatest Games of the 19th Century,* edited by Bill Felber, 228–230. Cleveland: Society for American Baseball Research, 2013.

Magazines

Baseball Analyst
Baseball Digest
Baseball Magazine
Baseball Research Journal
Collier's Weekly
DeWitt Base Ball Guide
Ebony
Jet
Journal of Sports Economics
Journal of Sports History
Life
Literary Digest
LOOK
National Pastime
Negro Digest
Reader's Digest
Saturday Evening Post
Smithsonian
Sport
Sporting News
Sports Illustrated
Time

Newspapers

Abilene (TX) Reporter
Adirondack (NY) Daily Enterprise
Akron Beacon Journal
Alabama Citizen (Tuscaloosa)
Alabama Tribune (Montgomery)
Alton (IL) Evening Telegraph
Altoona (PA) Tribune
Alva (OK) Review-Courier
Anaconda (MT) Standard
Arizona Daily Star (Tuscon)
Austin American
Ball Players' Chronicle (NY)
Baltimore Afro-American
Baltimore Sun
Bangor (ME) Daily News
Battle Creek (MI) Enquirer
Baytown (TX) Sun
Bedford (IN) Daily Mail
Benton Harbor (MI) News-Palladium
Berkeley (CA) Daily Gazette
Big Spring (TX) Daily Herald
Binghamton (NY) Daily Leader
Bismarck (ND) Tribune
Boston Globe / Sunday Globe
Bradford (PA) Era
Brooklyn Daily Eagle
Buffalo Criterion
Buffalo Evening News
Burlington (VT) Free Press
Capital Times (Madison WI)
Carolina Times (Durham NC)

Bibliography

Centralia (IL) Evening Sentinel
Charleston (SC) Daily Mail
Charlotte Messenger
Chattanooga (TN) Daily Times
Chester (PA) Times
Chicago Daily Herald
Chicago Defender
Chicago Tribune / Daily Tribune
Cincinnati Enquirer
Cincinnati Times-Star
Cleveland Call and Post
Cleveland Gazette
Cleveland Leader
Cleveland Plain Dealer
Colorado Springs Gazette / Gazette-Telegraph
Connellsville (PA) Daily Courier
Council Bluffs (IA) Nonpareil
Daily Deadwood (SD) Pioneer-Times
Daily Worker (NYC)
Dayton (OH) Daily Express
Dayton (OH) Journal Herald
Decatur (IL) Daily Review
Decatur (IL) Herald
Defiance (OH) Crescent News
Delaware County (PA) Daily Times
Des Moines Register
Detroit News
Detroit Tribune
Elmira (NY) Advertiser
Elwood (IN) Call-Leader
Emporia (KS) Gazette
Endicott (NY) Daily Bulletin
Estherville (IA) Evening News
Evansville (IN) Argus
Evening Statesman (Walla Walla WA)
Fort Wayne (IN) Daily News
Fresno (CA) Bee-Republican
Frostburg (MD) Mining Journal
Galveston (PA) Evening News
Gettysburg (PA) Times
Greeley (CO) Daily Tribune
Guardian (UK)
Harrisburg (PA) Evening News
Harrisburg (PA) Telegraph
Hattiesburg (MS) American
Hawaii Tribune-Herald (Hilo)
Holton (KS) Recorder
Honolulu Advertiser
Honolulu Star-Bulletin
Hope (AR) Star
Huron (SD) Daily Plainsman
Hutchinson (KS) News
Indianapolis Freeman Supplement
Indianapolis Recorder
Island Dispatch (Grand Island NY)
Janesville (WI) Daily Gazzette
Jefferson (TX) Jimplecute
Kansas (MO) City Star
Knoxville (TN) Journal
Knoxville (TN) News-Sentinel
Lafayette (IN) Courier and Journal
Larned (KS) Chronoscope
Lawrence (KS) Daily Journal

Lincoln (NE) Journal-Star
Lincoln (NE) Star
Logansport (IN) Pharos Tribune
Los Angeles Times
Louisville Commercial
Louisville Courier-Journal
Macon (GA) Chronicle-Herald
Massilion (OH) Evening Independent
Medina (NY) Daily Journal & Register
Meriden (CT) Morning Record
Metropolitan Pasadena (CA) Star-News
Milwaukee Journal
Milwaukee Sentinel
Moline (IL) Dispatch
Montana Standard (Butte MO)
Montgomery (AL) Advertiser
Montpelier (IN) Herald
Montreal Gazette
Mount Vernon (IL) Register News
Muncie (IN) Star Press
Munster (IN) Times
Muscatine (IA) Journal
New Castle (PA) News
New Jersey Herald News (Newton)
New York Age
New York Clipper
New York Daily News
New York Herald Tribune
New York Telegram
New York Times
Newark Evening News
Newark Journal / Daily Journal
Newark News
Newark Star-Ledger
Newark Sunday Call
Newport News (VA) Daily Press
Oakland Tribune
Ogdensburg (NY) Advance-News
Ogdensburg (NY) Journal
Oil City (PA) Derrick
Owensboro (KY) Messenger-Inquirer
Passaic (NJ) Herald-News
Paterson (NJ) Morning Call
People's Voice (Hamilton ON)
Philadelphia Inquirer
Philadelphia Record
Philadelphia Tribune
Pittsburgh Courier
Pittsburgh Daily Post
Pittsburgh Press
Plattsburgh (NY) Press-Republican
Portland (OR) Daily Press
Racine (IL) Journal-Times
Raleigh (NC) News and Observer
Richmond (IN) Palladium-Item
Richmond (VA) Afro-American
Richmond (VA) Times-Dispatch
Rochester (NY) Democrat & Chronicle
St. Louis Argus
St. Louis Globe-Democrat
St. Louis Post-Dispatch
St. Louis Sporting News
St. Louis Star and Times

St. Petersburg (FL) Times
San Francisco Examiner
San Mateo (CA) Times
Sandusky (OH) Register
Seymour (IN) Daily Republican
Shreveport (LA) Caucasian
Shreveport (LA) Journal
Somerset (PA) Daily American
Sporting Life (Philadelphia PA)
Steubenville (OH) Weekly Gazette
Syracuse (NY) Daily Standard
Syracuse (NY) Herald
Syracuse (NY) Post-Standard
Tampa (FL) Tribune
Tampa Bay Times (St. Petersburg FL)
Toledo (OH) Daily Blade / Weekly Blade
Toledo (OH) Evening Bee
Toronto Daily Globe
Toronto Daily Mail
Toronto Globe and Mail
Toronto World
Towanda (PA) Daily Review
Trenton (NJ) Daily True American
Trenton (NJ) Evening Times
Tyler (TX) Courier-Times
Virgin Islands Daily News
Washington (DC) Afro-American
Washington (DC) Evening Star
Washington (DC) Post
Washington (DC) Tribune
Waterbury (CT) Evening Democrat
Wichita (KS) Beacon
Wilmington (DE) News Journal
Winnipeg (MB) Free Press

Websites and Blogs

academia.edu
Access to Research
The Atavist
The Athletic
Babe Ruth Central
Baseball Almanac
Baseball Fever
Baseball Hall of Fame Digital Collection
Baseball History Daily
Baseball Joe
Baseball Prospectus
Beisbol 101
Bill James Online
Black Athlete
Bleacher Report
Canadiana
Cap Chronicled
CBS Sports
Center for Negro League Baseball Research
Chronicling America (US Library of Congress)
Cool Cleveland
CORE
Cut4
Deadball Era
The Digital Shoebox Project
Directory of Open Access Journals
Doug Wilson's Baseball Bookshelf
Encyclopedia of Baseball Catchers
encyclopedia.com
ericenders.com
ESPN
FanGraphs
Franklin D. Roosevelt Presidential Library and Museum
GeneaologyBank
Google Books
Google News Archive Search
The Hall of Merit
The Hall of Miller and Eric
The Hardball Times
HathiTrust
history.com
Hoosier State Chronicles
Illinois Digital Newspaper Collections
Illinois Newspaper Project
Inside Sources
Internet Archive Wayback Machine
JockBio
Joe Blogs
JRank
JSTOR
LA84 Foundation Digital Library
Library of Congress Digital
MLB.com
National Pastime Museum
NBC Sports
The Negro Leagues Up Close
newspaperarchive.com
newspapers.com
Newspapers
19c Baseball
nlbmuseum.com
oscarcharleston.com
Our Game
PBS
PICRYL
Pixabay
Project Gutenberg
ProQuest
ResearchGate
Royal Heritage
SABR
Salon
Saturday Evening Post
SBNation
SeanLahman.com
SF Weekly
Sports Illustrated
Stats Crew
UK Press Online
USA Today
Wikipedia
WorldCat
YouTube

Index

Numbers in ***bold italics*** indicate pages with illustrations

Aaron, Henry "Hank" 2, 36, 48, 55, 79–80, 88, 127, 141, 150–51, 157–58, 161, 174, 302
Abdul-Jabbar, Kareem 88
Acho, Emmanuel 305
Albright, Thomas 83
Alexander, Lisa Doris 340*n*1
Alexander, Pete 162
All-Star Game (MLB) 4, 71, 136, 145
Allen, Newton "Newt" 176; batting record 180–81
Alomar, Roberto 159
Alston, Tom 302
Alston, Walter 119, 123–24, 300
Altman, George 303
American Association (AA) 1, 16–17, 36–38, 67–68, 94, 97, 121, 123–24, 134–35, 270, 300, 308
American Baseball League 271, 300
American Basketball League (ABL) 143
American League All Stars (barnstorming team) 89
American Negro League (ANL) 66, 271, 273
American Stars 89
American Youth for Democracy 43
Amoros, Sandy 301
Anderson, Dave 342*n*13
Anson, Adrian "Cap" 7, 11, ***12***, 15–20, 24, 26–32, 34, 56, 90, 149, 157, 159, 307, 312
Appleton, Walter 19
Appling, Luke 159
Armour, Bill 71
The Artful Dodgers 117
Arundel, John "Tug" 18
Asburn, Richie 161
Ashford, Emmett 53
Ashwill, Gary 113, 177
Askew, Jesse 126

Associated Press (AP) 45, 51, 127, 134, 139, 325
Astroth, Joe 137
Atlanta Black Crackers 303
Atlanta Braves 329; *see also* Milwaukee Braves
Atlanta Crackers 52

Baby Ruth (candy bar) 103
Bacharach Giants 121
Bacharach Park (Atlantic City) 69
Bagwell, Jeff 58, 61, 159
Baker, Del 137
Baker, Gene 302
Baker, John "Home Run" 160
Baker Bowl 33, 56
balata-cored baseballs 59, 131
A Ball Player's Career 28
Baltimore Elite Giants 121–22, 124, 300–1
Baltimore Lord Baltimores 18
Baltimore Orioles 32–33, 302
Baltimore Sun 20
"Bama grapevine" 71
Bankhead, Dan 300
Bankhead, Sam 161, 176, 269, 302; batting record 182–83
Banks, Ernie 36, 48, 79–80, 159, 173–74, 301
Barkley, Sam 34
Barnes, Bill 83
Barnes, Frank 303
Barnes, Ross 31, 56–57
Barney, Rex 123
Barnhill, Dave 52, 121
Barrett, Dick 137
Baseball Digest 309
Baseball Encyclopedia see Macmillan Baseball Encyclopedia
Baseball Fever 89
Baseball Hall of Fame 4, 6, 11, 30, 125, 135–36, 164; proposed separate wing for Black players 100, 312

Baseball-Reference.com 6, 177
Batavia Pirates 302
Bates, Michael 157
Battin, Joe 25
Bavasi, Emil "Buzzy" 123
Beard, Ollie 22
Beckley, Jake 37
Beckwith, John 57, 59, 100–2, 160, 176; batting record 184
Beer, Jeremy 92
Bell, James "Cool Papa" 57, 72, 147, 154, 160, 174, 176, 269; batting record 185–86
Belle, Albert 58, 61, 101
"Bench 5" (Baseball Fever poster) 89
Bench, Johnny 105, 114–15, 118, 124, 158
Bennett, Charlie 115, 118
Bennett Park (Detroit) 71
Benswanger, William 44, 121–22, 315
Berardino, John 337*ch*10*n*8
Berkow, Ira 143
Berra, Lawrence "Yogi" 105, 114, 117–18, 124, 144, 146, 158
Bessick, Ed 153
Biggio, Craig 159, 164
The Bill James Historical Baseball Abstract 103; *see also The New Bill James Historical Baseball Abstract*
Binghamton Bings 23–24
Binghamton Daily Leader 23
The Bingo Long Traveling All-Stars & Motor Kings 86–87, 335*ch*6*n*3
Birmingham Black Barons 301–5
Bishop, Max 101
Bismarck Club 273
Bittman, Henry "Red" 22
Black, Joe 49, 301
"Black Sox" *see* Chicago Black Sox
Blackistone, Kevin B. 26

360 Index

Blackistone Hotel (Chicago IL) 323
Blackwell, Charlie 57
Blocker, "Fireball" 338n3
Bob Feller's Major League All Stars 89
Bock, Wally 134
Boggs, Wade 160
Bond, Tommy 84
Bond, Walt 304
Bonds, Barry 58–61, 91, 101, 147–52, 160, 340n1
Border League 112
Bordick, Mike 55
Boston, racial problems in 298
Boston Beaneaters 36
Boston Braves 300–1
Boston Buffeds 88
Boston Globe 28, 46
Boston Red Sox 47, 132, 144, 298
Boston Reds 36
Boudreau, Lou 143, 342n13
boxing 27, 121
Boyd, Bob 49, 301
Boyer, Cletis "Clete" 6
Boyer, Ken 160
Bracken, Herbert "Doc" 126
Bradley, Alva 46, 315
Brashler, William 4
Breadon, Sam 47, 313, 315, 342n23; *see also* MacPhail Report
Bregman, Alex 55
Bresnahan, Roger 115, 118
Bressler, Raymond "Rube" 72, 84
Brett, George 6, 54–55, 61–62, 160
Brewer, Chet 43, 82, 84, 137
Bridges, Marshall 303
Brissie, Lou 143
Britt, George *274*
Brock, Lou 107
Brockway, John 35
Brooklyn Bridegrooms 33–34
Brooklyn Daily Eagle 16
Brooklyn Dodgers 46, 51, 119, 123–24, 300–1, 303, 315; *see also* Los Angeles Dodgers
Brooklyn Grays 32
Brooklyn Tip-Tops 69
Brooklyn Ward's Wonders 32, 35
Brooks, Irwin "Chester" 176; batting record 187
Brouthers, Dan 37, 101, 159
Brown, Dave 101–2, 162, 176; pitching record 254
Brown, John 16
Brown, Ike 305
Brown, Ray 101, 162, 174, 176; pitching record 255

Brown, Willard "Home Run" 1, 36, 46, 48–49, 57, 110, 130, 143, 160, 174, 176, 178–79, 269, 300, 306, 334n20; batting record 188–89; profile 109–112
Brown v. Board of Education 39
Browning, Pete 56, 102
Bruton, Bill 301
Bryant, Howard 4
Buffalo Bisons 120, 133, 135–36, 138, 166
Buffalo Stadium (Houston TX) 145
Bulgliosi, Vincent 125
Bumpus, Earl "Lefty" 126
Bunker, Wally 84–85
Burbage, Knowlington "Buddy" 57
Burkett, Jesse 56–57, 107, 160
Burnett, Fred "Tex" 1931 Grays *274*
Burns, Ken 89
Burns, Tom 19
Burns, Willie 83
Burr, Raymond 11

Cabrera, Cucú 137
Caffie, Joe 303
California Angels 305
Call and Post 309
Camden Giants 141
Campanella, Roy 1, 36, 44, 48–51, 79, 94, 111, 142, 158, 168–69, 174, 178, 300, 306, 309, 314, 337n10; batting record 189–90; profile 113–24
Campanis, Al 52
Canada 67
Cannon, Richard 83
Carew, Rod 54–55, 61, 159
Caribbean Series Hall of Fame 165
Carlson, Tucker 333n23
Carlton, Steve 162
Carmichael, John 311
Carroll, Louis 316–26
Carrying Jackie's Torch 335n24
Carter, Gary 115, 118, 158
Casanova, Paul 305
Cash, Norm 60
Cater, Danny 54
Catholic Protectory Oval (CPO) (NYC) 69
Celler, Emanuel 317, 321, 323
Central League 302
Chalek, Eric 113–117
Chamberlain, Wilt "The Stilt" 88
Chandler, Albert "Happy" 316, 318, 320–22, 325–26, 343n13
Chappas, Harry 305
Charleston, Oscar 57, 59, 62–64, 88, 100–2, 147–52, 160, 174,

176, 273, *274*; batting record 192–93
Charlottesville riot 30
Chicago American Giants 301–2
Chicago "Black Sox" 29, 34
Chicago Colts 34
Chicago Cubs 32–33, 36, 47, 71, 166, 301–3, 315–16
Chicago Defender 40, 310
Chicago Pirates 32
"Chicago slide" 19–20
Chicago Tribune 28, 311
Chicago Urban League 310
Chicago White Sox 146, 155, 165, 300, 305
Chicago White Stockings 15–16, 27, 32
Chism, "Big" John 126
Chism, "Little" Eli 126
Chuinichi Dragons 146
Cincinnati Enquirer 129
Cincinnati Reds 32–33, 40, 52, 298, 302–3, 305, 315
Clark, Vibert "Webbo" 83–84, 303
Clarke, Fred 107–8, 303
Clarkson, James "Bus" 301
Clemens, Roger 102, 153, 162
Clemente, Roberto 153, 161
Clendenon, Don 304
Cleveland, Grover (US president) 103
Cleveland, Howard 121
Cleveland, Ruth 103
Cleveland Blues 15, 19, 27
Cleveland Buckeyes 300–1, 303
Cleveland Gazette 19, 26
Cleveland Indians 32, 132–34, 136, 139, 142–44, 154–55, 166, 299–305, 309, 311, 315, 326, 342n13
Cleveland Infants 88
Cleveland Plain Dealer 138
Cleveland Stadium 145
Cleveland Whites 13
Clifton, Nat "Sweetwater" 88
Cobb, Chris 113–16
Cobb, Tyrus "Ty" 3, 34–35, 55–57, 90–91, 96, 99–100, 120, 147, 150, 160, 164
Cochrane, Mickey 114, 118, 153, 158
Coleman, Clarence "Choo-Choo" 304
College Station Post Office Employees 43
Collier's Weekly magazine 127
Collins, Eddie 100, 159
Collins, Pat 50
Colored World Series 67; *see also* Negro World Series
Coltzie, Jim 137

Index

Columbus Buckeyes 15–16
Combs, Earle 50
Comiskey, Charles 37
Comiskey Park 1, 47, 69, 71, 169
Commissioner's office 40; see also National Commission
Committee on Unity 45, 334n16
Congressional Record 316
Conley, Gene 145
Connelsville (PA) *Daily Courier* 130
Connor, Roger 37
Cool Papas and Double Duties 176
Cooper, Andy 82, 174
Cooper, Chuck 88
Coors Field 56
Corbett, Warren 342n23
Corriden, John "Red" 91
Costas, Bob 93–94
Courtenay, Ed 154
Cox, Bill 309
Craig, Peter S. 317
Crane, Ed 21
Crawford, Sam 33, 161
Cronin, Joe 159
Crothers, Doug 23
Crowe, George 301
Cruchfield, Jimmy 121
Cuban Giants 18, 23; "champions of the world" 40
Cuban Hall of Fame 165
Cuban Stars 154
Cummiskey, Joe 41
Curtiss Candy Company 103
Cushman, Charley "Cush" 22, 25, 332n20

Daily Worker 41, 121
Dalkowski, Steve 153–54
Dandridge, Ray 6, 48, 57, 160, 174, 176–77, 269; batting record 194
Daniel, Dan 336ch9n1
Danley, Kerwin 53
Davis, George 159
Davis, Harry 33
Davis, Lorenzo "Piper" 176; batting record 195
Davis, Roosevelt 82
Day, Leon 83–84, 174, 176; pitching record 256
Day, Tom 19
Dean, Jay "Dizzy" 145, 153–54
Dean, Paul 154
Dees, Charlie 304
deGrom, Jacob 101, 153
Delahanty, Ed 37, 54, 56–57, 100, 107, 160
DeMoss, Elwood "Bingo" 159, 176; batting record 196
Denver Post Tournament 154

Derrington, Jim 82
Detroit Stars 154, 338n3
Detroit Tigers 35, 40, 71, 89, 298, 303, 305
Devlin, Jim 101
DeWitt, Bill 109, 111
DeWitt, Charlie 111
DeWitt Base Ball Guide for 1868 12
DeZonie, Hank 88
Dickey, Bill 114, 118, 158
Dickson, Paul 308
Dihigo, Martin 59, 72, 82–83, 161, 174, 176, 178, 269, 273; batting record 197–98; pitching record 257
Dillinger, Bob 337ch10n8
Dilworth, William 23
DiMaggio, Joe 101, 137, 140, 144, 153, 160
Dixon, Herbert "Rap" 57, 59
Dizzy Dean All-Stars 40
Doby, Larry v, 1, 36, 47–51, 68, 71, 77, 79, 92, 132–33, 136; as basketball player 77, 88, 142–43, 146, 155, 161, 165, 168, 174, 178–79, 299–300, 307, 312, 334n20, 335ch6n3, 339n1, 340ch14n7, 342n13; batting record 198–99; introduces batting helmet to AL 145; profile 141–46
Doerr, Bobby 130, 309
Donahue, Jim 34
Donaldson, John 176; pitching record 258; see also John Donaldson's All-Stars
Donoso, Lino 303
Doolittle, Brad 62
Doswell, Ray 110
Doyle, Jack 34
Dred Scott v. Sandford 12
Dressen's All Stars 89
Duffy, Hugh 34, 37, 54–56
Dugan, Joe 50
Dundon, Ed 15
Dunlap, Fred 56
Dunne, Edward 28
Durham, Joe 302
Durocher, Leo 40–41, 44, 123, 333n6
Duval, Clarence 28, **29**
Dyer, Eddie 342n23

East-West All-Star Game (*St. Louis Argus*) 127
East-West Game 71, 121–22, 127, 142, 154
East-West League (EWL) 66, 272–73
Easter, Luscious "Big Luke" 1, 48–51, 112, 159, 166, 178–79; batting record 200–2, 300, 309, 311, 338n6, 338n17, 342n11; profile 125–40; proposed Hall of Fame plaque 166
Easter, Virgil 134
Eastern Colored League (ECL) 66–67, 94, 271
Eastern Independent Clubs (EIC / EAS) 66, 271, 273; see also independent Black teams
Ebbets Field 69
Ebony magazine 47, 299, 307
Eckersley, Dennis 163
Eclipse see Louisville Eclipse
Edwards, Frank "Tenny" 126
Edwards, Johnny 118
Ellison, Ralph 3–4, 6
Enders, Eric 4
Erskine, Carl 119
Escalera, Saturnina "Nina" 298
ESPN 62, 298
Evans, Bill **274**
Evans, Darrell 160
Evers, Johnny 20
Ewing, William "Buck" 17, 37, 115, 118, 137, 158
Executive Order 8802 334n9
Exposition Park (Pittsburgh) **70**

Faber, Urban "Red" 155
Fain, Ferris 101, 135
Farnham Pirates 302
Federal League (FL) 37–38, 66, 69, 94, 271
Fenway Park 298
Feller, Bob 47, 85, 137, 153, 162
Ferrell, Wes 72
Fields, Wilmer "Red" 83, 137
Fiery, Ben 317–18, 326
15th Amendment to the US Constitution 14
Figueroa, Jose "Tito" 83
Finch, Frank 137
Fisk, Carlton 115, 118, 158
Flood, Curt 324
Floyd, George 30
Forbes Field 1, 121
Force, Davy 56
Ford, Edward "Whitey" 162
Fort, Dr. Rodney 313–14
Fort Wayne (IN) *Daily News* 18
Foster, Andrew "Rube" 66, 174, 178–79; pitching record 258
Foster, Willie 82–84, 102, 153, 162, 174, 176; pitching record 259–60
Fowler, Bob 19
Fowler, John "Bud" 12, **13**, 20, 26
Foxx, Jimmie 58, 100–2, 104, 115, 131, 158
Franklin, Cory 5

Freehan, Bill 115, 118, 158
Frick, Ford 47, 312, 315, 325, 342*n*23; *see also* MacPhail Report
Fuller, Charles 12

Gallagher, James 44
Galvin, James "Pud" 37
Garcia, Silvio 44
Garvey, Marcus 28
Gehrig, Lou 4, 50–51, 58–59, 100–1, 115, 138, 145, 148, 158, 161
Gehringer, Charlie 159
Genesee House (Buffalo NY) 23
George, Alex 82
Gerlach, Larry R. 35, 342*n*11
Gibson, Bob 162, 169
Gibson, Josh 3–5, 7, 40, 43–44, 57, 59–60, 90, 93–94, 96, **97**, 98–103, **104**, 105, 110, 114–15, 122, 124, 129–30, 132, 135, 138–39, 141–42, 147–52, 157–58, 174, 176, 269, **274**; batting record 203–24
Gibson, Vernon 309
Gifford, Andy 35
Giles, Warren 315
Gilliam, Jim "Junior" 49, 161, 301
Glass, George 338*n*3
Glasscock, Jack 36
Goebbels, Joseph 333*n*23
Golden, Clyde 83
Goldman, Steven 306
Goldstein, E. Ernest 317–23, 326
Goldstein, Harold "Spud" 299
Golenbock, Peter 343*n*13
Gonzales, Juan 61
Gooden, Dwight "Doc" 84–85
Gordon, Joe 309, 342*n*13
Goslin, Leon "Goose" 107, 160
Gossage, Rich "Goose" 162
Graham, Gordon 132
Grandfather *see* Petersen, Woodrow T. "Woody"
Grant, Ulysses "Frank" 20–21, 23, 25, 133, 174; batting record 205
Gray, Pete 43
Grayson, Harry 134, 137
Greason, Bill 302
Great Depression 66
Great Lakes Naval Air Station (Great Lakes NAS) 142, 168, 339*n*1
Green, Elijah "Pumpsie" 298
Greene, James "Joe" 176; batting record 206
Greenberg, Hank 85, 101–2, 104, 109, 131, 138–39, 143, 161; as progressive on civil rights 299
Greenberg, Stephen 299
Greenlee, Gus 68
Greenlee Field (Pittsburgh PA) 68
Greensboro Red Wings 302
Greenwood, Bill 19
Grich, Bobby 159
Griffey, Ken, Jr. 61, 161
Griffith, Calvin 52
Griffith, Clark 44, 51–52, 315
Griffith Stadium 1, 68, 143, 145
Grimes, Burleigh 40, 155
Grimm, Charles "Jolly Cholly" 308
Gromek, Greg 144
Gromek, Steve 43, 144
Grote, Jerry 118
Grove, Robert "Lefty" 90, 101, 153, 162
Gwynn, Tony 54–55, 58, 61, 161

Hack, Stan 160
Hackett, Charlie 20, 24
Hackett, Walter 55
Hafey, Charles "Chick" 107–8
Hairston, Sam 301
Hall of Fame *see* Baseball Hall of Fame
Hall of Merit 113, 116, 118, 120, 124
Hamilton, "Sliding" Billy 54, 56, 100, 161
Hamilton (Ontario) *Spectator* 23
Hamtramck Stadium (MI) 69
Haney, Fred 138
Hanlon, Ned 37
Hano, Arnold 145
Harlem Globetrotters 87–88, 309
Harlem Renaissance 3–4
Harmon, Chuck 298, 303
Harper, Bryce 61
Harrell, Billy 303
Harridge, William 47, 318, 320–21; *see also* MacPhail Report
Harris, Vic **274**
Harrisburg (PA) *Telegraph* 139
Hartman, J.C. 304
Hartnett, Charles "Gabby" 114, 118, 158
Havana Cuban Giants 302
Hawaiian Fall League (HFL) 128–29, 166
Hawkins, Burton 156
Hayes, Jackie 32
Heard, Jehosie "Jay" 302
Heath, Jeff 110–11, 337*ch*10*n*8
Hegan, Bob 342*n*13
Heilmann, Harry 101

Helton, Todd 61
Henderson, Rickey 107, 148, 160
Herrera, Juan "Pancho" 303
Herrman, August "Garry" 40
Heydler, John 44
Higgins, Robert "Bob" 22–23, 25–26
Hill, Pete 161, 174, 176; batting record 207
Hilldale Park (Darby PA) 69
Hillings, Patrick J. 317, 320
Hines, Paul 15
Hinton, Archie 83
History of Colored Baseball 18–19
Hobgood, Fred 83
Hoffman, Trevor 163
Hogan, Bob 32
Holland, Bill 82
Hollingsworth, Al 155
Hollis, John 143
Holtzman, Jerome 311
Holway, John 6, 89, 343*n*13
Homestead Grays 4, 121, 142, 154, 166, 300–1, 314; 1931 team 273, **274**
Honig, Donald 5
Honolulu Advertiser 130
Hoover, Billy 25
Hornsby, Rogers 55–58, 62–64, 100–1, 159
Hornsby's Major League Stars 89
Hoskins, Bill 57
Hoskins, Dave 301
Hotel and Club Union 43
Houk, Ralph 138
Houston Astros 305
Houston Colt .45s 88, 305
Houtteman, Art 145
Howard, Elston 48
Howard, Ryan 61
Howe, George W. 19, 307
Hoyt, Waite 50
Hubbell, Carl 99, 153
Hudson, Nat 84
Hughes, Mickey 24
Hughes, Sammy T. 121, 176, 269; batting record 208–9
Hundley, Johnny 126
Hunter, Torii 298
Husman, John R. 16
Hutchinson, Willie 83–84

Ichiro *see* Suzuki, Ichiro
independent Black teams (IND) 94, 136, 166, 271–73; *see also* Eastern Independent Clubs
Indianapolis Blues 32
Indianapolis Clowns 87–88, 299, 301–5
Indianapolis Hoosiers 36
inferred data recovery 179

Inter-State League 301
International League (IL) 15, 20, 23–26, 46, 120–21, 124, 127–29, 134–36, 155, 166, 179, 270, 300, 309
International News Service 41
international Workers Order 43
Irvin, Monte 1, 36, 44, 48–51, 67, 77–78, 142, 161, 165, 174, 176, 178, 300, 309, 333n6; batting record 209–10; profile 106–8
Izenberg, Jerry 143

Jackie Robinson's All-Stars 129, 142–43; see also Robinson, Jackie
Jackson, Reggie 60, 161
Jackson, "Shoeless" Joe 100–1, 161
Jacksonville Eagles 305
Jacobs, Mike 59
Jacobsen, Steve 335n24
James, Bill 1, 4, 6, 55, 65, 71, 77, 82, 106, 119, 122, 127, 135, 333ch2n4, 335n10
Jarbeau, Verona **29**
Jefferson, Willie 82
Jeffries, Jim 82
Jennings, Hughie 56
Jeter, Derek 159
Jethroe, Sam "The Jet" 48–49, 51, 126, 132, 176; batting record 210
Jersey City Skeeters 18, 20
Joe Judge's All Stars 89
John Donaldson's All-Stars 273; see also Donaldson, John
Johnson, Bert 57
Johnson, Byron "Ban" 40
Johnson, Connie 83–84, 301
Johnson, Grant "Home Run" 159; batting record 212
Johnson, Kevin 69, 113
Johnson, Lou 304
Johnson, Oscar "Heavy" 57, 59
Johnson, Randy 153, 162
Johnson, Walter 99, 101, 153, 162
Johnson, William "Judy" 153, 174, 176, 306; batting record 213–14
Jones, Adam 298
Jones, Hal 304
Jones, Larry "Chipper" 160
Jones, Sam "Toothpick" 48–50, 301
Jones, Stuart "Slim" 82–83; pitching record 260
Joost, Eddie 143
Joseph, Walter "Newt" 6
Joss, Adrian "Addie" 102
Joyce, Bill 100

Judge, Aaron 62
Judnich, Walt 337ch10n8
Juran, Edward "Eli" 82

Kaepernick, Colin 30
Kahn, Roger 325
Kaiser, David 39
Kaline, Al 127, 161
Kansas City Athletics 305
Kansas City Cowboys 33
Kansas City Monarchs 40, 51, 109–10, 126, 154, 166, 299–305
Kansas City Royals 166
Kauff, Benny 37
Keating, Kenneth B. 317–20
Keefe, Tim 37, 55, 90
Keeler, "Wee" Willie 56
Kelley, Joe 107–8
Kelly, Michael "King" 20, 37
Keltner list 135–37
Kennedy, Bob 134
Kennedy, John 303
Kent, Jeff 151
Kershaw, Clayton 101, 153, 155, 162
Killebrew, Harmon 161
Killefer, Bill 118
Kilroy, Matt 97
Kimbrough, Larry 83
Kiner, Ralph 107
King, Charles "Silver" 32
King, Hal 305
King, Dr. Martin Luther, Jr., 104, 124
Klein, Chuck 56
Knight, Lon 34
Knorr, Ted 88–89
Koenig, Mark 50
Korean War 149
Koufax, Sandy 153, 162
Kretlow, Lou 134
Ku Klux Klan 87, 90; see also Wichita Klan No. 6
Kuhn, Bowie 312

Lacy, Sam 44, 118
Lafayette (IN) *Courier and Journal* 132
La Grave Field (Fort Worth TX) **133**
LaGuardia, Fiorello 45
Lajoie, Napoleon "Nap" 56, 78, 91, 159
Landis, Kenesaw "Mountain" 37–39, **40**, 41–45, 52, 71, 307–8, 311
Lane, Thomas J. 317, 321
Lange, Bill 34
Larkin, Barry 159
Lawrence, David 305–6
Lazzeri, Tony 5, 50
League of Colored Base Ball Players 18

League Park (Cincinnati OH) 33, 69
Lebovitz, Hal 138
Lemon, Bob 342n13
Leonard, Walter "Buck" 44, 57, 59, 100–1, 130, 153, 158–59, 174, 176; batting record 214–15
Levin, Rich 90
Levy, Sam 308
Lewis (first name unknown) 35
Lewis, Ira 42–43
Lewis Park (Memphis) 69
Life magazine 117, 119
Light, Jonathan Fraser 49
Lloyd, Earl 88
Lloyd, John Henry "Pop" 88, 141, 159, 174, 176; batting record 216
Lockman, Carroll "Whitey" 302
Lombardi, Ernie 137
Lopat, Ed 138
Lopez, Al 132, 134, 144
Lord Baltimore Hotel 299
Los Angeles Angels 305
Los Angeles Dodgers 52, 303; see also Brooklyn Dodgers
Louisville, Kentucky 13–14, 17, 307
Louisville Buckeyes 301
Louisville Clippers 305
Louisville Commercial 13
Louisville Courier-Journal 14
Louisville Eclipse 13–14
Low, Nat 121
Lucas, Henry 36
Luke Easter's All-Stars **133**
Lundy, Dick 176; batting record 217–18
Luque, Adolfo "Dolf" 155
Lyles, John 126
Lynch, Tom 40

Macht, Norman L. 39
Mack, Cornelius "Connie" 37, 47
Mack, Roy 315
Mack Park (Detroit) 69
Mackey, James "Biz" 57, 114–15, 121, 158, 174, 176, 273; batting record 219–220
Macmillan Baseball Encyclopedia 3–4, 6
MacPhail, Leland "Larry" 44–47, 312, 316–25, 334n16; see also MacPhail Report
MacPhail Report 47–48, 269, 312–13, 315–26, 334n16
Maddux, Greg 153, 166
Maglie, Sal "The Barber" 138
Mah, Jay-Dell 67
Major League All Stars (barnstorming team) 89

Major League Equivalencies (MLEs) 1, 113–16
Malloy, Jerry 19
Manley, Effa 52, 107, 174
Manning, Gordon 127, 130
Mantle, Mickey 55, 58, 101, 131, 138, 145, 147, 150, 160
Manush, Henry "Heinie" 107
Marberry, Frederick "Firpo" 163
Marcell, Oliver "Ghost" 6, 176; batting record 221
Marichal, Juan 162
Marion, Marty 342n23
Marquez, Luis 300
Marr, Charles "Lefty" 22
Marrero, Connie 144
Marshall, William J. 316, 325
Martin Park (Memphis) 69
Martinez, Edgar 161
Martinez, J.D. 62
Martinez, Pedro 101, 162
Maryland Park (Baltimore) 69
Mason, Charlie 16
Mason, Hank 303
Mathews, Eddie 160
Mathewson, Christy 153, 162
Matthews, Bob 138
Mauer, Joe 158
Max Carey's All Stars 7
Maxcy, Dr. Joel 313–14
Mays, Willie 36, 48–51, 55, 79–80, 88, 94, 98, 127, 132, 137, 141, 145–52, 160–61, 169, 174, 178, 301, 314; batting record 222–23
Mazeroski, Bill 159
McAleer, Jimmy 34
McCarthy, Tommy 36
McCovey, Willie 130, 159, 166
McCutchen, Andrew 144
McDougald, Gil 161
McGee, James 138
McGlone, John 23
McGraw, John 100
McGuire, James "Deacon" 18
McGwire, Mark 58–59, 61, 101–2, 159
McInnis, John "Stuffy" 35
McIntyre, Matty 34
McKechnie, Bill 40
McKinley, Eric Garcia 6
McNeil, William 89, 175–76
McSkimming, Dent 109
McVey, Cal 56, 115, 118
Meany, Tom 44, 117
Medwick, Joe 107
Memphis Red Sox 300–1, 303, 305
Méndez, José 174
Metropolitans (1883 baseball club) 16
Meusel, Bob 50, 148

Mexican Hall of Fame 165
Mexican League (MEX) 66, 82, 114, 116, 120, 122, 177, 272–74; argument for consideration as Major League (1940–41) 269
Mexican Pacific Coast League (MPCL) 127–28, 134–36, 166
Miles, John "Mule" 152
Miller, Charles "Dusty" 33
Miller, Dorie 41
Miller, Jake 155
Miller, Marvin 324
Milwaukee Braves 301–2; see also Atlanta Braves
Milwaukee Brewers (AAA club) 308
Milwaukee Journal 308
Milwaukee Sentinel 308
Minneapolis Lakers (basketball team) 87
Minnesota Twins 52
Miñoso, Orestes "Minnie" 36, 48–51, 79–80, 160, 164–65, 174, 178–79, 300, 311; batting record 224–26
Mize, Johnny 101, 109, 159
Moffi, Larry 41
Molina, Yadier 118–19
Molitor, Paul 161
Monboquette, Bill 154
Monroe, Al 40
Monterey Industrials 122
Montgomery Advertiser 139
Montgomery bus boycott 52
Montreal Royals 26, 308, 325
Moore, Terry 145, 342n23
Moore, Walter "Dobie" 100; batting record 227
Moore, Wilcy 50
Morgan, Joe 55, 159
Morris, Barney 273
Morton, Charlie 15–16
Muehlebach Field (Kansas City) 69
Mullane, Tony 17
Murphy, Danny 33
Murphy, Howard 42–43
Murphy, Johnny 324
Murphy, Justin 126
Murray, Charlie 335n24
Murray, Eddie 159, 335n24
Murray, Jim 50
Murtaugh, Danny 302
Musial, Stan "The Man" 43, 58, 72, 88, 101–2, 107, 127, 137, 150, 160, 342n23
Mutrie, Jim 20
Myerle, Levi 56, 58
Myers, Henry "Hi" 55, 92

Nagashima, Shigeo 157
Nashua Dodgers 122–24, 300
Nashville Elite Giants 154

National Association (NA) 11, 56–57, 66–67, 92, 97, 270
National Association of Base Ball Players (NABBP) 11–12
National Association of Colored Baseball Clubs of the United States & Cuba 271
National Colored Base Ball League (NCBBL) 270
National Commission 40
National Football League (NFL) 27
National Pastime Museum 38
Neal, Charlie 303
Negro American Association (NAA) 272
Negro American League (NAL) 66–67, 112, 122, 126, 155, 269, 272
Negro American League All-Stars *133*
Negro Leagues Baseball Museum 175–76
Negro Leagues Committee (Baseball Hall of Fame) 166
Negro National League (first iteration, NNL) 66, 92, 94, 155, 271
Negro National League (second iteration, NN2) 66–67, 116, 120, 128–29, 141–42, 155, 179, 269, 272–73
Negro Newspaper Publishers Association 42
Negro Southern League (NSL) 66, 272
Negro World Series 68, 135, 142, 154; see also Colored World Series
Nettles, Greg 160
New Bill James Historical Baseball Abstract 65; see also *Bill James Historical Baseball Abstract*
New England League 120–21, 123–24, 300
New Orleans Eagles 302
New York Age 17
New York Black Yankees 301
New York Clipper 32
New York Cubans 51, 300–3
New York Gothams 16
New York Giants 18–20, 32–34, 49, 51, 89, 123, 300–1
New York Herald Tribune 15, 44, 308, 312
New York Yankees 4, 47, 68, 153, 302, 319, 324; 1927 team 49–51, 58
Newark Bears 18
Newark Daily Journal 20, 24
Newark Eagles 52, 107, 121, 141–42, 300, 303, 305, 307, 338n3

Index

Newark Evening News 24, 45
Newark Little Giants 20, 27
Newark Star-Ledger 44–45
Newark Sunday Call 24
Newcombe, Don "Newk" 46, 48–50, 83–84, 124, 178–79, 300, 337n10; pitching record 261
Newport News Dodgers 46
Newspaper Enterprise Association (NEA) 137
Neyer, Rob 6–7, 91
Nichols, Charles "Kid" 162
Nippon Pro Baseball 4
Noble, Ray 300
Nolan, Ed 32
Nolan, Gary 84–85
Northwestern League 15–16, 26–27
Nunn, Bill 142
Nuxhall, Joe 82

Oberlin College (OH) 13, 15–16
O'Brien, Tom 34
O'Connor, Jack "Peach Pie" 90
Odom, John "Blue Moon" 305
O'Doul, Francis "Lefty" 72, 100
Offerman Stadium (Buffalo) 166
Oh, Sadaharu 157
Ohtani, Shohei 72
O'Malley, Walter 122
Oms, Alejandro: batting record 229–30
O'Neil, James "Tip" 56
O'Neil, John "Buck" 71, 87, 138, *165*, 166, 174–76, 179; batting record 228
O'Neill's All Stars 89
O'Rourke, "Orator" Jim 37, 107
Orr, Dave 101–2
Ortiz, David 61, 161
Ott, Mel 161
Ottawa Nationals 112
Overfield, Joe 138

Pacific Coast League (PCL) 128, 133, 135, 155, 179
Page, Ted **274**
Paige, Leroy "Satchel" 3, 36, 44, 47–50, 71, 87, 90, 101–2, 105, 111, 132, 142, 144, 157, 162, 174, 176, 178–79, 273, 298, 300, 309–12, 314, 341n11; pitching record 262–64; profile 152–56
Painter, Alex 338n6
Palmer, Pete 4, 91
Parker, Billy 305
Parker, Tom 83
Parnell, Roy 57
Paterson Crescents (basketball team) 143
Paula, Carlos 302

Pedroso, Eustaquio 176; pitching record 264
Peeples, Nate 52
Peete, Charlie 303
Pendleton, Jim 301
Pennock, Herb 50
performance-enhancing drugs *see* steroids
Petersen, Woodrow T. "Woody" v, 3, 142, 150, **168**, 169, 339n1
Peterson, Robert 11
Peterson, Todd 89
Pfeffer, Fred 1, 307
Philadelphia Athletics 18, 33, 35, 40, 89, 301–2, 315
Philadelphia Independent 309
Philadelphia Phillies 33, 111, 143, 303, 305, 307–9
Philadelphia Pythians 11–12
Philadelphia Quakers 32–33
Philadelphia Stars 301–3
Philadelphia Tribune 122
Piazza, Mike 114, 118, 158
Pietrusza, David 39
Pike, Lippman "Lip" 34
Pittsburgh Courier 40–42, 120, 122, 139, 142, 153, 175–76, 325
Pittsburgh Crawfords 68, 148
Pittsburgh Pirates 32, 44, 121–22, 302, 305, 315
Pittsburgh Press 20
Pittsburgh Stogies 88
Players' League (PL) 37, 94, 270, 274
PNC Park (Pittsburgh) **70**
Poindexter, Owen 5
Poles, Spottswood "Spot" 161; batting record 231
The Politics of Glory 135
Polo Grounds 1, 47, 68, 137
Pompez, Alex 51, 174
Pope, Dave 301
Porter, Paul 316–19, 321–24, 326
Posey, Cumberland "Cum" 122, 174–76, **274**; batting and managerial records 232
Posnansky, Joe 88, 123, 126
Powers, Pat 18–19, 307
Prentice, Bob 134
Prescott, Bobby 304
Proctor, Jim 303
Providence Grays 13, 15
Puerto Rican Winter League (PRWL) 112, 127–29, 134–36, 142, 155, 166, 179
Pujols, Albert 61, 104, 159

Quinn, Jack 155
Quisenberry, Dan 102, 162

"Race Question report" *see* MacPhail Report
race suicide" 28

Radbourn, Charles "Old Hoss" 37, 55
Radcliffe, Ted "Double Duty" 153, 162, 273, **274**
Raines, Larry 299, 303
Raines, Tim 107, 160
Raleigh Tigers 303, 305
Ramirez, Manny 101, 160
Rawlings Sporting Goods 1
Redding, "Cannonball" Dick 162, 176; pitching record 265
Reese, Harold "Pee Wee" 44
Reese, Jimmie 138
Reid, Ambrose **274**
Reilly, Rick 151
Renfro, William 23
Rennie, Rutherford "Rud" 342n23
Restelli, Dino 138
Retrosheet 56
Rice, Jim 107
Richards, Paul 120
Richardson, Abram "Hardy" 34
Richmond, VA 17–18
Rickey, Wesley "Branch" 7, 42–43, 46–47, 51, 120–23, 298, 308, 311–12, 315–16, 324–25, 334n22, 343n13
Rickwood Field (Birmingham) 69
Ripken, Cal, Jr. 3, 159
Ripken, Cal, Sr. 153
Ritter, Lawrence 5
Rivera, Mariano 101–2, 163
Rixey, Eppa 155
Rizzuto, Phil 117, 146
Roberts, Curt 302
Roberts, Eric "Ric" 325, 343n13
Robeson, Paul 42–43
Robinson, Brooks 160
Robinson, Eddie 143, 312
Robinson, Frank 80, 111, 138, 146, 161
Robinson, Jackie 7, 12, 26, 29, 36, 39, 42, 44, 46, 48–53, 77, 79, 88, 104, 111, 122–24, 141–42, 145, 159, 174, 176, 178, 298–300, 307, 315, 317; batting record 233–34, 308–9, 312, 314, 325, 334n22; court-martial 15; *see also* Jackie Robinson's All-Stars
Rochester Red Wings 88
Rodney, Lester 40–41, 121
Rodriguez, Alex 61, 159
Rodriguez, Francisco 55
Rodriguez, Hector 301
Rodriguez, Ivan 115, 117–18, 158
Rogan, Wilber "Bullet Joe" 2, 57, 72, 101, 157, 161, 174, 176, 178; batting record 234–35; pitching record 266

Roosevelt, Franklin Delano 44, 103, 325, 334*n*9
Roosevelt, Theodore 28, 333*n*23
Rose, Pete 29, 127, 162
Roseboro, John 118
Rosenberg, Howard W. 16, 307
Ruel, Herold "Muddy" 109–10, 337*ch*10*n*8
Rule 691 40
Rusie, Amos 85
Ruth, George Herman "Babe" 3–4, 7, 11, 31, 50–51, 55–56, 58–59, 62–64, 88, 90, 92, 96, 99–103, **104-5**, 115, 130, 137–39, 143, 145, 147–52, 161, 169; as pitcher 62, 72, 150–52, 157–58
Ruth, Julia 105
Ryan, Nolan 97, 149

Sabathia, Carston "C.C." 298
Sain, Johnny 144
Saint Cloud Hotel (Louisville KY) 13
St. Louis Argus 125, 1135
St. Louis Browns 16, 32, 89–90, 109, 300, 336*ch*9*n*1
St. Louis Cardinals 47, 89, 150, 302–3, 312–13, 315, 336*ch*9*n*1, 342*n*13
St. Louis Maroons 36
St. Louis Post-Dispatch 109
St. Louis Star and Times 126
St. Louis Stars 69
St. Louis Titanium Giants 125–26, 338*n*3
St. Petersburg (FL) Times 309
Sampson, Tommy 121
San Diego Padres (AAA franchise) 138–39
San Francisco News-Call Bulletin 138
Sandberg, Ryne 159
Santiago, José 302
Santo, Ron 6, 160
Santop, Louis 158, 174; batting record 236
Saperstein, Abe 309–11, 342*n*11
Saskatchewan, Canada 67
Sauter, Al 35
Scales, George 59, 101, **274**
Scantlebury, Pat 303
Scherzer, Max 162
Schlemmer, Jim 138
Schmidt, Mike 111, 160
Schorling Park (Chicago) 69
Schott, Marge 52
seamheads.com 6–7, 69, 113, 154, 177
Seaver, Tom 162
Secades, Eladio 138
Senadores de San Juan 142

Sengstacke, John H. 42–43, 334*n*9
Shantz, Bobby 146
Sharsig, Bill 18
Sheeley, Earl 138
shin guards (wooden) 20–21
Siever, Ed 34
Simkus, Scott 89, 331
Simmons, Al "Bucketfoot" 58, 107
Simmons, Ted 115, 118
Simon, Hank 23
Simpson, Harry "Suitcase" 49, 301
Sisler, George 56–57, 72, 159
Slattery, Mike 22
Slide, Kelly, Slide (movie and song) **20-21**
Smith, Al "Fuzzy" 299, 301
Smith, Charles "Chino" 57, 59, 176; batting record 237
Smith, Clare 335*ch*6*n*3
Smith, Elmer 33
Smith, Eugene 338*n*3
Smith, Elvis "Hilton" 7, 101, 174, 176, 273; pitching record 267
Smith, George 305
Smith, George "Germany" 32
Smith, John "Phenomenal" 19, 32
Smith, Milt 303
Smith, Ozzie 148, 150, 159
Smith, Rick 138
Smith, Walter "Red" 308–9
Smith, Wendell 67, 138, 142
Smith, Willie 305
Smoltz, John 163
Snider, Edwin "Duke" 144, 161
Society for American Baseball Research (SABR) 35, 39, 56, 88, 126
Soderholm-Difatte, Bryan 124
Sosa, Sammy 58, 61
Southern Association 52
Southern League (minor league) 22
Southern League of Colored Base Ballists (SL) 270
Spahn, Warren 144, 153, 159, 162
Spalding 1
Spalding, Albert 16–17
Speaker, Tris 100, 120, 143, 148, 161
Spink, J.G. Taylor 45–46, 155
Sporting Life 15, 17–18, 21, 23, 25, 27
The Sporting News (TSN) 19–20, 23, 45–46, 137, 139
Sports Illustrated 151
Spriggs, George 305
standard deviation (StDev) 78–81, 96–99

Stanky, Eddie 309
Stanton, Giancarlo 61
Stargell, Willie 107, 130, 160, 166
Starr, Bill 138
Stars Park (St. Louis) 69
Start, Joe 12
Stearnes, Norman "Turkey" 59, 98, 100–2, 161, 174, 176; batting record 237–28
Stengel All Stars 89
Stephens, Vern 44, 109, 337*ch*10*n*8
Sterling (first name unknown) 35
steroids 29, 80, 135, 147, 151, 159–60, 162, 340*n*1
Stevens, John Paul 317, 322
Stone, George 34
Stovey, George 18–20, 24, 27
Strong, Joe 82
Strong, Ted "T.R." 176, 269; batting record 239–40
Sukeforth, Clyde 43, 122, 142
Suttles, George "Mule" 57, 59, 92, 101–2, 159, 174, 176; batting record 240–41
Suzuki, Ichiro 61, 149, 161, 341*n*11
Swaine, Rick 309, 336*ch*9*n*1
Syracuse Evening Herald 26
Syracuse Orange (basketball team) 88
Syracuse Stars 22, 24

Talbot, Gayle 139
Taney, Robert 12
Taylor, Ben 159, 174, 176; batting record 242
Taylor, "Candy" Jim 59
Taylor, Joe "Cephus" 302
Taylor, Johnny 83, 156
Terry, Bill 56
Texas League 112, 302
Tharps, Lori L. 305
Thomas, Arthur 18
Thomas, Clint 176
Thomas, Frank 58, 61, 101, 104, 159
Thomas, Herb 83
Thome, Jim 159
Thompson, Henry "Hank" 46, 109, 111, 300, 333*n*6, 337*ch*10*n*8
Thompson, Sam 54, 56, 92
Thorn, John 4, 69
Thurman, Bob 139
Thurston, Hollis 139
Tiernan, Mike 19
Tierney's All Stars 89
Time magazine 117
Tinker, Harold "Hooks" 148
Titanium Giants *see* St. Louis Titanium Giants

Index

Toledo Blue Stockings 15–18
Toledo Daily Blade 15
Toledo Maumees 88
Topps Trading Cards 127
Toronto Canucks 21–22
Toronto Daily Mail 25
Toronto World 22
Torre, Joe 115, 118
Torriente, Cristóbal 57, 102, 161, 174, 176; batting record 243
Total Baseball 106–107, 109
Trammel, Alan 159
Traynor, Harold "Pie" 160
Trenton, New Jersey 19
Trenton Daily True American 18
Trenton Evening News 16
Trenton Giants 19
Trice, Bob 301
Trinkle, Ken 123
Trouppe, Quincy 115, 269, 273, 301; batting record 244–45
Trout, Mike 55, 101, 161, 169
Turner, George "Tuck" 54, 56
Tygiel, Jules 311, 336ch9n1
Tyler, William "Steel Arm" 82

Umphlett, Tom 145
Union Association (UA) 1, 36–38, 55, 65, 67, 94, 270
Union League 14
United Office and Professional Workers of America 43
United Press/United Press International 122, 139, 315
United States Baseball League (USBL) 271
United States League (USL) 122, 272
University of California, Los Angeles (UCLA) 77

Vargas, Juan "Tetelo" 56–57
Vaughn, Joseph "Arky" 159
Veeck, Bill 46–47, 126, 132, 139, 142–43, 153, 307–12, 342n13
Venezuelan Professional Baseball League (VBPL) 128, 135, 166
Vincent, Francis "Fay" 335ch6n3
Virgil, Ozzie, Sr. 298, 303
Von der Ahe, Chris 24

Wagner, Honus 147–52, 159
Walker, Fred "Dixie" 342n23
Walker, Larry 58, 61, 101

Walker, Moses "Fleetwood" 11–13, *14*, 15–20, 24, *25*, 26–29, 123, 332n20; patents held by 27
Walker, Weldy 16, *17*
Walsh, Ed 102
Waner, Lloyd 145
Waner, Paul 140, 161
Ward, John Montgomery 18–19, 37, 72, 84–85
Wargo, Ron 118
Wasdell, Jimmy 154
Washington, Jasper *274*
Washington Afro-American 109, 118
Washington Elite Giants *see* Baltimore Elite Giants
Washington Park (Indianapolis) 69
Washington Post 99
Washington Senators 302–3, 305, 315, 336ch9n1
Watson, Amos 83
Wee Willie Keeler *see* Keeler, "Wee" Willie
Weimer, Jake 84
Wells, Willie "El Diablo" 57, 67, 159, 174, 176, 269; batting record 246–47
Welmaker, Roy 83
Welsh, Curt 24
Wertz, Vic 132–33
Wesley, Edgar 57, 59
West (first name unknown) 13
West, Milt "Buck" 23
Western League 302
Weyhing, Gus 32
Wheat, Zack 107
Whitaker, Lou 159
White, Charlie 302
White, James "Deacon" 92, 115, 118
White, Joseph "Jo-Jo" 299
White, Sol 18–19, 29, 87, 174; batting record 248
White, William Edward *13*
White Sewing Machine Company (Cleveland OH) 12
Whitney, Carl 126
Wichita Klan No. 6 90; *see also* Ku Klux Klan
Wichita Monrovians 90
Wilhelm, Hoyt 101, 163
Wilkinson, J.L. 174
Williams, Billy 88, 107
Williams, Charles Henry "Lefty" *274*

Williams, Charlie *274*
Williams, "Cyclone" Joe 72, 90, 101, 153, 162, 174, 176, 273; pitching record 268
Williams, Frederick "Cy" 116
Williams, Harry 57
Williams, Ted 3–4, 56, 58–60, 91, 100–1, 107, 127, 136–37, 139–40, 145, 147–52, 160, 178
Williamson, Ned 20
Willis, Edwin E. 317, 321
Wills, Maury 48, 303
Wilson, Artie 48–51, 57, 176, 178, 301; batting record 249–50
Wilson, Bob 303
Wilson, Ernest "Jud" 57, 59, 100–2, 160, 174, 176, *274*; batting record 251–52
Wilson, Lewis "Hack" 58, 145
Wilson, W. Rollo 122
Wilson Sporting Goods 1
Winfield, Dave 161
Winters, James "Nip" 82
Wolf, Willie "Chicken" 34
Woolner, Keith 117
Wood, "Smoky" Joe 72, 84, 102
Woodward, Stanley 15, 312–13, 342n23
Worcester Ruby Legs 88
World War II 60, 103, 106–7, 125, 127, 141–42, 149, 168
Wright, Taft "Taffy" 56
Wright, "Wild" Bill 59, 100, 176, 269; batting record 253–54
Wrigley, Phil 47, 71, 315, 325; *see also* MacPhail Report
Wrigley Field 41, 169
Wyatt, John 304
Wynn, Early 55

Yankee Stadium 1, 47, 68, 71, 145
Yastrzemski, Carl 54–55, 107, 127, 160
Yawkey, Tom 47; *see also* MacPhail Report
Young, A.S. "Doc" 133, 309–10
Young, Denton "Cy" 153, 162
Young, Dick 123
Young, Ed "Pep" 126
Young, Fay 310–11
Yount, Robin 161

Zimmerman, Ryan 61

www.ingramcontent.com/pod-product-compliance
Lightning Source LLC
Chambersburg PA
CBHW060334010526
44117CB00017B/2829